FOREIGN & COMMONWEALTH OFFICE

DOCUMENTS ON BRITISH POLICY OVERSEAS

EDITED BY

G. BENNETT, O.B.E., M.A.

AND

K.A. HAMILTON, Ph.D.

SERIES III

Volume III

WHITEHALL HISTORY PUBLISHING
in association with
FRANK CASS
LONDON • PORTLAND, OR

First published in 2001 in Great Britain by
FRANK CASS PUBLISHERS
Crown House, 47 Chase Side
Southgate, London, N14 5BP

and in the United States of America by
FRANK CASS PUBLISHERS
c/o ISBS, 5824 N.E. Hassalo Street
Portland, Oregon, 97213-3644

Website: www.frankcass.com

British Library Cataloguing in Publication Data

Documents on British policy overseas
  Series 3 Vol. 3: Detente in Europe, 1972–1976 edited by
  G. Bennett and K.A. Hamilton. – (Whitehall histories)
  1. Great Britain – Foreign relations – Sources
  I. Bennett, Gillian, 1951– II. Hamilton, Keith, 1942–
  III. Great Britain. Foreign and Commonwealth Office
  327.4'1

ISBN 0-7146-5116-8 (cloth)
ISSN 1471-2083

Library of Congress Catalogue Control No. 84-161776

Published on behalf of the Whitehall History Publishing Consortium. Applications to reproduce Crown copyright protected material in this publication should be submitted in writing to: HMSO, Copyright Unit, St Clements House, 2-16 Colegate, Norwich NR3 1BQ. Fax: 01603 723000.
E-mail: copyright@hmso.gov.uk

Typeset in 11/12 Monotype Baskerville by Vitaset, Paddock Wood, Kent
Printed in Great Britain by
Bookcraft (Bath) Ltd, Midsomer Norton, Somerset

DOCUMENTS ON BRITISH POLICY OVERSEAS

Series III, Volume III

Détente in Europe, 1972–76

PREFACE

East/West *détente* was a defining, though ill-defined, feature of international relations during the early and mid-1970s. The progressive easing of tensions between the superpowers, West Germany's pursuit of *Ostpolitik*, and France's commitment to the Gaullist trilogy of 'détente, de l'entente et de la coopération' in its relations with the Soviet Union, seemed for some to signal the end of cold war. Yet British diplomats were also very much aware that, according to current Soviet doctrine, *détente* necessitated an 'intensification of the political, economic and ideological struggle', and that it could serve as an instrument for furthering Moscow's global ambitions. In the opinion of the Eastern European and Soviet Department (EESD) of the Foreign and Commonwealth Office (FCO) 'the principal objective of Soviet foreign policy [was] progressively to shift the balance of power in the world in favour of the Socialist states', and Mr. L.I. Brezhnev, the General Secretary of the Central Committee of the Communist Party of the Soviet Union (CPSU), had 'selected Europe as the decisive front in this continuing struggle'. The Russians were perceived as pursuing policies aimed at achieving a Western Europe from which United States (US) protection had been largely withdrawn, and which would exist under the shadow of Soviet power. A brief prepared by EESD in the autumn of 1973 concluded: 'The word "Finlandisation" is not too strong for Brezhnev's European vision.' With a view to combating such aspirations, British officials recommended that Western governments must first defend their own national interests against Soviet encroachment even on very small points, and secondly, ensure that public opinion was 'alive to the realities of the situation'. Both the Conference on Security and Cooperation in Europe (CSCE) and its diplomatic sibling, the talks on Mutual and Balanced Force Reductions (MBFR) in central Europe, were in this context considered likely to prove 'highly educative' (No. 49). Volume II of Series III documents the role of the United Kingdom (UK) in the CSCE up until the conclusion of the Helsinki Final Act in August 1975. The first two chapters of this volume cover British preparations for, and Britain's contribution to, the MBFR negotiations in Vienna during the years 1972–76.

Exploring MBFR

Officials in Whitehall were, as initially with regard to the CSCE, highly sceptical about the value of MBFR. Talks on the subject were, on the Western side, very much an American-sponsored idea to which the British, unlike the French, subscribed in response to popular support for *détente* and in the hope that they could thereby assist the Administration in Washington to withstand mounting Congressional pressure for unilateral cuts in US forces in Europe. Mr. C.C.C. Tickell, Head of the FCO's Western Organisations Department (WOD) made the point succinctly in a minute of 13 March 1973. 'We', he recalled, 'do not like the MBFR … We are in the negotiations because we think this is the best way of helping the Americans keep their forces in Europe at acceptable levels, and because we think it enables us the more effectively to protect our own and European defence interests' (No. 4). Britain's approach to the talks was therefore from the first essentially defensive. FCO officials and their colleagues in the Ministry of Defence (MoD) feared that force reductions would weaken the Western Alliance and dismissed as a 'pipe dream' the notion that these could be compatible with undiminished security for all (No. 2). For most of the period covered by this volume the negotiations, which were to extend over the best part of sixteen years, seemed to offer Western diplomats few opportunities for making political or other gains at the expense of the Soviet Union. Nevertheless, in the aftermath of the CSCE summit at Helsinki the MBFR negotiations emerged as a measure of Moscow's continuing commitment to *détente* in Europe. And, as the documents in Chapter IV suggest, at a time when the barometer of Anglo-Soviet relations was once more in decline, and when Britain's defence spending was again under review, the rigid stance adopted by the Russians on MBFR served to alert public opinion to the parallel expansion of Soviet military might.

The Soviet leadership's interest in MBFR was considered by British service chiefs to be primarily political. 'It is', noted a Defence Policy Staff paper of 21 April 1972, 'one element in a worldwide campaign to show themselves as peace-loving pursuers of détente and beaters of swords into ploughshares.' Studies undertaken by the North Atlantic Treaty Organisation (NATO) also indicated that any satisfactory MBFR agreement in central Europe would require considerably larger force withdrawals and reductions by the Warsaw Pact than by NATO, and that there was a critical minimum of NATO forces, 'perhaps not very far below the present levels', at which the Alliance's strategy of flexible response ceased to be viable (No. 1). In addition, the ongoing US/Soviet dialogue on strategic matters appeared to put the Europeans 'constantly at risk of having matters of vital interest to their security settled over their heads'. The FCO did not, however, reject the option of an accord which would limit reductions to US and Soviet forces in central Europe, provided that it was arrived at through multi-lateral negotiations. Although such an arrangement might smack of 'bilateral-ism', it would avoid cuts in other Alliance forces and any consequential erosion of the basis of a future European defence system. If the Europeans were to join the Americans in reducing military expenditure it might demonstrate that they did not take defence seriously and precipitate further American reductions. Mr. Tickell thought the British should impress upon their European allies that MBFR must be seen in the context of the changing relationship between the US and Europe, the pressure on the Europeans to do more in their own self-defence, and the development of a future European defence identity (No. 2). These views were reflected in the steering brief prepared for the British delegation to the MBFR exploratory talks which opened in Vienna on 31 January 1973. It emphasised: (1) that the negotiations should initially concentrate on measures designed to create greater confidence between both sides, with appropriate measures for verifi-cation; (2) that the West Europeans must be left free to devise whatever new defence arrangements within NATO they judged right; and (3) that any reductions should, in the first instance, be confined to American forces in Europe and Soviet forces in Europe outside the Soviet Union (No. 3).

Progress in the exploratory talks was, from the Western point of view, far from satisfactory. The Warsaw Pact delegations opposed Western demands that Hungary, but not Italy, should be included in the force reductions area covered by the negotiations, and discussions at Vienna continued only on an informal basis until mid-May, when a formula was agreed to cover Hungary's status. Reluctant to delay the opening of the talks, the Americans had not insisted on prior agreement on participation and procedures and, much to the alarm of their NATO allies, they seemed all too ready to give way on Hungary in order to ensure the start of substantive negotiations in the autumn. After eight weeks of talks the Alliance was, according to Mr. W.F. Mumford, the UK Deputy Head of Delegation, in 'considerable disarray'; it seemed divided in its objectives and insufficiently prepared. Representatives of the European allies also resented the high-handed conduct of Mr. J. Dean, the US Head of Delegation, who very often appeared insensitive to their views and sometimes more in accord with his Soviet opposite number (No. 4). 'So much of the energy of the allies was devoted to negotiating among themselves', observed Mr. J.A. Thomson, the UK Head of Delegation, 'that it sometimes seemed as if the negotiations with the Russians were a secondary matter' (No. 6). The British held out longest against the concession of flank status to Hungary. Mr. Mumford thought that Western agreement to 'downgrade Hungary', a country which was 'indisputably part of Central Europe' and where four Soviet divisions and 200 aircraft were stationed, would be 'interpreted publicly as a major defeat for NATO at the outset of the negotiations' (No. 4). Yet, in the presence of an American ally who found a retreat on Hungary acceptable, and European allies who considered it tolerable, the British finally acquiesced in an understanding which, while it allowed for enlargement of the area under negotiation, designated Hungary a flank participant.

In Mr. Thomson's opinion the understanding on Hungary 'represented a victory for Soviet persistence over Western impatience' (No. 7). Allied conduct was, as a Joint Intelligence Committee (JIC) report suggested, such as to convince the Russians that they had no reason to make concessions to the West as a whole and that there were advantages to be had from protracted negotiations (No. 8). Already in April Mr. C.D. Wiggin, Assistant Under-Secretary (AUS) in the FCO, had returned from a visit to the United States worried by both the evident doubts of the Administration over whether it could hold to its intentions regarding MBFR and the 'appalling muddle' he sensed in Washington. Americans had argued that once substantive negotiations began they would 'be able to play things tough and long because the very fact that negotiations were taking place would contain Congress'. Some 'optimists' predicted that 'negotiations might drag on inconclusively for years' (No. 5). British diplomats nevertheless thought that sooner or later cuts in US forces were inevitable, and that, with a view to ensuring that adequate troop levels were maintained in Europe, they should, when the substantive negotiations began in October, 'be very careful not to oppose the Americans except for very good reasons'. A draft brief for the British delegation to the MBFR talks, prepared by the FCO in conjunction with the MoD, described the talks 'primarily as an exercise in damage limitation'. It listed amongst their general aims: being seen by Parliament and the public to be working seriously for a lowering of the level of armed forces and armaments in central Europe 'while maintaining undiminished security for all'; ensuring that the reductions in manpower that the Americans and others considered domestically unavoidable fell 'on logistic support rather than combat support troops ... and on both of these rather than on combat ready troops and equipment'; and the maintenance of Allied unity which would mean a 'sensitive and sympathetic attitude towards the domestic political problems of the Americans, and of our Western European Allies (especially the Germans)' (No. 9).

Negotiating MBFR

The British draft brief also insisted that any mutually satisfactory agreement must be based on asymmetrical force reductions. This was a key element in Western thinking about MBFR. In central Europe the Russians were quantitatively superior to NATO in conventional offensive equipment, especially tanks, and enjoyed short lines of communication over which they could reinforce quickly, and if these disparities were to be removed or neutralised there would have to be 'significantly larger reductions in Soviet forces in the agreed area compared with those of the Alliance'. NATO thus envisaged negotiations taking place in two phases: in the first, the parties would agree on a 15% cut in US and Soviet forces in the agreed reductions area, with Russian cuts of 68,000 men, including one tank army of five divisions, and American cuts of 29,000 men of which the proportion of combat troops was as yet undecided; and in the second, each side would make further cuts to bring their forces down to a common ceiling of 700,000 in the reductions area, representing a 10% reduction in NATO forces and a 20% reduction in those of the Warsaw Pact (*ibid.*). But on 8 November, barely a week after the opening of substantive talks in Vienna (now, in order to meet Eastern objections to the use of the adjective 'balanced', officially designated the negotiations on the Mutual Reduction of Armed Forces and Armaments and Associated Measures in Central Europe) and before the tabling of the Western proposals, the Soviet delegation submitted a draft agreement which provided for the reduction in three stages of all armed forces, including air and nuclear forces, in central Europe. Reductions were to be carried out in whole units of approximately similar types and were to fall on the forces of direct participants in proportion to their contribution to the total forces on each side, thereby creating permanent separate ceilings on the manpower and equipment of individual allies (No. 10).

Such terms were incompatible with Western objectives since their acceptance would confirm what NATO perceived as the existing imbalance of forces in central Europe. Whilst the Western Allies were seeking unequal reductions to a common ceiling, the Warsaw Pact countries were offering 'symbolic' reductions of equal quantity, to be followed by reductions of equal proportions; and instead of two-phased negotiations confined to ground forces, the East proposed a single negotiation with all the forces (including nuclear weapons and aircraft) of direct participants being reduced from the outset. Sub-ceilings on individual participants, which the Western powers feared would prejudice the evolution of future European defence arrangements (including the creation of a European defence community), would also become unavoidable. And the Warsaw Pact proposals said nothing about the verification and non-circumvention arrangements which the NATO participants wished to consider as 'associated measures'. Nevertheless, as Mr. C.M. Rose, the UK Head of Delegation, recognised, the Warsaw Pact proposals had a 'variety of apparent virtues well calculated to recommend them to Western, and in particular to American, public opinion': they were superficially easy to understand, superficially fair and superficially simple to execute. The Russians may also have hoped that the early tabling of their draft agreement would disrupt Western tactics and draw Western delegations into negotiations on the basis of Soviet proposals and concepts. The US delegation, now led by Mr. S. Resor, were at first impatient to make progress and to engage in detailed bargaining with the Russians. But Allied unity was maintained within NATO's Ad Hoc Group (the committee of Allied negotiators), and war in the Middle East and the ensuing energy crisis seemed to moderate domestic pressure on the administration in Washington for early force reductions in Europe. 'They are', Mr. Rose observed on 17 January 1974, 'resigned to a fairly long haul, and not disposed to make early concessions' (*ibid.*).

The British were determined to resist any attempt, either to impose sub-ceilings on non-US forces in Europe, or to restrict their own deployment of nuclear weapons. Such measures would inhibit future defence collaboration amongst European members of NATO and impede their efforts to make up for any shortfall caused by a reduction of US forces in Europe (No. 11). Meanwhile, the FCO welcomed an understanding reached at a multilateral dinner, hosted by Mr. Rose on 20 February, to extend the practice of regular informal meetings between NATO and Warsaw Pact delegates (No. 12). British and West German delegates henceforth alternated in accompanying US delegates and representatives of one other of the direct NATO participants at meetings, initially disguised as 'social gatherings', which allowed them to explore the attitudes, strategy and tactics of the Soviet and other Eastern delegations (No. 13). Mr. Rose was encouraged by these talks. When the second round of the negotiations drew to a close in April 1974 he felt that if, as he thought possible, the Russians were anxious for an early agreement, the outlook was 'not entirely unpromising'. He considered press reports of deadlock exaggerated and that *The Economist*'s recent reference to movement at 'a snail's pace' was nearer the mark. However, the Russians were still insisting on the inadequacy of Western proposals and that any agreement must cover all forces and armaments. They wanted assurances that both the *Bundeswehr* and the British Army of the Rhine (BAOR) would be brought within the scope of the reductions, and refused to accept general undertakings that the European forces would be reduced in a second phase (No. 13). 'In effect', as Mr. Rose subsequently admitted, 'the Warsaw Pact was seeking to codify the [East/West military] imbalance and to persuade the West to give it a certificate of respectability in the agreements which would eventually emerge from Vienna' (No. 14).

Mr. J.L. Bullard, Head of EESD, was equally pessimistic. 'All the evidence', he noted in a minute of 21 May, 'suggests that the Soviet leaders regard Vienna as a slow-moving and long-drawn out affair where early agreements are unlikely to be attainable' (No. 15). And a slackening of pace and interest on the part of the Eastern participants in the negotiations had by late July convinced Mr. Rose that they 'were digging themselves in for a war of attrition'. He suspected that the Russians might for the sake of their *détente* policy be prepared to go some way towards meeting American wishes, but that they would pursue any understanding by wedge-driving and that their primary object would be to achieve an agreement which would reduce the *Bundeswehr* and thereby obstruct the development of any European defence union in which West Germany might have a dominant role (No. 16). Fortunately, from the point of view of their European allies, the Americans seemed in no hurry. Mr. Tickell, who visited Washington in October for tripartite Anglo-US-West German discussions on the longer term aspects of Allied defence policy, returned under the impression that in the United States MBFR remained 'on the back burner' (No. 18). Yet the MBFR talks were about more than East/West relations. As Mr. Tickell later explained, Western governments were engaged in a dialogue with their own parliaments and domestic public opinion, and amongst themselves in trying to arrive at, and elaborate, agreed Allied negotiating positions (No. 25). This in part explains differences which arose between the FCO and the UK delegates at Vienna over the Western response to proposals put forward informally by Eastern participants on 15 October for 'first step' equal force reductions by each side, including Poland and West Germany, of 15,000 men with armaments and corresponding combat equipment. Mr. Tickell would have preferred to delay a formal response to this offer in order to 'enable governments to think about it, and be seen to be thinking about it, and to give [their] ultimate rejection greater weight'. But much to his evident irritation, at a meeting of the Ad Hoc Group on 6 November Mr. Rose agreed to the adoption of a Western plenary statement which omitted from a British compromise formula words indicating that the West might wish later to revert to the Soviet proposal (No. 19).

A subsequent visit by Mr. Tickell to Vienna revealed the extent to which the negotiations were being conducted in what he termed a 'curiously isolated atmosphere'. This, in his view, had encouraged the development of a series of 'overlapping group identities': delegates of East and West understood each other well, enjoyed good personal relations, went on coach trips together, and even had a song-book for their evening entertainments. On the Western side a tripartite group of British, US and West German delegates effectively provided the 'motor for the negotiations'. But while Mr. Tickell welcomed this close collaboration with the Americans, he was also wary of the dangers of European interests being too easily subordinated to the wishes of an overly-independent US delegation, and of local tactical considerations being given priority over broader matters of policy (*ibid.*). There were no easy solutions to these problems. NATO delegations in Vienna were responsible for deciding on day-to-day negotiating tactics, and Mr. Rose had only limited room for manoeuvre. The constraints imposed by alliance diplomacy could not be ignored, especially when Eastern participants followed up their 'first step' initiative with a proposal, tabled on 26 November, for a freeze on the manpower of both sides until the negotiations were completed. The proposal, whose very simplicity seemed calculated to appeal to public opinion in the West, once more put Allied negotiators on the defensive. Its acceptance would have confirmed the existing imbalance of forces in central Europe; its rejection, which the Americans favoured, would have presented the East with a considerable propaganda advantage (No. 20). Fortunately for Western delegates, the Russians chose not to exploit their proposal to the full. Influenced perhaps by the forthcoming official visit of the Prime Minister, Mr. H. Wilson, and the Foreign and Commonwealth Secretary, Mr. L.J. Callaghan, to Moscow, the Russians tended to play down the notion of a freeze when the fifth round of the talks began in January 1975, and they accepted without undue protest its formal rejection by the West (Nos. 21 and 23).

After fourteen months of negotiation Mr. Rose was convinced that if the Russians were ever going to make the concessions on MBFR thought essential by the West, they were unlikely to do so solely for anything the Allies might be able to offer them in Vienna. If an agreement were achieved, it would, he assumed, be because the Russians had 'taken a political decision that such an agreement [was] desirable for reasons partly or wholly extraneous to the negotiations themselves'. Nevertheless, he thought the consensus amongst Allied negotiators in Vienna was that the Russians might be persuaded to agree to asymmetrical manpower reductions if they were offered what the Americans had originally seen as a third negotiating option, notably a reduction of US nuclear systems in Europe in return for an equivalent percentage reduction in Soviet armoured attack capability (No. 20). The problem with such an offer was, as Mr. J. Mayne, Assistant Secretary of the Defence Staff, had already pointed out in a paper of 16 August, that it would mean the Allies conceding at an early stage that the principle of parity could be achieved by a 'by-and-large combat capability deal which would, to a considerable extent, short-circuit the measurement of parity in the basic currency of manpower numbers' (No. 17). A similar line was taken by Mr. Tickell when he, along with West German and other British diplomats, again went to Washington in February 1975, this time specifically to discuss the possible introduction of a nuclear package into the Vienna talks. There was by then little doubt in Mr. Tickell's mind that both air and nuclear forces would eventually be subject to negotiation. But at Washington he and his German colleagues argued that Option III was 'perhaps the most valuable negotiating card the Alliance had', and that it should be used to extract from the Russians, not just the withdrawal of a Soviet tank army and agreement to an undefined concept of a common ceiling, but a specific definition of a common ceiling in explicit numerical terms. He also questioned whether the deployment of Option III would lead to success in the negotiations. 'It might sugar the pill of the asymmetrical reductions we were asking in conventional forces; but', he added, 'it would not meet Soviet objections to the present Allied concept of phasing.' He wanted Option III to be delayed until conditions were right, and that he thought would not be the case until the latest round of US/Soviet Strategic Arms Limitation Talks (SALT II) was further advanced and Stage II (the negotiating stage) of the CSCE was nearer to its conclusion (No. 22).

In the event the whole of the fifth round of the talks was, as Mr. Rose noted, passed on the Western side 'under the shadow of Option III' (No. 23). Neither it nor the next round were particularly eventful. This could, to some extent, be attributed to political changes in North America and Western Europe. Pressure for force reductions was on the decline in Washington, and Herr H. Schmidt, the new West German Chancellor, was ready to take a tougher stance than his immediate predecessor in opposing measures that might obstruct future European defence collaboration. Even the Labour Government in Britain, which was committed to reducing military expenditure, insisted that cuts in British forces in Germany must depend on an MBFR accord. And within NATO it was accepted that MBFR were unlikely to yield substantial savings. Nevertheless, the gradual improvement of US/Soviet relations, the likelihood of a SALT II agreement, and the signing of the CSCE Final Act at Helsinki, encouraged British officials to think that the Soviet Union might make a fresh effort to achieve some kind of understanding at Vienna. Mr. Tickell, who left WOD in August 1975, thought the danger was that the Americans might settle with the Russians on Phase I terms affecting European interests in Phase II. In such circumstances, he believed that Britain should lean more towards the Germans than the Americans. 'We must', he minuted on 20 August, 'not expect the Americans to stay in Europe in their present numbers for ever, and the Germans, and with them the other Europeans, with whom we shall be increasingly associated, will constitute our essential shield' (No. 25).

The assumption that the successful conclusion of the CSCE would lead the Russians to modify their stance at Vienna soon proved illusory. As Mr. Rose acknowledged in a note of 17 November, their fundamental aims had not changed and, in his opinion, progress in SALT II remained a precondition for progress on MBFR. Nevertheless, he still believed there was a case for saying that the Russians needed and wanted an agreement. They wished, he reasoned, to maintain the momentum of *détente*; to satisfy the US desire for agreement on MBFR, to fulfil their own commitment to complement political with military *détente*, and to demonstrate either progress in MBFR or Western intransigence before the CSCE Review Conference scheduled for Belgrade in 1977. He also thought that they were still seeking a *droit de regard* over Western defence arrangements and a ceiling on the total of Western forces (No. 26). During the autumn of 1975 both sides at Vienna continued to reiterate their basic positions 'on familiar ground and in hallowed phrases', and only in the practical field of force definitions was any useful work done. Since, however, Eastern negotiators seemed to be well aware from press leaks that an important Western initiative was imminent, it was, in Mr. Rose's view, hardly surprising that 'they were content to sit tight and wait for it'. NATO had for some time had under consideration the tabling of proposals on the lines of Option III, and on 16 December the Western delegates formally offered to add to their existing proposals the withdrawal of certain US tactical nuclear armaments and the inclusion of air manpower in a combined common collective ceiling, within which the existing goal of a common ceiling on ground force manpower would be maintained. This was accompanied by a proviso, on which the British insisted and to which the US delegates initially objected, which stated explicitly that reductions in non-US Western equipment formed no part of the offer (No. 27).

The Western proposal represented in Mr. Rose's words the 'first substantive shift in the position of either side since 1973'. But few of the Western delegates were optimistic about Option III doing the 'final trick', and it was generally assumed that if there were to be an MBFR agreement on terms acceptable to the West further compromises would be needed (*ibid.*). Indeed, the Russians later claimed that the offer was inadequate, and when Dr. H. Kissinger, the US Secretary of State, visited Moscow early in the new year Mr. Brezhnev told him that the East intended to reject the Western offer and to put forward a new proposal. This, when it materialised on 19 February 1976, foresaw equal percentage Phase I reductions of US and Soviet forces, including specific weapons reductions, a 'freeze' in the size of the forces of all other direct participants, and equal national percentage reductions within a precisely defined subsequent phase. While the proposal thus went some way towards accepting the Western notion of phasing, it left the two sides as far apart as ever on such basic issues as asymmetric reductions and collective, as opposed to national, ceilings (No. 29). It also encouraged further speculation about the future of the talks. Mr. R. Hattersley, Minister of State for Foreign and Commonwealth Affairs, admitted at an Office meeting on 15 March that he remained sceptical about MBFR and feared that the Allies 'would be pushed into paying an unacceptable price for agreement'. Mr. Callaghan was, for his part, of the opinion that the political gain which the West had hoped to extract from the talks had largely been achieved: 'MBFR had enabled Western Governments to resist domestic pressures for unilateral force reductions'. The Soviet military superiority had in the meantime become much more of a reality; there had been a change of mood in the West with regard to *détente*; and Mr. Callaghan believed that the FCO should work on the assumption that time was on their side, at least until the CSCE Review Conference, and that they were in a position to bring pressure to bear on the Russians to 'adopt a more constructive attitude in Vienna'. He thought that he would have to convey to Mr. A. Gromyko, the Soviet Foreign Minister, the idea that Britain and its allies were in no particular hurry and could afford to play it long (No. 28).

Western participants may have appeared to have time on their side, but it was difficult to see how the Russians could be persuaded to move from their present stance. Mr. Rose wondered whether the UK should make MBFR a 'substantial issue in its relations with the Soviet Union' in the run-up the CSCE Review Conference, and whether they should take the lead in persuading other Western participants to do the same. There was, however, little enthusiasm in the FCO for the idea of establishing an explicit link between progress in the two negotiating fora. Mr. T.C. Wood of Defence Department (which had taken over responsibility for MBFR from WOD) was apprehensive lest the Soviet Union should then seek deliberately to embarrass the West by launching a new but unacceptable MBFR initiative on the eve of the Review Conference (No. 30). And others were of the opinion that such leverage as the West possessed in the CSCE ought to be used to exert pressure on the Russians on matters outside the military sphere. Certainly, there were those, like Mr. R.A. Hibbert (AUS), who thought that for propaganda purposes the West could exploit the Russian line that *détente* would have little meaning unless it produced progress in the military field, and that they might use the atmosphere surrounding CSCE to achieve progress in the MBFR talks. But Miss A.J.K. Bailes of the UK Permanent Delegation to NATO pointed to the obvious flaw in arguments in favour of linkage. 'There was', she told colleagues on 27 April, 'nothing that the East wanted to get out of the Belgrade meeting which would cause [the Russians] to be prepared to pay us a price in terms of MBFR.' The Russians had in any case not yet agreed that MBFR was at the centre of military *détente* (No. 31).

The evident reluctance of the Russians to go beyond their February proposals meant that when, in September 1976, the recently-knighted Sir C. Rose left Vienna to take up a new position in the Cabinet Office the same basic differences separated East and West. The former remained opposed to the concept of asymmetric force reductions, and the latter continued to insist that the existing relationship of forces was unsatisfactory since it was characterised by a serious imbalance in ground forces of the two sides to the advantage of the East. But the West's negotiating position had, as Mr. E. Bolland, Sir C. Rose's successor, explained in a letter of 3 November, been weakened by its inability to offer a satisfactory response to the Russians' tabling on 10 June of data on Warsaw Pact overall ground and air manpower in central Europe (No. 34). Western delegates had long argued that substantive progress in the negotiations would not be possible until the facts of the existing military situation in central Europe were known to both sides. The figures supplied by the East were, however, considerably lower than Western estimates, and purported to show that the size of NATO and Warsaw Pact forces in the area were 'broadly equivalent'. And France's opposition in NATO to the inclusion of its forces in any up-dated Western manpower data, obstructed the efforts of Western participants to draw their Eastern counterparts into any serious discussion of numbers. It was therefore impossible to make any progress in clarifying the basis on which the Eastern figures had been calculated, or towards understanding the discrepancies between data tabled and previous Western assessments (No. 32). Allied negotiators were for first time since the talks began unable to sustain their case with authoritative data and risked being pushed too far onto the defensive. They had finally drawn the East onto their negotiating ground, but found themselves unable to exploit the situation as they had once intended (No. 34).

Only on 16 December, the last day of the tenth round, were Western participants able to table up-dated figures on Allied manpower, but these did not include French forces in Germany which Paris continued to insist must be excluded from any common manpower ceilings. During the round both sides therefore spent much of their time 'restating and elaborating their respective positions', and Mr. Bolland was forced to conclude that there was at present little hope of there being early progress on the central issues of MBFR. Nevertheless, despite the stalemate in Vienna, by the end of 1976 the MBFR talks had, in the words of Mr. P.H. Moberly, AUS superintending the FCO's Defence Department, 'emerged as a prominent feature in the détente panorama' and were seen in the West as 'one of the means of testing the Soviet commitment to détente' (No. 36). Indeed, the Russians themselves contributed to this political elevation of MBFR.

Public opinion in the West may have long since lost interest in the negotiations, but the Russians seemed reluctant to envisage their demise, fearing lest this should demonstrate the limits of *détente* and represent a setback for their policies in Europe. Western governments meanwhile found in the Soviet Union's determination to maintain its military superiority in central Europe a motive and a pretext for avoiding damaging cuts to their own forces in the region. In consequence, the conference endured for another twelve years, and not until February 1989 were its seemingly fruitless labours brought to a conclusion. There was, as Mr. R.J. O'Neill, the last British Head of Delegation to the talks, later recalled, 'no moment when both sides really wanted an agreement, except on such one-sidedly favourable terms as to be unnegotiable; and for a number of years neither side was ready for an agreement at all'. Warsaw Pact participants had nevertheless come to accept the Western case for 'measures designed to promote the general goal of increasing security and stability'. And, as Mr. O'Neill also recognised, from the British point of view the talks had served their original purpose. They had forestalled any reduction of US troops in Europe, and the burden of unreduced military expenditure had contributed 'to the crippling of the Soviet economy', which by 1989 was the Soviet Government's 'greatest single problem' (Appendix III).

Cassandra to the Western Alliance

Throughout the MBFR negotiations British diplomats played a leading role in helping both to co-ordinate Allied strategy and tactics and to maintain a dialogue with Warsaw Pact participants. Yet, when the exploratory talks began in January 1973 the UK was, by comparison to other Western states, very much the 'odd man out' in its bilateral relations with the Soviet Union. Ever since the expulsion from London in September 1971 of 105 Russian diplomats accused of spying, the Soviet Government had, as Volume I reveals, assumed a distinctly cool attitude towards Britain. There were few contacts at Ministerial level and such relations as there were between the British Embassy in Moscow and the Ministries of Foreign Affairs and Trade tended to be devoid of content. This in the opinion of Sir J. Killick, the British Ambassador in Moscow, was due to more than KGB pique and the desire of the Soviet leadership to have Britain as a whipping-boy. Rather, he suspected it was because KGB and Soviet foreign policy interests were evolving in the same direction. Britain had just acceded to the European Community (EC), and Sir J. Killick thought that the Russians regarded the Conservative Government of Mr. E. Heath as the principal source of ideas which, if eventually accepted, could lead to the EC acquiring a significant defence identity. In addition, Mr. Heath was, as the Russians knew only too well, a strong advocate of greater economic and political integration in Western Europe. British aspirations were therefore, according to this thesis, at odds with Soviet objectives in Europe. FCO officials recognised, British interests could suffer if there were no improvement in Anglo-Soviet relations. 'At the least', Sir J. Killick observed, 'our lack of contact with and direct insight into top-level Soviet thinking may seriously undermine the credibility of our counsels within both NATO and the E[uropean] E[conomic] C[ommunity] and leave the three (or two) "main interlocutors" less open to our influence' (No. 37). It was also possible that the poor political relationship would have a detrimental affect upon British exporters, whose share of the Soviet market had diminished markedly during the previous five years (No. 38).

British Ministers were, however, in no mood 'to run after the Russians'. Experience suggested that this did not pay, and a memorandum prepared by EESD, and approved by the Cabinet Defence and Oversea Policy Committee on 6 April, asserted that any 'dramatic moves' on Britain's part 'would be interpreted by them as a sign of weakness' (*v. ibid.*). Sir A. Douglas-Home, the Foreign and Commonwealth Secretary, was ready to dissociate the Government from any misrepresentations of Soviet policy in the British press, but there were to be no concessions to the Russians on matters relating to the staffing of their mission in London, and, as Mr. Bullard affirmed, the British would not abandon their 'chosen role as a Cassandra to the Western alliance on the theme of the Soviet threat to Western Europe' (No. 40). Their stance seems not to have worked to Britain's disadvantage. During the spring of 1973 there were signs of an improvement in relations with Moscow, and in mid-April Mr. P. Walker, the Secretary of State for Trade and Industry, visited Russia for the second session of the Anglo-Soviet Joint Commission on trade and technology. Little resulted from this meeting beyond an understanding that both sides would aim to bring about a substantial increase in the volume of trade between Britain and the Soviet Union, and a British commitment to negotiate with the Russians a long-term economic cooperation agreement (No. 42). Indeed, Sir J. Killick was subsequently to complain over the way in which the pursuit of such cooperation agreements by Britain's EC partners seemed to circumvent the Common Commercial Policy towards the East which they were supposed to be establishing (No. 45). The welcome extended by the Soviet Government to Mr. Walker seemed, nevertheless, to demonstrate that the Russians had either accepted from the first that they could not keep Britain 'permanently in the doghouse', or had decided that it would be against their interests, with so much European diplomacy going on, to keep Britain 'totally at arm's length' (No. 42). And, following Mr. Heath's receipt on 25 July of a message 'from the [Soviet] leadership', stressing the importance of the two countries 'maintaining permanent contacts on a bilateral as well as a multilateral basis', Sir J. Killick wrote to Sir T. Brimelow, then Deputy Under-Secretary of State (DUS), that the spectacle of a major West European country coming to no apparent harm through remaining outside the Soviet embrace was inconvenient to the present leadership since it might start other countries looking too closely at what, if anything, they gained from being embraced themselves. He also guessed that during the multilateral preparatory talks for the CSCE the Russians had identified the British as one of the most effective delegations, and that they recognised that if they continued to keep Britain apart they had no hope of mitigating its influence during Stage II of the Conference at Geneva (No. 46).

Another explanation offered by Sir J. Killick for Soviet behaviour was Mr. Brezhnev's personal wish to have a meeting with the British Prime Minister in order to 'fill in the missing piece of his "summitry" jigsaw'. If matters were left to the Soviet Foreign Minister, Mr. A. Gromyko, relations would, he noted, remain on a 'level of surly inactivity almost indefinitely'. Other British diplomats were more wary. Mr. Bullard, suspected that the Russians aimed at 'cultivating the Prime Minister personally, in the hope of cutting out the hard-liners in the FCO' (*ibid.*) and, much to Sir J. Killick's irritation, in September Mr. Heath failed to respond to the Soviet resuscitation of an earlier invitation to him to visit Moscow (No. 48). Mr. Heath did, however, approve Sir A. Douglas-Home's acceptance of a similar invitation, and the Foreign and Commonwealth Secretary's reception in Moscow in December 1973 was regarded by British diplomats as signalling the end of Britain's virtual ostracism. Sir A. Douglas-Home insisted that it would be a disservice and would create an illusion leading to disappointment to gloss over Anglo-Soviet differences 'just for the sake of creating a "good atmosphere"' (No. 50). But Mr. Gromyko was evidently determined to avoid controversy: he offered no challenge to those aspects of British or Western policy which Soviet propaganda was currently attacking, and refused to be provoked. The visit, according to Sir T. Garvey, Sir J. Killick's successor in Moscow, 'not only buried the events of September 1971. It provided their final justification' (No. 52).

Sir T. Garvey was later to recall that both sides having drawn a line under past events, the Russians were at the beginning of 1974 ready to 'turn the page' in Anglo-Soviet relations (No. 72). But other international developments and Britain's own economic and political troubles stunted further initiatives. Barely two months after his arrival in Moscow Sir T. Garvey found it necessary to consider the impact of the energy crisis, itself a by-product of the latest Arab-Israeli war, and the associated inflationary pressures and industrial unrest in Western Europe upon East/West relations. From a Leninist perspective the West's economic problems seemed, as Sir T. Garvey pointed out, to confirm that 'what was foretold by the prophets [was], at last, verily coming to pass'. There may have been 'no let-up in pro-détente propaganda in the Soviet press', but predictions by Communist party ideologues of impending 'radical revolutionary transformations' did nothing in Mr. Bullard's judgement to remove underlying Western fears that 'one day doctrine and policy [would] coincide, and that the present separation between them [was] merely a question of tactics' (No. 53). It also seemed likely that rising fuel costs would check the economic growth of Western Europe and slow the process of integration. A paper prepared by the FCO's Planning Staff on future policy towards Eastern Europe, the final draft of which was approved by the Permanent Under-Secretary (PUS)'s Planning Committee on 12 February 1974, foresaw a consequent diminution of Western influence in the Soviet satellites. The 'magnetic attraction' which Western Europe had exercised upon the countries of the East would no longer be reinforced by a rise in material prosperity as rapid as that of the previous decades; and it was possible that 'economic depression and its social repercussions might dim the lustre of Western Europe while increasing the economic dependence of Eastern Europe on the Soviet Union' (No. 54).

In addition to these developments, the planning paper reckoned on a continuing shift in the strategic balance in Europe in favour of the Soviet Union and the further erosion of transatlantic unity. True, movements in Eastern Europe towards greater national independence, internal liberalisation and increased contacts with the West, would tend to reduce the Soviet Union's ability to bring pressure on Western Europe and ultimately stimulate some degree of beneficial change in Russia itself. But, as the paper recognised, if taken too far and too quickly, such changes might be regarded in Moscow as a threat to the *status quo* and increase the risk of Soviet aggression and renewed pressure upon the West. Military intervention by the Soviet Union in Eastern Europe 'might strike a useful blow against wishful thinking' in the West; it would also check progress throughout the region, and would certainly not advance British or Western European interests. All this in the view of the Planning Staff militated against any further extension of purely British efforts to stimulate change in Eastern Europe. British interests there were, in any case, 'insufficient to justify the diversion of resources from more remunerative employment or the running of risks'. For the moment, FCO Planners favoured efforts to encourage a more co-ordinated West European policy towards the East. It would advance EC integration, reduce unrestricted competition in Eastern Europe from which, given Britain's doubtful economic prospects, Britain stood to lose, and restrain the tendency of other EC members to adopt an unduly conciliatory policy towards East European governments and the Soviet Union. 'A common West European policy might', the paper asserted, 'be "softer" than we would wish, but it would certainly be less dangerously so than the kind of Ostpolitik which might be pursued by a future government of the FRG [Federal Republic of Germany] that had become disillusioned by the prospects for Western European unity' (*ibid.*).

Mr. J. Amery, Minister of State for Foreign and Commonwealth Affairs, was likewise of the opinion that sustained 'progress towards European political union and ... defence union' offered a means towards increasing the independence of the East European states from Moscow. A prosperous and united Europe would act as a magnet on the East European countries, it would reduce fears on their part of German 'revanchism', and they might find it easier to associate, and even 'converge', with a European Community which had an identity distinct from the broader Atlantic community. But Mr. Amery, who had been responsible for commissioning the Planning Staff paper, was far more pessimistic than some of his officials about the prospects for genuine *détente* in East/West relations. That, he argued in a paper drafted in February 1974, would be 'hard enough to achieve ... with a powerful but "have not" Muscovite Empire with no claim to universalism ... it is virtually impossible to do so with an Empire whose "establishment" depends for its own survival on its allegiance to and encouragement of a revolutionary doctrine and movement which have the overthrow of other established states and their subordination to Moscow as their declared aim'. Any accommodation with the West would, he thought, in the present circumstances be purely tactical, a truce rather than a peace. Mr. Amery believed that the problem might be solved if the Soviet leaders were persuaded to accept the concept of 'convergence', the then fashionable notion that the communist and capitalist orders would eventually evolve into a single system. The process of drawing the satellites away from the Soviet grip must, however, be gradual. It might even, Mr. Amery suggested, 'lead to the gentle decline of the Soviet Empire into a Soviet Commonwealth with its own Arnold Smith and Marlborough House' (No. 55).

This paper had been intended by Mr. Amery to serve as a basis for discussion amongst Britain's Ambassadors in Eastern Europe and the Soviet Union at their biennial conference, then planned for the spring. But Britain's domestic troubles, the challenge posed by a miners' strike to the Government's efforts to impose wages restraint, and Mr. Heath's decision to call a General Election, meant that it was to prove little more than an academic exercise—a reflection of Conservative thinking on East/West relations rather than a guide to future policy. The election, held on 28 February, the day on which Mr. Amery submitted his paper to Sir A. Douglas-Home, resulted in the Conservatives losing their majority in Parliament and Labour's return to power. Mr. Callaghan, the new Foreign and Commonwealth Secretary, seemed determined to assume a more positive attitude towards the East. On 19 March he told the Commons that the Labour Government would 'look for opportunities to build a safer and more productive relationship with the Soviet Union'. The statement was hardly inconsistent with the course on which the FCO had already embarked. Officials were nevertheless hard pressed to come up with new ideas with which to give substance to Ministerial aspirations and rhetoric. This was only too apparent in the preparation of a general position paper on the current state of Britain's relations with Eastern Europe and the Soviet Union, which Mr. Callaghan requested from Mr. Hattersley. 'To seek for "new" attitudes and initiatives may', Mr. Bullard commented on this exercise, 'be an understandable emotion, but it confuses the issue by obliging officials to ransack their minds and cupboards for types of action which have never previously been thought to be in the British interest, but which would now be so represented. Naturally, these do not exist.' Mr. Hattersley was evidently not convinced. In the final version of his paper, completed on 30 July, he asserted that too often in the past the FCO had 'confused the maximisation of British interests with the minimisation of the interests of the Soviet Union'; that traditionally the Office had believed that Britain could only secure adequate protection of its interests by adopting a 'purely defensive posture'; and that in his view Britain's interests could be better served by 'activity' (No. 65).

EESD officials had reason to question this remedy. The results of Britain's active participation in the multilateral processes of East/West *détente* had so far been disappointing. In Mr. Bullard's opinion 'the tightening of the Soviet screw all over Eastern Europe in the last 2 years [was] unmistakable' (No. 57). Moreover, in the face of divisions within the Western alliance and a Britain beset with economic and political difficulties, Moscow had seemed to lose interest in cultivating closer relations with London (No. 59). Mr. Gromyko did not even bother to reply to a personal message from Mr. Callaghan suggesting how bilateral relations might be improved through increased contacts between British and Soviet officials and politicians (No. 61). There was, in any case, as a JIC paper of 6 May contended, the danger that the Russians were simply using the policy of *détente* 'to soften up the West while maintaining their long term aims and improving their military strength' (No. 58). Mr. Hattersley, nevertheless, believed that the British should make it clear that they no longer regarded themselves as the 'sheet anchor of defence against the hurricane of détente'. He believed Britain could do more within the Western alliance to help the MBFR negotiations along, and he recommended that they should be ready to go further in blurring the distinction between the two phases of MBFR and be more forthcoming on the inclusion of nuclear weapons in any agreement. Yet, where bilateral relations with the Soviet Union and its allies were concerned, Mr. Hattersley's paper had little more to propose than increased Ministerial visits and more active trade promotion. As he recognised, the real success of any general plan for the improvement of East/West relations must be determined by the 'methodical application of small initiatives' each of which had to be worked out to ensure that it was suitable for the country at which it was directed. Moreover, Mr. Hattersley stressed the need for the UK to overcome its own domestic troubles, including those in Northern Ireland, and the importance of continued Western unity. Although the new Government were committed to renegotiating the terms of Britain's entry into the EC, and Mr. Callaghan was evidently sceptical about the whole European project, Mr. Hattersley felt Britain could 'avoid some of the self-inflicted wounds which are caused in part by our inability to solve our economic difficulties and in part by what has been our ambivalence towards the United States and may now become our detachment from the EEC' (No. 66).

The exact status of Mr. Hattersley's paper was to remain, in Mr. Bullard's words, 'a little ambiguous'. The Government was without a Parliamentary majority and an Office meeting on 9 September accepted that any decisions on the basis of the paper would have to await the outcome of another General Election in the autumn. This, Mr. Bullard observed, was 'a rather foggy outcome to what [had] throughout been a rather foggy exercise' (*ibid.*). British policy towards Eastern Europe had in any case to be viewed in the broader context of changes taking place in East/West, and more particularly US/Soviet, relations. Slow progress in the CSCE, virtual deadlock in the MBFR negotiations, uncertainties about what could be achieved in SALT II, differences between Moscow and Washington over developments in the Middle East and Cyprus, the debilitating affect of the Watergate affair on the American Presidency, and opposition in Congress to Dr. Kissinger's dealings with the Soviet Union, all seemed to threaten the future of *détente* (Nos. 62 and 63). In a minute of 15 July, Sir J. Killick (now DUS) speculated on whether British diplomats 'should start thinking privately about the possible consequences of a breakdown in the US/Soviet relationship, with or without the disappearance of the President and/or Dr. Kissinger' (No. 65). Yet, there were still those, like Mr. Bullard, who were concerned about the possible emergence of a US/Soviet 'condominium' and its potential for damaging the interests of America's European allies (No. 57). European fears about US intentions were not allayed by the *communiqué* issued at the end of President Nixon's visit to Moscow in June 1974 which appeared to endorse Soviet views on the CSCE. Sir J. Killick was nevertheless inclined to attribute lapses of this kind more to the devious methods employed by Dr. Kissinger, than to the policies he pursued, and he thought it wiser to avoid such emotive phrases as 'US/Soviet Hegemonism' which carried so many 'undesirable overtones' (No. 68).

The Russians might likewise have been wondering about the value of their relationship with the United States. Congress's refusal to grant the Soviet Union most favoured nation treatment, its withholding of commercial credits, American demands for the adoption of a more liberal Soviet emigration policy, and the expansion of US influence in the Middle East, provided them with what Sir T. Garvey called a '*prima facie* case for reassessing ... the assumptions of the policy of détente'. But Sir T. Garvey also believed that the Russians saw in *détente* a phase of peaceful coexistence which would allow them to make economic progress and gain access to Western technology. Sir J. Killick agreed. 'On a broader time-scale', he observed, 'I cannot see Brezhnev and his colleagues abandoning détente so long as they are able to assure themselves and the country at large that in a general sense it has lubricated the wheel of history (in their determinist sense) and will continue to do so better than any other known product' (No. 69). Mr. Bullard, nonetheless, claimed to detect a shift in Soviet attitudes towards the outside world. From the unhurried approach of the Soviet delegation to the resumption of Stage II of the CSCE in the autumn of 1974 and the 'Olympian tone' assumed by Mr. Gromyko in his September address to the UN General Assembly, he deduced that they might be entering a 'new phase' in East/West relations. The events of the past year had, he wrote in letter to Sir T. Garvey of 4 October, 'greatly strengthened the streak of self-reliance and self-sufficiency ... which [had] always been so strong in the Russians national character. During 1974 the international economic situation had been transformed to the detriment of the West, and the Russians had witnessed the removal of '3 glittering figures' (President G. Pompidou of France, Chancellor W. Brandt of West Germany, and President Nixon) prominent in the politics of *détente*. They might, Mr. Bullard suggested, be asking whether it was time 'to stop bothering about far-off countries of which [they knew] nothing, and to concentrate on events at home and within the Soviet empire'. However, he expected *détente* to remain the Soviet 'watchword', even if it were perhaps given a less active interpretation (No. 71).

The New Phase

In the autumn of 1974 bilateral relations between Britain and the Soviet Union were also seen as entering a 'new phase'. Labour's victory in the General Election of 10 October left Mr. Wilson free to accept a long-standing Soviet invitation to the Prime Minister to visit Russia, and on 13 February 1975 he and Mr. Callaghan travelled to Moscow for talks with the Soviet leadership. Sir T. Garvey anticipated that this visit, the first by a British Prime Minister to the Soviet Union since Mr. Wilson's visit in 1968, would be a 'landmark'. Its two main aims were, in the Ambassador's opinion, an improvement in the tone and atmosphere of Anglo-Soviet relations, and the achievement of a substantial increase in trade. But he reminded Mr. Callaghan in a despatch of 27 November 1974 that, while during the 'unproductive' period of Anglo-Soviet relations the British had not been able to take advantage of the extended range of contacts that *détente* made possible, in the eyes of Russia's leaders *détente* was neither open-ended nor applicable within the Soviet Union itself. Furthermore, he explained in language similar to that employed in Mr. Hattersley's paper that, unlike other middle-ranking powers which enjoyed specific advantages in Russia because of geography and history, such leverage as Britain possessed in Moscow depended in the final analysis upon its 'influence in West European and transatlantic counsels' (No. 72). 'The

Russians', he noted in a telegram of 16 January, 'do not regard good relations with us as essential. They can get on without us … Accordingly if we are to get anywhere we shall need to work our passage' (No. 73).

The visit was in fact preceded by a good deal of haggling on the part of the Russians about dates and press announcements. Soviet officials prevaricated over the form and contents of documents to be signed, and their counter-draft of an Anglo-Soviet Joint Statement proposed by the FCO was, according to Mr. Bullard, a 'scissors and paste job … using more scissors than paste'. There was also a question mark over whether Mr. Brezhnev would be fit enough to greet Mr. Wilson (No. 73). In the event, however, Sir T. Garvey considered the visit a notable success. Mr. Brezhnev attended three sessions of the talks (even finding time during the first of these to joke with Mr. Wilson over the election of Mrs Thatcher as leader the Conservative Opposition), a Kremlin dinner and the final document signing ceremony; the Soviet media gave exceptional coverage to the presence of the British Ministers in Moscow; and in an FCO guidance telegram of 17 February Mr. Callaghan observed that it seemed clear that the Soviet side 'wished to open a new phase, in which Britain [moved] up alongside France and the FRG in Brezhnev's pattern of détente diplomacy' (No. 76). True, much of the first formal meeting between the British and Soviet leaders on 13 February was taken up with the restatement by both parties of positions assumed in other fora: Mr. Brezhnev's complaint that in the CSCE 'people were digging around in the Third Basket [those issues dealing with human contacts and the freer dissemination of information] discussing tourism and questions of opening a bar or a café in someone else's country' was countered by Mr. Callaghan's assertion that Basket III was 'about the quality of peace' (No. 74). But in Sir T. Garvey's estimate the tough bargaining which accompanied the visit and the seven resulting documents worked, on balance, to Britain's advantage. They offered opportunities both for further political cooperation and for the expansion of British trade with Russia. In addition, the Russians explicitly endorsed the notion of a 'new phase' in Anglo-Soviet relations, and subscribed to a definition of 'peaceful co-existence' devoid of such references to a continuing ideological struggle as had previously made the concept so repugnant to Western diplomats (No. 76). It would, Sir T. Brimelow, now PUS, commented, henceforth be up to the British Government to try to impose on further developments in their relations with the Soviet Union a pattern which suited them and which was 'not dictated from the Soviet side' (No. 77).

The Soviet Union's policy towards Britain was nonetheless bound to be in part conditioned by its relations with the United States and other Western governments. Mr. Brezhnev may have wished to demonstrate the 'completeness' of his peace policy, and the warm reception extended to the British Ministers in Moscow may, as Sir T. Garvey suggested, have been directed towards silencing Britain's 'discordant voice in the choir of détente'. But the Ambassador also thought that Mr. Brezhnev wanted to reaffirm the Soviet Government's commitment to *détente* following its recent rejection of conditions set by the American Congress on the application of its projected trade treaty with the United States (No. 76). Indeed, in the early spring of 1975 British diplomats once more began to speculate about the future of *détente*. The collapse of US policy in south-east Asia, setbacks for Dr. Kissinger's diplomacy in the Middle East, the prospect of the Communists coming to power in Portugal, and divisions within NATO resulting from Turkey's military intervention in Cyprus, appeared to indicate that international developments were moving in Moscow's favour. There was always the possibility that the Soviet Union might seek to use this situation in order to expand its influence, and that this would in turn encourage opposition to *détente* in the United States (No. 78). For the moment, however, Sir P. Ramsbotham, Britain's Ambassador in Washington, considered that there were few indications that the present US Administration was either disillusioned 'with its relatively equable relationship with the Soviet Union' or contemplated alternative policies (No. 79). And although the SAL negotiations seemed beset with difficulties over verification and new weapon developments, progress in Stage II of the CSCE at Geneva opened the way to the Helsinki summit in the summer. Meanwhile, the docking on 17 July of the US *Apollo* and the Soviet *Soyuz* spacecraft seemed to offer scientific as well as symbolic proof of the achievements of *détente* (No. 80).

The conclusion of the Helsinki Final Act was soon followed by revived speculation amongst British diplomats about the future direction of Soviet foreign policy and Mr. Brezhnev's role in its management. The 25th Congress of the Soviet Communist Party was due to assemble in February 1976 and it was assumed that Mr. Brezhnev, whose state of health remained in doubt, would then want to report on his foreign policy successes. But plans for the summoning of a Conference of European Communist Parties also seemed likely to reveal significant differences between those Soviet party ideologists who wished to exploit the current 'crisis of capitalism' and Western communist party leaders committed to a democratic form of socialist society. FCO officials did not share the view of American analysts that Mr. Brezhnev and his colleagues were becoming impatient with the constraints of *détente* and were ready to encourage a more militant line. Mr. B.G. Cartledge, Mr. Bullard's successor as Head of EESD, admitted in a minute of 14 October that at a time when Soviet military power had never been greater and when Moscow might have been expected to exploit Western difficulties to good effect, the 'promotion of Soviet interests across the globe [seemed] to have slowed to a halt'. The American withdrawal from south-east Asia had led to increased Sino-Soviet rivalry; Dr. Kissinger had achieved a disengagement agreement between Egypt and Israel without Soviet participation; the Communists in Portugal had failed to consolidate their influence; a SALT II agreement had not yet materialised; in the MBFR talks the Russians risked being charged with opposing military *détente*; and, despite the euphoria initially generated by the CSCE, the Final Act had been greeted with widespread cynicism in the West. Some of the Soviet establishment might, Mr. Cartledge suspected, be asking whether in these circumstances Soviet national interests were not suffering as a result of the limits set by *détente*. He nevertheless thought that the majority in the *Politburo* would continue to consider the policy worthwhile. 'The over-riding Soviet objective of maintaining a sufficiently stable international climate to make a revival of the arms race unlikely and increased economic cooperation with the West possible is', he noted, 'still being achieved.' Sir T.

Garvey agreed. The abandonment of Mr. Brezhnev's 'peace policy' was, he argued, 'hardly on the cards' (Nos. 81 and 82).

There may in Sir T. Garvey's opinion have been 'no credible alternative to Westpolitik for the Russians to adopt', but their pursuit of a 'relaxation of world tension' was, the Ambassador insisted, conditional on their 'maintaining to the fullest extent practicable the imperial aims of old Russia and the revolutionary aims of the Marxist myth' (No. 85). Mr. Callaghan made the point himself when, on 10 November, he told the House of Commons that the CSCE had brought no overnight end to East/West tensions: there remained, he said, 'great ideological differences' and there was 'no armistice in the war of ideas'. And his Political Adviser, Mr. T. McNally, was equally emphatic in advocating Britain s engagement in a 'positive [ideological] war of movement—advancing our own ideas, challenging theirs' (No. 83). The same theme was taken up by British diplomats when the long-postponed Conference of Heads of Mission in Eastern Europe and the Soviet Union assembled in London during 17–19 November. A paper presented by EESD argued that there was no longer any point in telling the Russians that the ideological struggle was inconsistent with *détente*, and that the West should take advantage of the Final Act 'to make the contest more equal by widening and improving the channels through which Western ideas and objective information about the West [could] reach the citizens of the Soviet Union and Eastern Europe'. But Helsinki had also increased the threat of hostile propaganda from the East (No. 84). Already in a minute of 14 February Mr. G. Foggon, the FCO's Overseas Labour Adviser, had drawn Mr. Bullard's attention to the way in which, during a period of industrial unrest, increased contacts between trade union representatives from East and West tended to weaken the resolve of British trade unionists to resist communist infiltration and disruption (No. 75). Moreover, although monetary inflation had so far probably done more than *détente* to increase pressure on Western governments to reduce defence expenditure, the easing of East/West tensions made it all the more difficult for them to counter Soviet efforts to nurture in the West a public mood favourable to unilateral disarmament. Western societies were, according to the EESD paper, 'faced to a greater extent than at any time since 1939 with the complex task of maintaining their economic and social integrity, and their will to defend themselves, if necessary, in a relatively relaxed, non-confrontational situation' (No. 84).

British diplomats were, however, fully alive to the benefits to be derived from continuing with *détente*. Its prolongation reduced the likelihood of a nuclear war, and placed constraints on Soviet 'mischief-making': its replacement by confrontation would, according to EESD, 'quickly bring to a standstill those trends in the societies of the Soviet Union and Eastern Europe which [were] desirable from the Western point of view' (*ibid.*) This was endorsed by Mr. Callaghan in a despatch, drafted as a follow-up to the Ambassadors' Conference, and sent on 11 March 1976 to Sir H. Smith, the new British Ambassador in Moscow. He was also sceptical about the suggestion that Britain should give 'greater priority to dealing directly with the "management" in Moscow' rather than the governments of its East European allies. The development of a network of links between the two halves of Europe was, he reasoned, 'at least a marginal inhibition on the application of the "Brezhnev Doctrine", and [that was] in itself a worthwhile objective'. And Mr. Callaghan recalled with approval an earlier despatch from Sir T. Garvey in which the Ambassador had asserted that it was not only the communists who wanted to promote revolutionary change; 'we also heartily desire change in Soviet society and the others that emulate it'. Traditional attitudes and practices were unlikely to be modified or reversed overnight, but he was determined to use the CSCE Final Act to press for change. Mr. Callaghan was still, however, perturbed by the lack of progress in dealing with other aspects of *détente*. Although Soviet propaganda made much of the need to move from political to military *détente*, the previous five years had witnessed the greatest build-up of Soviet military power since the Second World War, and in the MBFR talks the Russians had seemed to resist all measures which might impair the superiority of Warsaw Pact forces in Europe. The Soviet Union's military might had meanwhile been deployed to swing the political balance in the former Portuguese colony of Angola in favour of the Marxist-orientated MPLA (*Movimento Popular de Libertacao de Angola*) (No. 87).

Soviet involvement in southern Africa (British reactions to which will be documented in a later volume) was taken up by Mr. Callaghan in exchanges with the Russians early in 1976. The massive military assistance given by the Soviet Union to the MPLA and the presence in Angola of Soviet-backed Cuban forces had already attracted considerable criticism in the West, and this in turn seemed destined to threaten the achievements of *détente*. 'You should', Mr. Callaghan instructed Sir H. Smith in a telegram of 29 January, 'impress upon the Russians that, while we have no objection to the contest of ideas, we object strongly to efforts to promote the solution by force of political problems arising in countries far from the Soviet Union's territory' (No. 86). The issue came up again when in March, during a visit to London by Mr. Gromyko, Mr. Callaghan emphasised that *détente* was 'indivisible', and that British public opinion was 'not likely to accept that détente in Europe should be immune from developments in the African continent' (No. 88). Southern Africa figured equally large in the continuing public debate in the United States on the merits of *détente*. American critics of *détente* were becoming increasingly vocal in expressing their concern about Soviet military might, the prospect of the Russians exploiting a SALT II agreement in order to secure a 'war-winning capability', and their rigid suppression of internal dissent, and Sir P. Ramsbotham reported that events in Angola had 'confirmed the pessimists' fears and deepened their anger at US impotence in the face of Soviet "adventurism"'. In a television interview on 1 March President Ford even announced that he was dropping the word '*détente*' as a description of US policy towards the Soviet Union: henceforth he would describe the process as a 'policy of peace through strength'. This did not in Sir P. Ramsbotham's opinion mean that the US Administration was intending to abandon the central core of Dr. Kissinger's policy towards the Soviet Union. However, he thought that it did reflect a change in atmosphere which would affect the conduct of US/Soviet relations during the remainder of the year (No. 89).

Other British diplomats took a rather bleaker view of the future for East/West relations. Mr. Cartledge thought that the Soviet Union would 'continue to endeavour both to have its détente cake and to eat it', and that the Russians would go on seizing such opportunities as offered themselves for extending their influence until the Americans were prepared to deploy the full extent of their power in the world and the Soviet leadership were made to believe in the American will to do so (No. 90). He was also very much aware of the fragility of Anglo-Soviet relations. Mr. Gromyko's visit to London in March had produced 'no surprises and no drama' and this, according to Mr. Callaghan, was 'exactly what was needed' for the 'consolidation of the improved Anglo-Soviet working relationship' (No. 88). But while 1975 had witnessed a doubling of British exports to the Soviet Union, the Russians had been slow to take up more than a small fraction of the commercial credit offered to them during Mr. Wilson's Moscow visit, and Mr. Brezhnev seemed in no hurry to pay a return visit to London. Indeed, on 7 September 1976 a Soviet diplomat in London, told Mr. McNally that 'there was a strong feeling on the Soviet side that Anglo-Soviet relations were somewhat in the doldrums, and … may have slipped back since the Wilson visit of 1975' (No. 91). The remark may have been triggered by HMG's denial, on security grounds, of a visa to the Counsellor-designate at the Soviet Embassy. But relations were also disturbed by a number of relatively minor bilateral difficulties regarding such matters as British objections to plans for a new Soviet Embassy building in London and the withholding of permission for Soviet 'research vessels' to visit British ports. There were signs too of increased public disillusionment with *détente* policies, in part, according to one senior official, 'the result of Soviet actions and in part the consequence of unrealistic expectations generated by CSCE'. And Mr. A. Crosland, who in April had succeeded Mr. Callaghan as Foreign and Commonwealth Secretary, was, Mr. Cartledge observed, 'somewhat disenchanted with the development of our bilateral relations with the East' (No. 92).

In essence, as a paper prepared by the FCO's Planning Staff made clear, it was difficult to see any way, apart from Western acceptance of Soviet hegemony, by which the confrontational element in East/West relations might eventually be eliminated. Negotiations between the two sides seemed inevitably to combine a cooperative approach towards solving difficult problems with a confrontational approach aimed at achieving unilateral advantages (No. 93). *Détente* may, as Mr. Crosland told an Office meeting on 6 December, have led to a *modus vivendi* between East and West, and it may also have defused tension (No. 94). Yet, even in the context of CSCE, measures such as those embodied in Basket III were evidently perceived by the Russians as potentially subversive. Moreover, despite initial British scepticism with regard to MBFR, in the view of the FCO's Planners *détente* in Europe could neither be stable nor complete until it was carried into the sphere of conventional armaments. Soviet armed forces in central Europe had over the previous five years been systematically re-equipped with more effective and sophisticated weapons, with the result that the qualitative advantage once possessed by NATO had been largely eroded. There was therefore 'a strong case for making MBFR the proving ground for détente', and for bringing the Vienna talks more to the attention of the public in order to make the maintenance of an adequate Western defence effort all the more easier (No. 93). 'In short', noted Sir

J. Killick (now Britain's Permanent Representative to NATO), 'we must somehow make credibly clear that not just [the CSCE Review Conference at] Belgrade, but the whole process of détente (its achievements as well as its future development) is at stake unless the present Soviet military build-up is at least halted.' Mr. Crosland was of much the same opinion. He readily agreed with the suggestion made by Sir M. Palliser, Sir T. Brimelow's successor as PUS, that the draft of a speech which he was due to make at a NATO Ministerial meeting and upon which he intended subsequently to draw, should be 'vulgarised' in order to make the public more fully aware of the situation at Vienna. Disturbed too by Soviet conduct in southern Africa, Mr. Crosland used the same speech to label the Soviet Union an 'imperialist power' (No. 94). By December 1976 the language, if not yet the mechanisms, of *détente* was in recession.

Acknowledgements

In accordance with the Parliamentary announcement cited in the Introduction to the Series, the Editors have had the customary freedom in the selection and arrangement of documents including full access to all classes of FCO documentation. There have, in the case of the present volume, been no exceptional cases, provided for in the Parliamentary announcement where it has been necessary on security grounds to restrict the availability of particular documents, editorially selected in accordance with regular practice.

The main source of documentation in this volume has been the archives of the FCO held, pending their transfer to the Public Record Office, by Records and Historical Department (RHD), and I should like to thank Mrs Heather Yasamee, the Head of RHD, and her staff for all their help and support. In this respect, I am particularly indebted to Ms. Joan McPherson, the former Head of Retrieval Services, and her colleagues at Hanslope Park for their diligence in dealing with our many enquiries and requests. I am also grateful to the Historical and Records Section of the Cabinet Office, and the Departmental Records Officers of the MoD and the Department of Trade and Industry, for permission to publish and cite documents in their custody; to Sir Clive Rose and Sir John Thomson for their advice and information; and to my colleagues, Dr. Nigel Jarvis, for his intellectual, and Mrs Diane Morrish and Miss Jackie Till, for their secretarial, assistance. Special thanks are finally due to the FCO's Chief Historian, Ms. Gill Bennett OBE, who has invariably been ready to offer guidance and support; and to my Research Assistants, Dr. Martin Longden, who raised the first two chapters from the deadlock of MBFR, and Dr. Kirsty Buckthorp, who brought new order to the 'new phase' in documenting *détente*.

KEITH A. HAMILTON

July 2000

LIST OF PLATES

CONTENTS

ABBREVIATIONS FOR PRINTED SOURCES

Cmnd 6932 | *Selected Documents Related to Problems of Security and Cooperation in Europe 1954–77* (London: HMSO, 1977)

Grenville | J.A.S. Grenville (ed.), *The Major International Treaties 1914–1973: A history and guide with texts* (London: Methuen, 1974)

Keesing's | *Keesing's Contemporary Archives* (London: Keesing's Publications, 1975)

Kissinger *Years of Upheaval* | H.A. Kissinger, *Years of Upheaval* (London: Weidenfeld and Nicolson and Michael Joseph, 1982)

Kissinger *Years of Renewal* | H.A. Kissinger, *Years of Renewal* (New York: Simon & Schuster, 1999)

Parl. Debs., 5th ser., H. of C. | *Parliamentary Debates (Hansard), Fifth Series, House of Commons, Official Report* (London: 1909f.)

Public Papers: Nixon, 1971, 1974 | *Public Papers of the Presidents of the United States* (Washington: GPO, 1965f.)

Volume I | *Documents on British Policy Overseas*, Series III, Volume I, *Britain and the Soviet Union, 1968–72* (London: TSO, 1997)

Volume II | *Documents on British Policy Overseas*, Series III, Volume II, *The Conference on Security and Cooperation in Europe, 1972–75* (London: TSO, 1997)

Treaty Series | *Treaty Series* (London: HMSO, 1892f.)

UNGA, A/PV 2240 | *Official Records of the Sessions of the UN General Assembly. 6th Special Session Plenary Meetings, A/PV 2240*

ABBREVIATED DESIGNATIONS

ACDD	Arms Control and Disarmament Department, FCO
ACDA	Arms Control and Disarmament Agency
APAG	NATO's Atlantic Policy Advisory Group
AUCCTU	All Union Central Council of Trades Unions of the USSR
AUS	Assistant Under-Secretary of State
BAOR	British Army of the Rhine
BBC	British Broadcasting Corporation
BW	Biological weapons
CBI	Confederation of British Industry
CCD	Conference of the Committee on Disarmament
CCMS	Committee on the Challenges to Modern Society
CCP	Common Commercial Policy
CDE	Conference on Confidence and Security-Building Measures and Disarmament in Europe
CDS	Chief of the Defence Staff
CDU	*Christlich Demokratische Union*/Christian Democratic Union
CENTO	Central Treaty Organisation
CFE	Conventional Forces in Europe Talks
CIEC	Conference on International Economic Cooperation
CMEA/ COMECON	Council for Mutual Economic Assistance
COCOM	Coordinating Committee on Exports to Communist Countries
CPGB	Communist Party of Great Britain
CPSU	Communist Party of the Soviet Union
CRE	Commercial Relations and Export Division of the DOT

CSCE	Conference on Security and Cooperation in Europe
CTB	Comprehensive Nuclear Test Ban
CW	Chemical weapons
DOAE	Defence Operational Analysis Establishment
DOP	Defence and Oversea Policy Committee
DOT	Department of Trade
DPC	NATO's Defence Planning Committee
DTI	Department of Trade and Industry
DUS	Deputy Under-Secretary of State
EC	European Community/ Communities
ECE	Economic Commission for Europe
EEC	European Economic Community
EESD	Eastern European and Soviet Department, FCO
EID	European Integration Department, FCO
EUO	Cabinet Official Committee on Europe
EPC	European Political Cooperation
ETU	Electrical Trades Union
FBS	Forward Based Nuclear Delivery Systems
FCO	Foreign and Commonwealth Office
FDP	*Freie Demokratische Partei*/Free Democrat Party
FRG	Federal Republic of Germany
GDR	German Democratic Republic
GATT	General Agreement on Tariffs and Trade
GLA	Guidelines Limitations Area
GNP	Gross National Product
HMG	Her Majesty's Government

ICBM	Intercontinental Ballistic Missile	OECD	Organisation for Economic Cooperation and Development
INF	Intermediate-range Nuclear Forces	PCP	Portuguese Communist Party
IPU	Inter-Parliamentary Union	PLO	Palestine Liberation Organisation
IRA	Irish Republican Army	PQ	Parliamentary Question
IRD	Information Research Department, FCO	PUS	Permanent Under-Secretary
ISC	International Student Conference	RCDS	Royal College of Defence Studies
IUS	International Union of Students	SACEUR	Supreme Allied Commander, Europe
KGB	*Komitet Gosudarstvennoi Besopasnosti*/Committee of State Security	SALT	Strategic Arms Limitation Talks
LSE	London School of Economics and Political Science	SCTS	State Committee for Science and Technology
MBFR	Mutual and Balanced Force Reductions	SHAPE	Supreme Headquarters Allied Powers Europe
MFA	Ministry of Foreign Affairs	SLBM	Submarine-launched Ballistic Missiles
MFN	Most Favoured Nation	SPD	*Sozialdemokratische Partei Deutschlands*/Social Democrat Party
MIFT	My immediately following telegram	SSM	Surface to surface missiles
MIRV	Multiple Independently Targetable Reentry Vehicle	START	Strategic Arms Reduction Talks
MIPT	My immediately preceding telegram	STD	Soviet Trade Delegation
MoD	Ministry of Defence	TUC	Trades Union Congress
MPT	Multilateral Preparatory Talks	UKDEL	United Kingdom Delegation
MRCA	Multi-Role Combat Aircraft	UKMIS	United Kingdom Mission
NAC	North Atlantic Council	UKREP	United Kingdom Representative
NASA	National Aeronautics and Space Administration	UN	United Nations
NATO	North Atlantic Treaty Organisation	UNCTAD	United Nations Conference on Trade and Development
NEM	New Economic Mechanism	UNGA	United Nations General Assembly
NGA	Non-Guidelines Area	UNCLOS	United Nations Conference on the Law of the Sea
NPT	Nuclear Non-proliferation Treaty	WFTU	World Federation of Trade Unions
NSC	National Security Council	WMD	Western Military Districts
NSWP	Non-Soviet Warsaw Pact countries	WOD	Western Organisations Department, FCO
NUS	National Union of Students	WPC	World Peace Council
NUSWP	Non-United States Western Participants		

CHAPTER SUMMARIES

CHAPTER I

Mutual and Balanced Force Reductions in Central Europe:
The Exploratory Talks, 21 April 1972–12 July 1973

CHAPTER II

MBFR: The Vienna Negotiations,
11 October 1973–22 December 1976

CHAPTER III

Détente in Anglo-Soviet Relations,
5 January 1973–4 October 1974

CHAPTER IV

The New Phase,
27 November 1974–7 December 1976

CHAPTER I

Mutual and Balanced Force Reductions in Central Europe: The Exploratory Talks 21 April 1972–12 July 1973

No. 1

Note by the Defence Policy Staff of the Chiefs of Staff Committee

DP Note 215/72 [*WDN 27/19*]

Secret   MoD,[1] *21 April 1972*

Mutual and Balanced Force Reductions
The Situation in NATO[2]

1. On 2 June 1971 the Chiefs of Staff approved a note by the Defence Policy Staff summarising the then current state of the MBFR[3] discussions in NATO. On 13 July they took note of a report on certain further developments in this field.

2. A progress report on MBFR is on the agenda for the meeting of the NATO Military Committee in Chiefs of Staff Session in Brussels on 25 April. MBFR also provides the theme for this years SHAPEX[4] Exercise on the following three days. This may therefore be an opportune moment to review the situation in NATO.

Political Developments Since July 1971

3. It will be remembered that the Meeting of NATO Ministers, held in Lisbon in June 1971,[5] was preceded by two events which renewed interest throughout the Alliance in the whole subject of MBFR. The first was Mr. Brezhnev's[6] Tiflis speech of 14 May in which he called upon the West to show the genuineness of their pursuit of détente by entering into immediate negotiations on force reductions in Central Europe. The second was the defeat in the American Congress of the Mansfield Resolution calling for substantial (but unilateral) reductions in US troop levels in Europe: a defeat which appeared to have been aided by implicit assurances on the part of the US Administration that negotiations on Mutual and Balanced Reductions would be undertaken without

---

[1] Ministry of Defence.

[2] North Atlantic Treaty Organisation.

[3] Mutual and Balanced Force Reductions.

[4] Supreme Headquarters Allied Powers Europe Exercise.

[5] See *Selected Documents Related to Problems of Security and Cooperation in Europe 1954–77*, Cmnd 6932 (London: HMSO, 1977), pp. 96–9.

[6] Mr. L.I. Brezhnev was General Secretary of the Central Committee of the Communist Party of the Soviet Union (CPSU).

delay.[7] In consequence the communiqué following the meeting declared the intention of all member Governments (except France) 'to continue and intensify the exploration of common ground with the Soviet Union as the object of MBFR and to proceed as soon as may be practicable to negotiations'.

4.   In October the NATO Deputy Foreign Ministers met in Brussels to appoint Signor Brosio, the retiring Secretary General,[8] as their 'Explorer' for this purpose, to agree a document which provided his general brief and terms of reference and to appoint a party of 'experts' (one British) to accompany him. The news of this move was conveyed to the Russians by the host country, Belgium, through their Embassy in Moscow.

5.   There has been little or no Russian reaction to this initiative, in spite of a number of public statements by Western statesmen and frequent reminders from the Belgians. The communiqué of the Moscow Pact [sic] Ministers, meeting in December, made no reference either to MBFR or Brosio,[9] and the reference to MBFR in the communiqué of their Consultative Committee, which met in January, was a very low key one.[10] Russian statements have made it clear that they particularly dislike the bloc-to-bloc approach implicit in the Brosio mission.

6.   Meanwhile attention in NATO has been partially diverted from MBFR as such to the prospects of holding a Conference on European Security and Co-operation (CSCE) in 1973. The shape and content of such a Conference are still far from clear, and so too is the possible link between a CSCE and the subject of MBFR.[11] It could be the prelude to an MBFR negotiation, it could provide the forum for exploratory talks, or it could establish the machinery for negotiation. But in the view of the UK and of most of NATO it is not an appropriate forum for actual negotiation. This is for a number of reasons, of which the most important is that the Conference will include nations (such as the neutrals) with only an indirect interest in MBFR in Central Europe. There are also limits to the extent to which it is good tactics to divorce the political aspects of MBFR from the military for negotiation in separate fora. It should not necessarily be assumed, however, that the holding of a CSCE will necessarily delay exploratory talks on MBFR.

7.   The MBFR issue is therefore neither dead nor dormant in NATO. It is bound to remain active because:

(*a*)   For political reasons NATO must be seen to be active in pursuing détente,

---

[7] In May 1971 the United States (US) Senate debated a resolution introduced by Mr. M. Mansfield (Democrat, Montana), calling for a reduction of US forces in Europe from 300,000 to 150,000. Mr. Mansfield argued that, with the onset of *détente* and Sino-Soviet rivalry, and with the Soviet Union keen to reduce its defence burdens, it was now opportune for the US to reduce its military presence in Europe. Although the resolution and subsequent compromise amendments were defeated, Congressional support for the Senator's views remained significant.

[8] Sig. M. Brosio was Secretary-General of NATO during 1964–71.

[9] See Cmnd 6932, pp. 102–4.

[10] *V. ibid.*, pp. 107–12.

[11] See Volume II, Nos. 1 and 9.

and MBFR is an aspect of arms control which is more meaningful for most NATO nations than eg SALT[12] or CTB.[13]

(*b*)   Some NATO nations still hanker perversely after MBFR in the hope that it will enable them to reduce the size of their Defence Budget.

(*c*)   There is a need for the Alliance to reach a common position on a number of unresolved issues against the possibility of a reviewed [*sic*] Soviet initiative on this front.

(*d*)   The American Administration is anxious to keep the prospects of MBFR in the public eye as a means of combating domestic pressures for unilateral troop reductions in Europe.[14] They may also want to keep all the options for improvements in East/West relations open at least until President Nixon returns from Moscow, though they have assured NATO that there is no question of any MBFR negotiation during the visit.[15]

8.   NATO therefore has a full programme of work on both the political and military aspects of MBFR extending well beyond the Ministerial meetings in the last week in May.

Progress of NATO Studies

9.   The focus in NATO for all work on MBFR not of an exclusively political nature is provided by the MBFR Working Group. This is chaired by the present Deputy Chairman of the Military Committee, who has just submitted a short progress report for the information of the forthcoming meeting of the Military Committee in Chief of Staff Session. The main elements of the internal studies undertaken over the past year have been:

(*a*)   Saceur's [16] Risk Assessment. This analysed the military implications of two possible MBFR options and concluded that none of the variants so far considered by NATO (with the possible exception of the British 'common

[12]   Strategic Arms Limitation Talks. These US/Soviet talks (SALT I) began in November 1969 and ended in May 1972 with the conclusion in Moscow of the Treaty on the Limitation of Anti-Ballistic Missile Systems and an Interim Agreement on the Limitation of Strategic Offensive Arms. See Cmnd 6932, pp. 122–34. New SAL talks (SALT II) began in October 1972.

[13]   Comprehensive [Nuclear] Test Ban.

[14]   The US President, Mr. R.M. Nixon, had repeatedly said that he would not reduce US forces in Europe except in the context of MBFR. Yet, as Lord Bridges (Head of Western Organisations Department (WOD) in the Foreign and Commonwealth Office (FCO), 1971–72) pointed out in a submission to Mr. C.D. Wiggin (Assistant Under-Secretary (AUS)) of 23 November 1971, it was uncertain whether, 'in order to keep Congressional opinion under control', Mr. Nixon would require 'the conclusion of an agreement, or merely the opening of negotiations'. 'It is, however, sensible', Lord Bridges reasoned, 'to plan on the assumption that the Americans will sooner or later feel bound to reach an East–West agreement enabling them [to] withdraw some forces; and that they would resent, and in the last analysis override, attempts by the Europeans to prevent them' (WDN 27/14).

[15]   Mr. Nixon visited the Soviet Union during 22–30 May.

[16]   NATO's Supreme Allied Commander, Europe.

ceiling' approach) could do other than result in a military disadvantage to NATO.

(*b*) Two US papers describing in general terms the US analytical approach to MBFR. These reached no conclusions, but were intended to provide a general 'insight' into various elements of the MBFR problem. Unfortunately both the data and the assumptions on which they were based differed in some respects from those accepted in NATO, and the different methods of analysis used produced some internal inconsistencies. Both papers presented a slightly more optimistic picture of the relative capabilities of NATO and the Warsaw Pact than the Alliance is accustomed to accept, and the second in particular failed to provide the clear indication of US views which her allies have been expecting.

(*c*) A German paper suggesting a 'Phased, Integral Programme' for MBFR, according to which negotiation would begin with declarations of principles, a force freeze and the introduction of collateral measures (constraints on troop movements, manoeuvres etc): only when confidence had been established by this means, and methods of verification had been proved, would negotiations move on to actual troop reductions and withdrawals. There is now general acceptance of this concept in NATO, though differences of opinion persist about the value in practical military terms of movement 'constraints'.

(*d*) A UK paper based on the model developed at DOAE[17] for the analysis of operations in the Central Region. The object of this paper was to illuminate in simple terms the problem of the force-to-task ratio, which has been insufficiently emphasised in other studies, i.e. the effect of MBFR on the ability of NATO forces to provide a meaningful defence over the whole of the required front, irrespective of comparable reductions on the Warsaw Pact side. It also suggested a method of attaching values to the reduction in military capability arising from any given MBFR option; this was expressed in terms of the time it would take for Warsaw Pact forces to break through the NATO defences. Since this is equivalent, in effect, to reduction in nuclear decision time it was hoped that this approach would provide a scale for assessing reductions in military security which would be readily appreciated in political as well as military circles. This paper was well received in NATO and may provide the basis for further studies.

10. On the organisational side, four sub-groups have been formed to deal with specialist aspects of MBFR work, as follows:

(*a*) *Verification*. Much of the basic work in this area has already been done, and little further progress can be made without knowing the terms of the MBFR agreement which has to be verified. Work is still in progress however on the possibilities of certain methods eg air photography, and the type and scale of inspection procedures which would be acceptable to NATO.

(*b*) *Constraints*. This sub-group is studying the kind of measures (mainly restrictions on movement) which could be introduced during the 'confidence-

---

[17] Defence Operational Analysis Establishment.

building' phases. (See 9c above.) The key questions here are the practical extent to which such measures might limit the offensive capability of the Warsaw Pact, the degree to which they might increase warning time, and the danger that they might inhibit NATO's own reinforcement plans in a crisis.

(*c*) *Tactical Air.* This sub-group is investigating the implications of MBFR for tactical aircraft: in doing so it is studying concepts which have not been considered in the context of land forces, eg the 'sterilisation' of forward bases. It is our view, and that of a number of NATO allies, that tactical aircraft should be kept out of MBFR negotiations for as long as possible: but we have to be prepared to meet Soviet insistence that they should be included.

(*d*) *Data Base.* Coherent discussion of MBFR in NATO is often inhibited because of disagreements over the basic facts and figures of force levels on each side. This sub-group is seeking to ensure that all discussion and analysis starts from a reasonably common basis.

11. In our view one of the most important gaps in the present NATO work programme is the lack of a study of the implications of MBFR for 'battlefield' nuclear weapons. We believe that this study can be undertaken without impinging on the sensitive areas of targetting and warhead numbers, and without prejudicing NATO's position towards the FBS [18] issue in SALT. Progress cannot, however, be made without the co-operation of the Americans, and this has not, so far, been forthcoming.

NATO Attitudes

12. National attitudes to MBFR are determined partly by the general 'hawkishness' or otherwise of a country's attitude and partly by geographical position. The original German enthusiasm for MBFR was an offshoot of Ost-politik, and is now considerably qualified by a more hard-headed appreciation of the military risks to NATO and of the particularly exposed position of the FGR. [19] The Canadians and Belgians are doves, reflecting the preoccupation of their Ministers with détente and their desire for a respectable excuse to reduce their defence effort. The Dutch are outwardly hard-liners, but their defence budget is equally under pressure. The Italians, being outside the probable area of reduction take a close, but mainly academic interest. The Scandinavians, also outside the area, are doves: but in the Norwegian case, their attitude is conditioned as is also that of the Greeks and Turks, by anxiety about the effect which reductions in the Central Region would have on the threat to the flanks. The French say frankly that MBFR is a trap, and have so far refused to have anything to do with the studies at all.

13. As will be seen from the preceding paragraphs, there is some ambivalence in the American attitude, though there has been a detectable hardening since the post-Mansfield enthusiasms of last summer. Their public position in NATO is best illustrated, however, by the terms of the President's assurance given to the

[18] Forward Based [Nuclear Delivery] Systems.

[19] Federal Republic of Germany (usually abbreviated to FRG).

December 1970 meeting of NATO Defence Ministers—'Given a comparable effort by our allies, there will be no reduction in American troop levels in Europe, except in the context of East/West negotiations'. The double condition indicates that they see MBFR as a mechanism for containing pressure for unilateral reductions at home, and also for discouraging unilateral reductions by their allies. Until these pressures and possibilities disappear (and perhaps until they are better able to assess Soviet attitudes as a result of the Nixon visit) they are determined to keep their options open and the MBFR pot on the simmer both within NATO and with Moscow.[20]

Soviet Attitudes

14. We ourselves have attempted an analysis of the Soviet attitude, and this has recently been circulated in NATO. Hard evidence is scanty, and the conclusions are based largely upon informed judgement; but broadly speaking they are as follows:

(*a*) The Russians have no economic or military reason for pursuing MBFR. Such reductions as we believe they might be willing to make would not be of a scale which would result in significant savings in money or manpower; nor would they be necessary to enable them to face more effectively the threat from the East.

(*b*) Taking into account the likely Soviet perception of the threat from the West, in conjunction with their need to maintain military control of the satellite countries, their assessment of the forces which they might have to maintain in Eastern Europe, even assuming comparable reductions by NATO, might be little less than the present level. Specifically their room for negotiation might not be greater than three of the 31 Divisions now deployed in the likely reduction area.

(*c*) Soviet interest in the MBFR concept is almost certainly primarily political. It is one element in a worldwide campaign to show themselves as peace-loving, pursuers of détente, and beaters of swords into ploughshares. The genuineness of their initiatives on MBFR must be judged alongside their sporadic enthusiasms for CTB, General and Complete Disarmament, CW[21] and BW[22] bans,

---

[20] In a letter to Sir T. Brimelow, Deputy Under-Secretary of State (DUS), of 18 February, Mr. D.C. Tebbit, British Minister in Washington, reported: 'We still do not know whether neo-isolationism has passed its peak or whether the withdrawal of all but a residual force from Vietnam will, as some people think, take the heat off the issue of US troops in Europe or whether, as others think, the Liberal Democrats will then turn the heat on Europe still more. There is certainly a tendency on the part of non-isolationist, moderate members of Congress who have so far voted against Mansfield to look for reasonable ways of securing partial withdrawals. Most people we meet, in and out of government, tend to say that the trend is still in favour of Mansfieldism.' Mr. Tebbit also pointed out that while the current Administration's line was that Mansfieldism could be defeated, he was hesitant about making any prediction for 1973, whatever the outcome of the forthcoming presidential elections in November (WDN 27/1).

[21] Chemical weapons.

[22] Biological weapons.

Naval Limitations and world nuclear conferences. In a more narrow sense they may also believe that MBFR is a means of exploiting the different national interests in NATO for divisive effect. In the past MBFR has also been a card of entry for one of their major political objectives, the CSCE; now that this is virtually achieved, their interest appears to be on the wane.

The UK Position

15. The military view on MBFR remains as set out in paras 33–41 of the note we circulated last year;[23] and indeed it has not altered in any significant particular since the general statements of view approved in 1969 and 1970. While our distrust of the MBFR concept is almost as deep as that of the French, our tactics have been entirely different, and considerably more successful. We have not turned our backs on the whole issue; neither have we thought it necessary or desirable to take initiatives or propose solutions.[24] But by playing a reasonably constructive part in the debate we have been able to retain some control over a muddled and reasonably fast-moving situation. The cautiousness of our approach, coupled with the lack of any apparent enthusiasm on the part of the Russians, has had its effect in NATO and is probably at least partially responsible for the more sophisticated and realistic approach reflected in current NATO Studies. The themes we have been emphasising may be summarised as follows:

(*a*) Three years of intensive study in NATO have shown that any satisfactory MBFR agreement related to the Central Region must require considerably larger withdrawals and reductions by the Warsaw Pact than by NATO (particularly of major types of offensive equipment). The degree to which the Russians are prepared to accept this will be an indicator of the genuineness of their desire to negotiate. There is no sign of this at the moment.

(*b*) Irrespective of the scale of force reductions on the side of the Warsaw Pact, there may be a 'critical minimum' of NATO forces, perhaps not very far below the present levels, at which the strategy of flexible response ceases to be viable.[25]

[23] In this note (DP Note 206/71 (Final)) of 25 May 1971 the Defence Policy Staff expressed their doubts about whether MBFR were 'the path to détente in Europe' as some Allies believed, and claimed that reductions could not 'be safely negotiated until that relaxation in tension ha[d] already been achieved'. They argued that in order to avoid jeopardising Western security, 'any new balance of forces in Europe must be struck at, or only slightly below the present NATO level. If NATO strengths were permitted to drop significantly below this 'critical minimum' the only logical course for NATO would be to adopt a different strategy, which would place greater reliance on the strategic nuclear deterrent; the political consequences of this would be considerable' (DP 1/579/14).

[24] Sir T. Brimelow summed up the British view of MBFR in a letter to Mr. Tebbit of 29 February. 'From our military studies', he wrote, 'we have concluded that MBFRs are likely only to do the Alliance military damage. We continue to work hard at the subject in order to try to ensure that, whether or not MBFRs come about, the political and/or military damage to the Alliance be minimized. We have no desire to promote MBFR' (WDN 27/1).

[25] Lord Bridges noted in his submission of 23 November 1971 (see note 13 above): 'It is the view of all the best qualified military experts that NATO's conventional forces are already at or near the "critical minimum", and that any reductions are bound to be dangerous ... it means that however

(*c*) If we ever get to the negotiating table NATO will therefore be bargaining a known military risk against only the prospects of détente. It is the duty of the military authorities to ensure that these risks are expressed in terms fully comprehensible to those who will negotiate for us. Hence the significance of the UK analysis paper, which demonstrates the link between NATO force levels and decision-time available to Governments.

(*d*) The military risks of MBFR can be offset in two ways:

(i) By negotiating force reductions in an atmosphere in which significant developments towards détente have already taken place rather than the other way round; this is the significance of the 'phased integral programme' approach in which the implementation of MBFR depends on the successful prior implementation of 'collateral', or 'confidence-building' measures. It would be a mistake, however, to attach too much military importance to such measures either as imposing practical constraints on the Warsaw Pact offensive capability or as a means of making their aggressive moves easier to detect. We must also beware of agreeing measures which might be more of a handicap to NATO in time of tension than to the Warsaw Pact.

(ii) By increasing the readiness and effectiveness of forces in qualitative terms. The prospect of MBFR places even more emphasis on the need to implement the AD 70 recommendations;[26] it does not provide an excuse for those who want to reduce their expenditure on defence.

(*e*) MBFR is therefore a politico-military problem. Sensible solutions will only emerge if both elements are kept in balance. There is therefore the necessity for the closest collaboration between the political and military authorities in NATO and in capitals.

US/Soviet Only Agreement?

16. There is one possible MBFR variant which requires special mention, because, for obvious reasons, it is not the subject of formal study in NATO at the moment. One can envisage an agreement which would affect US forces in Europe and Soviet forces in Eastern Europe only. Such an agreement could be reached on the US side with the tacit or explicit consent of its NATO allies. There is in fact much to be said for an agreement of this kind. MBFR is basically a problem related to US force levels in Europe, and a 'bilateral' agreement provides the only hope for the US of making a change in the present pattern of allied force contributions, which an overall MBFR agreement would merely perpetuate on a reduced scale. Moreover in the wider context of détente it is US and Soviet forces which provide the key elements in the East/West military balance.

17. But there are also dangers in such an arrangement. Firstly it would be a

many studies are done, the Alliance is unlikely ever to agree just how far NATO can afford to reduce its forces in negotiation without weakening its military posture.'

[26] This study of Alliance Defence Problems in the 1970s (AD 70) was launched in an effort to analyse NATO's deficiencies and produce recommendations for concerted action. The AD 70 Report was considered and approved by NATO Defence Ministers in December 1970.

divisive move, with more than an element of potential 'decoupling' about it (i.e. a weakening of US involvement in NATO defence and deterrence). Secondly there would be great and probably irresistible pressure on other NATO Governments to follow the American lead, point to the Soviet reductions and make reductions in their own forces, irrespective of any further reductions on the Soviet side. This could lead to a wholesale crumbling of the whole Allied military structure, already under considerable economic pressure.

18. It is impossible to reach a balanced judgement on the UK attitude to such a proposal without knowing the political and military context in which it might be made. If the Americans appeared determined to go ahead with such an agreement we should no doubt attempt to rationalise it to ourselves and our allies in a way which would discourage others from following the American lead. But if the Americans regard MBFR as a mechanism of control over their opposition and their allies, it can also be regarded as a NATO mechanism of control over the scale, nature and timing of unilateral initiatives by themselves. This control would be weakened by indications of allied acquiescence in advance. It has therefore been agreed with the FCO that for the present UK representatives should not speak in favour of a US/Soviet only agreement or give the Americans and our other allies the impression that we would find it acceptable.[27]

The Future

19. It is difficult to make any confident predictions about the way in which the MBFR situation will develop. For the moment it is impossible to look much beyond the NATO Ministerial meetings at the end of May, which are likely to be overshadowed by President Nixon's visit to Moscow, and dominated by the theme of the Security Conference. No doubt the communiqué will reiterate the invitation, already five times repeated to the Warsaw Pact, to talks about MBFR; but the terms will be conditioned by those greater considerations, and by any initiatives the Russians themselves may take (as on precedent they may) during the next few months.[28]

20. Meanwhile the only prudent course is to proceed methodically and rationally with the work programme in hand. The MBFR idea will not suddenly die or go away; on the other hand we have no fixed deadline for the completion of internal studies or the commencement of contacts with the other side. The one clear feature of the scene is that NATO is still very far from achieving a common view on the basic elements of an allied negotiating position; certain central issues (eg tactical aircraft) are still unresolved, and others (eg nuclear

---

[27] Mr. J. Godber, Minister of State for Foreign and Commonwealth Affairs, had already made clear in a minute to Sir T. Brimelow of 7 December 1971 that in his opinion the danger to the Alliance lay in a bilateral deal between the Americans and the Russians which would have a very disruptive effect on the UK's European allies. 'Our basic objective', he insisted, 'must be not to give the Americans any excuse to do a deal with the Russians over NATO's head, and not to encourage any of our European Allies in NATO to think that this exercise justifies them reducing their own forces committed to NATO. The solution therefore should be a bilateral reduction arrived at by multilateral agreement' (WDN 27/1).

[28] Cf. Volume I, pp. 477–8.

weapons) have not yet been tackled. While this is so, NATO remains vulnerable to any unexpected initiative, whether of a political or military nature, from the other side. The only method of achieving such a position is to think through the outstanding problems collectively, and try to assemble the results into some coherent sequence which would represent, as we suggested in our previous note, the extreme upper and lower limits of acceptable negotiation.

21. Such work will not be wasted, even if in the end no MBFR negotiation ever takes place. We have found already that MBFR studies have forced us and our allies to re-examine, in an analytical manner, the various elements of our current force structure and the value which each makes to the deterrent or defensive capabilities of the Alliance. MBFR studies represent the examination of various current security issues from the obverse side, and may have a positive value for defence planning quite separate from the arms control context.

Conclusions
22. The Chiefs of Staff are invited to take note of the current MBFR situation in NATO, as described in the foregoing paragraphs.

D.W. FRASER
MAJOR GENERAL
ASSISTANT CHIEF OF THE
DEFENCE STAFF (POLICY)

NATO Ministers meeting at Bonn on 30–31 May committed the Alliance to entering Multilateral Preparatory Talks for a Conference on Security and Cooperation in Europe (CSCE), and agreed that multilateral explorations for MBFR negotiations should be undertaken either before, or in parallel with, these talks.[1] The Americans were particularly concerned to avoid any procedural complication which might impede progress towards MBFR, and they responded positively to a Soviet paper handed to Dr. H.A. Kissinger, the US President's Special Assistant for National Security Affairs, when he visited Moscow during 11–13 September for talks with the Soviet leadership. The paper proposed that preparatory talks for the CSCE should begin in November, and that preliminary consultations on MBFR should start in January 1973 and be followed by negotiations 'on a non-block basis' in October.[2]

Meanwhile, NATO continued to prepare for the negotiations. A regular series of Anglo-German bilateral discussions on MBFR was inaugurated, and towards the end of September British officials travelled to Washington for secret talks with members of Dr. Kissinger's White House staff.[3] Still sceptical about the true value of the process, the British nevertheless recognised that it might serve to broaden and intensify cooperation amongst their European allies. During a meeting with West German officials in Bonn on 20 October Mr. C.C.C. Tickell, Lord Bridges's successor as Head of WOD, argued that it was 'time to inject into the debate on the future

[1] See Volume II, No. 9, note 2.
[2] *V. ibid.* Nos. 9, 12 and 13.
[3] See No. 2, note 2.

relationships of European countries some consideration of defence issues'. He said that he thought it cardinal that Western participants in MBFR should emphasise that there would be no unilateral reductions during the actual negotiations, and that they should make it known that force reductions would only be achieved, if at all, at the end of a long, tortuous and difficult process. 'The aim of the MBFR was', he affirmed, 'not only to produce a reduction in force levels but also to agree on measures such as constraints and enable us to maintain a dialogue with East European countries on security issues.'[4]

It was also evident that if the Soviet Union were to be held to its promise to negotiate, other more mundane issues must soon be settled. On 15 November those NATO countries which maintained forces in central Europe and which intended to be direct participants in the MBFR negotiations (Belgium, Canada, the FRG, Luxembourg, the Netherlands, the UK and the USA) addressed identical notes to their Warsaw Pact counterparts (Czechoslovakia, the German Democratic Republic (GDR), Hungary, Poland and the USSR) proposing that exploratory talks begin on 31 January. The notes stated that certain Allied flank countries (Denmark, Greece, Italy, Norway and Turkey) would also participate, but without full status, and suggested that exploratory talks should deal with matters of procedure, organisation and agendas for substantive negotiations. NATO's preference for Geneva as the site of these talks was later communicated bilaterally by the Netherlands. No Warsaw Pact replies were, however, received until 18 January 1973. These agreed to the proposed starting date, but suggested Vienna as the venue. And while the Warsaw Pact governments did not object to NATO participation as set out in the Allies' notes, they stated that other interested European states should have the right to participate on an equal basis and that participation in substantive negotiations should be decided during the exploratory consultations. The US was not, as discussions within NATO revealed, prepared to oppose the Soviet Union over where the talks should take place; nor were the Americans ready to risk delay by insisting that agreement must be reached on participation before the exploratory talks began. In consequence, the NATO reply of 24 January simply indicated that participation could be discussed during the talks. But Belgium, the Netherlands and some flank countries made it plain in the North Atlantic Council (NAC) that while they were ready to accept the presence of Bulgaria and Romania as flank participants, they would not attend the talks if neutral countries were included.

In their response of 27 January the Warsaw Pact states reserved the right to return to the question of inviting other countries during the course of the exploratory talks. They also indicated that direct participants would have an obligation to reduce their forces, and they avoided endorsing the West's use of 'MBFR' as a description of the negotiations. The NAC nonetheless considered their reply to provide a satisfactory basis on which to begin the talks. The next two documents reveal FCO thinking with regard to the prospects for MBFR and the objectives to be achieved.

---

[4] Record of Anglo-German talks on MBFR, 20 October (WDN 27/1).

No. 2

Minute from Mr. Tickell to Mr. Wiggin
[*WDN 27/1*]

Secret   FCO, *30 November 1972*

Mutual and Balanced Force Reductions (MBFR)[1]

We face the prospect of exploratory talks on MBFR in January, followed by negotiations next autumn. NATO must therefore decide urgently on the objectives to be pursued in the exploratory talks and on the tactics to be employed. Although a great deal of work has been done on MBFR to analyse the military implications of a range of possible reductions, NATO is still far from agreement on the essential policy objectives.

The MBFR Problem

2. The more we have studied MBFRs in any negotiable form, the less we have liked them. Like the French, we fear that force reductions would probably lead to a weakening of the Alliance and that the notion of reductions compatible with undiminished security for all concerned (at least on the Western side) is a pipe dream. Like the French we wish to see United States force levels in Europe maintained at their present level for as long as possible. Unlike the French we believe that the best way of persuading the Americans not to make unilateral cuts is to help them cope with their domestic critics by participating in negotiations which could, if they succeeded, lead to cuts on the Eastern as well as on the Western side. We have no reason to believe that the Americans are in a hurry for real cuts or indeed think them to be necessary; but we do know that the present US Administration feels it has 'a moral obligation to the Senate to negotiate on MBFR, and wants to be seen to be facing and then engaging in MBFR negotiations'.[2]

3. Even so, nothing would be more dangerous than for the Alliance to enter into exploratory talks and then negotiations, on the comfortable assumption that nothing would in fact happen in the end; and that 'the long drawn out technical negotiations' which the Americans want would prove inconclusive.[3] Once started

---

[1] This paper was prepared in conjunction with MoD officials, originally with the December NATO Ministerial meeting in view (cf. Cmnd 6932, pp. 137–40). The substance of it was written into the relevant briefs for Lord Carrington, the Secretary of State for Defence.

[2] Dr. H. Sonnenfeldt, a member of Dr. Kissinger's staff, conveyed this view to Mr. Tickell during secret Anglo-US talks held in the White House on 22 September. He added that the US wanted to be seen to be facing and then engaging in 'long drawn out technical negotiations' on MBFR. 'The prospect', he noted, 'of such negotiations, followed by the negotiations themselves, should enable the Administration to see things through the next financial year and keep Congress happy' (minute from Mr. Tickell to Sir T. Brimelow of 27 September covering record of Anglo/American talks on CSCE and MBFR). Cf. Volume II, No. 13, note 12.

[3] *V. ibid.*

MBFR negotiations could acquire an impetus of their own. Hence we now need clearly to decide where our own interests lie and what sort of MBFR arrangement—if there has to be one—would least damage the Alliance. The attitude of our other Allies towards MBFR will be of cardinal importance in making such an assessment.

European (and Canadian) attitudes towards MBFR

4. Governments have not as yet taken up firm positions on what MBFR would mean for them. Those in the Central Zone who would qualify for full participation in exploratory talks and subsequent negotiations on the Western side are (apart from the United States) Canada, Belgium, France and Great Britain (all of whom have forces stationed in the Federal Republic) and the West Germans, Dutch and Luxembourgeois (whose countries fall into the Central Zone).

(a) *Canada* The Canadians appear to have no plans to withdraw their single brigade from Germany. Indeed it can be argued that they would be reluctant to do so because this would weaken their foot in the door of European affairs; but the possibility that they might seek to reduce their air force contribution as part of MBFR cannot be entirely excluded;

(b) *Belgium* The Belgians would like to withdraw some of their forces based in Germany for domestic reasons, first to increase the proportion of home-based troops, and secondly to relieve pressure on defence expenditure. Although fairly firm in demanding a cast-iron MBFR arrangement, they would certainly hope to participate in it;

(c) *France* The French have refused to participate in either MBFR explorations or negotiations. It is conceivable that they might in the end have second thoughts but even if they did they would scarcely want more than observer status. They have, so far as we know, no plans to withdraw their forces from Germany;

(d) *Britain* We have no plans to reduce our forces in Germany. Moreover we are bound under the revised Brussels Treaty to maintain a certain level of troops on the mainland of Europe;[4]

(e) *The Federal Republic* The German attitude is equivocal: they have a conceptual approach to MBFR and tend to see it as an instrument of East/West dialogue on security matters. At the same time they would be most reluctant to jeopardize the continuing US presence in Europe, to which they attach the highest importance, by any premature move towards reductions. But there are pressures in Germany for troop reductions and for cuts in defence expenditure, and the Germans may be reluctant to abandon any hope of eventually reducing their own forces through MBFR;

(f) *The Netherlands* The Dutch are under domestic pressure to reduce defence

---

[4] Under the terms of the revised Brussels Treaty, negotiated at the London Conference of September/October 1954, the UK undertook not to withdraw from the continent its four divisions and tactical air force, then assigned to NATO, against the wishes of the majority of the Brussels powers, except in the event of an acute overseas emergency.

expenditure, and some may hope to see Dutch troop reductions in MBFR. The recent debate in the Netherlands over future defence policy seems likely to result in lower defence expenditure;

(g) *Luxembourg* The Luxembourgeois have few forces to reduce.

5. Of the remaining countries in the Alliance (who would not on present assumptions participate in force reductions) we need have no worries about the Greeks, Turks and Portuguese. The Norwegians do not appear to be contemplating any force reductions. The Italians are under no pressure to reduce their forces, and have recently told us that they believe that a bilateral American/Russian arrangement would be the best eventual outcome. The Danes have already proposed significant cuts in their forces and are reducing their defence expenditure.

The Alternatives

6. We are thus faced with a situation in which the Americans, for domestic and presentational reasons, are determined to press forward to substantive MBFR negotiations and in which some of our European Allies see MBFR as a respectable means for scaling down their own forces. Our own scepticism is only fully shared by the French who have decided to stay outside the game. Nor can we take comfort in the hope that the 'long drawn out technical negotiations' which the Americans want will eventually run into the sand. The new dimension in East/West relations created by the growing understanding between the United States and the Soviet Union in strategic matters puts the Europeans constantly at risk of having matters of vital interest to their security settled over their heads.

7. Western Europe is moving into an era when it both wants, and is expected by the United Sates, to become more self-reliant in defence. It would thus be inconsistent with that aim for Europe to latch on to MBFR as a device for cutting down the European defence effort. While we all hope that US forces in Europe will not be substantially reduced, it would be rash to count on their being held at present levels for all time. There is at least a possibility that over the next few years the Europeans, faced with the prospect of US withdrawals without sufficient compensating reductions on the other side, will have to choose between diminished security or plugging the gaps left by the Americans. Even if the Russians reduced their forces significantly more than the Americans, the present conventional balance would, given the Warsaw Pact's great facility in reinforcement, remain tilted against the West. In this situation it seems more important than ever that the Europeans should see MBFR in the context of the future needs of European defence.[5]

[5] In a minute to Mr. Tickell of 13 July, Mr. J.E. Cable, Head of Planning Staff, suggested that the MBFR negotiations could be linked with 'proposals for the expansion of European defence cooperation'. The 'moment of American force reductions will', he added, 'be the turning point, perhaps even the point of no return, in the future evolution of European defence. If this moment is not exploited to launch a new movement towards a more effective and self-sufficient European defence, then I fear that the departure of any substantial number of American troops will mark the beginning of an accelerated decline in European defence efforts, leading to a loss of political

8.   If reductions are ever to take place, they could, on present thinking, take one of three forms: a reduction limited to stationed forces (i.e. involving only American, British, Belgian and Canadian forces); reductions divided between stationed and indigenous forces within the agreed zone; and reductions limited to American and Russian forces in an agreement reached through multilateral negotiations.[6] Objections to the first two are obvious. Apart from the general considerations already advanced about the future needs of European defence, reductions confined to stationed forces would look discriminatory against indigenous ones; and reductions which included indigenous forces would amount to a measure of partial disarmament which would have serious implications for future European defence policy.

9.   The main arguments against reductions limited to American and Russian forces are:

(*a*)   American troops are among the most efficient and best equipped in Europe. The size of the American presence has a symbolic importance, and the more reductions can be shared among the less important (and militarily less efficient) countries, the better;

(*b*)   Without the pretext of reduction through MBFR there would be a risk of certain countries, in particular Germany and Belgium, taking unilateral action to reduce;

(*c*)   Such an arrangement would smack of bilateralism.

10.   The main arguments for are:

(*a*)   If reductions were to be made in West European forces, the basis of any future European defence system could be eroded and we would find it more difficult to promote our aim of giving the enlarged Community a defence aspect;

(*b*)   In order to maintain the American commitment to European defence, fend off Congressional pressures for more and greater reductions, and cope with demands for further burden-sharing, the Europeans must show that they take defence seriously and are ready to assume more responsibility with their increased prosperity. For them to join in reductions would have the opposite effect and might precipitate further American reductions;

(*c*)   The troops we want to see reduced on the other side are Russian. If reductions on our side were spread between Americans and Europeans, reductions on the other would be spread between all interested members of the Warsaw Pact (who would thereby be weakened in regard to the Soviet Union).

11.   The idea that our objective should be to limit reductions to Americans and

self confidence and to increasing reliance on accommodation with the Soviet Union as a substitute for effective defence.'

[6]   The Americans clearly welcomed this suggestion when it was put to them by Mr. Wiggin during the White House talks of 22 September (see note 2 above).

Russians has already received some Ministerial endorsement. Ministers in the Foreign and Commonwealth Office considered the arguments in November 1971, and the Minister of State agreed that if there had to be troop reductions, an arrangement limited to American and Russian ones would do Europe least harm.[7] The Foreign Secretary[8] subsequently indicated his agreement. For his part the Defence Secretary has expressed similar views in private meetings with European Ministers of Defence.[9]

12. It would be essential to the confidence of the Alliance that an outcome limited to American and Russian forces only should emerge as the result of a genuine multilateral negotiation. It would also be necessary to ensure that the size of reductions was not such as to leave gaps in NATO's defences that could not be made good, or to impair the credibility of the US commitment to Europe.

Her Majesty's Government's Objectives

13. Her Majesty's government's basic objective in MBFR must be to avoid any detriment to the security of the Alliance or to its present political cohesion; and to make the most of the braking effect of negotiations to thwart any tendency toward unilateral reductions. To achieve these objectives we must:

(*a*) Persuade our Allies to look at MBFR not simply in terms of force reductions alone but as an instrument of dialogue with the Soviet Union and its allies on the real issues of European security;

(*b*) Continue to emphasise that MBFR is a matter for the Alliance as a whole, and to discountenance any tendency that the Americans may have to treat it as a bilateral issue; and

(*c*) Impress upon our European Allies that MBFR should be seen in the context of the changing relationship between the United States and Europe; the pressures on the Europeans to do more in their own defence; and the development of a future European defence identity.

Presentation of the Case

14. Our first endeavour should be to persuade our Allies that while negotiations are in prospect or in progress there must be no talk of unilateral reductions in NATO's forces and still less in any actual reductions. The arguments we could deploy are briefly:

(*a*) The Russians can already be expected to exploit their knowledge of US

---

[7] In his minute to Sir T. Brimelow of 7 December 1971, Mr. J. Godber proposed that the initial aim of any MBFR negotiations 'should be, in the first instance, a relatively small—say 5%—reduction limited to "foreign" (e.g. American and Russian) forces' (see No. 1, note 27).

[8] Sir A. Douglas-Home

[9] But MoD officials had not initially shared the FCO's enthusiasm for force reductions restricted to the USA and the Soviet Union. In a minute to Mr. Wiggin of 7 July Mr. Tickell observed that the 'basic argument advanced by the Ministry of Defence [was] that the domestic pressures on European Governments [were] irresistible [*sic*], and that the alternatives [were] that European forces [would] be cut within the framework of an MBFR agreement, or that they [would] be cut unilaterally'.

domestic pressures for troop reductions. If they were led to believe that a number of Western participants intended either to reduce their forces uni-laterally while negotiations were in progress, or to use MBFR as a means for cuts which would take place irrespective of the outcome of MBFR, NATO's negotiating position would be seriously undermined;

(*b*) NATO could not assess the effects of its own negotiating ploys, or of proposals from the other side, if the basis of its present force levels were shifting or expected to shift;

(*c*) The prospect of MBFR negotiations provides no justification for dismantling or putting into cold storage NATO's efforts in the AD 70 exercise (and in the Eurogroup)[10] to improve its forces in relation to the continuing threat from the Warsaw Pact.

15. Our second main endeavour should be to move the emphasis in MBFR away from consideration of troop reductions alone towards examination of the various proposals for constraints, with accompanying verification measures to establish the seriousness of the negotiating intentions of the other side. We should advance the argument that such measures should be seen as an essential lead in to MBFR and that any later reductions should be a product of détente and not a means to it. We should also take this line in public. As part of this approach we should seek to blur any definition of the form reductions might take and of the final outcome of MBFR negotiations. In present circumstances it would be unwise to indicate too clearly that in our judgement the least damaging result might be Russian and American reductions multilaterally arrived at in the terms discussed in this submission. It would be better to help others to arrive at this conclusion themselves through appropriate emphasis on the future needs of European defence and greater European responsibility within the Alliance.

16. On bilateral discussion with the Americans we should avoid giving them any encouragement to regard MBFR as a means of providing public justification for reductions that the US Administration planned to make in any case. It would be most damaging for European confidence if it were thought that the Americans were determined, irrespective of the course of negotiations, to achieve reductions at any cost.

Conclusion

17. Ministers are invited to:

(*a*) Endorse the approach to MBFR suggested in this paper; and

(*b*) Agree that it should be drawn upon, subject to the need to adapt arguments according to the occasion, in discussion with our NATO Allies and in our contributions to NATO's preparations for MBFR negotiations.[11]

---

[10] The Eurogroup was a non-institutionalised grouping of the European members of NATO, founded in 1968, and tasked with improving European defence cooperation. See Volume I, No. 18, note 1.

[11] Mr. Wiggin endorsed Mr. Tickell's comments in a minute of 4 December: 'Our long term

18. My colleagues in the Ministry of Defence are making a submission in the same terms (less paragraph 11) to the Defence Secretary.

C.C.C. TICKELL

aim', he observed, 'can be fairly simply stated. (a) If there have to be Western force reductions they should if possible be balanced by Communist force reductions. (b) Any such reductions, while multilaterally negotiated, should if possible be limited to United States and Soviet forces, and should not, of course, be of such a scale as to affect the credibility of the American nuclear deterrent in relation to the European theatre.' But, he added, to 'tackle our European Allies head-on by saying that MBFR must in no circumstances lead to any reductions in Western European forces would, at this stage at least, be counter-productive'. Sir A. Douglas-Home noted on this minute his agreement that a 'modest reduction' of US and Soviet forces would best suit Britain; but he thought it would be 'hard to get them'.

No. 3

*Steering Brief for the British Delegation
to the MBFR Exploratory Talks*

[*WDN 27/1*]

Secret   FCO, *30 January 1973*

Background
The British delegation to the exploratory talks should adhere to the positions worked out in discussion among the Allies and defined in the three following papers:

(a) The Guidelines and Agenda paper (CM(72)87)[1] which serves as a steering brief for the Alliance and indicates the positions which the Allies should take on individual issue in the exploratory talks;
(b) The Consolidated Consultative Programme on MBFR (PO/72/413) Revised)[2] which sets out the arrangements for the co-ordination of Allied consultations on the spot with those in Brussels and national capitals; and

[1] According to this NATO paper, the participants in the exploratory talks were to be those 'countries maintaining forces in Central Europe': i.e. Belgium, Canada, the FRG, Luxembourg, the Netherlands, the UK and the USA, on the NATO side; and Czechoslovakia, the GDR, Hungary, Poland, and the USSR, on the Warsaw Pact side. It foresaw Denmark, Greece, Italy and Turkey being represented on a rotating basis, not participating directly in formal decisions reached in the talks, but having the right, on invitation, to speak on issues of direct concern to them. The attendance of other Warsaw Pact countries would be acceptable on the same basis as agreed for the NATO 'flank countries'. The paper also summarised the items the Allies wished to see included in the Conference's agenda: the geographical areas to be covered by agreements; the phasing of reductions; principles; constraints; forces, size and methods of reductions; and verification. 'In proceeding from explorations to negotiations', the paper asserted, 'the Allies should bear in mind the view that the implementation of reductions should be the product and not the cause of détente.'

[2] Not printed.

(*c*)   A position paper on procedures for MBFR talks (CM(72)91)[3] which deals with questions of chairmanship, rules of procedure, seating arrangements, facilities etc.

2.   On 18 January, after the approval of these papers, the Russians and their allies replied to the Allied invitations to MBFR exploratory talks, suggesting that participation at them should be widened to include all interested European States. The Allies replied on 24 January contesting this point, and on 27 January the Russians and their allies agreed that the talks should open with those the Allies had originally proposed (plus Bulgaria and Romania). But the issue is far from resolved, and its handling will require decision by the Alliance as a whole. The British delegation should be guided by whatever decision the Alliance reaches upon it.

British Aims

3.   There are certain specific British objectives towards MBFR negotiations which the British delegation should bear in mind during the exploratory talks. Our broad objective is the same as that of other members of the Alliance: to seek some way of lowering the level of armed forces and armaments in Central Europe while maintaining undiminished security for all. Even if we may be sceptical of the real possibilities of doing so, we believe that the attempt should be made. This is the least that Parliament and public opinion will expect. Any public statements we may make on this subject should reflect this fundamental view.

4.   It is an equally important objective, and essential to the security we now enjoy in Western Europe, that the Americans should maintain substantial military forces in Europe, preferably not much lower than their present levels. We therefore attach particular importance to President Nixon's assurance to the North Atlantic Council in December that, given a similar approach by the Allies, the United States would not reduce their forces in Europe unless there were reciprocal action by the other side. It follows that we wish to help the United States Administration cope with domestic pressures for reductions in Europe whether in or out of MBFR, and must in general accept the advice of the Administration on how best to do so. Hence we should give particular weight to the views of the United States and so far as possible co-operate with the American delegations.

5.   Our third objective is to maintain the unity of the Alliance. The preparations for MBFR have already created severe strains, which could get worse. We should in particular seek to bring our European Allies along with us, combat any tendencies to favour unilateral or inadequately compensated reductions, and persuade them of the need for a practical and realistic approach. In the preparatory talks and negotiations, we want them to co-operate in using the Alliance machinery as the chosen diplomatic instrument in such a way that the Americans are also happy to use it and are not tempted to deal bilaterally with the Russians.

[3] Not printed.

6. During the exploratory talks the British delegation, while doing everything possible to preserve Allied solidarity, should take care to avoid any commitment either to our Allies or to the Warsaw Pact participants which might prejudice our ability to promote specific points in our policy relating to the negotiations themselves. Three are particularly important. First we believe that the negotiations should initially be concentrated on measures designed to create greater confidence between both sides, with appropriate measures for verification, and that a greater degree of such confidence should precede any actual reduction of troops. (It may be that in the event we shall not be able to achieve this in the negotiations. But we must not surrender the right to try at this stage.) Secondly we are anxious to link in European minds the issues raised in MBFR with the future needs of European defence, and in particular to maintain the freedom of the West Europeans to devise whatever new defence arrangements within the Alliance they judge right. Thirdly we believe that any reductions should be confined, at least in the first instance, to the Americans in Europe on the one hand, and the Russians in Europe outside their frontiers on the other. For this reason we wish gradually to establish the idea that the distinction in MBFR should be not between 'stationed' and 'indigenous' forces but between American and Russian forces in one category and European forces in another.

Tactics

7. Day-to-day tactics in the exploratory talks will be worked out in the consultative machinery to be set up on the spot in the light of the decisions already taken by the Alliance. New, important or difficult points should of course be referred to the Atlantic Council and to capitals. The British delegation should in general be guided by the following considerations:

(*a*) We do not want to give the Warsaw Pact countries any excuse for refusing to agree to actual negotiations. This is a point to which the Americans attach particular importance. But we must also bear in mind that the Russians can be expected to have reasons of their own for getting into MBFR negotiations. They also know that MBFR must be seen in the general context of East/West relations and the development of their relationship with the United States. We should not during the preliminary talks give any indication of readiness to concede points of substance in exchange for Russian willingness to engage in actual negotiations.

(*b*) We should seek to resolve Allied differences within the consultative machinery or at least to avoid exposing such differences to the Warsaw Pact countries. From time to time it may be tactically desirable to indicate variations in Allied positions and for an Ally to put forward a particular point of view. But in this event action at the Conference table should be concerted and agreed upon beforehand.

(*c*) We must take care not to pre-empt any decision on points of substance which may arise at the exploratory talks before they have been thoroughly considered in capitals. Points of substance should normally be reserved for the negotiations themselves.

(*d*) With our Allies we must seek to establish some general criterion of admissibility for inscription on the agenda of the negotiations. If we are to have the sort of negotiations we want, we should seek to confine the agenda to questions arising from the military confrontation of the two Alliances in Central Europe, and the forces and armaments deployed in the countries fully participating in the talks.

(*e*) We should be on the watch for indications of Soviet and Warsaw Pact objectives and expectations in regard to MBFR, whether tactically or as a serious subject in its own right.

On 31 January 1973 delegates representing nineteen countries, including all the members of the Warsaw Pact and all the NATO member states except France, Iceland and Portugal, assembled in Vienna to begin exploratory talks on what Western governments continued to refer to as MBFR in Central Europe. The meeting was in accord with the timetable set by Dr. Kissinger and Mr. Brezhnev in the previous September. Since, however, the Soviet delegation were unable to accept NATO proposals on how the talks should be chaired and on what should be the seating arrangements, the first meeting was informal and unstructured and lasted barely half-an-hour. Another fourteen weeks were to elapse before the holding of the first formal plenary session. Talks meanwhile proceeded on a bilateral basis and, from 13 February onwards, these were assisted by what Mr. O.N. Khlestov, the principal Soviet delegate, termed 'plenary cocktails', a regular series of receptions, hosted alternately by Eastern and Western delegations. Discussions also proceeded between Mr. J. Dean, the US Head of Delegation, Mr. B. Quarles van Ufford, the Netherlands Head of Delegation and designated NATO spokesman, and Mr. Khlestov. This, in British eyes, was a far from satisfactory arrangement for, as Mr. D. Johnson (First Secretary in the British Embassy at Vienna) subsequently recalled, 'Quarles seemed unable to prevent himself going beyond agreed Allied positions while Dean, constantly motivated by the US concern to demonstrate progress, was always prepared to move quickly to fall-back positions thereby giving the East just cause to stonewall in the expectation of further Allied concessions'.[1]

The Soviet delegation made it clear from the start that they would not agree to any formal plenary until an understanding had been reached on participants and procedures. The critical issue was the status of flank countries in the talks and, in particular, the position of Hungary. Western governments considered Hungary part of the strategic area to be covered by the negotiations, whilst the Russians thought that Hungary should be able to opt for a special flank status corresponding to that which NATO demanded for Italy. If Hungary were to be a direct participant, then, in the Soviet view, so also must Italy. Within the Ad Hoc Group established by NATO representatives at Vienna (including Portugal) for consultation and co-ordination of tactics, the British advocated a firm stand on Hungary. They argued there and in the NAC that although the military advantage of Hungary's inclusion was marginal, the question had considerable political significance at this early stage in the talks. 'It seems to us', Sir A. Douglas-Home noted on 24 February, 'highly unlikely that the Russians would in fact be prepared to break off the talks even if there were continued stalemate on the Hungarian issue.'[2] *But Dr.*

---

[1] Report by Mr. Johnson on the Exploratory Talks on MBFR in Central Europe enclosed in No. 6.

[2] Telegram No. 523 to Washington of 24 February (WDN 27/4).

Kissinger thought the British 'wrong' on this point,[3] and, evidently anxious to avoid further delay, Mr. Dean suggested that the problem be solved by leaving Hungary's status in abeyance. He proposed that eleven direct participants (excluding Hungary) should be listed along with a statement to the effect that Hungary's participation in subsequent negotiations would be decided at a later stage. The British opposed this American 'abeyance formula' on the ground that it would make it impossible for the Alliance ever to negotiate full Hungarian participation. Nevertheless, during successive NAC meetings between 2 and 9 March they found themselves isolated in resisting its adoption. In consequence, they eventually gave way, but only on condition that the Allied proposal should not be presented formally to the Warsaw Pact until the two Allied emissaries had probed the Soviet position to ascertain whether an 'abeyance formula' might prove acceptable. The following report from Vienna was drafted almost a fortnight after this probe began on 13 March; it and the subsequent document highlight continuing intra-allied differences over negotiating tactics and objectives.

[3] Washington telegram No. 735 of 22 February (WDN 27/4).

No. 4

Report from Mr. W.F. Mumford[1]

[WDN 27/4]

Confidential. UK Eyes A   MoD, *22 March 1973*

MBFR Lessons from Vienna

NATO has embarked on a perilous voyage. It has divided objectives. Its preparations have been found wanting. The locusts are eating into the few months left for NATO's preparations for the substantive talks, under the inexorable timetable imposed by the Kissinger/Brezhnev agreement. The Soviet Union, who is in charge of its Warsaw Pact allies, is displaying no goodwill.[2]

2. This minute reviews briefly in Part I the progress of the exploratory talks and in Part II draws some lessons from them for the future negotiations. The conclusions I have drawn are my own, based on my experience as a member of

[1] Mr. Mumford was UK Deputy Head of Delegation to the exploratory talks. He was subsequently Private Secretary to the Secretary of State for Defence. His report was sent by Mr. Tickell to Mr. Wiggin under cover of a minute of 23 March.

[2] This lack of enthusiasm for MBFR negotiations was shared by Mr. J.A. Thomson, Deputy Permanent UK Representative to the NAC and Head of Delegation at the exploratory talks. In Vienna telegram No. 267 of 26 March he noted that NATO needed to rethink the objectives at which MBFR was supposed to aim. 'Over the last few years', he reasoned, 'we have got good mileage out of this Western proposal. It embarrassed the Russians after Czechoslovakia. It helped to hold off Mansfieldism. It also helped to convince Western public opinion that we had constructive proposals at a time when we were showing a good deal of caution if not dislike towards the Soviet proposals for CSCE. Circumstances have now changed, e.g. the Soviet acceptance of MBFR and the Western acceptance of CSCE. There is a danger that we may be hoist with our own propaganda.' In October 1973 Mr. Thomson became an AUS.

the British Delegation from the outset. But I discussed them with the head of our team (Mr Thomson) before leaving Vienna and he gave them his general endorsement.[3]

PART I: POTTED HISTORY

3.   The exploratory talks in Vienna are now in their eighth week. There was one 'unstructured' meeting of all 19 delegations on 31 January which lasted 32 minutes. Since then lack of agreement on procedures, notably those arising from the status of Hungary, has prevented the staging of plenary meetings. The conference room in the Hofburg, the expensively-hired interpreters and the elaborate Press centre have stood idle.

4.   As a result, all contact between the two sides has been informal and dispersed. The respective heads of the Netherlands team (Ambassador Quarles)[4] and of the American team (Mr. Dean)[5] have been the designated spokesmen when Western proposals on procedure have been put forward to the other side. Their contacts have been with the Soviet delegation, joined by the Hungarians when the question of Hungary has been under discussion. This channel has been supplemented by bilateral contacts between other NATO delegations with opposite numbers originally selected haphazardly.[6] There have also been weekly 'plenary cocktails' given in turn by NATO and Warsaw Pact delegations which have provided a forum for informal exchanges. There are other social occasions such as lunches and dinners when one or two delegations from each side meet. NATO's positions are co-ordinated in an Ad Hoc Group which meets almost daily in Vienna, with reference back to the Council in Brussels on any major new departures.

The Question of Hungary

5.   The prominence assumed by the Hungarian question in Vienna has been

---

[3] In a letter to Mr. Tickell of 21 February Mr. Thomson gave his initial impressions of the negotiations thus far: 'These exploratory talks have been justly compared to a premature baby. Nothing was fully prepared, no name had been agreed, the accommodation for the infant had to be improvised and the hastily appointed godparents were at odds. But I suspect the child will have a long life. Our three weeks of intensive and niggling discussions have been uncomfortable but they have served to show that there are some underlying interests shared by all 19 participants. Tedious though it will be to get some of these reduced to agreed language and mutual actions I am inclined to think that we all recognise that we are condemned to row in the same galley.'

[4] Mr. Thomson described Mr. Quarles in his letter of 21 February (*v. ibid.*) as having 'the appearance of a man who will do almost anything for a quiet life', but who also had 'a certain innate courtesy which [added] considerable tone to the group'.

[5] Mr. Dean, noted Mr. Thomson (*v. ibid.*), 'makes the proceedings of the Ad Hoc Group more exciting than they would otherwise be but also more acerbic. Indeed many members of the Group plainly feel that the tough negotiations are with him rather than with the Warsaw Pact. When Dean has been on the defensive, and under attack particularly from flank countries, I have been reminded of nothing so much as an owl mobbed by blackbirds.'

[6] Mr. Thomson commented (*v. ibid.*): 'If this present *impasse* over Hungary continues for very much longer these bilateral exchanges will become—indeed they have already tended to become— routine and enervating.'

largely of NATO's own making. Hungary was added to the NATO 'guidelines' area for MBFR agreements only late in the day, on the initiative of Belgium and with the strong support of the United States. NATO's military studies had shown consistently that the potential disadvantages in terms of demands for compensation for the inclusion of Hungary were likely to out-weigh the merits of trying to bring her in. None-the-less, NATO's MBFR invitations to the Warsaw Pact included Hungary as a full participant. On arrival in Vienna, NATO found to its surprise that, instead of the expected battle on the inclusion of neutrals, it was confronted with a determined bid by Romania for full status. The Soviets stood on the sidelines of the argument, although making it clear that they were prepared to give Romania a run for her money. NATO's tactics in dealing with Romania were to stress the clear-cut division in its thinking between the twelve direct participants who had forces or territories in Central Europe (in which we included Hungary) and the remainder who, while having a peripheral interest in MBFR, should not take part in actual agreements. After a week's fight, the Romanian delegation succumbed to the icy draught of isolation; but even before NATO had time to relish its victory the Soviet delegation gave notice of its intention that Hungary should also join the ranks of the secondary participants. They may have been forced into declaring their hand on Hungary earlier than planned because of Western insistence on two distinct categories of participants. Be that as it may, the exclusion of Hungary from the scope of MBFR agreements has emerged as a clear object of Soviet policy, with a view to ensuring that there will be at least one country outside the Soviet Union where Soviet stationed troops will not be subject to restrictions. The Soviet delegation has argued consistently that the Hungarian issue must be seen in strategic and not geographic terms. Initially they claimed that the counterpart of the Soviet forces deployed in Hungary, which they claim are oriented southwards, are NATO forces on the Southern flank notably those in Italy. More recently they have indicated that the compensation they would demand for the inclusion of Hungary in MBFR agreements could extend wider afield to France. These demands are almost certainly tactical, in order to convince NATO to drop the issue.

6. As a result of the negotiating history in Vienna, the Hungarian problem has assumed major political dimensions. The issue has been aired in public and it is well known that the two sides have been in conflict over it for many weeks. Western agreement to downgrade Hungary would be interpreted publicly as a major defeat for NATO at the outset of the negotiations. NATO would be exposed to the criticism that it was prepared to leave out of the reckoning a country that is indisputably part of Central Europe and where four Soviet divisions and over 200 aircraft are stationed.[7] The latest Western proposal now

[7] Mr. A.J. Ramsay (First Secretary, WOD), who was briefly a member of the British delegation at Vienna, added in a minute of 1 March to Mr. R.J.T. McLaren (Deputy Head of WOD) another reason for seeking to avoid an early resolution of the Hungarian issue in the Russians' favour. It would, he observed, have been to the Allies' advantage to have thereby loosened the Soviet grip on their Warsaw Pact allies, however slightly, both in the hope of being able to take tactical advantage of the subsequent situation in the negotiations, 'but also as a means of helping to realise the hope

Fig. 1 Détente in the Hofburg: a Plenary session of the MBFR negotiations.
Reproduced by the kind permission of Sir Clive Rose

Fig. 2 Détente in the Vienna Woods: Mr. Rose and Mr. Goodall with their Eastern and
Western MBFR colleagues.
Reproduced by the kind permission of Sir Clive Rose

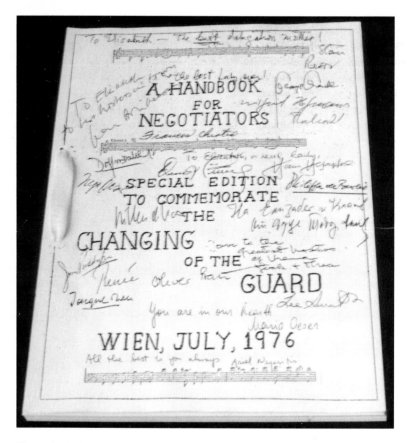

Fig. 3 *A Handbook for Negotiators*. The MBFR Song-book presented to Sir Clive and Lady Rose on their departure from Vienna.

Fig. 4 Mr. (later Sir) John Thomson.

Fig. 5 Sir Peter Ramsbotham.

Fig. 6 Mr. (later Sir) Edwin Bolland.

Fig. 7 Mr. (later Sir) Bryan Cartledge.

All figures supplied from the FCO photographic collection.

Fig. 8 Détente in Moscow. Mr. Wilson drinks a toast with Mr. Brezhnev and Mr. Kosygin during the Prime Ministerial visit to the Soviet Union, February 1975. *Reproduced by permission of Bettmann/CORBIS*

under discussion with the Warsaw Pact delegations in Vienna is that the Hungarian issue should be put in abeyance to be resolved at a later, unspecified, stage.

Allied Positions

7. The Hungarian issue has put NATO into considerable disarray. For the United States the over-riding objective in Vienna is to pin the Warsaw Pact down to starting substantive negotiations in the autumn and for that goal they are prepared to pay a high price, almost certainly including giving way to the Warsaw Pact on Hungary. They regard the lack of progress in Vienna as generally unhelpful to their efforts to persuade Congress that MBFR will provide a serious forum for the negotiation of US force withdrawals on a reciprocal basis.[8] The preoccupation of Greece, Italy and Turkey is to deflect Warsaw Pact pressures to upgrade the status of NATO's southern flank countries to full participation in return for the inclusion of Hungary. Thus they too are prepared to concede the point.[9] Denmark and Norway are not unattracted by the idea of taking part in some MBFR agreements and are therefore less sensitive and emotional than the southern flank in their attitude towards Hungary. The European full participants (Benelux, FRG and UK) are at one in holding out against the concession of flank status to Hungary. Forward of that position they have a mixed bag of ideas on means and tactics, ranging from hastily conceived demands for non-circumvention from the Netherlands to the British proposal to leave the Hungarian problem on one side temporarily while attempts are made in informal meetings of the 19 to reach agreement on other items hopefully less controversial. The UK is regarded in Vienna by both sides as the hardest-liner on Hungary.[10] Throughout the consultations, there has been a strong undercurrent of European

of encouraging the non-Soviet Warsaw Pact countries to move a little further out of the Soviet shadow'.

[8] In a minute to Mr. Wiggin of 13 March, Mr. Tickell declared that the 'present deadlock over Hungary has shown up the Alliance in a bad light', and complained that the US, after initially insisting upon Hungarian participation, 'have now been ready to abandon Hungary for the sake of getting the exploratory talks going and committing the Russians to substantive negotiations in the autumn. Their domestic political preoccupations have been more important to them than the maintenance of Allied positions.'

[9] Mr. Tickell further noted in his minute of 13 March (*v. ibid.*): 'The flank countries, which were originally desperate to be included somehow in MBFR, are now equally desperate not to have their territories included in the area under negotiation. They therefore support the American view that we should not insist on full Hungarian participation in case the other side should demand an Italian, Greek or Turkish *quid pro quo*.'

[10] In a letter to Mr. Tickell of 7 March Mr. Mumford, reported, with regard to the British stance on Hungary, that Mr. Dean 'clearly regards us as the nigger in the woodpile, holding up what would otherwise be a consensus in favour of the US abeyance formula'. To a suggestion from Mr. Dean that in the absence of Allied unity the majority view should be represented to Eastern delegations, Mr. Mumford replied that such a 'procedure would not only be quite alien to the way the alliance had settled its internal problems over the years but would seriously undermine the concept of multilateral MBFR negotiations'. He added that 'it would be difficult to think of a recipe that could be more readily exploited by the East to expose divergences in the allied ranks'.

resentment at the hustling, often bull-dozing tactics employed by the US with their allies, made manifest and accentuated by the personality of Mr. Dean.[11]

Soviet Tactics

8. The Soviet delegation in Vienna has been determined to reap the maximum advantage from NATO's position as demandeur. Their tactics have been to press the West to make all the proposals and to offer nothing in return. On the model of Mr. Mintoff,[12] they have sought to extract from the successive NATO offers those elements which they like, tucking them under their belts and then to continue to negotiate on the main issue on the basis of their original stand. In these tactics, they have achieved a measure of success. They have rightly assessed (with the almost certain assistance of a major intelligence effort) that they have got NATO on the run on Hungary. They have reason to be confident that NATO is not prepared, in support of its Hungarian position, to apply pressure outside MBFR notably at Helsinki.[13] They watch the US stance carefully and correctly read signals which indicate that the US are not fully backing NATO proposals e.g. lack of conviction or near-silence on the part of the US spokesman when the proposals were put forward or the absence of parallel US pressures through diplomatic channels. They have swiftly latched on to NATO's willingness in its latest abeyance proposals to designate 11 direct participants without including Hungary in the list, which they are seeking to exploit as a means of both eliminating any residual Western leverage posed by the threat of the withdrawal of the Benelux countries from full participation and of pinning down all the NATO direct participants as 'undisputed potential participants in future agreements'.[14] They have not given up their attempts to set up a bilateral link with the United States. Their first move on arriving in Vienna was to contact the United States leader and suggest that the two delegations should meet to discuss procedures. This was the genesis of the Quarles/Dean team. They may sincerely believe that the US is in the same position to dominate NATO as they do the

---

[11] Sir E. Peck, the UK Permanent Representative on the NAC, reported in UKDEL NATO telegram No. 198 of 8 March: 'I am becoming increasingly concerned at the risks for wider interests involved in a continuation of the current rather acrimonious disagreements within the Alliance. We are at the moment entirely isolated on the US abeyance formula and risk being accused of sabotaging the MBFR talks if we persist in our attitude despite my repeated explanations of our reasons for not acquiescing at this stage in excluding Hungary wholly or in part from MBFR measures. Below the surface, there lies the apprehension which has not so far been publicly expressed that if the wrangles continue, the Americans, despite President Nixon's undertaking to work with and through the Alliance, might well feel justified in dropping alliance consultation and proceeding to bilateral talks.'

[12] Mr. D. Mintoff, the Maltese Prime Minister, had caused consternation amongst Western governments when, in June 1971, he cancelled the Anglo-Maltese Defence Agreement of 1964, forcing tortuous negotiations over NATO basing rights that were concluded in March 1972.

[13] The Multilateral Preparatory Talks for the CSCE were currently taking place in Helsinki. See Volume II, No. 37.

[14] This phrase carried with it the implication that these states would have an obligation to reduce their forces.

Warsaw Pact. Mr. Kvitsinsky,[15] a former colleague of Mr. Dean from the Four Power negotiations on Berlin,[16] presented him with a Russian shirt in Vienna with the proposal that he should wear it in the NATO Ad Hoc Groups meetings 'in order to show the others who was boss'. The Soviets have given ample warning of the tough hand they will play in the negotiations proper. Reductions proposals based on asymmetry will be laughed out of court by reference to the global balance of military power. Attempts by NATO (*pace* the US) to broaden the concept of MBFR to include constraints as well as reductions must expect similar short shrift.

Prognosis

9. In contrast to its summary and precipitate rejection of NATO's earlier proposals, the Soviet Delegation has been willing to engage in a dialogue—if not a very constructive one—on NATO's latest abeyance proposals. This dialogue continues, although so far there has been no give on the Soviet side. Meanwhile, there has been no agreement among the allies to move ahead in parallel with an informal discussion of other items either among the 19 or in a smaller grouping. NATO is thus courting the danger of the development of a new highly unfavourable situation. This would be one in which eventually NATO's overtures on abeyance receive a formal rejection from the other side with the ball thrown back in our court. The Council would then once again become involved in an agonising debate this time between the US and the southern flankers (who would want to cede flank status to Hungary) and the central European countries who in varying degrees would want to stand firm on abeyance, with the northern flankers perhaps somewhere in between. Meanwhile, the Warsaw Pact would be happily sitting tight enjoying the spectacle of NATO's internal conflict and confidently expecting the Hungarian apple to fall into its lap.

10. With these factors in mind, there could be considerable advantage in setting in motion some discussion of other topics (the agenda items would be the obvious choice) while the probing exercise on Hungary continues. This could open up the possibility of reaching agreements, at present sorely lacking in the Vienna discussions; it would also enable discussions to continue between the two sides even if NATO runs into another brick wall on the Hungarian issue. Most of the Delegations in Vienna are well disposed to moving ahead in this way. It would, however, be necessary to convert the Italians who at present are vehemently opposed to discussions in any wider forum which might be prejudicial to the status of the NATO flank countries. It is just possible that Italy might acquiesce in smaller informal meetings of say four or five on each side. But on her present showing the chances are that Italy would not be prepared to broaden the discussion without taking the issue back to the Council.

[15] In his letter to Mr. Tickell (see note 3 above) Mr. Thomson described Mr. Y. Kvitsinsky, a Soviet delegate to the MBFR negotiations, as 'the nearest living approximation to Widmerpool, a character in Anthony Powell's novels, whose chief qualities were a distinct belief in his own indispensibility, extreme resilience and a rather sinister efficiency'.

[16] The final protocol of the four-Power agreement on Berlin was signed on 3 June. The quadripartite negotiations on Berlin are documented in Volume I.

PART II: CONCLUSIONS AND LESSONS FOR THE AUTUMN

11. A tempting conclusion to draw from what has happened at Vienna is that NATO's best course of action would be to call off the whole MBFR exercise, on the grounds that to continue offers no prospects of a satisfactory military outcome for the West and would impose undue strains on Allied unity. Would it not be better to negotiate any necessary reductions in US forces, together with any other changes in force structures that some of the European countries may have in mind, within the NATO family and not in the hostile environment of MBFR negotiations?

12. It is doubtful, however, whether abandonment is a real option. The issue has been joined and not only the United States but several of the European countries regard themselves as irrevocably and publicly committed to the enterprise. The breakdown of MBFR would be seen as a major failure of Western diplomacy, leaving the CSCE to dominate the multilateral East/West dialogue on security matters. The Warsaw Pact would be able to claim that NATO's MBFR invitation was devised merely as a counter-ploy to the CSCE and was never meant to be taken seriously.[17]

13. A more serious objection is that, without the inhibitions imposed by ongoing MBFR negotiations and subsequent agreements, there could be no end to the process of US force withdrawals. Under the 'keep it in the family' approach, there could be no guarantee that the US would not want to come along to NATO every two or three years with new proposals for reductions. On the other hand, if US reductions were made as part of MBFR, a link albeit informal would be established between the remaining levels of US forces and their Soviet counterparts. If there were further Congressional or public pressures, the existence of this link could be an important argument in the armoury of a well-disposed Administration, even one less favourable to Europe than the Nixon Administration.[18]

---

[17] In his minute of 1 March to Mr. McLaren (see note 7 above), Mr. Ramsay admitted that, with the risks inherent in MBFR negotiations, it was 'undeniably attractive' to try to reduce US Congressional pressure without recourse to discussions with the Russians. Nevertheless, despite the West having 'got off to a dismaying start', Mr. Ramsay suggested that 'there [was] no reason, given luck, patience and persistence, why the allies should not master the subject and their opponents'. Moreover, he added, there was 'no reason why the allies should not continue to attempt to reduce the level of Soviet forces in Eastern Europe. Although any withdrawal may be to a certain extent illusory in military terms insofar as troops could quickly be reintroduced, it could signify to a very real extent politically the shortening of the Russian shadow over Eastern Europe.'

[18] This point was made by Mr. Dean in his meeting with Mr. Mumford on 6 March (see note 10 above). Attempts to engineer a reduction in the US military presence in Europe 'within the NATO family as opposed to MBFR negotiations' had, Mr. Dean explained, the 'chief disadvantage' that 'there might be no end to the process so far as the US was concerned; NATO might be asked every few years to agree to a further scaling down of US forces in Europe. On the other hand, if US force reductions (which hopefully could be kept on a small scale) were negotiated under MBFR the resulting US force levels would be linked under contractual arrangements to the size of the Soviet forces remaining in Central Europe and thus a 'floor' would be established.' There would, Mr. Dean thought, be 'a good chance (if MBFR negotiations were successful) of introducing stability in NATO force levels in Europe over a long period which even an Administration of a different complexion in the United States would hesitate to upset. The prospect of having to engage

14 These arguments—which are commonly advanced by the Americans—are not completely water-tight. It may, for instance, turn out that MBFR is itself a continuous process and that the first agreements would merely prepare the ground for further scaling down of the US force presence in Europe. It has also yet to be proved that it would be possible to restrict MBFR even initially to reductions involving only US and Soviet stationed forces. There is evidence that some of the European countries will want to climb on the band-wagon from the outset.[19] The establishment of a link between US and Soviet force levels in Europe could have a serious disadvantage in terms of Allied freedom to manoeuvre. Nor does it necessarily follow that a link would be clearly established; some kinds of MBFR agreements, e.g. those involving a mixed package of identified capabilities on each side, would not necessarily be linked to overall force levels (the definition of which would be a major and highly controversial exercise).

15. On the assumption—which is probably the most realistic one—that NATO is saddled with MBFR, our aim should be to draw the right lessons from our experience in Vienna and apply them both to the preparations for and the conduct of the substantive negotiations which we must expect to begin in the autumn of this year. These lessons, as I see them, are as follows:

(1) Over the next few months, NATO must spare no effort to reach clear-cut agreement on its objectives in the substantive talks.[20] This applies not only to the nature, incidence and scale of force reductions proposals that NATO will want to put forward initially, but also to the major unresolved questions of the phasing of the negotiations and subsequent agreements and the place to be allocated to ancillary measures such as constraints. This would be a formidable task. At present the Alliance is awaiting a major new American study setting

anew in complicated MBFR negotiations in order to reduce US forces further could act as a powerful deterrent.'

[19] British officials were much exercised lest the MBFR negotiations impede attempts to secure new European defence arrangements. In a minute to Mr. McLaren of 27 March, Mr. Ramsay endorsed Mr. Thomson's view that one of the Soviet aims in MBFR would be to check and, if possible, reverse moves towards European defence unity. 'We may thus find', Mr. Ramsay observed, 'decisions with regard to future defence arrangements have been prejudiced not only by the letter of MBFR agreements but also by the spirit of East–West negotiations on reductions and other measures.'

[20] In a minute to Mr. Wiggin of 13 March (see notes 8 and 9), Mr. Tickell contrasted differing NATO attitudes towards the MBFR negotiations. The Americans, he claimed, wished to appear enthusiastic to reduce their forces to 'fend off domestic pressures'; the Belgians and the Dutch had 'an idealistic commitment' to the negotiations; and German opinion was divided between those who saw MBFR as a complement to *Ostpolitik*, and those who considered it 'to be militarily as well as politically dangerous'. However, he thought the British position clear: 'We do not like MBFR. We do not want Britain to be in a constraints area and we do not intend to reduce our forces. We are in the negotiations because we think this is the best way of helping the Americans keep their forces in Europe at acceptable levels, and because we think it enables us the more effectively to protect our own and European defence interests.' Mr. Tickell was not optimistic about the prospects for Allied agreement: 'Together these objectives scarcely add up. We are all playing a game of mirrors. It follows that the more we try to reach common positions, the harder it will be.'

out US ideas on the options; but this is not expected to be available until April at the earliest. Other countries including the UK are working on some studies but it will not be possible to make much progress until the American input is available.[21] It may not be possible to resolve in this period the delicate issue of whether NATO will be prepared to accept that at least initially MBFR reductions should be confined to US and Soviet stationed forces. But NATO should be clear on what scale of reductions on the US side would be consistent with the maintenance of NATO's military security; on what stage in the negotiations should NATO put forward proposals on reductions; and on whether NATO would be prepared to put forward a concept of constraints applying to a wider area than the potential reduction zone (in this context the question of Hungary could arise again in critical terms).

(2) NATO should also identify and seek to agree on the limits to which it is prepared to go on all aspects of MBFR, in response to Soviet counter-proposals. The hard lessons [*sic*] of Vienna is that sticking points must be those on which NATO is prepared either to break off the negotiations or to stomach a long period of delay notwithstanding the public consequences.

(3) In the substantive negotiations NATO must not operate under time pressures. We must avoid artificial deadlines.

(4) The criterion of success must not be allowed to dominate NATO thinking. This means that the Americans in particular will have to show a much greater sensitivity for Allied views and be prepared to conduct themselves as members of a team and not as the driver of the coach.[22]

(5) There must be trust in both the ability and the integrity of NATO's designated spokesmen. Once suspicion arises that deals are being conducted behind the scenes or proposals put forward in a way that causes misunder-

---

[21] In his minute of 27 March (see note 19 above) Mr. Ramsay argued that British policy should be more active than Mr. Mumford suggested. Britain, he argued, had the confidence of all her allies in the MBFR negotiations: 'They recognise that we do not operate under pressures, domestic or otherwise. They respect our military judgement and are quick to acknowledge that BAOR [British Army of the Rhine] is probably the most effective of all national contributions to NATO. If anyone is in a position to play an active role in formulating an Allied strategy for MBFR, we are. I think, therefore, that our earlier approach, namely that we could afford a relatively quietist role, has been to some extent overtaken by events. MBFR is clearly a hazardous enterprise. If it went wrong, it could have serious repercussions on the whole Western defence structure and consequently on our own security. We should do more to ensure that it does not. Among other things this will mean making our own views on MBFR more widely known.' Mr. Tickell, however, remained in favour of playing a waiting game. In a minute to Mr. Wiggin of 2 April, he explained that he was 'somewhat doubtful about whether we should come out entirely into the open in the immediate future. At present our somewhat insidious approach is making good progress, more indeed than seemed likely even a couple of months ago.' It would be better, he argued, to 'wait until we have discussed matters further with the Americans and can see the shape of their papers before attempting to change the time-encrusted mould of NATO thinking on MBFR'.

[22] In a minute to Sir T. Brimelow of 19 March, Mr. Wiggin confided that 'the Allied performance over MBFR to date has been pretty appalling. The Americans are by no means exclusively to blame. But the root cause of the trouble is that they have been in a hurry. There is no worse way to deal with the Russians.'

standings or gives signals to the other side that they are not fully backed by all members of the Alliance, NATO's negotiating position becomes untenable.

(6) The Alliance must improve its internal security. There is ample evidence in Vienna that the other side is well-informed of NATO's internal discussions. This calls for special handling of documents, restricted procedures for Council and other discussions, and generally a much greater degree of awareness of the security problem, which will be especially acute if, as seems likely, the substantive negotiations take place in Vienna where the NATO delegations are particularly vulnerable to intelligence efforts from the other side.[23]

(7) Satisfactory arrangements must be made within the Alliance between the negotiators on the spot and the North Atlantic Council. Tactics including the formulation of detailed texts should be left to the negotiators, within the broad guidance and criteria laid down by the Council. Once the objectives have been set out, the negotiators should be given a reasonable measure of flexibility on how they are achieved. They should not be placed in a position in which they have to refer back to the Council at every twist and turn of the negotiations.[24]

W.F. MUMFORD

[23] Mr. Wiggin noted on Mr. Tickell's covering minute: 'A very good report. I doubt, however, that the Russians need a major intelligence effort (though I do not doubt they have mounted it). The indiscipline in the Western camp is such that the Russians can get all they need by overt means!'

[24] But in a letter to Mr. Wiggin of 13 July, Sir E. Peck questioned whether the NAC had sufficient control over the negotiations. The West, he argued, had not extracted the best deal that they might have achieved. Allied delegations had been far too willing to fall back to reserve positions, conceding too much to the Soviet Union for too little gain. 'Some *tactical* flexibility must of course be left to the men on the spot', he wrote, 'but I fear that if they are also given flexibility on questions of substance and strategy, we shall find ourselves (as we did in the exploratory talks) giving away one position after another. The back-seat driver has a role to play in this sort of progress. This may all seem obvious to you and me, sitting in our rear echelons, but the temptations to some of our allies in the front line to yield points, whether for personal relief or domestic political considerations, are very considerable and the goodies are better kept from the eyes of the children, whatever charges of paternalism this may arouse.'

No. 5

Memorandum by Mr. Wiggin[1]

[*CAB 136/5*][2]

Secret. Eclipse FCO, *16 April 1973*

MBFR: Anglo/American Talks in Washington, 9–11 April 1973

I was accompanied to these talks by Mr. Nash[3] and Mr. Mumford, MoD, Mr Tickell, FCO, and members of our Embassy in Washington. Detailed records are being produced separately. What follows are some personal impressions of mine.

2. We saw the experts in the State Department, the White House, the Department of Defense, and ACDA[4] in that order, and finished with a round-up meeting in the State Department at which the above-mentioned Agencies, excluding the White House, were represented. In addition we had a variety of conversations with individuals on the side. All in all we saw a lot of people. The broad message that came across to me was both confused and depressing.

3. I am recording separately a summary of what we gleaned about the then current state of play (by no means necessarily final) on the Americans' outline reduction options, and will not discuss them in detail here. Broadly speaking the Administration's intentions struck me as good. One might pick holes in the options at length in detail and indeed some Americans we spoke to were themselves critical of certain aspects. And the Western percentage cuts, as we pointed out, are larger than we would ideally wish. But the options seemed to me pretty tough in principle, all involving more extensive Russian reductions than American ones. *Prima facie* they arguably corresponded with the repeated emphasis which the Americans placed on 'security first'.[5]

---

[1] Mr. Wiggin sent this paper and a memorandum on US outline force reduction options under a covering minute of 16 April to Sir T. Brimelow in preparation for the latter's forthcoming visit to Washington.

[2] The FCO copy of this document has not been traced.

[3] Mr. K.T. Nash was an AUS (Defence Staff) in the MoD.

[4] Arms Control and Disarmament Agency

[5] An American paper, 'The United States Approach to MBFR', communicated to NATO on 30 April, foresaw three possible force reduction approaches:

'1. Phased ten percent reductions in NATO stationed and then indigenous ground forces together with Soviet and [Warsaw] Pact stationed and then indigenous reductions, respectively, to common ceilings for both sides.

2. Reduction to parity in overall NATO/Pact ground force levels in the Center Region by means of US and Soviet reductions of one-sixth of their forces.

3. A mixed package illustrating an approximated 20 percent reduction of US nuclear systems for 20 percent reduction in Soviet armoured attack capability resulting in more defensively oriented postures and approximate stationed ground force parity on both sides' (WDN 27/10).

Commenting on this last proposal (which in earlier US draft papers had been listed as the second option), Mr. Wiggin noted in his memorandum on US outline force reduction options (see note 1

4.   However a series of basic questions arise from the options to which we were predictably unable to get clear or consistent answers. For example will the Americans be prepared to be tough over constraints, verification, and non-circumvention? (There are clearly divided views in Washington on collateral measures, with the Pentagon hawkish, the White House doveish.) How much of their initial positions do they regard as 'fat'? Will they, when the time comes in negotiation, hold out for asymmetrical common ceiling reductions or will they fall back to the type of equal reduction approach which the Russians are all too likely to favour? (The Americans argued, but without the appearance of deep conviction, that we should not under-estimate the possible attraction of their options to the Russians.) Will the Americans' position (or positions), whether or not eroded, constitute a once-for-all operation, or the start of a continuing process, i.e. a slippery slope? In other words how will they reconcile their negotiating positions with their Congressional requirements and actually play their hand in NATO and with the Warsaw Pact?

5.   On every side we heard that the key is Congress (though there were also warnings of budgetary difficulties and references to burden-sharing on the side); that there is now an unprecedented war across the board between the Executive and the Legislature which increasingly means issues are not judged on their merits; and that MBFR must be regarded as a part and parcel of that war. (Mr. Sonnenfeldt expressed the view that, in the light of hindsight, the Administration had 'overloaded' MBFR, which was by now sceptically regarded in Congress as a device; but they were stuck with it.)

6.   I have no doubt that this preoccupation with Congress is genuine, not something invented to put the wind up the Europeans. Opinions varied on the containability of Congress. Indeed one could extract differing opinions from an individual depending on how the question was put. Some optimists argued that negotiations might drag on inconclusively for years. But the answers added up to an overwhelming consensus that sooner or later some cuts in American forces are inevitable; that the important thing is to keep them minimal; and to mitigate their effect by qualitative improvements (both American and European).

7.   Inevitably we were subjected to a variety of arguments designed to rationalise the situation. We were told more than once that MBFR, if properly handled, should actually lead to enhanced security for the West (because the Russian withdrawals would be greater and because the West could improve quality and so on). We were also told by systems analysts in the Defense Department that their latest studies (not yet accepted throughout the Administration nor indeed in the Defense Department as a whole) suggest that current conventional NATO wisdom strongly overestimates the Warsaw Pact threat and strongly

above): 'An obvious disadvantage of this option is that it envisages minimal cuts in United States personnel and hence is likely to be the least attractive to Congress. Moreover there is recognition that some at least of the Western Europeans might fear this was the start of "decoupling". Nevertheless there are arguably attractions in "swapping" a relatively small part of NATO's tactical nuclear capability, which many consider both over-abundant and obsolescent, for a very large number of Soviet tanks. And the White House argued that it ought to be possible to persuade Congress that anything involving teeth arms on this scale was a very serious MBFR exercise.'

underestimates the NATO capability to contain a conventional attack by conventional means. Repeatedly the Americans placed emphasis on the importance of winding up the exploratory talks in Vienna as quickly as possible but insisted that when it came to negotiations in the Autumn they would be able to play things tough and long because the very fact that negotiations were taking place would contain Congress. (Yet the Americans had no real answer to the comment that the exploratory talks were supposed to establish whether a basis for negotiations existed; in reply they effectively pleaded expediency; they also argued that reductions must be *discussed* quite early in negotiations if Congress were to be contained; one could not sit for ever arguing about principles and constraints, even if the prior exploratory talks had been virtually a non-event.)

8.   As we already knew, all the Americans wanted to concede on Hungary as quickly as possible. They insisted (with some truth) that Hungary is not militarily all that important. Mr. Eagleburger[6] in the Department of Defense put the position bluntly. He said that the Alliance had got themselves into a mess over Hungary; for this the Americans (who had initially made the running in pressing for Hungary to be in the reduction zone) were primarily to blame; but in present circumstances, given also the Congressional problem, the Alliance must cut their diplomatic losses instead of losing further political face. If we continue to hold out against a Hungarian formula acceptable to the Americans and tolerable to the rest of our Allies—and we seem to be getting very near the point—we are likely to come under very heavy pressure indeed to 'display solidarity'.

9.   Within the Administration, the White House and the Defense Department struck us as the key ingredients. I was depressed, though not surprised, by the seeming 'deadness' of the State Department (even Mr. Rush)[7] and, to a somewhat lesser extent, of ACDA. The White House and Defense Department take a global view of the MBFR problem. For example, Mr. Eagleburger (who will shortly replace Mr. Sonnenfeldt in the White House) told me in terms that the Administration are not prepared to try to exert leverage on the Russians over Hungary if only because they need all the leverage they can get for much more burning issues, eg Cambodia.[8] However, we were subjected to comparatively little pressure on the wider scene (trade, monetary, burden-sharing, etc.).

10.   Both the White House and Defense Department spoke to us with frankness. (The latter were particularly frank on continuing differences within the Administration eg on one or two major questions relating to the negotiating options, partly because they wished to enlist our aid on their side!) Both also showed every indication of wanting to work very closely with us. The Defense Department also hope that the Americans, Germans, and ourselves will from now on be able to work together over MBFR on a continuing basis informally; we

[6] Mr. L.S. Eagleburger was an Acting Assistant Secretary of Defence and a Deputy Assistant to the President for National Security Operations.

[7] Mr. K. Rush was Deputy Secretary of State.

[8] Despite the arrangement of cease-fires in Vietnam and Laos during January/February 1973, Dr. Kissinger had so far been unable to end the conflict in Cambodia between the forces of the Khmer Rouge and those of the Lon Nol Government in Phnom Penh.

welcomed this idea, provided it were done discreetly, but it remains to be seen whether the State Department, who were clearly nervous, will seek to block it.

11. The Americans are acutely conscious that time is getting short if negotiations are to start in September/October. (We also heard November mentioned.) They hoped to get their options paper to NATO 'in a week or two'. They purported to think that no special machinery would be needed in NATO to process their options paper. They are evidently nervous that the more extensive the machinery the slower the process of evolving an Allied negotiating position will prove.

12. While on this occasion all our meetings were 'overt' we found ourselves faced with the usual procedural difficulties one experiences with this Administration. The fullest and most detailed account of the options we were given came from the White House with injunctions not to let anyone else (American or Allied) [know] that we had been given them in such detail. In practice this did not prove too difficult. Mr. Eagleburger sensibly proceeded on the assumption that we knew all we needed to know for the time being. The State Department were more concerned with pious generalities and fending off awkward questions defensively than with serious discussion of substance. And ACDA had little to contribute.

13. To sum up, it is not the Administration's basic intentions that worry me but their own evident doubts that they will be able to hold to them; and the appalling muddle one senses in Washington. (They are going through a highly incestuous time, and seemed to have given little visible thought, even, to what negotiating position the Russians are likely to adopt.)

Initial Soviet and Hungarian reactions to the formula agreed in the NAC and advanced by Mr. Dean and Mr. Quarles were discouraging. The Hungarians were opposed to an arrangement which singled them out for special mention, and during late March Warsaw Pact representatives began to press for agreement on a list of eleven direct participants, to be described as 'potential participants in future agreements', followed by a clause allowing for the co-option of other states (possibly including France) to their ranks, and a list of eight special participants, including Hungary. Meanwhile, Mr. Dean's will to hold out against Soviet tactics appeared to be sapped by the news from Washington that on 15 March Senator Mansfield had succeeded in persuading the Senate Democratic Caucus to adopt a resolution calling for a substantial reduction of American troops overseas during the next eighteen months. Other NATO delegations were in any case prepared, albeit reluctantly, to accept a tentative agreement negotiated by Mr. Dean and Mr. Quarles with the Russians. This listed eleven direct, and eight flank, participants, and included an enlargement clause and provisions for chairmanship, seating, equal rights of speaking, confidentiality of meetings and official languages; and was associated with an ad referendum agreement on the texts of two statements, one setting out the Western view of Hungary's status on the lines agreed by the NAC on 12 March, and the other, for delivery by Hungary, which stated that its participation in possible agreements could only take place as long as the 'appropriate conditions' were fulfilled—a thinly veiled reference to the link with Italy. When the NAC met on 18 April the British delegates objected to this understanding which seemed to prejudge the Hungarian issue in favour of the Warsaw Pact, and which exposed the Alliance to the risk of 'a major political and psychological set-back at the start of long and vitally important negotiations'.[1] *They floated instead the idea of going for an agreement on a simple agenda and for a brief communiqué, leaving the vexed question of participation and procedures to be settled through other diplomatic channels. But once more isolated within the Alliance, the British had by 27 April to make do with American assurances that the United States would join fully in Western efforts to prevent the circumvention of agreements and would keep open the question of Hungary's inclusion in a constraints area. They also acquiesced, in the interest of Allied solidarity, in a Soviet demand that the application of agreed procedures to the substantive negotiations should not preclude participation by other states.*[2]

The package on participation and procedures was approved at the first formal plenary session which was held in the boardroom of the International Atomic Energy Agency on 14 May. Subsequent plenaries on 15, 16 and 17 May revealed how far apart Eastern and Western delegations were on the objects and substance of the negotiations. For NATO, Canada proposed a detailed agenda consisting of: timing and stages; principles and criteria; the precise area to be covered; constraints; determination of forces to be addressed; size and method of reductions (including non-circumvention); and verification. By contrast, the GDR and Poland suggested on behalf of the Warsaw Pact that the agenda should consist of only three items: mutual reductions of armed forces and armaments in central Europe; the principle of undiminished security; and the creation of a working group. Two lengthy meetings between delegations representing each side failed to reconcile these widely divergent views and, following a plenary on 24 May, the Ad Hoc Group decided that the time had come to move on to the discussion of a brief communiqué which might incorporate language on the general objectives of the negotiations and cover certain cardinal points such as constraints on armed forces and the phasing of force reductions. A week of intensive negotiations resulted in an understanding on some controversial passages and agreement on a number of more difficult sentences, notably those covering general objectives and the right of direct participants to introduce for negotiation any topic connected with the subject matter of the negotiations. The latter was important for the Western delegates since, in the event of no formal agenda having been settled at the outset of the negotiations, it would allow them to insist on the consideration of such issues as constraints and the non-circumvention of force reductions in Hungary without being subject to the consensus procedure. There was also a tentative accord on how the negotiations should be described: Mutual Reduction of Armed Forces and Armaments and Associated Measures in Central Europe. This met Eastern objections to the use of the adjective 'balanced' which the West finally agreed to omit from the description, provided the concept was covered elsewhere in the communiqué.[3]

During two informal negotiating sessions on 7 and 8 June a communiqué was completed and agreed ad referendum. But the Russians were by then demanding that the negotiations should not commence until one month after the completion of Stage III of the CSCE. This seemed likely to postpone the negotiations until at least the spring of 1974. The Canadians, with support from the Dutch and Belgians, argued in the NAC that the West should block progress towards a CSCE until the Russians had conceded an acceptable starting date for MBFR. Others, particularly the

---

[1] Report by Mr. Johnson on the Exploratory Talks on MBFR in Central Europe enclosed in No. 6.

[2] *V. ibid.*

[3] *V. ibid.*

Americans, were not prepared to make such a formal link, but were ready to put pressure on the Russians to stand by their earlier commitment. Indeed, Soviet agreement to negotiations beginning in Vienna on 30 October was finally achieved during Mr. Brezhnev's visit to the United States in mid-June.[4] *This allowed for the formal adoption of the communiqué at a plenary on 28 June.*[5]

[4] See Volume II, No. 40, note 7.

[5] See Cmnd 6932, p. 142.

No. 6

Letter from Mr. Thomson (UKDEL Vienna) to Mr. Wiggin
[*WDN 27/4*]

Confidential   VIENNA, *29 June 1973*

Dear Charles,

MBFR

1.   In a separate letter to Crispin Tickell[1] I have followed a suggestion from Tom Brimelow and set out some of the conclusions I reached about Soviet techniques of negotiation as demonstrated in the MBFR Exploratory Talks in Vienna. This letter is intended as a more formal summing up of these talks from their beginning on 31 January to their closure on 28 June. I enclose three documents which together tell the story. The first is an historical account by Mr. David Johnson;[2] the second is the agreed record of the plenary meeting on 14 May;[3] and the third is the final communiqué.[4] The purpose of this letter is not to adorn the tale but to point some morals.

2.   The steering brief[5] for the negotiations instructed me to aim at three objectives: to seek some way of lowering the level of armed forces and armaments in Central Europe while maintaining undiminished security for all; to help the Americans; to keep the alliance together.

3.   The third of these objectives proved the most difficult. The lack of common substantive positions meant that in every document and in many discussions members of the Western Ad Hoc Group in Vienna were contending for somewhat differing policies. The debates on procedural questions were correctly seen as likely to influence the outcome of disputes on policy and were accordingly hard fought. Many of the most important words in the negotiation were highly neuralgic within the supposedly united body of the 13 allied representatives (including Portugal) not to speak of the various silent representatives

[1] No. 7.

[2] Not printed. See p. 21, note 1, and p. 36, note 1.

[3] Not printed. See p. 36.

[4] See Cmnd 6932, p. 142.

[5] No. 3.

of the Secretary General, Saceur and Deputy Saceur. For example it mattered considerably whether the word 'area' appeared in the singular or the plural. So much of the energy of the allies was devoted to negotiating among themselves that it sometimes seemed as if the negotiations with the Russians were a secondary matter. This resulted from the failure of the alliance to agree on a substantive policy covering basic matters in the MBFR field in advance of the Vienna talks. These basic questions have still not been resolved and it is clearly important for the harmony and effectiveness of the alliance that they should be soon. However I believe that it must be accepted that the considerations involved in MBFR touch the sovereignty and security of members of the alliance a good deal more closely than the CSCE questions and accordingly there will probably always be some questions on which one or more members of the alliance feels so strongly that they are not prepared to acquiesce in a consensus without a major struggle.[6] The history of the Vienna talks is discouraging to the extent that it shows these questions are fairly numerous but reassuring in that it shows that even so the alliance does in the end achieve a consensus.

4.   No question provoked more differences within the alliance or took up more of the time and energy of the negotiators than that of participation. The question of who was involved in what, to what extent and with what rights and responsibilities emerged in almost every discussion. In numerous telegrams I have described the attitudes—often inconsistent—taken up by the various countries and the vast expense of emotion which has been expended upon them. Again these are questions which are thought to involve so closely the sovereignty, self-respect and security of various countries that it will probably never be possible to draw up hard and fast rules to which there will be no exceptions. In dealing with these questions from a distance there is a great temptation when one or more allies feel passionately to allow them to have their way. But against this natural and generous impulse must be set the real risks to security and efficiency. For example, if the flank countries are really allowed to act as if they were direct participants we may all find that before long it will be hard to prevent their troops and armaments being brought into the negotiations. Once the geographic concept of Central Europe is blurred it would be an easy matter to bring in the territory of the United Kingdom on the grounds that British plans specifically provide for air and ground intervention in Central Europe. Hence the UK should be counted as part of the 'strategic area' of Central Europe—a phrase which the Russians were with some difficulty persuaded to drop from the final communiqué. Moreover it is simply not practical to draft in a plenary of 19 delegations involving some 150 people in the room. Even if it were practical the Russians have convincingly shown that in the presence of so large a group particularly of their

---

[6] In a letter to Mr. Tickell of 21 March Sir E. Peck argued that the UK had 'a crucial role to play' in maintaining Allied cohesion: 'Whether we like it or not, many of our Allies are going to look to us to speak with the voice of reason and moderation, to speak for the interests of the Alliance as a whole. Many of my colleagues feel, however much they understand the overall Alliance interest, that they have no choice but to reflect the domestic pressures to which their governments are subject'. Mr. Wiggin hardly enthused at this prospect. On 19 March he minuted to Sir T. Brimelow 'the lot of the honest broker in an Alliance in disarray is not always a happy one'.

allies they are unwilling to make any concessions. The real bargaining in Vienna has taken place in small groups often with only two a-side and in informal circumstances. We must expect that this pattern will largely hold true for the substantive negotiations as well. Any attempt to insist on conducting the essence of the negotiations in a plenary or some similarly broad forum will undoubtedly result in private Soviet/American meetings in which all the real business will be done. The consequence for European American relations and for the cohesion of the alliance could be serious.

5.   Accordingly it will be important that in discussing participation questions the alliance should avoid saddling itself with a Procrutean [*sic*] formula. Flexibility should be left to the negotiators on the spot. To accommodate the susceptibilities of all with the requirements of alliance security and efficiency it will be necessary to negotiate in a variety of different fora and groups. While the flank countries should have every opportunity to play a full and equal part in the Ad Hoc Group they should not be accorded a part in the negotiations equal to that of the direct participants. Even the Turks profess to accept this but unless they are held to their professed view from the very outset there will be serious internal allied squabbles. Plenaries should be a regular feature of the negotiations but they will be largely used for making speeches rather than for detailed negotiation. Smaller groups can be established for individual tasks. More generally I believe it will be valuable for each at least of the Western direct participants to be charged with some specific task in the context of the negotiations so that all may feel they have their own role within the team. Working groups (both open-ended and with a restricted membership) dealing with different aspects of the negotiation may prove a useful device.

6.   But in the end the nub of the negotiations will for practical reasons have to be conducted privately in a very small group. It is obvious that the Russians and the Americans will have to be in it. But in practice it will be undesirable that it should be restricted to them alone. Additions on the Western side can be provided by a system of rotation but that tends to be clumsy and inefficient. The only two countries which could in practice form part of the permanent Western negotiating team are Britain and Germany and I believe it will be right that they should do so or at any rate that they should rotate between themselves.

7.   The danger of Soviet/American bilateralism was borne constantly in mind by the Western negotiators and certainly not least by Mr. Dean. Yet there is little doubt that in practice the MBFR Exploratory Talks in a small way forwarded this bilateralism. There were occasions on which the two super powers obviously felt more comfortable in talking to each other than to their allies. I believe the British and German delegations did a good deal to help reduce this risk and I am sure that this will be a principle [*sic*] task of our negotiators in the substantive talks. Yet when all is said and done I suspect that in the long run it will be seen that MBFR is enhancing the tendency towards Soviet/American bilateralism.[7]

---

[7] Giving his 'worm's eye view' of the exploratory talks in his minute of 1 March (see No. 4 note 7) Mr. Ramsay observed that he did not think 'that the Americans, however tempted, [would]

8.   The second of the objectives set out in the steering brief was to help the Americans. The most important thing we could do in this respect was and is precisely to help them avoid both the appearance and the reality of bilateralism. But as I have suggested this is an uphill struggle. The Americans are so much the most powerful of the allies that they do not need ordinarily much help from the others. On some occasions when the Americans were in a minority of one or little more they managed to bring the whole alliance round to their point of view. And they disposed of splendid facilities which helped them in this task. For example they alone had a conference room which could comfortably accommodate the Ad Hoc Group. They alone had the staff and equipment to turn out voluminous records and simultaneously to prepare fresh proposals between one meeting and the next. The Vienna talks have certainly been conducted so far in an American ambience and the Russians by their constant consultation with the Americans in advance of any other Western country have encouraged this.

9.   Some European offset to the American dominance is required. In defence matters I do not think this can at present appropriately come from the Nine[8] and certainly as I have said elsewhere it is horrendous to think of the additional complications which France might introduce into the negotiations. Accordingly I believe that in the context of the MBFR negotiations the European offset must come from a continuance of the very close cooperation between the British and German delegations. In practice informal American/British/German meetings acted as a steering group for the Western caucus. It was in such meetings that the pros and cons of various moves were sorted out and that allied tactics were really determined. When the three of us were agreed we could always get the rest of the Ad Hoc Group to follow. It would be naive to suppose that the rest of the group were wholly ignorant of the tripartite meetings but their 'invisibility' made it easier for the rest of the Group to accept the results. I imagine that informal tripartite consultation of this sort will be equally essential for the substantive negotiations.

10.   The third[9] [*sic*] objective in the steering brief, namely to seek some way of lowering the level of armed forced and armaments in Central Europe while maintaining undiminished security for all hardly applied in a practical sense since it was accepted that the consultations were about procedure and not about substance. And as regards the latter I suggest that the balance sheet of our five months negotiation shows that both sides gained and lost about equally but with perhaps a shade of advantage to the West. On the one side the Western

ever deal bilaterally with the Russians on MBFR'. But he added that 'the American bell-wether is not a particularly sagacious animal and it is questionable whether it knows where it is leading the rest of the flock. The credibility of the future American negotiating position on MBFR, and of their professions that the interests of Western security are of the highest importance[,] risk being eroded by their apparent overwhelming sense of being under pressure and the lack of a sense of proportion evident in many of their attitudes on the Hungarian issue and others.' Mr. Ramsay concluded that in view of 'American behaviour over Hungary, it is not perhaps surprising that a number of allies have less confidence than hitherto in American promises of toughness in later stages'.

[8] The nine European Community (EC) member states. See Volume II, No. 1, note 14.

[9] This is evidently an error and refers to the first objective.

negotiators came to Vienna believing that Hungary would be fully involved as a direct participant in the substantive negotiations. Before they left they had had to concede that Hungary was a participant with a special status; in effect an observer. They had preserved their position to the extent that there was specific provision for enlarging the number of direct participants and that there was a specific Western statement acknowledged by the East that we reserved the right to bring Hungary into the negotiations. Nevertheless in the light of the agreement it is hard to believe that the Russians will be prepared to negotiate any reduction in their troops and armaments stationed in Hungary. This is perhaps not of vital importance for Hungary was not after all originally included in the area about which NATO wished to negotiate. Nevertheless the result of the battle over Hungarian participation must on balance be accounted a Russian victory. Against this the Russians came to Vienna with a concept which was limited to the mutual reduction of forces and armaments and in which there was no place for constraints, verification, step by step procedures and all the other safeguards and cautious procedures woven into the Western concept of a phased approach to MBFR. When the Russians left they had been obliged to accept a communiqué with their concept of mutual reduction of forces and armaments enlarged by the addition of the phrase 'and associated measures' which of course covers such Western desiderata as constraints and verification. They were also obliged to accept passages in the communiqué which spelt out the Western concept of 'step by step' and 'balanced'. Indeed paragraph 3 of the final communiqué probably contains a better description of the essence of the Western position than a great many of the earlier Western unilateral statements.[10] It remains to be seen how far these general agreements can be translated into acceptable practical measures. But at least the negotiators at the substantive talks will be proceeding from an agreed statement which owes more to the Western than to the Soviet concept of MBFR. Hence my belief that on balance the West has gained the advantage by a shade.

11. However MBFR remains a potentially dangerous negotiation: there are so many ways in which it can be turned against Western interests. The most serious risks are not military. Presumably the West will avoid entering into agreements which are seriously detrimental in military terms to Western security.[11] The real risks are more political. I have already drawn attention to the dangers posed

[10] See Cmnd 6932, p. 142.

[11] Mr. Ramsay was not confident that a militarily disadvantageous arrangement could so easily be avoided, fearing that domestic political pressure in the US might precipitate hasty force reductions. He warned Mr. McLaren in a minute of 9 March: 'If Senator Mansfield cannot be bought off with negotiations alone then the price must be raised to include early negotiation on reductions in which the focus would be on US troops. The Americans have not yet said that it would be necessary to reach an early agreement. But we now have abundant evidence that their commitment to keep Mansfield at bay includes a commitment to early consideration of reductions' (WDN 27/6). Mr. Tickell agreed. In his minute of 13 March to Mr. Wiggin (see No. 4, note 8) he observed that 'the Allies all feel public pressure in favour of a more relaxed relationship between East and West, and would like to enjoy undiminished security at lower expense'. Although privately Allied governments might 'believe a negotiable MBFR arrangement dangerous or unobtainable', he thought the 'gap between private and public attitudes [was] already evident'.

by the lack of agreed substantive positions, by the squabbles for place and prestige and by the growing degree of Soviet/American bilateralism. There is also the danger that the Russians will obtain a clear understanding of Western differences of opinion and will exploit them. For example they may be able to heighten American/European differences and thus reduce the credibility of the American guarantee to Europe.[12] They may also be able to establish a *locus standi* for interfering in European affairs particularly in European defence arrangements. In addition they will have opportunities to manoeuvre Germany into a special position.

12. The main moral to be pointed is that we must not allow ourselves to be carried incautiously forward by the momentum of policies established in different circumstances some years ago. We should think very hard and clearly about where the MBFR negotiation could take us, what options they will be closing off and what the balance of risk and advantage is likely to be. Some MBFR negotiations are inevitable and indeed for some purposes desirable. Yet for my own part I believe that the reorganisation of Western defence efforts is of greater importance than any attempt to achieve further relaxation of East–West tensions through MBFR.

13. There are also some administrative morals to be pointed. No one expected (except probably the Russians) that the negotiations would last five months and this was no doubt the reason why the British delegation had only one permanent member. The rest of us had other jobs in other capitals and we came and went at times that were often dictated by these and not by the MBFR situation. In the course of the five months four different people acted as my deputy. There were unexpected personnel changes in London which could not be avoided. In the circumstances I doubt whether this delegation could have operated at all without the generosity of Sir E Peck not only in loaning his deputy for an unconscionably long period but also in loaning on occasion other members of UKDEL NATO. Nor could this delegation have operated without the always cheerful and efficient assistance of HM Embassy Vienna. They were kindness itself in taking a cuckoo into the nest and in supporting and nourishing it at all hours of the day and night. But also it must be said that the peripatetic members of the delegation[,] as always the one stalwart Mr. David Johnson and my secretary Miss Christine Pealing[,] worked with a liveliness and determination which often enabled us to keep pace even with the Americans.

14. The conclusion I draw is that the Treasury having got a rather good bargain out of the exploratory talks should not take this as a precedent for the substantive negotiations. An adequate permanent staff with their own support

---

[12] In his minute of 9 March (*v. ibid.*) Mr. Ramsay noted: the 'difference in the European and American approach to MBFR is important. The Americans do not want their political difficulties exacerbated by European insistence on an approach to negotiations which would do little if anything to ease the Congressional pressures. Any temptations the US may have for dealing bilaterally with the USSR [in] a particular aspect of MBFR may be increased as a result. The Europeans do not wish to see a possible instrument of East/West dialogue on security matters used for the transitory political ends of the US Administration with the added risk that negotiations could, for all their multilateral appearance develop into a bilateral exercise.'

which they can call on as of right really makes a difference to efficiency. More-over they should have suitable entertainment allowances since with at least 19 delegations involved a great deal of the squaring and lobbying has to be done over meals.

15.   My final comment from Vienna is that the MBFR negotiations may prove to be typical of a great deal of diplomacy in the complicated multi-polar world in which we now exist. I have described above some of the frustrations and difficulties which are inherent in multilateral diplomacy. There is however a wealth of fascination in dealing with them. The techniques of this type of negoti-ation repay study but the main moral is clear: everything else can be managed if the alliance can be kept united.

Yours ever,
J.A. THOMSON

No. 7

Letter from Mr. Thomson (UKDEL Vienna) to Mr. Tickell

[*WDN 27/10*]

Confidential   VIENNA, *29 June 1973*

Dear Crispin,

Farewell from the Pension Nossek [1]

1.   Now that it is at last time to say farewell to Frau Rakowicz [2] and the Pension Nossek I do so with a tinge of regret that almost surprises me. When I flew to Vienna in January the ploughed fields of the Danubian plain were sharply etched in a powdering of snow. Vienna was drab and dowdy: it appeared to have reverted to its Roman role of an outpost on the edge of the civilised world.[3] But now the

---

[1]   The Pension Nossek was the small hotel used to accommodate the British delegation for the duration of the exploratory talks. The delegates were originally housed in the Astoria Hotel but were subsequently moved, on Mr. Thomson's insistence, both on grounds of economy and security (the hotel was also being used by Warsaw Pact delegates and was thought to be 'staked out' by the KGB (*Komitet Gosudarstvennoi Besopasnosti*)). As Mr. Thomson later recalled: 'The result was the Pension Nossek in the Graben. It was an admirable choice. It was approximately in the centre of the First District of Vienna in an historic setting; the building was more sympathetic and had much more light than the hotel; it was notably cheaper and we were all convinced that the proprietresses would have given short shrift to any permanent KGB eavesdropping' (letter from Sir J. Thomson to the Editor of 28 March 1999).

[2]   Frau Rakowicz, assisted by her sister, was the Pension Nossek's proprietress.

[3]   Mr. Thomson was mindful that this was not the first time Vienna had played host to a multilateral diplomatic conference. In a letter to Mr. Tickell of 21 February, he noted that Vienna's most recent conference did not perhaps compare, at least in style, to the one that had ended the Napoleonic Wars: 'Our grey little talks are no match for the Congress of Vienna. The Viennese have greeted us in friendly fashion but have probably been disappointed with our lack of glamour

same ploughed fields have burdgeoned [*sic*] in delicate greens and browns. Vienna has revealed undoubted charms. The Prunksæl[4] is a finer library even than Wren[']s at Trinity College Cambridge: Peterskirch[5] is the most perfect of restrained Baroque churches. And the collection of pictures rifled by the Habsburgs from every capital in Europe is one of the glories of Western civilization. But the impression remains that although Austria is a Western country, Vienna is a frontier outpost. I suspect that it is now about to become even more than in the past an East–West trading or negotiating station and the MBFR Exploratory Talks that are now concluding may prove to be typical of the commerce that will be done there.

2. Tom Brimelow suggested to me that it would be a modest addition to the store of knowledge if I were to note my impressions of the negotiating techniques used in the Vienna talks. This I now do pausing only to remind you briefly of the course which the talks took.

3. The initial stage was as barren and chilly as the fields on the Danubian plain. When the first agreement was finally reached (against strenuous British opposition) in the middle of May it represented a victory for Soviet persistence over Western impatience. In the next month the tables were somewhat turned. The West put the Russians under pressure and obtained from them some useful concessions which should later help the West to reach its objective of a phased MBFR programme, including not only troop and armament reductions but also 'associated measures'. During the final 3 weeks of the consultations nothing of importance happened in Vienna. The negotiators on both sides were waiting for the Nixon/Brezhnev summit[6] to confirm the date for the opening of the substantive talks, in accordance with the 1972 agreement between Kissinger and Brezhnev. The negotiators were under no illusion about the significance for the future of this dependence on super power agreement.

4. With the exception of this third and final phase, the talks were a valid and interesting exposition of two different types of negotiation—negotiating with Allies and negotiating with adversaries. One thing at least was common to both, and that was the importance of the personalities involved.

5. On the Western side the dominating personality was undoubtedly the leader of the US Delegation, Jock Dean. He is a man of many parts, of great

---

and our general 'invisibility'. We have been assigned the Hofburg as the site of our formal meetings whenever they may begin. But we are not destined to use the main salons. We drab bureaucrats are to gather in the room usually reserved for waiting footmen and coachmen in Franz Josef's time. The modern Metternich is not among us. His shadow does indeed fall darkly over us while he flits from Washington to Peking to Tokyo (everywhere but Europe in this 'year of Europe'. Nor do I discern a Talleyrand or a Castlereagh at our amiable 'plenary cocktails'. Instead we have hardworking lawyers and diplomats whose first thought is to engage in drafting and whose second is to avoid publicity' (WDN 27/4). Cf. H.A. Kissinger, *Years of Upheaval* (London: Weidenfeld and Nicolson and Michael Joseph, 1982), pp. 128–94.

[4] The Court Library was completed in 1737 and houses the *Österreichische Nationalbibliothek*.

[5] Completed in 1733, the Collegiate and City Parish Church of St. Peter was decorated by some of the most famous artists of the Baroque age.

[6] See p. 37.

force of character and yet he is insensitive to the impact he makes on others. He is more successful in thumping the table with Soviet adversaries than in cajoling Allies. The Germans were well served by Fred Ruth.[7] He was a loyal and generous colleague. He had the courage of his convictions, which were founded on an extensive knowledge of the subject. Yet, like some other German diplomats he was prone to abandon positions which he had hitherto held to be fundamental in exchange for some obscure and unlikely formula, the interpretation of which was certain to be disputed. Ambassador Quarles for the Netherlands was always professionally competent and showed himself a gentleman in every instinct but he had no stomach for a prolonged fight. Ambassador Grande for Canada was the one at whom we laughed while Ambassador Adriaenssen for Belgium was the one with whom we laughed. The former's stolidity was allied with obstinacy while the latter's quicksilver wit flowed from an instability of temperament which prevented him from pursuing the same policy for three days on end. The Northern flank representatives were silent and sensible; the Southern flank representatives were often vociferous and shrill. Although both Tulumen (Turkey) and Taliani (Italy) were personally agreeable they had only two themes: first, that they must be included to the full in all negotiations and second, that none of their countries' assets should be involved in any negotiations. It was to the credit of Sekeris (Greece) that he told his colleagues they could not have it both ways. By dint of daily meetings the Group evolved a high degree of cohesion and loyalty. It was an efficient or at any rate a necessary instrument for obtaining an agreed Allied position on objectives and tactics.

6. On the Eastern side the undoubted leader of the band was Professor Khlestov, the Head of Law and Treaty Department in the Soviet Ministry of Foreign Affairs. He was presumably appointed because of his ability to conduct a campaign of procrastination. He did this with success and was disappointed not to receive a Soviet decoration on his 50th birthday which came at the climax of the talks. However it was plain that Khlestov, the son of a former opera singer and with Jewish blood in his veins felt it necessary to pay much attention to the views of his two principal lieutenants. The sinister Kvitsinsky, the Widmerpool of my February letter,[8] was the hatchet man of the team while his successor Anatoli Movchan, who took over when procrastination gave way to constructive negotiation was the fixer. If he could be persuaded, the rest of the Soviet team almost always came round to that view. The function of Timerbayev (an Indi[a] rubber man to match the Belgian Adriaenssen) sometimes seemed to be to float ideas which could later be disavowed.

7. The other Warsaw Pact Delegations, when it came to the crunch, hardly mattered, although it must be said that Khlestov obviously felt that he had a difficult problem in handling some of them, especially the Hungarians who were given no notice at all of the unwelcome news that their country was not, after all, to be counted as a direct participant and the Romanians who were throughout courageous mavericks. Constantinescu, the leader of the Romanian team, was

---

[7] Herr F. Ruth was Head of the MBFR Department of the West German Foreign Ministry.

[8] See No. 4, notes 3 and 15.

clever and persistent but found it difficult to make bricks without straw. The Bulgarians were nonentities. Dr. Ustor,[9] the distinguished Hungarian international lawyer, made a dignified withdrawal to Geneva after ratifying his countries' [*sic*] demotion in status and his Delegation were of no account thereafter. Strulak, the Pole, was far and away the best informed of the Warsaw Pact leaders on the subject and showed himself subtle and able in argument. The East German, Brie, was plainly unsympathetic personally to the Soviet Delegation. So far as I could judge he was the only Warsaw Pact delegate who was a really devoted Communist and his ascetic attitude ('money is a matter of no importance') did not at all fit in with the jollity and hard drinking of the Russians in their off-duty moments. They much preferred to deal with the Czech Tomas Lahoda, a successful and convivial Vicar of Bray.[10] It was he whom the Russians chose to bring into the real negotiations, probably because Strulak and Brie could not be trusted to refrain from making awkward reports to their Embassies in Moscow.

8. In my brief and possibly untypical experience of face to face negotiation with the Russians, I found myself impressed by the techniques and attitudes required, so different from those that are usually successful in negotiation within the Alliance. A special effort was needed to understand the point of view from which the Russians were operating: it was in many respects so different from Western assumptions. It was necessary to explain the Western position and the reasons for it over and over and over again. In the end of course one used this repetition as a technique for boring the Russians and they proved just as susceptible to boredom as we did. But the first half a dozen times were often necessary simply to enable them to understand, for they too had to make an effort to comprehend our positions. When they understood it sometimes happened that they accepted the validity of the argument. Still more often it was only when they realised the seriousness of the Western attitude and the political or military requirements behind it that they could see that they would be obliged to make some concession to meet it.

9. This necessity for constant explanation and repetition meant that it was important that the Western negotiators should not become impatient. The Russians had to be made to understand that we could go on as long as they without moving. And the importance in their mind of the time pressures was demonstrated by the glee which they showed whenever they thought we were obliged to show a result by a given date.

10. Over time and with persistence the Western negotiators were able to feel they could piece together the Soviet instructions. It was apparent that the Russians had firm and clear instructions which however were probably not very detailed. It was also apparent that they did not like asking for fresh instructions unless they

[9] Dr. E. Ustor was Head of the International Law Department of the Hungarian Foreign Ministry.

[10] Tradition asserts that Symon Symonds, the vicar of Bray, Berkshire, preserved his incumbency of fifty years by becoming twice Protestant and twice Catholic under Henry VIII, Edward VI, Mary and Elizabeth I.

could report that they had achieved the objectives set them or that some well defined concession was absolutely essential in order to do so. Once one could discern the outline of the Soviet instructions it became possible to find ways round their immovable road blocks and to frame proposals in language which at the least was not forbidden by their instructions. In doing this it was helpful to point out to them the arguments which they could use with their own authorities in supporting such proposals.

11. The Socratic method was on occasion a useful technique. Feigned inability to understand the Soviet position sometimes led to useful explanations and admissions. When this happened it was desirable promptly to take note of the useful material thus elicited and to go on reminding the Russians of what they had said. Like other people they showed themselves uncomfortable in denying their own words.

12. If the Russians detected anything unprofessional or easy going they immediately discounted the seriousness of their interlocutor and pressed all the harder. For this, if for no other reason, it was essential to sell everything for a price. The watchword was no concession without a counter-concession. Generosity was out of place. The Russians were shameless in ascribing to Western negotiators proposals which they themselves put forward. The object was presumably to represent them in reporting to Moscow as Western proposals. Moreover, the Russians pulled fast ones whenever they could even after tentative agreements had been reached. In reaching tentative agreements it was desirable to arrange that the last point for discussion was one to which the Eastern attached more importance than did the Western side.

13. All this sounds a disagreeable process and certainly at times it was boring or unpleasant. But in fact there was much interest in observing the Russians at work and at play. The two were not entirely separate. Negotiations for them involved a strong element of game playing. They thoroughly understood the principles of horse trading and enjoyed it when they found a horse trader, such as Dean, who could manipulate the techniques. Well trained themselves in negotiation they admired virtuosity when they met it. Dean, Ruth and I saw a lot of Khlestov, Movchan and Timerbayev both off and on duty. We drank gallons of wine together to say nothing of Russian brandy (a drink I do not recommend) and this enabled us to get to know them rather well. This convivial process helped to establish confidence and made the Russians readier than they might have been to accept that when we said no we meant it. It also helped us to calculate what the most effective tactical approach might be. When we began the Russians wished to speak only to the Americans: when we ended they were content to talk with the British as well.

14. Each side has the strengths and weaknesses of their own societies. On the Soviet side, they were well drilled, patient and persistent, but their instructions allowed them little room for manoeuvre. Thus they were good at defending fixed positions but rather less good when it came to a campaign of manoeuvre. The Western side, however, was apt to be too impatient and too optimistic. Yet it was both more flexible and more confident in devising expedients to preserve the

essence of their Governments' positions while varying their presentation. The Western side profited on the whole from their greater ability to take the initiative and so to exploit the Eastern weaknesses.

15. Negotiating with the Russians bears the same sort of resemblance to negotiating with allies as water skiing does to skiing. Many of the same qualities are required but the element in which they are exercised is quite different. It made for variety to conduct one set of negotiation in the morning and the other in the afternoon. One was no easier than the other: indeed there were times when the Southern flank countries seemed the main obstacle to any progress. I have heard well-intentioned people deplore the absence of the French from the MBFR talks. This seems to me wrong-headed. It is a positive Western advantage that neither French territory nor forces should be involved. And had France been a member of the Ad Hoc Group I doubt whether we could have reached any conclusions: certainly the quarrels with the Americans would have been horrendous. As it was, even without France it took several weeks for the Ad Hoc Group to shake down and establish the necessary degree of trust between its members. Personalities as I have already said were of great importance. It was perhaps unfortunate that the United States which is so much the strongest of the Western countries should be represented by a man who is so strong willed as Dean. But he mellowed considerably and by the end he found that he got more by conciliation than by bulldozing. Nevertheless the inevitable dominance of the Americans does in my view require some European offset if a healthy exchange of opinions and concessions is to be maintained within the alliance. The European offset in this case was to a large extent provided by the extremely close collaboration between the German and British delegations. These two delegations had probably the closest and most harmonious working relationship of any within the Ad Hoc Group. The Germans were always generous and sometimes hesitant. The result was that the British who frequently had the firmest and clearest instructions of all played one of the more prominent roles in the Ad Hoc Group. It was generally noticed that when the British opposed the Americans as happened rather frequently in the first stage of the negotiations the way ahead was difficult and stoney [*sic*] but when the two delegations worked together as was usually the case in the latter part of the negotiations they almost invariably carried the rest of the group with them. The British lost nothing by having a view of their own and expressing it with some clarity.

16. The result of the negotiations was recorded in two short communiqués. The first tended to favour the Warsaw Pact and the second the West.[11] As I have

[11] Only one final *communiqué* was published at the end of the exploratory talks on 28 June (see No. 6, note 4). Mr. Thomson may, however, have had in mind the *communiqué* issued after the first plenary on 14 May and the published texts of the statements then made by Mr. Quarles and Mr. Ustor with regard to Hungary's future participation in the negotiations. An interpretative press statement made by Mr. Quarles on 28 June made it clear that NATO delegates understood the term 'associated measures', used in the final *communiqué* to describe the forthcoming negotiations, to encompass measures relating to constraint and verification; and that they regarded the 'principle of undiminished security', to which the *communiqué* also referred, as covering their concept of 'balanced' force reductions.

said in a separate letter I believe the balance of advantage lay by a shade with the West.[12] A huge number of words went into the making of these brief documents. Even a small delegation such as the Danes sent more than 250 telegrams. The US delegation sent over 700 (several of them 20 pages long) while at the other end of the scale the Belgians claim to have sent no more than 12, which may go a long way to explain discrepancies between Belgian attitudes in Brussels and in Vienna. Perhaps the Belgians like the Germans used the telephone a lot and this in turn may help to explain why the Russians were frequently so extremely well informed about the Western positions.

17. Now it is time to leave Vienna. The Russians left an hour after the final plenary. Shortly after the Ad Hoc Group adjourned after its 111th meeting and the British delegation went to pay its modest bills at the homely Pension Nossek.

Yours ever,
J.A. THOMSON

[12] See No. 6.

No. 8

*Report of the Joint Intelligence Committee
on the Soviet Attitude to MBFR*

JIC (A)(73)19

Secret   CABINET OFFICE, *12 July 1973*

Summary and Conclusions [1]

Introduction

1. The aim of this Report is to examine Soviet attitude to Mutual and Balanced Force Reductions (MBFR) in Europe, and to assess the Soviet approach to force reductions in the light of the Russians' past statements and behaviour at the preparatory talks in Vienna. The Report concentrates on the political factors involved, but also discusses military and economic issues, and places our assessments against the overall politico military background and the Soviet Union's present European policies. We do not try to present possible models for an agreement on MBFR, but we consider the aims and likely tactics of the Soviet Union as the negotiations proceed.

Summary

2. Soviet readiness to engage in negotiations on MBFR in response to Western initiative became clear only in 1971–72 at time when the Russians probably recognised the value of an offer of MBFR talks in persuading the West to participate in the Conference on Security and Co-operation in Europe (CSCE)

[1] Part II of this paper, the Main Report, is not printed.

and perhaps in assisting the United States administration to deal with domestic pressures for substantial reductions in American force levels in Europe, in return for favourable American reaction to other Soviet requirements of the United States.

3.   The Soviet attitude to MBFR must be seen against the background of the long term aim of the Soviet Union in Europe: to alter the existing balance of power to the advantage of the Soviet Union. In order to do this the Soviet Union wants, inter alia, to bring about reductions in the level of American forces in Europe, and to reduce the credibility of the American guarantee to Western Europe. The Soviet Union also wants to undermine the military and political effectiveness of NATO, and to hinder the further development of the EEC[2] into the political and defence fields. At the same time, the Soviet Union regards the successful development of its special relationship with the United States on strategic, economic and trade issues as of great importance, and this growing bilateral relationship will influence Soviet thinking on MBFR.

4.   Since they attach so much importance to their relationship with the United States there will be a continuing tendency for them to wish to deal directly with the Americans at MBFR talks. Their success at the preparatory talks in Vienna may have convinced them that they have no reason to make concessions to the West as a whole.[3]

5.   Although the Soviet obsession with China probably affects all Soviet foreign and defence policies, we do not believe that the Sino-Soviet dispute is at present a significant factor in Soviet decision-making on MBFR.[4] Nor do we believe that any economic savings brought about by reductions of forces or weapons in Europe can be an important factor, since these savings are likely to be very small.

6.   We believe that there are a number of factors which make it hard for the Russians to work for major force reductions in Europe, especially the kind of asymmetrical reductions favoured by NATO. These factors include the need to retain substantial forces in East Europe to keep Soviet hegemony there intact, to defend the Warsaw Pact area against NATO, (whose capabilities the Russians appear to over-estimate) and to give the Soviet forces the option of seizing the military initiative against NATO in the event of war in Europe.[5] Basically the Soviet Union wants to emerge, after a period of détente, as the dominant power, militarily, politically and economically in Europe. At the same time the Russians

[2] European Economic Community. See Volume II, No. 1, note 14.

[3] The Main Report elaborated on this point. It argued that the Soviet success on the issue of Hungarian participation would have encouraged the Russians in the view that they had no reason to make concessions. Moreover, it added, the exploratory talks must have made them more aware of the 'potential extent of divisions within the Western camp'.

[4] Although Soviet forces on the Chinese border had trebled since 1966, this, according to the Main Report, had not been achieved at the expense of forces facing the West: on the contrary, the Russians had effected significant improvements in their forces in Eastern Europe.

[5] The Main Report contended that it was a 'cardinal tenet' of Soviet defence doctrine that defence was 'a temporary expedient to be adopted only with reluctance and that war [could] only be won by offensive action', and that such a doctrine required superiority of force.

probably fear the impact of major force withdrawals on East European Governments and peoples. They would also find it difficult to accept an MBFR agreement which involved physical on-site inspection of Soviet territory; we are not sure, however, if this opposition extends to verification of this kind on non-Soviet territory, in view of the Soviet Union's continued tolerance of allied missions in East Germany.

7.   Although the Russians have not shown their hand directly on the kind of constraints which NATO would like to negotiate in connection with MBFR, it is possible that they would agree to prior notification of military exercises and the exchange of observers at such exercises. They would be most reluctant, however, to agree to any constraints on the movement of Soviet troops either from the Soviet Union to Eastern Europe or within the NSWP[6] countries.

8.   On the other hand the present Soviet leaders probably feel that negotiations on MBFR could bring dividends, although such talks will provide opportunities for NATO countries to highlight the military imbalance in central Europe to which the Russians would not wish attention to be drawn. The Russians will be aware that, mainly because of domestic pressures, (especially in the United States) NATO countries appear as the 'demandeurs' on force reductions; as time goes on, these pressures are likely to increase in the West. The Russians probably hope that negotiations will produce disunity on the NATO side and inhibit NATO's efforts to improve their defences. The Soviet leaders probably also believe that negotiations on MBFR may help to maintain the impetus of their campaign for détente after the CSCE process has been completed.

9.   Bearing these considerations in mind, we believe that the Soviet Union now favours lengthy negotiations with NATO on MBFR, possibly leading to a negotiated settlement which could give the Soviet Union some juridicial claim over certain aspects of West European affairs. Lengthy negotiations on MBFR have the advantage that there will be more time for domestic pressure to work on NATO Governments.

10.   The Russians have already made it clear, as the Brezhnev-Nixon communiqué indicated,[7] and as Mr. Gromyko said to the Foreign Secretary in Helsinki, that they do not accept the NATO concept of balanced force reductions.[8] When the talks begin the Russians will reject the idea that there is a military imbalance in their favour in central Europe and that geographical factors will work to their advantage if troops [*sic*] withdrawals are carried out. They will point to the substantial NATO forces outside the suggested area of reduction, and will probably argue that forces capable of intervening in the reduction area, eg strike fleets, must be taken into consideration.[9] They could offer a token unilateral reduction

---

[6] Non-Soviet Warsaw Pact.

[7] See Volume II, No. 40, note 7.

[8] Mr. A.A. Gromyko, the Soviet Foreign Minister, met Sir A. Douglas-Home at Stage I of the CSCE in Helsinki during 3–7 July. Cf. Volume II, No. 42.

[9] US troops withdrawn from the central region would, according to the Main Report, almost certainly have to be redeployed across the Atlantic, whereas Soviet forces could be redeployed in western Russia with much easier access to the central region.

of their own forces to encourage cuts in NATO while the talks are in progress, while at the same time calling for large-scale cuts on a 1 for 1 basis or some other form of reductions unacceptable to NATO.

11. The Russians are not after quick results in MBFR. Essentially they are ready to negotiate on MBFR not because they need to, but because they want to see what they can get out of it. If the answer turns out to be nothing, they will be prepared to reduce the MBFR to a long drawn-out propaganda exercise.

12. We therefore conclude–

(*a*) Soviet aims on MBFR are closely linked to the Soviet Union's overall policies which include altering the balance of power in Europe in the Soviet Union's favour, undermining the military and political effectiveness of NATO, and obtaining some substantial reduction in the American military presence in Europe, while inhibiting the development of closer West European defence co-operation.

(*b*) In formulating its MBFR policies the Soviet Union is likely to pay particular attention to its need for a special relationship with the United States. There will therefore be a tendency for them to want to talk to the Americans directly on MBFR.

(*c*) Neither economic factors nor the impact of China are likely to play a major part in Soviet thinking on MBFR in the foreseeable future.

(*d*) Most political and military factors relating to the Soviet position in Eastern Europe will tend to work against Soviet interest in a substantive agreement with the West on MBFR. Verification involving physical on-site inspection on Soviet territory is likely to provide a stumbling block in Soviet minds to such an agreement.

(*e*) The Soviet leaders, however, probably see a number of advantages in protracted negotiations with NATO on MBFR. These include expectations that existing domestic pressures in the NATO countries, for force reductions will intensify and disunity in NATO will be promoted. The negotiations themselves and a negotiated agreement would also give the Russians a permanent say in NATO force levels.

(*f*) The Russians who have already stated their opposition to the NATO concept of balanced force reductions, are unlikely to agree to the kind of asymmetrical reductions which NATO may offer. They are likely to press for reductions on a 1 for 1 basis (or other unacceptable forms), and also to try to secure consideration of NATO forces outside the reduction area which are capable of intervening in the event of hostilities.

GEOFFREY ARTHUR,
CHAIRMAN, ON BEHALF OF THE
JOINT INTELLIGENCE COMMITTEE (A)

CHAPTER II

MBFR: The Vienna Negotiations
11 October 1973–22 December 1976

No. 9

Draft Steering Brief for the British Delegation to the MBFR Talks [1]

[*WDN 27/10*]

Secret   FCO, *11 October 1973*

Background Documents ...[2]

Character of the Negotiations

2.   The substantive negotiations on MBFR[3] in Vienna will be governed by the following political and military factors:

Political

(*a*) The atmosphere of détente in most countries of the Western Alliance has led many to believe that the presence of large numbers of conventional troops in Central Europe is unjustified. There is public and parliamentary pressure on defence budgets, and a general wish at least to explore the possibilities of negotiated force reductions without sacrifice to security.

(*b*) These pressures are particularly strong in the United States, and much of the impetus to negotiate comes from the US Administration, which sees MBFR as one of the means of persuading Congress not to impose damaging cuts on US forces in Europe. The European members of the Alliance (excluding France) support MBFR for a variety of reasons: all prefer to attempt the negotiation of reciprocal cuts rather than to risk unilateral ones, and all want to help the US Administration to cope with its domestic critics. Some take an idealistic view of MBFR. Some (including ourselves) see it primarily as an exercise in damage limitation. Some, particularly the Germans, share the American view that MBFR provides a means for limiting and controlling cuts which they fear they will have to make in any case.

(*c*) We have detected no pressures on the Russians to negotiate comparable with the pressures on the West. On the contrary the Russians may see good reasons for maintaining large numbers of conventional troops in Central

---

[1] This paper was originally drafted by Mr. R.Q. Braithwaite (WOD) and subsequently revised in the light of comments made by other FCO and MoD officials. The final version has not been traced.

[2] Not printed.

[3] In discussions amongst themselves NATO countries still used the term 'MBFR' to describe the talks. 'It is shorter', explained guidance telegram No. 168 of 29 October, whilst 'its continued use helps to emphasize that the negotiations are taking place as a result of an Allied initiative.'

Europe, partly to cover NATO forces and partly to maintain order in their empire.

Military

(*a*) The military balance in Europe, and the strategic considerations which govern it, in the British view, shared for the most part by the US Administration, make any significant Allied reductions a matter of serious military concern. An MBFR arrangement could significantly damage Allied security and the Alliance's capacity to fulfil its strategic objectives of forward defence and flexible response.

(*b*) The Russians enjoy a number of military advantages which the West do not. They are quantitatively superior in conventional offensive equipment (especially tanks). And they enjoy short lines of communication to Central Europe over which they could reinforce quickly; Western reinforcements lie for the most part on the other side of the Atlantic.

(*c*) It will be difficult enough to establish satisfactorily the size of the armed forces and their equipment held by either side. It will be even harder to decide which aspects of the military confrontation should be included in the negotiation, which should be excluded, what their inter-relationships are, which collateral measures we need to insist on and which we can safely concede.

3. The negotiations in Vienna are thus likely to be dominated by a variety of strong and conflicting political pressures in the West, and a great deal of intellectual confusion. There is a danger that, at least on the Western side, the military aspects of the problem could be lost sight of; that domestic considerations will weigh too heavily; and that these, rather than the logic of the negotiations, will predominate in the framing of negotiating tactics and proposals.[4] The Russians on the other hand will have little incentive to make concessions or to negotiate on the basis of give and take. Mr Gromyko told the Foreign and Commonwealth Secretary in New York in September[5] that the Russians would come to negotiations with proposals. But their strategy will probably rather be to play their hand long and to avoid serious negotiation in the belief that this will benefit them and disrupt the West. They may have come to the negotiating table primarily to blunt a Western initiative. Now they are there, many tactics lie open to them, from deliberate prevarication to the launching of fair-seeming but unacceptable proposals carefully calculated to throw the West into disarray (Mr Dobrynin[6] is reported to have suggested 'a 5% reduction' on both sides). In these circumstances if the Russians are to be brought to make the concessions needed for agreement

[4] Mr. J. Amery, Minister of State for Foreign and Commonwealth Affairs, shared these anxieties. He minuted: 'The steering brief brings out the difficulties and dangers of this negotiation clearly. They are clearly greater than the advantages we are likely to derive' (minute by Mr. M.I. Goulding (Private Secretary to Mr. Amery) of 16 October 1973).

[5] Sir A. Douglas-Home was in New York for the opening of the 28th Session of the United Nations (UN) General Assembly.

[6] Mr. A.F. Dobrynin was the Soviet Ambassador in Washington.

based on genuine reciprocity, it will be necessary to exert pressure on them in fields not directly connected with the MBFR negotiations. This can only be done by the Americans.

4. The great complexity of the subject, the variety of political pressures on the West, and Russian reticence make it very hard for NATO to define and agree on clear negotiating positions. This difficulty is likely to continue until the negotiations are well engaged, and both sides have made preliminary proposals. It is therefore in general desirable that the Alliance should conduct the negotiations—especially at the beginning—with flexibility, and that it should avoid committing itself too early to proposals the full significance of which may be hard to foresee. The tempo of the negotiations must not accelerate to the point where the Alliance no longer has time to give such proposals a proper military and political evaluation.

British Aims
5. Our general aims in the negotiations will be as follows:

(*a*) To be seen by Parliament and public to be working seriously for a lowering of the level of armed forces and armaments in Central Europe while maintaining undiminished security for all.

(*b*) To impress on the Russians that their quantitative superiority in conventional offensive equipment, combined with their geographical advantages, justify significantly larger reductions in Soviet forces in the agreed area compared with those of the Alliance.

(*c*) To limit the military damage as far as possible. In practice this will mean seeking to ensure that the reductions in their manpower which the Americans and others may consider domestically unavoidable fall—to the extent which can be negotiated and is militarily feasible—on logistic support rather than combat support troops; and on both of these rather than on combat ready troops and equipment.

(*d*) In particular, to help the Americans through MBFR, to maintain an adequate level of American troops in Europe, which are vital to Western security as a whole, and our own in particular. We should be very careful not to oppose the Americans except for very good reasons.

(*e*) To maintain unity within the Alliance. This will mean a sensitive and sympathetic attitude towards the domestic political problems of the Americans, and of our Western European Allies (especially the Germans), and also to the fears of the flank countries, who are worried lest reductions in Central Europe will increase the Soviet threat to them.

(*f*) To avoid any MBFR arrangement which might limit the Western Europeans' freedom to devise common European defence arrangements, or which might give the Russians the handle for interfering in Western European military affairs.

(*g*) To keep in close contact with the French, who share our worries about the military implications of MBFR, but who are not participating in the talks. Their ground forces are among the most significant in Western Europe and the Russians may well insist that they be taken into account in calculating the effects of any reductions on the remaining Allied forces.

The Tactical Problem

6.   The central problem of the negotiations will be to get the Russians to accept (probably tacitly) that in any mutually satisfactory MBFR arrangement they will have to pay for their advantages and for any concessions the West may make. It will not be easy to persuade the Russians of this: they are likely to argue that, on a worldwide basis, the asymmetries are not in their favour. But if we fail to persuade the Russians of this central point, our chances of getting a satisfactory final agreement are remote. Negotiations (as the Russians accepted in the exploratory talks) are about the military confrontation in central Europe, where the concentration of Russian conventional forces is quite clearly superior to that which the Western Europeans and their American Allies can muster.

7.   It follows that we need not be too intimidated about stressing, in the negotiations, the military problems caused by the ability of the Russians to build up their forces on Soviet territory, and in other areas which may remain outside the agreed reductions area. But we must take account of American fears that, if this argument is pushed too far, the Russians will insist on extending the scope of MBFR to include naval and air forces in the Mediterranean, Britain and North America as well as French territory and forces.

The Negotiating Programme

8.   The Alliance has agreed that the first stage of the negotiation should take place in four steps:

(*a*)   The presentation of opening statements;
(*b*)   Development of main themes;
(*c*)   The presentation of the Alliance's 'framework proposal';[7]
(*d*)   The negotiation of 'Prereduction constraints'.

When these four steps have been completed the Alliance would propose to move to the negotiation of actual reductions.[8]

9.   This could be a practical and flexible arrangement. It makes no provision

---

[7] See paragraph 11 below.

[8] On 16 October the NAC approved a report on the 'Alliance Approach to Negotiations on MBFR' (C-M(73)83) outlining the Western objectives in, and negotiating strategy for, the MBFR talks: 'the Allies are not in a position', the document stated, 'to commit themselves to a negotiating strategy which requires frequent shifts in their basic position. While it might be theoretically possible to build a series of positions and fallbacks in order to maximize trading room, such an approach will not be feasible for a large, complex multilateral negotiation like MBFR'. The paper therefore concluded that 'the most effective general approach to the MBFR negotiations will be to take a firm basic position and to stick to it as the Western side attempts to move the negotiation through different levels of generalization down to the specifics of actual agreement. It will be a cardinal point of negotiating strategy for the Allies to maintain their agreed position with maximum consistency, determination and perseverance.'

for East/West discussion of fixed agenda, nor for argument about the size of the opposing forces, agreement on which might logically be regarded as a precondition for the negotiation of actual reductions. There are advantages in having no fixed agenda, since the Alliance can then raise points as they see fit, and the Russians will be unable to insist (as they sometimes do) that agreement on one agenda point must be reached before proceeding to the next.[9]

10. On the other hand, the programme could break down quite quickly. The Russians may attempt to force a discussion of an agenda. They may quickly introduce specious proposals, or proposals designed to enhance their own military and political position, which are incompatible with Allied objectives.[10] They may raise the nuclear issue. An early debate on the size of the opposing forces is almost inevitable, and from our point of view might be desirable since it should enable us to enlarge on the Russians' asymmetrical military advantages *before* discussing reductions. For their part the Americans will probably seek to curtail preliminary discussion in order that the West may—as the Americans prefer—table its 'framework proposal' before Christmas. We shall have to deal with the various possibilities as they arise.

The Allied Framework Proposal

11. The Allies have agreed that their initial proposals to the Russians should be:

(*a*) That the negotiations should take place in two phases.

(*b*) That in the first phase the parties should agree on a 15% cut in the American and Russian troops in the agreed reductions area: Russian cuts of 68,000 men to include one tank army of 5 divisions with its equipment including 1,700 tanks; American cuts to consist of 29,000 men, in which the proportion of combat troops is as yet undecided.

(*c*) In the second phase, each side would make further cuts to bring their forces down to a common ceiling of 700,000 in the reductions area. This would represent a 10% cut in NATO forces and a 20% cut in Warsaw Pact forces. The second phase cuts would focus on Western European forces.[11]

[9] Mr. Amery commented (see note 4 above): 'I hope we shall get down to "the argument about the size of the opposing forces" as of now, as soon as possible. The brief suggests later on that this is likely to happen. We should make sure that it does. It will reveal a lot about Soviet and Warsaw Pact thinking.'

[10] In guidance telegram No. 168 (see note 3 above) Sir A. Douglas-Home expressed his concern at the prospect of being hustled into ill-considered agreements with the East. 'The great complexity of the subject', he wrote, 'the variety of political pressures on the West, and Russian reticence have led us to believe that the Allies should conduct the negotiations—especially at the beginning—with flexibility, and that they should avoid committing themselves too early to specific proposals, the full significance of which may be hard to foresee. The tempo of the negotiations must not accelerate to the point where the Allies no longer have time to give such proposals a proper military and political evaluation.'

[11] The approach was agreed by the NAC on 16 October, to the obvious satisfaction of the British. 'Although we have had to accept a commitment to a second phase of negotiations with a

12. The Americans argue that this proposal satisfactorily establishes the principle of asymmetry in the first phase. We agree, but hope that American cuts fall mainly on support rather than combat troops. As a guide, we believe that reductions of US combat troops in the first phase should, if possible, be limited to the equivalent of about two US Brigades. So far the Americans have not formally confirmed that they share this view but have not disputed it.

The Common Ceiling

13. The 'common ceiling' is an attractive concept, easily appreciated by Western opinion, to which the Allies could hold during the negotiation. Furthermore, once the figure of 700,000 is established in the public mind, it could come to be seen as a floor by Western opinion (the Americans have in mind particularly the Senate). This could be a useful way of limiting pressure for excessive Western cuts. But the 'common ceiling' cannot serve these ends, unless the Alliance negotiates for it with great determination and with the firm intention to include in the final package significant asymmetries in terms of reductions in combat capability on each side. We should resist attempts to water it down in response to probable Russian objections.

14. We ourselves have accepted the idea of a common ceiling of 700,000, provided that the proportion of combat ready troops withdrawn on the Western side is kept to a reasonable minimum (e.g. two divisions) and that there is a satisfactory reduction of combat capability on the other side. We also believe that the figure should be formally put to the Russians only when the political and negotiating situation makes this appropriate. One cannot foresee when that will be but we expect it to be later rather than sooner. We believe it would be imprudent to initiate—or respond to Soviet attempts at—early negotiation of a link between Phase I and Phase II. The political context in which Phase II might be negotiated is at present quite unforeseeable, and it is likely to remain so until we are well into the negotiation of Phase I. Concessions made to secure a Phase I agreement could bulk unduly large as precedents in negotiations of Phase II. It is undesirable for the Allies to commit themselves in too much detail to something which in altered circumstances they might regret.

15. On the other hand the Germans, for domestic political reasons, are determined that there should be an early and precise East/West agreement to Phase II reductions in which they would participate. Only thus, they believe, can domestic pressure be averted for cuts in the Bundeswehr perhaps even in Phase I. There are unresolved disagreements here which we shall have to watch.

16. The figure of 700,000 has meanwhile leaked. (It is possible that neither the Germans nor the Americans really regret this.) We continue to argue that there is all the difference between speculation about the level at which a common

"focus" on European reductions', noted Mr. Tickell in a minute to Mr. Wiggin of 26 October, 'we have successfully resisted efforts to bind the two phases together and define the contents of the second. We have incidentally every cause to be pleased that the Allied [*sic*] should unequivocally have decided that they should aim for reductions of only US and Soviet forces in the first phase. This is an outcome for which we have worked long and hard.'

ceiling might be fixed, and formal confirmation by the Alliance of a definite figure. In publicising their policy between now and the tabling of an actual proposal in the negotiations, the Allies will need to keep this distinction in mind.

The Nuclear Issue

17. The Americans clearly believe that the Russians are unlikely to accept the Alliance's Phase I proposal unless we throw Western tactical nuclear warheads and launchers into the negotiations to balance the withdrawal of a Soviet tank army. Option III of the American paper of 30 April[12] sets out the figures which the Americans have told us are the limits to which they would go in securing the withdrawal of a Soviet Tank Army in exchange for 29,000 US troops. SHAPE[13] have commented very cautiously but not entirely negatively, on the military aspects. But the proposal could have serious politico-military implications for Forward Based Systems, dual-capable aircraft (which would lead to the inclusion of air forces in eventual reductions), and German fears of 'de-coupling'. Nuclear cuts in Phase I could lead by precedent to undesirably large nuclear cuts in Phase II (and there could be implications in terms of nuclear ceilings on both sides). All these are difficult problems which require urgent study.[14] Meanwhile we need to ensure that:

(*a*) these implications are thoroughly understood by the Allies and if possible some agreed position on them reached before the subject arises in Vienna;
(*b*) the nuclear make-weight is not meanwhile, by leaks and indiscretions, insensibly but irrevocably added to the Alliance's opening proposal, which at present involves only conventional forces, although the Russian tank army has nuclear weapons integral to it, which would presumably depart with the rest of the army's equipment.

Collateral measures: General Considerations

18. The Alliance's position on measures which might be negotiated in support of a reductions agreement is still very muddled. Such measures could include movement constraints, inspection and verification, and various forms of freeze: NATO's terminology has hitherto been confusing. We ourselves are particularly worried lest movement constraints wrongly defined could inhibit the development of European defence co-operation. Our aim, at least in phase I, is to see that constraints are applied only to the movement of American and Russian

---

[12] See No. 5, note 5.

[13] Supreme Headquarters Allied Powers Europe.

[14] NATO had no agreed position on the possible inclusion of tactical nuclear weapons in the MBFR negotiations and, as Mr. Wiggin confessed in a minute of 30 October, 'much homework still [had] to be done on it'. He added: 'Sooner or later I believe this will figure large in the negotiations. In his recent public pronouncement on MBFR Mr. Brezhnev mentioned nuclear weapons. And we ourselves are inclined to believe that it may well pay us to dispense with some of NATO's large tactical nuclear armoury if we can get enough Russian tanks out in return. I have no doubt that the basic NATO proposals, without any nuclear incentive added to them, will prove unnegotiable.'

forces into the reductions area and for European forces to reinforce the area from outside. At the same time, we have to accept that we shall be unable to achieve our ideal fully: for example, once a common ceiling in the reductions area has been fixed we will only be able to reinforce BAOR within the limit thus laid down.[15] Some of our European allies are, however, keen to participate in constraints even during Phase I, which would otherwise be confined to the Americans and the Russians: they believe that their public opinion expects it of them.

19. These matters are under urgent study in the Alliance, where those who have proposed particular measures are being asked to justify them politically, militarily and technically. The British aim is again to prevent the Alliance committing itself prematurely to inadequately considered proposals until a firm Allied position is evolved. The delegation in Vienna should avoid speculation on this subject in dealing with the Warsaw Pact.

20. The subject can be divided into three parts, known in the current NATO terminology as

(*a*) Pre-reduction stabilising measures
(*b*) Stabilising measures, including non-circumventions provision (paragraph 22 below)
(*c*) Verification (paragraph 23 below)

The first of these would operate during the negotiation of reductions. At their most elaborate, they would involve an inspected freeze on the opposing forces at their present level. The Russians, who have always opposed 'inspection before disarmament', would doubtless reject this, and the Americans would dislike anything which would be so hard to negotiate and would so long delay actual cuts. The proposals in para. 32 of CM(73)83 are far less ambitious.[16] In practice we may well end up with something much more like a moratorium—by unilateral announcement or by agreement—on reinforcements or other military activities in (or near) the reductions area which are incompatible with the purposes of the negotiation. In all cases, it is important that no 'pre-reductions constraints' be agreed with the East which could prejudice the substantive content of negotiations on actual reductions.

21. The Germans have recently proposed the adoption of appropriate MBFR 'pre-reduction stabilising measures' of the 'Confidence Building Measures' now under negotiation in the CSCE in Geneva. These measures would be voluntary,

---

[15] Whilst accepting that a common ceiling would affect European defence forces, Mr. Amery minuted (see notes 4 and 5 above) 'it is important that this should be expressed in terms of numbers or categories but *not* nationalities. Looking ahead to an eventual European Defence Union, the Nine must remain free to move their troops around e.g. more Belgians in Germany, balanced by more Germans in Belgium.'

[16] In this paragraph, the NATO report (see note 8 above) explained that agreements with the East on verification measures were necessary 'to ensure that the provisions of agreements [were] being carried out, to build mutual confidence, and to enhance warning in the event of a Pact build-up'. The document stressed, however, that any Western proposals for verification measures 'should be designed in such a way as not to give the Soviets means of interference in Western defence and foreign policies'.

not mandatory, and would cover the advance notification of military movements and manoeuvres and the exchange of observers at manoeuvres. We are dubious about the German proposal. The formal adoption by those concerned in MBFR of the vaguely defined Geneva measures would inevitably give them a more concrete character: for example, details such as the size of force involved, the method of notification, rules governing the behaviour of observers would have to be worked out rather fully. Yet the measures would probably not be very effective. The problem is not simple. Moreover precedents created by the negotiation of these measures in Geneva might be cited in Vienna by the Russians to frustrate Allied purposes there. The delegation should therefore be cautious about accepting any facile comparisons between the two sets of negotiations.

22. Once reductions have been agreed, both Alliances will clearly be bound not to reintroduce withdrawn, or reactivate disbanded, forces. The final agreement will also need to contain a generalised non-circumvention provision, which would provide for adversary challenge, and if necessary the denunciation of the treaty, if either side had reason to believe that the other was taking military measures incompatible with the purposes of the treaty. This is likely, in the final analysis, to be our only control over threatening Russian military moves in the Western Military districts and on the flanks, or on non-Soviet territory outside the reductions area. Our flank Allies are likely to want more stringent constraints on Soviet territory, but are unlikely to get them. We must be careful that measures negotiated in connexion with Phase I reductions do not create undesirable precedents for Phase II.

23. National technical means of verification and other sources of intelligence available to the major members of the Alliance may be adequate to detect major Soviet breaches of a treaty, although in certain cases over a period of three months or more on-the-spot inspection (as set out in CM(73)83) would provide useful additional intelligence.[17] Moreover those of our European allies who have no technical means of verification attach considerable political importance to sharing in inspection arrangements. It should therefore be our object to obtain the best inspection arrangements which can be negotiated.[18]

24. The Russians are of course unlikely to accept inspection arrangements so stringent that they embarrass us. But if the Allies agree to reduce their nuclear warheads (see para 17 above) the Russians might—for this one case—insist on

---

[17] The NATO report (see notes 8 and 16 above) recommended that ground observers should monitor the agreed withdrawals as they happened. In the post-MBFR period, 'special mobile inspection teams' would operate in the reductions area to ensure continuing adherence to the agreement.

[18] In a minute to Mr. Tickell of 12 October Mr. Ramsay explained that the Americans were unwilling to argue with the East over verification measures before actual force reductions had been secured: 'The conclusions that the Americans have drawn from their analysis of the measures proposed seem fairly modest. Their aim appears to be to avoid complicated arrangements. I do not think that we would wish to quarrel with this approach, but the very modesty of some of the arrangements proposed, e.g. for the observation of withdrawals and mobile inspection, may prove insufficiently dramatic for some of our European Allies, notably the Belgians, who attach importance to multilateral inspection arrangements mainly for presentational reasons.'

unacceptable measures of intrusive inspection. This is a point we shall need to watch.

The Reductions Area

25. The area to which the Vienna discussions may initially be directed consists of the two Germanies, the Benelux countries, Poland and Czechoslovakia. The Germans do not wish it to be reduced, since this would concentrate attention on them. The Americans do not want it to be increased, since this could bring into the question France and US forces in the Mediterranean and Britain. The Russians have threatened to demand that the area be vastly extended, so that they deploy their 'global balance' argument more convincingly (see para 6 above). The question of Hungary remains open.

26. The record of the plenary meeting of 14 May in Vienna records an Allied statement that the arrangements for Hungary's participation in the Exploratory Talks (subsequently carried over by general agreement for the negotiations as noted in the communique of 28 June) were 'without prejudice to the nature of Hungary's participation in future negotiations, decisions on agreed measures … and that, in particular how and to what extent Hungary will be included in future decisions, agreements or measures must be examined and decided during … negotiations'. Paragraph 31 of CM(73)83 says that an important goal of the Allied approach will be to ensure that any agreement will not be circumvented or undermined for example by means of an increase of Soviet forces in Hungary. The British delegation should support strongly Allied efforts to safeguard their position over Hungary.

Permanent Machinery

27. At some point, probably rather late in the negotiations, it may be necessary to tackle the problem of how the agreement is to be administered, which body should receive complaints about apparent breaches, interference with arrangements for inspection, notification of movements, and so on. The simple bilateral arrangements set up under SALT I would not be appropriate. Alternatives might be:

(*a*) neutral Control Commission;
(*b*) a permanent East/West organ;
(*c*) a more informal arrangement.

The first two alternatives are unattractive: a) would be cumbersome; b) would give the Russians too much opportunity to interfere in our affairs. An informal arrangement might be better, such as a committee of the ambassadors in Vienna of signatory countries, meeting under a rotating chairman, either monthly or at short notice on the request of four signatories.

Procedures for Negotiations

28. We can accept the procedural arrangements set out in 'The Alliance Approach to Negotiations on MBFR'. One aspect may cause trouble. Confidential negotiations outside the plenary meetings will, it is envisaged, take place between

'emissaries' from both Alliances. The Americans have indicated that, since Phase I negotiations concern them most directly, they will expect to be present at all such confidential exchanges, flanked by one or more of their Allies, perhaps on a rotating basis. Some of our European Allies may object to the appearance of American dominance which might thus be given. But the American claim is not unreasonable, at least for Phase I, and we should do what we can to minimise discord. We ought to be able to secure arrangements which will give us our full say.

No. 10

Mr. C.M. Rose[1] *(UKDEL Vienna) to Sir A. Douglas-Home*
[*WDN 27/1*]

Confidential. Eclipse   VIENNA, *17 January 1974*

Summary ...[2]

Sir,

MBFR: The First Round

The Christmas recess afforded the Allied MBFR negotiations [*sic*] in Vienna their first opportunity since the substantive talks opened on 30 October, 1973, to stand back a little from the negotiations and to take stock, with their Governments, of what has been happening. At the same time they have been able to reflect on the lessons learned, and on the tactics to be followed in the next round. In the few days between the resumption of Allied consultations in Vienna and the first formal encounter of the new session with the other side (who have presumably used the recess in the same way) we therefore stand at a vantage point from which it may be useful to review the ground covered since October and peer a little way into the murk ahead.

The proposals

2. The proposals which the Allies brought to Vienna reflect their conviction that the existing military relationship between NATO and the Warsaw Pact in Central Europe is potentially unstable and needs correcting. The purpose of the Allied proposals is to achieve reductions which will remove or neutralise the dangerous disparities in ground force manpower, tanks and geography which favour the Warsaw Pact, and thus to strengthen stability in Central Europe. The proposals also take account of the domestic pressure on the American Government for early and substantial withdrawals of US ground forces from Germany.

3. The central concept of the Allied proposals is that each side should reduce its overall ground force manpower in Central Europe to a common ceiling, which might be set at 700,000 men on either side. This ceiling would be reached in two

---

[1] UK Head of Delegation to the MBFR talks in Vienna.

[2] Not printed.

phases, each of which would be governed by a separate agreement. In the first phase the Soviet Union would withdraw a tank army comprising 68,000 men and 1,700 tanks, while the US would withdraw 29,000 soldiers (these figures representing in each case 15 per cent of each country's ground force manpower in the area of reductions). Because of the disparity in the relative distances over which US and Soviet forces would withdraw, the former could be withdrawn either as individuals or in units, at the discretion of the US, whereas the latter would be withdrawn in entire designated units; and the American units withdrawn could leave their equipment behind, whereas the Soviet forces would take theirs with them. In the second phase of negotiations for which specific provision would be made in the first phase agreement, the participants would agree to reductions which would complete movement to the proposed common ceiling.[3] On the NATO side, second phase reductions would focus on non-US forces. Reductions in both phases would be supplemented by 'associated measures' governing troop movements and manoeuvres and including specific verification and non-circumvention provisions. The memorandum in which these proposals were tabled at the Plenary meeting on 22 November is at Annex A to this despatch.[4]

4. Before the start of the negotiations it was decided within the Alliance that, before presenting their detailed proposals to the other side, the allied representatives would begin by explaining the reasoning behind them in a series of carefully co-ordinated statements. The Warsaw Pact made no effort to respond in kind, and kept their opening statements to a high level of generality. But they achieved considerable tactical surprise when, as early as 8 November, the Soviet Delegation, in the name of the four direct participants on the Eastern side, tabled specific proposals of their own in the form of a draft agreement. The text of this draft agreement is at Annex B.[5] A Soviet representative later claimed that their proposals had been drafted in full knowledge of the contents of those of the Allies. This is almost certainly true. Presentationally, the Warsaw Pact proposals form an effective counter to the Allied approach; and by courtesy of the *Los Angeles Times*, the Russians received advance notice of the substance of the Allied position by September at the latest.[6]

---

[3] The FCO were wary lest Allied negotiators too readily accept the notion of second-phase reductions. As Sir A. Douglas-Home reminded Mr. Rose in telegram No. 8 to UKDEL Vienna of 21 January, the agreed Alliance approach to the negotiations envisaged a first-phase agreement limited to reductions of US and Soviet forces and Soviet agreement to the concept, though not the precise figure, of an eventual overall common ceiling. 'We accept', he noted, 'that in order to obtain such agreement, it will probably be necessary for us to agree that second phase negotiations will begin within a fixed period after the conclusion of a satisfactory Phase I agreement.' But to concede the principle of second-phase reductions without Soviet acceptance of the concept of an overall common ceiling would, he argued 'be bad negotiating tactics'.

[4] Not printed. This memorandum contained the Allied proposals outlined in No. 9, paragraph 11.

[5] Not printed. The Eastern proposals are summarised in paragraph 6 below.

[6] In an article published in the *International Herald Tribune* of 14 September, Mr. R. Toth, a *Los Angeles Times* journalist, reported that NATO was to propose a cut in East/West forces in central Europe 'to the same level of about 700,000 men' (WDN 27/10).

5. Both in their general approach and in detail, the Warsaw Pact proposals are fundamentally incompatible with those of the West. Whereas the Allies wish to see the existing imbalance in ground forces corrected, the Warsaw Pact's guiding principle is that the existing relationship of forces in Central Europe must be maintained. Their contention is that it is the product of historical evolution; that it satisfactorily guarantees the security of all concerned; and that any attempt to adjust it would diminish the security of the Warsaw Pact countries and give NATO a unilateral military advantage.[7]

6. In detail, the Warsaw Pact proposals envisage a single agreement providing for the reduction in three stages of all armed forces—including air and nuclear forces—in Central Europe. In a first 'symbolic' stage, each side would reduce its forces by 20,000 men. The second and third stage would further reduce the forces of each side by 5 and 10 percent successively. Reductions would be carried out in whole units of approximately similar type (whatever that may mean) and would fall on the forces of the individual direct participants in proportion to their contribution to the total forces subject to reduction on each side, thereby in effect creating permanent separate ceilings on the manpower and equipment of each direct participant in the area of reductions. The proposals thus take no account of the disparities in the existing situation, nor of the Allied contention that to maintain the existing numerical disparity at a lower level of forces would, in strategic terms, have the effect of aggravating it. No mention is made of associated measures in the sense in which these are understood by the Allies.

7. In sum, the main points of difference between the two sides' proposals are:

(*a*) the Allies wish to redress the existing imbalance in ground forces, whereas the Warsaw Pact wish to preserve and, in effect, aggravate it;

(*b*) the Allies propose unequal reductions to a common ceiling, whereas the Warsaw Pact propose 'symbolic' reductions of equal quantity, to be followed by reductions of equal proportions;

(*c*) the Allies propose a two-phase negotiation, with reductions in the first phase confined to US and Soviet forces, whereas the Warsaw Pact propose a single negotiation, with the forces of all the direct participants being reduced from the outset;

(*d*) the Allies would confine reductions to ground forces, whereas the Warsaw Pact would include air and nuclear forces;

---

[7] In UKDEL Vienna telegram No. 8 of 10 January, Mr. Rose suggested arguments that the West could advance to counter the Soviet position: 'Our objective is surely to demonstrate the fairness of the common ceiling goal. For this purpose we need to show that:

a) the fact that the present relationship between forces on the two sides has been "shaped by history" does not, as the Russians suggest, make it acceptable:

b) merely to perpetuate the present relationship at a lower level will not provide for greater stability:

and

c) the disparities have been, and are still being, increased by the Warsaw Pact build up which has been going on since NATO first proposed MBFRs in June 1968.'

(*e*)   the Allied proposals are so framed as to avoid the creation of sub-ceilings, within the common ceiling, for the forces of non-US NATO countries (and thus to avoid prejudicing the future evolution of European defence arrangements), whereas the Warsaw Pact proposals would make such sub-ceilings unavoidable;

(*f*)   the Allied proposals for the disposition of equipment belonging to forces withdrawn take account of the geographical disparities, whereas those of the Warsaw Pact do not;

(*g*)   the Allies make provision for 'associated measures', including verification and non-circumvention arrangements, whereas the Warsaw Pact do not.

8.   Although the Warsaw Pact proposals have attracted relatively little attention in the Western Press so far, they have a variety of apparent virtues well calculated to recommend them to Western, and in particular to American, public opinion. They are superficially easy to understand, superficially fair and superficially—although this is more questionable—simple to execute. By comparison with earlier Soviet disarmament and troop reduction proposals, the order of magnitude of the reductions proposed is not unduly exaggerated, and has a realistic ring.

The negotiations

9.   In addition to making a favourable impact on Western public opinion, the Russians no doubt hoped that, by tabling these proposals early in the negotiations (and leaking their contents almost immediately to the Press), they would throw the Allies off balance, disrupt the ordered exposition of the proposals on which we had embarked, and draw us into negotiation on the basis of Soviet proposals and thus of Soviet concepts. If this was the Soviet calculation, Allied cohesion and good sense proved equal to it. After some feverish nocturnal consultation, the Ad Hoc Group (as the Committee of Allied negotiators in Vienna is called) decided to proceed with the exposition of the Alliance approach as already planned, merely bringing forward slightly the tabling of the memorandum on Allied proposals to which I have already referred. (Since agreement had not by then been reached in the North Atlantic Council on the details of the stabilising measures to be proposed, these were put forward separately in a statement made by the Head of the German Delegation,[8] as Allied spokesman at the Plenary meeting on 11 December). The Russians had no more surprises in store, and both sides devoted the remaining bi-weekly plenary meetings until the recess to repeating and expanding on the merits of their own proposals.

10.   The plenaries, with their long and frequently sterile exchanges of set speeches, are ill-adapted to serve as a forum for dialogue and interest has to a large extent centred on informal bilateral contacts between representatives of the two Alliances. In these the Russians have probed the Western position vigorously for any sign of weakness or divergence of view between the Allies. The points they have appeared most anxious to establish are that air and nuclear forces

[8] Herr W. Behrends.

should be included in any reductions, and the West European forces (particularly the Bundeswehr) should not slip through the net. They have pressed hard for an indication of what the Alliance would be prepared to pay for a first-phase agreement limited to US and Soviet troops in terms of a firm commitment on the timing and content of a second phase agreement; but without revealing the terms, if any, on which such an agreement would be acceptable to them. They have avoided outright rejection of the common ceiling concept, and have hinted that this 'iron pole' of the Allied negotiating structure might be twisted into a shape compatible with their own proposals, possibly by extending the reductions to include air force manpower.

11. In probing the Western position on these points, the Warsaw Pact has not, in my view, shown any genuine flexibility on the real issues of substance which separate the two sides, and in particular has given no sign of readiness to adjust the existing military imbalance in Central Europe. The Russians have given the impression of operating from a rigid but not very detailed brief, which has given them some tactical flexibility on points of detail but none whatever on points of substance. Until they have exhaustively investigated the Allied position, they have no basis for recommending to Moscow any revision of their brief. If this is right, the long hours spent patiently repeating the same arguments over and over again could bear fruit in the detailed negotiations which lie ahead.

12. The absence of movement, or indeed of any real dialogue, during the opening session should be regarded as neither surprising nor disappointing. Each side came to Vienna with a prepared position conceived, on the Allied side at least, in ignorance of what the other side might propose and with little reference to what the other side might reasonably be thought likely to accept. Prolonged and repetitious exposition of these two sets of proposals, reflecting fundamentally irreconcilable approaches, has been judged necessary by both sides in order to establish that the concerns which lie behind them are to be taken seriously. In other words, what we have witnessed so far has been a preliminary exchange of fire from entrenched positions, rather than the beginning of a general engagement.

13. During this 'phoney war', the atmosphere between the two sides in Vienna has been curiously and artificially relaxed. In plenary sessions, the exchanges have for the most part been courteous and businesslike. Away from the conference table, East and West have lunched and dined and sung songs together with an elaborate parade of bonhomie which has rarely been disturbed by the need for substantial discussion of potentially divisive topics. This cannot last much longer, and indeed some Eastern representatives were already beginning just before the recess to show signs of exasperation at the Allies' continuing refusal to be drawn into detailed discussion of the Warsaw Pact proposals.

The Warsaw Pact
14. The Warsaw Pact can have few problems in maintaining its cohesion. The Russians are in undisputed charge. In their Head of Delegation, Ambassador Khlestov (who has retained his position as Head of the Legal Department in the Soviet Foreign Ministry), they have an experienced negotiator whose affability is matched by his shrewdness. He is ably backed by the last Soviet Ambassador in

London, M. Smirnovsky,[9] and by the enigmatic but self-assured M. Kvitsinsky, one of the wiz-kids of the Soviet Foreign Service, whose features seem to relax most naturally into an unappealing sneer. Like actors in a play, the individual non-Soviet Eastern participants may be given a part to act, and may even be permitted a limited degree of ad-libbing. But they all speak from the same basic script, which they did not write. The East Germans, although privately agreeable and even civilised, are the only ones so far to include in their plenary statements, any genuinely polemical passages, while their Allies have consistently adopted tones of sweet reasonableness. The Poles have occasional well-rehearsed attacks of frankness and indiscretion. The Czechoslovaks provide a chorus of dutiful orthodoxy, and the Hungarians and Bulgarians have walk-on parts only. The Romanians provide the light relief; anxious to display their independence without suffering its penalties, they have taken as their theme the need to keep interested outsiders systematically informed, and have tried to avoid committing themselves publically on any other subject. Nobody agrees with them, but nobody feels his interests threatened either, and the Western participants are usually ready to express their sympathy and respect for the Romanian position—which at this stage is all the Romanians appear to want.

Relations with the Alliance

15. With none of the Warsaw Pact's inherent advantages in this respect, the NATO Ad Hoc Group—thanks in large measure to the habit and procedures of constant consultation established during the preparatory talks—has developed and maintained an admirable cohesion The strains through which the alliance has been passing have echoed only distantly in Vienna and have in no way affected the mutual understanding and excellent personal relationships which have been built up among the allied representatives here during their long and almost daily meetings. We were all gratified to learn from Mr. Secretary Schlesinger's[10] remarks to the North Atlantic Council in December that this cohesion had been noted and welcomed in Washington.[11]

16. At the same time it is only fair to point out that the cohesion of the Allies on MBFR has not yet been exposed to severe strain. During the first negotiating stage, we have not had to venture significantly outside the common ground agreed in advance by the North Atlantic Council. The Allied representatives have therefore been able to work out the modalities of their corporate operation in relatively favourable conditions, without having to face up to the underlying differences of policy and interest which the NATO negotiating mandate circum-navigates. In the process, the Group has developed an *esprit de corps* which should prove of great value in the more testing negotiations ahead.

17. Give the nature of the Allied proposals and the extent of the American interest in them, it has been inevitable and right that the Americans should take the lead and set the pace (which has been a brisk one) in the Ad Hoc Group.

[9] Mr. M.N. Smirnovsky was Soviet Ambassador in London during 1966–73.

[10] Mr. J.R. Schlesinger was US Secretary of Defense.

[11] The NAC met in Ministerial session in Brussels on 10 and 11 December.

Moreover the sheer size of the American Delegation enables them to produce drafts, reports and analysis for the Group at a rate, and in a quantity, which no other delegation could conceivably emulate. We and to a lesser extent the Germans, as the only other Delegations capable of undertaking this kind of work, have done our best (with some success) to moderate this American preponderance, but we cannot change it and do not want to. Although all members of the Group accept this situation without overt resentment, suspicions of possible super-Power collusion between the Americans and the Russians are never entirely absent from their minds; and it is no secret that the forceful personality of Mr. Jonathan Dean, the Deputy Head of the American Delegation, is not best adapted to allaying such suspicions. Although a formidable ally when it comes to hard bargaining with the other side, he is not temperamentally suited to the difficult and frustrating task of coaxing rather than bulldozing his colleagues, (many of whom have a less than total command of English) along what the Americans regard as the right road. Moreover, although Mr. Stanley Resor, the Head of the American Delegation, has by and large succeeded in smoothing any feathers which have been ruffled, he had not, by the time of the recess, given the impression of asserting his authority as fully as one would expect within his own Delegation. It is clear that the Americans are going to need all Mr. Resor's patience and tact if the Ad Hoc Group is to maintain its harmony and cohesion during the next, more critical, stage of the negotiations. I am glad to report however that first indications since the Allied representatives re-assembled here are that both the senior Americans are more relaxed—possibly because they are under less urgent pressure from their own authorities to achieve quick results— and that Mr. Resor appears to be more effectively in charge.

18. The Germans have done their best to play a role in the Group proportionate to their substantial stake in the negotiations, and I have found Herr Behrends an agreeable and helpful colleague. He suffers, however, from a division of opinion in Bonn between the Ministry of Defence and the Auswärtiges Amt[12] on both the tactics and the objectives of MBFR. In consequence, his interventions tend to be indecisive, and he displays a marked reluctance either to take the initiative in the Group or to stick firmly to a position in the face of pressure.

19. There is no doubt that when we, the Germans and the Americans can agree on a course of action before the Ad Hoc Group meets, a more satisfactory result can be obtained in the Group with a great saving of time. Unfortunately our regular tripartite meetings have not always succeeded in achieving this. The causes of failure have sometimes been American impatience, sometimes the confused and contradictory instructions received by the Germans, and sometimes (as on stabilising measures) a combination of the two. We have nevertheless developed a good working relationship and the omens for a more effective co-operation during the forthcoming session are so far favourable. (I should perhaps add that, for obvious reasons, the fact that the three major Allied participants meet regularly together to discuss tactics has not been disclosed to the other Allies and should not be mentioned to them.)

---

[12] The West German Foreign Ministry.

20. Besides this informal and unavowable tripartite group, two other group-ings on the NATO side have a discernible influence on Allied deliberations in Vienna. The first of these comprises the representatives of those member countries of the EEC which are participating in the negotiations. Its *raison d'être* is to ensure that the negotiations do not develop in any way which could prejudice the future development of European defence co-operation (by, for example, imposing separate national sub-ceilings on the forces of Western European participants in the reduction area), a possibility which it has become clear that the Russians have constantly in mind. This 'European reservation' was expressed by the participant EEC members in their opening statements, and its importance has become increasingly apparent as the Allies have begun to consider what assurances on the substance of a second phase they may have to offer as the price for a satisfactory first phase agreement.

21. The European grouping, in which my Italian colleague has made a great deal of the running, is strictly informal and meets only over working lunches and dinners. The Americans are kept fully informed of its deliberations and we have firmly headed off all attempts to institutionalise it or turn it into a formal European caucus, the effect of which could only be divisive. Provided it can be kept within these limits, it will provide a useful and unobjectionable sounding board for points of special European interest. Although the French Embassy here, consistent with its strict instructions from Paris, has refused to be drawn into any multilateral contact with members of Delegations of EEC countries, the French Counsellor maintains close and regular bilateral contact with this Delegation and through us (and the Germans) keeps fully in touch with the development of the negotiations.

22. The second informal grouping is that of the Flank countries. Here there is little evidence of cohesion, since the interests (to say nothing of the tempera-ments) of the Northern and Southern flanks are not identical; and the Italians in any case stand somewhat aloof, rightly judging that their stake in the outcome of the negotiations is larger than the other so-called 'special status participants'. Nevertheless, the Greek representative, M. Dountas, has emerged as an effective watch-dog of the collective Flank interest and makes their point—nearly always the same one—not only tirelessly but with considerable tact and humour.

The role of the UK

23. Our own Delegation is well placed to play a constructive part in the Ad Hoc Group. We are not hampered by contradictory instructions or by pressing domestic demands for early troop reductions. Except by comparison with the Americans, we have a relatively large permanently resident staff. The language of the Ad Hoc Group is English—more or less. We can act as nobody else can to assuage the mutual suspicions both of the Americans and of the older members of the EEC. As I have already mentioned, we effectively share with the Germans the responsibility for initiating drafts which will reflect other than American thinking: a contribution without which the American predominance would become overwhelming and could eventually threaten the cohesion of the Group. For all these reasons, as well as because of our major interest in the outcome of

the negotiations, it is inevitable as well as right that we should play, after the Americans, the most prominent and active part in the Ad Hoc Group's work. This is what we have so far done and expect to continue to do as the negotiations develop.

The next stage

24. The Allies have returned to Vienna after the Christmas recess in a resolute frame of mind. The only discernible change has been in the American Delegation. Before Christmas, they were impatient to press ahead and engage the other side in detailed bargaining. This desire remains: but it seems clear that events in the Middle East and on the international economic front[13] have temporarily at least taken some of the steam out of the domestic pressure on the US Administration for early force reductions in Europe, and that Washington are no longer (if they ever were) looking for immediate progress in Vienna. They are resigned to a fairly long haul, and are not disposed to make early concessions. Some at least of the urgency has accordingly gone out of the mood of the American Delegation here, with the beneficial effects to which I have already referred.

25. But the Americans are still keen to get down to business with the other side, if this can be done at a reasonable cost. Preliminary discussion of tactics has revealed a consensus in the Ad Hoc Group for continuing to present in plenary sessions the main elements in the Allied proposals, stressing in particular the importance we attach to the establishment of a common ceiling in ground force manpower. At the same time, it has been agreed that we should in parallel with these plenary statements, embark on a series of informal 'probes' with the other side in order if possible to start them talking, at least in private, on the basis of the Allied rather than the Soviet approach. In particular, it is hoped that these probes may induce the Russians—without prejudice to their formal position—to begin to discuss Soviet and American forces. If this can be achieved, it would under the guise of what the Americans refer to as 'a limited procedural agreement', represent a substantive tactical gain for the Allies.

26. Whether the Soviet Union will accept such an arrangement without seeking to exact an unacceptably substantive price in terms of firm commitments by the Allies on both the timing and content of the second phase of the negotiations is of course very much open to question. First tentative contacts with the Soviet representatives do not suggest any softening in their pre-Christmas position: but they do contain more than a hint of readiness to supplement the regular plenary exchanges with some more organised system of informal contacts. Any such informal contacts will, under one guise or another, in effect

[13] The fourth Arab-Israeli war began on 6 October 1973 when Egyptian and Syrian forces attacked Israeli military positions. The US was instrumental in ensuring that Israel was able to withstand the initial assault and launch a counter-offensive. In retaliation, Arab members of the Organisation of Petroleum-Exporting Countries (OPEC) restricted oil supplies to Western states considered sympathetic to Israel. The price of crude oil escalated and the resulting 'energy crisis' shook international business confidence and led to a severe downturn in Western manufacturing economies.

mean the re-introduction of the 'emissary' system which proved an indispensable negotiating instrument during the preparatory talks last spring. This system inevitably raises hackles within the Alliance, because it involves entrusting the actual business of negotiation to a restricted number of national representatives (the number suggested is three), one of whom is bound to be American; and in practice this would exclude the Flanks. But it is clear that some such system, even if heavily disguised as a series of apparently fortuitous social gatherings, will be essential if serious business is going to be done. I am fairly confident from the soundings I have taken among my colleagues so far, that, on the Allied side, we shall probably end up with an arrangement whereby the Allied team will always include the Americans; my German colleague and I will alternate in second place; and the remaining direct participants will take it in turns to provide the third member of the team. But it will not be easy to sell this idea to the flank countries.

27. We cannot yet tell whether the Russians will be prepared to accept a procedure of this kind. In any case it will not be possible, or indeed desirable, to start on it until some way into the new session and our first probes are even then likely to be cautious and tentative. It would be surprising if they led to rapid progress. The most we are likely to achieve by the Easter recess is an indication of the areas in which there might possibly be some flexibility on the Warsaw Pact side. If we achieved this we should at least be able to assess whether the Russians were interested in finding a basis on which agreement might be reached. This in turn could lead to the start of actual bargaining during the summer session. With the prospect of a visit by President Nixon to Moscow in the summer, we may at that point be under American pressure to force the pace. The Russians also may by then feel a similar need to produce some early results. But the difference between the Western process of full consultation and the relative absence of any corresponding process among the Warsaw Pact countries will provide the Russians with yet another unilateral advantage when we get down to detailed bargaining. While I am aware of the objections to examining anything in the nature of a fall-back position, I believe nevertheless that, if we are to be adequately prepared for this bargaining, we should within the Alliance very soon start trying to identify the limited number of elements in our position which might, when the time comes, be used to buy concessions from the other side. I hope to make some suggestions about this in correspondence with the Department during the next few weeks.

28. This report would not be complete if I did not end by expressing my appreciation of the way in which Her Majesty's Ambassador and his staff have coped with the considerable inconvenience caused them by the arrival of this Delegation. We are very grateful to them for their forebearance, assistance and hospitality.

29. I am sending copies of this despatch to Her Majesty's Representatives at Washington, Bonn, Moscow, Paris, Ottawa, Brussels, The Hague, Rome, Luxembourg, Copenhagen, Oslo, Ankara, Athens, Lisbon, Vienna, East Berlin, Warsaw, Prague, Bucharest, Budapest, Sofia, Belgrade and Stockholm, to the UK Permanent Representative to the North Atlantic Council; and to the Heads of

the UK Mission to the Conference on Security and Co-operation in Europe and of the UK Delegation to the Conference of the Committee on Disarmament in Geneva.

I, have etc.,
CLIVE M. ROSE

No. 11

Letter from Mr. Tickell to Mr. Rose (UKDEL Vienna)

[*WDN 27/1*]

Secret   FCO, *17 January 1974*

Dear Clive,

MBFR

In submitting to Ministers the draft of our telegram No. 3[1] to you giving you instructions on negotiating tactics for the forthcoming stage of the MBFR talks, we also drew Ministers' attention to two Soviet objectives which have been revealed in the line taken so far by the Soviet negotiators in Vienna. These were:

(*a*) The Russians are trying to ensure that as a result of the negotiations individual ceilings are set on the forces and equipment holdings of all direct MBFR participants; and
(*b*) The Russians are insisting that nuclear weapons and aircraft must be included within the scope of the negotiations.

2. We pointed out that although Allied decisions on how to deal with these two points were not likely to be needed in the immediate future, it would be worth

---

[1] In this telegram of 8 January Sir A. Douglas-Home, after recalling meetings with Mr. Rose and Sir E. Peck on 17 and 18 December, and with Mr. Dean on 29 December, advised that during the next session 'the negotiations should proceed at a natural pace' without any artificial urgency or time pressure. 'The Allies', he observed, 'should, in our view, continue to explain in greater detail the main elements in their framework proposal and seek generally to probe the Soviet position further. Although we must retain flexibility and be ready to exploit any openings, we should work on the assumption that real progress in the negotiations is unlikely during the forthcoming session.' The telegram also recommended that the Allies should highlight their proposed 'stabilising measures', and that, since these were likely to be unwelcome to the Russians, they should seek to build on requirements common to both the NATO and Warsaw Pact approaches for some kind of data bank. Discussion of data would, it was thought, lead inevitably to the consideration of those disparities of military strength to which the West had already drawn attention, and could permit the examination of Allied proposals for a common ceiling. Mr. Tickell noted in a submission to Mr. Wiggin of 4 January, covering the draft of this telegram, that despite Mr. Dean's known preference for forcing the pace in Vienna by engaging the Russians in detailed discussion of the concept of a first phase limited to US and Soviet troops, the inclination of the US authorities seemed to be to 'let the negotiations take their natural course and avoid any attempt to go for quick results'.

setting out the particular dangers, as we saw them, for British interests and to draw a couple of conclusions for future policy. We set out the dangers and the conclusions in the following terms:

(*a*) The establishment of individual sub-ceilings on all direct MBFR partici-pants would severely handicap, if not rule, out the development of any West European defence entity or European defence community. The Allied frame-work proposal, which envisaged an aggregate common ceiling on NATO manpower in the Reduction Area and within this ceiling a sub-ceiling on US manpower, was designed to leave the European members of the Alliance free to combine, deploy and improve their forces, and even to increase them if the US total fell below the US sub-ceiling. If European national sub-ceilings were imposed, this freedom would be lost, and if in the near future US forces were for any reason to be further reduced, the Europeans would be unable to make up the shortfall. We concluded therefore that we should firmly oppose any suggestion that there should be individual sub-ceilings on British or other European forces.

(*b*) Similar considerations applied to the Soviet desire to include a nuclear element in the negotiations. We recognised that if there were reductions of warheads and/or delivery systems on the Allied side in the first phase of MBFR, this would probably mean the imposition of at least a *de facto* ceiling on American, and perhaps even total Allied, holdings of nuclear warheads and delivery systems. But we might be faced with the problem of how to cope with a Soviet attempt to include British nuclear weapons in a nuclear component of the second phase, if such a component were to be added to that phase as well. We would of course wish to oppose any *de jure* ceiling on British forces, and hence on British nuclear delivery systems. But even more important, if British warheads were to be subject to a ceiling as well, our ability to deploy nuclear weapons as we thought best for the defence of Europe would be restricted as would be the freedom of the Europeans to collaborate in this field and, if necessary, make up any shortfall caused by reductions in American weapons deployed in the area. We concluded therefore that we should refuse to allow the possibility of reductions in British nuclear warheads to be brought into the negotiations (systems held under two-key arrangements would fall into a different category) or to accept any ceiling, explicit or implicit, on British nuclear warheads deployed in the Reductions Area.

3. Both Mr. Amery and the Secretary of State approved these conclusions,[2] which have also been endorsed by Ministry of Defence Ministers and the Chief of Defence Staff. We do not suggest the time has necessarily come to make use

---

[2] On 7 January Mr. Amery minuted on Mr. Tickell's submission of 4 January (*v. ibid.*) that its contents and that of the attached draft telegram were 'thoroughly sound'. Sir A. Douglas-Home subsequently noted: 'I agree. Sub-ceilings are clearly very dangerous for conventional forces. The nuclear is rather more difficult. What valid excuse do we have if the ceiling proposed for these weapons is enough to saturate but not to over-saturate?'

of these conclusions with our Allies. As you know, we are not inclined to emphasise the 'European' point any further in the East/West context. Paragraph 4 of Washington telegram No 136[3] suggests that Dr. Kissinger[4] understands our preoccupations and it may be that there will be no disposition among our Allies to take a different line on either point. There would be no harm however in you, or other recipients of this letter, telling your Allied colleagues that the first of these points, the avoidance of European sub-ceilings, is an issue of cardinal importance for us.[5] I have already spoken privately in this sense to Ambassador Roth[6] in Bonn. The second point, about British nuclear warheads, is perhaps more sensitive and we would not want to encourage any consideration of it among our Allies for the time being.

Yours ever,
C.C.C. TICKELL

[3] In this telegram of 11 January, Lord Cromer, the British Ambassador in Washington, reported that the US delegation at Vienna were under instructions that they 'should continue to oppose the inclusion of air force and nuclear elements [in the negotiations] and [that they] should make clear to the Soviets that the US were not prepared to address these issues'. There was, Lord Cromer added in paragraph 4, 'firm agreement' in Washington 'that no national sub-ceilings should be accepted in MBFR other than those for US and Soviet forces in the guidelines area'.

[4] Dr. Kissinger succeeded Mr. W.P. Rogers as US Secretary of State on 22 August 1973.

[5] In a minute of 7 January Sir J. Killick (DUS) argued that to weaken on either the issue of setting individual sub-ceilings or the inclusion of a nuclear element in the negotiations 'would horrify the French and have ... a very adverse effect on the prospects for future cooperation with them in the defence field'. Sir J. Killick was Ambassador in Moscow, 1971–73, DUS 1973–75, and Ambassador and UK Permanent Representative on the NAC, Brussels 1975–79.

[6] Herr R. Roth was Head of the Disarmament Division of the West German Foreign Ministry.

No. 12

Sir A. Douglas-Home to Mr. Rose (UKDEL Vienna)

No. 34 Telegraphic [*WDN 27/1*]

Confidential   FCO, *25 February 1974*

Repeated for information to UKDEL NATO, Routine Moscow, Washington and Bonn.
Your tel[egram]s Nos. 62, 64, 66 and 67:[1]

MBFR: Informal Contacts

1.   We share the Ad Hoc Group's view that some progress was made at the dinner on 20 February, and agree that the informal discussions between the two sides should continue.

[1] These telegrams of 19–22 February dealt with a multilateral dinner held at Mr. Rose's house on 20 February and attended by Mr. Resor, Mr. Quarles, Mr. Khlestov, Mr. Smirnovsky, Mr. Strulak and the Czechoslovak delegate, Mr. Klein. This was the third in a series of informal emissary

2.   In the discussions which have taken place so far, the Warsaw Pact representatives have been able, without modifying their own position, to obtain useful information about the Allied approach to the negotiations. We see no reason why we should not now do correspondingly. Provided that Allied representatives do not depart from agreed Allied positions there would be some advantage in obliging the Warsaw Pact representatives to explain—and justify—their own proposals in more detail.

3.   We can therefore accept the definition of the agenda set out in para 4 of your telegram No. 64, namely a) ground forces of the direct participants and b) other topics, on the understanding that reductions of US/Soviet ground forces will be discussed first under item a) (para 2a of your telegram No. 66).[2] Item a) goes beyond the topic for discussion envisaged in para 2 of the tactics paper[3] but we accept that the concession involved is purely procedural.

4.   We think it important that the Allied representatives should firmly rebut any Soviet attempt to categorise the forces in the area as 'foreign' or 'national'. We would not want the Soviet contention that this is an 'unbiased' description (para 3 of your telegram No. 64)[4] to go unchallenged. A letter from Tickell on this point is in the confidential bag, arriving in Vienna on 25 February.[5]

dinners (the first and second having been held on 6 and 13 February) initiated with a view to achieving a procedural understanding and promoting a more constructive East/West dialogue at Vienna.

[2]   During the dinner on 20 February Mr. Rose had indicated that Western delegations were willing to expand the definitions they had suggested for initial discussions to include: (a) US and Soviet ground forces; (b) the inclusion of the ground forces of other direct participants; and (c) phasing. Mr. Khlestov, however, proposed instead two agenda items: (a) ground forces of direct participants; and (b) air forces and nuclear weapons. Western delegates objected to the latter because it did not represent a 'common element'. They did, however, manage to persuade Mr. Khlestov that his item (a) should include 'phasing'; and that the title of item (b) should be 'other topics', with the understanding that, at the wish of the East, air forces and nuclear weapons would be raised first, and, on Western insistence, that other topics might be raised such as 'associated measures'. Mr. Rose's provisional view was that this represented a 'considerable advance' (UKDEL Vienna telegram No. 64 of 21 February). At their meeting on 21 February the Ad Hoc Group generally welcomed the progress made at the multilateral dinner, but they insisted that item (a) must begin with a discussion of US and Soviet ground forces (UKDEL Vienna telegram No. 66 of 22 February).

[3]   This paper, 'Next Tactical Steps in MBFR Negotiations', was agreed by the Ad Hoc Group on 29 January. It proposed that the Allies seek 'to probe hints of possible Soviet willingness to discuss a two-phase negotiation in order to bring the Soviets to defer, if only temporarily, for the practical purpose of beginning discussion at some specific point, their interest in coverage of non-US NATO forces, air and nuclear forces'. To this end, paragraph 2 of the paper recommended that the Allies seek an 'informal understanding' with the Russians that the process of East/West discussion would begin by talking about US/Soviet ground forces. The proposed understanding, to be presented to the Russians as a 'limited procedural one, without prejudice to or acceptance of the substantive elements of the program of either side', would, it was hoped, 'open the way for detailed discussion of, and exploration of Eastern attitudes toward, the entire Phase I Western negotiating program'.

[4]   Mr. Khlestov suggested at the dinner on 20 February (see note 2 above) that the subject matter of the talks should be divided between two items, 'foreign armed forces and national armed forces'.

[5]   In this letter of 19 February, Mr. Tickell noted that Mr. Khlestov had recently argued that Belgian troops deployed in the FRG could be regarded as 'foreign' for the purposes of the negotiations. 'As you know', he explained, 'we have always taken the view that unqualified use of

5.   During the discussions on item a) of the agenda it will no doubt be necessary to offer the Russians some assurance that there will be a second phase of MBFR including European reductions on the lines already agreed by the Alliance in the tactics paper. It is important that Allied representatives do not go beyond this. The Russians must be left in no doubt that we will not negotiate MBFR in terms of individual reductions (and hence implied individual force ceilings) by all Allied countries but only in terms of overall Alliance reductions and US reductions. It is for this reason that we are opposed to giving the Russians any commitment about which particular Allied forces will be included in the second phase of MBFR. This may well turn out to be a key issue in the negotiations and we believe it should be faced squarely by the Allies, if necessary at the outset of the informal discussions.

6.   As for item b) of the agenda we have always accepted that the Russians could not be prevented from raising the issues of air forces and nuclear weapons. This possibility is recognised in para 8 of the tactics paper.[6] Allied negotiators should listen to whatever the Russians have to say on these subjects and should be prepared to ask searching questions on what sort of reductions the Russians have in mind. We believe it would be possible to do this, and thus perhaps to get a clearer idea of whether any compromise in these fields is likely eventually to be attractive to us, without prejudice to the Alliance's present position.

7.   We do not see any particular need for Allied negotiators to raise the issue of associated measures in these informal discussions (para 1b of your telegram No. 66)[7] but we would not wish to oppose this idea if your colleagues thought it useful. We assume that the Allies' detailed proposals on stabilising measures will in any case be put forward as scheduled in the plenary sessions.

8.   We share your hope that these discussions can proceed without undue haste or time pressure. We think it important also to maintain their informal character without commitment on either side. As for the composition of the team we doubt whether an Allied group consisting of Resor/Dean, Behrends and Quarles will necessarily take as clear and firm a position on some issues (e.g. the point in para 4 above) as we would like.[8] We realise that it would be difficult and

the adjectives "foreign" and "national" to describe the forces which might be reduced as a result of the negotiations has disadvantages from the European point of view ... [W]e do not regard European forces stationed on European territory as in any way "foreign"; hence our preference for dealing separately with US and Soviet forces on the one hand and European forces on the other.'

[6] Paragraph 8 of the Allies' 'Next Tactical Steps' paper (see note 3 above) proposed that in response to Soviet questions on the inclusion of air and nuclear forces the Allies could say that their main interest was in starting an active dialogue on US and Soviet ground forces, and by agreeing now to discuss these the Russians would not be foregoing their right to raise 'subjects of interest to them'.

[7] This is evidently a typographic error. In paragraph 2(b) of this telegram Mr. Rose reported the Ad Hoc Group's requirement that that the East should recognise the West's right to raise under item (b) any topic, such as associated measures, which was of concern to them.

[8] The question of who should participate in these dinners was a particularly sensitive issue in the Ad Hoc Group, especially for those delegates who were bound by their instructions to oppose any formalised 'emissary' system (notably the Belgians, Greeks and Turks). A compromise worked

embarrassing for you now to try to change the team but we have in mind the danger alluded to in the last sentence of para 2 of your telegram No. 62 of a shift in the centre of gravity of the negotiations.[9] You may think it worth making the point in the Ad Hoc Group that the present procedure for informal discussions should be regarded as experimental for the time being and not as a permanent feature of the negotiations. We may wish in due course to review it. This is a point that we would like to see reflected also in the speaking notes in your telegram No. 67, with which we are otherwise content.[10]

9.   As explained to you by telephone, we would find it difficult in present financial circumstance to justify a visit to London by Goodall (para 4 of your telegram No. 62).[11] In any event we assume that you would not now think this necessary.

out after the first dinner in effect meant that at subsequent dinners the Allied team would be composed of an American, with the UK and FRG taking it in turns to occupy the second place, and Belgium, Canada and the Netherlands rotating in the third. As Mr. A.D.S. Goodall, a member of the UK delegation, noted in a letter to Mr. McLaren of 14 February, the issue was 'potentially explosive and [was] almost certain to lead to further disagreement if and when the emissary dinners [became] a channel for substantive negotiation'.

[9] In his telegram No. 62 (see note 1 above) Mr. Rose explained that the Americans wished to give Allied representatives at the dinner discretion to accept Eastern procedural proposals. Some Allied delegates feared this would herald 'a decisive shift in the centre of gravity of the negotiations from plenary sessions to restricted emissary meetings'.

[10] Mr. Rose's draft speaking notes recapitulated the procedural agreements reached at the dinner on 20 February for clarification with the Eastern delegations (UKDEL Vienna telegram No. 67 of 22 February).

[11] Mr. Rose had suggested in this telegram (see notes 1 and 9 above) that if the dinner on 20 February were to prove as unproductive as was expected, Mr. Goodall should return to London to discuss the situation with WOD.

No. 13

Mr. Rose (UKDEL Vienna) to Mr. L.J. Callaghan[1]
[*WDN 27/1*]

Secret. Eclipse   VIENNA, *11 April 1974*

Summary ...[2]

Sir,

MBFR: The Second Round

Today is, formally, the last day of the 'Second round' (this description has also been adopted by the Warsaw Pact). I enclose a memorandum summarising developments since Delegations reassembled in January.[3] The 'Third Round' is due to start in the week beginning 6 May. It has been agreed provisionally that the first plenary session after the recess, which will mark the official *reprise* of East–West contacts, will take place on 10 May.

2. Judging by the plenary statements by Eastern representatives, reports in the Press of deadlock may appear completely justified. This impression is reinforced by the increasing number of attacks in the Eastern media on the Western position in the talks. Yet the impression is a false one. *The Economist*'s reference to movement at 'a snail's pace' is nearer the mark.[4] It is also more

---

[1] The General Election of 28 February deprived the Conservative Government of its Parliamentary majority, and on 4 March the Labour leader, Mr. H. Wilson, became Prime Minister. The next day Mr. Callaghan succeeded Sir A. Douglas-Home as Secretary of State for Foreign and Commonwealth Affairs. In a letter of 8 March Mr. Tickell advised Mr. Rose the 'accent of the new Government is on the importance of the Alliance and the American connexion, and the need closely to associate defence and détente. If anything therefore we may find that MBFR have a higher priority than before.' A Labour Party National Executive Committee document of 1973 had proclaimed that 'MBFR discussions should be widened to include discussion of the nuclear aspects of European defence', and Mr. Tickell warned Mr. Rose that they could not be sure that new Ministers would take the view that British nuclear weapons should necessarily be excluded from any nuclear reductions. For the present, he suggested to the UK delegation that 'it would be as well for you to proceed fairly gently in Vienna', avoiding 'anything that could represent a change of policy'.

[2] Not printed.

[3] Not printed. In this summary memorandum Mr. Rose noted the 'good working relations established within the Ad Hoc Group during the opening round have been consolidated and improved during the round under review. Visitors from capitals and from NATO have alike been struck by the businesslike and friendly atmosphere, and by the absence of any discernible reflection in Vienna of the disagreements and misunderstandings between the United States and the European members of the Alliance which have attracted so much attention elsewhere.' Cf. Kissinger, *Years of Upheaval*, pp. 700–35.

[4] In a minute to Mr. Wiggin of 26 April covering this despatch Mr. Tickell commented: 'despite the serious and businesslike atmosphere of the informal contacts, the Warsaw Pact countries have shown no inclination to compromise on the basic elements of their proposals. In particular, there has been no lessening of their insistence that air and nuclear forces must be included in the negotiations and that forces of all direct participants must be reduced simultaneously from the outset.'

consistent with the extreme complexity and sensitivity of the subject matter of these negotiations. The Russians' illusion last autumn, if it was ever seriously entertained, that they could hustle the West into a quick, easily concluded, all-over-by-the-spring negotiation has long since been abandoned.[5] Now Ambassador Khlestov, the Head of the Soviet Delegation, is saying—perhaps with equally exaggerated emphasis—that the East are in no hurry and that his authorities are quite happy for him to carry on indefinitely defending his original position.

3. When reporting on the First Round, in my despatch of 17 January,[6] I analysed the points of difference between the Western and Eastern proposals. I suggested that the Second Round would see the establishment of more systematic informal contacts between the two sides and that, while these contacts were unlikely to lead to rapid progress, they might enable the West to identify possible areas of flexibility in the Eastern position. This prediction has, on the whole, been fulfilled.

4. Formally, the Eastern representatives have stood firm on their proposals tabled on 8 November last year and maintained that whereas these proposals are wholly consistent with the terms of the communiqué of 28 June, 1973, which provides agreed 'terms of reference' for the negotiations, those put forward by the West are not.[7] This emerges clearly from the heavily-slanted comparison of the positions of the two sides in the Soviet statement made in the final plenary session on 9 April.[8] At the same time, the informal sessions have demonstrated that the Eastern position may not be as inflexible as these formal statements imply. It would be wrong to suggest that there has been any positive indication so far of Eastern willingness to compromise on the basic elements of their proposals. But in the course of many hours of wide-ranging debate in this restricted and informal framework several pointers have emerged as to areas in which it may

---

[5] In a minute to Mr. Tickell of 3 May, Sir J. Killick disagreed with Mr. Rose's assessment of the Soviet Union's original intentions. The Russians, he wrote, 'have *never* for a moment thought of a "quick, easily-concluded … negotiation." Their unexpected first proposal was a pure propaganda device to enable them to claim a "positive" attitude over a long haul.'

[6] See No. 10.

[7] In discussing ground forces the East confirmed that according to their own three-stage proposal about 17% of tank holdings would be reduced on either side, but stressed that this would be conditional upon the agreement covering all forces and armaments. They also rejected the Allied concept of a disparity in ground forces, claiming that it was inequitable and artificial to isolate one force element in this way, and that if all types of forces were taken into account, overall parity in the present East/West force relationship in the reductions area already existed. Reductions necessary to reach a ceiling in ground force manpower alone would in their view be asymmetrical and thus give NATO unilateral advantages, and the common ceiling would in any case neither provide a guarantee of West European reductions in Phase II, nor carry any assurance that forces (particularly non-US forces) would not be increased between the two phases (see note 3 above).

[8] In his statement, Mr. Khlestov attacked the West's two-phased approach to reductions, insisted on the inclusion of air and nuclear weapons in the negotiations, and generally 'dwelt on the inequitability and inadequacy of the Western proposals' (UKDEL Vienna telegram No. 124 of 10 April).

be useful to consider elaborating the Western proposals in order to improve their negotiability with the East.[9]

5. The Russians were originally reluctant to embark on these informal sessions. They told the Americans that they thought more progress would be made on a bilateral basis and that they would be inhibited from speaking freely in the presence of their Warsaw Pact colleagues. They were only persuaded to accept them by American refusal of the bilateral bait. In practice, the Russians, who have played the predominant, almost exclusive, role on the Eastern side, have not shown themselves noticeably inhibited in what must, even in the context of current East–West contacts, be a fairly unique forum for exchanging views on such highly sensitive topics. They have demonstrated the seriousness of their interest in reaching some form of agreement, have claimed that they find the informal sessions useful and have made it clear that they wish to continue them in the next session.[10]

6. On the Western side, the informal sessions were, at the start, regarded with mixed feelings. There was considerable resistance to the introduction of any formal 'emissary' system, involving the appointment of representatives to negotiate on behalf of the NATO countries. This was overcome, procedurally, by holding the sessions, in the guise of 'social gatherings' in the house of one of the participants; and, substantively, by the use of Western representatives of speaking notes which had been agreed in the NATO Ad Hoc Group and by the very full record of the proceedings which the US Delegation produced with remarkable despatch for presentation to the Ad Hoc Group on the day following each informal session. As a result, this method of informal contact has been accepted by the Group and its value as a means of probing Eastern attitudes is

[9] In his minute of 3 May (see note 5 above) Sir J. Killick described Mr. Rose's optimistic conclusion as 'overstated'. He added: 'Such areas of flexibility as *may* have appeared do not seem to me to get to the real substance.' The Allies had sought, so far without success, to draw the East into a discussion of data. But while the Russians had continued to insist that agreement must first be reached on the size and nature of reductions, they had also indicated their readiness to consider what each side meant by 'ground forces' and to discuss whose forces should be reduced from the outset.

[10] As a result of the procedural agreement reached at the multilateral dinner on 20 February (see No. 12, notes 1 and 2) it was decided to hold seven informal meetings: the first three were to be on the subject of the 'ground forces of the direct participants', with the understanding that reductions of US and Soviet ground forces would be considered at the first meeting; the next four meetings were to be on 'other topics', it being understood that the East would raise air and nuclear forces at the first three of them, while at the fourth the Allies would be free to raise topics of their choice (UKDEL Vienna telegrams Nos. 70 and 71 of 26 February). This, as Mr. Rose explained in his enclosed summary memorandum (see notes 3 and 7 above), was seen by the Western Allies as being to their advantage since they had secured Eastern agreement: (1) to separating the question of ground forces from other force elements; and (2) to start by discussing US and Soviet ground forces. In addition Allied representatives were 'in practice … able to concentrate most of the discussion on Western ground'. NATO representation in these informal sessions continued on same basis as for the previous multilateral dinners, on the understanding that flank representatives retained the right to be present if a subject of direct concern to them was to be discussed.

recognised.[11] Its continuation is subject to review after the recess. My view is that our advantage lies in continuing it, because:

(*a*)   the session has proved a useful forum for informal dialogue between the two sides;

(*b*)   both the Americans and the Russians want to continue them; and

(*c*)   if they are discontinued, the Americans will be strongly tempted to develop a bilateral dialogue with the Russians, on which their Allies will have much less influence or control.

I believe my colleagues in the Ad Hoc Group will go along with this, so long as the emphasis remains on the 'probing' as distinct from the 'negotiating' aspect of the discussions. But, if we reach the point of substantive bargaining, pressure may grow for it to be conducted in a less restricted forum.[12]

7.   What are the prospects for the next session? All participants are 'agreed that security in this area of the European continent can and must be assured at lower levels of armed forces and that no one should gain unilateral advantages as a result of the negotiations'.[13] This quotation comes from Khlestov's plenary statement on 9 April. It represents not only the agreed aim of the two sides but also virtually the limit of the common ground which so far exists between them. But it goes no further, in substance, than the communiqué of 28 June, 1973. Whether it can be translated into a concrete first agreement before the end of 1974, which is the timetable the Russians have set themselves, will depend on:

(*a*)   the pressures on the Soviet leaders to reach an agreement and thus to modify the unacceptable features of their present proposals;[14]

(*b*)   the ability of the US Administration to resist pressures for unilateral withdrawals of US forces and to maintain its insistence on reciprocity; and

(*c*)   the extent to which NATO countries, especially the European direct participants, can find ways of meeting Eastern criticisms of the current Western proposals which would not damage existing security arrangements or give dangerous hostages for the future of European defence.

[11]   Plenary sessions continued in parallel with the informal meetings, but at a diminished rate. Although initially resistant, the Eastern side eventually acquiesced in moving from two plenaries a week to one. Arguments advanced in these sessions were frequently stilted versions of those used in the informal meetings.

[12]   Of this 'thinly disguised system of "emissaries"' Mr. Rose wrote in his summary memorandum (see notes 3, 7 and 10 above) that it was difficult to see how it could be significantly modified or improved. He added: 'It suits the UK reasonably well and, as a result of the close working relations we have developed with the German delegation, it has enabled us to play a prominent and effective part in the conduct of the informal meetings.'

[13]   'Surely', minuted Sir J. Killick, (see notes 5 and 9 above) 'the Russians in fact are only agreed on "can"—but not on "must", whatever Khlestov says'.

[14]   On this point Sir J. Killick commented (v. ibid.): 'The only "pressure" on the Russians to reach agreement which I can identify is the desire to cut the Bundeswehr.'

As regards (*a*), there are signs, from the way in which they have played their hand during the second round, that the Russians may be under pressure to produce positive results. I cannot speculate on whether this pressure is strong enough to persuade them to make any substantive concessions since this would involve considerations going well beyond the scope of these negotiations.[15] As regards (*b*), I would note that whereas, in the first round, the US Delegation were anxious to maintain a fast pace with, evidently, their eye on achieving positive results within a definite (though unspecified) timetable, their emphasis in this round has been much more on the need to demonstrate that steady progress is being made in serious negotiations without any particular deadline for their conclusion. But I am not qualified to assess how far this reflects changing priorities in Washington.

8. The point at (*c*) involves decisions by NATO countries. Basically the question is whether we can obtain the benefits in political and military terms, from mutual force reductions while at the same time limiting the damage to an acceptable degree. It is clear that, if we wish to secure reciprocal and asymmetrical Soviet reductions in a first phase in return for US reductions, we shall have to commit ourselves definitely to a second phase in which the forces of the direct participants would be reduced. On its own, such a commitment will not be enough. In the context of the Western proposals, the Eastern representatives have demanded assurances that:

(i) all direct participants would reduce their forces;

(ii) second phase negotiations would be completed;

(iii) while second phase negotiations were taking place, the forces of the Western direct participants would not be increased to compensate for American withdrawals; and

(iv) the agreements would cover nuclear and air as well as ground forces.

During the next few months we shall have to consider whether, and if so to what extent, we can meet these demands. Some aspects of them are already being studied in NATO. It seems possible that we may be able to reach agreement with our Allies on assurances—or modifications to the existing Western proposals—which would go some way to meet these demands, although it is difficult to see at present how we could give an assurance on (i) firm enough to satisfy the Russians without pre-empting the result of the Phase II negotiations. Even if we

---

[15] In a letter to Mr. Rose of 14 May, Mr. Tickell observed: 'it is, as you say, a matter for speculation whether such pressure, if it exists, will prove sufficiently strong to force them to modify their own position. In a strictly MBFR context there seem to be two possible forms of pressure on the Russians. One is their apparent obsession to get the Bundeswehr reduced. The second is their apparent continuing desire to maintain a fruitful relationship with the Americans. But neither of those two forms of pressure has so far caused the Russians to modify their approach to MBFR. You will recall from our conversation with Jock Dean that the Americans reckon the Russians are content to mark time in MBFR until the CSCE is out of the way. If that is right, and it sounds feasible, then there seems little prospect of any significant breakthrough in the negotiations between now and the summer.'

could, it is far from clear that such assurances would be sufficient to buy Eastern acceptance of the two basic features of the Western proposals, namely the two-phase approach and the common ceiling for ground force manpower. Acceptance of these features would mean abandonment of Eastern insistence on reductions by all direct participants from the outset and the maintenance after reductions of the existing relationship between the forces of the two sides. If, however, the Russians are anxious to reach an early agreement and we can avoid having to negotiate under threat of an American deadline, the outlook is not entirely unpromising.[16] But it would be rash, at this stage of the negotiations, to attempt to make any more optimistic prediction.[17]

9.   I am sending copies of this despatch to Her Majesty's Representatives at Washington, Bonn, Moscow, Paris, Ottawa, Brussels, The Hague, Rome, Luxembourg, Copenhagen, Oslo, Ankara, Athens, Lisbon, Vienna, East Berlin, Warsaw, Prague, Bucharest, Budapest, Sofia, Belgrade and Stockholm; to the UK Permanent Representative to the North Atlantic Council; and to the Heads of the UK Mission to the Conference on Security and Co-operation in Europe and of the UK Delegation to the Conference of the Committee on Disarmament in Geneva.

I have, etc.,
CLIVE ROSE

[16] Sir J. Killick concluded his minute of 3 May (see notes 5, 9, 13 and 14 above): 'A broader point, which I did put to Mr. Rose, & which I think he accepted, is my conviction that the Russians will want to keep MBFR in phase with SALT, because they (unlike any other participants except the Americans) are determined to keep the *global* balance of forces in perspective. Specifically, they want to keep both options open for F[orward]B[ased]S[ystems]. This is *not* to say they wouldn't buy some agreement which made the West weaker in Central Europe. It is up to us to prevent this.'

[17] In his enclosure (see notes 3, 7, 10 and 12 above) Mr. Rose struck an optimistic concluding note: 'In sum this has been a useful, and on the whole encouraging, session. Relations between the Allies have been generally harmonious. The Eastern side has shown itself ready for serious business, and the negotiations themselves have shown some slight hints of directions in which movement might be possible. The task of the next session will be to see whether these hints represent genuine flexibility in the Eastern position which the Allies can turn to their advantage and, if so, to find ways of responding which will not prejudice or erode the main elements in the Allied approach.'

No. 14

Record of Discussion between the Defence Secretary and Mr. Rose,
held at the Ministry of Defence on 29 April 1974

MO 13/1/4 [WDN 27/1]

Secret   MoD, *1 May 1974*

Present:

Mr. C.R. Rose CMG,   The Rt Hon Roy Mason MP,
HM Ambassador to the   Secretary of State for Defence
Vienna MBFR Negotiations

                                      Mr. W.F. Mumford,
                                      PS/Secretary of State

Mr. Rose began by explaining the way in which the negotiations in Vienna were being conducted by means of a combination of plenary meetings and informal sessions. The Allies' positions and tactics were closely co-ordinated in what was known as the Ad Hoc Committee which met frequently in Vienna and was, in his view, an excellent example of NATO co-operation. The informal sessions, which were usually arranged around a social occasion, were a recent innovation but one which was proving most valuable as a means of allowing both sides in a restricted but multi-lateral group to gain a greater insight into the background thinking and basic approach of the other side to the complex issues involved. In these informal sessions the US and the Soviet Delegations invariably took part; on the NATO side the other participants were either the FRG or Britain and one other NATO Delegation and the Soviet team was supported by one or two other Warsaw Pact Delegations. They took place in homes and the discussions often extended for three or four hours.

2.   On the substance of the negotiations, Mr. Rose said that NATO and the Warsaw Pact were still poles apart. The NATO approach was based on the disparities between NATO and the Warsaw Pact ground force levels in the central region of Europe and we were looking for a solution which would correct current discrepancies. The Warsaw Pact, on the other hand, argued that the present balance of forces was satisfactory and that it was not necessary, in MBFR reductions, to upset the current ratio between the two Alliances. In effect, the Warsaw Pact was seeking to codify the imbalance and to persuade the West to give it a certificate of respectability in the agreements which would eventually emerge from Vienna.

3.   *The Secretary of State* said that it was clear that the significance of the Vienna negotiations for the future of Western security could not be over-stressed; and that major NATO interests were at stake. What were the prospects of getting the Warsaw Pact to accept the NATO concept of the reductions in the first instance being restricted to the US and Soviet forces with the other participants becoming involved in the reductions in a second and later stage? He would also welcome Mr. Rose's views on the impact of the defence review now under way in the

Ministry of Defence on Britain's negotiating stance in MBFR.[1] Were the Russians still pressing hard for the inclusion of nuclear weapons in the negotiations? *Mr. Rose* agreed that the outcome of MBFR would indeed set the pattern for the European security system for many years ahead. Much hard negotiation would be needed to persuade the Russians to agree to NATO's ideas of phasing; they were seeking assurances that the Bundeswehr and BAOR would be brought firmly within the scope of reductions and so far had set themselves against merely general undertakings that European forces would be the subject of reductions in the second phase. The announcements that had so far been made about Britain's defence review had not caused the Delegation in Vienna any embarrassment. If the review should—and he hoped it would not—indicate reductions in BAOR (or of British air forces in Germany), it would be most important that the MBFR angle should be borne very closely in mind. The willingness to include British forces in the reductions had not so far been declared in the negotiations and was a card, if we wished to play it, which should not be thrown away without obtaining something in return from the Warsaw Pact. He also advocated strongly—again on the hypothesis that the review might call for some reductions in our forces in Germany—that the Government should announce that they would be sought in the context of the MBFR negotiations and subject to the achievement of generally satisfactory agreements in that forum. Otherwise, we should ourselves be wide open to the criticism that we were undermining the allied position, by contemplating uni-lateral reductions in our forces while MBFR negotiations were in progress. Mr. Rose recalled the repeated assurance given by the US Administration that American forces in Europe would not be reduced except as part of reciprocal agreements with the Warsaw Pact.

4. *The Secretary of State* said that on present forecasts the defence review would be completed during the summer and the outcome presented to Parliament in the autumn. How would this fit in with the MBFR timetable? *Mr. Rose* said that it was unlikely that the negotiations would have made any great progress by the autumn and he could only underline his previous remarks about the handling of any possible cuts in our forces in Germany.[2] As for nuclear weapons, these had

---

[1] On 21 March, Mr. Mason announced in Parliament the initiation of 'a review of current defence commitments and capabilities against the resources that, given the economic prospects of the country, we can afford to devote to defence', to be completed later that year. Although he stressed that NATO would remain 'the lynchpin of our security', he suggested that 'the burden which we bear in support of the common NATO interest should be brought into line with that of our major European allies'. As a result of the General Election in October and the initiation of the review, there was no 1974 Defence White Paper, but certain reductions in defence expenditure for 1974–75 were made by the Government, over and above those cuts proposed by the previous Conservative administration (Robert Fraser (ed.), *Keesing's Contemporary Archives* (London: Keesing's Publications, 1975), pp. 27221; *Parl. Debs, 5th ser., H. of C.*, vol. 870, cols. 153–154.

[2] In a minute to Mr. Tickell of 3 June, Mr. P. Lever (First Secretary, WOD) pointed out that if they accepted as axiomatic that some reductions in BAOR would be required by the Defence Review and that these should be fitted into the MBFR framework, the question of timing would be of crucial importance. 'The obvious implication of this', he commented, 'is that we may be running out of time if we wish to maintain our proposal of a two phase reduction, particularly if

so far not been the subject of any substantive negotiations. The Warsaw Pact had stated its claims for them to be included and it was possible that NATO might indicate, before the summer recess, as willingness to discuss them at a later stage.

5. *The Secretary of State* said that he noted Mr. Rose's views on the need to keep the MBFR dimension very much in mind during the defence review and he would ensure that this was done. He asked whether the West felt itself on the defensive in the negotiations? *Mr. Rose* replied that, to the contrary, NATO was able to make a good deal of capital in the negotiations by reference to the massive build-up of Warsaw Pact strength over the last five years since NATO first launched its MBFR initiative.

6. In conclusion *the Secretary of State* wished Mr. Rose well in his difficult task; he would be most welcome to call on him next time he was in London to inform him personally about developments.

we wish there to be any sort of gap between the two phases. We may come to regard the Soviet proposal of a single negotiation but with staged implementation as more suited to our domestic political requirements.'

Mr. Tickell took 'a less gloomy view—at least for the moment—of the likely consequences of the Defence Review'. He minuted on 5 June: 'I certainly don't want to plan how to cross this bridge before we know it exists. MBFR is a classic device by which Western gov[ernmen]ts resist pressure for unilateral cuts: we shall have to use it as others have used it' (WDN 27/17).

No. 15

Minute from Mr. Bullard[1] *to Sir J. Killick*

[ENS 2/1]

Confidential   FCO, *21 May 1974*

The Soviet Union, MBFR etc

1. This minute examines 2 separate but connected questions: how much pressure the Soviet Government are under to reach agreements in MBFR, and how far the West should take account of Brezhnev's personal position in formulating our own policies.

The Soviet Government under Pressure in MBFR?

2. In paragraph 7 of his despatch of 11 April[2] Mr. Rose said: 'There are signs, from the way in which they have played their hand during the second round, that the Russians may be under pressure to produce positive results'. This is the reverse of what was agreed at the 6-monthly NATO experts' meeting in Brussels last week, when the consensus was that the Russians are in no hurry on MBFR. Mr. Rose does not quote his evidence. He could mean either that the Soviet Government are under pressure to reduce defence expenditure, and see the Vienna talks

---

[1] Mr. J. Bullard was Head of Eastern European and Soviet Department (EESD).

[2] See No. 13.

as a way of doing this; or that they are under pressure to reach agreements with the West, and look upon Vienna as one place where this may be possible.

3. To take the first of these 2 possible interpretations first, I agree that there must be constant argument within the Soviet leadership over the distribution of the country's scarce resources of money, energy, labour, raw materials etc. It is thought that this was the chief reason why the 24th Party Congress was postponed for almost a year. But of all the possible lobbies in Moscow, the one least likely to secure its objective is the group which seeks reductions in Soviet defence spending. There is an old-fashioned patriotism about the Soviet Union which makes Russians believe that they should spend on defence whatever may be necessary in the country's interests, and that the military are the best judges of how much this ought to be. Senator Kennedy ran into this mood recently at Moscow University, where the audience was only partly hand-picked.[3] It is true that in the early sixties Khrushchev[4] took issue with the Soviet military establishment on this point. We were well aware of this at the time. But Khrushchev's relationship with Marshal Malinovsky[5] was very different from Brezhnev's with Marshal Grechko.[6] Brezhnev brought Grechko into the Politburo in April 1973, and the 2 men are known to be extremely close. Mr. Malcolm Mackintosh,[7] the leading Western student of Soviet military thought and personalities, has said that Grechko's main task in recent years has been to secure the maximum advantage for the Soviet Union out of the interval between SALT I and the expected SALT II agreement. This has involved huge expenditure on defence, and there is no sign that Brezhnev or any other Soviet leader has opposed this. Either there is a consensus, or Khrushchev's successors have his fate in mind.

4. In these circumstances it seems difficult to speak of the Soviet Government as being 'under pressure' to cut defence expenditure. I do not doubt that they would like if possible to reduce it, or at least to put a brake on its growth. That was certainly one of the reasons why they accepted SALT I. But any defence cut must be a balance of opportunities and risks, and the traditional Soviet approach is to insure (and often to over-insure) against the risks rather than to snatch at the opportunities. The Soviet leaders have no free press or Parliament to agitate for defence cuts, or to whom defence spending has to be justified. If there is pressure for cuts, it can only be internal, i.e. inside the Party. And the middle rank Party members are among the most conservative elements in the whole of Soviet society.

[3] On 21 April Senator E.M. Kennedy, addressing an audience of 800 staff and students at Moscow University, asked the assembled gathering: 'Do you think that in the Soviet Union more or less money from the budget should be spent on defence?' *The Times* reported: 'When he then requested the audience to raise their hands, there was an embarrassed shuffling. A white-haired professor said loudly in Russian: "That question is a provocation", and waved his fist at the senator' (*The Times*, 22 April, p. 1).

[4] Mr. N.S. Khrushchev was First Secretary to the Communist Party of the Soviet Union (CPSU), 1953–64, and Chairman of the Council of Ministers, 1958–64.

[5] Marshal R.Y. Malinovsky was Minister of Defence during 1957–67.

[6] Marshal A.A. Grechko succeeded Marshal Malinovsky as Minister of Defence in 1967.

[7] Mr. J.M. Mackintosh was Assistant Secretary in the Cabinet Office.

5.   If however I have misread the evidence, and there really is pressure upon the Soviet Government to cut defence spending, the possibility of significant savings looks much greater in SALT than in MBFR. In SALT the argument is about whole new generations of weapons systems: in MBFR it is about a possible redeployment of up to 15% of Soviet strength from Eastern Europe to Western Russia. We know from our own studies how small are the financial savings to be expected from this kind of movement.

6.   The other possible interpretation of Mr. Rose's remark (that the Soviet Government want agreements with the West over force reductions, for the sake of the agreements rather than the reductions) also seems open to question. Sir T Garvey's[8] recent telegrams point out that the chief Soviet interest at the moment seems to be in relations with the USA (as always) and in winding up the CSCE in what Brezhnev considers appropriate style. The Vienna talks are a long way down in the Soviet list of priorities—indeed they only agreed to go to Vienna because this was part of the price of coaxing the rest of us to go to Helsinki. All the evidence suggests that the Soviet leaders regard Vienna as a slow-moving and long-drawn-out affair where early agreements are unlikely to be attainable. The first informal contacts at the opening of the current session do not suggest that the Soviet delegation came back from the Easter break with new and more flexible instructions.

Brezhnev the best Soviet Leader we've got?

7.   The idea that the West should make concessions or show flexibility towards the Soviet Union in order to help to keep the current Soviet leadership in power is not a new one. This was said by some people in the West about Khrushchev, about Malenkov[9] and (for all I know) about Stalin[10] in his day. The Russians have naturally encouraged these ideas, since they tend to lead to the conclusion that current Soviet proposals should be accepted by the West.

8.   The objections to this line of thought have always been as follows:

(*a*)   We do not know for sure who are the alternatives to the current Soviet leadership;
(*b*)   even if we did know this, we could not predict their policies;
(*c*)   even if we were able to give positive rather than negative answers to the first 2 questions, it would not be easy in practice to frame policies for Britain on the basis of their likely effects upon a superpower with interests much broader than our own and for the most part contrary to ours.

9.   To apply these considerations to the present day, most observers believe that Brezhnev will probably be succeeded by Kirilenko, Kosygin by Mazurov or Polyansky and Podgorny perhaps by Kulakov or Grishin.[11] To list these names is

---

[8]   Sir T. Garvey succeeded Sir J. Killick as HM Ambassador in Moscow in November 1973.

[9]   Mr. G.M. Malenkov became Soviet Premier and Party Secretary in 1953.

[10]   Generalissimo J.V. Stalin was the President of the Soviet Council of Ministers, 1946–53.

[11]   Mr. A.P. Kirilenko was a secretary of the Central Committee of the CPSU; Mr. A.N. Kosygin was Chairman of the Council of Ministers of the USSR; Mr. K.T. Mazurov was a candidate

to make the point that they are not exactly familiar. The line-up could easily be otherwise. Brezhnev is more likely to be removed by illness or death than in any other way, so that the dauphins may have more years of waiting in the wings ahead of them. What line these men would pursue in foreign policy, when eventually they did come to power and whoever they might be, is consequently far from certain. Most observers think that a new Soviet Government would have little choice but to continue the Brezhnevian policies of détente in the West, firmness in the East and opportunism in the Third World. But Brezhnev's successors will be the first Russians to take office in a country that is already a superpower, and they may therefore be more willing to take risks than he was. I have heard this argued by some Americans. Others point out that, judging by experience over the last 50 years, a new Soviet leadership tends to act cautiously and by consensus, producing a single leader only some years later. A third theory is that the next generation of leaders in Moscow will not be prepared to give the security apparatus the free hand which they have hitherto enjoyed, so that a second round of de-Stalinisation could then be in prospect. Thus we cannot say for sure whether Brezhnev's successors will be better from our point of view, or worse. They might well be better in some ways and worse in others. Brezhnev, after all, is not all dove. His name is connected with summitry and détente, but also with the invasion of Czechoslovakia, the doctrine of limited sovereignty and the exile of the Nobel prize-winner whose novels Khrushchev allowed to be published.[12] The evidence is thus too obscure and contradictory to permit us to judge whether this or that action that we might take will promote or hinder the kind of evolution in the Soviet leadership which would suit us best.

Conclusions

10. Unless there is evidence to the contrary that I have overlooked, I conclude that:

(a) if the Soviet Government are under pressure to cut defence spending, this is a factor that is likely to operate only marginally and in the long term, and with relevance to SALT rather than to MBFR;

(b) we know too little about the workings of the Kremlin and the shades of opinion within the Soviet leadership to be able to draw reliable conclusions as to the policies we should adopt in order to strengthen the more sympathetic and combat the less favourable trends.

11. WOD and Research Department (Soviet Section) agree.

J.L. BULLARD

member of the *Politburo* and first deputy Chair of the Soviet Council of Ministers; Mr. D.S. Polyansky was Soviet Minister of Agriculture; Mr. N.V. Podgorny was Chairman of the Presidium of the Supreme Soviet; Marshal V.G. Kulikov was Chief of Staff of the Soviet armed forces and first deputy Soviet Minister of Defence; Mr. V.V. Grishin was a full member of the *Politburo* and head of the Moscow city Party organisation.

[12] Mr. A.I. Solzhenitsyn had been expelled from the Soviet Union earlier in the year. Cf. Volume II, No. 45.

No. 16

Letter from Mr. Rose (UKDEL Vienna) to Mr. Bullard

[EN 2/18]

Confidential and Eclipse   VIENNA, *4 July 1974*

Dear Julian,

Trends in the Soviet Union and Eastern Europe

1.   I am sorry that it has taken me so long to comment on your letter of 3 May to Terence Garvey.[1] We found this a most useful and cogent commentary on the present situation, and one which helps to put our own preoccupations and efforts here into a salutary perspective.

2.   Our view here is inevitably limited, since negotiations bearing so directly on the security of the Soviet Union are probably the last place in which any signs of stress or change within the Warsaw Pact are likely to become apparent. So far as it goes however our experience here is consistent with most of the main elements in your analysis.

3.   You will have gathered that, when the negotiations resumed after the Easter recess,[2] the Eastern line appeared to have hardened. The signs of flexibility, perhaps even of some anxiety to reach an agreement quickly, which had begun to become apparent during the informal sessions in March were no longer there: instead Eastern representatives seemed to be insisting once again on the totality of their original proposals. They laid great emphasis on the references to the Vienna negotiations in the communiqué of the April meeting of the Warsaw Pact Political Consultative Committee, and especially on the importance of the principle of undiminished security, which they presented as a conclusive argument against the possibility both of asymmetrical reductions and of Phase I reductions confined to US and Soviet forces. While maintaining this hard line in plenary statements, they have subsequently, in the informal sessions, reintroduced a limited degree of movement into their position. The Russians are now pressing for a limited 'first step' agreement, which they claim represents a compromise. This letter is not the place in which to analyse their position in detail: it is sufficient to say that the degree of Eastern movement which it represents is slight; that the compromise is more apparent than real; and that it remains our impression that for the moment the Russians are in no serious hurry to make progress.[3] This letter is of course being written before we know the outcome, or, more important, before my Soviet colleagues have felt the impact, of any

---

[1]   See No. 57.

[2]   The Ad Hoc Group reassembled for the third round of MBFR negotiations on 6 May and finished its business on 23 July.

[3]   In a despatch to Mr. Callaghan of 26 July Mr. Rose recalled: 'In my despatch of 11 April about the second round (see No. 13), I expressed the view that progress was in fact being made albeit at a snail's pace. It has turned out to be a very slow snail.' Eastern representatives, he concluded, 'gave the impression that they were digging themselves in for a war of attrition' (WDN 27/1).

discussion which may have taken place about MBFRs between President Nixon and Mr. Brezhnev.[4]

4. If we are right in thinking that on the Eastern side there has been some slackening of pace and interest in the negotiations since before Easter (and even this is by no means clear) it is impossible to do more than guess at the reasons for it. It may be, as the Americans were at first inclined to think, that the Russians want to see some results from the CSCE (or of Nixon's visit to Moscow) before making a substantive move on MBFR.[5] Another possibility is that the Russians judge that the strength and cohesion of the Western negotiators in Vienna bear little relation to the realities either of the state of NATO or of the pressures for force reductions in some of the Western participant countries; and that, if they slow the pace sufficiently, these outside forces are bound to make themselves felt in Vienna. Either of these interpretations, or a combination of both, may be right, and would be consistent with your main thesis.

5. The Eastern Europeans continue to provide the faithful echo of their master's voice which I described in the passage which you quoted from my January despatch. Indeed the echo is even more faithful than it was then, since the Romanians seem to have abandoned their claims to an independent position on MBFR and have made no plenary statements during the current negotiating round. In private, they now advance orthodox Warsaw Pact arguments; and we understand that Khlestov has started to include them in his briefing sessions for the other Eastern indirect participants Characteristically, it is only the Poles who continue to give token hints that they have a mind of their own, usually by claiming that one or other feature of the standard Eastern position (e.g. reductions in the Bundeswehr or in nuclear weapons) is of special importance to them. They are assiduous cultivators of their Western opposite numbers; and, from our own informal contacts with them, we would agree with the judgement in paragraph 12 of your letter that, provided one recognises their limitations in terms of ability to influence Soviet policy, they can be useful and even rewarding people to talk to.

6. Soviet-American 'bilateralism' with which you deal in paragraph 9(a) of your letter, has so far been less evident in the Vienna negotiations than the fear of it among certain Western European Delegations, most notably the Belgians.

[4] Mr. Nixon had talks with Mr. Brezhnev when he visited the Soviet Union during 27 June–3 July (cf. Volume, II, No. 89). The Russians seem, however, to have evaded all discussion of MBFR, and Dr. Kissinger subsequently reported to Allied representatives to NATO in Brussels that the Soviet Government had demonstrated 'no desire to make real progress at Vienna until the CSCE was concluded'. He added that 'the Americans had themselves not wished to press the subject there either' (UKDEL NATO telegram No. 349 of 4 July, WDN 27/1).

[5] Mr. Tickell agreed with Mr. Rose's view that the Warsaw Pact countries were unlikely to be more forthcoming in the MBFR talks until the conclusion of the CSCE was at least in sight, and, as this was unlikely before the end of the year, he was far from optimistic about what would emerge during the autumn session. 'Timing', he warned Sir J. Killick in a minute of 13 August, 'is, of course, of more importance to the West than to the East. MBFR is a Janus-headed negotiation, and the face turned towards the West has to take account of domestic pressures for force reductions, and in particular those in the United States' (WDN 27/1).

It is of course true that the Americans maintain much closer informal contacts with the Russians than do any other Western representatives here, and we naturally know no more of what takes place on these occasions than the Americans choose to tell us. So far as we can judge however the Americans have firmly rebuffed any Soviet attempts to deal direct with them over the heads of the Allies.

7.   There was a difficult period during the opening weeks of the negotiations last autumn, when the Americans—particularly Dean—seemed bent on fostering Allied suspicions by a combination of tactlessness and impatience; but since then, thanks in large part to Resor, the US Representative, whose prudence and integrity have made the best possible impression on all his Allied colleagues, the Americans have gone to great lengths to maintain the cohesion and confidence of the Ad Hoc Group and have, in addition, spent many hours of every week seeking to arrive at agreed positions with the Germans our ourselves [*sic*]. (This regular tripartite consultation, which enables the three of us unofficially but fairly effectively to steer the proceedings of the Ad Hoc Group, should not be referred to in conversations with officials of any other countries.) No doubt it has been easier for them to do this because MBFR has to some extent been temporarily relegated to the 'back burner' in Washington; and the situation may change for the worse if Congressional pressure for an early MBFR agreement with the Soviet Union should revive.[6] If that happens, we have grounds for hoping that the habits of cooperation and consultation which have been developed here over the past eight months will stand us all in good stead.

8.   Not that the special relationship between the United States and the Soviet Union has been altogether without its impact on the style and presentation of the Allied case in Vienna. The Americans have what often seems to us an excessive regard for Soviet sensibilities. This has not only prevented us from responding to the more belligerent Eastern statements in language which we think the Russians will understand; it has also at times inhibited the Allies from developing important elements in their case (for instance from spelling out the extent of the Soviet force build-up in Central Europe since 1968). But this is a matter of presentation rather than substance, and on the whole there has been gratifying little sign of any Soviet-American 'condominium' in Vienna.[7]

9.   In paragraph 5 of his letter of 29 May commenting on yours, Nicko Henderson suggested that the Russians were no longer particularly keen to hasten a large-scale reduction of US military forces in Europe, and probably attached

---

[6] In his despatch of 26 July (see note 3 above) Mr. Rose warned Mr. Callaghan that 'the US Delegation here—and Ambassador Resor in particular, who has his own lines to both houses of Congress have argued strongly that the situation is temporary; that Congressional pressure will shortly revive; and that the Autumn elections may tip the balance in the House of Representatives towards those who would favour unilateral US troop withdrawals from Europe'. The US delegation believed it was essential for the Allies to use the next round to develop their position so far as possible so as to be ready for a rapid advance towards an agreement as soon as the Russians showed any signs of loosening up. And Mr. Rose felt that to reject the logic of Mr. Resor's timetable 'could eventually place a considerable strain on Allied cohesion, if the pressures he [postulated], both in the United States and elsewhere, [did] materialise and in the end prove[d] irresistible'.

[7] Cf. No. 57, note 20.

more importance, at any rate in the MBFR context, to trying to ensure FRG reductions.[8] I am inclined to agree. But I do not think that this is because the Russians are genuinely afraid of the Bundeswehr on its present scale. Of course the Russians have an atavistic fear of the Germans; and they no doubt wish to insure against any revival of nationalism and irredentism in Germany by imposing a permanent ceiling, at the lowest practicable level, on West German forces, with an inbuilt Soviet legal right to police such a ceiling. In the past, they could have achieved this only by imposing a peace treaty on a defeated Germany; today they may be able to achieve it without accepting any greater reciprocal obligation than a limit on the deployment of Soviet troops in part of Central Europe. But I believe that the main explanation of their desire to see the Bundeswehr reduced is their wish to prevent the development of a Western European defence union, combined with their fear that the FRG would assume the dominant role in such a union. The Russians have always seemed to take a more serious view of an eventual Western European defence union than its immediate prospects seem to warrant (no doubt because its emergence would fundamentally alter the pattern of power on which the Soviet détente policy is predicated); and their evident determination to secure an MBFR agreement which would have the effect of inhibiting Western European defence cooperation and imposing a Soviet *droit de regard* over it leaves little room for doubt that fear of a West European defence union is a major element in Soviet interest in MBFR.

10. From the point of view of our negotiations in Vienna, the chief conclusion which I draw from your letter is that any early Soviet concessions of substance on MBFR, and in particular any concession in the direction of asymmetrical reductions, seem highly unlikely.[9] Yet Terence Garvey, in his telegram No 507,[10] refers to the Vienna talks as 'the touchstone of Soviet intentions'. In the wider interests of their détente policy the Russians may wish, and indeed find it necessary, to go some way to meet the interests of the Americans. It is perhaps on this rather tenuous prospect that the hope for a breakthrough in the Soviet approach to MBFRs which might provide the basis for an agreement acceptable

[8] In this letter to Mr. Bullard Sir N. Henderson, HM Ambassador in Bonn, explained that he rather fell for the 'fashionable view' that Moscow was no longer particularly keen to hasten a large-scale reduction of US military forces in Europe. He suspected that the Russians probably attached more importance to trying to ensure reductions in West Germany's armed forces, and that they were concerned about Germany's role and influence in an EC moving towards union. 'It is', he suggested, 'the old question of the Soviet Union trying to obtain a *droit de regard* in questions of future Western European defence organisation.' Cf. No. 67, notes 1 and 2.

[9] Mr. Rose reported in his despatch of 26 July (see notes 3 and 6 above): the Russians 'missed no opportunity of impressing on the Allies that they regard the Western objective of asymmetrical reductions leading to a common ceiling for ground force manpower as totally unacceptable'. Meanwhile, at the penultimate informal session on 9 July Allied negotiators put to the Soviet representatives a carefully qualified commitment that, given a satisfactory Phase I agreement covering US and Soviet ground forces, all of the non-US direct participants, other than Luxembourg, would reduce their forces in Phase II. 'We shall', Mr. Rose observed, 'have to wait until the Autumn before we can assess whether the assurances offered have been enough to edge the East into tentative acceptance of the Allied two-phase approach.'

[10] See No. 59.

to the West will continue to depend. Should such a breakthrough materialise, the Russians will undoubtedly try to drive the hardest possible bargain against the interests of the West Europeans; and to this end they can be expected to use every opportunity of wedge-driving—and there will be many—that the negotiations offer. Short of a policy change of this order, I have no doubt they will keep trying for a force reduction agreement so long as they judge that there is any chance of obtaining one on terms satisfactory to them. But they must surely reckon that time is on their side, and will be in no hurry to buy expensively today what they may be able to pick up for nothing tomorrow.

11. In this connexion, perhaps I could question one point in Terence Garvey's interesting despatch of 12 June about US–Soviet relations.[11] I am puzzled at the suggestion in paragraph 13 of that despatch that, since the Russians may no longer regard it as in their interests to obtain a rapid withdrawal of US forces from Central Europe, they can be expected to seek the inclusion of FBS in SALT II and, if successful, will have no further incentive to bring the MBFR negotiations to a positive outcome. As seen from here, Soviet reluctance to see the Americans withdraw too many troops from Europe too quickly is not a new development. So far from lessening Soviet interest in MBFR, it seems more likely to have been one of the considerations which prompted them to enter into the negotiations in the first place instead of just sitting back and waiting for the Americans to reduce unilaterally. Nor, as will be clear from paragraph 8 above, do I believe that the Russians fear the development of West European defence cooperation only in the context of a rapid withdrawal of US forces. Even given the present uncertain outlook for European political and military integration, my own hunch is that the Russians see the possible acquisition of a *droit de regard* over European defence arrangements, including those of the FRG, as a substantial prize; and one which will continue to provide them with one of their major incentives to work for some form of MBFR agreement. This is also incidentally a factor which may mitigate the risk of any US–Soviet deal at European expense, since the Russians must know that the Americans are not in a position to 'deliver' the Europeans. If this is right, however, we must bear in mind the possibility that, if the prospects of integrated West European defence arrangements recede, Soviet interest in security [*sic*] a force reductions agreement which would inhibit such a union may recede.

12. I give you a thought about the implications for the MBFR negotiations of the personalities of the two Soviet negotiators, Khlestov and Smirnovsky. They are very difficult characters.[12] Khlestov is a lawyer and an experienced negotiator with an ingenious and agile mind. Within the strict limits of his brief he is

[11] See No. 62.

[12] This should perhaps read 'different' rather than 'difficult'. In an enclosure to his despatch to Mr. Callaghan (see notes 3, 6, and 9 above), Mr. Rose reported: the 'hardening of the Eastern negotiating position has not been accompanied by any corresponding chill in the personal relations between Western and Eastern delegates. On the contrary, these have reached new levels of cordiality and conviviality. Not only has there been intensive East/West hospitality of both a bilateral and multilateral character; there have also, under the impetus of Mr. Dean's forceful personality, been joint excursions of various sorts at which much bad wine has flowed and a great

constantly trying to probe for ways of making progress. I am not suggesting that 'progress' means anything but progress in the Soviet direction and of course his efforts are directed at drawing the Allied representatives onto his ground. Nevertheless one has the definite impression that he is aiming at finding solutions. Smirnovsky is well known to you. He is dour, shrewd, deceptively mild, and has a pretty good understanding of the Anglo-Saxon mentality and sense of humour. He is also temperamentally suited to the task of stonewalling. In a sense these two complement one another. Nevertheless so long as Khlestov remains in charge it may be legitimate to suggest that the Soviet Government is interested in achieving some positive results from these negotiations. If he were to be withdrawn and his place taken, as leader of the Soviet Delegation, by Smirnovsky I would be tempted to draw the conclusion that the Russians had decided to shut up shop and either drag out the negotiations indefinitely or look for an opportunity to break them off. For the moment this does not seem likely to happen. Khlestov for a long time wanted to get back to Moscow and, during the last recess, applied to be transferred from his appointment here to the leadership of the Soviet Delegation to the Law of the Sea Conference at Caracas.[13] But, although I understand he is the leading Soviet Government expert on the Law of the Sea, his application was turned down on account of the importance of the job he was doing in Vienna (his account, of course).

Yours ever,
C.M. ROSE

number of songs have been sung in a variety of European languages. A twenty mile walk through the Vienna woods, which resembled, in its latter stages, a sequence from a film of Napoleon's retreat from Moscow, enabled some eleven of us to discover our common humanity and forget our ideological differences in shared discomfort. All this has generated an atmosphere of remarkable friendliness and informality between the two sides. Unfortunately, however, as the East German Representative remarked at a recent cocktail party, friendliness between negotiators (even if genuine) is not enough to produce progress in the negotiations.'

[13] The third UN Conference on the Law of the Sea (UNCLOS III) met in Caracas during 20 June–29 August.

No. 17

Note by Mr. J. Mayne[1]
D/DS22/13/15 [WDN 27/1]

Secret MoD, *16 August 1974*

MBFR

The Western negotiating position contains three main elements, (none of which the East accepts):

[1] This paper was attached to a personal letter of 16 August from Mr. Mayne, Assistant Secretary to the MoD's Defence Secretariat, to Mr. Tickell. In it Mr. Mayne explained: 'Returning from leave

(i) the concept of parity of forces as the objective of reductions;
(ii) confinement to ground forces only;
(iii) phasing—initial reductions confined to US and USSR forces.

2.   These elements are not of equal importance. There are very good reasons why (ii) and (iii) form part of the Western position; but:

(i) the Warsaw Pact negotiators have already demonstrated, to the West's discomfort, the anomalies which our attachments to the 'ground forces only' principle gives rise. Although we can argue convincingly that the most threatening elements on the Warsaw Pact side are their unreasonably large and offensive ground (and especially armoured) forces, there is an ultimately more convincing logic in the East's position that a true balance of forces in Europe can best be achieved only if all forces in the area were taken into account. (And we would be going a long way towards conceding as much in principle if we played the nuclear card);
(ii) it is very desirable from the Western point of view to reduce US and USSR forces in the first phase, leaving European reductions until later; but it is difficult to advance a convincing rationale for the position other than in terms of the West's self-interest. And the Soviet Union clearly regards phased reductions on the Western model as highly undesirable from their national point of view. In neither case is it possible to demonstrate convincingly in public that the West would be justified in breaking off the negotiations in the face of Eastern intransigence, because each is, from the Western point of view, a desirable means to an end, and not the necessary end itself. In short, on these two elements of our position, we are ill-equipped for a long, slow negotiation, in which Western Governments may come under pressure for results not only from the East but also from their own legislatures and public opinion.

3.   The principle of parity (paragraph 1(i) above) is very different. We can argue rationally and persuasively—and hence maintain our position publicly in the face of pressures both from the East, from Congress and from European domestic parliaments—that it is unreasonable for the East to continue, in an era of détente, to maintain grossly asymmetrical forces in the Guidelines area. And it is inherently unreasonable for the Soviet Union to argue—as they must to justify equal percentage reductions—that parity of forces is thinkable only when the forces of both sides are reduced to nil. The common ceiling is therefore the fundamental element of the Western position, on which we should consider no concessions until all other concessions on less important elements have been exhausted.

4.   The question then arises as to how the common ceiling should be measured. The Western position that this should be done in terms of manpower,

refreshed, I have dictated the attached note on MBFR concessions, as a mind clearing exercise prompted by our need to prepare for the trilateral talks [see No. 18, note 1], discussions with Clive Rose and the next negotiating session.' He added a post script: 'I have marked this letter "personal" because I am not in a position to put thoughts, such as those in the attached note, to you officially.'

taking account of combat capability is wholly defensible. To measure it in terms of manpower alone could lead to concessions which would wholly undermine the concept of real parity at a reasonable level of forces. On the other hand, an attempt to weigh the two sides primarily in terms of units and equipment would immeasurably complicate the negotiations. So it seems most reasonable to use manpower as the basic unit of measurement of the common ceiling, but, during the course of the negotiations, to find practical ways of taking account of combat capability elements, possibly including units and equipments in ground forces, aircraft in terms of conventional air forces and aircraft and missiles in dealing with nuclear combat capability.

5.   What does this tell us about concessions in the Western negotiating position? It suggests that, initially, any concessions should be concentrated in the following, less important areas:

(i) phasing;
(ii) inclusion of air force manpower.

It is arguable that the inclusion of air force manpower in the common ceiling would be of more fundamental importance than any concession on phasing, because of the inherent strength of the arguments in paragraph 2 (*a*) above and because the inclusion of air forces manpower would inevitably bring aircraft into the negotiations, a combat capability element which we might well wish to leave out. For these reasons alone we should not consider such a concession at this stage. But it is predictable, given the Eastern position that we will be pressed to include air force manpower; and that we may have to concede this. This points to completing the NATO study on air manpower and air forces urgently.[2]

6.   Concessions on the principle of parity of forces are of a quite different order, because they would undermine the fundamental element of the Western position. Once we start undermining the principle of parity we can expect the negotiations to end in disaster. Because, for a variety of reasons, some of principle and some of practice, the basic unit of account by which the common ceiling must be measured is manpower, concessions involving changes in the numbers in the allied proposal (paragraph 2e (i), and probably 2e(v) of Christopher Makins' letter of 8th August)[3] should be the very last that we should concede, and then only if they formed part of a deal which would inevitably lead to parity; eg different rates of progression to an accepted common ceiling, or a different common ceiling (750,000?). Symbolic reductions which were not demonstrably a progression to parity of forces at a reasonable ultimate level, or equal percentage reductions, cannot be contemplated, especially not at this stage.

[2] Mr. Mayne observed in his covering letter to Mr. Tickell (*v. ibid.*): 'I would personally abandon the phasing and include air force manpower in the computation of the common ceiling (in that order) before I would consider playing the nuclear card or making concessions of substance over the common ceiling and the principle of parity of forces at a reasonable level.'

[3] In this paragraph of his letter to Mr. Tickell, Mr. C.J. Makins, First Secretary in HM Embassy, Washington, outlined the American fallback position. This included the possibility of reducing the scope of the original Allied proposal for Phase I reductions from 68,000 Soviet and 29,000 US troops to 40,000 and 20,000 men respectively.

7. Concessions over combat capability may be less directly associable with the undermining of the concept of parity. For example, a broad deal of a tank army in exchange for Option III could, when added to manpower reductions towards a common ceiling, be defended against stiff opposition as representing a reasonable combat capability package reducing equally threatening elements on each side. But all we need to establish at this point in time is that any concessions on combat capability elements—and this includes not only compromises about the composition of ground force reductions, ground force equipments and aircraft (if air force manpower is included), but also the nuclear option—should form part of the final negotiations on how to express parity at a reasonable level of forces; in other words, before concessions on these elements are made, the Soviet Union should have accepted the principle of parity at a reasonable level of forces and of the common ceiling.

8. It may be argued that a first phase 'ground-forces-manpower-only' deal might be possible if the US nuclear Option III were thrown in. This seems to be a widely held US opinion, and there is a real danger that we may have to agree to it. But, to make such a deal possible:

(*a*) the Russians would have to make concessions on phasing which there seems no reason for them to do;

(*b*) they would have to concede that, the nuclear element apart, ground forces only should be dealt with at least in the first phase. This could put them at a negotiating disadvantage in trying to include air forces in later stages. There seems no reason, after the first negotiating year, why they should make such a concession;

(*c*) the West's position on the content, and even the numbers, of subsequent reductions, could be undermined: we would have conceded at an early stage that the principle of parity could be achieved by a by-and-large combat capability deal which would to a considerable extent, short-circuit the measurement of parity in the basic currency of manpower numbers.

Before any nuclear option is even suggested to the Soviet Union, we would need to be convinced that the Alliance would be satisfied with such a broad deal (with few manpower reductions, especially for the Europeans), and that the Soviet Union was prepared to forego the real negotiating advantages which they may expect to gain by remaining intransigent over phasing and the inclusion of all forces in the GLA.[4]

Conclusion

9. At this stage our objective should be to confine any concessions we make in the next round of negotiations strictly to concessions on phasing. We should press ahead urgently with the study of including air manpower in the negotiations. We should come to a firm British conclusion on the nuclear option.[5]

[4] Guidelines Limitations Area.

[5] In a minute to Sir J. Killick of 26 July Mr. Tickell observed: 'I am afraid that the explanation that we usually give for excluding air forces and nuclear weapons from MBFR is not entirely

convincing [i.e. that the principal source of instability was the preponderance of Soviet ground forces in central Europe, and to introduce air and nuclear forces would needlessly complicate the negotiations]. For this reason among others I have little doubt that they will eventually be brought in. It is very hard to refute the proposition that each side should call for reductions in that aspect of the other side's forces and armaments which it finds most threatening.'

No. 18

Mr. Callaghan to Mr. Rose (UKDEL Vienna)

No. 71 Telegraphic [WDN 27/304/1]

Secret. Eclipse   FCO, *14 October 1974, 7 p.m.*

Repeated for information to priority UKDEL NATO, Washington, Bonn, Moscow.

Washington Discussions on MBFR[1]

Following from Tickell.

1.   You may like a preliminary somewhat personal account of our discussions in Washington on MBFR. The formal meeting with the agencies on 9 October did not get us very far.[2] But we did the rounds within the administration and on the hill, and, although people spoke with many voices, I have tried to put their main points together. Please treat this account with the utmost discretion. Records follow.

2.   For the time being Congressional interest in MBFR and pressure for early reductions in US forces in Europe seem to be off. The shadow of the coming mid-term elections made people chary of predictions. All agreed that the economic situation might reinforce demands for reductions, but few could be sure about it. Senator Nunn[3] spoke about the possibility of unilateral US cuts in the spring if the negotiations remained deadlocked, and seemed to think that the Europeans could make up for any American short-fall. I hope we disillusioned

---

[1] Mr. Tickell, along with MoD and other FCO officials, visited Washington during 7–12 October for tripartite talks with their US and West German counterparts on the longer term aspects of Allied defence. Whilst in Washington Mr. Tickell also had bilateral discussions with the Americans on MBFR.

[2] In a meeting with Mr. Tickell on the afternoon of 9 October, Mr. J. Lowenstein, Deputy Assistant Secretary for European Affairs in the State Department, apologised for the 'rather wooden character of the formal talks on MBFR' in which they had both engaged that morning. These, he explained, 'had been for show and to keep the experts happy. ACDA was a pretty useless organisation' (minute from Mr. Tickell to Mr. H.T. Morgan (AUS) of 24 October).

[3] Senator S. Nunn (Democrat, Georgia) was a prime mover in promoting an amendment to the 1975 Defense Appropriation Authorization Act which limited the deployment of US warheads to their existing levels and directed the Secretary of Defense to study: (1) the overall concept for the use of tactical nuclear weapons in Europe; (2) how the use of such weapons related to deterrence and to a strong conventional defence; (3) possibilities for the reduction in the numbers and type of nuclear warheads inessential to the defence structure of Western Europe; and (4) the steps that could be taken to develop a rational and coordinated nuclear posture consistent with a proper emphasis on conventional defence forces.

him. Lowenstein (State Department) also seemed gloomy about the Congressional prospects for next year, and was inclined (as was Aaron in Senator Mondale's[4] Office) to despair of MBFR altogether.[5] But most whom we saw inclined the other way. For example Congressman Jones was almost unrealistically optimistic. He said that with greater scepticism about détente and a decline in isolationism there was better understanding in Congress of the force level issue, and in any case an inclination, which he hoped would continue in the new House, to leave it to the professionals. Sonnenfeldt, Hyland[6] and Vest[7] (State Department) all seemed relatively confident that Congressional pressure next spring could be held.

3. Nor did I detect any impatience within the Administration for early progress in Vienna. The proposition that changes in the Allied position should in present circumstances be designed to improve it rather than to lead to concessions (which would almost certainly be unrequited) found no challengers. At the formal meeting the Americans said that the Allies should simply maintain the momentum of the negotiations and press all the points in the current approach, in particular the common ceiling, the two phases and the withdrawal of the Soviet tank army. According to Vest, the effect of Resor's and Dean's presence in Washington in August had been to create a temporary sense of urgency, but this was no longer the case, and the Germans had been in an unnecessary flap in expecting early movement on such delicate matters as the nuclear aspects. No-one whom we saw expected substantive progress during the current round.[8]

4. The Americans declared their unreadiness for discussion of our paper on the nuclear aspects, but I gathered from all sides that it had made a good impression.[9] Hyland told me in confidence that Kissinger had given instructions

[4] Senator W.F. Mondale (Democrat, Minnesota).

[5] Mr. Lowenstein told Mr. Tickell (see note 2 above) that the MBFR negotiations were 'both hopeless and potentially dangerous. The Phase I proposals as they stood would not be acceptable to the Russians and, if they were, would not be acceptable to Congress. Verification was all nonsense … If, as he believed, there had to be cuts in US forces (and Congress would demand them sooner rather than later), the best policy would be to make a relatively small cut by way of a gesture, and promise a larger one if the small one was reciprocated in appropriately asymmetrical fashion.'

[6] Dr. Sonnenfeldt was now Counsellor in the State Department. Mr. W.G. Hyland was in charge of the Department's Bureau of Intelligence and Research.

[7] Mr. G.S. Vest was Director of the Bureau of Political-Military Affairs in the State Department. He was formerly US Head of Delegation to the CSCE.

[8] On 18 September, at the first tripartite (UK–US–FRG) meeting of the fourth round of the MBFR talks at Vienna, Mr. Resor had stated that there was a general consensus in the US Administration that the Allies must reach agreement with the East in principle by May 1975 when Congressional hearings on the Defence Authorisation Bill were due to begin. Otherwise, he asserted, the 'Alliance would at least need to be by then in a public posture which put the onus for deadlock squarely on the Russians'. No decision, he added, had yet been taken on Option III, but at working level there was a consensus in favour of using it (UKDEL Vienna telegram No. 207 of 19 September, WDN 27/1).

[9] This paper, based upon an FCO draft, amended by the MoD and the West German Government, was passed to the US Government on 8 October. Mr. Tickell explained to Mr.

that no-one should think and even less speak about the nuclear aspects and in particular Option III. Despite this injunction Hyland said that he thought the United States would want to play the nuclear card sooner or later, and Sonnenfeldt indicated the same. All emphasised that no decisions had yet been taken. But at the formal meeting the Americans indicated that they believed there should be some measure of reciprocity although they had not decided what: they thought only US and Soviet nuclear systems should be involved: they admitted that they had not fully studied the problem of the dual capable aircraft, but took the point that if air force manpower and perhaps aircraft were to be included in reductions this would put the F4[10] component of Option III in a different light. Lodal[11] (NSC staff) was particularly concerned about the problem of the dual capable aircraft, and raised the question of whether a ceiling should be imposed on F4s, all dual capable aircraft or all aircraft.

5. As for Kissinger's forthcoming visit to Moscow,[12] Sonnenfeldt said that Kissinger hoped he might pick up some 'vibrations' on MBFR, and Vest said that all would depend there on 'the sensation'.[13] Hyland went further. Speaking personally he said that it was not impossible that Kissinger would want to touch on the nuclear aspects in Moscow. A possible scenario would be for him to demand progress in MBFR, suggest that the Russians might find things easier in Geneva if there were movement in Vienna,[14] and offer to consider bringing in nuclear elements in exchange for progress in Phase 1 of MBFR. Hyland doubted if Kissinger would consult officials if he decided to act in this way.

6. Hyland and Lowenstein separately asked if I had any particular message we wished to get across to Kissinger. I replied that we attached great importance to the nuclear aspects of MBFR, and hence had tried to define our preliminary thoughts on the subject. It would be useful if Kissinger could be aware of the

Morgan in a minute of 2 October, the paper 'does not contain many surprises but it does record the firm view of the Ministry of Defence (endorsed by the Chiefs of Staff) that a nuclear package of the order of magnitude of Option III (i.e. that proposed by the Americans in their paper of 30 April 1973) is one which the United Kingdom could accept subject to consultation in the Alliance as a whole' (WDN 27/4).

[10] The American F4 Phantom fighter was the most widely used Western combat aircraft. It had been developed for use in many roles from long-range interceptor to medium-range bomber. The original Option III package foresaw the withdrawal of 54 US nuclear-capable F4s from central Europe, along with about 1,500 associated airmen.

[11] Mr. J. Lodal was systems analyst with the National Security Council (NSC).

[12] Dr. Kissinger visited Moscow during 23–27 October.

[13] During a conversation with Mr. Tickell on 9 October, Mr. Sonnenfeldt confessed that he 'could not say whether and when Dr. Kissinger would eventually decide whether it would be right to play the nuclear card (in the shape of Option III) in MBFR'. He thought, however, that Dr. Kissinger could well feel that Option III would prove useful in both SALT and MBFR. When Mr. Tickell suggested 'it might be difficult to sell the same horse twice, Mr. Sonnenfeldt said that he did not see that we shouldn't have a try. He thought it unlikely that there would be early progress in SALT (and implied that for that reason the use of Option III in MBFR would not be considered soon)' (minute from Mr. Tickell to Mr. Morgan of 14 October).

[14] Stage II of the CSCE was then proceeding at Geneva. Cf. Volume II, No. 100 on the prospects for a CSCE/MBFR link.

importance we attached to it. I then repeated the main points in our paper.[15] Lowenstein promised to brief Kissinger accordingly, underlining our hope for further consultation before the matter was discussed in the Alliance or propositions were put to the Russians.

7.   Our paper on further work[16] was reasonably well received. The Americans had clearly given little thought to the idea of blurring the distinction between the phases, and wanted maximum concentration on Phase 1. In doing so they tended to shelter behind the Germans. They did not conceal their primary interest in achieving US reductions and hence did not want the prospect of ultimate European reductions to delay or confuse the issue. Hence they were unhappy at the idea that the content and allocation of Western reductions in Phase 2 should be raised in the Alliance. Instead they suggested, and we agreed, that the Allies might first look at the question of what Soviet and Warsaw Pact reductions to expect in Phase 2. I put our usual arguments on phasing, and emphasised that the German idea of converting Phase 2 of MBFR into a semi-permanent dialogue on security issues would have little appeal for us, or probably the Russians.

8.   No American official questioned the value of the common ceiling as the iron pole of the negotiations but I detected some doubts (eg in the NSC staff) about the prospects of our achieving it. At the formal meeting the Americans said that they thought it would be hard to secure agreement on the concept in Phase 1 without either changing the vocabulary or devising some such means as a joint NATO/Warsaw Pact declaration of intent, or, failing that, a unilateral NATO declaration. We were not of course able to ascertain whether the Americans intended to demand agreement on the common ceiling as well as the withdrawal of a tank army in exchange for the introduction of the nuclear elements in Option III.[17]

---

[15] At the formal Anglo-US discussions on 11 October Mr. Tickell emphasised that the British believed the 'nuclear card' to be important not only to the negotiations but also to the Allied case *vis-à-vis* Western public opinion. He meanwhile expressed his doubts about the American suggestion that they might offer air force manpower reductions in order to obtain something from the Russians. 'The Russians', he contended, 'had no need to respond to Allied initiatives or make any move in Vienna. They probably thought that the apples would fall from the tree without their having to bother to shake it' (record of Anglo-US discussion held in the State Department, Washington, on 11 October).

[16] This working paper, prepared by the MoD in consultation with the FCO, was sent by Mr. Tickell to Mr. Makins under cover of a letter of 19 September. Based on the premise that the Russians were unlikely to negotiate seriously on MBFR until the final stage of CSCE was in sight and probably not until they had a clearer picture of their SALT II discussions with the Americans, it nevertheless assumed that they had an interest in ensuring a contractual arrangement for force levels in central Europe and in adding a further multilateral element to the process of *détente*. It proposed that the Alliance explore and reconsider: (1) possible modifications to the concept of phasing, including the 'blurring' of the distinction between the projected Phases I and II; and (2) the allocation and content of the reductions envisaged under the existing Allied approach (WDN 27/1).

[17] During Anglo-US discussions on 11 October on MBFR (see note 15 above) the Chairman Mr. D. Linebaugh (ACDA) said, speaking personally, 'it would place a heavy load on Option 3 if it were to be used to secure the Soviet tank army, asymmetrical reductions and the common ceiling

9. At the formal meeting the Americans asked for our support for their proposal for a no-increase agreement limiting Allied and Warsaw Pact air force manpower between Phases 1 and 2. They said this was quite different from their other four proposals under this heading, and regretted that this had not been made clear in Vienna and Brussels. They thus wanted early action only on the no-increase commitment. They were convinced that air force manpower could be included, perhaps in an overall common ceiling, without prejudice to Allied aircraft. This would have the advantage of meeting Soviet criticisms of Allied insistence on ground forces only. It would also have the more positive advantage of constraining Soviet air forces through MBFR. They seemed worried about the buildup of Soviet air power in the reductions area over the last year or so. They also expressed doubts about the competence of the MBFR working group. I said that if they were dissatisfied we should consider raising its calibre or revising its functions.

10. Perhaps my overriding impression is that in Washington MBFR remains on the back burner.[18] It could be brought forward if Kissinger judged it appropriate in Moscow. In this case we would be in a new situation. But on the assumption that the Russians give no sign of early willingness to negotiate, the Americans seem content to play MBFR long and let the Russians know it.[19] In the meantime I imagine that the US delegation in Vienna will be given a fairly free hand over tactics, but no-one in Washington seemed concerned about the day to day conduct of the negotiations or the need to stick to any particular timetable.

concept'. Mr. Tickell pointed out that the 'nuclear card was the most valuable in the Allied hand', that it could 'only be played once', and that the Allies should then buy all they could with it.

[18] Mr. Rose was less certain. 'As regards the American position', he noted in a letter to Mr. Tickell of 17 October, 'it is almost a case of *"quot homines, tot sententiae"*. But I do not think we should be entirely reassured by your general impression that MBFR is for the time being on the back-burner. The point made by Resor and Dean has never been that there is urgent pressure now for an MBFR agreement but that we have to reckon with such pressure developing by the early Summer [*sic*] of 1975 and get ourselves in the right posture to resist it.' Mr. Tickell replied in a letter of 25 October that he still considered it less likely than it had seemed earlier that the Americans would suddenly confront Her Majesty's Government (HMG) 'with far-reaching proposals requiring quick decisions between now and the end of the year'.

[19] During the Anglo-American talks on 11 October (see notes 17 and 15 above) Mr. Tickell drew attention to the 'fundamental flaw' in the MBFR negotiations. 'We were', he claimed, 'engaged in two sets of negotiations—one with the East and one in the West with our own domestic and parliamentary opinion. So far there had been an admirable degree of consultation within the Alliance. But we must ensure that we were not so obsessed with the Western aspect of MBFR that we neglected the Eastern aspect. If there were no progress in Vienna by the spring of 1975 and no break-through by then in the CSCE the Alliance would have to decide what to do next.'

No. 19

Minute from Mr. Tickell to Sir J. Killick

[*WDN 27/1*]

Personal and Secret　　　　　　　　　　　　　FCO, *27 November 1974*

MBFR: Visit to Vienna 19–21 November 1974

I visited Mr. Rose and our MBFR Delegation in Vienna from 19 to 21 November. I am preparing a separate note of the various detailed points which arose in my meetings with the heads of other Allied delegations, but I thought you might like a personal account of my impressions of the British Delegation and the character of the MBFR negotiations generally.

2.　As you know I had long hoped to pay a visit to the Delegation and had obtained authority to go. But the immediate cause of my present visit was the difference which arose between the Office and the Delegation on the handling of two broad issues: the timing and tone of our reply to the Soviet first step proposal of 31 October;[1] and the distinction which we think should be observed between the informal meetings (attended by a limited number of MBFR negotiators—not always including us—from each side) and the plenary sessions (at which all are represented).[2] In passing I should emphasise that although Mr. Rose made it clear that he did not like the instructions he received, he carried them out effectively, and we received satisfaction on the points to which we attached importance.

3.　So I went to Vienna with two main objectives in mind: first to hear out Mr. Rose and the Delegation on the events of the last three weeks, give them the chance of subjecting me to the views of colleagues and the Ad Hoc Group, and make them feel better understood and appreciated; and secondly to take them through British policy, explain the wider perspectives of East/West relations of which MBFR is only a part, and gently insist that Allied governments—and not a group of their representatives—make policy and hence must in certain

---

[1] This proposal, first raised informally by the Eastern delegates on 15 October, foresaw reductions by each side of 20,000 men with corresponding armaments and combat equipment during 1975. Soviet and US forces would be reduced by 10,000 men, and Poland and West Germany might each make force cuts of 5,000 men, with remaining reductions spread across the two alliances.

[2] In informal Conference sessions the US delegation had argued strongly against the Soviet proposal. But, as Mr. Tickell recalled in a minute to Sir J. Killick of 29 November, WOD preferred to delay a formal Western response to the proposal in order to 'enable governments to think about it, and be seen to be thinking about it, and to give [their] ultimate rejection greater weight'. He did not think the UK delegates should feel bound by what was said in informal discussions, and he rejected the American contention that non-opposition to the Soviet proposal in plenary session would be misinterpreted by the East as a softening of the Western position. Much however to Mr. Tickell's evident irritation, at a meeting of the Ad Hoc Group on 6 November Mr. Rose agreed, without having secured proper authority from London, to the adoption of a Western plenary statement which omitted from a British compromise formula words indicating that the West might wish later to revert to the Soviet proposal (minute from Mr. T.C. Wood (First Secretary, WOD) to Mr. McLaren of 7 November, WDN 27/7).

circumstances determine tactics at Vienna.[3] I think it fair to say that after prolonged but never acrimonious argument these objectives were generally met. The problems I encountered in the Delegation were partly psychological, and I think arose from the peculiar circumstances of these negotiations.

4.   MBFR negotiations are being conducted in a curiously isolated atmosphere. So far as I could judge most of the Allied negotiators (and certainly the British ones) see virtually no-one who is not concerned with MBFR. The same is probably true of the Warsaw Pact negotiators. The result has been the development of a series of group identities. First there are the negotiators from both East and West: they understand each other well, enjoy good personal relations on and off duty and even have a song-book for use in the evenings.[4] To-day they have gone off on a collective bus trip to Czechoslovakia. Secondly there is the Ad Hoc Group where the Allied negotiators meet at least twice a week. This body is not unlike a committee in the political co-operation machinery of the Nine[5] except that it contains the representatives of one of the super-powers and imposes a measure of discipline on its members which, at the present slow pace of the negotiations, is both effective and laudable (it may not last when the pace quickens). Thirdly there is the British Delegation itself headed by a highly competent and conscientious Ambassador and staffed by people of the highest quality. The effect created by these overlapping group identities is far from bad; but it explains why interference from outside is not always welcome and why local tactical considerations sometimes seem paramount.

5.   Mr Rose and his colleagues welcomed my visit in some respects but I fancy may have resented it in others. The number of times we went over the same arguments indicated the strength of their feelings rather than their arguments. I doubt if it is worth going into the substance of the points at issue, but I record three impressions:

(*a*) I think Mr. Rose exaggerated the damage which he told me had been done to Allied cohesion by our insistence on the points of policy mentioned in paragraph 2 above. Cohesion was, he suggested, damaged 'perhaps irretrievably' when we did not go along with the consensus in the Ad Hoc Group. I found no evidence that this was so. In the course of talks with the heads of nearly all Allied delegations the only person who raised the subject was myself. I went briefly through the reasons for our actions, and encountered no argument, let alone disagreement. This may have been because, as Mr. Rose suggested, no-one wished to be rude or to rake over the embers. But my own

---

[3]   In his minute to Sir J. Killick of 29 November (see note 2 above) Mr. Tickell reported that in Vienna he had 'deployed the thesis that it was unlikely that the MBFR negotiations would produce results on their own. There was no internal logic or momentum as in SALT. Any MBFR agreement would depend on the general state of East/West relations and above all the willingness of the Americans to exert leverage on the Russians in terms of their bilateral relationship.' Hence he thought 'it would be unwise to attach too much importance to local negotiating conditions in Vienna'.

[4]   See Appendix IV.

[5]   On the machinery of European Political Cooperation (EPC) see Volume II, No. 1, note 26.

impression was that we had, as one of the three main Allied countries in MBFR, registered our points and that these would now be understood and respected without resentment.

(*b*) I think that the very conscientiousness with which Mr. Rose and his Delegation do their business causes them sometimes to lose their sense of perspective. To some extent this goes for other Allied negotiators, in particular the Americans who have a notably free hand and for most of the time make as much as carry out US policy in this respect.[6] Things may well change when the negotiations become faster-moving.

(*c*) It is of course one of our objectives in MBFR to maintain the closest relations with the Americans who have the biggest stake in the negotiations on the Western side and on whom depends all hope of progress. Mr Rose is rightly very close to Messrs Resor and Dean; and with the German representative, Herr Behrends, participates in a tripartite group which effectively provides the motor for the negotiations. This is fine so far as it goes. But there are occasions when the European interest may require us, with the Germans, to mobilise support from the lower table where the Belgians, Dutch and Italians sit. I do not think that Mr. Rose much enjoys doing this, but it is something which on certain issues requires and will require to be done.[7]

6.   The faults to which I have drawn attention are those of a group or groups who are almost too good at their job. Hence I am chary of complaining about them. I think myself that we should in future:

(*a*) Ensure that someone relatively senior from the Office (next time it might be an Under-Secretary) should endeavour to visit the Delegation for two or

[6] In a minute of 2 December, Sir J. Killick noted 'MBFR is not in the forefront of the minds of President [G.] Ford [who succeeded Mr. Nixon as US President on 8 August] and Dr. Kissinger'. The American delegation was, he thought, 'rather like a satellite in orbit—transmitting like mad to Washington, but not being heard by, or receiving replies from, Dr. Kissinger himself'. And while he considered Mr. Resor 'sensible', he thought that he needed to be 'more careful (under the influence of Mr. Dean) to avoid doing anything, or acting in a manner, which [was] out of tune with Dr. Kissinger's concept of the US–Soviet relationship overall'.

[7] Mr. Tickell minuted Sir J. Killick on 8 November: 'The Ad Hoc Group has a strong sense of esprit de corps, and understandably dislikes criticism or interference from outside: the unquestioned leaders of the Ad Hoc Group are Messrs Resor and Dean who are given an extremely free hand by the US Government (and will continue to have it until MBFR becomes politically important again). Most European governments are intimidated by both the complexity of the negotiations and the personal authority of Messrs Resor and Dean, and their representatives in Vienna are extremely reluctant to take an independent line. This makes it all the more important that from time to time we should insist that the tail should not wag the dog, and attract the attention of other governments (including the United States) to what is being done in their name … We have no wish to challenge American leadership in the negotiations as a whole; but we must protect the European interest, and make sure that the wider perspectives in East/West relations are held clearly in view. In future this is going to be more rather than less necessary.' Sir J. Killick agreed. He noted on 11 November: 'I am sure that Messrs Resor and Dean are *not* playing this the way Dr. Kissinger would wish. I know it is not for us to save the Americans from themselves, but I am confident that Dr. Kissinger will be on our side if there is bad blood' (WDN 27/7).

three days at least once during each negotiating round. The visits of Mr. Rose and other members of his Delegation to London between rounds must of course be maintained;

(*b*) Take pains in our telegrams to put MBFR points into the wider perspective, and give all the general policy guidance which we can. This may mean being more liberal in copying papers to Vienna (for example the new US paper on Ministerial Guidance on the long-range defence concept for NATO, to which I had to refer several times during my visit);

(*c*) When the time comes replace the two Counsellors at our Delegation (which I gather will be next summer) with people who have among their other qualities that of detachment and if possible several outside interests.[8]

At the end of my visit Mr Goodall asked me whether I had any advice to give the Delegation. All I could reply was to say that he should, in a phrase I found current in Washington in October: stay loose.

C.C.C. TICKELL

[8] Mr. Rose wrote to Sir J. Killick on 21 November with regard to Mr. Tickell's visit: 'It would not be right to give you the impression that we were able to sort out all our differences either of approach or of interpretation. I do not think you would expect this to be possible in so short a time … The problem lies in the inevitable difference of perspective between those who have to look at our activities here as one facet in the wider canvas of East–West, and specifically UK/Soviet, relations, and those on the spot who are conducting the tactical negotiations as members of a team operating within the framework of an agreed Allied position. Most of the time these different approaches should not prove difficult to reconcile, but occasionally, as we have seen recently, they will diverge.'

No. 20

Mr. Rose (UKDEL Vienna) to Mr. Callaghan

[*WDN 27/1*]

Secret. Eclipse   VIENNA, *18 December 1974*

Summary …[1]

Sir,

MBFR: The Fourth Round

Our assessment of the prospects for the fourth round, as reflected in my despatch of 26 July,[2] was that the East were unlikely to show any substantive flexibility, and could be expected to pursue stonewalling tactics at least until the

[1] Not printed.

[2] See No. 16, notes 3, 6, 9 and 12. The first plenary session of the fourth round took place on 24 September.

end of the year. As can be seen from the calendar of events during the round annexed to this despatch,[3] the first part of this forecast has been borne out by events: the second part—that the East would stonewall throughout the round—has not. On the contrary, while the Allies have sought to continue the orderly development of the Western programme—stressing the significance of the 'all participants' commitment, offering to revise their definition of ground forces,[4] pressing the East to exchange data, and finally offering a no-increase commitment on air force manpower[5]—the East have managed, without departing from their basic position, to capture the tactical initiative by tabling avowedly new proposals.

2.   The first of these—the so-called 'first step' reductions proposal,[6] which was introduced at the informal meeting on 15 October and confirmed at the plenary session on 31 October—was little more that a revamped version of ideas which the East had been floating since before Easter, and which the Allies had made clear during the summer would meet none of the Western requirements. Nevertheless, it was not without difficulty that the Alliance reached agreement on a sufficiently prompt and definitive rejection of this 'new' proposal to prevent the East from establishing it as a focus for discussion during the remainder of the round.

3.   No sooner had the East digested the considered Allied reaction to the first step proposal than they came up, at the informal meeting on 26 November, with a proposal for a manpower freeze for the duration of the negotiations. This was formally confirmed at the plenary on 5 December.[7] With this proposal, the East for the first time succeeded in making a move to which the Allies were unable to agree on a definitive response within the time scale of the same negotiating round. Although Allied representatives were authorised by the Council to put on record the difficulties which they see in the Eastern proposal, they were also instructed to tell the East that it was being carefully studied.[8] This implied undertaking to

[3] Not printed.

[4] In an informal meeting of 15 October the US delegate offered to exclude from Western estimates of Warsaw Pact ground forces Polish and Czechoslovakian air defence units. This would, he explained, 'result in a sizeable decrease in the Eastern ground force total which would be used as a basis for computing overall ground force reductions' (record of informal session with Eastern representatives on 15 October, WDN 27/7).

[5] This Western proposal, for a commitment from both sides not to increase their air force manpower in the reductions area between the two phases, was put to the East at an informal meeting on 26 November.

[6] See No. 19, note 1.

[7] This proposal required the eleven direct participants in the negotiations to undertake not to increase the numerical strength of their armed forces in central Europe for the duration of the negotiations.

[8] On 9 December Mr. R. Hattersley, Minister of State for Foreign and Commonwealth Affairs, told Mr. A. Hartman, of the US State Department: 'the British delegation had, on instructions, taken a rather different line from their American colleagues on how the Alliance should respond to the Eastern freeze proposal. We did not want to accept it but at the same time we did not think that our response should be too negative. Our approach had encountered some opposition in the Ad Hoc Group but he had asked Mr. Rose to persevere. There was increasing political and Parliamentary interest here in the MBFR talks and he would not want to have to announce in

give a substantive response on completion of the study was welcomed by Khlestov in his otherwise negative statement at the concluding plenary on 12 December, a statement in which he upbraided the West for inflexibility and seemed to betray a certain anxiety at the lack of concrete progress. The reality of their hope that the West will be drawn into serious discussion of a freeze during the next round is perhaps demonstrated by the care the East have so far taken not to leak details of it to the Press. The round has thus closed with the ball firmly in the Western court.

4. The Eastern ability to conduct what has amounted to a war of movement without giving any indication of genuine flexibility stems in large part from the absolute control exercised over the Eastern participants by the Soviet Union. This contrasts with the necessarily cumbersome procedures of NATO consultation on the Allied side and gives the East an advantage of which they have made effective use during the fourth round. As a result, Alliance cohesion has been exposed to its first serious test; and although the Allies have on the whole stood the test well, signs of strain have undoubtedly appeared. In Vienna, for example, members of the Ad Hoc Group now invoke their national authorities more frequently than was the case earlier on; and in Brussels, the compromise reached on the initial response to the Eastern freeze proposal missed the advantages both of a straight and prompt counter-proposal (which we and the Germans had advocated) and of a quick rejection (as preferred by the Americans). The maintenance of Allied cohesion, both in Vienna and Brussels, will henceforward require special attention if we are to prevent the initiative from passing to the East and are to continue to be successful in resisting Eastern attempts at wedge-driving.

5. Despite the advantages which the launching of two official proposals undoubtedly gave the East, the discussion in the fourth round has not by any means gone all their way. When discomfited by Western arguments, Eastern representatives tend to ignore or bypass them; their 'new' proposals have helped them in pursuing this tactic. Nevertheless on the question of data, we have succeeded in keeping the East on the defensive for most of the round and they have shown some unease at their inability to find effective arguments with which to reject repeated Allied suggestions that both sides should put their figures on the table and thus seek to establish the facts on which a reductions agreement can be based. This is an area in which the Allies should maintain pressure during the fifth round. From the purely national point of view, we can congratulate ourselves that our Allies' suspicions of British intentions in the Defence Review, which produced a number of misunderstandings earlier in the round, were largely removed when the content of our proposals was disclosed to NATO on 3 December.[9]

Parliament that we had simply rejected the Eastern proposal (Annex to record of conversation, WDN 27/304/1).

[9] The preliminary results of the Defence Review were announced by Mr. Mason on 3 December. In an address to the House of Commons he indicated HMG's intention to reduce defence spending over a ten year period from 5.5 per cent of Gross National Product (GNP) to 4.5 per cent, a saving of £4,700 million over the decade. As the publication of the full Defence White Paper on 19 March was later to make clear, the review had determined that HMG would 'continue to maintain an army force level of 55,000 and a tactical air force on the mainland of Europe in

Although the Germans in particular have registered their concern at certain aspects of these proposals, the overwhelming Allied reaction has been one of relief that we have ruled out any reductions on the central front in advance of an MBFR agreement; and from now on I hope that any suggestions we make about the conduct of the negotiations will be taken at their face value and judged on their merits.

6. Also on a national note, I should like to record my warm appreciation of the visit which the Minister of State, Mr. Roy Hattersley, paid to this Delegation on 3 December. This visit, which included attendance at the plenary session on that day, was the first to the negotiations by any Minister from either side. The grasp of the central problems of the negotiations which Mr. Hattersley showed in his talks with my American and German colleagues, and the robustness with which he handled my Soviet opposite numbers, made a valuable contribution to the British effort in these negotiations and were an effective demonstration of the importance which Her Majesty's Government attach to them.

7. Looking to the future, the most immediate question which the Alliance now has to answer is what our considered reaction should be to the Eastern freeze proposal. It will be recalled that in Brezhnev's statement of 26 October, 1973, (the *locus classicus* of Soviet policy on MBFR) reference was made to the Soviet readiness to implement reductions 'as early as 1975'.[10] The same deadline was set in the Warsaw Pact draft agreement of 8 November 1973[11] and has been constantly invoked by Eastern representatives since. It also appears in both their first step reductions proposal and their freeze proposal; and the urgency underlying Khlestov's concluding plenary statement of 12 December[12] is consistent with a genuine Soviet anxiety to have something concrete to show from the Vienna negotiations during 1975, in order to maintain the momentum of the Soviet peace offensive.

8. In the light of this requirement, there is an evident logic in the successive Soviet proposals, all of which have been framed with an eye to Western opinion and to wedge-driving between the Allies. Their draft agreement of 8 November, 1973, reflects their optimum objectives. The first step reductions proposal is a limited, interim measure which would still give them much of what they want without prejudicing their full reductions programme. The freeze, which is the most clearly calculated of the three to appeal to Western public opinion and would be the simplest to negotiate, would, at virtually no cost to themselves, achieve their essential objectives: confirmation of the existing force relationship

accordance with [its] Brussels Treaty commitments, making no reductions below this level in advance of mutual and balanced force reductions' (*Keesing's*, 1975, pp. 27221–7); *Parl. Debs., 5th ser., H. of C.*, vol. 882, cols. 1351–69); see *Statement on the Defence Estimates*, 1975, Cmnd 5976 (London: HMSO, 1975).

[10] See Cmnd 6932, pp. 172–4.

[11] See No. 10, note 5.

[12] In this summary of the fourth round, Mr. Khlestov lamented the lack of serious movement in the negotiations, accused the West of attempting to secure unilateral military advantages, and urged the delegates that it was now 'time finally to go from words to deeds, and to work in real earnest for the search for concrete solutions' (statement by Khlestov on 12 December, WDN 27/7).

in Central Europe and the establishment of some degree of control over European defence arrangements. Once they had achieved this, the pressure on them to make progress would be relieved and they could probably afford to sit back and wait for the Alliance position to unravel.

9. It is this analysis of Soviet intentions which has led Mr. Resor, the Head of the US Delegation in Vienna, to argue so strongly for a decisive Allied rejection of the Soviet freeze proposal at the outset of the fifth negotiating round and to oppose suggestions for an Allied counter-proposal, which he thinks that the East would be able to adapt to their own requirements. He believes that Allied objectives in the MBFR negotiations would be better served by disposing of the freeze proposal and exploiting whatever concern the Russians may have for concrete results to put pressure on them to negotiate on the basis of the Allied reductions programme. In strictly negotiating terms it is difficult to disagree with Mr. Resor's assessment, though he may underestimate the wider political implications of the Soviet proposal. Whether his approach commends itself to the Alliance or not, it is clear that we shall need to respond definitively to the freeze proposal one way or the other early in the fifth round; and that, if we decide to do this by means of a counter-proposal, the question of a manpower freeze and the form it should take is liable to become the principal negotiating topic for the whole of the fifth round.[13]

10. On the assumption however that the Allies can avoid being drawn into detailed negotiation about a freeze, the wider question confronting the Alliance is how to advance the reduction negotiations in the face of the continued Eastern refusal to take any account of essential Western concerns: the need to correct the present unequal relationship in ground forces and to avoid the establishment of national ceilings on Allied forces.

11. In its reports to the Council[14] of 28 November and 12 December, 1974, the Ad Hoc Group identified two possible courses of action: either to continue to

[13] In telegram No. 62 to Washington of 10 January 1975 Mr. Callaghan maintained that HMG did not believe a categorical rejection of the Soviet freeze proposal feasible. 'We continue to think', he wrote, 'that the most effective response would be to put forward a counter-proposal designed to expose the defects of the Eastern draft and exploit the Warsaw Pact's vulnerability on the data question. Our reasons are primarily political. We think that if the Allies were to reject the Eastern proposal out of hand, as advocated by the US delegation in Vienna, the Warsaw Pact countries would almost certainly go public and exploit the undoubted propaganda advantages of their proposal. A freeze would be regarded by many people in Western Europe as a logical prelude to reductions. Moreover even an Allied rejection of the proposal could not be relied upon to discourage the Warsaw Pact countries from continuing to press it in the negotiations and to make political capital out of it in publicity.' But this telegram also explained that, although HMG had initially advocated a counter-proposal entailing a freeze on manpower prior to the conclusion of negotiations on Phase I reductions along with a clear limit on its duration and an agreement on exchange of data, they now felt this would risk side-tracking the negotiations into the discussion of proposals which would perpetuate existing force disparities and which might result in a freeze which it would be politically difficult to end if no real progress were made in the negotiations. They therefore recommended as a counter-proposal a ground and air manpower freeze which would come into effect from the moment a Phase I agreement was reached (WDN 27/304/1).

[14] i.e. the NAC.

elaborate details of the present Allied position while maintaining its substantial elements unchanged; or to add further elements to the Allied reduction proposals. Of these alternatives, the first would mean in effect that the only significant modification of their position which the Allies might be able to offer for the time being would be to bring air force manpower within the proposed common ceiling. The second alternative would mean offering to reduce US and Soviet Air Force manpower and to introduce a nuclear element into the reductions package—the so-called Option III.

12. The experience of the past 14 months has confirmed me in the view that if the Russians are ever to make the concessions on MBFR which would be required for essential Allied objectives to be met, they are unlikely to do so solely in return for anything which the Allies may be able to offer in the context of the Vienna negotiations. If we achieve an agreement on terms which the West can afford, it will be because the Russians have taken a political decision that such an agreement is desirable for reasons partly or wholly extraneous to the negotiations themselves. Nevertheless, I think it is the consensus of the Allied negotiators in Vienna that if there is any card in the Allied hand which might conceivably tempt the Russians to consider asymmetrical reductions in ground forces, it is Option III. This is certainly the strongly held view of the US Delegation here, who have made no secret of their conviction that, until this card has been played, the Allied negotiating position will remain critically incomplete and no real test can be made of Soviet seriousness of purpose. For this reason, and also because they believe that the public debate in the US about the American nuclear arsenal in Europe is converting Option III into a 'wasting asset' in negotiating terms, Mr. Resor and his staff favour the introduction of this option (and of an offer to reduce air force manpower) into the negotiations as soon as possible. More precisely, they advocate that the Allies should give to the East during the fifth round at least a preliminary indication of Western readiness to include nuclear elements in Western first phase reductions.

13. To judge from his remarks at the NATO Ministerial Meeting on 13 December, however, Dr. Kissinger has apparently come down against any early use of Option III and seems to be thinking in terms of a third course of action which the Allies have so far refrained from examining, namely a scaling down of the Western reduction proposals.[15] This despatch is not the place to weigh all the pros and cons of the various possibilities. My preliminary reaction, however, is to welcome the brake which Dr. Kissinger seems to be applying on the use of Option III, but to be sceptical of any suggestion to scale down the Allied reduction proposals—a course which could mean tacitly abandoning the common ceiling objective and prejudicing the interests of the Europeans. This will need very

[15] 'If nuclear weapons (in the form of Option III) went into MBFR', Dr. Kissinger said, 'this would be a decision to be taken by the Alliance as a whole. In his personal view it was the wrong time to propose it so soon after Vladivostok [see note 16 below]. The Russians had enough to digest already. Although he thought the current Allied approach was ridiculous in some respects, he thought it would be better to review Option III in the New Year and hold up any action for some months' (UKDEL NATO telegram No. 698 of 13 December 1974, WDN 21/8).

careful scrutiny when we have a clearer idea of just what Dr. Kissinger has in mind.

14. If we are right in thinking that Option III is the main negotiating card in the Western hand, there are obvious dangers in playing it before we judge that the East are ready to make substantial concessions in response. There is no sign of this yet, and it seems more likely that the Russians will want to wait until there has been a positive outcome to CSCE and further progress towards a SALT II agreement[16] before they are even prepared to contemplate substantive moves in MBFR. Once CSCE and SALT are within sight of conclusion, MBFR will be the only major East/West negotiation in being; and its significance as a vehicle for Brezhnev's *détente* policy will thereby be enhanced. It is at that point, if at all, that the wider political considerations referred to in paragraph 12 above might induce the Russians to think in terms of concessions in MBFR, especially if it has by then been demonstrated that the Allies are not to be tempted by such limited alternatives as a manpower freeze.

15. A further important consideration in favour of delay in introducing Option III is the need to establish with the Americans, before the option is broached, exactly what it should be expected to buy. There have been some suggestions, both in the US Delegation here and in Washington, that it should be used solely for the purpose of securing asymmetrical Soviet and US reductions in Phase I. This could result in our having to embark on a Phase II negotiation without a Soviet commitment to the common ceiling concept and without adequate leverage to obtain the further asymmetrical reductions needed to reach approximate parity in ground forces.[17] This is a crucial issue which has still to be thrashed out; and I hope that there will be no question of introducing Option III into the negotiations until we have an agreed understanding in the Alliance of what we aim to achieve with it.[18]

---

[16] During 23–24 November President Ford, accompanied by Dr. Kissinger, met Mr. Brezhnev at Vladivostok. There the American and Soviet leaders arrived at a provisional agreement on the form and content of a new Strategic Arms Limitation agreement, SALT II, covering the period from the termination of SALT I in 1977 until 1985. See Kissinger, *Years of Renewal* (New York: Simon & Schuster, 1999), pp. 291–7.

[17] In a minute of 6 January 1975 Sir J. Killick expressed his doubt about the maintenance of a common ceiling which 'must on any analysis involve highly asymmetrical reductions'; and he questioned 'whether a defender really [needed] parity of force to conduct successful defence'. He was also 'struck' by 'the potential Soviet ability to change course rapidly and improve both defence production and manpower almost overnight if they chose, with no possibility of an effective Western response'. In these circumstances, Sir J. Killick suggested 'Dr. Kissinger may come to abandon the "iron pole" of the common ceiling in favour of the argument ... that the Western interest might now be to "put a cap" on the military capabilities of the two sides in central Europe as they now stand on the grounds that the Russians are capable of making disparity much worse and on the argument that, with the present degree of disparity, the defender/aggressor ratio is just about tolerable' (WDN 27/2).

[18] Mr. Tickell argued in a minute to Mr. Morgan of 1 January 1975 covering this despatch that it was not yet time, from a tactical viewpoint, to use the nuclear option. He was pleased that Dr. Kissinger was in no hurry to deploy Option III, which he thought could only be justified if it were likely to evoke a positive Soviet response (WDN 27/2).

16. When the implications of the various alternative courses of action now open to us are being considered, much will depend on the decisions reached by the Americans during the Recess in the light of the attention which Dr. Kissinger— perhaps for the first time since the substantive negotiations began—now appears to be giving to MBFR. But these decisions will have critical implications for European—and British—interests in the negotiations, and it is imperative that we should not be hustled by the Americans into tactical moves of which the consequences have not been fully thought through or accepted by the Alliance. Both from this point of view, and because of probable Soviet reluctance to make any concessions of substance, it looks as if the best tactic for the Allies during the fifth round may be to sit tight on their present position with only very minor modifications, and allow some impatience for progress to make itself felt on the Soviet side.[19] This would not be an easy hand to play, either in the Ad Hoc Group or *vis-à-vis* the East. It would not at all accord with the temperament and inclination of the leading members of the US Delegation, though it would probably find support from the Germans and other Europeans. But, in the light of paragraph 13 above, the Americans may in practice have to reconcile themselves to it. I look forward to discussing future tactics with the Department in January.

17. I am sending copies of this despatch to Her Majesty's Representatives at Washington, Bonn, Moscow, Paris, Ottawa, Brussels, The Hague, Rome, Luxembourg, Copenhagen, Oslo, Ankara, Athens, Lisbon, Vienna, East Berlin, Warsaw, Prague, Bucharest, Budapest, Sofia, Belgrade and Stockholm; to the UK Permanent Representative to the North Atlantic Council; and to the Heads of the UK Delegation to the Conference on Security and Co-operation in Europe and of the UK Delegation to the Conference of the Committee on Disarmament in Geneva.

I have, etc.,
C.M. ROSE

[19] In his minute of 1 January (*v. ibid.*) Mr. Tickell maintained that he thought it right that the Allies should sit tight on their present position and offer only very minor concessions. But he thought that even without the deployment of Option III a significant new element would be added to Western proposals if the Alliance were to agree to further offers covering air forces and air force manpower. On 6 January Mr. Morgan noted on this: 'We expected the East to stonewall throughout the fourth round and, as far as I know, we did not think it would do them any great harm in the eyes of world opinion. So we should not be afraid of sitting tight ourselves for the fifth session, though a counter-proposal on the freeze and some further movement on air-force manpower would certainly help us in the Western press and parliaments. In general, however, we should not allow ourselves to be fussed about the ponderous movements of the Western side as compared with the nimbleness of the East, which has evidently been depressing Mr. Rose. The comparison was just as bad in the 'fifties, in fact worse, and it has not done us any harm in retrospect' (WDN 27/2).

No. 21

Mr. Rose (UKDEL Vienna) to Mr. Callaghan

No. 19 Telegraphic [*WDN 10/2*]

Immediate. Confidential   VIENNA, *12 February 1975*

Repeated for information to Washington, Bonn, Moscow, UKDEL NATO.

MBFR: Prime Minister's Visit to Moscow[1]

1. Although it seems unlikely that much time will be spent on MBFR, Smirnovsky has again told me that the Russians intend to raise the subject with you. The following assessment of the situation after the first two weeks of this round[2] may therefore be useful as a supplement to the brief prepared by the Department.

2. Eastern representatives have so far shown themselves completely unyielding, both as regards their own proposals and in their attitude towards the Western ones. This is not unusual or unexpected but they have this time adopted tougher language when referring to Western proposals than previously. For example the Polish representative, in a plenary statement, referred to the common ceiling concept as 'deceitful' and 'totally unacceptable'. Epithets which would have been avoided last summer. A similar tendency has been noticeable in the informal meetings. Although Eastern representatives still talk about the importance of reaching agreement in 1975, there is no sense of urgency and they give the impression of digging in for a long haul.[3]

3. The Western charge in the last round that the East were giving priority to 'symbolic' or 'limited' proposals over the negotiation of substantial reductions appears to have gone home. As a result Eastern representatives have emphasised the continued importance of their draft agreement of November 1973 (which contains their full reduction proposals),[4] have not pushed their first step 'symbolic' reductions proposal of October 1974 and have tended to play down the importance of their pre-reductions 'freeze' proposal (or 'no-increase' as they prefer to call it) of last December, although they have been careful to keep it on the table.

[1] Mr. Wilson and Mr. Callaghan visited Moscow during 13–17 February. See Nos. 73 and 74.

[2] The first plenary session of the fifth round of the negotiations was held on 30 January.

[3] But reports from British missions in Brussels (UKDEL NATO), Moscow and Washington suggested that US diplomats were less pessimistic about Soviet intentions, and that they no longer believed it necessary to wait until more progress had been made in the CSCE before putting forward a substantive new offer on MBFR. Mr. Wood was sceptical about this American analysis of the situation and could see no evidence of a change in the Soviet position. In a minute to Mr. R.A. Burns (First Secretary, EESD) of 10 February he observed: 'Our own feeling is that the Americans are deliberately understating Soviet resistance to progress in MBFR in order to generate support in the Alliance for two proposals—airforce manpower reductions and the nuclear package—and to overcome any argument that the time is not yet ripe for such major concessions by the West' (WDN 27/509/1).

[4] See No. 10, note 5.

4.   The East may still mount a propaganda campaign in favour of it in the hope of embarrassing Western Governments. But, from the way the discussion has gone in the informal meetings, I am inclined to think this may not happen at least at this stage. The East will have realised from the prompt and firm Western response delivered at the first informal meeting of this round that their hopes of dividing the Alliance have not been fulfilled. But the Russians are likely to urge you to seek a reconsideration of the Western rejection of their proposal (they may even express surprise that I—as Western spokesman—was responsible for delivering the negative response on 4 February).[5]

5.   Aspects of the Western position which the Russians may raise are:

(*a*) the Western attempt to 'seek unilateral advantage' by changing the relationship of forces between East and West:
(*b*) the failure of the UK (and other Western participants except the US) to say when and how much they intend to reduce:
(*c*) Western refusal to agree to national force ceilings and insistence that the forces of each side should be subject only to a collective ceiling.

These are the main themes which have been emphasised by the East in plenary and informal meetings during this round.

6.   The theme at (*a*) goes to the heart of the difference between East and West: the refusal of the East to admit the need to reduce the force disparities which at present strongly favour them. The East have rejected the Western offer to exchange data on force levels. Eastern negotiators are conscious of their vulnerability on this point and it would be helpful if the Soviet leaders could be reminded of the importance of establishing the facts as a basis for any agreement on reductions.

7.   The West have gone as far as they are prepared to at this stage to meet (*b*) by the undertaking that all Western participants would reduce their forces in the second phase and by indicating the total Western reductions down to the common ceiling. We have frequently told the Russians that before Western participants other than the US can accept any more specific commitments about the time and scope of their reductions, they must have confidence in Russian intentions. This can only come from the example of substantial Soviet withdrawals in phase I and Soviet acceptance of parity, in the form of a common ceiling for the ground force manpower of each side as the goal of the negotiations.

8.   As regards (*c*) the East want national ceilings on Western forces in the area of reductions so as to inhibit the development of defence cooperation in Western Europe and, in particular, to restrict the Bundeswehr. They have recently begun

---

[5] In addressing the Eastern delegates, Mr. Rose dismissed both the 'freeze' and the 'first step' proposals as 'no more than another reshuffle of the components of the existing Eastern proposals'. Their proposals, he said, 'still failed to address the crucial problem of the negotiations, the disparities in ground forces and tanks: it would worsen these disparities and contractualize them. The Eastern proposals would still set an unacceptable pattern of symmetrical reductions in place of the only equitable goal for the negotiations, which was the achievement of approximate parity in ground forces' (UKDEL Vienna telegram No. 38 of 5 March, WDN 27/12).

to argue that collective ceilings are unacceptable because their inclusion in an agreement would perpetuate the 'bloc-to-bloc' approach, which it is the aim of *détente* to eliminate. This is nonsense. The reality is that the negotiations are being conducted between the two alliances, and Eastern as well as Western, proposals and statements are all made on this basis. This reflects the fact that it is the force balance between the two alliances which matters: and Western participants cannot accept restrictions on their freedom to organise their defence within their own Alliance as may be required for their security.[6]

9.   The above paragraphs summarise the line which my Western colleagues and I have taken with Eastern representatives. If the questions in paragraph 4 are raised, I recommend that the answers given should follow the same general line.[7]

[6] On 12 February Mr. Tickell minuted the Private Secretary (Mr. A.A. Acland): 'If we were to agree to national force ceilings it would prevent the Allies from combining to make up any deficiencies which one or other among them might have, and in particular from replacing any American forces which might one day be withdrawn as a result of any unilateral cuts imposed by Congress. It would also have dangerous implications for the future of European defence co-operation. For this reason the Allies have firmly refused to accept the straightjacket which national force ceilings would impose, and have insisted that ceilings should apply to all NATO and Warsaw Pact ground forces in the designated area, with sub-ceilings only for American and Soviet ground forces.'

[7] On 20 February Sir J. Killick briefed the NAC on the Moscow visit of Mr. Wilson and Mr. Callaghan (see note 1 above). According to UKDEL NATO telegram No. 99 of 21 February, he 'confirmed that the Russians had made no explicit statement on the relationship between CSCE and MBFR: they had treated the latter in a low key which implied relatively lower priority'. He also pointed out that 'at present the USSR were still pressing the idea of political and military détente as separate phases'.

No. 22

Sir P. Ramsbotham[1] *(Washington) to Mr. Callaghan*

No. 758 Telegraphic [*WDN 27/304/1*]

Secret   WASHINGTON, *1 March 1975, 7.15 p.m.*

Repeated for information to UKDEL NATO, Vienna, Bonn, Saving Moscow.

MBFR: Trilateral Discussion on Option III

Following from Tickell.

Anglo-German-American talks on the possible introduction of a nuclear package (Option III) into the MBFR negotiations took place in Washington on 27 and 28 February. All the agencies concerned were represented in the American team, which was headed by Ikle, Resor and Klein (ACDA).[2] The German team

[1] Sir P. Ramsbotham was appointed HM Ambassador at Washington in March 1974.

[2] Mr. F.C. Iklé was Director, and Mr. D. Klein Assistant Director, of the ACDA.

was led by Roth and Ruth and included representatives from the Federal Ministries of Foreign Affairs and Defence and the German Delegation in Vienna.

2. The agenda of the meeting was the US paper circulated to us and the Germans on 14 February,[3] and most of the time was devoted to British and German efforts to further elucidate American thinking. Over the whole field [*sic*].[4] We made some progress, but in the end we had to remit the most difficult problem—that of ceilings and constraints—to a working party for further examination. The Americans clearly wanted to retain as much flexibility as possible and to avoid excessive commitment on points of detail. But with the Germans we argued strongly that the devil lay in the detail and that without better understanding of implications, in particular on points touching vital European interests, we would not be in a position to make the necessary recommendations to our Ministers. The Americans were, I think, sympathetic, and will now make a fresh effort to meet our points. They do not want a dispute between us within the Alliance. However they argued that complete agreement on all details is not necessary before opening up the general discussion in the Alliance.

A. Composition of Option III

3. Both we and the Germans emphasised that our Ministers had not yet taken decisions on the general question of introducing nuclear weapons into the negotiations nor on the specific package represented by Option III; but we were content to use Option III as a working hypothesis. In the course of discussion about its specific elements, the Germans expressed disquiet about the inclusion of dual-capable F-4s, and suggested a number of alternative approaches.[5] The

---

[3] The FCO had been aware since late January that the NSC were reviewing strategic options for MBFR and that in Washington the tide was 'once again running in favour of the fairly early use of Option 3' (Washington telegram No. 284 of 22 January, WDN 27/2). A steering brief of 24 February, prepared by WOD for the tripartite talks with the Americans and West Germans, explained that the most important point in the paper resulting from this review, 'US Views on Next Steps in MBFR', was its conclusion that 'the time [had] come for the Alliance to make an offer to bring nuclear weapons within the scope of MBFR, and that this offer should take the form of the package originally put forward by the Americans within the Alliance in April 1973 (the so-called Option III). This would involve the withdrawal from the reductions area of 1,000 nuclear warheads, 54 dual capable F4 aircraft, and 36 Pershing surface-to-surface missile launchers in return for Warsaw Pact acceptance of the principal Allied objectives for Phase I of the negotiations: in short the withdrawal of a Soviet tank army and agreement to the concept of a common ceiling within the reductions area'. In addition, the Americans proposed that Option III should be combined with an offer to bring air force manpower within the common ceiling, leaving open the possibility of proposing reductions of US and Soviet air force manpower in Phase I.

[4] The punctuation here is unclear.

[5] The West Germans were, as the steering brief (see note 3 above) explained, particularly concerned about the inclusion of dual capable aircraft (i.e. 54 F4s) in the US package, especially as the Americans intended to deploy Option III in conjunction with a proposal for including air manpower in a combined ground/air common ceiling. But British officials believed that the exclusion of dual capable aircraft, or the reduction of their numbers, would seriously detract from the value of the offer. The Americans seemed, in any case, unlikely to be ready to alter the mix of their Option III components.

Americans were clearly most reluctant to alter any of the specific elements, but undertook to respond to the German suggestions. They also gave good answers to questions on such points as gaps in allied targetting plans created by withdrawal of the F-4s and the use of aircraft as a tool in crisis management. The Germans indicated privately to us that they were sure their government would in the end accept the package as it was.

B. What Option III should buy

4. With German support we argued that Option III was perhaps the most valuable negotiating card the Alliance had. In our view there was a clear danger that if Option III were used, as at present envisaged, to buy the withdrawal of a Soviet tank army in Phase I and agreement to an undefined concept of the common ceiling, the Alliance would have nothing of sufficient bargaining power left to persuade the Warsaw Pact later to reach a common ceiling at a particular level and in ways militarily acceptable to the Alliance. This danger would be mitigated if the Russians were required to commit themselves to a specific definition of the common ceiling in explicit numerical terms. The Americans said that they thought the Warsaw Pact countries were in no doubt about what would be involved by acceptance of the concept of the common ceiling, but we argued that the Allies could not afford to leave any ambiguity on this point and that an acceptable definition must go into a Phase I agreement. The Americans took careful note of this statement and agreed to think further. Although they were clearly not anxious to lengthen the Allied shopping list, they seemed reluctantly to acknowledge the force of the argument.

C. Phasing

5. We argued that although Option III might be the most important Allied negotiating card we doubted if by itself it would lead to the success of the negotiations. It might sugar the pill of the asymmetrical reductions we were asking in conventional forces: but it would not meet Soviet objections to the present Allied concept of phasing. Although it might be better in tactical terms to deal with Option III first, we should at least give thought to ways and means of modifying our present ideas about phasing without sacrificing the vital distinction between US/Soviet reductions on the one hand and reductions of European (and Canadian) forces on the other. To this effect we produced an illustrative scheme. The Americans were clearly divided among themselves about the idea but did not reject it. Nor did the Germans, although they expressed strong reservations. All agreed that the time had not yet come.

D. Constraints

6. There was an inconclusive discussion of American ideas about ceilings and constraints. The Americans distinguished three categories: ceilings on US nuclear systems specifically covered by Option III and on Soviet tanks; possible constraints on US tanks and Soviet Nuclear weapon systems; and constraints or non-circumvention arrangements to cover non-US and non-Soviet weapon systems. After a lengthy analysis of the possibilities it became clear that much

more work needed to be done. The Americans maintained that such work should only be directed to 'clarifying' their ideas, but we and the Germans said that so far as we were concerned, the subject remained open and the purpose of future work should be to find the best solution to an extremely complex problem. At the end it was agreed that on production of further papers by the three delegations, experts would meet probably in Bonn on 12 March to pursue the matter further.[6]

E. Timing and Tactics

7.   Although the Americans argued in their paper that the Alliance should aim to deploy Option III in Vienna before the end of the current round, it was clear that they were divided on the subject themselves.[7] In the margin of the meeting Sonnenfeldt and his staff made plain to us that Kissinger and he had no wish to rush the Allies and, while there were arguments for proceeding this round they saw no decisive need to do so. We argued that Option III should only be deployed when negotiating conditions were right, and that we did not believe this would be the case until SALT II was further advanced and the second stage of the CSCE was near its conclusion. At present we saw no evidence that the Soviet leadership was ready to focus on MBFR. Apart from further examination of the problem among ourselves, consideration of it within the Alliance would also take time and care if the other Allies were to be brought along.[8] In the end it was agreed to leave the calendar fairly open. When the time came we should seek the advice of our respective Ambassadors on how the problem might best be dealt with in the Alliance.

8.   At an early point in the talks we established that the Americans did not intend to put their current paper (or an amended version of it) into the Alliance, and were thinking of proceeding there by means of a statement by their Ambassador. We agreed that it would probably not be possible for the three of us to agree on identical positions, and that we would retain our freedom of action

[6] In a letter of 18 April to Sir J. Barnes, HM Ambassador in The Hague, Mr. Tickell pointed out that the immediate problem was whether, in agreeing to reduce US nuclear weapons, the Allies should seek to impose some measure of constraint on Soviet nuclear weapons in the reductions area. He also recognised that it was inevitable that the Russians would regard Option III as having little value unless it were accompanied by assurances that other NATO countries would not seek to compensate for the withdrawal of US aircraft and missile launchers by increasing their own holding of these systems (WDN 27/510/1).

[7] 'Dr. Kissinger', the steering brief (see notes 3 and 5 above) stated, 'holds broadly to the thesis he set out at the [December] NATO meeting, and in particular does not want to see Option III deployed until SALT II has made further progress and the end of CSCE is in sight; while Dr. Schlesinger (possibly supported by the President) wants to make a visible move forward, partly perhaps to enable him to set in train certain reductions in the US nuclear armoury in Europe which he thinks justified on military grounds; and partly in order better to resist congressional pressures.'

[8] In UKDEL Vienna telegram No. 16 of 7 February Mr. Rose also expressed his doubts as to whether it would be logistically feasible to table the US package in this round. Nor could he see 'any tactical requirement for haste'. In his opinion all available evidence seemed to suggest that MBFR was not near the top of the Soviet list of priorities, and was only likely to become so when CSCE was effectively out of the way. It would, he believed, 'be tactically disadvantageous to introduce Option III in Vienna until the summer round', which was likely to start in mid-May.

when the matter came up in the Council: at the same time we should obviously do all we could to align our views without making it too obvious to the other Allies.

9 I suggested on a personal basis that in view of the special character of Option III there was something to be said for a high level American approach to the Russians before its deployment in Vienna to explain the nature of the package, the importance the United States attached to it, and how we intended to handle it in the negotiations. I also suggested that we would be deceiving ourselves if we thought that the Warsaw Pact countries would accept or reject it as a unique and untouchable package (as implied in the US paper).[9] Instead they would probably treat it as a basis for negotiation, do their best to unravel it, and try to use it to establish a precedent for subsequent reductions in non US nuclear forces. This meant that even if it would be better not to go into this aspect with our Allies in the coming NATO debate we should at least try among ourselves to distinguish the hard core of Option III, about which we were not prepared to negotiate, from those parts of it which we might be prepared to discuss and modify. Neither the Americans nor Germans made any substantive comments.

10. See my MIFT.[10]

[9] According to the steering brief (see notes 3, 5 and 7 above) it was implicit in the American paper and also in the current thinking of some officials in Washington that Option III should be regarded as a 'litmus test' of Soviet good faith. 'If', the brief asserted, 'the Soviet response were negative, then it is argued the Allies would be in a good position to go public and break off the negotiations. Indeed on page 13 of the American paper circumstances are envisaged in which a rupture of the negotiations would be preferable to an unsatisfactory MBFR agreement. We doubt whether Option III will prove quite the litmus paper the Americans suppose. Even if the result were wrong and the Russian reaction negative, we doubt if the Allies would be willing to break off the negotiations. Too much political capital is invested in them.'

[10] My Immediately Following Telegram. In Washington telegram No. 759 of 1 March Mr. Tickell reported that the British, German and US delegations had agreed that they should make no particular secret of their meeting to the other NATO allies, but that they should avoid specific reference to Option III, and stick firmly to the line that there had simply been a discussion on MBFR as a whole.

No. 23

Record of a Meeting held in the Secretary of State's Room at 10.00 on Friday 9 May 1975 between the Defence Secretary and HM Ambassador to MBFR negotiations in Vienna

MO 13/1/16/4 [WDN 27/2]

Secret

Present:

Rt Hon Roy Mason, MP
Secretary of State

Mr. J.F. Mayne
PS/Secretary of State

Mr. Clive Rose
HM Ambassador to MBFR
Negotiations, Vienna

Mr. Rose said that it was no surprise to either side in the negotiations that little progress had been made during the last round.[1] Somewhat to our surprise, the Eastern side had not exploited their 'freeze' initiative,[2] and the Western side had confined itself to setting out the fundamental arguments underlying the West's position and to impressing on the East that, if there was to be progress in the negotiations, it could not be on the basis of equal percentage reductions such as the East was proposing. The Prime Minister's visit to Moscow may have been a factor in the East's failure to exploit their initiative to the full, but there had been little chance of progress before the CSCE summit.

2. The timing of the CSCE summit might well slip from July into September, and it might therefore coincide also with the next meeting between President Ford and Mr. Brezhnev on SALT. It was clear that the Russians would not be ready to turn their minds to MBFR seriously at least until progress on CSCE and SALT was evident, and consequently it would not be sensible for Option III to be played until the autumn round of negotiations.[3]

3. *The Secretary of State* asked whether in the light of this MBFR might, by the end of the year, become a matter of active public interest; and whether, in that event, we would be well prepared to present the West's position clearly to the public. *Mr. Rose* said that it was possible that MBFR would begin to hit the headlines towards the end of the year, and that the arrangements for briefing on the West's position as a whole, backed up by individual background briefings such as he himself, and his other colleagues in Vienna, gave from time to time, should be sufficient to deal with intensified public interest. But there was much to be

[1] The final plenary session of the fifth round was held on 17 April.

[2] The Allied rejection of the manpower freeze proposal was given informally to the East on 4 February and confirmed in a plenary session on 13 February.

[3] Mr. Rose considered that the best time to deploy Option III was likely to be at the beginning of the seventh round in September, provided that Stage II of the CSCE had by then been successfully concluded (summary of MBFR: FCO/MoD discussions on 5–9 May enclosed in letter from Mr. Tickell to Mr. Rose of 15 May).

done both before Option III could be tabled in the negotiations, and there would be some considerable delay between the tabling of Option III and a substantive reaction from the Eastern side. Although the United States were anxious for progress in the negotiations through the tabling of Option III, they would first have to discuss the matter very fully within the Alliance; and agreement within the Alliance would not be easy.[4] For Congressional and other reasons, the US were anxious to link Option III with a Phase I agreement, possibly with a commitment to negotiate Phase II, but without any imperative to get on with the negotiations. We would not be alone in the Alliance in seeking not only a Phase I agreement but also a commitment to the common ceiling as the price for tabling Option III. Moreover, the Warsaw Pact would not agree to a Phase I agreement unless there was a firm commitment to Phase II reductions; and sooner or later the US and the Federal Republic of Germany would have to face up to this. The resolution of these difficulties within the Alliance would probably not be achieved until Option III had been tabled and the Warsaw Pact had reacted by arguing that Option III by itself was insufficient to buy the disparities in reductions inherent in the common ceiling. The alliance would at that stage be faced with the necessity for modifying or abandoning its proposals for negotiations in two phases.[5]

4.   In answer to a question by the Secretary of State, *Mr Rose* said that he had been delighted by the outcome of the Defence Review. During the run-up to the Defence Review, there had been suspicion of our motives by many of our Allies, but the undertaking that we would maintain our Brussels Treaty commitments in advance of a successful outcome to the MBFR negotiations had completely allayed these suspicions. And the Russians were correspondingly disappointed by the result of the Review.[6]

[4]   In a despatch to Mr. Callaghan of 23 April, reporting the fifth round, Mr. Rose observed: 'On the Allied side, the whole of the Fifth Round has been passed under the shadow of Option III—the nuclear reductions package which everyone has known that the Americans have up their sleeves but which, even now, is not quite finalised to the point at which the Americans can put detailed proposals on it to the Alliance.' Allied governments had, in consequence, been reluctant to focus on other, less far reaching modifications of NATO's position.

[5]   Mr. Rose argued in his despatch of 23 April (*v. ibid.*) that Option III should be presented as 'a self-contained package, designed to secure Eastern agreement to the Allied Phase I programme including asymmetrical US and Soviet ground force reductions, and commitment to the concept of a common manpower ceiling as the eventual outcome of Phase II'. But he advised against seeking Eastern acceptance, at the same time, of the numerical level of the common ceiling since this had not previously been included in Western Phase I proposals. On phasing, he noted, 'we are up against a determined and, to some extent, understandable reluctance on the part of the Soviet Union to reduce its forces until the West Europeans, and above all the Federal Republic of Germany, are expressly committed to reduce theirs. As the negotiations have developed, the importance of this issue for the Russians has become increasingly clear; and I do not myself believe that it will prove possible, even with Option III on the table, to bring the East to accept the Allied two-phase approach in its present form.'

[6]   From a meeting between Mr. Rose and Mr. W.T. Rodgers, Minister of State for Defence, on 6 May, it emerged that it 'remained firm Government policy that no reduction in BAOR would be made in advance of a satisfactory MBFR agreement with the Warsaw Pact, but this might well not

5.   In answer to a further question, *Mr. Rose* said that the Netherlands' statement on tactical nuclear weapons and the publicity given by the US to their examination of the numbers of tactical nuclear weapons in Europe had been a temporary embarrassment in the negotiations; but they had done no lasting damage to the basic Alliance position.[7]

6.   *Mr. Rose* hoped that the next round of negotiations would be able to concentrate on data rather than definitions, and that this might entail our tabling figures of forces on both sides, possibly on a unilateral basis, in order to pre-empt the Russians from focusing on broad definitions in an attempt to demonstrate a rough parity of forces in the guidelines area. We would want to pin down the Russian[s] to talking about specific forces and specific numbers.[8]

7.   *Mr. Rose* said that he was looking forward to the Minister of State's visit to Vienna,[9] and hoped that the Secretary of State might himself be able to manage a visit, possibly next year.

J.F. MAYNE,
Secretary of State's Office,
12 May, 1975

materialise until 1978/79 and it had to be recognised that the Defence Budget would continue to be under severe pressure in the intervening years' (record of a meeting held in Minister of State's room on 6 May).

[7] *The Times* reported on 12 December 1974 that the Dutch had suggested to NATO's Defence Planning Committee (DPC) that the Alliance reduce its 'undue dependence' on its 7,000 tactical nuclear weapons in Europe. Mr. Mason and Dr. Schlesinger had both emphasised the importance of the tactical nuclear weapons as the third element, along with strategic nuclear and conventional forces, of the 'triad' of NATO's defence; and Mr. Mason was reported as having voiced his concern over the United States' review of its own tactical nuclear forces in Europe (*The Times*, 12 December 1974, p. 4).

[8] Mr. Rose was cautiously optimistic with regard to the Soviet Union's interest in making progress, both on the specific question of data and in the talks generally. He wrote in his despatch of 23 April (see notes 4 and 5 above): 'As if to reinforce the impression thus created of a continued desire to maintain the serious and non-polemical character of the negotiations, they [the Russians] closed the round with a series of informal indications that they would be ready, in the Sixth Round, to engage in a discussion of force definitions and data—something which the Allies have been urging them to do for over a year.'

[9] Mr. Rodgers was due to visit Vienna on 25–27 June.

No. 24

Minute from Mr. Goodall to Mr. Rose

[*WDN 27/12*]

Secret   VIENNA, *27 June 1975*

MBFR: Conversation with M. Shustov [1]

1.   M. Shustov invited me to lunch with him at his hotel in Baden [2] on 25 June. No one else was present.

2.   As usual, M. Shustov was a most civilised interlocutor, with none of M. Smirnovsky's zest for scoring debating points. While being, as always, careful to safeguard the negotiating position of his own side, he manages to give the impression of a man seriously interested in identifying the real difficulties with a view—eventually—to reaching an agreement. He has, of course, a long experience of disarmament negotiations and of dealing face-to-face with his Western opposite numbers.

3.   We agreed that the negotiations looked as though they might be about to enter a more interesting phase. M. Shustov said that we had not yet entered the bargaining stage. When we did—which he described as probably being 'Stage III' of the present negotiations—progress would depend on each side's readiness to take greater account of the basic concerns of the other side than had been shown so far.

4.   We agreed that, despite the apparent lack of progress up to now, we had not been wasting our time. We had at least succeeded in identifying the basic differences of principle which would somehow have to be resolved if agreement was eventually to be reached. I said that, although it was never possible to lay down priorities as between different elements in a negotiating position, we detected that two main Eastern concerns were (a) to secure reduction commitments from the outset by all the Western direct participants; and (b) to include nuclear and air forces in reductions. The East had probably detected that, on the Western side we saw particular difficulty about Eastern insistence on proportionately equal reductions which would codify the existing disparities favouring the East, the Eastern failure to distinguish adequately between the two super powers and the rest, and Eastern insistence on separate national ceilings.

5.   M. Shustov agreed that these appeared to be the fundamental problems. As regards ceilings, it had not been part of the original Eastern concept to achieve national as distinct from collective ceilings: the East had simply started from the position that all participants would have to commit themselves to reductions. But their understanding of what Western representatives had been saying to them recently—namely that individual non-US Western participants would at no point even specify the reductions they would make—constituted a major difficulty. These

---

[1] Mr. V.V. Shustov was Deputy Head of the International Organisations Department in the Soviet Ministry of Foreign Affairs.

[2] A town to the south of Vienna.

statements had been made despite Eastern efforts to make clear that the question of ceilings could be considered separately from the question of reductions. I asked whether this distinction was intended to be taken theoretically (in which case, although valid, it was hardly helpful from the Western point of view) or whether we were intended to draw practical consequences from it: i.e. that the East would accept a collective ceiling if the NUSWP[3] would specify their reductions. M. Shustov said that it was intended to make a practical contribution to the discussion. The most important thing was to establish a reduced level of forces for either side (*sic*). The East understood the interest of the NUSWP in being able to compensate for reductions by any one of them, up to the level of the Western overall ceiling. If the NUSWP would agree to specify their individual reductions, this would be a helpful step. I said that this was a chicken-and-egg situation: it was unreasonable to expect us to specify our reductions unless we knew that the East would accept the collective nature of the resulting ceiling. Was this what M. Shustov was implying? M. Shustov smilingly said that this was a question to which I could hardly expect him to give an outright answer. (Despite this disclaimer, his earlier remarks carried the very strong implication that, provided the NUSWP specify their individual reductions, the East will eventually accept a collective ceiling.)

6.   Turning to the Eastern proposal for a definitions discussion, I said that we welcomed this as something we had ourselves proposed over a year ago. As he knew, we regarded a discussion of definitions as incomplete without a discussion of the data to which the definition related. But at least we would now be getting down to discussing practical issues. M. Shustov said that this was an important point. There would have to be a common understanding of definitions before reductions could be agreed; and, even if we could not arrive at agreed definitions, we could at least acquire an understanding of the basis on which each side categorised its forces. Some Western colleagues had suggested to him that the definitions discussion would not take very long, and this might turn out to be the case, but until we embarked on it it was difficult to know where or how far it might lead.

7.   On procedure, he was inclined to favour devoting a full informal meeting to definitions, followed by a meeting on other questions, rather than trying to divide each informal meeting in half. I agreed. He thought that the presence of military advisers would be valuable because it would associate them more closely with the negotiations and give them the feel for what was going on. Whether they would actually need to intervene in the discussion remained to be seen; but at least they would be present to provide explanations if needed. I said that I was sure it would also be educative for all our military advisers to have first hand experience of what their political colleagues were up against. M, Shustov said with feeling 'I agree with you one hundred per cent'. Asked how he saw the discussion developing, M. Shustov said that the Eastern side would definitely table their own definitions at the next informal meeting.

8.   M. Shustov asked why the West, having been so keen to get the negotiations

[3] Non-US Western Participants.

started, had now become so static. Were we losing interest in reaching an agreement? I said that this was certainly not so. But the first requirement for negotiating with the Soviet Union was patience. This was especially true of so complicated and important an issue as force levels, which directly affected the security of all of us. It was illusory to expect rapid progress. (M. Shustov agreed.) The Allies had nevertheless already made a number of modifications to their proposals to meet Eastern criticisms. The East did not seem to think much of these modifications and we did not think much of theirs. At the present stage we judged it essential to get across to the East what our fundamental concerns were, of which they would have to take account if they on their side genuinely wanted an agreement. A prime requirement was for the Soviet Union to abandon its attempt to codify the *status quo*. Whatever Western statesmen might say in public from time to time, the Europeans were profoundly aware of their military inferiority vis-à-vis the East, and of the disadvantage they were at from having their principal ally on the other side of the Atlantic Ocean, as contrasted with the immense military might of the Soviet Union camped on their borders. Whatever the Russians might profess to think, we ourselves knew that it was inconceivable that we could ever, either collectively or individually, launch an offensive war against the Soviet Union. But to speak frankly, we could not have the same confidence that the Soviet Union would never use its military might against us. We had to take into account the history of the past 25 years and the expansionist character of the Soviet ideology. Disparities we could live with as long as we retained the right to make them good whenever we judged it necessary for our security took on a totally different appearance when we were invited to codify them in an agreement. This was something we would certainly never do. If the Russians wanted an agreement—which would bring them significant advantages and still leave them militarily impregnable—they would have to pay the price of accepting approximate parity in ground forces in the area of reductions. In our view, this would be the test of whether their détente policies were real or (as we suspected) simply a means of getting the West to accept and codify a power relationship which, since the war, had evolved to Soviet advantage.

9. M. Shustov listened attentively to this lecture, but did not comment on it. But without wishing to ask a question to which he was not entitled to know the answer, what about nuclear weapons? Did not Secretary Schlesinger's recent remarks about Western first use of nuclear weapons illustrate the importance of including nuclear weapons in reductions?[4] I said that, on the contrary, they illustrated the validity of our thesis that it was the imbalance in ground forces which was destabilising. If the Soviet Union did not have the present great preponderance in ground forces which could make it difficult for the West to fight a defensive war with purely conventional forces, the situation envisaged by Mr. Schlesinger could never arise.

10. With reference to armaments, I asked M. Shustov how, under the Soviet

---

[4] On 21 June the *New York Times* reported Dr. Schlesinger as having confirmed 'that the United States retained the option to use nuclear weapons or introduce more ground troops in the event of a North Korean invasion of South Korea'.

programme, they saw the two sides reaching agreement on the comparability of armaments and equipment to be reduced. M. Shustov said, a shade uneasily, that this would be a matter for the military experts. I said that the Soviet proposals for reducing forces by units and formations presumably meant that all the related equipment would be reduced too, down to the last rifle. Did this mean that the Russians foresaw residual ceilings on rifles, bayonets, land rovers, etc.? If not, where would they draw the line? M. Shustov said, again rather uneasily, that it would be contrary to commonsense to expect ceilings to be applied to every single item of equipment however small. Clearly there would have to be some understanding on this point; but he did not suggest what it might be.

11. On personal matters, I did not learn anything about M. Shustov that we do not already know. He is married, but has no children, and his wife is temporarily staying with him in Baden. He is an avid reader of the American and English press, from which he quotes freely. He is clearly a serious and thoughtful person, with a pleasant sense of humour, and is a considerate host. The entire Soviet Delegation, including technical staff, are housed and fed in the Park Hotel, and M. Shustov and his wife have a two-roomed flat there. The only exception is Ambassador Khlestov, who has now taken a villa 15 minutes walk away.

A.D.S. GOODALL

No. 25

Minute from Mr. Tickell to Mr. S. Barrett [1]

[*WDN 27/2*]

Confidential   FCO, *20 August 1975*

MBFR

When we were in Helsinki for the third stage of the CSCE,[2] the Secretary of State invited me to set down my thoughts about the prospects for MBFR as a sort of last will and testament after my three years on the subject.[3] This arose from a conversation in which I had suggested that whereas the CSCE—a Soviet initiative—had been on points a success for the West, MBFR—a Western initiative—carried many dangers and could, unless we took the greatest care, be turned to Eastern advantage.

---

[1] Private Secretary to the Secretary of State.

[2] See Volume II, Nos. 138 and 139.

[3] Mr. Tickell began sabbatical leave as Fellow of the Centre of International Affairs, Harvard, in September 1975. As a result of FCO structural changes, involving the dissolution of WOD, departmental responsibility for the MBFR negotiations was subsequently transferred to Defence Department. Mr. Wood, who assisted Mr. Tickell in the preparation of this paper, informed Mr. P. Mehew (Deputy Head of Delegation, UKDEL Vienna) in a letter of 1 September: 'Although ... the paper is intended only as a personal statement it reflects many of the ideas which we have jointly developed over the last few years.'

2. The idea of Mutual Force Reductions, whether Balanced to our taste or not, represents a more than honourable objective. After a quarter of a century of military confrontation involving almost 2 million men in Central Europe in which war was probably avoided only because both sides possessed nuclear weapons, it is reasonable and right that both sides should wish as part of the general improvement in their relations to reduce the forces and armaments each has deployed against the other, and to divert badly needed resources to other more productive purposes. It is also reasonable that the weaker side should wish to negotiate these reductions in such a fashion as to remove or mitigate the disparity in military power which has long been one of the principal causes of instability between them.

3. It is at this point that the difficulties begin. Both sides may want better relations and greater stability but neither see them in the same way. It may be unwise to speculate on the intentions of others but in broad terms Soviet policy seems to be to establish a special relationship with the United States as the other super power, and with the help of the Americans hold the present European system in place as it is. In this light better relations for the Russians means, as we have seen at the CSCE, closer co-operation between governments—i.e. 'inter State relations' each side of the line, and stability means the maintenance of Soviet military preponderance (designed for garrison duties as well as attack and defence), and the frustration of any attempt to build up Western Europe as a new collective power in its own right with matching defence arrangements. By contrast the Western countries see better relations and greater stability as a dynamic process leading to closer co-operation between peoples as well as governments in Europe, the breakdown of ideological blocs as such, the free evolution of Europe, including the European Community, the continued association of the United States with its underpinning of European defence, and the achievement of a broad military balance sufficient to rule out the threat or use of force in European affairs.

4. Thus MBFR, like the CSCE, represents a meeting place, or rather a battle ground, between quite different philosophies, attitudes and policies. Because it touches vital questions of national security and mixes foreign and defence policy between European states as well as the super powers, it is a great deal more difficult than either the CSCE or SALT although it has connexions with both. So far the United States on one side and the Soviet Union on the other have made most of the running, and although some Americans and most Russians would probably like that to continue, it is unlikely to do so, at least on the Western side, if and when negotiations move into an active phase.

5. Although MBFR was a Western initiative which the Russians had to be persuaded to accept, there has long been confusion about Western aims in it. Looked at dispassionately and with some benefit of hindsight, MBFR, is less one negotiation than three inter-locking sets of negotiation, not all consistent with each other. These may be broadly distinguished as follows:

(a) From the beginning MBFR was used by Western governments to justify to their parliaments and public opinion the need for maintaining existing defence expenditures and military deployments. For the Americans under

President Nixon it was an admirable way of dealing with the Mansfield lobby and demands for release from American global responsibilities; and for the Germans under Chancellor Brandt and to a lesser extent for the other West Europeans it was a way of containing similar pressure for reductions in defence expenditure, when the threat to Western Europe seemed out of tune with the times. MBFR was a dyke against demands for unilateral reductions, and is likely to remain so.

(*b*) The elaboration of negotiating positions in MBFR led to a complex and on the whole fruitful negotiation within the Alliance on the nature of the West European defence system, the use of Allied military resources and the character of Allied deployments. By identifying problems long obscure, causing debate on central military issues and disseminating knowledge about the Allied and Warsaw Pact defence systems, MBFR led to new thinking within the Alliance, which made its contribution to the Ottawa Declaration[4] and the latest Ministerial Guidance to major NATO force commanders.

(*c*) But fundamentally MBFR is a negotiation between NATO and the Warsaw Pact. Its scope is so wide, it involves so many incompatibles, it so often demands the weighing of like against unlike that as in SALT it was obvious from the start that it would take a painfully long time even to clear the ground for progress. Moreover the Russians made clear their primary interest in the CSCE, while the Allies were at first more interested in working out their own positions. For both sides it seemed better to travel hopefully than to arrive. Their respective opening proposals were incompatible.[5]

6. Over two years of negotiation the circumstances surrounding the interlocking points described above have changed:

(*a*) The end of the Vietnam war and the new more hard-headed relationship between the United States and the Soviet Union has caused a change in congressional attitudes. Although MBFR has its uses and could well regain its former political importance, the power of the Mansfield lobby has declined and the continued American military presence in Europe needs less excuse. In Germany Chancellor Schmidt[6] takes a tougher attitude than his predecessor, and is more conscious of the implications both for the Federal Republic and for Western Europe as a whole of any agreement which discriminated against

---

[4] The NAC met in Ottawa at Ministerial level on 18 and 19 June 1974. See Cmnd 6932, pp. 182–6.

[5] Sir J. Killick noted in a minute to Mr. Barrett of 27 August that he personally had always been sceptical of the 'likelihood of serious Soviet interest in agreement on its merits and on terms tolerable to the West'. Furthermore, he thought that while there was an undoubted economic incentive for the Russians in SALT, which could avoid a further and costly arms race involving a new generation of strategic weapons, they would derive no such advantage from an MBFR agreement. The manpower and other resources which would become available to the Soviet economy from the withdrawal of 20–30,000 men from central Europe would, he reckoned, 'be no more than a drop in the bucket'.

[6] Herr H.H.W. Schmidt succeeded Herr W. Brandt as West German Chancellor in May 1974.

the countries in the reductions area, led to constraints on the NATO defence system, or prevented the emergence of a greater European defence co-operation within the Alliance.[7] In this attitude Chancellor Schmidt has the full support of President Giscard,[8] who like his two predecessors regards MBFR as a thoroughly bad and dangerous business likely to lead to greater Soviet influence in Western Europe. By contrast the present British, Dutch and Belgian governments are keener than their predecessors to reduce forces, if not in the immediate future at least in the longer term, but have undertaken to do so only within the framework of MBFR. It is fair to say that in no NATO country is there at present unmanageable political pressure for unilateral cuts or instant progress in MBFR.

(b) The debate within the Alliance is incomplete. But there is new emphasis on the need for standardisation of weapons and division of labour in defence planning and tasks. Because there is little prospect of substantial savings through MBFR, the pressure for greater efficiency, redeployment of forces, standardisation and inter-operability of equipment and so on tends to make MBFR look less of a cure for all ills. It has for example been possible to determine force levels below which it would not be feasible, taking political as well as military considerations into account, to plan any sort of conventional defence for Western Europe. Without such a defence we would of course be forced back into excessive dependence on nuclear weapons, and thus revert to the discredited doctrine of the tripwire.

(c) In the Vienna negotiations themselves the issues between the two sides are at least clearer. Whereas the NATO participants want agreement on approximate parity of manpower below a common ceiling within the reductions area (thus requiring greater Warsaw Pact than NATO reductions), the Warsaw Pact participants want equal or equal percentage cuts on both sides (thus perpetuating—and consecrating—the existing disparities between them). Whereas the NATO participants place emphasis on reductions in the forces of the two super powers within the area as a first step, the Warsaw Pact participants want all participants to reduce from the outset and have focussed their efforts on the reduction of European and in particular German forces. Whereas the NATO participants insist on collective undertakings (in order to protect their right to compensate for hypothetical American reductions in the future and leave open the possibilities of European defence co-operation), the Warsaw Pact participants insist on national undertakings with national force ceilings. Whereas the NATO participants have tried to limit the negotiations to ground force

[7] In a note of 8 August, drafted at Mr. Tickell's request, Mr. Wood recalled with regard to this change of attitude on the part of the West Germans: 'They no longer face domestic pressure and have become increasingly pre-occupied by the dangers of MBFR. The manifest Russian desire to limit the Bundeswehr has increased German distaste for MBFR; while they will not seek to impede a Phase I agreement confined to US and Soviet Union their interest in Phase II remains very uncertain. Their present position is not unlike that of the French.'

[8] On 19 May 1974, following the death of President G. Pompidou, M. V. Giscard d'Estaing was elected President of the French Republic.

manpower and armaments, the Warsaw Pact participants have demanded the inclusion of nuclear weapons and aircraft.

7.   In these circumstances the prospects may look forlorn. But they are not so bad as they appear.[9] First among the imponderables influencing this negotiation is the gradual improvement in US/Soviet relations and the prospects for a new SALT agreement. The Americans have not recently given MBFR much priority in their relations with the Russians, but if as seems likely they now do so there could well be a positive response. Secondly the Russians have said (whether sincerely or not we cannot judge) that with the political framework for future relationships in Europe now established in the Final Act of the CSCE, they will be ready to make a fresh effort.[10] MBFR must anyway figure in Brezhnev's prospectus for détente in Europe. Thirdly the Allies are planning to meet Warsaw Pact demands for the inclusion of nuclear weapons and aircraft by putting forward a nuclear package, including dual capable aircraft, in the shape of Option III, together with a proposal to bring air force manpower into the common ceiling.[11] None of these factors need make for early progress; but together they may push the negotiations forward in the autumn.

8.   This is not a bad time to consider Western priorities in the negotiations. In my judgment there are three main priorities:

(*a*)   We must continue to hold on to what Dr. Kissinger has described as the iron pole of the Western position: in short a collective common ceiling of ground (and now air) force manpower in the reductions area. To set our hands to an agreement involving unequal forces in Central Europe would tend to contractualise disparities, and constrain our freedom in the future to deploy our men and resources as we think best—with or without the Americans—for the defence of Western Europe. The demand for a common ceiling in manpower has simplicity and is easily understood by public opinion. It might one

---

[9]   In a despatch to Mr. Callaghan of 23 July, chronicling the sixth round of the negotiations (16 May–18 July), Mr. Rose characterised the previous two months as 'the least eventful so far'. With the NATO Allies engaged in active consideration of the implications of introducing Option III into the negotiations, it had not been possible for the NAC to formulate new guidance on other less crucial areas of the Western position; and Eastern negotiators had evidently exhausted the range of presentational moves which they had discretion to make in advance of some substantial new Western initiative.

[10]   But Mr. R.A. Sykes, who, having been appointed DUS in May 1975, assumed responsibility for MBFR in August, thought that 'despite the conclusion of the CSCE, MBFR negotiations [were] still going to be lengthy, protracted and tedious' (letter to Mr. Rose of 11 August).

[11]   In his despatch of 23 July (see note 9 above), Mr. Rose considered it probable that the East, like the West, were hopeful that the introduction of Option III would 'move the negotiations into the bargaining phase'. Nevertheless, he also expressed his scepticism about the value of Option III and whether the Russians could ever be brought to accept an agreement providing for 'substantial, asymmetrical Soviet force reductions in advance of any reductions by the Bundeswehr and in the absence of any explicit limitation (other than that imposed by the collective common ceiling) on the future size of the West German forces'.

day be extended to tanks. It already corresponds to the ceilings established for certain weapons systems in SALT. As a concept it is hard for the Russians to rebut on grounds of equity, particularly as they have the advantage of the Americans in reinforcement capability. Moreover the Russians, who used by all accounts to regard conventional superiority in Central Europe as necessary to offset US nuclear superiority world wide, may now feel with SALT that some balance in conventional forces in Western Europe could be acceptable in terms of their general strategy.

(*b*) We must continue to resist all demands for the establishment of national ceilings on European forces. In addition we must continue to draw the vital distinction between the positions of the super powers from outside the area who could accept ceilings and constraints on their forces and armaments within it without damage to their defence strategies as a whole; and the positions of the Europeans for whom reductions would in most cases mean disarmament and for whom constraints would permanently limit their freedom to organise, deploy and equip their forces as they think best within the Alliance.[12]

(*c*) We must take proper account of the different effects of an MBFR agreement on the open societies of the West and the relatively closed societies of the East. On our side we shall fully respect any undertakings into which we may enter; our troop movements, deployments and reinforcements will be known to all; and our public opinion will be vulnerable to accusations about breaches of undertakings, and of course to demands for further reductions in defence expenditure. On the other side the Warsaw Pact countries may—to judge from the SALT precedent—respect the letter but not always the spirit of agreements reached; we shall be little wiser than we are now about their troop movements, deployments and the rest; and their public opinion will scarcely be a factor. Moreover it will be far easier for the Russians to reinforce in relative secrecy in an emergency than it will be for the Americans to bring forces across the Atlantic, or for the Europeans to call up reserves. In these circumstances I think that our priority must always be to consider the effects of constraints upon ourselves before thinking about their effects, real or theoretical, upon the Warsaw Pact countries.

9. Finally it may be worth saying a word on the British role in the negotiations. So far there has been an effective but unofficial steering group of the Americans, Germans and British on the Allied side. The Americans have unquestioned primacy in the conduct of the negotiations, and the basic papers have all

---

[12] Mr. Wood thought it difficult to see what further concessions of substance the Allies could offer beyond Option III and the combined ground/air common ceiling without putting vital interests in jeopardy. A larger nuclear package would, he believed, raise doubts about the strength of the US nuclear commitment to Europe and would have grave implications for Western European armaments. Moreover, he added in his note of 8 August (see note 6 above): 'To surrender on the vital principle of avoiding national force ceilings (in order to meet the Soviet pre-occupation with the Bundeswehr) could be the first step on a very slippery slope, destroying the prospects for closer European defence co-operation and leaving the European members of the Alliance dangerously exposed if at some future time the Americans were to withdraw further forces from Europe.'

been American. In Washington Dr. Kissinger has taken only an intermittent interest in MBFR which he sees as subsidiary to SALT; but from the beginning MBFR has been under Presidential direction and has an important place in US foreign policy as a whole. The Germans have played a crucial but largely negative role. They are more certain of what they do not want than of what they do. I suspect that with Chancellor Schmidt's increasing scepticism the Germans will present more and more of a problem for the Americans in the management of the Allied case. We for our part have contributed many of the central ideas (including the common ceiling), have worked behind the scenes to refine and improve American papers, and with the Germans have defended what we have sought to define as the European interest. So far our influence has been out of proportion to the number of troops we have in the reductions area and our general contribution to NATO defence. In this respect our independent nuclear capability is of importance.

10. In these circumstances I think there are four main points for us to watch.

(*a*) We should be unable to continue to exert the influence we have so far enjoyed if we were to get too far out of line from the Americans and Germans. If both combined on some point against us, we could well find ourselves isolated within the Alliance, and would have to reckon with the consequences and the price to be paid. This means among other things that we should be very careful about insisting on the need for purely British reductions in Phase II before the time to negotiate European reductions within the Alliance arrives.

(*b*) Circumstances could arise in which we might have to choose between the American desire for the conclusion of a Phase I agreement on terms which affected European interests in Phase II, and the German desire to limit MBFR as much as possible to Phase I and avoid commitments, above all commitments affecting Europe in Phase II. Obviously it would be our purpose to avoid such circumstances arising. But if they did and depending on the case, I think we should lean more to the German than to the American side. We must not expect the Americans to stay in Europe in their present numbers for ever, and the Germans, and with them the other Europeans with whom we shall increasingly be associated, will constitute our essential shield.[13]

(*c*) As our independent nuclear capability could be of great importance in the future of European defence, and already gives us a special position in that respect, we must make sure that we do not accept any constraint upon our right to deploy British nuclear weapons and warheads as we think best in the reductions area, and in particular refuse the imposition of national equipment ceilings upon any but the US nuclear systems specified in Option III.

(*d*) In military terms it would be better to have no MBFR agreement at all than one which constrained future arrangements for European defence or

---

[13] Sir J. Killick strongly endorsed this conclusion in his minute of 27 August (see note 5 above). 'We need', he added, 'many things from the Germans—not least a new agreement on Offset [to assist cover the costs of British forces in the FRG]—and they are perfectly capable of establishing "linkage" between MBFR and these other issues.'

damaged the security of the Alliance as a whole. But circumstances can be imagined in which some reductions of British forces became necessary for political or economic reasons. If this should happen, it might be better for us to endure the odium of making once and for all unilateral reductions than to press our Allies to enter into arrangements for mutual reductions which in some sense mortgaged our—and their—future freedom of action.[14]

11. It may be worth recalling that when the Tsar Alexander I first raised the idea of negotiations on force reductions after the Napoleonic wars, it was Lord Castlereagh, then Foreign Secretary, who rejected the idea in the following terms. He said:

'It is impossible not to perceive that the settlement of a scale of force for so many Powers—under such different circumstances as to their relative means, frontiers, positions and faculties for re-arming—presents a very complicated question for negotiation: that the means of preserving a system if once created are not without their difficulties, liable as States are to partial necessities for an increase of force: and it is further to be considered that on this, as on many subjects of a jealous character, in attempting to do much, difficulties are rather brought into view than made to disappear.'

Lord Castlereagh therefore suggested that each state should on its own responsibility reduce its arms to the minimum it considered necessary and then:

'explain to Allied and Neighbouring States the extent and nature of its arrangements as a means of dispelling alarm and of rendering moderate establishments mutually convenient.'

Lord Castlereagh's words have force and relevance to-day.[15]

C.C.C. TICKELL

[14] In his letter to Mr. Rose of 11 August (see note 10 above) Mr. Sykes noted that while the British must avoid being manoeuvred into a position where they appeared too negative and were not supported by public opinion, 'we may well have to stonewall; and I do not think that we should be too apprehensive at the prospect of having to do so. After all, the Russians do it constantly.'

[15] Mr. Braithwaite was responsible for drawing Mr. Tickell's attention to this advice offered by Lord Castlereagh in a memorandum despatched to St. Petersburg on 28 May 1816 (minute from Mr. Tickell to Mr. Wiggin of 27 February 1973, WDN 27/4). Cf. C.K. Webster, *The Foreign Policy of Castlereagh, 1815–1822. Britain and the European Alliance* (2nd edn., London: G. Bell and Sons, 1958), pp. 97–9.

No. 26

Paper by Mr. Rose [1]

[*WDN 27/2*]

Confidential   VIENNA, *17 November 1975*

Soviet and Warsaw Pact Objectives and Policies in Europe after CSCE [2]

1.   The first thing to be said is that Soviet and Warsaw Pact strategic and military objectives after CSCE remain exactly the same as before it. That is, fundamental purposes of Soviet military policy have not changed—to provide military support for the Soviet Union's foreign policy objective of changing the balance of power in the world in general and in Europe in particular in favour of socialism, and to provide an invincible war-fighting capability for defence against attack by the West. Certainly no sign that the so-called 'peace-policy' has had any moderating effect on these purposes. Rather the reverse: the past five years has seen a greater Soviet military build-up than in any previous five year period.

2.   In global terms these purposes require at least the maintenance of strategic parity with the US and if possible the achievement of superiority. In Europe they mean three things:

First, maintenance by the Warsaw Pact of military superiority over NATO;
Second, pursuit by all available means of attempts to weaken the defence of Western Europe and the American commitment to it;
Third, a strong enough military presence in Eastern Europe to provide a credible guarantee for Soviet political domination of its Warsaw Pact allies.

Global strategic parity is the subject matter of SALT. I do not intend to discuss SALT now. Not because it is not vitally important. But it is a negotiation in which we are not directly involved at present and can only marginally influence the course of events. If a SALT II agreement is achieved, we are likely to be more directly concerned in SALT III, both because our own nuclear forces may be involved and also because of the effect that any agreement to reduce strategic systems could have on the credibility of the US commitment to European defence (higher nuclear threshold, greater reluctance to use tactical nuclear weapons, risks of No First Use). This is not the time to develop this line of thought. But if a SALT II agreement is not achieved, the hardening of the Soviet attitude which this will imply will make it even less likely that the Russians will be prepared to make the sort of concessions in Vienna which will be required to reach a MBFR

---

[1] This paper, evidently drafted in Vienna, served as the basis of Mr. Rose's opening statement to the Conference of HM Ambassadors in Eastern Europe and the Soviet Union which assembled in London on 17 November (see No. 84). A copy was sent to Mr. W.J.A. Wilberforce (Head of Defence Department) under cover of a letter of 20 November.

[2] The Final Act of the CSCE was signed in Helsinki on 1 August. See Volume II, No. 139.

agreement. (This of course leaves out of account the question whether it would, in these circumstances, be in the West's interest to make the moves needed to find a compromise.)

3.   The three objectives in Europe are familiar enough. The third—military guarantee of Russian domination of Eastern Europe—has been effectively demonstrated often enough during the last 20 years. Although CSCE may in theory make it harder to repeat action of this kind—Czechoslovakia, Hungary—in the future, I imagine that no-one in Eastern Europe would have much doubt about where Soviet priorities would lie if the occasion arose in the foreseeable future. In theory again, this objective could set a limit to the number of forces the Russians might be prepared to withdraw under a MBFR agreement. But in practice it does not seem likely that the level to which either side would reduce under any conceivable MBFR agreement will be affected by considerations of this kind. (It should be remembered that the Soviet Union has more than 50% of the Warsaw Pact combat divisions in Poland, Czechoslovakia, and the GDR and as many again immediately available in the WMD's.)[3]

4.   As for the other two objectives in Europe—Warsaw Pact superiority and weakening Western defence—the Russians clearly see the MBFR negotiations as a valuable forum for promoting them. Their aims in MBFR, which are reflected in every statement and proposal they make are directly designed to achieve these objectives. Let us look at them:

First, they want to get the present Warsaw Pact military superiority in Central Europe formally written into an agreement, or 'contractualised'. They call this 'maintaining the existing relationship of forces' which they claim has provided a stable balance for the past 30 years. Thus they insist that reductions should be symmetrical. They criticise the West for trying to change the relationship of forces to their advantage (which we are doing). They accuse us of seeking 'unilateral military advantage' and claim that this is contrary to the principle of 'undiminished security', which all governments accepted during the pre-liminary talks.

Second, they aim to include commitments in the agreement which would disrupt NATO's defence arrangements and prevent, or at least inhibit, any future development of European defence cooperation. They know they will get a certain *droit de regard* over Western defence in any agreement—the right of challenge, complaint, interpretation. But they have refused to accept that commitments should be collective; that is to say they are insisting on individual national reduction commitments resulting in national ceilings for each Western country. This would mean, as the Russians intend, that NATO countries would be deprived of the right collectively to offset any shortfall in the common ceiling due to future reductions by one member of the Alliance.

Third, they want to obtain reductions in, and permanent limitation of, the Bundeswehr. Often this seems to have the highest priority of all their aims in

[3]   Western Military Districts.

the MBFR negotiations. It is of course an aim behind which they are able to rally the wholehearted support of the other Warsaw Pact participants (the Czechs are equally anxious to see the East German army reduced and limited). It seems improbable that the Warsaw Pact countries would accept any agreement which did not give them the substance of this aim.

Fourth, they hope that a MBFR agreement will contribute to their longer term aim of weakening the American military presence in Europe. I include this as being a constant of Soviet policy. But I do not really think it plays a very prominent part in the MBFR negotiations. Indeed they may see a continued American presence as a desirable stabilising element in what they hope will be a period of disintegration in Western European defence arrangements. Certainly they would like to see the Germans limited and the other Europeans deprived of the possibility of taking effective compensating action before the Americans withdrew altogether.

These aims have not changed as a result of CSCE. They have been pursued unremittingly by the Russians and their allies since the negotiations started just over two years ago. Where there may be a change is in the prospects for progress. We cannot yet tell whether this is so. There was, in my view, never any possibility that we would make progress in Vienna before the conclusion of the CSCE. Since Vladivostok,[4] I have also thought that, if progress was possible in Vienna, it would have to await a SALT II agreement. In July, it looked as though both these preconditions would be fulfilled by about now. Helsinki is over but SALT II is not and, for the time being at least, has suffered a setback. The implications of this, for the MBFR negotiations, are still not clear; my own view is that because of the priority both parties attach to it, progress in SALT II is likely to remain a precondition for progress in MBFR.

5.   Given that these preconditions are fulfilled, what *are* the prospects for progress? Is there any basis for an agreement? Many people will say no; the Russians have no need or incentive to moderate their aims in such a way as to find a compromise: unlike the West, which is negotiating from weakness, they are under no time pressure; given the economic problems of the NATO countries,[5] the Russians have only to sit back and wait for Western reductions to take place without having to pay anything for them. These are persuasive arguments. But I believe there is also a case for saying that the Russians both need and want an agreement:

'*Needs*'
(*a*) Need to maintain the momentum of détente, to avoid Western disillusionment with Soviet performance.
(*b*) Need to satisfy American wishes for a MBFR agreement, once MBFR assumes a high place in American priorities (perhaps post-SALT II).

[4]   See No. 20, note 16.
[5]   Cf. No. 84.

(c) Need to fulfil the commitment, so frequently and publicly reiterated since Helsinki, to complementing political détente with military détente. Is anything needed before the February Congress?[6]

(d) Need to demonstrate either progress in MBFR or Western intransigence before the 1977 CSCE review conference.[7]

'Wants'

(e) Gains from any agreement: *droit de regard* over Western defence arrangements, ceiling on total Western forces, geographical advantages vis-à-vis US withdrawn forces.

(f) Given difficulties of precise verification, Western 'open societies' ensure that NATO more likely to observe the letter of the agreement than the Warsaw Pact.

Whether the Russians will see these arguments as sufficiently compelling to justify their making the concessions necessary to reach an agreement is impossible yet to tell. Probably the point which will be most difficult for them to accept will be asymmetrical reductions. But the basic question still is whether they really want to conclude a MBFR agreement. On this the verdict so far can only be 'not proven'.

[6] The 25th CPSU Congress was held in Moscow from 24 February to 5 March, 1976.

[7] See Volume II, No. 137 and Appendix III.

No. 27

Mr. Rose (UKDEL Vienna) to Mr. Callaghan

[*WDN 27/2*]

Secret   VIENNA, *23 December 1975*

Sir,

MBFR: The Seventh Round [1]

1. The new Western offer, formerly known as Option III, was tabled in Vienna on 16 December.[2] Its effect is to add to the existing Western reduction

[1] The seventh round of the negotiations lasted from 26 September to 18 December.

[2] Western participants offered, in return for Eastern acceptance of NATO's outline proposals of 22 November 1973, the withdrawal from the reductions area of 1,000 US nuclear warheads, 54 US nuclear-capable F4s, and 36 US Pershing ballistic missile launchers. In addition, the common collective ceiling for ground force manpower, which might be set at approximately 700,000 men, would be combined with air manpower in the area in such a way as to result in a combined common collective ceiling (to be defined in Phase I) of about 900,000 men on either side. Within this the ceiling on ground force manpower would be maintained. Guidance telegram No. 224 of 18 December emphasised that this offer was 'unique', that it was intended as a 'makeweight' to induce

proposals the withdrawal of certain US tactical nuclear armaments and to include air force manpower in a combined common collective ceiling, within which the existing goal of a common ceiling on ground force manpower would be maintained. This move followed a prolonged period of discussion within the Alliance, which was punctuated by all too frequent leaks in the Western press. With it, new blood has been injected into the negotiations for the first time since the initial proposals were tabled by each side in November 1973. Whatever arguments there may have been for postponing this offer until the next round, to delegations of both sides in Vienna it was something of a relief that the transfusion, long debated in the West and long awaited by the East, took place before the Christmas Recess.[3]

2.   Inevitably, the attention of Western negotiators throughout the seventh round was directed as much to the debate within the Alliance in Brussels as to the Vienna talks. For it was in the Political Committee at Senior Level (SPC) and, later, in the North Atlantic Council that the instructions for the tabling of Option III were hammered out. The substance of the additional reductions to be offered remained unchanged from the US proposals put to the Alliance in June. During the succeeding six months the Alliance debate concentrated on related issues, of which the most important were armaments limitations and the definition of the common ceiling. In this debate the principal role of this Delegation was to advise on negotiating tactics and procedures. These aspects assumed major importance in Vienna and aroused considerable controversy in the Ad Hoc Group once the decision was taken by Alliance Ministers on 12 December that the new offer should be tabled before the end of the round.[4]

---

the East to accept the original Western position, and that it did not 'constitute a surrender by the Allies of their basic thesis'.

[3] At a meeting with US officials in Washington in October, Mr. Thomson (AUS since October 1973) had said: 'we had no strong views about the timing of the presentation of Option III. We had a marginal preference that it should follow the SAL Agreement for the sake of logic, but that was not a point of great importance. However, we attached great importance to the point that Option III should be properly prepared and agreed between the Allies before it was presented' (record of a conversation about MBFR held at the Executive Office Building in Washington on 20 October 1975, WDN 27/304/1). Disagreements over the details of the presentation of the offer (see note 4 below) led HMG to press for the postponement of Option III until the beginning of the next round in January. But on 12 December NATO Ministers meeting in Brussels agreed to introduce Option III before the end of the current round.

[4] Because they considered it important, both from a military point of view and with regard to the debate on defence expenditure in several European countries, the British argued unsuccessfully in the NAC for the addition to the Western presentation of a paragraph which would state explicitly that reductions in non-US Western equipment were not part of the offer, and that limitations on such equipment, whether ground, air or nuclear, were unacceptable to the West. Although the US delegation in Vienna thought it undesirable from a tactical point of view to accompany a positive offer of further reductions with negative and detracting conditions, Dr. Kissinger supported the British position. Mr. Rose was thus eventually able to secure Allied backing for the British proviso. As, however, he confessed in a letter to Mr. Thomson of 18 December, he was disturbed by the extent to which the British delegation had had to '[ride] roughshod through Alliance and Ad Hoc Group procedures and understandings in order to get what [they] wanted'. Mr. Thomson was, for

3.   Meanwhile, until the last week of the round, the efforts of the negotiators of both sides in Vienna were mainly devoted to reiteration on familiar ground and in hallowed phrases of their basic positions. Eastern negotiators continued to insist that the negotiations must not change the existing relationship of forces in Central Europe, which, they claimed, is the result of historical circumstances and reflects each side's view of its security interests. They maintained that an agreement which did not commit all participants to specific reduction commitments from the outset would be inequitable and that the West's demand for a collective ceiling for its ground forces is intended to provide legal cover for individual countries, such as the Federal Republic, to increase their forces in contravention of a reductions agreement. Nor, they claimed, is it possible to confine reductions to a single element of the forces, as the Western proposals do: all forces and all armaments must be taken into account and all should be reduced by equal national percentages.

4.   For their part, Western negotiators maintained their emphasis on the force disparities which favour the East, as the principal destabilising factor on which the negotiations should focus. The massive Warsaw Pact, and especially Soviet, superiority in ground force manpower and main battle tanks should therefore be reduced from the outset. The final outcome should establish parity in ground force manpower between the two sides. An agreement in two phases, the first of which would be confined to reductions of US and Soviet forces and the second of which would establish a common collective ceiling for the ground force manpower levels of each side, remains the basis of the Western position.

5.   The seventh round brought no hint of a shift in the substance of the Eastern position on any of these issues. It would, indeed, have been surprising if it had. Eastern negotiators were well aware that an important Western initiative was imminent and they were content to sit tight and wait for it.

6.   In the absence of progress on the central issues however, some useful work was done in the practical field of force definitions. Although this is essentially a technical matter, the manner in which the two sides define the forces to be addressed in the negotiations and determine the basis on which these forces should be categorised as ground or air forces has a direct bearing on the substantive issues. Discussion of this matter during the seventh round centred on the principles applicable to any agreed definition. There is now a general, but informal, understanding between the two sides on two principles: first, that the definition should be comprehensive, that is, it should cover all military forces in the area; and, second, that it should distinguish between ground and air forces. However, before discussing the precise formulation of these principles, over which there are still some important differences between East and West, the East insist that the West should accept a third principle: that similar types of forces on each

his part, not overly concerned. 'I do not think we should take this situation too seriously', he remarked, 'and there may after all be a silver lining. It is not entirely a bad thing that from time to time our NATO allies should notice that when the chips are down it is the British position that prevails even when it appears (though not in this case in reality) opposed to the American position' (minute to Mr. J.O. Kerr (Private Secretary to the Permanent Under-Secretary of State (PUS)) of 19 December).

side should be placed in the same category, either ground or air. This seemingly innocuous principle conceals a conflict between the Western method of categorising forces by uniform and the Eastern method of categorising them by function. Although some anomalies undoubtedly arise under either method, the Eastern proposals for dealing with them, under their 'third principle', are patently designed to promote their aim of categorising as air forces as much as possible of their manpower, thereby reducing on paper the large Warsaw Pact superiority in ground forces on which the Western case for asymmetrical reductions rests. Thus the West, while recognising the need to resolve the problem on the anomalies actually identified by the East (which concern only a relatively small proportion of the total forces), have insisted that, before they are prepared to discuss how this should be done, there must be an exchange of data. In logic this requirement is difficult to defend; its justification lies in the complete refusal of the East to discuss data since the West tabled their figures for the strengths of ground forces in the area of reductions in November 1973. Nevertheless the US Delegation, who consider that the existence of these anomalies detracts from the credibility of the Western case for asymmetrical reductions based on disparities, are likely to press for this requirement to be reconsidered in the Alliance. There is I believe some scope for modification of the present Western position. But any modification should only be made in return for a countervailing concession by the East. I shall be discussing this problem separately with the Department.

7.   Essential though it is to any agreement, the working out of a definition of forces is a subsidiary aspect of the negotiations. The Western offer to reduce US tactical nuclear armaments, presented on 16 December in a plenary statement by the Head of the United States Delegation, was the first substantive shift in the position of either side since 1973. During the earlier part of this round, Western negotiators were asked constantly by their Eastern colleagues when the offer was to be tabled and the Head of the Soviet Delegation expressed the hope that he would have it in time for his authorities in Moscow to study during the recess. When however the decision to table the offer before the end of this round was announced in the NATO Ministerial Communiqué, Eastern representatives attempted to dissuade Allied negotiators from presenting it in a plenary session. They claimed that, if this course were followed, they would have to seek authority from their Capitals before they could discuss the offer in any subsequent informal meeting. Professor Khlestov said he feared that, in view of the publicity campaign in the Western press, which led some people in Moscow to write the offer off as a propaganda move, he might receive instructions to reject it outright. Since however the West stuck firmly to their right to call a plenary session and to present the offer in this forum, Eastern negotiators had no alternative but to accept. But they made it clear that, once the offer had been tabled, they would not be prepared to discuss it at informal meetings so as to avoid prejudicing their Governments' reactions. In one sense this Eastern attitude made it easier for us to secure the inclusion in the document incorporating the Western offer of the important proviso that limitations on European equipment were not acceptable to the West: since, in the absence of informal meetings, there was no other occasion before the end of the round on which this point could be made to the

East, it had either to be included in the initial presentation or left in abeyance until next round. The former was not achieved without a struggle in the Ad Hoc Group and then only thanks to the reluctant support which the US Delegation were instructed to give us.[5]

8. The first official Eastern reaction, in the statement by the Head of the Soviet Delegation at the final plenary session on 18 December, was awaited with interest and some anxiety. In the event it was as restrained and devoid of polemics as we could have hoped. Professor Khlestov predictably pointed out that the Western offer did not match the Eastern proposals and omitted non-US armaments. But by agreeing to study the offer during the recess, the East met our immediate concern. Bilateral conversations with Eastern representatives on 18 December have left me in no doubt that they understand the importance of the Western offer. But it cannot be assumed that these views are shared by all concerned in Eastern capitals. The series of press leaks which preceded presentation of the offer, some of which were pretty near the mark, have not served the Allied negotiating interest and may be seized on to support their case by advocates of a negative response.

9. Outright rejection of the offer at the beginning of the next round is an improbable reaction. But so also is unqualified acceptance. The best we can expect is the start of a lengthy process of cautious and critical probing which, while indicating Eastern willingness to regard the Western move as a serious one, will fully reserve the Eastern position on its adequacy and on the acceptability of the Western goals. In short, the East will try to pocket the concessions without paying the price. More specifically Eastern representatives will wish to be certain that they understand the fine print. Much of this has not yet been shown to them. So as to be ready to deal with questions Allied negotiators will need to be able to draw soon on the material in the Alliance Position Paper[6] which is at present embargoed for use with the East. While it is important not to allow the negotiations to be sidetracked into detail, the West should not be constrained from giving the East a clear and authoritative explanation of the implications of the new offer.

10. The East will continue to hammer away at those aspects of the Western offer which they claim provide no satisfaction to their interests. They will criticise it for defects in both quantity and quality. They will insist that non-US Western armaments must be reduced and subject to limitation. They will continue to resist Western demands for a data exchange. They will maintain their position that all forces must be reduced from the outset and that for this reason the Western concept of phasing is unacceptable to them. They can be expected strongly to attack the Western refusal to discuss non-US reduction commitments in advance of Phase II and Western insistence on the collective nature of the common ceiling. Finally—and this has the greatest immediate importance for us—they will seek to portray the Western offer as a deal involving a swap between American nuclear equipment and Soviet battle tanks.

[5] *V. ibid.*
[6] See No. 9, note 8.

11. The terms of the new offer provide the East with no satisfaction on any of these points. If there is to be any prospect of securing a modification of the East's attitude on any of them, it will be essential that, during the next phase of probing, the East should perceive no chink in the Western armour. Least of all should they be given any grounds for thinking that the offer to reduce US nuclear weapons may be the first in a series of Western concessions and that they have only to sit tight, refuse it and ask for more for the whole game to swing slowly but surely in their favour. There are few illusions among the Western delegations in Vienna that Option III will do the final trick and it is generally assumed that if there is to be a MBFR agreement on terms acceptable to the West, further compromises will be needed. But no hint of this should be given to the East until we have extracted the maximum that Option III will bear. This means standing absolutely firm for at least the next and probably the next two rounds.

12. The maintenance of Alliance cohesion is therefore, all important. This means that the West must continue, not only to speak with one voice, but also to be silent with one voice; the East must not be allowed to perceive that on certain issues there are disagreements within the Alliance. These disagreements are likely to become apparent during the elaboration of Option III and still more when the time comes to consider possible further moves. On each of the main points in the Eastern position, individual members of the Alliance can be expected to take different, sometimes diametrically opposite, views on how far the Alliance can afford to go. The Germans can be expected to remain adamant that Western reductions must be collective in nature and that the Bundeswehr should under no circumstances be singled out for special treatment. The Americans (at least the US Delegation in Vienna) are openly attracted to the concept of the Western offer as a 'nucs-for-tanks' deal, a concept which has unfortunately been given credence by ill-informed press leaks. These are but two examples of future problems.

13. So far Alliance cohesion has held up well, both in Vienna and in Brussels. But it will need constant vigilance to maintain it if the negotiations now begin slowly to move out of the present deadlock. In the next period we will need more than ever to ensure that on points where important British interests are involved we secure the widest possible measure of support within the Alliance.[7]

---

[7] In a minute to Mr. Thomson of 7 January 1976 covering this despatch, Mr. Wilberforce observed that much of the argument in Brussels concerning the latest Western offer could be attributed to European suspicions of the 'dominant rôle' played by the US delegation in Vienna, sometimes independently of guidance from Washington, and 'thus to a feeling that it was necessary to tie down the Americans very precisely on the content and handling of the new proposals'. Mr. Wiberforce suspected that Mr. Rose feared that the US delegation might still try to reopen, or to blur, issues in Vienna already settled in Brussels and that, in consequence, Allied unity would break down just when it was most needed. Nevertheless, Mr. Wilberforce did not feel too pessimistic. 'One lesson from the Option III debate was', he commented, 'that our close contact with the Americans at a high level in Washington ensured that, on points of major concern to us, we could if necessary, secure the attention of Dr. Kissinger or Mr. Sonnenfeldt and even get specific instructions sent to the US Delegation in Vienna to toe the line with us. Since we will practically always have the Germans supporting us in any future difficulties with the US Delegation, I feel fairly confident of

14. I attach as Annex A to this Despatch a Calendar of Events in the Seventh Round and as Annex B the text of the Western offer presented to the East on 16 December.[8]

15. I am sending copies of this despatch to HM Representatives at Washington, Bonn, Moscow, Paris, Ottawa, Brussels, The Hague, Rome, Luxembourg, Copenhagen, Oslo, Ankara, Athens, Lisbon, Vienna, East Berlin, Warsaw, Prague, Bucharest, Budapest, Sofia, Belgrade, Stockholm and Peking; to the United Kingdom Permanent Representative to the North Atlantic Council; and to the Head of the United Kingdom Delegation to the Conference of the Committee on Disarmament in Geneva.

> I have the honour to be Sir
> Your obedient Servant
> CLIVE M. ROSE

our ability, through intervention in Washington, to stop any manoeuvres by the US Delegation which we consider seriously unwise' (EN 021/628/1).

[8] Annexes not printed.

No. 28

Letter from Mr. Sykes to Mr. Rose (UKDEL Vienna)

[*DPM 081/6*]

Confidential   FCO, *26 March 1976*

My dear Clive,

MBFR: Office Meeting, 15 March 1976

The Secretary of State called a meeting last week to discuss **MBFR**. This was primarily in response to a suggestion made some time ago by Mr. Hattersley that there would be value in examining the overall prospects in MBFR and looking in broad political terms at its likely developments. From the Department's point of view we thought we should also take this opportunity to engage the Secretary of State's attention on one or two questions which seemed particularly relevant not only to the forthcoming visit of Mr. Gromyko[1] but also to the run-up to the 1977 [CSCE] Review Conference in Belgrade. These were set out in a short submission (copy attached).[2] You and the other recipients of this letter may find

[1] See No. 88.

[2] Not printed. In this submission of 12 March Mr. Wilberforce pointed out that whereas in October 1973 the US and other Western governments were worried about domestic pressure to reduce the size of their forces, the mood had recently changed on both sides of the Atlantic to 'one of some disenchantment with "détente" and a correspondingly greater awareness of the need for sound NATO defences'. If it could be assumed that the current relative absence of pressures on Western governments for force reductions would last through the run-up to the Belgrade CSCE

it helpful to have, strictly for your own information, the following note of what took place.

2. Mr. Hattersley was invited to open the discussion. He admitted that he remained sceptical about MBFR and feared that the Allies would be pushed into paying an unacceptable price for agreement. He referred to the exchange of minutes he had had with the Department and with yourself at the beginning of the year and said that none of the replies he had received to his questions had really convinced him that MBFR could end in anything other than a breakdown or an agreement detrimental to the West.

3. In reply to the Secretary of State's request for comments on Mr. Hattersley's *exposé* I said that it would be very helpful for us to know what value the Secretary of State attached to MBFR. Did he regard it as essential to have success in these negotiations or, if the worst came to the worst, would he be prepared to see them wound up?

4. In reply the Secretary of State said that the political gain which we had hoped so far to extract from MBFR had largely been achieved: MBFR had enabled Western Governments to resist domestic pressures for unilateral force reductions. But the perception of Soviet military superiority on which we had based our approach to force reductions had in the meantime become much more of a reality. There was a change of mood about détente in the West. He believed that we should work on the assumption that time *was* on our side between now and the May 1977 Belgrade Review Conference and that we were therefore in a position to bring pressure to bear on the Russians to adopt a more constructive attitude in Vienna.[3] When he met Gromyko on 22 March he would try to convey the impression not that Britain had no interest in MBFR but rather that we and our allies were in no particular hurry and could afford to play it long. (You will be getting a record of the talks with Gromyko shortly.) At one point John Thomson suggested that we might have to aim at turning the MBFR negotiations into something like the CCD negotiations in Geneva,[4] i.e. into a continuing process. The Secretary of State, while not specifically giving the idea his blessing, did not dissent.

5. We then turned to the question whether the common ceiling objective was the right one. The Secretary of State said that if it did not prove acceptable to the other side then he could see no reason for the Allies to offer any further concessions. He was not entirely convinced that the common ceiling was anything more than a useful means to an end; but he recognised that it had considerable presentational attractions; and he therefore believed we should stick

Review Conference, then, he contended, time would be on their side and they could 'mount quite considerable political pressure on the Russians over MBFR'.

[3] Mr. Wilberforce thought that it was probably not worth putting public pressure on the Russians over MBFR until the SALT II negotiations had been completed. 'Thereafter', he noted in his submission (see note 2 above), 'we might be able to let the pressure for Soviet concessions in MBFR build up fairly naturally, as public attention—and preparatory discussions—start focussing on the East/West issues for Belgrade.'

[4] The UN-sponsored Geneva Conference of the Committee on Disarmament, the establishment of which was first announced in August 1959.

to it.[5] He was, however, less sure about the national ceiling point, particularly as it affected the FRG. He was not personally keen to see a situation arise in the future in which the Germans could increase their strength out of all proportion to that of their Allies; but that was a much longer term problem and not one that need concern us now.

6. Finally we asked whether the Secretary of State attached much political importance to ensuring provision in an MBFR agreement for overt measures of verification. He did not see this as a political issue; it was, he believed, essentially a technical question.

7. In short, the consensus of the meeting was that while we did not need the MBFR negotiations to succeed at any cost, we should play things long and try to avoid outright failure. We were not under time-pressures; and as 1977 approached, the Russians might be.

Yours ever,
R.A. SYKES

[5] 'The common ceiling is the "iron pole" of the Western approach', observed Mr. Wilberforce (see notes 2 and 3 above), 'and there is no sign of the Americans or any other ally wanting to do other than hold firmly to it. But is it a realistic negotiating objective (including for public purposes), to get the Russians to agree to a common ceiling and, moreover, a *collective* common ceiling, (i.e. one in which there would be no specific ceilings on the forces of each individual country)? On the basis of Allied data the common ceiling would require the Warsaw Pact to agree to reduce three times as many troops as the West. This is a steep demand.'

No. 29

Mr. Rose (UKDEL Vienna) to Mr. C.A.R. Crosland[1]

[*DPM 081/6*]

Secret   VIENNA, *13 April 1976*

Summary ...[2]

Sir,

MBFR: The Eighth Round[3]

1. It was clear from the start of the round that the Western offer of 16 December 1975 to include US nuclear armaments in the Western reduction proposals[4] was not likely to result in an early Eastern move towards the Western position on any point of substance. In the Ad Hoc Group the Head of the

[1] Mr. Callaghan succeeded Mr. Wilson as Prime Minister on 5 April. Four days later Mr. C.A.R. (Tony) Crosland was appointed Secretary of State for Foreign and Commonwealth Affairs.

[2] Not printed.

[3] The eighth round lasted from 30 January until 8 April.

[4] See No. 27.

American Delegation confirmed in detail what Dr. Kissinger had told the North Atlantic Council on 23 January; that Mr. Brezhnev had told him in Moscow earlier that week that the East would reject the Western offer and put forward early in the round a new proposal on behalf of the Warsaw Pact.[5]

2. This negative reaction to the new Western proposal was reflected in Eastern statements at the beginning of the round. Although Eastern representatives described the nuclear offer as a move in the right direction in that the West showed readiness to include nuclear weapons in its reductions proposals, they claimed that the Western offer of 16 December was unacceptable both because it did not go far enough and because it was made conditional upon acceptance by the East of all other elements of the proposals previously put forward by the West. Throughout the eighth round the East has elaborated these criticisms. Their representatives have in particular focussed on those elements of the Western position which remain unchanged by the nuclear offer. They have continued to claim that the Western requirement for larger reductions by the Warsaw Pact than by NATO is unjustified, and that this requirement is aimed at changing the existing relationship of forces in the area to the unilateral advantage of West. They object to the absence in the Western proposals of any specific and binding commitment by the Western European countries and Canada to reduce their forces. They are critical of the Western 'mixed package' approach under which the components of the reductions undertaken by the two sides would be different, claiming that there is no means by which the military value of different components can be compared. They complain that, by its insistence on collective ceilings, the West is seeking to retain the right for individual NATO countries to increase the size of their armed forces even above present levels. They have strongly criticised the Western refusal to reduce or limit the nuclear armaments of non-US Western participants.

3. In my despatch of 23 December 1975[4] I suggested that the best we could expect from the new Western offer was the start of a lengthy process of critical probing by the East. So far this cannot be said to have materialised. Although there has been more discussion of the Western offer, in parallel with the new Eastern proposal, in the second half of the round than in the first, the Alliance has not needed to draw on the fine print of the Western position so meticulously elaborated in Brussels in the last half of 1975. Western negotiators have therefore concentrated on emphasising the military value of the nuclear offer. They have insisted that any reduction agreement must deal effectively with the crucial sources of military instability in Central Europe: the vast Eastern superiority in ground force manpower and tanks. They have stressed that the Western move of 16 December is a once for all offer designed to gain Eastern acceptance of the basic Western proposals which would eliminate or reduce this superiority.

4. The new Eastern proposal, of which the text is at Annex A,[6] was formally

---

[5] Dr. Kissinger visited Moscow during 21–23 January.

[6] Not printed. This began by proposing: 'In the first stage—in the course of 1976—the reduction is to be carried out in Central Europe of the armed forces only of the USSR and the USA by an equal percentage (approximately 2–3%) of the overall numerical strength of the armed forces of

tabled by the Head of the Soviet Delegation at the Plenary Session on 19 February. This timing was clearly designed to allow Mr. Brezhnev to refer to the importance of the new Eastern initiative in his speech to the 24th Congress of the Soviet Communist Party on 24 February. The broad lines of the proposal were similar to those which Mr. Brezhnev had outlined to Dr. Kissinger in January. Although the text of the proposal contained a number of significant and probably deliberate ambiguities many of these have been clarified, either explicitly or implicitly, in subsequent informal meetings and bilateral conversations with the East. Although the essential elements of the Eastern position remain unchanged, the East claim that their new proposal takes into account certain major Western interests and thus represents a positive move towards the Western position.

5.   The basis on which the East make this claim is that the new proposal adopts the main elements of the Western two phase procedure. They argue that their proposal provides for two separate, but linked, agreements, to be negotiated in sequence; and that in the first stage US and Soviet forces only would be reduced, while the other direct participants would undertake only general commitments to reduce their forces in the second stage. If these points could be accepted at their face value, they would represent considerable changes in comparison with the Eastern draft agreement tabled in November 1973, or even with subsequent modifications of that draft. Although these changes may be largely presentational, because they are closely linked to unacceptable elements in the Eastern proposals, it may however be possible at a later stage in the negotiations to exploit them to Western advantage.[7]

6.   Nevertheless the East have made no move towards any of the West's essential requirements. The East have not dropped their demand that from the outset the Western European direct participants and Canada should undertake firm commitments on the scope and the timing of their reductions. Their new proposal requires all direct participants to commit themselves in the first stage to

the countries of the Warsaw Pact and of NATO in this area.' It then outlined specific US and Soviet weapons reductions (e.g. an equal number of operational-tactical missile launchers). Within this US/Soviet framework all other states with forces in central Europe were 'to assume clearly formulated obligations to "freeze" at the present level the numerical strength of their armed forces and to reduce these forces in the subsequent stage (1977–1978) so that as a result of the reductions in both stages all states participating in them [would] have reduced their armed forces by an equal percentage'.

[7] In a minute of 3 February to Mr. Wood, Mr. P.M. Nixon (also of the Defence Department) speculated that the Soviet initiative could prove attractive to the Americans. Although the counterproposal did not explicitly provide for asymmetrical reductions, it had, he noted, 'many of the features of the "quick and dirty" approach contemplated earlier by the Americans'. If they wished to be able to show some results soon in MBFR, it might serve as a 'basis for a compromise', despite its containing 'several features … unlikely to prove acceptable to the Alliance as a whole'. Mr. Wood evidently agreed. 'We know', he minuted on 3 February, 'that Dr. Kissinger earlier expressed irritation with the "absurd asymmetries" of the Allies' Phase I approach and that the Americans have long contemplated the possibilities of a less substantial Phase I arrangement than that envisaged in the present Allied approach. Whether or not there is a SALT II agreement they might take the view that some sort of exchange of US for Soviet withdrawals would be a good thing for détente generally and for the US/Soviet relationship in particular' (DPM 081/5).

make reductions by a specific equal percentage in a second stage to be completed in 1977/78. The West, in order to meet Eastern concerns, made an offer in 1974 by which all Western direct participants would commit themselves to take part in the second phase reductions. This was however dependent on the conclusion of a satisfactory first phase agreement including agreement on a common collective ceiling for ground force manpower as the goal of the second phase reductions and it has always been an essential element of the Western approach that non-US Western participants would undertake no binding commitments until the second phase. An essential difference between the position of the two sides on phasing is, therefore, that of timing. If the East is to secure binding obligations from the outset from the non-US Western direct participants, it is essential for it that any first agreement should set a time limit by which such obligations must be executed. In the last weeks of this round Eastern negotiators have been at pains to emphasise the importance, not of the precise dates of 1977/78 which figure in their proposal, but of their need for a commitment to some specific and not too distant date by which participants would be legally bound to execute the reductions for which they had contracted in the first stage.

7.   Another small change, which has been virtually unsung by the East, should also be noted. This is that the East have abandoned the requirement in their 1973 draft agreement that all armaments, equipment and units, as well as manpower, should be reduced by equal percentages. Although Western negotiators had for long pointed out that this requirement was quite unworkable in practice, it continued to be part of the Eastern position. Eastern negotiators have now made clear their intention that manpower is to be the basic yardstick by which reductions will be measured in both stages. But the East maintain their insistence that the actual reductions of manpower should be taken in the form of complete units or formations with their associated armaments and equipment.

8.   Moreover the East's reduction proposals remain unchanged. They continue to insist that, since participants are negotiating as individual sovereign states, their reductions, and the resulting ceilings, should be on a national basis. They also maintain their insistence that these reductions should be carried out by equal percentages by each participant. They argue that the existing relationship of forces is a stable one, resulting from historical developments and that, therefore, it should not be changed. They claim that the Western case that there exist in Central European vast disparities in ground force manpower and tanks is artificial and a distortion of the true situation, which requires all forces and armaments to be taken into account and reduced.

9.   Thus, at the end of the eighth round, the two sides remain as far apart as ever on the basic issues. If there has been any progress it has been in narrowing the focus of discussion. In this respect, the continuing debate at informal meetings on a definition of forces has been of practical value. Although technical and complicated, this subject is of central importance to the negotiations. Agreement on a force definition will provide a set of agreed counting rules specifying the manpower to which agreed reductions or limitations will apply and will, for this purpose, provide a method for dividing military personnel between ground and air forces. From the Western point of view, a force definition, when taken with

the relevant data, will show the size of the disparities in manpower favouring the East. The definitions discussion therefore provides a forum in which the West can establish its case for larger Eastern manpower reductions to a common ceiling.

10. Eastern negotiators on the other hand see the definition discussion as a means for undermining the Western case for larger Eastern force reductions. In the seventh round their efforts were spent on trying to secure Western acceptance of the so-called 'third principle' (see paragraph 6 of my despatch of 23 December 1975)[4] and they claimed that the West had wrongly allocated certain types of forces in order artificially to increase the ground force disparity between the two sides. The US Delegation, fortunately, did not pursue their idea of making a move towards the East on this issue and Eastern agreement on 12 March temporarily to leave it on one side, as the West had long argued, and to discuss first the main issue of what personnel should be included in and what personnel excluded from an agreed definition was therefore a welcome move, although it involved no concession of substance. Eastern representatives subsequently proposed to exclude from the manpower totals of the Warsaw Pact certain military personnel who, they claimed, perform the same functions as certain civilian employees of NATO armed forces in the area of reductions. The Eastern objective is clear: to write off some of the Warsaw Pact manpower in order to reduce the disparities on which the Western case for asymmetrical reductions is built. Western negotiators have been able effectively to resist the Eastern argument. They have maintained that a force definition must in logic include all active duty military personnel in the reductions area, and only such personnel. Civilians, reservists and members of para-military organisations should be excluded as a package. They have told Eastern representatives that if they wish to undo this package of exclusions the West will have to reconsider its position on the exclusion of para-military forces which are vastly more numerous in the East than in the West. There are signs that this line or argument has embarrassed Eastern negotiators, particularly the East Germans and the Poles who maintain large full-time para-military forces, many of which are under direct control of their Ministries of Defence. The Western case is, I believe, logical and defensible. I see no need to fear Eastern attempts to undermine it because I do not think that the East can substantiate its case.

11. The US Delegation appeared to be convinced, possibly as a result of indications given during Dr. Kissinger's visit to Moscow in January, that the East intended to table data on their force strengths in the course of the eighth round. In the event, despite strong Western pressure, the East have not done so. The continued absence of Eastern data puts Warsaw Pact negotiators on the defensive on this issue, particularly because, under their new proposal, the first stage reductions of US and Soviet forces would be calculated as a percentage of the overall manpower strengths of the two sides. Western negotiators have also pointed out that the discussion on definitions is unproductive in a factual vacuum, and they have told the East that no agreement on a force definition is possible until an understanding on data has been reached. Eastern negotiators have conceded that they will in due course have to produce figures, but they say that the time is not yet appropriate. At one stage in the eighth round they dropped

hints that they might table data in the course of the next round, though they gave no indication that the figures would be complete. The US Delegation still consider that Eastern data may well be forthcoming in the near future. But it seems more likely that the East will try first to make progress in the discussion on a force definition and that only when they feel they have solid grounds for their case that the West has exaggerated the force disparities will they then produce the corresponding data to prove it.

12. Alliance cohesion has been well maintained in the eighth round. There is no disposition among my Western colleagues in Vienna to look at this stage for further concessions or compromises. In the second half of the round, the United States, in particular, took a much harder line than in the past. This may be a reflection of a trend in United States domestic opinion on East–West relations; but I believe that the Americans also entertained greater hopes than the rest of us that the Western nuclear offer would produce a substantive shift in the Eastern position and were correspondingly more disappointed by the Warsaw Pact's dismissive reaction to it. I believe that all my colleagues regard the Western position as sound, coherent and defensible and that there is no reason to consider any new Western move at least for some time ahead. This view is reflected in the Ad Hoc Group's recommendation in its report prepared for the NATO Ministerial meeting in May.

13. Whether the Warsaw Pact is prepared to make substantive moves towards the West in 1976 is an open question. Dr. Kissinger told the North Atlantic Council in January that he thought the new Eastern proposal would be merely an opening bid and that the Soviet Government wished to make some progress in the course of this year. There were signs, following the tabling of the Eastern proposal in February, that Eastern negotiators were under instructions to increase the pace of negotiations; but this was probably little more than a tactical device designed to draw attention to the importance of their latest initiative. The formulation of their new proposal is, however, flexible enough to allow further modifications which, in presentational terms, could be represented as moves towards the Western position. I have suggested a number of such possibilities to the Department and shall be discussing them during my consultations in London later in the present recess. But none of these possible Eastern moves constitutes a substantive shift. It seems to me unlikely that in the closed season before the United States Presidential elections and the elections in the Federal Republic,[8] the East will choose to make a move which goes much beyond an optical improvement in its present negotiating position.[9]

[8] German federal elections were held on 3 October and the US presidential elections on 2 November.

[9] In UKDEL Vienna telegram No. 48 of 15 March, Mr. Rose had commented: 'Any positive elements in the new Eastern proposal and in their move on force definitions are limited and largely procedural. There is still scope for the East to make further moves of a cosmetic or presentational character without detriment to their basic objectives. If the East wish to maintain the appearance that the negotiations are being intensified, more such moves may be expected. But unless the East show readiness to meet the substantive elements of the Western position—and there is no sign of this yet—there is no prospect of progress towards an agreement.'

14. The position may, however, change thereafter. By the end of 1976 the negotiations will have entered their fourth year. Faced by the resolve of Western participants not to make concessions which entail any risks for the Alliance, the Warsaw Pact participants may begin to feel themselves under some pressure to make substantive progress in military détente, a field which is as much of their choosing as of the West's and on which Eastern leaders have placed increasing emphasis in their public utterances since Helsinki. Already a certain nervousness is discernible in the reactions of Eastern negotiators to Western suggestions that the talks have reached an impasse. The Russians, in particular, may see the need early in 1977 to make a significant gesture towards a new United States President. They may also be casting a none-too-confident eye towards the CSCE Review Conference in the middle of 1977. If there has been no progress towards a SALT II agreement by the turn of the year they might choose this as a field in which to make a move. SALT is however essentially a bilateral negotiation between the United States and the Soviet Union. While the conclusion of a SALT II agreement would be seen as a success for détente, any move which did not have this result immediately would probably not have the same impact on participants in the CSCE Review Conference as a substantive Eastern move on MBFR.

15. For the reasons given in the preceding paragraph, it is possible that the Soviet Government may be faced, at the end of this year or early in 1977, with the need to make a difficult choice on MBFR. At that stage, Soviet willingness to pay the price we ask may indeed be the acid test of their commitment to military détente. Is there anything the Western participants can usefully do to exploit this situation? I am encouraged by the view recorded in Mr. Callaghan's despatch of 11 March to HM Ambassador in Moscow[10] that:

'The Soviet Government must not be allowed to engage us in a further marathon of European negotiations until they have first established their credentials by making material—not simply presentational—contributions to the consolidation of détente, both through the implementation of the provisions of "Basket III" and by adopting a more constructive approach in the MBFR negotiations in Vienna.'

This view prompts the question whether it would serve Western interests if Western participants were to make MBFR a substantial issue in their relations with the Soviet Union in the run-up to the Review Conference. It has always seemed unlikely that the Soviet Government could be induced to move towards an agreement on MBFR on anything like Western terms except under pressure of some external political factor. The imminence of the Review Conference and the Soviet desire to extend the scope of détente into other areas of negotiation could possibly provide such a factor. I recognise the difficulties, both within the Alliance and in terms of past experience of Soviet behaviour. The probability of success may not be high. But the opportunity which will present itself next year is not likely to recur and the question is therefore in my view worthy of serious

[10] See No. 87.

consideration. I shall hope to discuss this with the Department during my visit to London later this month.

16. I attach as Annex B to this despatch a Calendar of Events in the Eighth Round.[11]

17. I am sending copies of this despatch to HM Representatives at Washington, Bonn, Moscow, Paris, Ottawa, Brussels, The Hague, Rome, Luxembourg, Copenhagen, Oslo, Ankara, Athens, Lisbon, Vienna, East Berlin, Warsaw, Prague, Bucharest, Budapest, Sofia, Belgrade, Stockholm and Peking; to the United Kingdom Permanent Representative to the North Atlantic Council; and to the Head of the United Kingdom Delegation to the Conference of the Committee on Disarmament in Geneva.

> I have the honour to be Sir
> Your obedient Servant
> CLIVE M. ROSE

[11] Not printed.

No. 30

Minute from Mr. Wood to Mr. Thomson

[*DPM 081/6*]

Confidential   FCO, *23 April 1976*

MBFR: Mr. Rose's Letter of 14 April [1]

1. The following comments which I should like to make on this letter are as follows:

(*a*) it seems to me important to distinguish between the pressures which the Russians may feel they are facing as the CSCE Review Conference draws near and the pressure which we and other Allies would be able to bring upon the Russians to be more flexible in MBFR. I think it is conceivable that the Russians, particularly if there is no SALT II agreement and if there is continuing disillusionment in the West about détente, might think it politic to make some gesture in MBFR. But that is not to say that such a gesture would necessarily amount to a genuine concession to the West. The Russians could equally well make some move which, like their 19 February proposal, constituted no real change in their basic approach to force reductions.

(*b*) There could thus be some risk involved if the Allies were to make any very explicit linkage between the Review Conference and progress in MBFR; and

---

[1] In this letter, written in reply to Mr. Sykes's letter of 26 March (see No. 28), Mr. Rose stated how very much encouraged he was by the 'firm line adopted by Ministers both to East/West relations generally and to MBFR in particular'.

it could be embarrassing for the West, on the eve of the Review Conference, to have to reject some Eastern initiative in MBFR which the Russians would inevitably announce to the world in general as a genuine concession.[2]

(c) There seems to me a particular danger in Mr. Rose's suggestion that the UK should make MBFR a substantial issue in its relations with the Soviet Union; would this not encourage the Russians to try to deal with us on MBFR behind the backs of our Allies? Moreover, if we were to take the lead in persuading our Allies to do the same this might be misinterpreted, particularly by the US and FRG. But Mr. Rose himself acknowledges that these ideas raise a number of difficult problems which would require very careful consideration.[3]

(d) Finally, it is not clear to me what Mr. Rose has in mind when he talks of the Soviet Union retaining 'a great deal of flexibility' in tactics and in substance; presumably he means that the Russians have at their disposal a wider range of negotiating options than do the Allies. Admittedly that is flexibility of a sort but it is not necessarily synonymous with the type of flexibility which we require the Russians to demonstrate if there is to be any prospect of an agreement which genuinely 'creates a more stable relationship'.

This brings us back to the consideration in (a) above, namely, that there is considerable scope for 'constructive' gestures in MBFR by the Russians, many of which would probably be of little practical value to the West. But we have had little difficulty hitherto in exposing the limitations of Soviet proposals in MBFR and I do not think we need be as pessimistic as Mr. Rose in assuming that in the longer term the credibility of the Western position will 'wither on the vine'.[4]

[2] Mr. Thomson agreed with Mr. Wood. 'When talking about détente and the significance of the CSCE', he minuted on 25 April, 'we can and should refer to the inadequacy of the Soviet position in MBFR, but this is significantly different from making a direct linkage between the substantive progress in the two negotiations.' To insist on such a linkage would, he thought, be to 'risk being hoist with our petard'.

[3] 'Solely in military terms', Mr. Rose conceded in his letter of 14 April see (note 1 above), 'the Western reduction proposals may remain unacceptable at least to the Soviet military establishment, and perhaps more widely: if this is so a plus factor will be required in political terms in order to achieve an agreement on the basis of Western reduction proposals.' That 'plus factor' might, he reasoned, have previously been developed in the context of the US/Soviet bilateral relationship, but this no longer seemed the case 'given the check apparently imposed on any development of this kind by the presidential election and by the lack of progress in SALT'. He therefore wondered whether it fell to the UK to 'make MBFR a substantial issue in its relations with the Soviet Union in the run-up to Belgrade, and whether [they] should take the lead in persuading other Western participants to do the same'.

[4] 'The Soviet Union', Mr. Rose opined (see notes 1 and 3 above), 'retains a great deal of flexibility both in terms of tactics and substance which they will no doubt go on exploiting for as long as the negotiations continue. The West does not have, and cannot expect to have, flexibility of this sort. In this situation there must be a risk that over the long haul (and, given the timing of the German and American elections, we recognise that this is inevitable in any case), the credibility of the Western position will wither on the vine and with it the prospects of an agreement on the basis of the existing Western negotiating position.'

No. 31

Record of Discussion in the FCO

[*DPM 081/557/1*]

Confidential   FCO, *27 April 1976*

CSCE/MBFR

1.   The following records the main points of a discussion which took place on this subject in the FCO on 27 April.[1]

2.   *Mr. Sykes* said that in his view the Russians would be under more pressure than would we to have some progress to show in the MBFR field by the time of the Belgrade review meeting. The West are unlikely to expect much to come out of the Belgrade meeting whereas the Russians would want to create an impression of détente moving forward.[2] He was therefore inclined to be cautious about the question of directly linking CSCE and MBFR; if we overplayed this aspect of our policy, the Russians might retire into their shells in a huff and from then on simply stone wall. We should also bear in mind that public opinion in the West was perhaps more likely to concentrate on Basket III than on Basket I.[3] He was in favour of our placing considerable emphasis on the question of MBFR, but he did not think that we would get very much out of the idea of linking it with the CSCE directly.

3.   *Mr. Rose* (UKDEL Vienna) said that he understood that view. The problem for him was that we were saying that Soviet willingness to pay the price we asked on MBFR would be the acid test of its commitment to military détente (see para 16 of FCO despatch no EN 408/548/1/ of 11 March to Moscow).[4] He understood that this statement should not be taken too literally, but what did it in fact mean? In order for progress to be made on MBFR, a new stimulus was needed. There were a number of further proposals which the Russians could make in line with the MBFR framework they had been using since late 1973; we knew in advance

---

[1]   Present at this meeting were: Mr. Sykes, Mr. Rose, Mr. R.A. Hibbert (AUS), Mr. Thomson, Dr. M.J. Harte (MoD), Mr. C.R. Budd (First Secretary) and Miss A.J.K. Bailes (Second Secretary, UKDEL NATO).

[2]   But Sir H. Smith, HM Ambassador in Moscow since January 1976, doubted if the Russians felt 'particularly vulnerable' with regard to those provisions of the CSCE Final Act which were concerned with increasing confidence in the military sphere. 'There are', he reported, 'signs that they hope to keep the Belgrade Conference in a low key, but I do not believe that fear of criticism at Belgrade if there is no movement in MBFR by the end of 1976 is or is likely to be a significant factor in clearing what policies should be adopted in Vienna.' There had, he added, 'certainly been no sense of urgency, or of concern at the lack of progress, in Soviet press comment on the negotiating round which has just ended. The line has been that the ball is now in the Western court and that it is the NATO participants who are responsible for holding up progress' (letter to Mr. Thomson of 28 April).

[3]   The Basket I issues covered by the CSCE Final Act included Confidence Building Measures and certain aspects of security and disarmament. See Cmnd 6932, pp. 234–7.

[4]   See No. 87.

that none of these would satisfy us, and we therefore needed to find some stimulus which would get the Russians to depart from their present framework. Since there was no likelihood that the West would make concessions, we were left with the question of whether there was any prospect of the East making concessions on their own or of their being forced to do so. It seemed to the delegation in Vienna that the first half of 1977 would provide a historic opportunity for the West to try to encourage the Russians to adopt a more constructive approach towards MBFR: the new US administration would just have come into power, and there was the prospect of the CSCE Review meeting later in the year, at which the Russians would want to be able to ward off any criticism that they were not genuine about military détente.

4.   *Mr. Hibbert* said that he wished to emphasise that the CSCE was and had always been only one of several means to the overall end of keeping the Soviet Union under control. It had never been central to East–West relations, and it would be difficult to handle should it be made so. Only secondary things were involved in it, and it should not be elevated to any more prominent position.

5.   It was also important to remember that the West's tactics for the Review meeting would inevitably have to be determined by the political events of the coming winter and spring; it was impossible at this stage to be dogmatic about what our approach should be. All we could say was that at present the Russians were taking the line that if détente were to mean anything it had to be extended into the disarmament field. This was a proposition with which the EESD side of the Office could only agree. For propaganda purposes it suited us well to put pressure on the Russians by saying the same i.e. that détente would have little meaning unless it produced progress in the military field; without progress in the MBFR field the CSCE did not amount to very much. Such a line might well not cause the Soviet Union to make any concessions on MBFR, but it would enable us to expose to public opinion the Soviet Union's hypocrisy in the defence field, and to maintain Western defence budgets. No linkage was possible between CSCE and MBFR, and there was no mileage to be made out of any such linkage: the two were simply not on the same plane of importance. But if we could use the atmosphere surrounding the CSCE to achieve progress in the MBFR field, we should by all means do so.

6.   *Mr. Rose* said that this was all very well, but he hoped that we would be able to get Ministers to say to the Russians that where MBFR was concerned cosmetic changes in the Soviet position were really quite pointless, and that what the West needed was a substantive change which would prove the Soviet Union's good intent.

7.   *Mr. Thomson* said that he very much agreed with Mr. Hibbert on this subject. There was no direct linkage between the two topics, and no particular mileage in trying to develop one. Mr. Callaghan, when Secretary of State, had taken the line that time was now on our side in the MBFR context; but he had taken this line not exclusively or even mainly because of the imminence of the CSCE Review Meeting. He had been thinking rather of the change in the attitude of public opinion towards the subject. We needed to use the word linkage very carefully; it was partly a question of timing. We should certainly use the Soviet

proclamation of the need for military détente to press the Soviet Union to make concessions on MBFR. They might make an effort in this field because of the CSCE, but we should be very careful about instituting any linkage between the two things. We would not get anywhere by doing so, because our CSCE leverage was not strong enough for the purpose. It was arguable that we should use what leverage we possessed to press for improvements in the Basket III area. There was also the danger that in response to any demand for such linkage the Russians might come back with specious but superficially impressive MBFR proposals which would then put the West under pressure to make concessions in other fields.

8. *Dr. Harte* (Head of DS 22, MOD)[5] at this point suggested that it was quite possible that by the time of the Belgrade meeting public opinion would be more concerned about the military aspects of détente than about Basket III type questions.

9. *Mr. Budd* pointed out that in so far as it was possible to predict at this stage what would happen at the Belgrade meeting, we thought it likely that the neutrals would make a determined attempt to push the question of military détente into the foreground. EESD were anxious that there should not be any linkage between the CSCE and MBFR, because we thought it undesirable that the Belgrade meeting should in any way come to be dominated by questions of military détente; where there was linkage there was usually spill-over, and this would be better avoided. There was moreover the risk that by focusing on the question of military détente the West might appear to acquiesce in the Soviet claim that political détente had already been satisfactorily achieved.

10. *Miss Bailes*, representing UKDEL NATO, said that Sir J Killick was also of the view that there was no chance of our being able to make a convincing linkage between the two topics. There was nothing that the East wanted to get out of the Belgrade meeting which would cause them to be prepared to pay us a price in terms of MBFR. Moreover, we should remember that the CSCE involved a number of countries who were not members of NATO; there were political questions involved which went well outside the military field. Another point was that the Russians had not yet agreed that MBFR was at the centre of military détente; the latter, after all, could be said to incorporate not only SALT but also all the general Soviet initiatives such as their proposal to ban weapons of mass destruction. They would no doubt be only too happy to make great play in propaganda terms of vague but superficially impressive ideas.

11. *Mr. Rose* concluded by saying that he had in fact been thinking of a less organic linkage between the two topics. He hoped at least that there would be no question of excluding military détente completely from the line which we would take at the Belgrade meeting. Mendelevich,[6] the roving Soviet Ambassador, had recently been visiting a number of neutral capitals and had apparently been

[5] Defence Secretariat division 22 of MoD was responsible for longer term defence studies and disarmament.

[6] Mr. L.I. Mendelevich had been a leading member of the Soviet delegation to the CSCE negotiations at Geneva.

taking the line that the Russians wanted the Belgrade meeting to be a very quiet affair. It was important that we should not let them get away with this; there were weaknesses in their case which we should not be afraid to expose.

No. 32

Sir C. Rose [1] *(UKDEL Vienna) to Mr. Crosland*
[DPM 081/548/1]

Secret   VIENNA, *23 July 1976*

Summary ...[2]

Sir,

MBFR: The Ninth Round and Valedictory [3]

1. The end of the Ninth Round marks the conclusion of the third year of these negotiations. It also marks the end of my own period as Head of this Delegation.[4] In this despatch I intend first to review the events of the Round and then to add some more general reflections on the negotiations.

2. Two events dominated the Ninth Round: the tabling by the East of data on Warsaw Pact manpower levels in the reductions area; and the subsequent French intervention in the NATO Council which has made it impossible for Western negotiators to respond to the Eastern move by tabling up-to-date Western figures on NATO and Warsaw Pact manpower.

3. The figures for Warsaw Pact overall ground force manpower in the reductions area, tabled by the Head of the Soviet Delegation in Plenary Session on 10 June, revealed large discrepancies when compared with up-to-date Western assessments of Warsaw Pact manpower strengths. The East's figures of 987,300 for combined air and ground force manpower is nearly 160,000 lower than current NATO assessments and their figure of 805,000 for ground force manpower only is 144,000 lower. Although the current NATO assessments have not yet been given to the East, the latter are aware of the order of magnitude of the discrepancy from the published Western figure for Eastern ground force manpower (925,000) which was tabled in November 1973.

4. Despite these discrepancies the Eastern move has positive aspects. There can be little doubt that it came as a result of strong pressure from Western negotiators who had over a long period insisted repeatedly that substantive progress in the negotiations was not possible until the facts of the existing military

[1] Sir C. Rose received his KCMG on 12 June 1976.

[2] Not printed.

[3] The ninth round began on 19 May and ended on 21 July.

[4] In his farewell statement at the plenary session of 21 July, Sir C. Rose recalled that in his three years as UK Head of Delegation there had been 111 plenary sessions and 182 plenary statements, twelve of which he had made himself (DPM 081/4).

situation in Central Europe were known to both sides and that, without data, the negotiators could not get down to concrete discussion. Eastern negotiators in private conversation with Western colleagues have been at pains to make clear that the decision to present figures for Warsaw Pact manpower was not lightly taken and that it represented a significant victory over those elements in the Eastern hierarchies which have always regarded the MBFR negotiations with disfavour and have sought to maintain the traditional Eastern reserve about military data. They claim that it therefore constitutes a significant and encouraging sign of Eastern interest in the effective prosecution of the negotiations. I believe that there is a measure of truth in such assertions. This is, I believe, the first occasion in East–West disarmament talks on which the Soviet Union has been ready to disclose data on Warsaw Pact force levels. That the East have now done so reveals, at least, that Eastern interest in keeping alive the possibility of substantive progress is genuine.[5]

5.   On the other hand, by presenting data formally in Plenary Session, the East have put the West on notice that their figures are ones to which they are firmly attached. It is therefore not likely to be easy to persuade the East to accept substantial modifications in their data. Yet without such modifications the West will not be able to secure agreement on the asymmetrical reductions required in order to establish the common ceiling on military manpower which is the West's principal negotiating objective. It is evident that the data the East has tabled represent a further attempt to undermine the basis of the Western position (a previous attempt was the argument about Western civilian manpower, which was described in paragraphs 9 to 11 of my despatch of 13 April on the Eighth Round).[6] Eastern figures purport to show that manpower levels of NATO and the Warsaw Pact in the area of reductions are broadly equivalent. They are thus a clear rejection of the basic Allied negotiating contention that there are large disparities between the two sides, particularly in ground force manpower, and that the outcome to the negotiations must provide for their elimination or substantial reduction.

6.   Since tabling Western data on NATO and Warsaw Pact ground forces in November 1973, Western negotiators had repeatedly given assurances that when Eastern data was on the table the West would provide up-dated figures. Western negotiators therefore considered it important to respond rapidly to the Eastern statement of 10 June, which had included a request for up-dated NATO figures covering both NATO overall and ground force manpower levels in the area of reductions. In addition, my Western colleagues accepted my proposal that the West should at the same time table up-dated figures on Warsaw Pact manpower levels. This is necessary in order to substantiate quickly and in concrete terms the Western case on disparities and in order to bring the East to a serious discussion

[5] In a minute to Mr. Thomson of 4 August covering this despatch Mr. Wilberforce opined that Sir C. Rose was too sanguine in his judgement of Eastern intentions. The most he thought that could be said on this subject was that 'it would be contrary to the general Soviet interest for the MBFR negotiations to reach a deadlock for which Soviet policy would be held to blame'.

[6] See No. 29.

of the reasons for the discrepancies between Western and Eastern figures for Warsaw Pact manpower.

7. The Ad Hoc Group therefore requested the North Atlantic Council to release figures for NATO force levels in the area and indicated that Western negotiators intended at the same time to table figures for the Warsaw Pact which had been previously agreed in the Alliance. On 17 June the French representative in the NATO Political Committee at Senior Level (SPC) announced that the French wanted their forces excluded from new Western data tabled in Vienna and from the common collective ceiling on manpower. This French position has been maintained unchanged in all subsequent French interventions.

8. The full implications of the French intervention for the Western negotiating position are serious. I have sent the Department a detailed assessment of these implications, together with a paper produced jointly with my United States and Federal German colleagues on the effect on the negotiations of excluding French forces from data and from the common ceiling.[7] This paper concluded that if Western negotiators were now to take the position that, since France was not a participant in the Vienna negotiations, the effects of possible increases in the level of French forces in the reductions area could not be addressed in the negotiations, then no satisfactory MBFR agreement was likely to be negotiable. If the West is to preserve intact its concept, which has formed the basis of the agreed Alliance position since the start of the negotiations in 1973, that the outcome of negotiated reductions should be parity in military manpower in the area, then it is essential that French forces should be included both in Western data and under a common collective ceiling. As they have so far been presented, the French requirements are tantamount to a demand that the West should make a radical change in the basis on which they have negotiated over nearly three years with the full knowledge of the French, who have been present at all meetings of the North Atlantic Council and the SPC when MBFR have been discussed. The argument that Western interests can be safeguarded only by the maintenance of the existing Western negotiating position, including a common collective ceiling on all the active duty military personnel of both sides in the area of reductions, is a compelling one. Together with my United States and Federal German colleagues I have examined a number of alternative courses of action. But I am bound to say that, unless the French can be brought to accept that their interests would be adequately met by a formal Western statement to the East that since the French are not participants in the negotiations (the so-called 'disclaimer' solution), France can accept no obligations under a MBFR agreement, I see little prospect of finding a compromise which would be both satisfactory for the West and negotiable with the East. This is not only a question of whether there is any

---

[7] Sir C. Rose's assessment, in a letter to Mr. Thomson of 8 July, concluded that 'the French position has been imposed from the top, quite probably on the authority of the President himself, and regardless of what might be the implications for the rest of the Alliance', and he suggested that Dr. J.M.A.H. Luns, NATO Secretary-General, approach the French at 'the highest level'. The agreed text of the tripartite paper is contained in UKDEL Vienna telegram No. 116 of 3 July (DPM 081/1).

alternative outcome which would be militarily acceptable to the Alliance; the credibility of the Western negotiating position would be weakened by a substantive change of objective at this stage and this would seriously undermine the efforts of the Western negotiators to convince the East of the essential soundness of the Western case.

9.   Bilateral contacts with the French in capitals have, at the time of writing this despatch, revealed no sign of movement in the French position. It is accepted by the Tripartite group in Vienna that if we are to shift the French from their present ground this will take time and a good deal of well-orchestrated lobbying, the first objective of which must be to bring home to the French the precise implications of the change of course on which they are now insisting. An early priority should be to ascertain whether the French objection is based on the view that a MBFR agreement on the lines proposed by the West would seriously impair their freedom of action with respect to French forces stationed in Germany and, if so, whether some form of assurance from the Western participants might offer the best hope of a compromise which would leave the Western position undamaged.

10. Many of my colleagues are of the view that the Eastern negotiators are aware of our difficulties on this matter and have so far deliberately refrained from taking advantage of them. During the last few weeks of the Round, Eastern representatives told their Western colleagues several times in private conversations that they did not expect the West to reciprocate with up-dated figures before the end of the Round. But Eastern forebearance is not likely to be prolonged far into the next Round. Western negotiators will therefore find themselves hard pressed if they have to return to Vienna at the end of September with the French issue still unresolved. If such a state of affairs were to continue for any length of time thereafter and if, pending resolution, it were to be suggested that Western negotiators should avoid using argumentation which might be regarded as prejudicial to the French position, the West would be hard put to maintain a credible negotiating stance at all. These difficulties would be greatly exacerbated if it proved impossible to keep the French problem from the press.

11. The East have firmly declined to discuss, or answer questions on, their data until such time as the West have tabled up-to-date and reciprocal figures of their own. No progress has therefore been made on clarifying the basis on which the Eastern figures have been calculated or on the reason for the discrepancies with Western assessments. The principal subject of discussion in the Informal meetings has been the nature of the reduction commitment to be undertaken by the Western direct participants other than the United States. This is a complex subject. In brief, the East demand that, before any Soviet reductions take place, the Western European countries and Canada should provide concrete guarantees both as to the scope of their reductions and the date by which they will be completed. Thus they require these countries to undertake, in a first stage agreement, precise commitments not only on the size and nature of their reductions in the second stage but also on their timing. The West, on the other hand, continue to argue that the Western European countries and Canada will only have the confidence necessary for them to reduce their forces if the Soviet Union has first

made withdrawals of its own and there is agreement by all participants that the outcome of the negotiations should be approximate parity in ground forces. Thus the West insist that the Western European countries and Canada can give only a general commitment in the first phase to participate in second phase reductions towards a common collective ceiling in military manpower and that the precise form and timing of their reductions must be left for negotiation in the second phase. There is no sign at present of any compromise between these two positions.

12. At the end of the Ninth Round the same basic differences exist between the approaches of the two sides as were present at the end of the First. The East still maintain that the present relationship of forces in Central Europe is satisfactory because it is stable, and stable because it is the result of 'historical development'. Thus the purpose of the negotiations is to ensure that this relationship is maintained at a lower level, and it is on the method of reductions, by equal percentages designed to secure this, that the negotiators should concentrate their efforts. The West maintain that the present relationship of forces is unsatisfactory because it is characterised by a serious imbalance between the ground forces of the two sides, to the advantage of the East, and that this imbalance is the key source of instability. The negotiations should concentrate on removing this source of instability and thus on the outcome of reductions, which should be based on the principle of parity.[8]

13. There is no sign of an imminent breakthrough. Even if it were not for the French problem, the second half of 1976 would be unlikely to see any substantive movement. Any possibility of this will have to wait until the new United States Administration is in office. Thereafter, in the first half of 1977, it is not inconceivable that Belgrade might cast its shadow before and persuade the Soviet Government of the desirability of making some substantive move in Vienna towards the Western position. Such a move would be intended partly as a gesture to the new Administration and partly in the hope of diverting Western attention at the CSCE follow-up from, or meeting Western criticism of, Soviet failure to live up to their obligations in Basket III of the Helsinki Final Act.[9] But if any move of this kind were to set the scene for progress in Vienna towards a MBFR agreement, the West will at the minimum still need to find ways of meeting two basic Eastern requirements:

(*a*) for firm assurance, before any Soviet withdrawals take place, that they will

---

[8] In UKDEL Vienna telegram No. 101 of 24 June Sir. C. Rose reported that the West had continued to stress the military importance of its 16 December proposals. 'They have', he observed, 'argued that the East's 19 February proposal meets no major Western interest and cannot be regarded as a serious response, particularly since the East's answers to questions have shown that the East still expect Western participants to accept all the essential aspects of the East's reduction approach in a first agreement. The West have repeated that taking everything into account, including reductions, limitations and the Soviet geographical advantage deriving from proximity to the area of reductions, the West are offering at least as much as they are asking from the East.'

[9] The Basket III issues covered by the Helsinki Final Act of the CSCE were those relating to human contacts, the freer dissemination of information and cultural and educational cooperation. See Volume II, No. 137.

be followed by reductions by the Western European countries (especially the Federal Republic) and Canada. This is the problem of phasing;

(*b*) for some form of limitation on the rights of individual Western European countries (especially the Federal Republic) to increase their forces in order to compensate for reductions by their Allies. This concerns the nature and definition of the common collective ceiling.

If ways could be found to meet the essence of these Eastern requirements, the basic issue of parity would remain. It is here that there is least scope for movement by the West and it is therefore in this area that we must hope the East will indicate their willingness to show flexibility. If they are genuinely interested in making progress towards an agreement, it should not be impossible for them to do so. But if not, the prospects for progress in Vienna must be regarded as slight.[10]

14. These thoughts are for 1977, the year in which Chancellor Schmidt has said he believes there will be a good chance of progress in the MBFR negotiations. That we have not made such progress in the first three years should not be regarded as an indication of failure, or that time spent in Vienna so far has been wasted. When the negotiators assembled in October 1973, they had, in the communiqué of the Preparatory Talks, agreed guidance in only the most general terms on the principles and objectives of the negotiations. This is in no way to belittle the efforts of those who fought hard over five months to achieve the limited amount of agreement on substance and procedure which the communiqué represented. But I do not think they would dissent from the view that, in order to get that agreement, many problems had to be papered over or left for subsequent resolution in the negotiations. Thus each side has claimed—and has been able to do with a reasonable degree of plausibility—that its proposals are consistent with the principles agreed in the Preparatory Talks. Thus, also, the gap which nonetheless remains between the two sides. If in three years we have not succeeded in bridging this gap, we can, I suggest, chalk up a number of other successes.

15. First among these is the fact that there have been no unilateral reductions by NATO countries. The successful resistance of the United States' Administration to Congressional pressures going back as far as Reykjavik[11] has undoubtedly been assisted by first the prospect of MBFR and then by the fact that the negotiations were in progress. Other NATO countries have similarly avoided cuts, recognising the importance of not rocking the MBFR boat and strengthened by the American example. It would be rash to suggest that these pressures have

---

[10] In his minute of 4 August (see note 5 above) Mr. Wilberforce concluded: 'Barring some Soviet decision for wider political reasons, perhaps in the first half of 1977, to make a substantive move towards the Western position that would transform the prospects for the negotiation ... it is a long slog facing us in Vienna; and the data discussion that lies ahead will be an arduous instance of this.' But Mr. Hattersley was relieved to read that a 'long slog' was likely. 'I have', he noted on Mr. Wilberforce's minute, 'always feared that the Western desire for "results" would lead us to accept proposals which were not in our interest. The previous Foreign Secretary agreed that a breakdown was better than a disadvantageous conclusion. From every point of view ... a "long slog" is better than either.'

[11] See Cmnd 6932, pp. 54-5.

wholly subsided, though for the time being they appear to be less acute. Moreover there are wider factors which, especially in the case of the United States, have influenced the change of climate in the Congress. But I believe it is fair to claim that MBFR negotiations have played a part, and an important one, in helping the Alliance through what might otherwise have been a dangerous period.[12]

16. Second, we have, in the course of many hours of concentrated East–West discussion, learned a good deal about Eastern, especially Russian, attitudes, preoccupations and methods in a field in which there has hitherto been very little East–West contact. I do not suggest that we have learned any important secrets. But the East have engaged with us in a dialogue week in and week out, about military security in Central Europe. Not many of those engaged in this negotiation would have imagined, four years ago, that it would be possible to talk even with the limited degree of frankness that we have done about this sensitive subject. In the course of doing so, Eastern and Western negotiators have established—and have consciously set out to establish—a degree of personal confidence in one another which I am sure will prove of benefit if there is ever a substantive break-through enabling progress to be made with the negotiation of an agreement. Although I, and my Soviet and Canadian colleagues, all of whom have been here since the start of the negotiations, are leaving Vienna before the next Round starts, the habit is by now well enough grounded for our successors to find little difficulty in adopting it.

17. Finally, the conduct of the MBFR negotiations has benefitted the Alliance in more ways than the one described in paragraph 15. The Alliance has had to work out its position in depth and in detail, and the Western negotiators have had to support that position with arguments and explanations which they can defend against critical examination and questioning by the East. This has involved the whole Alliance, the political as well as the military bodies, in a rigorous assessment of priorities and scrutiny of assumptions. Greater attention has had to be paid to the preparation of accurate and up-to-date assessments of the size and nature of the threat, and, if this has resulted in the refinement of some intelligence procedures, this is an added bonus. Most important, however, is the example the negotiations have given of the Alliance in action. In this respect they are unique. Never before has the Alliance—at least the greater part of it—embarked on a multilateral negotiation with the East on any subject let alone on one which goes to the heart of the Alliance's purpose. The degree of cohesion maintained among

---

[12] In his letter of 28 April (see No. 31, note 2) Sir H. Smith had argued that this hardening of American attitudes towards *détente* policy in general might even assist the MBFR process. 'It is not inconceivable', he observed, 'that the threat of a continuing tough US line on questions outside the armaments field, eg trade and technological cooperation, would incline the Russians to take a more accommodating position on MBFR where, after all, they can make concessions without weakening their military position at all dangerously. But it seems more likely that Soviet concern about growing American military strength could be used by the Americans to persuade them that it is in their interest to be a bit more cooperative over MBFR and SALT. They certainly have shown some concern about the size of the US defence budget for 1977, with the prospect of an increase in US armed forces personnel as well as new weapons systems and they probably see their earlier hopes of Mansfield type unilateral reductions fading' (DPM 081/557/1).

the negotiators in Vienna has been remarkable. It has been a heartening experience to participate in achieving this through the proceedings of the Ad Hoc Group and I share the view, expressed to me by several of my colleagues, that this achievement makes (because it is continuing) a valuable contribution to the strengthening of the Alliance as a whole. There is no doubt, too, that the solidarity of the Alliance position and of the Western negotiators—whether direct participants or flanks—in defending it has impressed the East. Any idea they may have had that democracy meant disunity has been a little shaken; some of the East Europeans have even privately expressed their envy not so much of Western solidarity (the East have this too) but of the process by which it is achieved.[13]

18. I leave Vienna with a natural regret that we have not yet succeeded in concluding even a first agreement. I am well aware that the decisions which will be required if progress is to be made will not be taken here. But I believe that much valuable groundwork has been done in Vienna, so that, if the moment comes, the experience gained in the past three years will be able to be used to good effect. I cannot end without recording my appreciation of the loyalty and support I have received throughout my time here from my Delegation. I do not intend to single out anyone for special mention because the tribute is deserved by all members, both past and present and at all levels. They have worked together as a splendid team in circumstance where a team was needed, and it is this factor above all which has ensured that the Delegation has made a contribution to the handling of the Western position which, I think it is fair to claim, has been second only to that of the United States.

19. I attach as Annex A to this despatch a Calendar of Events in the Ninth Round.[14]

20. I am sending copies of this despatch to HM Representative at Washington, Bonn, Paris, Moscow, Ottawa, Brussels, The Hague, Rome, Luxembourg, Copenhagen, Oslo, Ankara, Athens, Lisbon, Vienna, East Berlin, Warsaw, Prague, Bucharest, Budapest, Sofia, Belgrade, Stockholm and Peking; to the United Kingdom Permanent Representative to the North Atlantic Council and to the Head of the United Kingdom Delegation to the Conference of the Committee on Disarmament in Geneva.

I have the honour to be Sir
Your Obedient Servant
CLIVE M. ROSE

[13] 'I agree with most of Sir C Rose's general reflections (para 12 onwards)', minuted Mr. Wilberforce (see notes 5 and 10 above), 'which are fairly orthodox in his analysis of the lack of progress, and of the degree of consolation which may still be felt. In particular, I would endorse what he says in para 17 about the "heartening experience" of the work of the Ad Hoc Group of the Allied Delegations in Vienna. The thoroughness with which they prepare themselves for their encounters with the Warsaw Pact Delegations, and the degree of unity which they have maintained (despite some European concern, latent at present, about American over-eagerness), make a strong impression on the visitor—and I think Sir C Rose is right to claim, on the Warsaw Pact Delegations too!'

[14] Not printed.

No. 33

Minute from Mr. Wood to Mr. E. Bolland[1]
[DPM 081/6]

Confidential   FCO, *6 September 1976*

MBFR: Western Objectives

1.   You said you would find it helpful to have a brief summary of our essential objectives in MBFR.

2.   First it is necessary to distinguish between two sets of aims which might be broadly characterised as 'military' and 'political'. The latter are concerned with wider issues such as our relationship with the East and the interest of both sides in maintaining the negotiations as an element in the East/West dialogue and in the general process of détente. These factors provide a backcloth to the negotiations and may at times affect their course. But for the Allied negotiators in Vienna the principal task is to secure an agreement which, while politically acceptable, also satisfies certain military criteria.

3.   These military criteria are set out in CM(73)83[2] and have been further elaborated in subsequent guidance to the Ad Hoc Group. The key points could be summarised as follows:

(*a*) It is the military judgement of the Alliance that Western reductions in MBFR should not exceed 10% of the total ground force manpower. This on present estimates is 791,000 and reductions should not therefore exceed 79,000.
(*b*) The West is prepared to undertake these reductions only in return for disproportionately greater reductions by the East which take account of the Warsaw Pact's combat capability and geographical advantages.
(*c*) The West cannot quantify precisely the reductions to be taken by the East (this depends on whatever understanding is eventually reached on the size of the disparities) but has proposed asymmetrical reductions of ground force manpower in two phases culminating in a common ceiling which (on the basis of 1973 NATO estimates) might be set at around the 700,000 level.
(*d*) The West is concerned primarily with the Warsaw Pact's preponderance in ground force manpower and main battle tanks and, in particular, with *Soviet forces* which constitute 50% of Eastern forces in the reductions area. The Allies are not prepared to agree to reductions expressed simply in terms of manpower. To do so would be to invite the Soviet Union to take reductions of 'tail' rather than 'teeth' forces, thus leaving their combat formations intact. That is why the West's Phase I proposals call specifically for the withdrawal of a five division Soviet tank army including 68,000 men and 1,700 main battle tanks. Our Phase II proposals have yet to be elaborated but are unlikely to include further specific proposals for reductions by units.

[1] Mr. Bolland was HM Ambassador in Sofia during 1973–76. In September he succeeded Sir C. Rose as UK Head of Delegation to the MBFR talks in Vienna.
[2] See No. 9, note 8.

4. Let us now consider what these proposals would mean in practice, in terms both of reductions and of constraints:

(a) Phase I

Soviet Union Soviet withdrawal of 68,000 men in the form of a five division tank army and 1,700 tanks. These would represent a 15% reduction of Soviet manpower and impose permanent ceilings on residual levels of both Soviet ground force manpower and of main battle tanks. These ceilings could be further adjusted downwards if there were further withdrawals of Soviet manpower and/or equipment in the second phase.

US A withdrawal of 29,000 men (equivalent to 15% of total US ground manpower) some of whom might be taken in formed units (though this would not be specified in the agreement and there would be no specific constraints on units). The ceiling on residual US ground manpower, like the Soviet one, would endure throughout the agreement. Additionally, in accordance with the West's nuclear proposals of last December, there would be specific reductions of, and constraints upon, residual levels of, US F4 aircraft, Pershing SSMs[3] and nuclear warheads, (though limitations on the latter would in practice be unverifiable).

(b) Between the Phases

The West has also proposed, in the event of a satisfactory Phase I agreement, provisions to cover the interval between Phase I and the conclusion of Phase II. These would include a no-increase commitment by both sides to ensure that US and Soviet ground force withdrawals in Phase I were not circumvented by, for example, increases in the ground forces of non-US Allies or non-Soviet Warsaw Pact countries. There would thus be a 'freeze' on each side's ground force manpower between the Phases within which there would be the subceilings on Soviet and US manpower, together with constraints on specific equipment (see (a) above).

(c) Phase II

Further reductions by both sides down to the common ceiling. In the Western case these would be taken mainly by the European participants and presumably the Soviet Union would also prefer further reductions to be taken by NSWP rather than by Soviet forces. How many forces the East would in fact reduce in Phase II in return for the reductions which the West would wish to take depends crucially on whatever understanding is reached between the two sides on the size of the manpower disparities. On our estimates the East should reduce by some 150,000 men of which 68,000 would be accounted for by the Soviet tanks army in Phase I.

(d) Post Phase II

The Western proposals of last December also included the idea that each side's air manpower (roughly in balance at around 200,000) be incorporated in a combined ground/air common collective ceiling. This would therefore be set at around the 900,000 level, within which there would be a common ceiling

[3] Surface to surface missiles.

on ground forces at around 700,000. There would also be subceilings on US and Soviet ground forces and on those items of their equipment (Soviet tanks, US nuclear weapons) specified in Phase I. The West also envisages certain 'exceptions' to the manpower ceilings to accommodate major exercises, force rotations etc. and possibly a margin of flexibility between ground and air. In practice the overall ceiling level might be 900,000 plus or minus 50,000, with some permitted margin to enable each side to vary the ratio of ground to air within that overall ceiling.

(e) Verification
The East has so far refused to discuss this or any other type of 'associated' measure. It may be assumed that both sides would agree to non-interference with national technical means (i.e. satellites) though this would not by itself be sufficient for effective monitoring of manpower levels. Mobile inspection teams are unlikely to be acceptable to the East and, because of German objections,[4] the West are in any case unlikely to propose them. But a small number of static check points on each side might be installed for the purpose of monitoring actual withdrawals/reductions. For the West the main task of any verification arrangements will be to monitor Soviet compliance, and our requirements might be met if we could be reasonably sure that Soviet tanks were not reintroduced and that there was no major build-up of Soviet forces in the NGA.[5]

T.C. WOOD

[4] A paper attached to a minute from Mr. Wood to Mr. R. Westbrook (Private Secretary to Dr. D. Owen (Minister of State)) of 26 November explained that the Germans had 'made clear in the Alliance their strong opposition to the idea of mobile inspection teams which would give Warsaw Pact inspectors access to German territory and installations'.

[5] Non-Guidelines Area (i.e. territory not covered by the geographical remit of the negotiations).

No. 34

Letter from Mr. Bolland (UKDEL Vienna) to Mr. P.H. Moberly[1]
[DPM 081/6]

Confidential   VIENNA, *3 November 1976*

Dear Pat,

Mutual and Balanced Force Reductions

1.   We are approaching the half-way stage of the present Round.[2] I am, like you, new to these negotiations and (most ably assisted by my staff) still feeling my

[1] In October Mr. Patrick Moberly succeeded Mr. Thomson as AUS superintending Defence Department.

[2] The tenth round began on 30 September.

way. But the time has, I think, come for me to ask: where do we stand now? Is there any action we should be taking to advance our interests in these talks?

2.   Perhaps first we should ask ourselves precisely what are Britain's interests in the MBFR talks. Unlike my predecessor, I have not grown up with the talks and cannot, therefore, like him have an instinctive feel for the direction we should take. And Clive Rose himself, just before leaving Vienna, suggested we needed to up-date the original Steering Brief of 1973[3] to take account of developments since then. Since that time, there have been changes in the negotiating situation, some of which have amounted to substantial revisions in the Western position on which the 1973 Brief was based. My predecessor also had the cumulative benefit of a series of consultations in London in the intervals between Rounds providing him with continuing guidance. It would certainly be helpful to me and to the Delegation if, at a convenient moment, a fresh look could be taken at our position as a whole as it has now developed so as to provide us with a clear indication of what HMG is currently trying to achieve in these talks.

3.   I am of course already fully aware of the notorious complexity of the talks and of the procedures which collective action as an Alliance imposes upon Governments and negotiators. This complexity is due not only to the nature of the talks themselves and the important defence issues involved, but also to the fact that all participants in Vienna negotiate as members of an Alliance whose collective instructions must pass through the mill of the NATO machinery in Brussels. In addition there are extraneous factors such as, for example, the French intervention on data and the common ceiling. None of these factors should, however, prevent us from having a clear view of what attitude HMG should take towards these talks and of the objectives we are seeking to achieve.

4.   As I see it—and expressed in the simplest terms—British interests will be served if we continue to work for an MBFR agreement which brings about a substantial reduction in the vast Warsaw Pact preponderance of ground forces in Central Europe: only in the context of such reductions in Warsaw Pact superiority will NATO be able to reduce its forces in the area without endangering Western, and therefore British, security. On this essential objective I am assured there is no difference of view within the Alliance.

5.   For the past three years the Alliance has been able to sustain its case in Vienna based on a premise which is both simple and unequivocal: that the Warsaw Pact maintain in the Eastern part of the reductions area a vastly superior number of ground forces, particularly men and tanks. By tabling figures for the ground forces of both NATO and the Warsaw Pact at the outset of the negotiations, the Alliance was able clearly to demonstrate this aspect of the military realities in Central Europe. The package of reduction proposals which the Alliance developed since October 1973 flowed logically from this premise. The Western case it seems to me, has been coherent in negotiating terms and should have been readily comprehensible to public and parliamentary opinion. We have said that the military situation in Central Europe is characterised by instability, arising from the important Eastern superiorities which we have demonstrated;

[3] See No. 9.

that if the MBFR negotiations are to create a situation of greater stability, it follows that there must be a reduction in Eastern ground force superiorities; and that the only satisfactory outcome is therefore one of approximate parity in the ground forces of the two sides in the reductions area.

6.   This presentation of the Western position, which I have described, has proved remarkably resilient. It has stood up well to constant attack by the East over three years of negotiations. Furthermore, the self-evident equity of the outcome which the West proposes has, as far as I know, meant that public and parliamentary opinion in Western countries has never seriously challenged the objectives which Western Governments have set themselves. Dr Kissinger's description of the common collective ceiling as the 'iron pole' of the Western position is singularly apt.

7.   For the first time since these negotiations began Allied negotiators now, however, find themselves unable to sustain their case with the authority which they have displayed so far. By preventing the West from tabling up-dated data, the French intervention on the inclusion of its forces in data and the common ceiling has meant that the Allies are not able at present clearly to demonstrate the premise on which their case is built: the existing disparities between Eastern and Western ground forces. This, in my view, is a measure of the seriousness of our inability to secure NATO's authority for the West to table data as it requested over four months ago. For, in order to put forward and to sustain our case, we must use numbers. Over more than two years we urged the East to stop talking about concepts and instead to produce their own data and to discuss and compare them with us. Because the East have refused to engage in any discussion on the data which they tabled on 10 June until after we have tabled our own, we find ourselves in the position of having finally drawn the East on to our negotiating ground and then of being unable to exploit this new situation as we had intended. Furthermore, Eastern negotiators told us last week that until we have put down our own data we should refrain from making unsubstantiated claims about the disparities. Of course, such an assertion will in no way prevent us from restating our case, but it will certainly sound increasingly hollow to Eastern representatives and the longer we wait to table data the easier it will be for the East to push us on to the defensive and to attack the premise on which the whole edifice of the Western reduction programme is constructed.[4]

8.   I am here, of course, expressing the point of view of a Vienna negotiator. I fully realise the complications caused by the French attitude and the problems to be faced in extricating ourselves from this position.[5] But if we are to maintain

[4] In a letter to Mr. Bolland of 19 November Mr. Moberly confessed to sharing his anxieties about the damage which continuing prevarication over the tabling of new data was likely to do to the Western position in general and to their case on disparities in particular.

[5] During tripartite consultations with the Americans and West Germans, following the end of the ninth round, the British suggested that it might be possible to devise an interim tactical solution to the data problem by tabling figures representing only the forces of direct Western participants and leaving the issue of French force numbers to be settled in the longer term. But the West Germans insisted that it should first be made clear to the French that this did not imply any change in the Allies' common ceiling objective, and disagreement over how this message might be conveyed

the united, coherent and logical case which the West has presented throughout the negotiations we must, I and others here think, be authorised to present our data soon. Whatever doubts we may have about the likelihood that a data discussion will bring early and substantive progress in the negotiations, only the tabling of up-dated Western data for NATO and the Warsaw Pact can re-establish unequivocally the premise which provides us with the rationale for our whole reduction approach (see my telegram no. 153).[6]

9. I am of course very much aware that it has been recognised in London that, in these negotiations, we are in for a long haul. There are, I agree, sound reasons for taking this view (e.g. the wide and substantial gap between the basic position of East and West, the grave risks to Western security which are likely to be involved in accepting compromises, and the very complexity of the problems we face) but I do not think that any of these factors constitute sound reasons for not engaging the East as soon as possible in detailed discussion on data, which is, after all, ground of our own choosing.

10. First, although as I have suggested above I do not think that such discussions are likely to result in rapid and substantial progress, we would, through a data discussion, be able to probe more deeply Eastern intentions in these talks.

11. Second, even the most optimistic must be on guard against getting into a stalemate, responsibility for which could be made convincingly to appear to be ours and not the East's. A failure to produce revised data would provide the East with an excellent weapon should this situation arise.

12. Third, we must also take into account the fact that, with Belgrade looming on the near horizon and with the East looking for distractions and scapegoats to conceal or excuse their failure to measure up to the Final Act, it is clearly not in our interest to allow Moscow to use our alleged conduct of the MBFR talks to secure these ends.

13. Another factor affecting timing is Brezhnev's proposed meetings in the New Year with Chancellor Schmidt, President Giscard and possibly other Western leaders. Brezhnev has referred twice recently, in the context of the MBFR talks, to meetings at the highest level. It is clearly in the Western interest that we should be in a good negotiating posture in Vienna before this round of summit talks takes place.

to the French delayed further action at Vienna. Finally, on 25 November, the Belgians explained the Allied position to the French Government (see No. 35), and on 16 December Western delegates presented the East with data on totals of Western direct participants' ground force and combined ground and air force personnel in the reductions area as of 1 January 1976 (see No. 33, note 4).

[6] In this telegram of 22 October, Mr. Bolland suggested that if the Western delegations tabled their own figures of allied numbers without challenging the Eastern estimates of their own forces, the effect would be, after the French figure of 60,000 men had been taken into account, 'to show an overall disparity between the West's Blue data and the East's Red data of only 7,300 men (i.e. 980,000 and 987,300 respectively). Western negotiators would be able, of course, to say that they do not agree with the Eastern figures, but the fact would remain that in this situation, the East would extract considerable advantage, both in negotiating and propaganda terms, from renewed emphasis on their contention that revised Western figures demonstrate precisely what the East has always maintained: namely that there is no significant disparity and that Western demands for asymmetrical reductions are totally inequitable' (DPM 081/1).

14. There is another new issue which Western negotiators have had to consider this Round, viz. the implications of what we have called the 'Tarasov formula'. Its latest expression was given by Tarasov[7] when, in concluding his Plenary statement of 21 October, he said:

'It is necessary to concretise the negotiations to the maximum which is to say in one way or another to strengthen those provisions on which we have succeeded in reaching general understanding and to define precisely those questions where it is necessary to seek compromise solutions. This is fully attainable if like us the Western Delegations will be guided by the principles of genuine mutuality and by the other principles concerning the reduction of forces which were agreed in the preparatory consultations.'

The Ad Hoc Group has taken the view that we should not be drawn into negotiating on this Eastern terrain since an exercise of this kind might:

(*a*) compromise the West's basic positions; and
(*b*) afford tactical negotiating advantages to the East rather than the West.

The US Delegation, which seems less inclined than others to see the risks in such an exercise and indeed appears to think that it might be turned to the West's tactical advantage, are prepared to discuss the 'Tarasov formula' with Western participants and have circulated a draft paper, in the first instance only to the Germans and ourselves (copy attached to Gillmore's[8] letter of 21 October to Wood).[9] My present view is that the Ad Hoc Group's collective reaction was right: indeed, I argued strongly in favour of it.[10] At the same time, we must be careful not to reject out of hand an offer which seems reasonable, especially after three years of talks. It seems likely that, whatever our reaction the East will continue to pursue this line, either optimistically as a negotiating tactic or perhaps more

---

[7] Mr. N.K. Tarasov was Mr. Khlestov's successor as Soviet Head of Delegation.

[8] Mr. D.H. Gillmore was Counsellor and Head of Chancery to UKDEL Vienna.

[9] The US paper of 15 October comprised a draft list of areas of agreement and disagreement between the two sides. But in his letter of 21 October Mr. Gillmore remained 'extremely cautious', arguing that he could not 'see any advantage to be gained from allowing the East to take the initiative now in breaking up into separate components the package which the West is proposing and to select from it only those items which serve their purposes' (DPM 081/309/2).

[10] Mr. Moberly agreed. In his letter of 19 November (see note 4 above) he wrote that he too saw 'distinct risks' in the West allowing itself to be drawn into this sort of exercise. He also hoped that the Americans could be dissuaded from going further if there were a need to respond to more moves by the East on the lines of the Tarasov formula. 'As you know', he added, 'we have always considered that to accede to Eastern requests to conclude "partial agreements" *viz* agreements on individual aspects of MBFR, would make it impossible for us to secure our fundamental objectives. It is far more prudent to try and advance the negotiations as far as we can across the whole spectrum (several segments of which are still virgin territory since the East have refused to discuss them), withholding commitments to any part until we are in a position to see the shape of the package as a whole.'

realistically for its propaganda value, especially with Belgrade in mind. Whatever Eastern motives may be, Western negotiators need to be clear on whether there has been sufficient progress on the substance of the negotiations to justify the kind of exercise Tarasov has proposed or whether Western interests would not be better served by declining to be drawn into it until the East has come forward with moves of real substance. On balance, I still think that such an exercise is not justified by the moves the East have so far taken to meet our basic requirements. But we are continuing to study this question, partly to be able to comment on the US Delegation's paper should they return to this subject.

15. In much of what I have written there is an important publicity aspect. It is a British interest to establish that we should not be held responsible in the public mind, especially in a Britain faced with serious economic difficulties, for any failure of these talks. Equally, if the talks eventually succeed, we need to be able to show that we have played an appropriate and hence significant role in achieving this outcome. To these ends, I suggest that it would be helpful if anything said by Ministers could let it be known we are working with our Allies for a successful conclusion to these talks and that delays in reaching this outcome are entirely the responsibility of the East. It would, however, obviously be counterproductive for us to say much if anything in public on MBFR until we have been able to present our up-to-date data. And, even then, we would need to consider carefully the implications any public statements by Ministers might have on the negotiations here.[11]

16. These are the main thoughts which occur to me half-way through my first Round. I would welcome any reactions from you and other recipients of this letter.

Yours ever,
EDWIN BOLLAND

[11] Mr. Wood doubted if HMG's 'public relations posture on MBFR' was quite as shaky as Mr. Bolland suggested. He minuted Mr. Moberly on 18 November that he did not imagine that a breakdown of negotiations 'would create a public uproar in the West (except perhaps in the Netherlands)'. In his letter of 19 November (see notes 4 and 10 above) Mr. Moberly observed: 'I agree that we have to bear in mind the general public relations posture of the West and I am sure this will become even more important as the Belgrade Review Conference draws nearer. At present, however, publicity does not seem to pose much of a problem for us here. There continues to be little active interest on the part of Parliament and of the press in MBFR generally and none whatsoever in the day-to-day problems encountered in Vienna … For the record, our usual briefing for public statements by Ministers continues to put the blame for the lack of progress firmly upon the Warsaw Pact. In this our greatest asset is, of course, the common ceiling concept which is readily comprehensible and a far more effective selling point than any feature of the East's approach.'

No. 35

Mr. Bolland (UKDEL Vienna) to Mr. Crosland
[DPM 081/548/1]

Secret   VIENNA, *21 December 1976*

Summary ...[1]

Sir,

MBFR: The Tenth Round

1. No substantial progress was made in the Tenth Round which ended here on 16 December. All participating delegations agree that East and West marked time. The hopes expressed to me in the Department before I came to Vienna in September that the talks were about to enter an active negotiating phase did not, unfortunately, materialise.[2]

2. The reasons for this lack of progress were twofold. Firstly, neither side offered to change its basic proposals, put forward in their up-dated form by the West on 16 December 1975 and by the East on 19 February 1976. Each side insisted that it continued to await from the other a serious and positive response to its proposals. Secondly, the discussion of data and definitions foreshadowed by the East's tabling of their figures for Warsaw Pact forces on 10 June, could not get under way because the East would not enter into such a discussion until we had tabled our up-to-date figures. We were not able to do this until the very last day of the Round, 16 December, because of difficulties with the French.[3] Even then, the compromise agreed with France was far from satisfactory: they refused to allow us to include in Western totals the number of French forces in the Federal Republic and continued to insist that their forces should also be excluded from the common manpower ceilings. The latter obstacle, unless removed or circumvented in some way, will cause us great difficulties as the talks continue.

3. On balance, the West rather than the East was on the defensive during this Round. Although our basic positions remained sound, we were not able, without our data, to engage the East in a discussion on our ground *viz*. the East's large superiorities in Central Europe particularly in soldiers and tanks. On the other hand the East could insist that, by failing to table our figures, we were holding up the talks and that, meanwhile, we should not refer to the 'fictitious' Eastern numerical superiorities, the existence of which we could not sustain. The East were able, therefore, to call for movement whilst making no moves themselves. No doubt this suited their book as they awaited the results of the elections in the United States and the Federal Republic and for possible signals

---

[1] Not printed.

[2] In a covering minute to Mr. Moberly of 13 January 1977, Mr. Wilberforce observed Mr. Bolland's despatch was 'rather on the pessimistic side—and not unnaturally since his first round in the negotiations happened to be one of the least rewarding since they began'.

[3] See No. 34, note 5.

of changes in the West's negotiating position. Recent public statements by Chancellor Schmidt and Herr Brandt that the MBFR talks should be removed from the 'web of experts' and given some higher political impulse certainly encouraged Eastern negotiators to believe that the West might offer concessions in 1977.[4] The East were thus able to sit tight and wait.

4. In the absence of any major move until we presented our data on 16 December, both sides spent this Round restating and elaborating their respective positions. This was not altogether time wasted as we were able to clarify our understanding of each other's points of view and the positions to which each attached most importance.

5. The West concentrated above all in this Round on distinguishing between the *outcome* of our negotiations and the *reductions* leading to it, stressing the greater importance of the former. We argued, I think effectively, that our major concern must be the outcome to an agreement, i.e. the military relationship between the two sides when agreed reductions and force limitations had taken effect, which would constitute the new security situation in Central Europe in which East and West would have to live. We emphasised that the Allies would settle for nothing less than an outcome of approximate parity with the East in manpower and that we were not prepared to contractualise in an agreement the large numerical superiorities at present enjoyed by the East, not only in manpower, but also in nearly all major armaments. None of the modifications made to the East's positions since the negotiations began had brought, we noted, any substantive change to the outcome which the East asked us to accept. This was in sharp contrast to our proposals of 16 December 1975 which, by including certain United States nuclear armaments and Western air force personnel, offered a substantial compromise to the East.

6. For their part, Eastern negotiators emphatically reiterated their determination not to accept greater reductions by the East than by the West. They developed the contention, stated authoritatively by Brezhnev at the Conference of European Communist Parties on 29 June, that, in spite of certain differences in military profiles, there already existed a more or less identical level between Eastern and Western armed forced in Central Europe. They, therefore, rejected the Western case for asymmetrical reductions and insisted on their method of reduction by equal percentages.

7. More specifically, they firmly rejected our call for the withdrawal in Phase 1 of a tank army of five divisions. This would make, they said, an unacceptable breach in their defences. Second, they called for across-the-board reductions in armaments, focussing particularly on aircraft and nuclear weapons. On the latter, they argued strongly that the Western offer to reduce and limit United States nuclear armaments would be of little military significance if it could be circumvented by, e.g. nuclear armaments of other Western participants, including Britain. Third, they called for 'contractual guarantees' in Phase 1 for specific reductions in Phase 2 by all direct participants other than the United States and

[4] See No. 36, note 11.

the Soviet Union. These reductions must be carried out within a specified period. The East rejected our argument that Western countries other than the United States were not prepared to take final decisions on these questions until a substantial move towards approximate parity in ground forces had been made through United States and Soviet reductions. The East replied that, until all the Western direct participants had given clear and binding assurances that they would reduce in Phase 2, the Soviet Union could not be expected to withdraw a single soldier in Phase 1. Here, as in the continued Eastern insistence on national rather than collective ceilings, Eastern eyes remained riveted on the Bundeswehr and its future role in West European defence.

8. So, the Tenth Round came to an end, with each side having restated in Plenary and Informal sessions its position, repetitively and exhaustively. Faced with this continuing stalemate, what are the chances of forward movement in the next Round? There are some, but they are, I think, slim.[5]

9. The tactical accommodation we have reached with the French, enabling us to present figures of Western manpower, means that we should be able to discuss Eastern and Western data when we reconvene in February. An encouraging sign is that, although obviously aware of our problems with the French during this Round, the East did not choose to exploit them. So, if the assurances given by Eastern representatives that they are now ready to discuss the 'counting rules' which each side has used in the calculation of its figures turn out to be genuine, the negotiations could be brought on to solid ground of the West's choosing. The United States Delegation is hopeful that, by patient and detailed questioning of Eastern counting rules, it will be possible to prove that certain categories of Warsaw Pact military personnel have been omitted from the Eastern figures and that, consequently, they are incomplete. There must, however, be serious doubts whether the East will allow a discussion of actual figures to undermine their basic premise that, in broad terms, parity of force levels already exists in Central Europe. The 'impromptu' remark made by Tarasov, the Head of the Soviet Delegation at the final Plenary session of the Round, that the proposed data study would enable the negotiators to remove such distractions as 'so-called disparities and asymmetrical reductions', strongly reinforces these doubts. Even the Americans think it unlikely that in a discussion of data the West will be able to demonstrate conclusively that the disparities on which so much of the Western case is built are as large as we assess them to be. But a start on a discussion of the existing military facts could strengthen our position in the negotiations.

10. There have also been recent hints that the East might be ready to make

[5] In his covering minute (see note 2 above) Mr. Wilberforce observed: 'While sharing Mr Bolland's scepticism that the Warsaw Pact countries will be prepared to admit that they do in fact outnumber NATO in the reductions area it is, I think, quite possible for our negotiators to succeed in driving the Russians into an awkward corner on this, in the same way as we did in the first round last year over the related issue of "force definitions". These tactical battles in Vienna will not in themselves determine the eventual outcome of the negotiations. But unless our negotiators go on winning them, our general political leverage for getting the Russians to move towards our position will be diminished.'

moves next year towards reaching a first agreement, if only for propaganda reasons. Following up the repeated Soviet statements that political *détente* in Europe must now be supplemented by military *détente*, Brezhnev made this call more specific on one or two occasions during the last few months when he expressed his willingness to discuss force reductions in Central Europe with Western leaders at the highest level. At the beginning of this Round and sub-sequently, Tarasov suggested that we should draw up a balance sheet, identifying those points on which the two sides had approached an understanding and those on which compromise should be sought. In his final Plenary speech, Tarasov said:

> 'already in the next Round we should be able to achieve substantial progress in the matter of an agreed draft agreement covering the first stage of reductions.'

He called also, as the East have done repeatedly during the Round, for an agreement in the next Round to 'freeze' our forces in Central Europe for the duration of the negotiations. These statements seem, however, to have more propaganda than negotiating content and could be intended mainly as part of the current Soviet disarmament campaign designed probably to distract attention from Eastern failures to live up to the CSCE Final Act which are clearly worrying the Communist leaders as the Belgrade review conference approaches. Certainly, the East have given no indication in the negotiations this Round that they are prepared to make a substantial move which would make an agreement possible, even for the first Phase. Their basic rigidity renders completely nugatory Tarasov's suggestion that the time had come to begin to draw up the bases of an agreement.

11. Regrettably, therefore, I must conclude, that there is at present little hope of early progress on the central issues of MBFR. The East seem most unlikely to offer substantial concessions in the near future. The West have little room for manoeuvre within the existing guidelines established by the North Atlantic Council.[6] There remains, in fact, a deep divide between the two sides firmly entrenched in their opposed positions.

12. For the Western negotiators, our most important task in the next Round will be to try to draw the East into a discussion of the facts of military manpower in Central Europe. This discussion will provide a serious test of the East's willingness to acknowledge the real military situation on which an acceptable agreement must be based. Should the East show that they are prepared to work with us to establish an objective and agreed data base for military manpower reductions, we could then look forward to a purposeful summer Round.

13. Meanwhile, there would I think be advantage in considering now, as a UK-Eyes Only exercise, what modifications, if any, we could make to Western positions to meet further legitimate Eastern concerns without prejudicing Western security. After three years of negotiations, such a study should ensure

---

[6] Mr. Wood noted that this assertion betrayed 'a fundamental misunderstanding of Allied procedures' (minute to Mr. Wilberforce of 12 January 1977).

that any possibilities there may be of further advance have not been overlooked.[7] Furthermore, we must have in mind early next year that the new United States Administration, and perhaps the Germans too, will be reviewing the course of the MBFR negotiations and possibly suggesting some new moves.[8] It would be useful also to have completed such a study before the East, as they may well do next year, put forward further, superficially attractive 'initiatives' allegedly to achieve an early agreement in the Vienna talks. This study could cover, *inter alia*, the two issues, of phasing and a variation of the collective ceiling, towards which my predecessor suggested in his despatch of 23 July[9] the West might one day have to adopt a more flexible attitude; and perhaps also it could consider whether we should support any possible United States proposal to take a fresh look at the question of withdrawing their soldiers in Phase 1 in complete units rather than as individuals.

14. However, until the East have shown their willingness to negotiate on the basis of the realities of the present military situation in Europe, we should not, I submit, even hint, either in our tripartite discussions with the Americans and Germans or in the Alliance as a whole, that any modifications in the Western positions should be considered. The West's overriding concern in Vienna during the next Round will be, I suggest, to make clear to the East that progress will be possible only when Eastern negotiators are prepared to accept these realities.

15. I enclose as Annex A to this despatch a Calendar of Events during the Tenth Round.[10]

16. I am sending copies of this despatch to Her Majesty's Representatives at Washington, Bonn, Paris, Moscow, Ottawa, Brussels, The Hague, Rome, Luxembourg, Copenhagen, Oslo, Ankara, Athens, Lisbon, Vienna, East Berlin, Warsaw, Prague, Bucharest, Budapest, Sofia, Belgrade, Stockholm and Peking; to the United Kingdom Permanent Representative to the North Atlantic Council; and to the Head of the United Kingdom Delegation to the Conference of the Committee on Disarmament in Geneva.

> I have the honour to be Sir
> Your obedient Servant
> EDWIN BOLLAND

---

[7] According to Mr. Wood, the MoD, who were provided with advance copies of this despatch, were 'particularly worried by Mr Bolland's implication that there [were] real ways of modifying the Western position which, without detriment to [Western] security, would meet some of the East's "legitimate" concerns, and that if only Brussels and capitals would approve these modifications the prospect of a successful outcome to MBFR would be enhanced' (*v. ibid.*).

[8] Mr. Wilberforce thought it very unlikely that any review would result in the Americans proposing that NATO should follow an entirely different tack in MBFR, given the overriding importance which the new administration would surely attach to the requirements of Allied 'military security and political solidarity' which had so far dictated the principal features of the West's negotiating position (see notes 2 and 5 above).

[9] See No. 32.

[10] Not printed.

No. 36

Letter from Mr. Moberly to Mr. Bullard (Bonn)[1]

[*DPM 081/6*]

Confidential   FCO, *22 December 1976*

Dear Julian,

MBFR

1.   Thank you for your letter of 10 November.[2] You will have seen from my reply of 19 November to Eddie Bolland that we intend to start work in the New Year on a longer term assessment of MBFR in which we shall need to address ourselves, *inter alia*, to the fundamental questions which you raise. The Department has also been asked by Dr Owen to prepare for him two study papers (Terence Wood's letter of 7 December to David Gillmore) one of which will be an attempt to look at the negotiations through Soviet eyes in the sense suggested by paragraph 7 of your letter.[3] A key element in this process of reappraisal will undoubtedly be the position of the Germans and, more importantly, any forecast which we are able to make, with your assistance, of likely developments in German thinking in 1977/78.

2.   The view of MBFR as three negotiations rather than one seems to me still to hold good, provided we bear in mind that these three exercises are interlocked.[4] Perhaps it would be more accurate to describe MBFR as a three-dimensional undertaking or even, post-Helsinki, four-dimensional, to take account of the fact that, whether we like it or not, MBFR has emerged as a prominent feature in the détente panorama and, with the approach of the Belgrade Review Conference, is increasingly regarded in the West as one of the means of testing the genuineness

---

[1]   British Minister in Bonn since June 1975.

[2]   In this letter Mr. Bullard commented on the contents of No. 34.

[3]   In his letter of 7 December, Mr. Wood explained that 'Dr. Owen [had] said he would like to see if ways could be found to break the present deadlock'. Dr. Owen asked the Defence Department to prepare two study papers, one on 'the problems associated with those weapons systems not covered by SALT or MBFR, eg forward based systems', and the other on 'an analysis of MBFR from the Soviet viewpoint'. Mr. Bullard agreed in paragraph 7 of his letter of 10 November (see note 2 above) that it would be useful to examine 'where the MBFR talks [were] seen nowadays as fitting in the general East–West picture, whether as looked at from the Soviet side or from our own. It seems a longish time since I saw anything much on this theme.'

[4]   In his letter to Mr. Moberly (*v. ibid.*) Mr. Bullard recalled Mr. Tickell 'used to say that MBFR was not one negotiation but three–

(*a*) It is a negotiation with the Warsaw Pact which may or may not lead to something concrete but will at least serve to educate the Soviet leaders and the top military men in Moscow.
(*b*) It is a dialogue between the United States and its European allies for their mutual enlightenment and harmony.
(*c*) It is also a dialogue between the governments in the Western democracies and their own peoples, because the very existence of the MBFR talks helps to take the steam out of pressure for unilateral cuts in Western defence budgets' (cf. No. 25).

of the Soviet commitment to détente.[5] The Secretary of State emphasised this point in the East–West relations chapter of his speech at the restricted session at the NATO Ministerial Meeting on 9 December (UKDEL NATO telegram No 441).[6]

3. As you say, MBFR has proved a remarkably successful bulwark against domestic pressures in the West for unilateral force cuts. It has also helped to a considerable degree in fostering a more open and constructive dialogue on defence and security matters between the United States and the other members of the Alliance; and in our own case it has brought the additional benefit of a close working relationship with the Germans and Americans in the tripartite forum in Vienna and in capitals. Paradoxically the lack of substantive progress in the negotiations and the generally inflexible line pursued by the East have strengthened Western determination to stand firm on their position and to resist easy political compromises. So far so good. But whether we can expect this state of affairs to continue indefinitely is another matter. I find it hard to imagine that Western Governments will be content to see the stalemate continue in Vienna for a further two or three years. The time is bound to come when we have to decide whether to call off the talks and/or to devise a new approach. The alternative, which the Germans have seemed to favour from time to time, would be to transform the talks from negotiations towards an agreement into some form of continuing East/West dialogue on security matters rather on the pattern of the CCD. But while that may suit German needs it has never seemed to us a realistic option so long as we and other Western European countries have domestic and economic reasons to try to secure actual reductions in MBFR. In short, our experience over the past three years since the negotiations began suggests that MBFR is a useful and even beneficial undertaking so long as we can keep its basic elements (paragraph 2 above) closely interlocked, and that the key to the whole exercise is the maintenance of Western cohesion.

4. The next stage is likely to depend upon what conclusions emerge from

---

[5] Mr. C.L.G. Mallaby (Counsellor in HM Embassy, Moscow) offered the following analysis of Soviet intentions in a letter to Mr. Wilberforce of 8 December: 'The Russians have definite military objectives in MBFR. They hope to weaken NATO's defences, *inter alia* by securing some US withdrawals from Europe without compensating increases being allowed in the Bundeswehr; to obtain a *droit de regard* over West European defence arrangements; and to create new obstacles to any possible moves towards West European defence integration. They could live without these gains. But MBFR has come to assume a political value too. The Russians have built it up as a central element in military détente, and their propaganda is still maintaining that success is perfectly possible if the West would only argue on a reasonable basis and not seek unilateral advantage. They would be very reluctant to see the talks break up, mainly because this would be a setback for current Soviet foreign policy since it would demonstrate the limits on détente especially in the military field. Thus, while for the Russians MBFR is much less vital than SALT and while military détente involves other elements including many proposals advanced by the Russians, Moscow wants the Vienna talks to continue and is likely to maintain in public the view that they can succeed. Part of the calculation is that as time goes on Western solidarity about asymmetry may crumble and the chances of the Russians gaining military advantage thus increase. Alternatively the negotiations may get entirely bogged down in which case the West can be blamed.'

[6] See No. 94, note 17.

Washington once the new US Administration[7] have completed their own appraisal of MBFR and of the other processes which directly or indirectly affect it, such as SALT and developments in the overall US/Soviet relationship. On the little evidence we have at the moment it seems on balance unlikely that the US Government intend to propose any radical departures from the present Western position on MBFR. But of course we cannot be sure. Even so, the Americans could not get very far without clearing their lines with the Germans. And so we come back to the fundamental question, namely what do the Germans want out of MBFR?[8] As you say, in the first place they saw it as the best means of ensuring that any withdrawal of US forces would be orderly and limited and reciprocated by withdrawals of Soviet forces.[9] At the same time the German Government were concerned about domestic pressures for cuts in the Bundeswehr and were enthusiastic about making progress towards a second phase in which the focus would be upon European reductions. But having completed their own restructuring programme for the Bundeswehr the Germans no longer seem prepared to look beyond Phase I; and they have implied on several occasions that their support for a Phase I agreement is in any case conditional upon its being an exclusively bilateral US/Soviet undertaking which establishes no precedents for Phase II and which involves no specific obligations by the FRG and the other European participants beyond the collective commitment to reduce to an eventual common collective ceiling.[10] Various questions which we have put to the Germans as to what this would mean in practice, for example as regards the commitments which the non-US participants are expected to give with regard to the link between the phases, have never been answered in wholly satisfactory terms. In other respects, notably in their attitude towards verification, the Germans have been totally unco-operative; they have not budged an inch despite the arguments which the Americans, let alone ourselves, have advanced in favour of such measures as mobile inspection. Nor have the Germans been prepared to discuss, even

---

[7] The US presidential elections on 2 November resulted in victory for the Democrat candidate, Mr. J. Carter.

[8] Mr. Moberly noted in his letter to Mr. Bolland of 19 November (see No. 34, notes 4 and 10) that it was 'becoming increasingly clear that the Germans [were] key figures in MBFR, with the capacity to make or break the negotiations'. But he thought it hard to see 'which way they [would] jump and what in the end Schmidt [might] have in mind'.

[9] In his letter of 10 November (see notes 2, 3 and 4 above) Mr. Bullard observed that the 'Germans' main reason in agreeing to MBFR talks in the first place ... was that they saw these as a device for preventing a unilateral reductions [*sic*] in American forces in Europe'. 'This motive', he added, 'receded into the background as Congressional pressures for US troop reductions eased (itself an indication of the success of this stratagem?), but it remains generally valid and would quickly re-emerge if the danger of a unilateral US troop reduction were to reappear. The Germans are watching anxiously to see whether President Carter will encourage any movement in this direction.'

[10] Mr. Bullard warned Mr. Moberly (*v. ibid.*) 'the recent history of the negotiations has done nothing to allay [the German Government's] three main worries about the Vienna talks, namely that they might result in a limitation on the size of the Bundeswehr, the creation of a special zone in Central Europe of which the FRG would be a part, and the erection of additional obstacles in the way of eventual European defence co-operation'.

theoretically, possible ways of accommodating the not altogether unjustified concern of the Soviet Union to secure some form of limitation on the Bundeswehr. That is not to say that we or any other member of the Alliance are prepared to contemplate national ceilings in MBFR; nonetheless, we have always thought that the common ceiling would not prove negotiable unless we were able to give the East some kind of assurance that it would not permit unlimited expansion of the Bundeswehr. I think it no exaggeration to describe this last problem as a potential breaking point in the negotiations.

5. Against this background, Chancellor Schmidt's pronouncements during and after the election campaign have caused a good deal of puzzlement.[11] It now looks as though his idea of 'raising the talks to political level' was an off-the-cuff remark. We have been told by Horstmann[12] of the German Embassy (please protect) that the Federal Chancellery have been at a loss to explain to enquirers what Schmidt meant by this and that they have beseeched the NATO Department in the Auswaertiges Amt to provide them with some kind of 'explanation' which would appear plausible in MBFR terms! The most plausible explanation we have seen was provided by Fred Ruth. He said that Schmidt meant simply that he, and other Western leaders, should take every opportunity in bilateral talks with their Soviet and East European counterparts to impress upon them the need for progress in MBFR and, Ruth emphasised, this in turn meant pressing them to agree to the West's proposals for asymmetrical reductions leading to the common collective ceiling. We thought it significant that his later interview with 'Der Spiegel' Schmidt talked in terms of 'partial success'; this seemed to us to reflect the usual German line that the FRG would not be averse to a Phase I agreement while leaving uncertain any continuing German commitment to a second phase.

6. Further interest has been generated by Brandt's references to MBFR in his speech in Amsterdam to the Socialist International.[13] Dr Owen's soundings of Brandt during his recent visit to Germany tend to confirm our impression that the German Government (or at any rate the SPD), are keen to ascribe greater political importance to MBFR; but nothing emerged from this exchange to raise expectations of some dramatic German initiative. Brandt referred to the possibility of the Germans' wishing to co-ordinate a new position on MBFR with their

---

[11] The Federal German elections, held on 3 October, confirmed the coalition of the *Sozialdemokratische Partei Deutschlands*/Social Democratic Party (SPD) and the *Freie Demokratische Partei*/Free Democrat Party (FDP) in power, but with a reduced Bundestag majority. Herr Schmidt spoke 'both before and after the elections, about the need to "get the cow off the ice" and lift MBFR from the expert to the political level'. But, as Mr. Bullard reported (*v. ibid.*), 'the Germans [did] not always speak with one voice'. As well as the Chancellor's impatient pronouncements there existed 'the orthodox Roth/Ruth line which [implied] that the FRG [was] prepared to continue the Vienna talks till the cows [came] home'. However, other senior 'German officials admittedly more remote from the talks in Vienna' thought otherwise, and one had remarked to Mr. Bullard that he 'hoped the MBFR talks would in due course peter out'.

[12] Herr H.H. Horstmann was Second Secretary in the West German Embassy in London.

[13] Herr Brandt was Federal German Chancellor during 1969–74 (cf. No. 25, note 7). His speech was delivered to a Conference on Peace and Security, organised by the Netherlands Labour Party, on 5 and 6 November.

Allies in the autumn of 1977. This would seem to preclude the idea of any unilateral initiative by the FRG, while the timescale envisaged accords with our own expectation that the Allies will in any case probably wish to re-examine their whole approach later next year in the light of whatever reappraisal is undertaken by the new US Administration.

7. As for the substance of Brandt's speech in Amsterdam we have now seen the complete text and discern little in it which presages any radical change in German thinking. Bearing in mind that Brandt sometimes pursues an idiosyncratic line and that his views are not always consistent with Federal Government policy his references to MBFR were remarkably orthodox. His warning against unilateral initiatives and his emphasis upon the need for close co-operation within the Alliance in the interests of common security sounded a suitably cautious note. He held out no hope of rapid progress and dampened any expectations of early savings in defence budgets. He confirmed that first phase withdrawals of US and Soviet forces would have to precede reductions by the European participants and made even that degree of progress in MBFR dependent upon the achievement of a SALT II agreement. In only two respects could he be said to have diverged from the standard Allied line. First, in his apparent advocacy of a freeze on both sides' forces while the negotiations are in train: 'die in Zentraleuropa vorhandenen Streitkräfte für die Dauer der MBFR-Verhandlungen quantitativ jedenfalls nicht wesentlich zu verstärken'.[14] That could be interpreted as endorsing the Eastern freeze proposal but could equally be a carelessly worded reference to the West's own proposal for a no-increase commitment between the phases. Secondly, he referred to 'eine erste Begrenzung nationaler Streitkräfte'[15] following US and Soviet withdrawals. John Whitehead's[16] letters of 6 and 10 December to Terence Wood reporting the outcome of enquiries in Bonn tend to support our assumption that Brandt was probably using the word. 'nationaler' in the sense of indigenous ('einheimlicher'); that is certainly the interpretation placed upon it by the German Embassy here, although I note that John did not exclude the more literal sense of 'national ceiling' being what Brandt meant.[17] On the other hand Genscher[18] made a point of saying at the recent

---

[14] 'not, in any case, to strengthen significantly the number of forces available in central Europe for the duration of the MBFR negotiations'.

[15] 'a first limitation of national forces'.

[16] Counsellor and Head of Chancery in HM Embassy, Bonn.

[17] In his letter of 6 December, Mr. J.S. Whitehead concluded that it was impossible to be certain whether Herr Brandt really was, contrary to the Allied position, willing to concede national sub-ceilings to the Soviets. It could not, he warned, be ruled out altogether though as 'Brandt has pursued an idiosyncratic line on MBFR in the past'. Dr. Owen, who had called on Herr Brandt on 1 December, 'believed [that] Brandt and Schmidt would like to make progress on MBFR on political grounds'. Mr. Whitehead concurred: 'The conclusion we draw from this is that the Chancellor and his closest political colleagues would very much like to see some movement in the MBFR talks, whatever officials may say. There is pressure for this within the SPD', he noted, and since 'the prospects in other fields of détente [were] not bright', there was now a 'renewed political interest here in the MBFR talks' (DPM 081/309/1).

[18] Herr H-D. Genscher was West German Foreign Minister.

NATO Ministerial meeting that there must be no national limitations but only collective ones (UKDEL NATO telegram No 440).[19]

8.   You suggested in the final paragraph of your letter that Gehlhoff's[20] recent talks with the PUS might provide an opportunity to obtain a high level view of German thinking. You were there so you will know, but I understand in the event he said nothing of note other than to confirm that there had been no change in the German position on MBFR. Nor, as I see from Bonn telegram No 1189, was any further clue provided in Schmidt's statement of Federal Government policy.[21]

9.   Finally, may I comment on the point in paragraph 6 of your letter where you questioned the utility of an agreement based upon manpower ceilings in an age of rapid technological development.[22] An essential point here, I think, is that military equipment, however advanced, still depends on manpower for its deployment and maintenance; manpower ceilings would therefore inevitably limit the Soviet Union's capacity to make the best use of modern equipment in the reductions area. Moreover, the array of weaponry is so vast that the practical problems of comparing one item with another and deciding on their equivalence in negotiating terms would probably be insurmountable. But there is a more fundamental consideration which has hitherto dissuaded the West from extending their equipment reduction proposals to the East beyond the specific demand for the withdrawal of Soviet main battle banks in Phase 1. This is that to ask for such reductions and constraints would inevitably entail reciprocal limitations upon Western equipment.

Yours ever,
P.H. MOBERLY

[19] In his address to the NAC on 9 December (cf. No. 94), Herr Genscher argued that as 'we wished MBFR to be a centre of public interest next year, it was necessary to restate briefly the principles we should follow. First and most important, these negotiations were a joint matter: it was hard to conceive of a negotiation which was less suitable as a vehicle for solo national performances. Secondly, we must retain parity as an inalienable objective. Thirdly, there must be no national limitations but only collective ones, in order not to impair either co-operation in the Alliance (including with members who did not participate in the military organisation) or future European developments in the defence field' (UKDEL NATO telegram No. 440 of 9 December, DPN 060/13).

[20] Herr W. Gehlhoff was State Secretary in the German Foreign Ministry.

[21] This telegram of 17 December reported that references to MBFR in Herr Schmidt's address were 'perfunctory' and that there was 'no reflection of earlier statements by Brandt and Schmidt himself on the need to raise them to the political level' (WRG 011/1).

[22] See notes 2, 3, 4, 9, 10 and 11 above. Mr. Bullard wondered whether by the time an MBFR agreement was signed it would have been frustrated 'either by advances in military technology or by dispositions deliberately made by the Warsaw Pact'. He gave as a possible example 'the vastly higher tank-man and gun-man ratios achieved in the Soviet forces in Central Europe within the last few years [which tended] to cast doubt on the value of an agreement based upon manpower ceilings'.

CHAPTER III

Détente in Anglo-Soviet Relations
5 January 1973–4 October 1974

No. 37

Letter from Sir J. Killick (Moscow) to Sir T. Brimelow

[*ENS 3/548/2*]

Personal and Confidential   MOSCOW, *5 January 1973*

Dear Tom,

Anglo-Soviet Relations

As I have said in my Annual Review (copy of relevant section enclosed for ease of reference)[1] I believe we should be well enough satisfied with the progress made in 1972 in returning towards 'normal' in Anglo-Soviet relations.[2] All the same, I think we must, at the outset of a new year, take a look ahead. This has been a difficult letter to write, as you can imagine. It has been in my mind since mid-December and has been through a lot of different thought-processes. Now it has been hurriedly revamped to make account of last night's bag, while yet catching today's return bag in the knowledge that the problem is already before Ministers. In particular I have tried to take account of the draft DOP paper[3] which George Walden kindly sent. The revamping has not been all that difficult, insofar as, not greatly to my surprise, the draft shows that we were thinking on much the same lines.

2.   The following is the basic analysis from which I proceed. At a time when all our major partners are more or less deeply 'engaged' with the Soviet Union

---

[1] Not printed.

[2] In his Annual Review for 1972, despatched on 2 January 1973, Sir J. Killick observed: 'The year has vindicated our policy, best summarised as deliberately eschewing any running after the Russians in supplication or apology, while at the same time showing ourselves ready, on every suitable occasion and in every possible field, to resume normal business.' He admitted that the 'general coolness' in bilateral relations had been prolonged by what would seem to have been a deliberate Soviet political decision, and that only muted criticism of the Soviet Union by the governments of Britain's three principal allies meant that the UK had been 'cast in the role of the West's leading and unrepentant "reactionary"'. Nevertheless, he thought Britain had been able to 'move forward gradually from the total "deep freeze"' at the beginning of 1972 through the steady and patient resumption of working relations (ENS 1/2). Cf. Volume I, pp. 351–512.

[3] The Cabinet Defence and Oversea Policy Committee. This draft paper, submitted by Mr. G. Walden (First Secretary, EESD) to Sir T. Brimelow on 29 December 1972 and copied to Sir J. Killick, reviewed the advantages and disadvantages for HMG of their currently 'cool relationship' with the Soviet Union and pressed for a Ministerial decision on whether Britain should maintain or modify the present course. It proposed, if Ministers decided for change, 'certain calculated procedural steps', such as inviting the Soviet Ambassador to call on Sir A. Douglas-Home for a 'long talk'.

bilaterally, as well as through CSCE, MBFR, etc., we must ask ourselves whether any concrete British interest is liable to come under threat if, during the coming twelve months, we fail to make further significant progress on the bilateral net, and remain confined to such bilateral contact as arises from or in the corridors of continued multilateral European negotiation. (I deliberately leave out of consideration contact of a similar nature at the United Nations or elsewhere, since it is generally liable to be rather *ad hoc* and self-contained, without much prospect of useful 'spin-off' on the bilateral relationship as such.)[4]

3. A few months ago, I would not have thought the question necessary, because it was my belief that the return to normal would prove an ineluctable process; however much the Russians might wish to delay it or restrict it solely to channels of their own choice, they would progressively find it essential to carry us along in the interests of a successful CSCE. Equally, with the enlargement of EEC[5] and the ever increasing interlocking of Western European commerce and industry, as well as the common commercial policy[6] and the harmonisation of foreign policy, they would find it more and more unrealistic to try to deal with us in a separate compartment.[7] More recently I—indeed all of us here in our various ways—feel we detect a distinct and rather fundamental setback, at least insofar as we have lost the expectancy that a further significant step forward is in the offing. (This may explain why I have, I am afraid, sounded a rather uncertain trumpet in correspondence with Peter Preston[8] about his forthcoming visit.) The press campaign against us is the main indicator, culminating in Brezhnev's remarks in his 50th Anniversary speech (see particularly my telegram No. 1946).[9]

[4] The draft DOP paper (*v. ibid.*) cited as advantages of the present UK–Soviet relationship: (1) HMG's attitude towards the USSR was an 'honest one'; (2) it was consistent with the position assumed by Sir A. Douglas-Home and other Ministers during the 1960s; (3) the Soviet 'espionage machine' in Britain had been cut to a level 'almost certainly lower than in any allied country'; (4) the British Embassy in Moscow was still functioning 'satisfactorily'; and (5) there was no tangible evidence that Anglo-Soviet trade had suffered. According to the paper, the disadvantages were: (1) the UK's exclusion from the kind of talks its allies enjoyed; (2) as competition for the Soviet market increased the handicap of a cool political relationship might be reflected adversely in Britain's balance of trade; (3) poor relations could place a brake on relations with 'all but the most daring countries of Eastern Europe'; and (4) there was a risk that policy towards the Soviet Union might become a matter of party dispute in Britain.

[5] The UK, along with Denmark and the Republic of Ireland, became a full member of the European Community/Communities (EC) on 1 January 1973.

[6] The EC's Common Commercial Policy (CCP) disallowed bilateral trade negotiations between EC member states and the state-trading countries of Eastern Europe (including the USSR) after 1 January 1973, and required the termination of all existing bilateral trade agreements between members of the two groups by 31 December 1974. Cf. Volume II, No. 1, note 36.

[7] In a letter to Mr. J.O. Wright (DUS) of 5 January Sir J. Killick observed that one of the merits of the EEC was 'the important fact that the Russians fear[ed] its magnetism and [were] vulnerable to economic comparison'.

[8] Mr. P.S. Preston, Deputy Secretary at the Department of Trade and Industry (DTI), was due to arrive in Moscow on 22 January.

[9] In this telegram of 22 December 1972 Sir J. Killick commented on references in a speech by Mr. Brezhnev on the fiftieth anniversary of the USSR to the British Government's conducting 'a

4. What this means in practice is that relations with the Ministry of Foreign Affairs and the Ministry of Foreign Trade are perfectly friendly, but have no real content. Relations with the SCST[10] are somehow rather negative but at the same time pregnant, though I do not know with what (I shall be seeing Gvishiani[11] next week, I hope, now that Mr. Walker's[12] plans are known.) It remains to be seen whether anything useful can be done in the cultural negotiations. Peter Preston's visit and the Joint Commission[13] meeting are to be welcomed and on the trade front generally things are not unpromising. But it is significant that major prospects in the offing have not emerged from inter-Governmental, still less Ministerial, exchanges. There is the suspicion that Sternberg[14] is being used for political purposes, and we shall somehow have, before the Joint Commission meeting, to establish whether Ministerial involvement will help specific potential deals. We have to reckon with a continuing exceptionally negative press and no prospect of Ministerial meetings on the foreign policy front. (Visa difficulties also continue and there has been some underhand sniping at members of my staff, but I cannot be sure how relevant these are.)

5. These unsatisfactory features of life are not, in my opinion, to be wholly explained as a hangover from the expulsions.[15] There is room for discussion about their continuing effect. I confess that I seem to have been over sanguine, mainly because I have over the years seen the Russians swallow so much, perhaps after what seems to them a decent interval, when it is in their interests to do so. My feeling from my contacts with the MFA[16] during the latter part of last year was that the anniversary of September 1971[17] would prove to be a sort of 'magic' date. However, it looks now as though the KGB, as the most powerful single Soviet executive organ, is still having its way to an important extent, perhaps still feeling the need to deter others from dealing it as decisive and comprehensive a blow as

cruel war against the people of Northern Ireland', and Britain's omission from 'Brezhnev's prize giving to the West European class'. This was, Sir J. Killick thought, 'a striking and probably accurate indication [of] how far we still have to go to reach anything resembling normality in Anglo-Soviet political relations' (ENS 3/548/3).

[10] State Committee for Science and Technology.

[11] Professor D.M. Gvishiani was Deputy Chairman of the SCST.

[12] Mr. P.E. Walker was Secretary of State for Trade and Industry.

[13] A Joint Commission to review UK–Soviet trade and technological agreements and to promote cooperation in the areas they covered was established in 1970. See Volume I, No. 41, note 2. Mr. Walker was due to attend the next scheduled meeting of the Joint Commission in April (cf. No. 42).

[14] Sir Rudy Sternberg was Chairman of both the Sterling Group of companies and the British Agricultural Export Council. The draft DOP paper (see notes 6 and 7 above) pointed out that the Soviet authorities were seeking, through Sir R. Sternberg, to engage British interest in a number of large projects in the USSR. 'Even a fraction of this business', the paper explained, 'would make a big difference to the Anglo-Soviet trade statistics.' But the basic facts of trading with the USSR remained unchanged, and the economic situation did not suggest trade with the West was about to increase.

[15] See Volume I, Nos. 75–81.

[16] Ministry of Foreign Affairs.

[17] See note 15 above.

HM Government did. I hope this is only a question of time, but it may be still quite a long time.

6.   Certainly the situation is not the result of the sort of extraneous and fortuitous issues I refer to in the Annual Review like espionage in Hong Kong[18] or Soviet-made weapons in Northern Ireland.[19] Such things arise in Soviet bilateral relations with others, and are not allowed to affect them substantially (*par excellence* Vietnam for the Americans, but also Mitterand/Abrasimov,[20] continued nuclear testing and a negative line on force reductions in Europe and disarmament for the French, Maddelena[21] for the Italians, the islands and the Japanese/American Treaty for the Japanese and so on. Not to mention relations with Peking for all of them).

7.   So my next question is whether there is any concrete reason in our foreign policy why we should be singled out for treatment so different from the others. I ran into Smirnovsky at the Kremlin reception on 22 December and taxed him on the point. I pointed out for example that HM Government said and thought nothing essentially different from other Western Governments as regards the need for caution and the maintenance of our security, until true détente was achieved; President Nixon's message to NATO was a case in point,[22] yet it had not been criticised. Smirnovsky tried to suggest that there was some qualitative difference in HM Government's attitude, though he could only refer lamely to Hong Kong and to the manner in which the British press had played up the story of Soviet weapons in Ireland.

8.   I think the Russians do in fact now see a qualitative difference between the 'English Tories' whom Brezhnev singles out for attack and the rest of our Allies. It is one which the Russians of course dislike very much indeed, because it is clearly and publicly expressed, and it runs directly counter to their long-term European aims, which we discussed at the Heads of Mission Conference last

[18]   On 24 November 1972 the British authorities in Hong Kong deported a stateless Chinese man on suspicion of spying for the Soviet Union.

[19]   British newspapers reported in December 1972 that rockets seized from the Provisional Irish Republican Army (IRA) appeared to be of Soviet origin. Mr. Walden held these allegations in large part responsible for the 'new note of recrimination … pervading many fields of Anglo-Soviet relations'. In a minute to Sir T. Brimelow of 5 January he noted: 'I suspect that many Soviet officials, headed of course by the KGB, have seized on the opportunity offered by the Irish affair to convince senior Soviet leaders, including quite probably Brezhnev himself, that the Conservative Government are doing everything possible to wreck the policy of détente with which Brezhnev has so closely associated himself.'

[20]   In a letter to *l'Humanité* of 5 September 1972 Mr. P.A. Abrasimov, the Soviet Ambassador in Paris, criticised a recent statement by M. F. Mitterrand, the French Socialist leader, condemning the Soviet invasion of Czechoslovakia in 1968. A visit which M. Mitterrand was planning to make to the Soviet Union was subsequently cancelled.

[21]   Soviet and Italian Communist Party leaders had been particularly critical of the Italian Government's decision to provide the US Navy with a nuclear submarine support base at La Maddalena.

[22]   In his address to the NAC on 7 December 1972, Mr. Nixon had stressed that 'prospects for peace … must rest on a foundation of continued military preparedness' (AMU 13/4).

April[23] and which I refer to again in my despatch in this bag commenting on Nicko Henderson's despatch on Ostpolitik.[24] The Russians, in all probability, rightly regard the present British Government as being the principal source of ideas and policies which could, if eventually accepted by our European partners, result in the EEC acquiring a significant defence identity. This, of course, is the aspect of potential development of Western Europe which the Russians are most concerned and even determined to prevent. Short of this they cannot be much less unhappy about the very credible determination of HM Government, and the Prime Minister in particular, to develop the EEC both economically and in the field of foreign policy. Progress of this sort would to them be undesirable both in its own right and as the necessary foundation for defence capability. I am now forced to conclude therefore that there is more to the situation than just a Soviet wish to have HM Government as a whipping boy.

9. The consequence is that KGB and foreign policy interests are evolving in the same direction. The former alone might slowly evaporate, and could have been overborne by now if foreign policy interests ran counter to them. This will now only happen if current tactics prove unproductive or even counter-productive. Obviously the Russians do not at present think they are. They are apparently encouraging their allies to follow the same line. Nor do they think they are damaging their own practical interests by pursuing it; they do not want much from us, and probably think they can bank on getting enough of what they do want in the field of trade in particular as a result of our natural wish not to be outstripped by our competitors.[25]

10. By contrast the Americans, French and Germans, all in their different ways and whether consciously or not, have confirmed the Russians in their expectations of the political advantages to be gained from an effective bilateral relationship. I need not enlarge on the nature of the advantages seen in the American case. In the case of the French and Germans (now that what Brandt's Ostpolitik had to

[23] See Volume I, No. 95.

[24] Sir N. Henderson considered in a despatch of 4 December 1972 the results of West Germany's *Ostpolitik.* 'It has', he noted, 'not settled the German question but opens it up to new influences and new adjustments in which the aspiration to be once more a nation may begin to assume more practical forms' (WRE 3/309/1). In his despatch of 4 January, in which he expressed doubts about the potential benefits of *Ostpolitik* for intra-German relations, Sir J. Killick asserted: 'The Russians use the expression "detente" as a presentationally useful portmanteau term to embrace a series of objectives which in fact are not necessarily conducive to a genuine relaxation of tension at all: these objectives include the consolidation of the Soviet sphere of influence in Eastern Europe and Western acquiescence in it; the perpetuation of the division of Germany; the obstruction of West European integration in the name of "pan-Europeanism"; and the creation of a framework of economic collaboration through which they hope to tap Western technology more effectively than they have done in the past.' He added that *détente* was an 'essential ingredient of Soviet long-term security planning ... while beyond pure security lie vague hopes of political and ideological advance' (WRG 3/303/1).

[25] Sir J. Killick explained, in his letter to Mr. Wright of 5 January (see note 7 above), that he was 'concerned at the "bicycle race" going on to conclude long-term economic agreements on a bilateral basis with the USSR and Eastern European countries on the specious argument that they [were] outside the CCP'. See note 6 above.

offer in terms of what only the Federal Republic could give has been pretty well sucked dry) it looks as though the Russians still see possibilities of sabotaging the development of the expanded EEC through the exploitation of the appeal of national economic advantage and the rivalry between the two for the role of '*interlocuteur valable*' in East–West relations in Europe. I hope that this will be proved an illusion when the chips are really down, but it will be some time before we come to such a 'crunch' situation. Meanwhile Pompidou's visit may prove an important touchstone.[26] In this situation, however, the Russians can calculate that we are the odd man out, that we are a negligible force within the Western Alliance, and that we shall have no alternative but to come into line with the others.

11. Therefore my worry (and my answer to my own question in paragraph 2 above) is that our partners may come to share the Soviet belief that we do not matter and that we are out of step. If the Russians think that Britain, as 'odd man out' in Europe, will in the end always go along with the majority, the thought may prove contagious. At the least, our lack of contact with and direct insight into top-level Soviet thinking may seriously undermine the credibility of our counsels within both NATO and the EEC and leave the three (or two) main 'interlocuteurs' less open to our influence. This is what the Russians may well hope to see as the outcome of their present campaign, NB Mayevsky's article reported in my telegram No. 1972[27] where he says of the British, ' … still imbued with the imperial spirit, they claim a special role in Western Europe and hope to play it in the expanded Common Market'.[28] Quite a clever line to take. If doubt can be sown about our intentions coupled with doubt about our attractiveness as a new partner in [the] EEC (Northern Ireland, domestic industrial and other problems) the chances of our becoming a sort of European leper are enhanced. More specu-latively I would even hazard the guess that the intention could be to prolong this campaign up to the next General Election and a possible change of Government.

12. So, as I see it, we have got to exert ourselves 'pour se fair valoir' in practical ways and to make it difficult, if not impossible, for the Russians to go on treating us as they are. If my foregoing analysis is broadly correct the means for doing this do not lie in the bilateral Anglo-Soviet relationship itself. (Nor of course can they be found in anything on the Anglo-American net.) We need to show that, far from being odd man out in the enlarged EEC, we are playing a leading role and effectively so, in pressing forward with its development. I realise that this is something which must be pursued in substance on its merits and tactically (vis-

---

[26] The French President, M.G. Pompidou, and Foreign Minister, M.M. Schumann, visited Byelorussia during 11–12 January. On the morning of 12 January M. Pompidou and Mr. Brezhnev met in Minsk and discussed, amongst other topics, progress in the preparatory talks for the CSCE (Paris telegram No. 72 of 15 January, MWE 5/303/2).

[27] Not traced.

[28] When, at a cocktail party on 5 January, Mr. J.A. Dobbs, the British Minister in Moscow, questioned Mr. V. Mayevsky on why the UK was singled out for so much unfavourable criticism in the Soviet press, the latter referred to HMG's statements about the need for the UK and other Western European countries to increase their military spending. He said that 'Britain had in history been hostile to the Soviet state. The Soviet Union had never attacked Britain' (minute from Mr. Dobbs to Sir J. Killick of 9 January, ENS 3/548/3).

à-vis the French and Germans in particular) in the light of considerations separate from and perhaps more important than relations with Moscow, but I would hope that the latter angle can always be borne in mind. By 'effectively so', I of course mean, from my own point of view, that it should increasingly be seen by Moscow that our views and influence are, in respects important to them, reflected in what actually is done by the EEC and result from the over-persuasion, if necessary, of our major partners. The most obvious immediate practical fields of activity seem the evolution of the common commercial policy, and more generally the harmonisation of foreign policy. Much as I agree with the need for a European defence capability, on the other hand, I must say frankly that I think it is a mistake to continue to press it so publicly and uncompromisingly. This not because it attracts Soviet reactions, but because it does not look to me as though it would be effective in any demonstrable sense over the coming twelve months at any rate. Least of all does it look as though the idea of an Anglo-French nuclear force would get anywhere in this time scale. So to keep publicly advocating policies and courses of action which our European partners do not adopt amounts to fostering precisely the public image of being out of step and irrelevant which the Russians want to encourage. (None of what I say here is intended to imply that we should not go on quietly doing solid and useful work in NATO and the Euro-group.)

13. Another field of activity, closely related to but potentially broader than the foregoing, is of course CSCE/MBFR. Here too, if we can demonstrate in practical ways that we have real and effective influence, not only with our allies but with important neutrals as well, the Russians will surely find it necessary to change their tune and re-engage with us politically. I am *not* suggesting that we should take a strongly anti-Soviet line as such of course. And the effectiveness of this sphere of activity can be rated no higher than Soviet interest in CSCE. Can we perhaps make a start even at MPT[29] by putting forward important proposals which are at once supported by at least the French and the Germans? Would we envisage taking the initiative in further bilateral exchanges of substance with the Russians between MPT and CSCE?

14. Of course we must not neglect the bilateral field meanwhile. Without abasing ourselves in any way or making concessions on policy, I think there is much we can and should do to demonstrate continually that we are 'open for business' and that it is the Russians who are being negative. In all this, it is right to emphasise that the target for Russian antipathy is very much *Ministers* and not officials; not Britain in general nor even the British press except insofar as certain papers are regarded as 'mouthpieces of the Tories'. 'Certain calculated steps' (in terms of George Walden's draft),[30] though not necessarily only procedural ones, would be the right approach. With this in mind I am all for the Secretary of State having a good talk with Smirnovsky, though we must always be careful not to approach the subject of the bilateral relationship as such in a way which gives the impression of unease and weakness on our side, and avoid giving hostages to fortune. George Walden's DOP paper seems fine to us up to the end of paragraph

[29] Multilateral Preparatory Talks for the CSCE. See Volume II, Nos. 17–38.
[30] See notes 4 and 5 above.

21. We are thinking about the specific steps proposed in paragraphs 22 and 23[31] and will telegraph some recommendations.[32]

15. So really the possibilities lie largely outside the field of foreign affairs. I have written separately to Julian Bullard by this bag in response to a circular enquiry from him inviting suggestions for Ministerial exchanges.[33] We should not aim high this year. We have the Joint Commission in prospect anyway, which is an event of great importance in itself, whatever comes out of it. A propos of that, I sympathise fully with a point of Peter Preston's in his letter to me of 2 January[34] —'I would hate to push my Secretary of State into making a major effort in April only to find that the Russians had already decided not to play the game.' It is too early to forecast whether they will, and Peter's visit will, I hope, give us some indication. However, I am not pessimistic—only uncertain—because the Russians have all along played the trade relationship pretty straight. Even though Mr. Walker may well find his visit a disappointment there can in any case be no doubt that if the British side were to take the initiative to call it off, this would do considerable damage and would be used by the Russians to delay the return to 'normal' still further.

16. Below Ministerial level, there are other things we can do. George Walden has mentioned the Parliamentary Exchange. The GB/USSR Association might revive its earlier plans or think up some new ones. We are thinking about the suggested possibility of an exchange of journalists. And, of course, all the regular scientific and cultural exchanges will no doubt go ahead. I am rather

---

[31] Paragraph 22 of the draft DOP paper (*v. ibid.*) suggested that during a 'long talk' with Mr. Smirnovsky (see note 5 above) Sir A. Douglas-Home should, after expressing regret that his meeting with Mr. Gromyko in Berlin in June 1972 (see Volume I, No. 98) had not been followed by a 'comprehensive improvement' in Anglo-Soviet relations, propose that: (1) each side should give full governmental support to a programme of 'Anglo-Soviet events'; (2) any 'incidents' occurring should be handled by each side in such a manner as to cause least public difficulty for the other; (3) in their public statements each side should respond to what it found most positive in the other's public statements; and (4) each Ambassador should be received once a month for a general talk by the other side's Foreign Minister or his deputy. Whitehall would then, according to paragraph 23, seek to dissuade the press from publishing what the Russians would regard as unwarrantably anti-Soviet articles.

[32] In Moscow telegram No. 33 of 8 January Sir J. Killick argued that he thought recommendations (2) and (3) of paragraph 22 of the draft paper (*v. ibid.*) would offer 'unnecessary and potentially troublesome hostages to fortune' without bringing the very practical results HMG would be seeking. He was also opposed to any attempt to influence the press since it would give a 'misleading impression' to the British press and to the Russians if they learnt of it: 'We should stand pat on having a free press which HMG cannot control.'

[33] Sir J. Killick noted in this letter of 4 January that he was not sure whether in the present state of UK–Soviet relations a visit to Moscow by an FCO Minister or a visit to London by a Minister from the Ministry of Foreign Affairs would serve any useful purpose. He, nevertheless, thought the projected visits to Moscow by Mr. Preston and Mr. Walker to 'represent a good advance on the situation in early 1972', and to balance them he 'strongly recommend[ed] an invitation to either the Soviet equivalents to Ministers for Health or Housing to pay an official visit' to the UK in the late summer or early autumn (EN 22/5).

[34] Not printed.

disappointed that you have discouraged the idea of an RCDS visit (Julian's letter of 21 December).[35] Although I had not expected the whole College to come, and I agree they would not get much out of it, we in the Embassy would get some useful mileage out of the occasion. So we would out of a naval visit.[36] I don't see why an obligation to reciprocate should worry us, I thought we were trying to foster reciprocal exchanges.

17. For the second half of the year, please think seriously about the Duke of Edinburgh.[37] All I say in this letter makes no difference to what I said about the desirability of this going ahead on its merits in my last letter to Julian on the subject. If His Royal Highness came to Moscow as well, it would give our standing a tremendous boost and surely involve some interesting contacts with the Russians at the top. The sooner he can indicate acceptance, if he so decides, the better.

18. Looking ahead to 1974, and the possibility of a visit by the Prime Minister,[38] which I discussed briefly with Julian before Christmas, of course we support the idea warmly. But against all the foregoing background, I am bound to conclude that it is unrealistic to try to evolve any sort of effective scenario for 1973 leading up to its realisation. We must in no circumstance do anything to solicit it or risk a rebuff; through the sort of activity suggested in paragraphs 11 and 12 above we must hope to make the Russians feel a need to talk to him. Perhaps he will meet Mr. Brezhnev at the third stage of a CSCE, if it even happens in 1973, and something might come of that. Otherwise I feel we can only await developments and review possibilities from time to time, and I am honestly not very optimistic about the prospects.

Yours ever,
J.E. KILLICK

PS Very welcome news in today's telegram CREDA 2.[39] I ought of course to have mentioned the invitation to Patolichev[40] both in my separate letter on Ministerial visits and in paragraph 15 above. It is very much part of the Joint Commission complex.

[35] In this letter Mr. Bullard informed Sir J. Killick that the FCO were averse to a proposal from the Commandant of the Royal College of Defence Studies (RCDS) that the 1973 course should visit the Soviet Union. Mr. Rose (then AUS) explained in an enclosed copy of a letter to the MoD of 20 December 1972 that, while he doubted if the RCDS would be shown anything of value, the UK would incur an obligation to reciprocate. 'Moreover', he added, 'so long as the Soviet Government continue to refuse to reply to a suggestion for a visit to Moscow by a FCO Minister we think it would be quite wrong to propose a visit by the RCDS' (ENS 22/9).

[36] Sir J. Killick informed Mr. Bullard in a letter of 11 January that he had understood that a visit by the Royal Navy to Leningrad had been under consideration (ENS 22/9).

[37] A proposed visit by the Duke of Edinburgh to a three-day horse-jumping event in Kiev was under review. Cf. No. 40, note 3, and No. 48, note 6.

[38] Mr. E.R.G. Heath.

[39] Not traced. CREDA telegrams originated from the Commercial Relations and Export Division of the DTI.

[40] Mr. N.S. Patolichev was Soviet Minister of Foreign Trade.

No. 38

Memorandum by Sir A. Douglas-Home for the
Cabinet Defence and Oversea Policy Committee[1]

DOP(73)5 [CAB 148/129]

Confidential   FCO, *18 January 1973*

Anglo-Soviet Relations

1.   After the expulsion of the Soviet spies we hoped that:

(*a*)   the Russians would eventually stop sulking;
(*b*)   they would gradually allow relations to return to normal;
(*c*)   they would eventually stop trying to assign known intelligence agents to this country;
(*d*)   Ministerial visits and other Anglo-Soviet exchanges would, after a time, gradually return to traditional levels.

2.   The improvement in Anglo-Soviet relations has been slow and incomplete. HM Ambassador in Moscow does not enjoy the access to Ministers which the Soviet Ambassador enjoys in London. The Soviet Foreign Ministry continues occasionally to submit visa applications for known intelligence agents, and we have difficulty in obtaining Soviet visas for some Russian-speaking British officials. There have been no visits to the Soviet Union by FCO Ministers since September 1971, when the spies were expelled. There are signs that commercial relations will be allowed to return to normal, but to judge from the current rate of Soviet orders, the decline in British exports to the Soviet Union is likely to continue. Many non-political factors are contributing to this decline.

3.   Since the NATO Ministerial meetings last December 'Pravda' has published several criticisms of statements by me about Western European defence and about the foreign policy of the United Kingdom. Three times in 1972 the Prime Minister made speeches which included friendly references to the Soviet Union. The first reference was twisted by the Russians to make it appear anti-Soviet; the other two were ignored.

4.   The volume of recent Soviet criticisms of the United Kingdom may have been influenced by Soviet irritation at articles in the British press suggesting that

---

[1] Mr. Bullard informed Sir J. Killick in a letter of 17 January that the line taken in EESD's original draft DOP paper (see No. 37, notes 4, 5, and 33) had 'not been endorsed at higher levels in the FCO'. Ministers, he explained, felt there was no case for modifying HMG's present stance towards the USSR, 'or rather, they considered that the most important thing was to hold fast to the points which really matter to us including the paramount need to maintain the defensive capability of Western Europe, whether with US assistance or without it'. Mr. Bullard noted that he would have been more inclined to resist the 'changed slant of the Paper' had reports from Moscow not led him to conclude that perhaps EESD had been too quick to detect a real change in the Soviet attitude towards Britain (ENS 3/548/2).

Soviet involvement in the Irish troubles and in the supply of Soviet rockets to the IRA has been considerable.[2]

5. But this apart, it is clear that the Soviet authorities dislike the British Ministerial practice of speaking frankly about the realities of defence and European security, and are content to cast HMG in the role of their current whipping-boy.[3] The Russians also view our plans for the political and defence development of the EEC with suspicion and believe they go beyond French and German intentions.[4] Simultaneously, the Soviet authorities are trying to develop contacts with the Opposition, the Trade Unions and other individuals not closely connected with HM Government.[5]

6. Officials of some East European countries have recently been hinting to us that their own Governments are inhibited in the development of their relations with us by the chill wind blowing from Moscow.

7. This state of affairs entails the following disadvantages:

(*a*) the United Kingdom cannot conduct with the Soviet Government a

---

[2] See No. 37, note 20.

[3] On 17 January, during a lunch with Mr. Smirnovsky, Sir D. Greenhill (PUS) said that the FCO were ready 'to try for better relations', indeed they sometimes wondered why the UK was set apart from certain other Western European countries since on the majority of East/West issues the British position was very much the same as their allies'. 'It seemed to him', the PUS observed, 'that a point of difference was that we were ready to say to the Russians' face what others only said behind their backs' (telegram No. 38 to Moscow of 17 January, ENS 3/548/2).

[4] The publication in *Izvestia* of 17 January of an article by Mr. V.D. Osipov about Britain and the EC was followed by what Mr. Bullard termed a 'further spate of virulent anti-British commentaries on the same theme'. Mr. Osipov accused the British of wishing to transform the EC into a 'military/political alliance opposing the countries of the Socialist commonwealth', and went on to argue that since the British were now disqualified from the leadership of Europe by their internal weaknesses, they were forced to rely on their nuclear capability to assert themselves. Hence, he contended, Britain's advocacy of a European nuclear force and its tougher attitude towards the East, since the 'nuclear trump' would clearly count for less if *détente* continued. These criticisms of HMG, along with remarks made to Mr. Dobbs by Mr. V.M. Vasev, the Deputy Head of the Second European Department of the Soviet Foreign Ministry, to the effect that it was British public pronouncements which irritated the Russians most, led Mr. Bullard to conclude that in order to improve the atmosphere of Anglo-Soviet relations they must avoid 'public expressions of views which [were] known to be anathema to the Russians and disturbing to some of our allies' (minute from Mr. Bullard to Sir T. Brimelow of 24 January). On this Sir T. Brimelow noted his reluctance to make any recommendation 'which might limit our freedom to say what we think appropriate' (ENS 3/548/2).

[5] In Moscow telegram No. 93 of 22 January, in which he commented to Sir T. Brimelow on this paper, Sir J. Killick argued that basic Soviet objectives towards Britain were threefold: (1) to devalue and sabotage HMG's views and policies in the eyes of its principal EC partners by categorising them as inimical to *détente*; (2) to erode the UK's *locus standi* as interpreter of East/West relations by reducing Anglo-Soviet political contacts to a minimum and keeping bilateral relations largely in cold storage; and (3) to bring about a modification of HMG's European policies and stance on East/West relations by inducing in HMG a concern at being odd man out and frustration with bilateral immobility, and by stimulating domestic political pressure for a 'more malleable line'. He added: 'It is difficult to judge from Moscow the extent to which we can regard our relations with our EEC partners as being permanently invulnerable to Soviet wedge-driving' (ENS 3/548/2).

dialogue of the kind now conducted by the Americans, the French, the West Germans and the Canadians. Whether the content of these dialogues is valuable is open to doubt. But the United Kingdom is beginning to look the odd man out and cannot claim first-hand knowledge of Soviet thinking.[6]

(*b*) As was pointed out in DOP(72)6,[7] competition for the Soviet market has increased to a point where the extra handicap of a cool political relationship may come to be reflected adversely in our balance of trade.

Ministerial exchanges with some of the countries of Eastern Europe may be inhibited.

(*c*) Policy towards the Soviet Union is becoming a subject of Party controversy. Preference is being clearly given by the Russians to contacts with the Opposition and left-wing organisations.

8. It is therefore for consideration whether we should continue in our present policy, or whether we should make a demonstrative effort to improve our relations with the Soviet Government. Experience suggests that it does not pay to run after the Russians. Any dramatic moves on our part would be interpreted by them as a sign of weakness. Their reaction would be stiff and might be coupled with unacceptable demands. They would certainly imply that we had been in the wrong to expel their officials in 1971 and to speak so plainly in public about defence and security.

9. I should like my colleagues to agree that between now and the opening of the Conference on Security and Cooperation in Europe we should continue, quietly but firmly, to make known our views on defence and security, while dissociating ourselves from any misrepresentations of Soviet policy in the British press, and making plain our continuing readiness to improve relations with the Soviet Government and with the Warsaw Pact Governments of Eastern Europe. In the meantime we should not be deterred from developing our relations with China, Yugoslavia and Romania.[8]

A.D-H.

---

[6] In a minute to Mr. G.D.G. Murrell (Research Department) of 30 January Mr. Bullard recalled that he and Sir J. Killick had argued recently to Sir T. Brimelow that 'the prolonged absence of contact with the Soviet Union at high and upper-middle levels may in time affect the quality and depth of [British] understanding of Soviet policies' and this could lower the UK's standing in the eyes of its allies. Sir T. Brimelow questioned the validity of this assertion (ENS 3/548/2).

[7] See Volume I, No. 89.

[8] Sir J. Killick warned Sir T. Brimelow in his telegram No. 93 (see note 5 above) that the Soviet Government would 'desist from its present behaviour only when this [could] be clearly shown to be unproductive', and this involved 'getting the message across to them that HMG [had] no intention of changing its policies ... that these policies [contained] no hidden threat to European security or to legitimate Soviet interests ... and that there [was] no incompatibility between these policies and moves toward general détente or between them and the restoration of normal, realistic and constructive Anglo-Soviet relations'. See No. 41.

No. 39

Letter from Sir T. Brimelow to Mr. Dobbs (Moscow)

[*ENS 3/548/2*]

Confidential   FCO, *6 February 1973*

Anglo-Soviet Relations

In John Killick's absence on leave, we have been considering how to answer the points made in his letter of 26 January to me.[1] We appreciate their importance.

2.   The Ambassador's first point was that we need high-level contacts with the Russians in order that they should have a direct insight into the minds of members of HMG. This point is reinforced in your letter to Julian Bullard 3/5 of 2 February.[2] It is clear from both letters that in the Embassy you are thinking of the need to work towards meetings between Brezhnev and Mr. Heath. The Prime Minister would, I know, like to meet Brezhnev in Moscow, preferably in 1974, if mutually satisfactory conditions for this could be created. It is a question of ways and means and of timing. I shall return to these points later in this letter.

3.   The Ambassador's second point was that we are important to the Russians, who think that if it were not for us, they would find the Western Alliance an altogether softer proposition to deal with.[3] The Russians might or might not be right in so thinking; but this assessment of the nature and extent of our influence

---

[1] In his letter Sir J. Killick put the case for a 'round of PUS/Deputy Foreign Minister talks as a first step towards a political ministerial meeting'. He argued that the Soviet leaders were 'not getting a direct insight into the minds' of HMG, and that they were 'too dependent on their Ambassador's reports and a mass of press-cuttings, with no doubt the most obviously anti-Soviet ones on the top of the pile'. Sir J. Killick added that Mr. Brezhnev was the man who mattered in Soviet foreign policy, and that this was significantly influenced by the personal relations he had established with other Western leaders. But Mr. Brezhnev had never met Mr. Heath or Sir A. Douglas-Home: 'Great Britain, and especially Conservative Britain, is associated no doubt in his mind with intervention, Winston Churchill and past imperial splendour. He has no conception of modern Britain or modern Conservatism.'

[2] Mr. Dobbs reported in this letter a recent conversation with Mr. Vasev during which the latter had indicated that the British Embassy were 'not getting through to the Soviet leadership' when they spoke to senior officials of the Foreign Ministry. 'We are', Mr. Dobbs wrote, '... up against this new tendency for the more important aspects of foreign policy, which certainly include (because of the strategic implications) Britain and Britain's relationship with the EEC, to be concentrated more and more, it seems, in the hands of the Soviet "White House"—the Central Committee Secretariat and Brezhnev's personal staff.'

[3] Sir. J. Killick had argued (see note 1 above) that the Russians resented the British policy of 'combining East/West negotiations with a proper concern for our collective defence precisely because we appear to be taking the lead within the Western alliance on this aspect of Western policy', and believed the British were 'stiffening the Western position at Helsinki'. Although he conceded that the UK was 'a useful whipping boy' for Moscow, he did not believe it was attacked 'because the Russians *must* have a whipping boy'. He thought the 'Soviet attitude to HM Government could change quite quickly once the Soviet leaders, in effect Brezhnev, came to the conclusion that this important leader in the EEC was, in the Soviet interest, more worth cultivating than reviling'.

on the Alliance is not in itself an argument in favour of Mr. Heath's visiting Moscow. Ministers in this country would certainly not wish to help the Russians to bring about any softening of the Western Alliance. Questions concerning the future defence of Western Europe are very much on the minds of the Prime Minister, Sir Alec and Lord Carrington. This is no time for us to appear to be going soft on questions concerning the defence of Western Europe. You will have seen the blunt tone adopted by the Prime Minister in answering questions at the National Press Club in Washington.[4]

4. The rest of John Killick's letter stated the case for our taking the initiative in going for the establishment between Brezhnev and Mr. Heath of a relationship of the kind which Brezhnev already has with Pompidou and Brandt (though I am not completely satisfied that the two latter relationships can be accurately described as being of a kind).[5] We think the Ambassador is probably right in believing that any initiative will have to come from us. We are not opposed to such an initiative. But the tactics, timing and content of any such initiative give rise to many difficulties.[6]

5. On content there is room for some scepticism. Pompidou publicly takes pride in his personal relationship with Brezhnev, but in one private conversation he has said that he has obtained little in the way of concrete results from this relationship. In other private conversations Pompidou has expressed apprehension about the extent of Soviet influence through the French Communist Party, and has stressed the need for vigilance. He is clearly anxious about the effects on French public opinion of the apparent moderation of Soviet diplomacy at a time when the military strength of the USSR is increasing. If this is the assessment of the favoured French, we in the United Kingdom could hardly expect to gain material advantage from talks between Brezhnev and Mr. Heath. We should no doubt be able to say afterwards that we had recent and immediate acquaintance with the expressed views of the Soviet leaders and that we had been able to put our own views to them in direct discussion; but this kind of benefit is hard to

[4] In an interview with NBC Television on 4 February, Mr. Heath referred to the Soviet Union as a 'hostile power'. Mr. Dobbs suggested in a letter of 1 March to Sir T. Brimelow that Mr. Heath's comment was a 'slip of the tongue', since the Prime Minister had evidently been thinking of the Soviet Union as 'potentially hostile'. But, he added, 'this use of the word "hostile" does seem to have been given the worst possible interpretation here'. Indeed, in an article in *Izvestia* of 26 February, Mr. Osipov argued that British statesmen were still making a fuss about the 'threat from the East', and that this owed much to their desire to regain prestige for Britain by taking the lead in military expenditure and preparations and by sabotaging the process of *détente* (Moscow telegram No. 288 of 27 February).

[5] 'In short', Sir J. Killick observed (see notes 1 and 3 above), 'there is not likely to be an end to the present excessive coolness in Anglo-Soviet relations and a return to normal until this top-level relationship is established.'

[6] Sir J. Killick advised (*v. ibid.*) that the Russians would 'not want to seem to be running after us: and indeed they may well feel even more inhibited by this than we are because it was the British side which initiated strong and public action against them in September 1971 and they might feel, understandably in some ways, that for them to make the first move in a restoration of normal relations—or *a fortiori* to initiate a process designed to lead to a meeting between Messrs. Heath and Brezhnev—would give an impression of weakness and contrition'.

quantify. From the point of view of the UK, the chief advantage of such a meeting would be the public knowledge that Brezhnev had heard at first hand what Mr. Heath had to say. We agree that this is desirable. It is one of the reasons why we argued a year ago that Ministers should intensify their contacts with both the Soviet Union and Eastern Europe—a recommendation that was accepted but has proved far from easy to put into practice. If the price of a meeting between the Prime Minister and Brezhnev were an eventual visit by Brezhnev to London with all the honours of a Head of State, we accept at official level that this would probably be a price worth paying, though he would have to wait a bit for his visit to London, given the length of the queue for State Visits. If Brezhnev were willing to accept something less than a State Visit, the problem would be easier.

6. On timing, we agree that, leaving the unforeseen, 1974 would be the best year for a visit by Mr. Heath to Moscow. But Mr. Heath wishes to visit China. Given Soviet sensitivity to the development of our contacts with China, and given our own wish that these should not lead to a further deterioration in Anglo-Soviet relations, we should be happy if it could be arranged for the Prime Minister to go to Moscow before Peking. This might render his journey to China more acceptable in Soviet eyes. But a visit by the Prime Minister to China may well take place before a visit by him to Moscow can be arranged. The best we might be able to do would be to give the Russians advance warning of it. We are proposing to tell the Russians in advance about a visit which the Chinese Foreign Minister is expected to pay to Britain (among other countries) later this month. You will be receiving separate instructions about this.

7. On tactics, there is the problem that the Russians may seek to exploit our interest in a visit by Mr. Heath to Moscow to extract concessions which we shall not feel inclined to make. These could be either in international questions such as CSCE or MBFR, or on the line which British Ministers take in public about détente and the defence of Western Europe, or about the small but knotty problems which we have here in London: the size of the Soviet establishment, their claim that the STD[7] should be exempt from rates, the continued attempts to introduce intelligence officers through the normal visa machinery, etc. We could not, without serious and possibly unacceptable disadvantages, give way on such points as these. An encounter between Mr. Heath and Brezhnev before these minor points had been dealt with would be very different from the kind of meeting which Pompidou was able to enjoy in Minsk.[8] I am not saying that these minor difficulties are insurmountable; only that the arrangement of a successful visit to Moscow by the Prime Minister may not be easy if we have not been able to get them out of the way beforehand.

8. There is another important point of a general kind. We want to find some way of discouraging the US Government from withdrawing troops from Europe, and we want to encourage our partners in the EEC to maintain and, if necessary, increase their own defensive capacity as part of the quest for détente. This is one of the most important tasks confronting British Ministers at the moment. It would

[7] Soviet Trade Delegation.
[8] See No. 37, note 28.

be essential to manage a visit by the Prime Minister to Moscow in such a way that it did not manifestly contribute to any weakening of NATO.

9. To sum up, I am sure that the Prime Minister would be happy to make a visit to Moscow in 1974 provided the circumstances were right; but there are risks as regards the effect on public opinion in this country and in Western Europe; tactics and timing present difficulties; and the content is likely to be disappointing. When the PUS and Mr. Amery considered the first draft (which you saw) of a recent DOP paper on Anglo-Soviet relations,[9] they were not in favour of our taking the initiative at the moment. As for the suggestion that the PUS should invite Kozyrev[10] to pay a second visit to London, I am tempted to comment that Kozyrev's visit in 1971 could hardly be described as fruitful. The circumstances will obviously have to be right if a second visit by him is to do any good. We are considering the question now in the context of the meeting which the Secretary of State will presumably have with Gromyko at the Conference on Vietnam later this month.[11] I will let you know the outcome.

THOMAS BRIMELOW

[9] *V. ibid.*, note 4.

[10] Mr. S.P. Kozyrev was Soviet Deputy Minister for Foreign Affairs.

[11] The international conference on Vietnam, a provision of the peace agreement signed in January, opened in Paris on 26 February 1973.

No. 40

Letter from Mr. Bullard to Sir J. Killick (Moscow)

[*ENS 3/548/2*]

Confidential FCO, *28 March 1973*

My dear John,

Anglo-Soviet Relations

1. I should like to sum up, in the light of recent developments in Anglo-Soviet relations, the themes touched on in Joe Dobbs' letter to Sir T. Brimelow of 1 March[1] replying to his letter to you of 6 February.[2]

[1] In this letter (see No. 39, note 2) Mr. Dobbs reminded Sir T. Brimelow that there had been 'indications' that the Soviet Government had decided 'to mark time so far as Anglo/Soviet relations [were] concerned until after the next election, which they presumably regard[ed] the Labour Party as standing a good chance of winning'. EESD's draft DOP paper of December 1972 (see No. 37, note 4) had already suggested that Soviet cultivation of Opposition leaders and trade unionists appeared 'designed to outflank the present Conservative administration'. Visits by Mr. Callaghan, then Chairman of the Labour Party, and Mr. V.G.H. Feather, the General Secretary of the Trades Union Congress (TUC), to Russia, and a speech by the former in the Commons Foreign Affairs debate on 14 December, were regarded as indicating that these tactics were achieving some success.

[2] No. 39.

2.   We are satisfied that, broadly speaking, Anglo-Soviet relations are moving in the right direction. We are getting on better with the Russians and are being seen to do so (Parliamentary delegation, Joint Commission, Prince Philip).[3] At the same time we are not shrinking from firm action in sensitive fields such as security (the visa war, intelligence activities), nor are we abandoning our chosen role as a Cassandra to the Western alliance on the theme of the Soviet threat to Western Europe (Defence Debate). I think this is a pretty satisfactory à la carte menu.

3.   Our hope is that present trends will continue in such a way as to generate a sensible and businesslike atmosphere in which a preliminary, ice-breaking meeting can take place between the Prime Minister and Mr. Brezhnev at the third stage of the CSCE (if this takes place at such a level, which now seems highly probable), which in turn would make it possible for Mr. Heath to visit Moscow in 1974, either at Soviet invitation or at his own suggestion (which could be represented as by mutual agreement).

4.   The missing ingredient, as you point out, is Ministerial visits at a lower level. I see these as desirable, but not any means essential. The Secretary of State has had several useful meetings with Mr. Gromyko on neutral territory since the expulsions, though I doubt whether the Russians are ready to invite him to Moscow yet. This in itself need not stand in the way of a visit by Mr. Heath in 1974. The Russians' increasing interest in conducting foreign affairs at a high level may make them ready to overlook the intermediate stages once Brezhnev himself decides that he is ready to welcome the Prime Minister to Moscow. This does not mean that we should not watch for opportunities to encourage a resumption of visits by FCO Ministers. But we can hardly assume the posture of demandeurs after the Godber affair.[4] Nor can we invite Gromyko here when it is clear that it is the Russians' turn to have an FCO Minister in Moscow.[5]

5.   Visits by 'non-political' Soviet Ministers to this country seem to us rather less important. Would a visit by a Soviet technical Minister to Britain really be very useful, either as an indicator of the Soviet attitude to Mr. Heath or as a rung in the ladder leading to his visit to Moscow? I am not against such visits, but I think they must justify themselves mainly on technical grounds. In the case of the Minister of Housing there are two difficulties. The first is that the Russians included Mr. Amery's visit (then Minister for Public Building and Works) in the list of events cancelled in reprisal for FOOT.[6] Secondly, Mr. Channon,[7] the

---

[3] Six Soviet parliamentarians visited the UK in March. The Anglo-Soviet Joint Commission on Trade and Technology was scheduled to meet in Moscow during 16–18 April 1973, and it had been settled that the Duke of Edinburgh would visit Moscow and Kiev during 3–9 September 1973 (cf. No. 37, note 37).

[4] See Volume I, Nos. 93 and 103.

[5] In his letter of 1 March (see note 1 above) Mr. Dobbs suggested that the next rung in the ladder of Ministerial visits should presumably be a meeting of Foreign Ministers either 'in London or in Moscow for rather more substantive discussions than are possible at international occasions like the Vietnam Conference'.

[6] See Volume I, No. 80, note 1.

[7] Mr. H.P.G. Channon was Minister for Housing and Construction.

present Minister, already has a series of engagements with his opposite numbers in Eastern Europe this year, and we are not sure that this is the right time to try to add Moscow to the list. The prospects for a visit by the Soviet Minister of Health look better. There has been no formal return visit this way since Mr. Robinson[8] visited Moscow in 1967, and it seems possible that the Department of Health and Social Security may agree to sign an agreement on Medical Co-operation. We will keep an eye on this.

6. Next there is the question of inviting Brezhnev to London, or Kosygin as your letter of 23 March[9] suggests. We will consider this as part of the preparations for Mr. Walker's visit,[10] but I myself am not much attracted by the idea. The maxim that if you want to get on with the Russians, you must show that you can get on without them, surely applies to high-level visits as much as to any other aspect of relations. The Prime Minister is also known to believe very strongly that any such visit, inward or outward, must have a specific and important purpose. I doubt whether he would think it appropriate to invite either Brezhnev or Kosygin here in 1973 simply to pave the way for his own return visit in 1974. In Brezhnev's case it is in any case almost certainly too late to fit in a Head of State-type visit this year, and I agree that nothing less would be suitable for him. Altogether I should prefer you not to hint at any such possibility when you see Gromyko to hand over the memorandum on Anglo-Soviet trade.[11]

7. Finally, Joe Dobbs mentioned the tone of British Ministerial statements.[12] Here you will bear in mind the point which we made when the same complaint was voiced at last year's meeting of Ambassadors from Eastern Europe,[13] namely that these speeches are directed more at the audiences to which they are delivered and at the public opinion in this country than at hypothetical readers in the Foreign Ministry in Moscow. To take the concrete case of the Prime Minister's visit to Washington, the good effect of this in Anglo-American terms was surely such as to outweigh by far the consequences of any irritation that may have been caused in Moscow by Mr. Heath's choice of adjectives. Nevertheless I do admit that the choice of words in some British Ministerial speeches over the last couple of years has on occasions been a little crude. If you read last week's Defence

---

[8] Mr. K. Robinson was Minister of Health during 1964–68.

[9] In this letter to Mr. Bullard Sir J. Killick suggested that, since 'it would in principle be desirable for the Prime Minister to visit the Soviet Union in 1974', Mr. Walker might, during his forthcoming visit to Moscow, seek to promote this by giving Mr. Kosygin an invitation from Mr. Heath to visit London in 1973.

[10] See No. 37, notes 13 and 14.

[11] During a luncheon at HM Embassy in Paris on 27 February Sir A. Douglas-Home responded to Mr. Gromyko's queries regarding the implications of Britain's membership of the EC for Anglo-Soviet trade by promising him a memorandum on the subject. The resulting paper, which was drafted in consultation with the DTI, stated that the UK's membership would not 'have a detrimental effect on the level of trade between the two countries in the coming years', and that no sectors of Soviet exports to the UK were likely to be reduced significantly by the application of the EC's Common External Tariff (MWE 3/303/1). Cf. No. 42.

[12] See No. 39, note 4.

[13] Cf. Volume I, No. 95.

Debate (when the Hansard strike is over), I hope you will notice that we have been trying to achieve a style of presentation which would be, in Duncan Wilson's[14] phrase, 'more nuancé'. But Victor Louis' trial balloon about a State Visit to the Soviet Union by HM The Queen seems to me a gross miscalculation of the British public mood, inviting the riposte from the Daily Telegraph.[15] The day is surely not yet come when leader writers on a British newspaper need to consider the effect of their words upon the sensitivity of the Soviet leaders, or when the FCO ought to ask them to do so. We can leave that to our opposite numbers in Finland.

8. Tom Brimelow has seen the foregoing and agrees with it. This will be part of our brief for the discussion on Anglo-Soviet relations which Ministers are to have (at last) on 6 April.[16]

Yours ever,
J.L. BULLARD

[14] Sir D. Wilson was HM Ambassador in Moscow during 1968–71.

[15] The *Evening News* of 23 February carried on its front page a report from its Moscow correspondent Mr. Louis, whom the FCO regarded as an unofficial Soviet mouthpiece, that the Kremlin was hoping that the Queen would pay a full state visit to the Soviet Union. Mr. Dobbs subsequently complained (see note 1 above) that he was appalled by *The Daily Telegraph*'s reference on 24 February to the present Soviet leaders as the 'spiritual heirs' of the men who murdered the Queen's relatives in '1917' and countless others since. The 'point', Mr. Dobbs noted, 'is not whether this is true or not; it is more that the present Soviet leaders would be deeply wounded by this accusation, and all the more so because of the portion of truth in it'.

[16] See No. 41.

No. 41

Record of Ninth Meeting of the Cabinet Defence and Oversea Policy Committee

[*CAB 148/129*]

Secret   CABINET OFFICE, *6 April 1973*

Anglo-Soviet Relations

The Committee had before them a memorandum by the Foreign and Commonwealth Secretary (DOP(73)5) on Anglo-Soviet relations.[1]

The Foreign and Commonwealth Secretary said that the climate of our relations with the Soviet Union had recently shown some improvement. Soviet Press comment had become less bitter towards us; the Embassy in Moscow was being granted

[1] No. 38. In a brief, submitted to the Private Secretary on 5 April, Mr. Bullard noted that since the circulation of the DOP paper in January there had been a 'considerable improvement in the Anglo-Soviet atmosphere' (ENS 3/548/2).

better access to Soviet officials; the Russians had reacted sensibly by withdrawing their Military Attaché and one of his assistants who had been engaging in activities unacceptable to us, and had thus not obliged us to proceed to the expulsion of these men. The Secretary of State for Trade and Industry would shortly visit Moscow for a meeting of the Anglo-Soviet Joint Committee and the Duke of Edinburgh would be visiting Kiev in the autumn.[2] The man appointed as the new Soviet Ambassador in London had a good reputation.[3] On the other hand, the Russians had not of course abandoned their spying operations in this country and they were using other Communist Embassies, notably the Czecho-slovakian and Cuban, to help them. The Russians undoubtedly regarded us as the hardliners among the West Europeans and we had this reputation among the West Europeans themselves.[4] But the present Soviet policy of détente was directed to longer term aims hostile to Western interests and it was necessary that we should try to prevent Western opinion from being misled into weakening its political and military defences. We must also pursue such relations with other countries, for example China, as we conceived to be in our interest and we should not be deterred by the prospect of incurring Soviet displeasure. It might indeed sometimes be useful to us in dealing with the Russians that we should be developing our relations with China. While, therefore, we should be ready to contribute to any improvement in relations with the Soviet Union which the Russians themselves made possible, we could not sacrifice our fundamental interests elsewhere in order to please Moscow.

In discussion it was suggested that we might on occasion have taken, or appeared to take, an unnecessarily hard-line attitude and that although it was necessary to talk plainly, (however unpalatable this might be to the Russians) we might lose influence with our own allies if we earned the reputation of always being the odd man out. It was also suggested that if, as a result of maintaining openly an unduly rigid line in contrast to that of our allies, our trade with Russia continued to decline while that of our allies improved, our voice in European affairs and within the North Atlantic Treaty Organisation might come to be increasingly disregarded. A vigorous effort should be made to improve our trad-ing performance. It was also noted, however, that the possibilities of increasing trade with the Soviet Union could easily be exaggerated. The pursuit of this trade had always been a frustrating task.[5]

[2] See No. 40, note 3.

[3] In May Mr. N.M. Lunkov, formerly Head of the Second European Department in the Soviet Foreign Ministry, succeeded Mr. Smirnovsky as Soviet Ambassador in London.

[4] Mr. Bullard explained in his brief of 5 April (see note 1 above) that the progress so far made in relations with the USSR had been achieved 'without any sacrifice of principles'. He added: 'We have continued to state the facts about the Soviet military threat as we see them … In the intelligence field, which is important both in itself and as a test of will, we have not admitted any identified Soviet intelligence officers to this country since the expulsions of September 1971, and we have maintained the ceilings imposed at that time on the Soviet establishment in Britain. It is almost certainly our firmness which has led the Russians to modify their attitude in recent weeks.'

[5] Mr. Bullard had thought it possible that Mr. Walker might suggest to the Committee that there was a stronger case than the DOP paper allowed for making political concessions to Moscow

The Prime Minister, summing up the discussion, said that the recent indications of an improvement in the Russian attitude were welcome. The Secretary of State for Trade and Industry on his forthcoming visit to Moscow should pursue vigorously the possibilities of increasing trade with the Soviet Union; dramatic results were not to be expected; past performance showed that trade talks with the Russians often produced grandiose proposals which were not matched by subsequent performance. In the past the Russians had sought to justify the imbalance in our trade by claiming that their trade with the rest of the Sterling Area should be taken into account. This line of argument must be firmly resisted. A naval visit to Leningrad would probably take place later this year; this too could add to a climate of improved relations. But while visits of various kinds were useful in this way it was important not to exaggerate their effect upon the reality of our relations with the Soviet Union. He would himself invite the departing Soviet Ambassador in London, Mr. Smirnovsky, to a farewell talk.

The Committee:

Took note, with approval, of the Prime Minister's summing up of their discussion.

in order to secure commercial benefit. But, as he pointed out in his brief (*v. ibid.*), this was questionable on the grounds that: (1) the part played by politics in Soviet trade had never been precisely established; (2) Soviet imports were and would be limited by an acute shortage of foreign currency; (3) Western European exports to the USSR were likely to suffer as a result of increased US and Japanese competition; and (4) the Russians could not give commercial bounties to all Western European countries simultaneously and they had special reasons for conciliating many of Britain's competitors. 'It would', Mr. Bullard concluded, 'in any case be difficult to give Moscow much satisfaction without appearing either to retract our views on "détente" or taking a more tolerant attitude to Soviet intelligence activities in this country.'

No. 42

Sir J. Killick (Moscow) to Sir A. Douglas-Home

[*ENS 6/548/3*]

Confidential   MOSCOW, *7 May 1973*

Summary ...[1]

Sir,

Anglo-Soviet Relations and Mr. Brezhnev's Economic Diplomacy

I have set out for the record in a separate despatch an account of the second session of the Anglo-Soviet Joint Commission held in Moscow from 16–18

[1] Not printed.

April,[2] together with certain comments and conclusions directly related to it.

2.   It would be wrong not to supplement this from the broader political point of view, with particular regard to its implications for Anglo-Soviet relations in general. It was, after all, the most important development in Anglo-Soviet relations since the events of September, 1971.

3.   Following the imposition of the 'freeze' by the Soviet side which followed those events, and which specifically included the cancellation of the second session of the Joint Commission itself, scheduled for February, 1972, Her Majesty's Government adopted a position which amounted in essence to willingness to return to normal at any time, while refraining from running after the Russians as if in supplication or repentance. Although this left in Soviet hands control of the timing and manner of the return to normal, which was sooner or later bound to come, there was no alternative in practice. British overtures to the Russians would either have been rebuffed or regarded as a sign of actual or potential weakness.

4.   The chosen Soviet route of return has been through the Joint Commission. They took the initiative in sending Mr. Pronsky, of the State Committee for Science and Technology (which provides the Chairman of the Soviet side of the Commission) to London in October of last year, and he proposed that the cancelled meeting should be held this spring. Mr. Preston, of the Department of Trade and Industry, responded by paying a valuable return visit to Moscow in January of this year. However, this exchange of visits, and subsequent follow-up in Moscow, failed to reveal any clear or satisfactory picture of what, in practical terms of Anglo-Soviet commercial and economic relations, might emerge from the meeting of the Commission, although its political significance was not in question.

5.   Thus as our own steering brief said, its most important aspect was that it was taking place at all. I suspect that this was true of both sides, and it certainly did not appear from the Soviet performance, as described in my accompanying despatch, that the Soviet side had any specific objectives of importance in mind beyond the restoration of contact and the picking up of threads—in itself a desirable operation two and a quarter years after the Commission's first meeting had taken place.[3] Nobody on the Soviet side gave me any sensible answer before the session to the question what they would regard as a successful outcome, and

[2] In a despatch of 4 May Sir J. Killick described the meeting of the Joint Commission on 16–18 April. It was co-chaired by Mr. Walker and Academician V.A. Kirillin, Chairman of the State Committee of the Council of Ministers of the USSR for Science and Technology. 'The revival of the Joint Commission and its related activities after a year of "punitive" inactivity', Sir J. Killick noted, 'will not automatically bring benefits, although the Russians have agreed that it should meet again in a year's time and must know that that the British side will then want to review progress. The Commission cannot conclude actual business deals, but only create a favourable climate for them through formulae on paper.' As Sir A. Douglas-Home pointed out in telegram No. 290 to Moscow of 11 April (ENS 3/548/2), Mr. Walker was the 'first British Cabinet Minister to visit Moscow on bilateral business since the present administration came to power'.

[3] Sir J. Killick wrote in his despatch of 4 May (*v. ibid.*): 'The proceedings took the form of the usual rather dreary, prepared Soviet statements followed by refreshingly original and provocative contributions by Mr. Walker, backed up as appropriate by other members of the British delegation.

Mr. Manzhulo,[4] Deputy Minister of Foreign Trade, went so far as to assure me that they had 'nothing up their sleeves'.

6.   Not so on the British side. The Secretary of State for Trade and Industry came against the background of a general Governmental desire to see a major effort made to restore Britain's place in the pattern of Soviet foreign trade. The Soviet side ought to have been prepared for this, but seem to have been taken somewhat off balance.[5] Perhaps they had not expected such a forceful and effective approach from Mr. Walker, although I had made some effort to awaken them to what they should expect, in the general context of my long-standing attempts to bring home to Mr. Gromyko and others that the present British Government believes in actions rather than words.[6]

7.   The question inevitably arises, what led the Soviet Government to make this move, which must clearly have resulted from a political decision at the highest level and to what further developments it may lead. One must proceed from the assumption that the Russians either accepted from the first that they could not keep us permanently in the doghouse or came to the conclusion last year that it would be against their interest, with so much European diplomacy going on, to keep us totally at arm's length. If they wished only to make a symbolic gesture, with no real content, the commercial-economic field was the most appropriate as involving the least public appearance of a climb-down on their side. It may stop at that, and lead to no follow-up in the foreign policy field with the resumption of normal bilateral contacts between Foreign Ministers. There is certainly not the slightest indication of any Soviet move in this direction, still less of any interest in 'summit-type' meetings at Head of Government level. (In all this, I have not overlooked Mr. Lunkov's visit to London last year,[7] but now that he has been appointed Ambassador, it looks more than ever as though he was mainly interested in 'casing the joint'.) I do not exclude the possibility that such moves will in due course come, but it may equally well be that the Soviet Government is banking on the resumption of contacts of this sort coming about less deliberately through the expected stages of the proposed Conference on Security and Co-operation in Europe. Meanwhile, the UK remains conspicuously absent from the list of countries continually set out in Soviet propaganda as those with which relations are developing satisfactorily: the Federal Republic of Germany, France, Japan and the US.

For the most part the Russians appeared incapable of response or debate and hardly went beyond unimaginative regurgitation of points from their formal statements.'

 [4] Mr. A.N. Manzhulo.

 [5] According to Sir J. Killick (see notes 2 and 3 above), 'it was left to Mr. Walker to put life and substance into the proceedings' relating to trade and economic cooperation. 'The Russians', he reported, 'could not rebut his [Mr. Walker's] vivid and carefully chosen examples of the success of British exports in almost every other market—and thus laid themselves open to the implication that the fault must be on their side, possibly because of deliberate diversion of their purchases elsewhere for the past four years.'

 [6] In telegram No. 290 to Moscow (see note 2 above) Sir A. Douglas-Home wrote of the Joint Commission meeting: 'I hope this meeting will open the door to rescuing Anglo-Soviet trade from the state of stagnation where it has languished since 1969.'

 [7] See Volume II, No. 14.

8.   The presumed ultimate Soviet objective is to bring about some change in Her Majesty's Government's present main lines of policy, both in terms of our healthy scepticism about 'detente' and East–West relations and of our ideas and influence on the future development of the expanded European Economic Community. They cannot realistically hope to achieve much by keeping us at a distance and offering us no sweeteners or inducements. It would be foolish of them to suppose that they can get anywhere just through the superficial device of holding the Joint Commission meeting and perhaps concluding a long-term economic co-operation agreement. They ought at least to be prepared next to try to give us enough satisfaction, through the conclusion of some actual commercial contracts, despite their foreign currency and other difficulties, to keep us interested and in play. Otherwise we shall stand out as a glaring example of failure of their 'economic co-operation' overtures to the West, as a major industrial country which has not only found no substance in them, but does not mind.

9.   On the other hand, Mr. Walker's admirably firm line of counter-attack on a number of fronts ought to leave them with no illusion that they can make even a small dent on Her Majesty's Government's political position, however forthcoming they try to be with offers of trade and economic co-operation. The choice before them is between conducting their trade with us mainly on commercial merit, renouncing any efforts to offer us carrots in this field with political objectives in mind, or continuing to dangle glittering commercial and economic prospects before us with the implied condition that we become more 'co-operative' in our foreign policy. They no doubt have some reason to hope for success with these tactics with others of their trading partners and now with the US, but they cannot deliver adequate rewards to them all. It may turn out to be no exaggeration to speak of a 'Siberian bubble'.

10.   Probably they do not yet accept that, with us, the second alternative has no future. Politically, we should not mind. The trouble is that it may lead to a good deal of time- and money- wasting effort by British firms before the Russians decide that Her Majesty's Government have not been sufficiently 'co-operative' and that the British shall not be given contracts. I am increasingly struck by the fact that the new era of 'economic co-operation' is so evidently part and parcel of Mr. Brezhnev's foreign policy, and perhaps a controversial one domestically at that. In other words, the risk of political considerations interfering with the genuine trading interests of the Soviet Union seems greater than ever.

11.   At all events, Mr. Walker spoke to the Russians so clearly and frankly that they have no excuse for failing to understand Britain's position. In particular, we are in no sense *demandeurs*. For example:

(*a*) He underlined the lowly position of Anglo-Soviet trade in Britain's overall trading pattern.

(*b*) He drew attention to the risk that British firms would lose interest in the market if the Soviet side did not give them adequate encouragement and proper treatment.

(*c*)   In reply to questions from Mr. Kosygin,[8] he said categorically that Britain would be self-sufficient in North Sea gas from 1980, 50 per cent self-sufficient in oil from the same source, and was already and for the foreseeable future well-supplied with nuclear fuel. (From this the Soviet side should readily see that we have not the same incentive for the sort of deals concluded or under negotiation with France, Germany, Italy, Japan or the US in these areas.)

(*d*)   Perhaps most importantly of all, he answered Mr. Kosygin's questioning about Britain's entry into the European Economic Community in confidently positive terms. He was able to cite the conclusion of the memorandum on this subject which I handed to Mr. Gromyko on 11 April, and go over to the counter-attack.[9]

12.   It was remarkable that his Soviet interlocutors seemed at a loss for answers to all this, and I was particularly struck by the manner in which Mr. Kosygin dropped the subject and did not press home any kind of attack or criticism as regards the EEC. Nor was there any difficulty in resisting a Soviet suggestion of incorporating in the final Protocol a British assurance that the 'necessary measures' would be taken if, as a consequence of UK membership of the EEC, circumstances were to arise which might impede the access to the British market of Soviet exports. I would hesitate to conclude that the Russians have been completely floored or are convinced by the cogency of all our arguments. How-ever, it looks as though they have been given food for thought. When they have digested it, they may well come back with new tactics and new lines of attack. I begin to detect the outline of one possible campaign in the statement and Press comment following last month's Central Committee Plenum, with its references to the strengthening of the 'defensive' capability of the Council for Mutual Economic Assistance (CMEA).[10] This has all the appearance of a bargaining counter to be used as the basis for the suggestion that the Soviet Union will call off its integration of the CMEA for defence purposes if the EEC will do the same.[11] However, we must wait and see. For the present I have no hesitation in claiming the round of exchanges on these subjects as a British victory on points. The Soviet side may derive some satisfaction from our agreement to negotiate a

---

[8]   Mr. Walker met Mr. Kosygin in the Kremlin on 18 April.

[9]   See No. 40, note 11.

[10]   The Plenum of the Central Committee of the CPSU met during 26–27 April. In Moscow telegram No. 524 of 28 April Sir J. Killick observed that Mr. Brezhnev's objective in convening the Plenum must have been to secure a demonstration of total support by a united party leadership for 'his forays into the capitalist camp and the commitment of his colleagues to his strategy and tactics'. The Plenum's resolution, reported in Moscow telegram No. 522 of 28 April, referred to the special importance of 'perfecting … economic cooperation with the CMEA countries' and the strengthening of the 'economic and defensive power of the socialist community' (ENS 1/5).

[11]   In a letter to Sir J. Killick of 21 June Mr. Bullard pointed out that the *communiqué* issued on 8 June, after the 27th session of the CMEA in Prague, had stated that socialist economic integration would 'ensure the further strengthening of economic and scientific-technical potential and defence capability of the CMEA member states' (EN 5/2).

long-term economic co-operation agreement, and they are welcome to do so. We are fully aware that their objective in this is to undermine the integration of the EEC, and shall ensure that the content of the agreement gives them no opportunity of achieving that objective.

13. As regards trade itself, it was an achievement to secure, as a result of Mr. Walker's 'hard sell', Soviet agreement to two propositions in the Protocol:

(*a*) That the Working Groups established under the aegis of the Joint Commission are to so promote scientific, technological and economic co-operation as to facilitate the development of trade. While this will not prevent the State Committee for Science and Technology from using them, as hitherto, as a vehicle for the one-way transmission of information on non-commercial terms, it should help to mitigate it, and gives us a point of reference for complaint.
(*b*) That both sides agree the aim of bringing about a substantial increase in the volume of trade in both directions.

14. It remains to be seen whether the will exists on the Soviet side to give real effect to these formulae. It also remains to be seen whether British industry is willing or able to devote organised and effective effort to exploiting them. I am bound to say, I hope not unfairly on brief acquaintance, that it did not strike me that the Chairman of the Confederation of British Industries [*sic*] [CBI],[12] who was a member of the British delegation, had any very impressive or forward-looking ideas on the subject. He will certainly have left an impression reinforcing Mr. Walker's point that this is not a market of first importance for British industry. However, there are of course many firms, large and small, with irons already in the fire here, and they could and should do better. They deserve, and will continue to have, our full support. The Soviet economy is expanding and the need to import is, albeit with reluctance, accepted, if only as an unfortunate necessity and not as a desirable end in itself. Comecon autarky remains the aim, but a vague and doubtful prospect for the foreseeable future.[13] Meanwhile, the foreign trade cake ought to grow larger, despite foreign exchange difficulties, and although there are more countries after a slice of it and the slices are consequently percentage-wise smaller, our share is well below what it should be in terms of British exports. A doubling of our exports to say £200 million per annum over the next few years should not be an unrealistic target and would presumably be well worth having,

---

[12] Sir M. Clapham.

[13] In a personal message to Sir T. Brimelow, in Moscow telegram No. 542 of 4 May, Sir J. Killick dubbed 'premature and dangerous' the tendency of some of his Western colleagues to conclude that 'Brezhnev's foreign policy line [involved] Soviet abandonment of economic autarky'. He considered it highly probable that Mr. Brezhnev approached economic cooperation with the West 'from the position that it is necessary only as a temporary means (albeit over ten years or so) of redressing Soviet economic backwardness while at the same time serving to promote an atmosphere of détente in which the West becomes militarily weaker'. At the end of such a period, he thought Mr. Brezhnev might envisage a reversion to Soviet pressure tactics from a position of relative strength based upon Soviet plus COMECON economic and military power (ENS 2/1).

even if some proportion had to be on a counter-trading or industrial co-operation basis.

15. On the other hand, it cannot be said too often that the potential of this market falls far short of what it might seem on the surface, judged by the size and population of the Soviet Union, its crying need for advanced technology and equipment, consumer goods and light industry, and the immensity of its under-developed natural resources. Apart from the doctrine of autarky and the probable continuing problem of foreign exchange, the whole system militates against the creation of anything closely resembling what might in Western terms be regarded as an inviting investment climate. The danger of 'strategic dependence' on the capitalist world is probably a more cogent factor here than the reverse proposition in the West. Ingrained secrecy coupled with plain bureaucratic inefficiency will militate against the timely or adequate provision of information. The possibility of the admittance of Western management is so remote as to be virtually ruled out. The creation of effective Soviet management, particularly in areas involving the acceptance of market forces, seems little less unlikely; yet will not the Western entrepreneur involved in 'industrial co-operation' need to be satisfied that Soviet management can assure him of his return in full measure and on time, whether in kind or cash? In any case, it will not be easy to identify appropriate products or commodities for counterpurchase; raw materials are all very well if one needs them and if the problem of our strategic dependence does not arise. Yet the Soviet Government clearly aims at carving out markets for its finished products and is unlikely to be satisfied with the inherently second-class status of provider of basic natural resources to the Western world. Its present apparent willingness to con-template this only strengthens the suspicion that the objective may be to bring about a significant degree of Western strategic dependence. I have the impression that considerations of this sort are steadily attracting wider attention in the US and beginning to put into better perspective the true prospects for US–Soviet economic relations. Yet the Soviet political will to make progress in US–Soviet relations is evident—to the extent of disregarding the major political differences which exist between the two Governments (though undoubtedly with the hope of removing them).

16. So it would appear that there is no need whatever to pay any political price for trade with the Soviet Union. It is the Russians who need economic co-operation with the West, not the reverse. This is the strength of the position of the US and Japan, if they choose to use it; it is also the potential strength of the EEC, if only we can organise ourselves to use it. There is, I fear, considerable illusion on the Soviet side about Western need for Soviet markets and about the effect of the obstacles to further development to which I refer in my preceding paragraph. This means that there is something fundamentally unsound in this aspect of Mr. Brezhnev's foreign policy, but he must be left to find this out for himself. It is not for us to go to any trouble to save him from himself.

I have, etc.,
J.E. KILLICK

No. 43

Letter from Sir J. Killick (Moscow) to Mr. Bullard

[*ENS 3/548/2*]

Confidential   MOSCOW, *13 June 1973*

Dear Julian,

The Queen's Birthday Party 1973

1.   I thought you might like to have a short note on the level of Soviet representation at our Queen's Birthday Party this year (7 June) as an indicator of the extent to which we have climbed back to respectability in Soviet eyes. In brief, my assessment is that in this purely formal and protocol context we have been moved up two notches, as compared with last year, but certainly no more.[1]

2.   Despite the repeated and fervid protestations to which all of us were subjected by members of Second European Department and others concerning the bright new horizons which are opening up for Anglo-Soviet relations and the desire of the Soviet side to press on towards them, we still rated no more than one Deputy Chairman of the Council of Ministers, N.A. Tikhonov (a former engine-driver, who looked and behaved like one, on the whole), to supplement last year's turn out of M.P. Georgadze (Secretary of the Praesidium of the Supreme Soviet) and Deputy Foreign Minister Kozyrev. The improvement was a little more marked on the military side, which gave us nine three-star Generals, as compared with three in 1972, and an Engineer Admiral; there was, however, no Air Force representation of significance. The Orthodox Church was unaccountably absent altogether; the explanation may lie in the fact that our Party took place on Ascension Day, but, even so, it is curious that no apologies for absence or expressions of goodwill were sent. The Proto-Deacon George Ustinov of the Old Believers came, bringing with him a nice letter from Archbishop Nikodim of Moscow and All the Russias. Trade was adequately represented but, given the recent session of the Joint Commission,[2] no more than that. Deputy Minister of Foreign Trade Manzhulo attended and the All-Union chamber of Commerce made a good showing. All in all, Soviet attendance was just good enough not to give us cause for complaint but fell some way short of the level which the proclamations of a new dawn by Second European Department and others might have led us to expect.

3.   If I can say so without immodesty, the Party was in every other respect a

---

[1] In a letter to Sir J. Killick of 14 June Mr. Bullard observed that he felt a 'strong temptation' to advise Sir A. Douglas-Home against attending the next Soviet Embassy invitation in order to 'drop a hint to the Russians that we mean to preserve reciprocity in these matters'. But, he added, Sir T. Brimelow thought this to be 'one of those cases where "it is no good getting into a stinking match with a skunk", and that the right course [was] to continue to behave courteously on our side, and await an opportunity of drawing the attention of some suitable Soviet official to the difference between their behaviour and ours'.

[2] See No. 42.

very considerable success. The weather was reasonably kind, letting us off with one short thunder-shower. The presence of the Labour Party delegation and even more so (if I may say so without making invidious comparisons!) the arrival half way through the Party of Sir Alf Ramsay[3] [*sic*] and the England football team gave it additional lift. When I called on Suslov[4] in the Second European Department on the following morning, he told me that he wished to make 'a stern protest'; I had, he alleged, made all his staff so drunk at my Party that they were incapable of work.[5] He then produced a bottle of Armenian brandy as a hair of the dog!

4. Among other social notes at random, I would only mention my quiet enjoyment of the efforts (viewed through my upstairs window after my own departure) of a British businessman trying to connect a cigarette with his mouth, and then a match with his cigarette, before falling gracefully into a flower bed. And of Viktor Sukhodrev's assiduous collection of footballers' autographs, which he amply repaid by watching the match on the following Sunday from a seat in the middle of the British Embassy contingent, with whom he cheered as heartily for England as befits an 'old Highgatian'.[6]

Yours ever,
J.E. KILLICK

[3] Sir A. Ramsey was Manager of the England Football Association national side.

[4] Mr. V.P. Suslov was Mr. Lunkov's successor as Head of the Second European Department of the Soviet Foreign Ministry.

[5] In a letter to Mr. Bullard of 13 June Mr. Dobbs described conversations he had had with two other guests at the party, Mr. Vasev and Mr. V.V. Karyagin, Deputy Head of the Cultural Relations Department, both of whom 'had had a good many whiskeys'. Mr. Vasev gave Mr. Dobbs to understand that the Soviet Government had concluded that the British were taking the CSCE 'seriously' and 'now wished to be much more positive towards relations with the UK'. Mr. Karyagin's 'message seemed to be that Gromyko's personal pique over his involvement with the Secretary of State in the spy problem was still a considerable obstacle to full normalisation of relations'.

[6] Mr. Sukhodrev was a Counsellor in the Second European Department of the Soviet Foreign Ministry. The son of a Soviet diplomat in London, he was educated at Highgate school. England played the Soviet Union on 10 June in the Lenin Stadium, beating the home side 2-1.

No. 44

Sir A. Douglas-Home to Sir J. Killick (Moscow)

No. 498 Telegraphic [*ENS 3/548/2*]

Immediate. Confidential   FCO, *3 July 1973, 2.40 p.m.*

Following for Ambassador from EESD.

Lunkov's call on the Prime Minister

1.   As you will see from our brief for the Secretary of State's talk with Mr Gromyko in Helsinki, (copy follows by bag),[1] our preliminary analysis of Lunkov's talk with the Prime Minister was that we may have reached a point where each side is waiting for the other to take the next step forward in Anglo-Soviet relations. Lunkov said very firmly that 'the ball was in our court'.[2] There are grounds for thinking that the Russians would like an exchange of high level visits, probably at Prime Minister-Brezhnev level. But the message from Brezhnev which Mr. Lunkov delivered to the Prime Minister on 29 June showed that the Russians are not yet prepared to issue a firm invitation to Mr Heath, although there was a fairly broad hint that if Mr Heath were to ask to come to Moscow the reply would be favourable. The Russians may calculate that Brezhnev's recent visits to Bonn, Washington and Paris will highlight our position as the odd-man out, and increase pressure on us to ask for a visit. Mr. Lunkov rather implied that we should have to pay a price for it both in our bilateral relations and in our attitude to East–West relations as a whole.[3]

2.   The Prime Minister has now told the PUS that he wants his talk with Lunkov followed up urgently in order that the ball may be returned to the Soviet court. In particular, the Prime Minister would like a specific proposal for some joint industrial enterprise to be put to the Russians, if this is possible. There may be some other way that the tables could be turned on the Russians, but the PUS believes that a joint industrial venture would be the most acceptable way to do this.[4]

[1]   Not printed. Cf. Volume II, No. 40, note 4 and No. 42.

[2]   During his first meeting as Ambassador with Mr. Heath on 29 June Mr. Lunkov stated: 'The Soviet leadership favoured improved contacts between Britain and the Soviet Union at all possible levels, particularly at this time, in a period of change from the cold war. In this new phase the two countries were in a position to make a substantial contribution to détente and the improvement of international relations.' When Mr. Heath questioned him as to the meaning of his assertion that the 'ball was in our court', he responded that what was needed was 'positive and practical measures' to improve Anglo-Soviet relations (note by Mr. R.T. Armstrong (Principal Private Secretary to the Prime Minister) of 30 June).

[3]   In Moscow telegram No. 769 of 5 July Sir J. Killick observed that he and his colleagues felt sure that, although Mr. Brezhnev would now like to establish contact and was probably uncomfortable without it, he would be reluctant to do so unless he had some assurance of a positive political outcome which could be presented in the Soviet Union and elsewhere as 'another triumph'. He thought that some move to give political content to a visit could be devised.

[4]   Mr. Bullard had minuted Sir T. Brimelow on 22 June that he had 'the impression that Anglo-

3.   We are consulting the DTI urgently, and would be grateful for your views by immediate telegram before close of play on 5 July.[5]

Soviet relations [had] turned a definite corner and [were] now set on a more amicable course'.

[5] Sir J. Killick pointed out in his telegram No. 769 (see note 3 above) that the logic of the Soviet position was that economic cooperation and major deals were not steps towards an improved political relationship, but could be a consequence of it. 'It follows', he added, 'that to suggest a joint industrial venture would not succeed in turning the tables. The Russians are notoriously slow negotiators. It could take several years before the two sides got close enough to be fairly confident that a viable enterprise would see the light of day.'

No. 45

Letter from Sir J. Killick (Moscow) to Mr. J.O. Wright
[*MWE 3/303/2*]

Confidential   MOSCOW, *1 August 1973*

Dear Oliver,

Whatever became of CCP?[1]

I am afraid I neglected to thank you for sending me, as long ago as 16 February, a copy of a draft FCO/DTI note for the European Unit on this subject.[2] Although you invited comments, I had none of substance. It seemed to cover the essentials of the early thoughts on the content of the CCP which I put to John Mason, then in EID(1),[3] in a letter of 11 May, 1972, following last year's Heads of Mission meeting.[4]

2.   A good deal of water has flowed under the bridge since then, and I do not think I am up to date on developments in Brussels. But as seen from here, there has been little progress in elaborating the CCP (and indeed serious backsliding by e.g. the Italians over credit policy)[5] while the extension of economic, ostensibly

[1] See No. 37, notes 7 and 27.

[2] This draft paper, prepared for the Cabinet Official Committee on Europe (EUO), dealt with the implementation of the CCP.

[3] European Integration Department (1) had been primarily responsible for overseeing the negotiations for the UK's entry into the EC.

[4] In this letter Sir J. Killick warned Mr. Mason that the Soviet Union might seek to undermine the CCP even before it was established. 'The important thing', he observed, 'is to exploit the relative strength of the Western position before the Russians make any more progress with "socialist integration"' (MWE 5/303/1).

[5] A DTI memorandum of 8 May, drafted for the Cabinet Ministerial Committee on Europe, noted that the only significant EC measure affecting export credits to CMEA (COMECON) countries had been the institution of a consultation procedure between member states on all officially supported transactions involving credit in excess of five years. Italy had, however, 'flagrantly disregarded' its requirements by 'granting to the USSR massive credits involving abnormally long repayment periods and heavily subsidised interest rates' (EUM (73) 33).

non-commercial, relationships with the Soviet Union has proceeded apace. Now we are confronted with an important initiative from the CMEA side[6] which challenges us in effect to clarify our minds and decide what we want. To me, this is a welcome, if different development.

3. I have been wanting to take stock for some time, and had hoped it would be possible to put together a paper summing up our knowledge of the whole network of bilateral relationships which has now been created, but my Commercial Department, with people on summer leave, has been overwhelmed with current trade promotion work. No doubt you and the DTI have all the information anyway. However, I think certain general points emerge fairly clearly.

Economic Cooperation Agreements

4. *Politically*, one's whole instinct has been against them, at any rate with the Soviet Union. We all know that the Soviet Government's underlying intention is to try to use them to get round or inhibit the CCP or its further development.[7] It is noteworthy that the Soviet Union has only concluded them with or suggested them to members of the EEC or countries associated with or intending to associate with EEC. Although vis-à-vis the United States and Japan, for example, there is heavy emphasis on long-term co-operation, there does not seem to have been any suggestion that formal agreements are needed with those countries, nor that their trade will suffer in their absence. (Consequently I question the statement in the second sentence of paragraph 9 of the Secretary of State's despatch to me of 26 July.)[8] However, I trust that our determination to continue with the development of the EEC will remain strong enough to defeat any Russian machinations. Our agreements give them no real handle in substance to do so.

5. *Commercially*, however, I entirely accept the argument that when our partners (and competitors) in the EEC or elsewhere have concluded long-term economic co-operation agreements with the Soviet Union, we would be foolish

---

[6] On 27 August Mr. N.V. Faddeyev, the CMEA's Secretary-General, visited Copenhagen and proposed to the Danish Ministers of Foreign Economic Affairs and Foreign Affairs that the CMEA and the EC should 'take up contact with the broad objective of furthering détente and cooperation' and that the two organisations should appoint delegations 'to discuss the framework and content of further talks' (brief for Ad Hoc Group: 3–4 September, EN 5/1). Cf. Volume II, No. 55, note 7.

[7] The EC Commission had made various proposals regarding policy co-ordination on such cooperation agreements. But the DTI memorandum of 8 May (see note 5 above) commented: 'While at national level Cooperation Agreements are negotiated by Governments their implementation is essentially a matter for industry and the proposed involvement of the Commission in the implementation of Community Agreements, covering as it would the discussion of specific commercial opportunities with the CMEA countries, assumes an identity of interest among the industries of the Community that does not in fact exist; it would therefore also be difficult to operate.'

[8] This despatch set out the views of Sir A. Douglas-Home and Mr. Walker on the results of the April meeting of the Anglo-Soviet Joint Commission (see No. 42). In the second sentence of paragraph 9, which dealt with Soviet proposals for a ten-year cooperation agreement, Sir A. Douglas-Home wrote: 'The Soviet authorities clearly see such an agreement as providing a guaranteed framework for their planners, establishing a stable relationship between our two countries for at least 10 years' (ENS 6/548/3).

to risk harming our interests and prospects by not following suit. We have done so, and are successfully and promptly following up Mr. Peter Walker's assent, at the Joint Commission meeting in April, to the negotiation.[9] I do not think he, any more than I, is under any illusion about how much material effect this will have on our trading prospects; but at least it ensures that we are not at a built-in disadvantage by comparison with our European competitors.

6. It has also been suggested in correspondence from the DTI that we could not very well resist an agreement with the Soviet Union when we already have them with Hungary, Romania, Czechoslovakia and Poland. Perhaps so, but I do think it important to make a clear distinction between the Soviet Union on the one hand and the Eastern Europeans on the other. The latter certainly do not share, at any rate in the same degree, the sinister Soviet aim referred to above. Both for them and for us, bilateral long-term co-operation agreements can serve the purpose, emphatically not shared by the Soviet Union, of keeping open a line to Western Europe and inhibiting their further integration in CMEA. They are thus a Good Thing, whereas with the Soviet Union they have become more of a somewhat regrettable necessity.

The Development of the CCP

7. As I said in my letter to John Mason under reference, however, if a truly common EEC spirit and philosophy are lacking, formal agreements in the CCP are going to be pretty fruitless. The French were the first to show the way in concluding and defending their long-term economic co-operation agreement with the USSR of October 1971.[10] We have all sooner or later followed suit without, so far as I am aware considering in Brussels where this is all leading. Now the French have gone a step further with the ten-year programme, in further implementation of their agreement, signed by Giscard in Moscow during the French Grande Commission this month.[11] The French say that that it is non-commercial but their refusal to publish gives rise to suspicion, and it is difficult to believe that we do not get ever closer to the commercial bone at each stage of the further elaboration of these agreements. Are we all now going to follow the French this stage further without looking further down the road? It looks from Nicho Henderson's telegram No. 823 as though the Germans well might.[12]

---

[9] See No. 42.

[10] This provided for a ten-year programme of economic and industrial cooperation between France and the USSR.

[11] M. Giscard d'Estaing, then French Minister for the Economy and Finance, visited Moscow during 1–11 July for the eighth session of the Franco-Soviet *Grande Commission* and in order to sign the Franco-Soviet cooperation programme (*v. ibid.*). In Moscow telegram No. 802 of 13 July Sir J. Killick complained that his French colleagues had 'at all levels been evasive' about the contents of the documents signed. But he noted that the cooperation programme, however vague its language, was regarded by both sides 'as in effect an outline trade agreement' providing for a large increase in the volume of trade turnover (MWE 3/303/1).

[12] Sir N. Henderson explained in this telegram of 18 July that the Germans were disenchanted with the EC, largely because of its failure to make any sort of political progress. He noted: 'if the Germans begin to have doubts about the prospects of achieving European Union and if they

8.   The problems and dangers of doing so do not of course arise from the *content* of all this. Of course we all want and should have more trade with the Soviet Union on a sound and profitable commercial basis. But what we are doing is furthering the Soviet purpose of keeping it all in separate bilateral channels, enabling them to play each of us off against the other, drive the hardest of hard bargains, exploit national rivalry to chip away at COCOM,[13] and make Western Europe as a whole less competitive with the United States and Japan in this market. They even gain a political bonus through propagating the idea that political concessions bring better commercial prospect. One such political concession—a favourite apparently with the French—is the belief that we must not press the CCP issue for fear of bringing about closer integration in CMEA. (I believe this to be a phoney argument. The Russians are going to press the integration of CMEA to the limit of the possible whatever EEC does; and the limit is a fairly tight one because of the resistance of their partners like the Romanians.) Perhaps the French do not really believe the argument themselves, but merely use it as a pretext for continuing to exploit a bilateral relationship with the Russians which they think brings them national advantage. This seems to me short-sighted. As the German industrialists apparently said to Brezhnev in Bonn, the sort of major industrial co-operation projects the Russian have in mind are too big to be undertaken by individual Western European countries. If we allow Brezhnev to continue to play the purely bilateral game, the danger of the Americans, perhaps with the Japanese in Siberia, walking off with the plums is all the greater. Conceivably the French hope to play the role of 'chef de file' in negotiating such deals and carrying along with them in consortia participants from other Western European countries. Renault have got into something of this role over the Kamaz project.[14] But this seems to me a rather cumbersome, time-wasting and inefficient way of going about this, and it remains to be proved that it is even profitable.

9.   However, it is not for me to go into detail about what the content of CCP should be, although I continue to believe that credit policy and practices, including common reviews of Soviet creditworthiness overall, must be a, if not the, key element in it. What does seem to me important is to get away from the superficial formalities of such things as whether and how the Commission should play a role under Basket II at CSCE,[15] or whether the Soviet Union and others will be willing to sign largely mea[n]ingless and unnecessary trade agreements with the Commission. This sort of thing will only encourage the Russians to respond in kind by establishing matching counterparts from the CMEA which,

remain unconvinced about the absolute reliability of the US commitment to European defence, a dangerous gap could develop between their national interests and those of their Western partners. They could be tempted to pursue their aims by more direct dealings with the East' (WRG 2/1).

[13] Co-ordinating Committee on Exports to Communist Countries.

[14] A vast car and truck manufacturing plant on the Kama River with which the French car maker, Renault, became associated.

[15] CSCE Basket II issues were those relating to economic and technological cooperation. Cf. Volume II, No. 55.

however meaningless in content, will only alarm and distress the Romanians et al.

10. Surely all we have to do is to decide for ourselves what common policies and practices we need, and go ahead and apply them. This can be done without necessarily involving additional formal responsibilities and functions vis-à-vis non-members on the part of the Commission; simply harmonised action and full pooling of information (subject to the protection of legitimate commercial interest) on the part of member states, with the Commission perhaps discharging, internally, a co-ordinating and monitoring role. So far as the Soviet Government is concerned, they can take it or leave it, and so can their CMEA associates. If their reactions are substantially different, so much the better. There is no question of formal public acts of acceptance or rejection. Indeed I do not see why our policies should not differentiate between the Soviet Union and other CMEA members. Nothing new will emerge which will give the Russians pretext or cause to go for a greater measure of CMEA integration than they are already trying and will continue to try to achieve. We simply start applying our agreed lines of policy in practice, and it need not even emerge straightaway what those lines of policy are.

11. Does this kind of approach make any sense to you? Does it offer any hope of making the progress we want on the substance of CCP without having to fight empty formalistic battles over extending the competence of the Commission? It seems to me the only possible way, now that we are on the verge of coming to grips with CMEA, of ensuring that we can assure the interests of EEC without damaging the interest of the Eastern Europeans.

Yours ever,
J.E. KILLICK

No. 46

Letter from Sir J. Killick (Moscow) to Sir. T. Brimelow

[*ENS 3/548/2*]

Personal and Confidential   MOSCOW, *14 August 1973*

Dear Tom,

Anglo-Soviet Relations

1. In my letter of 8 August to George Walden about our response to the message 'from the leadership' which Lunkov delivered to the Prime Minister on 25 July,[1] I said that I would write again about the related questions of Soviet

---

[1] A message from the 'Soviet leadership', which Mr. Lunkov read to Mr. Heath on 25 July, noted Sir A. Douglas-Home's recent statement in the House of Commons that HMG regarded relations with the USSR as an 'important element in its foreign policy' (see *Parl. Debs.*, 5th *ser.*, H. *of* C., vol. 860, cols. 1601–2), and affirmed the Soviet Government's wish 'to develop relations with Britain in

motives in taking the initiative towards an improvement in our relations and the possible content of the meeting between Mr. Brezhnev and Mr. Heath which may eventually result.

2.   To take the question of Soviet motives first, I would guess that the basic reason for what is evidently a top-level Soviet decision to reactivate our relations is simply that they have failed to achieve their objectives by keeping us in the freezer.[2] Not only have we continued to speak our minds in European fora but there are indications that our European partners have become more, rather then less, attentive to what we have to say. Not only have we shown no disposition to be the first to extend the olive branch, but we have shown no signs of even mild discomfort while Anglo-Soviet relations have been in limbo. The spectacle of a major West European country coming to no apparent harm through remaining outside the current Soviet embrace is inconvenient to the Soviet leadership since it may start other countries looking too closely at what, if anything, they are gaining from being embraced themselves. There are already signs of dissatisfaction and impatience in Soviet-French and Soviet-German relations. For these reasons, the leadership has evidently decided, in proper Leninist style, to abandon zig in favour of zag and to approach the British problem from another direction. In short, in the terms of my letter of 5 January[3] to you, we have made ourselves '*valoir*' and the Russians have found the cold-storage tactic counter-productive. They may have concluded from the experience of the last two years that (as some of their own experts on Britain may very well have been telling them all along) we are least vulnerable to overt attack and unpopularity but possibly more receptive to the smile and outstretched hand. I think that this is, in fact, a very fair assessment.

3.   It might be wrong to discount altogether the influence of personalities on the Anglo-Soviet equation. The minus quantity is, and probably has been since the Secretary of State's pre-Operation Foot letters to him, very evidently Gromyko. If the matter was left entirely to him, I have no doubt that Anglo-Soviet relations would remain on a level of surly inactivity almost indefinitely.[4] It

---

various fields'. Mr. Lunkov said that his Government were prepared to enter into 'political consultations' particularly devoted to British and Soviet proposals for the work of the CSCE, and stressed the importance of 'maintaining permanent contacts on a bilateral as well as multilateral basis' (record of conversation on 25 July). Sir J. Killick wrote two letters to Mr. Walden on 8 August recounting a conversation he had with Mr. Suslov on 3 August during which the latter had emphasised that the CSCE would be the 'touchstone' for future Anglo-Soviet relations. Sir J. Killick inferred from Mr. Suslov's remarks that he was aiming ultimately at a meeting between Mr. Heath and Mr. Brezhnev.

[2] In a letter to Sir J. Killick of 28 July Mr. Bullard noted: 'The Russians seem to be trying to convey to us that the sun of their favour will shine upon us if only we will try just a little bit harder to be good boys. They are not going to put anything on paper which could make them appear to be the demandeur or which could be quoted against them later ... They are cultivating the Prime Minister personally, in the hope of cutting out hard-liners in the FCO and of leading up to an eventual visit by Mr Heath to Moscow, with the Secretary of State present only as a member of his entourage.'

[3] No. 37.

[4] See Volume I, No. 71. In the second of his letters to Mr. Walden of 8 August (see note 1 above)

seems possible that his influence may, however, now have been outweighed both by Brezhnev's impatience to fill in the missing piece of his 'summitry' jigsaw puzzle and by Lunkov's own activist approach to his appointment which is, perhaps, a reflection of his very considerable self-esteem. As one whose career has been based in the party as well as in the bureaucracy and has included close contact with the top leadership Lunkov could, as I suggested before his arrival in London, be expected to have reasonable lines of communication to the Central Committee *apparat* and I would not be surprised if current developments owed at least something to them.

4. The timing of the change in the Soviet approach is obviously determined in part by Stage II of the CSCE. I would guess that the Russians have identified our delegation as one of the most effective and influential at the Conference and also one of the most professionally competent. If they continue to keep us at arms length, they can have no hope of mitigating our influence during Stage II. On the other hand we would be the most effective channel for putting across whatever deal the Russians may have in mind for an outcome to Stage II with which they could live. The very fact that the British have until so recently been least-favoured nation in the Soviet eyes and most active in reminding Europe of the realities behind Soviet words would make anything which we could be persuaded to say in favour of reasonableness and moderation towards Soviet initiatives doubly effective.[5] In the longer term, the Soviet leadership may be applying the same analysis to intra-EEC relations. They must realise that none of the developments within the Community which they most fear—e.g. moves towards greater political cohesion and the acquisition of a defensive capacity—can take place without the wholehearted support of both the British and the French. They have tried to divide us from the French. They evidently believed for some time that they would succeed in diminishing our credit with the French by giving us the 'European leper' treatment but this got them nowhere. They have now doubtless concluded that the possibilities for wedge-driving and mischief-making in general are very limited unless they are on good speaking terms with both governments.

5. Given that the Soviet analysis is likely to be roughly along the above lines, what should HMG's response be to 'positive initiatives' thus motivated? It seems to be out of the question for us simply to retreat into our shells and to dig in behind a kind of political Maginot line. Apart from the obvious requirements of domestic politics, reflected in the Prime Minister's own wish to work towards a meeting, a negative response could damage our currently high standing with our

---

Sir J. Killick observed: 'It is clear that Gromyko, in spite of being in the Politburo, is still not the person who counts here in foreign affairs. Although he does Brezhnev's bidding, I would not discount the possibility that he is less enthusiastic than Brezhnev about mending fences with us. We must accept that the ball-game now is a prospective meeting between the Prime Minister and Brezhnev, without preparation at Foreign Minister level.'

[5] Mr. Suslov told Sir J. Killick on 3 August (see note 1 above) that he knew it was Mr. Gromyko's opinion that if cooperation in the CSCE were successful there would be better prospects in other fields. 'I', Sir J. Killick reported, 'chose not to probe him on what he meant by this, since the answer is obvious enough—"Lay off Basket III and help us to get the thing over quickly".'

European partners since it would tend to confirm the Russian version of the recent freeze in Anglo-Soviet relations rather than ours.[6] The main point, however, is that we surely have definite objectives of our own which seem to me to satisfy the Prime Minister's desire that any meeting must serve a useful political purpose. The first is a significant improvement in Soviet imports from the UK; the Russians have hinted that we suffer commercially from continuing bad relations, and however phoney this argument, the trade figures are bad. We are fully entitled to suggest that a concrete sign of returning to normal should be improved exports to the Soviet Union. (I have already had one go at Suslov on this subject, in accordance with the Secretary of State's instruction in his despatch of 26 July.)[7] Secondly, we should—particularly as none of our allies seem inclined to do so—use the opportunity of a top-level meeting to bring home to the Russians that they cannot have it both ways—détente in Europe and the continued undermining of our interests elsewhere; economic, scientific and technological co-operation conducted with the maximum openness on the Western side and the maximum secrecy and 'vigilance' on the Soviet side; long-term economic co-operation with the capitalist world coupled with continuing hostility to and ideological warfare against the capitalist system, and so on. Thirdly, we might endeavour to turn the tables on the Russians in terms of their 'touch-stone' arguments: in response to their line that HMG's policies during Stage II of CSCE will show whether a genuine improvement in Anglo-Soviet relations is possible, we should argue that the Soviet attitude to Agenda Item III will show us and the rest of Europe whether Soviet professions of a desire for a lasting 'relaxation of tension' in Europe are genuine or not.[8] Fourthly, we have a continuing interest in the improvement of our bilateral relations, commercial and otherwise, with the other countries of Eastern Europe and it seems probable that even the appearance of a turn-around in Anglo-Soviet relations will make it easier for the East European governments to meet us half way. Finally, I think that the Soviet leadership would benefit from the kind of exposition of our objectives within and

[6] Sir A. Douglas-Home told Mr. Lunkov on 27 July that 'basically' there were three obstacles to the development of Anglo-Soviet relations: (1) the ideological outlook of the Soviet leaders who appeared determined to undermine the capitalist system; (2) the Soviet 'closed society' which made it impossible for people in the West to know what was going on in the USSR; and (3) the military policy of the Soviet Union and the build-up of Warsaw Pact forces 'in spite of the demands of the Eastern Front' (minute from Sir D. Greenhill to Mr. Acland of 27 July).

[7] In this despatch (see No. 45, note 8) Sir A. Douglas-Home instructed Sir J. Killick to 'take every appropriate opportunity to impress upon the Soviet authorities the political need for early and substantial new business to be seen to follow' from the April meeting of the Anglo-Soviet Joint Commission. When during his conversation with Mr. Suslov on 3 August (see notes 1 and 5 above) Sir J. Killick expressed his disappointment at the lack of progress on commercial matters, Mr. Suslov replied that the 'improvement of trade was a mutual task', and expressed the hope that a ten-year economic cooperation agreement, envisaged during Mr. Walker's visit, could be signed as soon as possible (cf. No. 42).

[8] Mr. Bullard commented in his letter to Sir J. Killick of 28 July (see note 2 above) the Russians 'really would be prepared to make substantial atmospheric concessions in Anglo-Soviet bilateral relations if we could help them out of the pit that they have dug for themselves over the CSCE, by co-operating in moves to sterilise and cut short the Second Stage'.

for the EEC which Mr. Heath is perhaps better able and qualified to give than most of his present European colleagues.

6. There need be no shortage, therefore, of material for political exchanges of importance and substance. But, as we have seen in Moscow a year ago and more recently in Bonn and Washington, Mr. Brezhnev does not see the purpose of top-level meetings as consisting primarily in the exchange of views.[9] Apart from his predilection for interminable and emotional monologues, to an almost obsessive extent he wants 'trophies'—lists of treaties and agreements to recite in speeches and reports, pieces of paper to publish. Unless we can hold out some prospect of satisfying this craving, I would rate the chances of a visit by Brezhnev to London as low, although the importance of trophies might be less crucial if Mr. Heath were to come to Moscow. Nevertheless, we should perhaps be giving some thought even at this stage to the kind of trophy which we might be prepared to consider. It is common ground between us that any kind of association with the US–Soviet agreement on the prevention of nuclear war[10] must be excluded. Quite apart from the substance, there could presumably be nothing better calculated to cause suspicion and ill-feeling between us and the French and Germans. We might manage to dig up one or two 'co-operation agreements', e.g. on the environment, for signature during the visit but these would not really be suitable for signature by principals. It seems to me, therefore, that we are driven back to the possibility of a 'declaration of principles' on the same lines as those already negotiated by the Russians with the French and the Americans but, hopefully, with rather different content. This, however, will depend very much on the timing of the meeting. If it takes place before Stage III of CSCE—which seems on the face of it unlikely—it will clearly be impossible to predict the outcome of the Conference with sufficient accuracy to avoid discrepancy or conflict between its declaration of principles and ours, or the use of the latter to influence the former. If the meeting were to take place after Stage III of CSCE, and in addition to whatever top-level contacts may take place at the Conference, it should be possible, if not very valuable, to produce a version of the principles emanating from the Conference suitably tailored to the Anglo-Soviet bilateral relationship. The essential emptiness of such an exercise would not really matter if it enabled the meeting to take place, and there might even be some value in reaffirming bilaterally whatever we get out of the Russians under Basket III.[11]

7. I am not necessarily suggesting that Brezhnev should be given a cast-iron assurance in advance that he will get the 'trophy' he wants. There might be some preliminary discussion of the possibility, and conceivably a draft of some sort

[9] President Nixon visited Moscow during 22–30 May 1972, and Mr. Brezhnev visited Bonn during 18–21 May 1973, and Washington during 17–25 June 1973.

[10] See J.A.S. Grenville, *The Major International Treaties 1914–1973. A history and guide with texts* (London: Methuen, 1974), pp. 541–2. The message Mr. Lunkov delivered to Mr. Heath on 25 July (see note 1 above) referred to statements by the Soviet *Politburo* and the Supreme Soviet emphasising 'the importance which the Soviet Government attached to the willingness of other States to subscribe to the declaration on the renunciation of the use of force, and the agreement about the use of nuclear weapons'.

[11] See No. 32, note 9.

might be proposed from the Soviet side. But if the pre-negotiation of some document were pursued to the point where all that was left was for the principals to sign it, there would be no incentive for Brezhnev to embark seriously on discussion of the sort of subjects suggested in paragraph 5 above. I imagine that the Prime Minister would not, in the last resort, mind too much if there were no outcome beyond a communiqué, possibly expressing disagreed positions, provided that ground of this sort had been covered in frank discussion. If, on the other hand, the discussion did demonstrate a measure of progress in the direction of 'constructive co-existence', Brezhnev might be given his trophy to take away.

8. This leads me to the question of mechanics. I have the strong impression that the Russians do not want preparation at Foreign Minister level, and that further exchanges between the Secretary of State and Gromyko are unlikely to be much more rewarding than past ones.[12] Before Brezhnev's visit to Paris in 1971, a great deal of preparatory work was done here between Seydoux[13] and Gromyko and at lower levels between the French Embassy and the MFA. But this was on the basis of a common desire that a number of documents should be signed, and our aim is different. In our case, it might well be better to go on dealing with Lunkov. It is premature to take any firm decision on the modalities, but it would be helpful to know to what extent, as a matter of principle, the Prime Minister would want a meeting to be thoroughly prepared in advance. If you agree with my suggested line in paragraph 5, perhaps the less preparation the better, and even an agenda might be unnecessary if not positively undesirable, as liable to frighten Brezhnev off. But, as regards a 'trophy', the Russians must surely need a certain amount of preparation, and I do not see much harm in leaving the initiative to them. Depending on what they came up with, we could say something to the effect that the Prime Minister would consider something on these lines, but would take a final decision in the light of the full and frank discussion he hopes to have with the General Secretary.

9. Of course I realise that a meeting is not yet 'in the bag', but I do not think it is too early for us to be clearing our minds about the way ahead, since I have a feeling that things may begin to move fairly fast now that the logs in the jam are beginning to shift a bit. I should be very grateful for your comments.

Yours ever,
J.E. KILLICK

---

[12] Sir A. Douglas-Home told the House of Commons on 25 July that during his meeting with Mr. Gromyko in Helsinki (cf. Volume II, No. 42) he had expressed the hope that the Soviet Foreign Minister would be able to visit London before long: 'If he can do so', he added, 'we shall be very glad' (see note 1 above). A month later, on 23 August, Mr. Heath told Mr. Lunkov that he would be pleased to meet Mr. Gromyko if he passed through London on his return from the United States, where, in September, he would be attending the UN General Assembly (telegram No. 630 to Moscow of 24 August, ENS 3/548/13). But only on 18 September did Mr. Lunkov indicate to Sir A. Douglas-Home that this was impossible in view of Mr. Gromyko's workload (telegram No. 695 to Moscow of 18 September; letter from Mr. Acland to Lord Bridges (since January 1972 Private Secretary (Overseas Affairs) to the Prime Minister) of 21 September).

[13] M.R. Seydoux was French Ambassador in Moscow during 1968–73.

No. 47

Letter from Sir T. Brimelow to Sir J. Killick (Moscow)

[*ENS 2/1*]

Confidential   FCO, *23 August 1973*

Dear John,

Soviet Foreign Policy

1.   We were most grateful for your well-timed, well balanced and complementary despatches of 13 August on 'The Leninist Strategic Course of Soviet Foreign Policy'[1] and of 14 August on 'Mr. Brezhnev's 'Personal Contribution'.[2] Both have been sent for printing as diplomatic reports.

2.   I think you are wise to attempt to extract Brezhnev's 'personal contribution' from the more impersonal elements of Soviet policy. One might say that your despatch of 13 August deals with the objective needs of the USSR under Soviet rule, and that of 14 August with Brezhnev's personal needs. I should like to comment on the impersonal aspects first.

3.   Your analysis of the impersonal elements in current Soviet foreign policy does not attempt to analyse the general political strategy of the CPSU. It concentrates on the current requirement of the Soviet economy and the Soviet people in a phase which may be fairly prolonged. I agree with most of your analysis: but it raises three questions in my mind. First, do you make adequate allowance for the conjuncture of external circumstances favouring the present Soviet policy of détente; second, how far are Soviet aims at domination over, or division of, Western Europe conscious, or indeed actual;[3] and third, is the deliberate elimination of autarky[4] now a basic principle of the Soviet economy,

---

[1]   Sir J. Killick argued in this lengthy despatch that the 'historic motivations' of Soviet foreign policy were the quest for security and the endeavour to translate economic potential into economic strength. Mr. Brezhnev's contribution to enhancing Soviet security had, he maintained, been 'directed more towards the consolidation of favourable positions than towards attempts to improve them'.

[2]   In this analysis of Soviet foreign policy Sir J. Killick concluded that: (1) Mr. Brezhnev was 'now for practical purposes the sole valid interlocutor for the Soviet Union in international affairs'; (2) account had to be taken of his 'personal foibles and vanities, as well as the strength of his wish to "represent" the Soviet Union in the world'; and (3) since he was in a hurry and still wanted more successes, the West was in a favourable tactical position from which it might extract advantage.

[3]   Sir J. Killick observed in his despatch of 13 August (see note 1 above) that Mr. Brezhnev's preoccupation with buttressing the European *status quo* did not signify the abandonment of greater ambitions for the longer term. 'At their most extreme' he thought these 'might be expressed by the proposition that if the security of the Soviet state is improved by its control of half of Europe it would be improved still further by establishing domination over the rest.' But, he noted, Mr. Brezhnev 'must know that anything like the "Finlandisation" of Western Europe belongs to a phase of Soviet policy over which he cannot expect to preside'.

[4]   Mr. Brezhnev stated in a West German television address on 21 May 'our plans are far from being based on autarky'.

or merely another 'phase' largely conditioned by developments outside the USSR?

4. From the Soviet viewpoint, 'peaceful existence' [*sic*] has always had the virtue of flexibility. There are 'hard' and 'soft' definitions. There are also more or less auspicious circumstances for the implementation of either 'hard' or 'soft' interpretation. Your despatch rightly emphasises that the deficiencies of the Soviet economy are a major element in the Soviet decision to concentrate for the moment on the more liberal interpretation of this policy.[5] But it is worth recalling that Soviet 'détente' policies would have no prospect of success, and would probably not have been launched, if the external circumstances had not been right. These circumstances were of course the Vietnam War and neo-isolationist feeling in America; Gaullist foreign policy; Herr Brandt; and China.[6]

5. This relates to my second point. It seems to me of doubtful utility to attempt to establish a 'primary motivation' in the present phase of Soviet policy. You suggest that Brezhnev's primary motive is consolidation.[7] But ultimately, the consolidation of the Soviet position in Eastern Europe is only secure so long as Western Europe is weak and divided. Soviet policy, like a glacier, can appear to be frozen while continuing to be mobile.[8] I think there is no doubt about the direction in which Brezhnev intends the glacier to move. I should also note that the suggestion in paragraph 11 of your despatch that the Soviet urge to dominate is 'almost somnambulent' would be queried throughout Eastern Europe. Moreover, it is to some extent belied by the quotation from Lenin with which your despatch begins: '... to utilise the conflict of interest amongst one's enemies' suggests a perfectly conscious motivation.

6. Finally there is the question of autarky. Perhaps the difficulty is that this word has too finite a ring, but we should I think remember that total Soviet external trade at present as a percentage of Soviet GNP is about 3%. Even if this were doubled soon (which would be a remarkable achievement given that most

---

[5] Sir J. Killick was also of the opinion that Mr. Brezhnev saw Western economic involvement in the USSR 'as a means of giving the capitalist powers a degree of self-interest in accepting that the state of détente is indeed irreversible, at least until the Soviet Union is ready to reverse it'.

[6] Sir J. Killick deliberately made only one mention of China in his despatch of 13 August (see note 1 above). 'I think', he wrote to Sir A. Douglas-Home, 'it is common ground between us that the "China factor" is not the main driving force behind Mr Brezhnev's West-politik, although it is of course closely relevant to it and a fundamental consideration in all Soviet thinking ... Mr Brezhnev's line of policy towards Western Europe and the Atlantic Alliance still seems to me to have a dynamic of its own.'

[7] In his 13 August despatch (*v. ibid.*) Sir J. Killick insisted that he did not subscribe to the view that the primary and immediate objective of Mr. Brezhnev's *détente* policies was to tempt the West to lower its guard and to divide and weaken the Western Alliance. 'They look to me', he observed, 'much more like a reaction to a situation in which various threats and shortcomings make the Soviet Union feel distinctly vulnerable, and hence under compulsion to take defensive action.' However, he added that he did not 'believe for a moment that the Soviet regime [had] lost interest in, or hope of, changing the balance of power in Europe to the advantage of the Soviet Union and the global balance in favour of the socialist camp'.

[8] Sir J. Killick disliked this metaphor because, as he explained in a letter to Sir T. Brimelow of 3 September, 'a glacier is not well-equipped to be opportunist: Soviet tactics certainly are'.

of the major projects now discussed are very long term indeed), it would still be possible to describe the Soviet economy as extremely autarkic, by comparison with Western or even Eastern European economies.

7. As I say, I agree basically with your conclusions. Your final sentence suggests that time is short to benefit from Brezhnev's policies.[9] Without wishing to suggest that we should not be cautiously forthcoming in our response to them, I think that we should also remember that any benefits obtained during this period of relative relaxation of tension may be equally short-lived. We are always leaning gently against the door, and when it opens another inch we should take the chance to insert another toe in the gap. But we should never be surprised if it is stamped on and we are obliged to withdraw.

8. I enjoyed your despatch on Brezhnev's 'personal contribution' of 14 August, and I note that its conclusions are similar to those of your earlier despatch. Brezhnev is certainly eager to produce results from his foreign policy for personal reasons.[10] But these policies also reflect the natural impatience of a newly fledged super power to exert its influence in the world. To that extent Brezhnev's eagerness is a potential cause for concern, as well as providing opportunities from which the West could benefit if it plays its cards very carefully. To revert for a moment to your earlier despatch, and at the risk of sounding complacent, I admit sharing your view that HMG have contributed significantly to the 'counsels of realism' in Western Europe during a difficult period. The problem now is to continue to do so while developing our own dialogue with the man you rightly describe as 'the sole valid interlocutor of the Soviet Union in international relations'. He wants us to pay a price for giving him another triumph. This may lead to some tricky bargaining. The Soviet technique of beating about the bush does not help.

9. The final thought must always be: how long will he last? When I saw the photograph of Brezhnev, his back to the camera and his feet a good foot off the ground, in the arms of an American actor whose name I forget, I wondered how Brezhnev's more staid colleagues on the Politburo would react.[11] It inevitably recalled Khrushchev's shoe-banging exercise, which became a symbol of a style which was later repudiated by his colleagues. I cannot help wondering whether that photograph might not one day be used against Brezhnev. (Khrushchev at least was the active party!)[12] But here again I agree with the implied conclusion of your despatch: that we could do worse than Brezhnev, and that his downfall would not necessarily be in our interests.

Yours ever,
THOMAS BRIMELOW

[9] Sir J. Killick considered that Western Europe appeared to have achieved what had always been 'a basic objective of its collective foreign policy, namely the creation of a powerful and cohesive economic pole of attraction for Eastern Europe while remaining militarily secure and politically, for all its defects, proof against effective subversion'. This, he thought, had forced the Russians into a policy of manoeuvre which held out greater opportunities for the West than it contained dangers. 'Mr. Brezhnev', he asserted in his concluding sentences, '... risks making the discovery that the climate of détente is uncongenial to a monolithic and repressive political structure which has hitherto drawn both its strength and its justification from national crisis and international tension.

He may have to pull in his horns or pay the penalty, and the period of opportunity for us may not be long.'

[10] In his despatch of 14 August (see note 2 above) Sir J. Killick noted that Mr. Brezhnev's recent visits abroad, and especially his visit to the United States, had 'greatly increased his general popularity and served to strengthen his already very considerable internal standing'.

[11] During his visit to the USA in June Mr. Brezhnev travelled with Mr. Nixon to San Clemente in California. There he spotted Chuck Connors, a television Western star, in the crowd and rushed up to greet him. Mr. Connors grabbed Mr. Brezhnev under the arms and, to the delight of press photographers, lifted him bodily off the ground.

[12] During a speech by the British Prime Minister, Mr. H. Macmillan, to the UN General Assembly on 29 September 1960, in which Mr. Macmillan defended Western conduct in Africa, the Soviet leader, Mr. N. Khrushchev, after making several noisy interruptions, began banging his shoe on the desk. The scene was recorded and received widespread media coverage.

No. 48

Letter from Sir J. Killick (Moscow) to Mr. Bullard
[*ENS 3/548/13*]

Confidential   MOSCOW, *10 October 1973*

Dear Julian,

Secretary of State's Visit [1]

1. Thank you very much for your letter of 5 October with its enclosures [2] We seem to have arrived at a rather infelicitous situation.

2. First, I am really not at all happy that the Prime Minister said nothing to Lunkov about Podgorny's revival of the invitation to him to visit the Soviet Union, [3] especially as he referred approvingly to Gromyko's invitation to the Secretary of State. [4] For my money, he should have been advised to note this new

[1] On 25 September, whilst in New York for the UN General Assembly, Sir A. Douglas-Home met with Mr. Gromyko. The latter then renewed an earlier invitation for Sir A. Douglas-Home to visit the Soviet Union, proposing that the visit take place at the end of November or in early December. Sir A. Douglas-Home's 'own fairly strong inclination' was to accept (UKMIS New York telegrams Nos. 957 and 958 of 25 September, ENS 3/548/2).

[2] With this letter Mr. Bullard enclosed the record of a meeting between Mr. Heath and Mr. Lunkov on 3 October. The Prime Minister used the occasion to say how glad he was that Sir A. Douglas-Home had been invited to Moscow.

[3] In Moscow telegram No. 997 of 3 September Sir J. Killick reported on a conversation that day in Moscow between the Duke of Edinburgh and Mr. Podgorny, during which the latter affirmed that 'an invitation extended at one time in the past to the Prime Minister remained valid', and expressed the hope that 'at an appropriate time' there would be an opportunity for Mr. Heath to visit the Soviet Union (ENS 26/1).

[4] Already in Moscow telegram No. 1114 of 26 September Sir J. Killick had advised against acceptance of Mr. Gromyko's invitation, since it would mean two high-level UK Ministerial visits to Moscow in succession, and these the Soviet Government could portray as evidence of a 'change of heart' by HMG. He insisted that Britain's 'present primary objective' in the development of

development with appreciation and say that he would be thinking further about it, without waiting for Lunkov to raise the question (paragraph 3 of Alexander's[5] letter of 2 October to Tom Bridges).[6] In fact, for practical purposes, Lunkov in effect did raise the subject by enquiring about my report on the conversation between the Duke of Edinburgh and Podgorny, in which the only precise point of importance was the renewed invitation. Could you find out whether the Prime Minister had any particular reason for saying nothing?[7] My recommendations in paragraph 8 below are perhaps dependent on the answer to this. But in essence I feel that we are safely beyond the point at which a positive response looks like 'running after the Russians'.

3.   Meanwhile, on this front, the Russians must be feeling somewhat puzzled, if not worse, at the lack of response, particularly since, as you rightly recall in your paragraph 8, the Prime Minister has not yet replied to the message which Lunkov gave him as long ago as 25 July.[8] They presumably do not think that I neglected to report accurately since (my telegram No 998 of 4 September)[9] I reverted to the subject with Lunkov after the event and emphasised that I had already taken action. They may think that in doing so I advised against any response. I hope not, because I have been taking a fairly strong line lately on a number of fronts and I would not like them to conclude, with my future job in mind,[10] that I am also concerned to sabotage the development of high level contacts. More importantly, however, the Russians are surely bound to feel that, whether on the basis of advice from me or not, the Prime Minister has been at

Anglo-Soviet relations was to bring about a meeting between the Prime Minister and Mr. Brezhnev. (ENS 3/548/2).

[5] Mr. M.O'D.B. Alexander was Assistant Private Secretary to the Secretary of State.

[6] Mr. Bullard suggested in his draft of this letter that if Mr. Lunkov raised the subject of the Prime Minister visiting the Soviet Union, Mr. Heath should say that he had taken note of President Podgorny's statement to Prince Philip, and that if he were then pressed to go further he might say that Sir A. Douglas-Home could discuss this with Mr. Gromyko in Moscow (ENS 3/548/2).

[7] Mr. Bullard replied in a letter to Sir J. Killick of 12 October that he 'frankly [did] not know the answer to this question'. He thought that Mr. Heath would, at the time of the conversation, have been strongly influenced by the argument that 'we should not seem to be running after the Russians'.

[8] See No. 46, note 1.

[9] Sir J. Killick recalled in this telegram that on the evening of 3 September he had informed Mr. Lunkov that he had reported to London Mr. Podgorny's remark regarding a visit from Mr. Heath (ENS 26 /1). In a submission to Sir T. Brimelow of 10 October Mr. Walden noted that No. 10 had agreed that they should await a Soviet response to Sir A. Douglas-Home's invitation to Mr. Gromyko (see No. 46, note 12) before replying to the message delivered by Mr. Lunkov. Mr. Walden thought Sir J. Killick's arguments in favour of pursuing a top-level exchange of visits by direct contacts between Mr. Heath and Mr. Brezhnev 'impressive'. But he foresaw two difficulties: (1) the risk that Mr. Heath's willingness to visit Moscow or receive Mr. Brezhnev might be interpreted as reflecting a 'new anxiety of being the only major Western country who is not dining at the top table'; and (2) if Mr. Heath were to write to Mr. Brezhnev this 'might strengthen the impression of concern in London, and mislead the Russians into thinking that we may after all be prepared to pay a price for a visit' (ENS 3/548/2).

[10] In November Sir J. Killick was appointed DUS in the FCO.

least discourteous and perhaps deliberately negative in failing to acknowledge what Podgorny said.

4. Second, as regards the Secretary of State's visit, I understand what you say about the 'key element'. I had assumed that the situation was changed by the fact that we now have a definite invitation to the Prime Minister to pick up. However, I certainly do not dispute the value of a visit by the Secretary of State, on the timing at present envisaged, in terms of the knowledge and impressions which he may gain and be able to pass on to the Nine and the Fifteen. But I do think it important to its success that it should be based on some forward movement on the Prime Minister's part.[11]

5. In this connection I am still not clear whether the Prime Minister wants thorough preparation in advance of his meeting with Brezhnev and if so to what extent the Secretary of State's visit should also seek to focus on this (paragraph 8 of my letter of 14 August to Tom Brimelow).[12]

6. I entirely agree with your paragraph 6, that it is not a practical possibility to envisage the Secretary of State signing any Anglo-Soviet Agreements when he comes. We are going to have quite enough difficulty in scraping together enough for the Prime Minister and Brezhnev to sign and it would in my view be wrong to take the Ten Year Economic Co-operation Agreement away from the Peter Walker/Patolichev channel. I am keen that Patolichev should visit London and the prospect of signature of that Agreement is the strongest inducement for him to go.[13]

7. Before going on to suggest what we might now do to clarify the situation I would just say that I am sorry if my telegram No 1150[14] was ambiguous in its first paragraph. The meaning intended was certainly not that Brezhnev would wish or expect to be involved with the Secretary of State's visit but that Gromyko would be going to India with him. (It is incidentally interesting to speculate now with hindsight whether Gromyko's refusal to come to London was connected with discussion here of the Middle East situation and Egyptian/Syrian intentions.)[15]

8. You will not thank me for getting back to the tennis match,[16] but it seems to me that although there is now one ball in the Soviet court (a response to our suggestion of dates for the Secretary of State's visit), there are two balls in our

---

[11] Telegram No. 654 of 26 September to UKMIS New York stated that the FCO had originally envisaged a visit by Sir A. Douglas-Home to Moscow as a 'key element' in the restoration of Ministerial contacts with the Russians. In his letter to Sir J. Killick of 5 October (see note 2 above) Mr. Bullard further explained that, although the FCO had been wrong in assuming that Mr. Gromyko would not revive this invitation, Mr. Gromyko had seemed to be 'acting under superior orders and with personal reluctance' (ENS 3/548/2).

[12] No. 46.

[13] Cf. No. 45.

[14] In paragraph 1 of this telegram of 5 October, Sir J. Killick noted that the preceding evening Mr. Suslov had 'muttered' that there were 'difficulties' over the timing of the Secretary of State's visit, 'connected with Brezhnev's forthcoming visit to India. However it *must* happen, and he hoped I would do everything possible to facilitate it.'

[15] Cf. No. 10, note 13.

[16] See No. 44.

court—Podgorny's reaffirmation of the invitation to the Prime Minister and the leadership's message of July. I am less concerned about the latter than the former in so far as Gromyko elected not to come to London, where he would have had an assured meeting with the Prime Minister and consequently a reasonable expectation of receiving a reply. Nevertheless, I think it is high time for us to take some action on both, and a response to the 'message' need not be a reply but could be useful as a statement of our position.[17] There are essentially two possibilities. I agree with you that to leave this to Terence Garvey following his arrival would indeed be rather late, and would be difficult to fit in before the Secretary of State's visit, except with Podgorny following presentation of credentials. I see two possibilities. They are not necessarily alternatives, but could be tried in succession. They are:

(*a*) to give me a reply to the July message, incorporating a response in principle to Podgorny's invitation, for me to use a means of trying to secure a call on Brezhnev before I leave. I could take the opportunity of establishing that the invitation is for a meeting with Brezhnev himself; Podgorny did not specifically say so, and we must be certain that the Prime Minister is given equal treatment with Pompidou, Brandt and Tanaka.[18] This would be somewhat contrived but entirely justified on the basis of the treatment Lunkov has had since his arrival in London. If I were soon able to say that I had some such message, Soviet curiosity might be excited and any damage done by the failure to respond to Podgorny's invitation would to some extent be neutralised. The device might not work, but then it would be in essence the fault of the Soviet side that they had not responded;

(*b*) to save all this for the Secretary of State's visit. Here again, there would be no point in doing this except as a lever for getting the Secretary of State a meeting with Brezhnev. In my view the device in this context would be much more undignified and transparent, and the implications would have to be regarded as a good deal more significant if it did not work, unless Brezhnev was definitely known to be out of Moscow at the time. Otherwise it seems to me to have no utility since the Secretary of State is assured of his meeting with Gromyko in any case (unless it should emerge that the Soviet side is so taken aback by the Prime Minister's failure to respond to the Podgorny invitation

---

[17] Mr. Bullard agreed with Sir J. Killick's advice (minute to Mr. Wiggin of 12 October), and Mr. Heath sent the text of a personal message to Mr. Brezhnev in telegram No. 805 to Moscow of 25 October. In this he stated that there existed 'no obstacle to the further development of relations between Britain and the Soviet Union, and to the attainment of the level of the relations which each already enjoy[ed] with allies of the other'. Mr. Heath added that he had 'taken note with appreciation' of Mr. Podgorny's statement that the invitation to him to visit the USSR, first made in 1970, remained valid, and that he hoped to take up this invitation in 1974. However, as Sir J. Killick was unable to deliver this message to either Mr. Podgorny or Mr. Brezhnev before his departure from Moscow on 31 October, his successor, Sir T. Garvey, was instructed to hand it to President Podgorny when he presented his credentials on 29 November (telegram No. 889 to Moscow of 26 November and Moscow telegram No. 1453 of 30 November; ENS 3/548/2).

[18] Mr. K. Tanaka was Prime Minister of Japan.

that they are considering running out on the invitation to the Secretary of State by creating difficulties over dates. Although Gromyko might not be averse to this, I have no reason at present to suppose that it is the case.)

9. A third possibility would of course be through Lunkov again. I agree with you that he seems to have run out of arrows and to be rather deflated[19] but am bound to say that this hardly surprises me in the light of what I say in paragraph 2 above. I feel he now has some legitimate reason to be surprised at his failure to extract any reaction from the Prime Minister on 3 October. But my main reason for objection to this possibility is that he has had a more than good run for his money and it is fair enough to put the Russians in the position of having to give me a slice of the cake.

10. Finally, thank you for the text of the Secretary of State's speech to the American Newspaper Publishers.[20] You will see from my separate letter about the visit of the Chairman of Reuters that I referred to the only part of it which had come to my attention through normal press channels at the dinner party I gave for Barnetson.[21] The passage which I quoted was perfect for my purposes and paragraph 7[22] as a whole fits in admirably with what I said to Zemskov[23] when I took Anthony Elliott[24] to call on him. For my part, I really cannot find anything unnecessarily conciliatory in it at all.

Yours ever,
J.E. KILLICK

[19] In his letter of 5 October (see note 1 above) Mr. Bullard noted in parenthesis: 'Lunkov incidentally gives the impression of a man who has shot off all his arrows, some of them several times, and has nothing left in his quiver except a lot of flannel.' He subsequently remarked that while it would be possible to 'concoct' a reply to the Soviet message of 25 July (see No. 46, note 1), the FCO would prefer not to channel this through Mr. Lunkov 'who wears the air of an exploded balloon at the moment'.

[20] Mr. Bullard enclosed with his letter of 5 October (see note 2 above) the advance text of this speech, scheduled for 3 October.

[21] Sir W. Barnetson, Chairman of Reuters Ltd., arrived in Moscow at the end of September for a brief visit to the Soviet Union. In a letter to Mr. Bullard of 8 October Sir J. Killick described a dinner which he gave for Sir W. Barnetson on 4 October, during which Sir J. Killick urged on another of his guests, Mr. Suslov, the abolition of restrictions on the movements of foreign diplomats and resident journalists in the Soviet Union. 'In general', he said, 'our working links with the MFA were still on the basis of a sort of adversary relationship, which accorded ill with what was supposed to be a period of détente' (ENS 13/10).

[22] Sir A. Douglas-Home stated in paragraph 7 of his speech (see note 20 above) that while the means for East/West *détente* were 'undoubtedly available', what had yet to be proved was that the Soviet Union really intended 'to bring about cooperation in the sense that we understand it'. He noted with regard to the CSCE negotiations: 'We are not trying to subvert or undermine. We are trying to build a better relationship and the proposals are modest. The surest way to progress in East/West relations is one step at a time.'

[23] Mr. I.N. Zemskov was Deputy Minister of Foreign Affairs for the Soviet Union.

[24] Mr. T.A.K. Elliott was HM Ambassador in Helsinki and Head of the UK Delegation to the CSCE.

No. 49

Letter from Mr. Bullard to Sir T. Garvey (Moscow)

[*EN 2 / 25*]

Confidential   FCO, *2 November 1973*

My dear Terence,

Britain's Relations with the Soviet Union and Eastern Europe

In one of the briefs written for the visit of Herr Bahr,[1] the architect or assistant architect of Ostpolitik, we were asked to define our general attitude to the Soviet Union and Eastern Europe, and to what is attainable in relations with those countries.

I enclose a copy of the paragraphs which we wrote. It seemed to me that you might find it of interest to have this summary of our views.

Yours ever,
J.L. BULLARD

ENCLOSURE IN NO. 49

(*a*) *UK and FRG Relations with the USSR and Eastern Europe*

(*i*)   *British Policy*

9.   British policy towards the Communist countries is based on our analysis of Communist motives. In our view the principal objective of Soviet foreign policy is progressively to shift the balance of power in the world in favour of the Socialist states. Brezhnev has selected Europe as the decisive front in this continuing struggle (unlike Khrushchev who believed that the decisive battles would be fought in the fields of production and in the Third World).

10.   The Soviet goals in Europe for the 1980s have been clearly defined as follows. The two military alliances either will have been abolished or will have lost most of their military significance, like CENTO.[2] US forces will have been largely or wholly withdrawn, leaving the Soviet Union infinitely the strongest power in the continent. The talks in Vienna will have led to the establishment of de-nuclearised, de-militarised or neutralised zones. The idea of defence against the Soviet threat will be increasingly regarded in Western Europe as futile or irrelevant or both. The two economic groupings will have continued

---

[1]   Herr E. Bahr, Minister without portfolio attached to the German Federal Chancellor's Office, visited London during 29–30 October. He had talks there with Mr. Heath, Sir A. Douglas-Home and Mr. Amery.

[2]   The Central Treaty Organisation. On 24 February 1955 Iraq and Turkey concluded a mutual security and defence treaty in Baghdad, to which Iran, Pakistan and the UK subsequently adhered. Originally known as the Baghdad Pact, it adopted the acronym CENTO after Iraq's formal withdrawal from the agreement in August 1959.

their internal integration, but the EEC will not have developed a political personality, still less a military one. The development of the Common Commercial Policy (CCP) will have proceeded slowly, thanks to the distracting mirage of all-European economic co-operation. All these developments will be monitored and encouraged by the all-European organ set up by the first or the subsequent CSCE. Meanwhile Eastern Europe will remain rigidly subject to the Soviet grip exactly as at present.

11. In other words, the Russians envisage a Western Europe from which US protection has been largely withdrawn; which exists under the shadow of Soviet power and which is obliged to adjust its policies accordingly. The word 'Finlandisation' is not too strong for Brezhnev's European vision.

12. This strategy appears to have a much better chance of succeeding than Khrushchev's ever did. The West could help to realise Brezhnev's vision not by taking the wrong decisions, but simply by failing to take the right ones, or by taking no decisions at all. The first task of Western governments must be to defend their own national interests against Soviet encroachment even on very small points. The second task is to ensure that public opinion is alive to the realities of the situation and especially to the Soviet record in Europe, the position of East Europe today and the current Soviet doctrine that détente necessitates an intensification of the political, economic and ideological struggle. The CSCE, and the Vienna talks when these begin, could be highly educative.

13. This is the background of British policies towards the Communist world. It will be seen that we interpret good relations with the Soviet Union in a rather limited sense. The natural relationship of Britain with the Soviet Union is a rather cool one, given our totally different world outlooks. The most we can hope for with Moscow is a political dialogue, yielding revealing glimpses of Soviet thinking from time to time and serving to educate the Soviet leaders in the real state of the Western world; expanding trade, though at great cost in private and official effort; technological contacts, in which the balance of advantage will tend to be on the Soviet side; and cultural contact, which we must recognise will leave the great bulk of the Soviet population untouched. This is the direction in which Anglo-Soviet relations are moving, now that we seem to be emerging from the freeze caused by Soviet intelligence activities and our attempts to deal with them.

14. In Eastern Europe we have a different analysis and therefore different objectives. With the exception of Bulgaria, the association of the East European states with the Soviet Union seems to us unnatural and in the long run unstable. We have no ambition to turn East European peoples against their governments, but we try to practice policies which make it easier rather than harder for those governments to exercise whatever degree of independence from Moscow they may feel to be in their power. This involves above all treating each East European country (in spite of much evidence to the contrary) as a fully sovereign entity with an international status in its own right. We try to push the political dialogue beyond the conventional level to a point where views are exchanged of which the Russians are not aware and would definitely not

approve. In trade, we want the maximum of direct contact with end-users in Eastern Europe. Industrial co-operation serves to ensure that Western rather than Soviet technological standards are regarded throughout Eastern Europe as the goal to aim at. In cultural activities we try to offer the East Europeans the maximum contact, subject to limited resources, with the heritage of civilisation which they too regard as their own. We do not expect dramatic events, e.g. that Rumania will walk out of the Warsaw Pact or Hungary out of COMECON. But we believe that Western Europe can play a role by showing sympathy and patience, against the day when events may weaken the Soviet grip upon Eastern Europe or when the links binding those countries to Moscow may become less vital to Soviet security.[3]

[3] In a minute to Mr. Bullard of 15 November Mr. P.J. Goulden (First Secretary, Planning Staff) questioned whether there was not a contradiction between Mr. Bullard's description of Soviet policy and his view of Eastern Europe as a place where there was 'scope for dialogue and for helping Governments to weaken the Soviet grip'. He thought that if Soviet policy towards Western Europe continued to be 'aggressive and based on strength', as the brief predicted, the Russians would presumably have little difficulty in preserving their position in the East. HMG could, he reasoned, do nothing to influence the underlying pace of change in Eastern Europe, and he wondered if it were therefore worthwhile devoting any extra resources to pushing the dialogue further than the Russians would approve.

No. 50

Sir A. Douglas-Home to Sir T. Garvey (Moscow)

No. 876 Telegraphic [ENS 3/548/13]

Priority. Confidential   FCO, *22 November 1973*

Repeated to UKMIS Geneva, UKDEL Vienna, UKMIS New York. Repeated for information to Priority to Washington, Bonn, Paris, UKDEL NATO, UKREP Brussels, Saving to Warsaw, East Berlin, Budapest, Prague, Bucharest, Sofia, Helsinki and Belgrade.

My visit to the Soviet Union 2–5 December[1]

1.   There can be no doubt that the Soviet decision to invite me to Moscow was based on the conclusion that it was in the Soviet interest to do so. No price was asked or paid. However, there have been several recent indications that the Russians hope to take advantage of the visit to modify British policies, especially

[1] In a submission to Sir J. Killick of 21 November, covering a draft steering brief for Sir A. Douglas-Home's forthcoming visit to the Soviet Union (cf. No. 48, note 1), Mr. Bullard stressed that he thought it very important 'not to drift into the position of supposing that it is our duty to modify our position on international questions for the sake of unspecified favours from Moscow or in the interest of improving the atmosphere for the Secretary of State's visit'. He added: 'The Prime Minister is on record as endorsing our view that we should not seek to modify our line towards the USSR just at the moment when it is commanding respect elsewhere.' Sir J. Killick agreed, and drafted this telegram largely on the basis of Mr. Bullard's advice.

on 'détente' in general and some aspects of CSCE in particular,[2] by using the argument that certain British positions are 'inappropriate' at a time when a meeting between two Foreign Ministers is about to take place. It is not my intention to seek a 'successful' outcome to my visit on these terms.

2.   It is therefore important to discourage Soviet suggestions in this sense before the preparations for the visit reach their final stage. In any conversations with representatives of the Soviet Union or their allies which take such a turn you should by [*sic*] by the following points, which can be made explicitly if necessary:

(*a*)   I do not regard an invitation from one Foreign Minister to another for a meeting in the former's capital as a favour to be requited by anything more than acceptance. I am not expecting Mr. Gromyko to modify his policies as the price of my acceptance of his invitation, and he will know better than to expect this of me.

(*b*)   A meeting of two Foreign Ministers is an occasion useful to both sides for identifying and recording points of agreement and we shall certainly hope to do this in Moscow. It will, I hope, also provide an opportunity of discussing and clarifying points of disagreement. If progress can be made towards reconciling them, I shall be glad, but I consider it would be a disservice and would create illusions leading to disappointment and recrimination later, to gloss over them just for the sake of creating a 'good atmosphere'.

(*c*)   There is a certain tradition of clear thinking and plain speaking in British diplomacy, which has been reflected in my public statements over a long period, and I intend to adhere to it.

(*d*)   This is not to say that I wish to be provocative or pick quarrels, and I see no incompatibility between this approach and the development of the kind of businesslike and mutually beneficial contacts, based on mutual respect, with the Soviet Union which we enjoy with many of their allies.

---

[2] See Volume II, No. 56. In his submission (*v. ibid.*) Mr. Bullard also referred to a complaint made by Mr. Khlestov on 20 November at the MBFR talks in Vienna that the British had attempted 'to distort the foreign policy of the Soviet Union and other Warsaw Pact states' (UKDEL Vienna telegram No. 115 of 20 November, WDN 27/19).

No. 51

Letter from Mr. Wright to Sir T. Garvey (Moscow)

[*MWE 3/33/2*]

Confidential   FCO, *23 November 1973*

Dear Terence,

1.   We still owe a reply to your predecessor's letter of 1 August entitled 'Whatever became of the CCP?'[1]

---

[1] No. 45.

2.   The Community is making very slow progress on filling in the details of the Common Commercial Policy which it said it would apply to East Europe from 1 January 1973. As will be clear, I hope, from the paragraphs which follow we agree on the need for the Community to apply an effective policy; but I think Sir J Killick's letter underestimates—notably in paragraph 10 which says 'Surely all we have to do is to decide for ourselves what common policies and practices we need, and go ahead and apply them'—the problems involved in securing agreement on such policy. Without being too sure about this, we think it may be possible to make better progress in 1974 than we did in 1973.

3.   We agree with the views expressed in earlier letters about the political importance of a genuine common commercial policy for the Community in its commercial dealings with the Soviet Union and Eastern Europe. An effective CCP would be a powerful obstacle to the Soviet Union's attempts to secure a weak and divided Western Europe amenable to Soviet pressure. It would reduce the ability of the Soviet Union and its allies to play one Member State off against another. This would in turn give the Community confidence in broader political dealings with the Soviet Union. We want to move forward to common positions of the Nine on both the political and the economic fronts. We therefore favour the further development of the CCP and, in a number of particular fields, we would like our partners in the Community to move faster towards this than they seem prepared to do.

4.   It is quite clear that the Soviet Union's analysis of the political importance of the CCP is similar to ours. It therefore wishes to inhibit the further development of the CCP. It has seized upon 'cooperation' agreements as an obvious loophole in the common policy. And for both political and commercial motives, the latter shared by the other East Europeans, it plays the West Europeans off against each other in a brazen way.

5.   The problem for the Community is not simply one of procedures but of finding a common will to operate as a single unit in intergovernmental commercial dealings (in the broad sense) with the Communist countries. So far, though our partners are in general alive to the political considerations, the will has not yet made itself apparent. There are a number of reasons for this.

6.   The first and much the most important reason is the conviction on the part of some countries, notably of course France, that they can derive more national commercial benefit by negotiating separately than they can collectively. At any time some members of the Community are doing relatively well, in comparison with their partners, in East/West trade and they will be tempted to argue that a pooling of their efforts would be against their national interests. Michael Palliser's letter to me of 2 October admirably describes the practical effect of this in EEC discussions on cooperation agreements, export credits, quotas etc.[2]

---

[2]   Sir M. Palliser, HM Ambassador and UK Permanent Representative to the EC, pointed out in his letter of 2 October that, in the context of the CCP towards Eastern Europe, both tariffs and quotas were of little significance since the Community operated a Most Favoured Nation régime and quotas on imports from Eastern Europe were 'on the way out'. The terms of export credits were, by contrast, 'vastly more important', since member states felt themselves to be in competition

7.   Secondly there is a simple fact that the Common Commercial Policy, in spite of the commitment in the Paris Summit Communiqué, has not been top priority for the Community. The work-load in Brussels is heavy. Questions of international monetary reform, the GATT[3] multilateral trade talks, Regional Policy, Economic and Monetary Union, Relations with the Associables and with the Mediterranean have more than filled up the Council's time in the first part of this year.

8.   Thirdly there is the French doctrinal opposition to extending the competence of the Community in general, and the Commission in particular, into new fields such as industrial cooperation. This is a separate reason from the commercial one I have already mentioned, for French opposition to putting flesh on the CCP. Our general view of the development of the Community is less restrictive than that of the French. We have always made it clear that we want a dynamic Community (the French go along with the letter of that but not the spirit) and that we expect new common policies to be agreed on new subjects making full use of the EEC Institutions.

9.   Finally there is the argument sometimes used against developing the CCP which Sir J Killick mentions, namely that we must not press the CCP for fear of bringing about closer integration in CMEA. He says he finds that the French argument on this to be a phoney one. We agree. Our general view is that our policies are unlikely to have much effect on the integration of COMECON but that, if it arises, we should avoid adopting policies which would positively encourage integration in CMEA. They should not, however, be at the cost of holding up desired Community policies. We must rely on the East Europeans to fight their own battles within the CMEA as they see fit. I will comment below on Michael Palliser's suggestions, in his letter of 2 October to me, on the scope for doing business with CMEA in the longer term.[4]

10.   In discussions on this subject a general economic argument is sometimes brought in, namely that West Europe must now compete with the US and Japan for the expanding East European markets and that Europe will be more competitive if it operates as a single unit and uses new procedures, perhaps involving the Commission, to handle the grandiose new projects for industrial cooperation which the Russians seem to envisage. We are not altogether convinced by this argument. First of all there are limits to the scope which East European markets afford. As you know, trade with CMEA countries represents only a small proportion (less than 4 per cent) of the total foreign trade of the enlarged Community. We do not think that this is likely to increase substantially in the coming years. The constraints imposed by East European economic

with each other and, consequently, they had 'not made a Gadarene rush towards self-denying ordinances when they [had] felt that there was a national interest at stake in helping their exporters'. Likewise, he thought that bilateral economic cooperation agreements 'suited all parties'.

[3] General Agreement on Tariffs and Trade.

[4] Sir M. Palliser observed in his letter of 2 October (see note 2 above): 'The view I take at present is that the advantages of our gaining access to information through CMEA and of using a relationship with it as a juridical basis for economic ventures in Eastern Europe are persuasive arguments in favour of receiving the CMEA approach rather more warmly and encouragingly than most of my colleagues have so far viewed it.'

systems are still important; (the current 1971/75 Five Year Plans, except for those of Hungary and Romania, schedule a much more rapid increase in trade with COMECON partners than they do with the rest of the world). Export earnings in hard currency are unlikely to go up steeply without widespread measures of reform to update their commodity structure; and few if any of us see convincing signs of this. Cooperation, which essentially means making imports of technology pay for themselves, is in our view unlikely to make such rapid progress as the Communists seem to hope. The thing which, much more than new inter-governmental procedures, really will help West European businessmen to operate competitively in the East is the gradual fusion of national markets within the EEC into a genuine Common Market with the economies of scale which that will provide. This is a different thing from coordinated bidding through the Commission, and in our opinion much more likely to be effective.

11. So much for the excuses. In spite of the problems there are signs that pressure in the Community for action on the CCP is now building up. We take the view that it falls primarily to the Commission to make proposals. They are in a much better position to do this than Member States which have national commercial interests and their relations with the Russians to consider. So it is encouraging that Sir Christopher Soames[5] is now pursuing the subject (see Luxembourg telegram No 346 reporting the discussion in the EEC Council on 15 October[6] and the attached copy of a record of a meeting between Soames and Scheel[7]—which you should not quote to your German or other colleagues). There will almost certainly be action on the Common Commercial Policy in the coming months and we will encourage the Commission to see to it that there is. The Council's discussion on it on 6 November should be regarded as the beginning of the process.

12. To come to the substance of the CCP: What kind of policy do we want? The draft EUO paper to which Sir J Killick refers in paragraph 1 of his letter was considerably amended in interdepartmental discussion.[8] There is now an agreed paper which, as a Cabinet document, we cannot send you but which you saw while you were in London.[9] Meanwhile it may be helpful for you to have the following notes on our views on the main subjects which are bound to be discussed in the context of the CCP:

[5] Sir C. Soames was Vice-President of the EC Commission.

[6] In this telegram of 15 October Sir M. Palliser reported on Dutch complaints in the EC Council over the lack of progress in defining a CCP towards the East.

[7] Not printed. During this meeting with Herr W. Scheel, the West German Foreign Minister, on 8 October, Sir C. Soames insisted that cooperation agreements, 'while remaining national, must be brought within some sort of consultation and coordination on a Community basis'.

[8] See No. 45, note 2.

[9] This memorandum, 'EEC Common Commercial Policy towards the USSR and Eastern Europe', of 8 May (EUM (73) 33) endorsed the view that 'an effective CCP would be a powerful obstacle to the Soviet Union's attempts to secure a weak and divided Western Europe amenable to Soviet pressure'. It also insisted on the 'need to avoid adopting policies which would encourage integration in the CMEA though not at the cost of holding up desired Community policies'. The paper was discussed in the Ministerial Committee on Europe on 17 May (EUM (73) 10th Meeting).

(a) Cooperation Agreements

In view of the growing importance of economic and industrial cooperation in relations with the CMEA countries the Commission have made various proposals covering not only the coordination of Member States' activities in this field but also the negotiations with the CMEA countries of Community supplementary framework agreements on cooperation. The Commission have also recently been taking individual Member States to task for the short-comings of their cooperation agreements with East Europeans. Our general view is that cooperation agreements are a necessary evil which we must play along with so long as our major trade partners and rivals insist on having them. At the moment there is no doubt that cooperation agreements provide a glaring loophole in the operation of a Common Commercial Policy. The East Europeans make no secret of their satisfaction at this. There is not much we can do about existing cooperation agreements. When we ourselves have signed cooperation agreements we have taken full account of the provisions of the CCP and have been careful not to include references to such subjects as most favoured nation treatment. Others, particularly the Italians, have been less scrupulous. We agree that the Commission should establish such common rules and procedures as are necessary to satisfy itself that national cooperation agreements are consistent with the CCP. Indeed we see positive advantage in this and will take a constructive part in the efforts which the Commission are now making to put these into practice.

(b) The Handling of Quota Negotiations

There has been some discussion in the Community about arrangements to be followed for establishing quota levels for imports from the CMEA countries in 1974. Brussels telegram No. 3536 of 5 July repeated to Moscow recorded our so far unsuccessful efforts to persuade other members of the EEC that it would be better not to have bilateral talks on the 1974 quotas and to agree that there should be a concerted announcement of the 1974 quota lists (preferably by the Commission).[10] We got little support. Now the DTI are stuck with the worst of both worlds having some kind of discussions with the East Europeans about 1974 without having the right to negotiate quotas with them. The actual arrangements for 1974 quotas are that Member States will decide unilaterally on what they are prepared to give after a series of consultations in an EEC Working Group to consider and agree on Member States' proposals. 'Discussions' with the CMEA countries are permitted, but 'negotiations' including such things as agreed minutes and exchanges of letters are firmly ruled out. A separate exercise in the EEC has the horrible title of 'uniformisation of liberalisation measures towards state-trading countries'. The aim is to work

[10] In UKREP Brussels telegram No. 3536 Sir M. Palliser described how at a meeting of the EC's Eastern Countries Group on 4 July the UK representatives had, following statements by Benelux and West German representatives to the effect that member states might bilaterally discuss quotas with Eastern states, asked whether this implied that in general member states expected to discuss quota levels with the Eastern countries. 'When', Sir M. Palliser observed, 'an eloquent silence followed we said that it answered our question and that we did not need to pursue it further.'

out a list common to all EEC countries of imported items subject to quotas. But agreement on that is a long way off.

(c) Export Credit Policy

I agree with you that this is an important area. We support as a priority objective within the Common Commercial Policy the establishment of a binding agreement within the Community setting overall rules for maximum credit terms for Community exports to the CMEA countries. Any agreement will need to be sufficiently flexible to take account of competition from other countries such as Japan and the USA and ensure that the Community exporters are not placed in a disadvantageous position which a unilateral action by the Community, in advance of wider international agreement, might otherwise create. We are at the moment considering the legal aspects of the Community's competence in the credit field. We are also taking full account of course of the effect on our commercial interest of this 'Communautaire' approach, ie how much we stand to gain on balance from the advantages of a joint (and therefore stronger) bargaining position, set against any lost opportunities of bringing off bilateral deals.

(d) Agriculture

We realise that the development of the Common Agricultural Policy has raised some trading difficulties for the CMEA countries (though not for the Soviet Union). Our interests in this respect are different from those of other Member States. We will have to be careful on this because of the sensitivities within the Community. But we will do our best to ensure the continuation of agricultural imports from Eastern European countries.[11]

EEC Relations with CMEA

13. I will not go here into our general policy on the handling of EEC/CMEA relations. You will be aware of this from telegrams dealing with Faddeyev's approach[12] and discussion of this in the EEC council. It was satisfactory that there was a very wide measure of agreement in the EEC on how we should react. It may however be worth commenting briefly on the interesting ideas in Michael Palliser's letter of 2 October and the possible advantages of practical contacts between the Community and CMEA.[13] I fully agree with the view that we must not reject the possible advantages of such contacts out of hand. But we do not think that the potential advantages, which are frankly nebulous and of the kind

---

[11] The UK was a major importer of food from Eastern Europe and its adoption of the EC's Common Agricultural Policy put CMEA exports at risk. As the agreed Cabinet paper on the CCP (see note 9 above) pointed out, in addition to British consumer interest in the continuing availability of East European agricultural produce, the CMEA countries still thought bilaterally, and the expected loss of earnings arising from a fall in their agricultural sales to the UK was already having adverse consequences on the UK's export prospects in CMEA markets.

[12] See No. 45, note 6.

[13] See notes 2 and 4 above.

to which I have already referred in paragraph 10 above, would justify the Community's actively encouraging the CMEA as such to do business with it. Such a policy would run counter to the one agreed in the EEC Council and would face the disadvantages Michael Palliser sets out well in his letter.[14] I think that the sensible and most likely pattern we should envisage is that over the years some practical business will be done between the EEC and CMEA but that it is up to the East Europeans to decide what kind of contacts they want CMEA to offer. They are already beginning to do this. If they come up with suggestions which seem attractive to our businessmen, trade ministries etc. we will of course encourage the EEC to take them seriously.

Political Cooperation

14. Finally, we are proposing to try to follow up the success so far achieved in the 'European Identity' exercise by getting the Nine to write a paper defining their 'identity' (by which we mean broadly their common interests and policies) viz-à-viz [*sic*] the Soviet Union and Eastern Europe.[15] If we can get this done, it may help to make agreement on filling out the CCP easier just as an effective CCP would help to achieve our aim of a common political position.

Yours ever,
J.O. WRIGHT

[14] These were: (1) Britain's partners might benefit more from improved access and possibly stronger influence on East European planning; (2) it might raise premature expectations of cooperation amongst firms of different member states; (3) the EEC would be contributing to the CMEA's supranationality; and (4) it would encourage the development of new competences for the EEC.

[15] EC Heads of Government, meeting in Copenhagen during 14–15 December, formally adopted a declaration on the 'European Identity'. The preparation of a paper on this subject, in the context of the EC's relations with the USA, had originally been suggested by Mr. Heath to M. M. Jobert, the French Foreign Minister, in July, and the idea was subsequently discussed within the European Political Cooperation machinery of the nine EC member states. In its final form the declaration foresaw the progressive definition of the identity of the member states in relation to other countries or groups of countries (guidance telegram No. 197 of 13 December, MWE 3/304/8). See *Political Co-operation by the Member States of the European Communities. The European Identity*, Cmnd 5516 (London: HMSO, 1973).

No. 52

Sir T. Garvey (Moscow) to Sir A. Douglas-Home

[*ENS 3/548/13*]

Confidential   MOSCOW, *11 December 1973*

Summary ...[1]

Sir,

Visit of the Secretary of State for Foreign and Commonwealth Affairs to the USSR—2–5 December

1.   Accompanied by Lady Douglas-Home, you paid an official visit to the Soviet Union, at the invitation of the Soviet Government, arriving in Moscow on the evening of Sunday, 2 December, spending two days here and leaving from Leningrad on the evening of Wednesday, 5 December. Records of your three sessions of talks with the Soviet Foreign Minister, and of your call on President Podgorny,[2] are already with the Department. For convenience, I attach copies of the programme which you and Lady Douglas-Home carried out, and of the joint communiqué issued at the end of your stay.[3] In this despatch, I offer general conclusions on the handling of the visit by your Soviet hosts, and some comments on the content of your discussions.

2.   In the words of the communiqué, your talks 'took place in a friendly and businesslike atmosphere'.[4] Russian officials were already using the word 'friendly' before the visit began, and it was indeed obvious that it had been programmed for a successful outcome. In all the lesser details that accompany such an occasion, the Soviet authorities went out of their way to create a favourable impression. The Soviet Press had prepared in a minor key for a successful visit, at least to the extent of toning down the amount of critical comment (the Press follow-up to the visit has also been minimal). Soviet hospitality was ample, extending even to the provision of a large block of seats for members of the Embassy at the ballet performance in the Kremlin Palace of Congresses on the Monday night, and of suitable entertainment for this large party in the interval. Generous provision was made for accommodation and transport of your large delegation, including the cost of their travel to Leningrad. A lavish banquet was given by Mr. Gromyko in the Soviet Government's hospitality villa on the Lenin Hills, at which the guest

---

[1] Not printed.

[2] In a personal message to Mr. Heath transmitted in Moscow telegram No. 1480 of 4 December, Sir A. Douglas-Home described Mr. Podgorny as 'almost [an] exact replica of Douglas Houghton [the Chairman of the Parliamentary Labour Party] only three times as verbose'.

[3] Not printed.

[4] The *communiqué* stated that the two Ministers 'noted with satisfaction positive trends in the international situation, particularly in Europe, which create opportunities for the further development of friendly and peaceful cooperation between states irrespective of their political, economic and social systems'.

list on the Soviet side included one Deputy Prime Minister, Mr. Lesechko, four other Ministers of the Soviet Government: Foreign Trade, Culture, Higher Education, and Merchant Marine; besides Mr. Lapin, Chairman of the State Committee for Broadcasting and Television, who is also a member of the Council of Ministers. Two of these, Mr. Guzhenko, the Minister for Merchant Marine, and Mr. Elyutin, the Minister for Higher Education, also attended the lunch which you gave on the Tuesday in the Embassy.

3.   The Soviet handling of the communiqué also turned out to be a lot more accommodating than is usual on such occasions. The Russians failed to carry out an agreement to negotiate the communiqué in London, but once work started on it in Moscow on the evening of your arrival, it was concluded without major difficulty, though at the cost of some burning of midnight oil. I think this was only partly due to the operation of the principle that work expands or contracts to the time allotted for it. There could have been much more wrangling. Mr. Suslov, Head of the Second European Department, who led the Soviet side, was clearly authorised not to insist on any formulations which would cause us particular difficulty. The result was the kind of neutral, reasonably short document to which Her Majesty's Government could, without shame or dissimulation, subscribe.

4.   The Soviet Government's intention to make the blandest possible impression was also reflected in Mr. Gromyko's handling of your discussions. He laid himself out to be as civil as possible, to avoid controversy, even to avoid argument. He made no attempt whatever to challenge you on any of those aspects of British or Western policy which Soviet propaganda is currently attacking, notably current moves to strengthen the European element in Western defence. Mr. Gromyko was in general content to leave the running to you. You yourself came with no intention to avoid difficult or controversial questions, but even when these were raised, for example the debate which you initiated on the difference between the British and the Soviet outlooks on the world, and our different ideas on détente, or your proposals for closer contacts and exchanges between the peoples of Europe under Basket III,[5] or the restrictions operated by the Soviet Government on movements of foreign diplomats—on all these questions Mr. Gromyko replied with a notable absence of acrimony. He showed an iron refusal to be provoked. It was as if battle was offered but never engaged.

5.   One problem which could have caused some bad feeling at this time had been our refusal of a visa to Mr. Pronsky, at present Head of the Foreign Relations Department of the State Committee for Science and Technology, whom the Soviet Government wished to nominate as Minister-Counsellor at their Embassy, to work ostensibly as the Committee's representative in London. The application had presumably been timed in the hope that Mr. Pronsky's nomination would have a better chance of being accepted during the run-up to your visit. But there was no mention of this matter by anyone on the Soviet side throughout the visit. The Soviet Government's, or at least the State Committee's, pique, was silently demonstrated by the absence of any representative of the Committee at either

[5] See No. 32, note 9.

of the functions already referred to. The Chairman of the State Committee, Academician Kirillin, would have been the normal choice among the Soviet Deputy Prime Ministers to be present on such an occasion; and it was no doubt because of his demonstrative absence that Mr. Lesechko, the Soviet Deputy Prime Minister, who normally deals with CMEA affairs, was brought in to represent the Soviet Government at that level. The essential point however, is that the Soviet authorities did not wish to spoil the atmosphere of your visit by any more direct expression of displeasure.

6. Your visit, then, appeared as the final act of burial for the virtual ostracism to which we were subjected immediately after the expulsion of the 105 in September 1971. The Russians seemed more concerned to create an atmosphere for the further development of our relations than to reach any specific agreements with us or even to try directly to influence our thinking on those international problems such as the Middle East, CSCE, or MBFR,[6] in which both the Soviet Union and the UK are now particularly involved. The Soviet aim was simply to restore amicable relations at government level. Such relations, they must believe, will serve their interests at a later stage. I think they have two prospects in mind.

7. First, they are concerned for the part which USSR/UK relations can play in their general policy of détente in Europe. It must make no sense for them to have excellent relations with France and good relations with Germany, and at the same time to leave the UK as a potential troublemaker for them inside the European community. They have already seen at Helsinki, Vienna and Geneva that the UK has a significant and, for them rather troublesome, part in the working out of Western positions in European questions. They may not have much hope of turning any British Government towards sympathy for Soviet policies, but they probably wish to avert the negative effect which a Britain still in bad relations with the Soviet Union could have on the general development of Western policies. A closer dialogue with us might also be useful to them in wider international questions such as the Middle East. In short, their aim has been to re-establish normal relations between the USSR and the UK in pursuit of Mr. Brezhnev's policy of general détente.[7]

8. Secondly, there may well be a more personal element in Soviet moves to improve their relations with us. Mr. Brezhnev has his own human weaknesses, curiosity, ambitions. He has before him an obviously limited period of life at the top. He appears to enjoy the panoply of summitry, the meetings with his peers

---

[6] In Moscow telegram No. 1486 of 4 December Sir A. Douglas-Home reported that Mr. Gromyko had been at pains to avoid controversy over MBFR: 'He made no attempt to rebut my remarks about Soviet military superiority, nor to probe the Western position. He said that he could not accept the Western idea of "balance". The fundamental principle was that neither side should seek unilateral advantage: not all the Western interventions in Vienna recognised this.'

[7] In guidance telegram No. 193 of 7 December Sir A. Douglas-Home remarked that the 'main obvious significance' of his visit had been for Anglo-Soviet relations: 'We now have a basis for the kind of relations with the Soviet Union which we ought to have with a power of its importance and for which we on our side have always been ready. We have made no concessions to achieve this.' The Russians, he concluded, 'have abandoned their attempts to isolate and neutralise Britain as a force in European politics'.

on the international stage, and the adulation of the Soviet media which accompanies all his foreign travels. And these repeated diplomatic successes are put to good use in strengthening his political position at home. A visit to the Soviet Union by Mr. Heath, to be followed by a visit to the UK by Mr. Brezhnev could provide in due course another of those valued occasions. We need not be modest for the prestige of Downing Street or Buckingham Palace. These considerations would not weigh very heavily against those of Soviet State interest; but when they point in the same direction they could be powerful stimuli for the moves which Soviet diplomacy is now making to bring the UK into the circle of Mr. Brezhnev's favour.

9. I need not recapitulate here the content of your discussions. Even though Mr. Gromyko did little more than repeat well-known Soviet positions on the matters raised, it was enlightening to hear the structure described by the architect himself; and I imagine each member of your delegation will have carried away from the talks and from the social occasions some new and valuable personal insight. But the aspect of Mr. Gromyko's exposition which most impressed me and others from the Embassy was the evidence he provided of the weight given to the Soviet internal interest in foreign policy matters. Mr. Gromyko showed an iron immobility on anything touching on Soviet security or Soviet internal requirements and regulations. He replied politely to your explanation of the difficulties caused us by the Soviet concept of inevitable 'struggle' but made it clear that in his view nothing could come out of any discussion of the Soviet ideology. Ideology, one might conclude, is as much a part of the protective shield around the Communist order inside the USSR as are the Soviet Armed Forces themselves.[8] When you referred, in the context of Basket III, to proposals for a joint magazine, or joint television programmes, Mr. Gromyko was completely negative. He was negative because any joint enterprise in such matters would amount in the Soviet view to admitting peaceful co-existence in the ideological field: it would be surprising if we encountered any flexibility on this at Geneva. Most revealing of all was his manner of rejecting your suggestion that there should be a mutual abolition of travel restrictions for Soviet diplomats in London and British diplomats in Moscow. The practice in other countries, even 'socialist' countries, was of no interest to him. If the Soviet practice changed, we would be informed. But the Soviet Union and the Soviet Union alone would be the judge of what rules and regulations were required at any time in this field. Behind all Mr. Gromyko's remarks on these subjects we had a grim picture of how the Soviet leaders see security in ideological and political as much as in military terms.[9]

[8] During his conversation with Mr. Gromyko on the afternoon of 3 December, reported in Moscow telegram No. 1480 (see note 2 above), Sir A. Douglas-Home explained how Western countries were irritated by the 'consistent harping of the Communists on the ideological struggle and their determination to achieve victory over rival ideologies'. But Mr. Gromyko insisted that the Communists fully believed that their system would triumph and, according to Sir A. Douglas-Home, 'he argued rather unconvincingly that not too much attention should be paid to emotive language. "Struggle" could be equally well described as "differences".'

[9] Sir A. Douglas-Home observed in Moscow telegram No. 1480 (*V. ibid.*): 'All in all I am encouraged by the fact that they [the Russians] clearly set store by good relations. It gives us some little leverage. But on anything even faintly related to liberalism the door is firmly locked.'

10. Apart from what has already been said in your guidance telegram No. 193,[10] I would suggest two conclusions from the experience of this visit. First, it is clear that the Soviet Government, for reasons which I have tried to analyse above, see a need for Anglo-Soviet relations to be seen to be improving rather than to be stagnant or deteriorating. Mr. Gromyko spoke at your lunch party of the further rungs on the ladder. This may give us a modest amount of leverage with the Soviet Government to make some progress in matters of interest to us, notably in trade.

11. Secondly, I think we had confirmation that the West need not hesitate to turn to its own advantage the Soviet regime's insistence on being the absolute judge on matters concerning the Soviet Union's security or internal order. The Russians give us in their own example the strongest possible justification for the thesis that good political relations with the USSR are entirely compatible with our looking to our own security as judged by our own exclusive criteria. There is no field in which the Soviet authorities, on the basis of their own practice, can less expect indulgence in others. Your visit not only buried the events of September 1971. It provided their final justification.

12. I see I have barely mentioned your trip to Leningrad. I hope and trust that it may have provided some small relaxation and pleasure in the midst of an intolerably busy month. For those of us who travelled in the Leningrad underground, with the British Foreign Secretary at the footplate, it was a memorable as well as a happy occasion.

13. I am sending copies of this despatch to Her Majesty's Representatives at Washington, Bonn, Paris, Helsinki, UKDEL NATO and UKREP EEC.

I have, etc.
TERENCE GARVEY

---

[10] Sir A. Douglas-Home pointed out in this guidance telegram (see note 7 above) that the 'chief practical results of the visit' were that Mr. Heath hoped to visit the Soviet Union in 1974 and Mr. Gromyko would subsequently visit the UK. 'A less obvious benefit of the visit was', Sir A. Douglas-Home noted, 'that it demonstrated that it is possible for a Western Minister to conduct a frank and outspoken dialogue with the Soviet Government without adverse reactions.'

No. 53

Sir T. Garvey (Moscow) to Sir A. Douglas-Home

No. 79 Telegraphic [ENS 2/1]

Restricted   MOSCOW, *22 January 1974*

My tel[egram] No. 69.[1]

Crisis of Capitalism

1.   Leninists have for 50 years maintained, in face of all the evidence, that capitalism must disintegrate: and we should not underrate inspirational effects on Soviet thinking of recent confirmation (as they see it) that what was foretold by the prophets is, at last, verily coming to pass.

2.   Nevertheless I note that the business end (as opposed to the claptrap end) of the Soviet Government continues to pursue and make medium and long term collaboration arrangements with US, German, French and, indeed, British partners: which suggests that it does not contemplate the very early disappearance of the other form of society.

3.   There is currently no let-up in pro-détente propaganda in the Soviet press, e.g. comment continues to express optimism about the eventual outcome of CSCE and force reduction talks. My impression remains that the Russians will continue to seek détente in inter-state relations with capitalist countries but will combine this with possible increased support and attention for Western Communist parties as the leading force in the class struggle which they now see as having entered a more promising stage.[2] It is some comfort that they cannot but be hampered by the essential contradiction in this policy as also in the policy of combining 'unity of action' in the workers' movement with continuing struggle against the social democrats.[3]

---

[1] In this telegram of 21 January Sir T. Garvey described a high-level ideological meeting held in Moscow on 18 January to mark the 50th anniversary of Lenin's death. Professor B.N. Ponomarev, the Secretary of the Central Committee of CPSU, informed participants that there was such a sharpening of all the contradictions in bourgeois society that one could speak of 'a definite qualitative shift in the development of the general crisis of capitalism'. This, he contended, involved: an economic crisis going beyond the bounds of cyclical recessions; a currency crisis; a crisis in the relations between 'imperialist' countries and their former colonies, and between the USA, Western Europe and Japan; an energy crisis which assumed the nature of a real calamity; and a political and ideological crisis reflected in the general sharpening of the internal class struggle within capitalist countries. Prof. Ponomarev added that because of all these factors a situation which would 'open the door to radical revolutionary transformations might arise at any moment in some part of the system', and that the Communist party's 'correct and effective' policy would play an immeasurably greater role.

[2] Mr. Bullard noted in a minute to Mr. Wiggin of 28 January that he did not dissent from this view. 'But', he continued, 'Ponomarev's speeches do once again throw into relief the contradiction between Soviet dogma and Soviet practice. Such statements do nothing to remove the underlying fear in the West that one day doctrine and policy will coincide, and that the present separation between them is merely a question of tactics.'

[3] In a minute to Mr. Bullard of 2 January Mr. Murrell observed with regard to Soviet policy towards the West: 'The West's current economic and political difficulties may have strengthened the hand of any elements in the Soviet Party opposed to the détente policy. With a genuine crisis of capitalism in prospect the ideologists and hardliners may press for a more aggressive Soviet foreign policy strategy to exploit the situation. But there is no evidence as yet of any dissension in the Soviet leadership, or change of Soviet attitude towards the West.'

No. 54

Planning Paper on Future Policy towards Eastern Europe by the Foreign and Commonwealth Office[1]

[*ENS 2/4*]

Confidential   FCO, *12 February 1974*

I INTRODUCTION

Questions

1   This paper seeks to answer certain questions originally posed by Mr. Amery. These may be summarised (full text at Annex A)[2] as follows:

(*a*) What evolution in the internal systems of East European countries, and in their relations with the Soviet Union, would, over the next decade:
    (i) best suit British and West European interests?
    (ii) be most likely to occur in practice?
(*b*) What action might we, and our partners in Western Europe take, either to promote the ideal solution or to cope with any problems posed by likely developments?[3]

[1] This paper was approved by the PUS's Planning Committee on 12 February. It was requested by Mr. Amery on 19 July 1973 and, after consultations between Mr. Cable, Mr. E.E. Orchard, Director of Research, and Mr. Bullard, an outline draft was circulated within the FCO on 16 August. Planning Staff subsequently worked closely with EESD in the preparation of the paper, the first draft of which attracted a good deal of adverse comment following its despatch, on 2 November, to posts in Eastern Europe. Mr. Bolland, HM Ambassador in Sofia, thought it 'unduly pessimistic' (letter to Mr. Cable of 12 November), and Mr. R.J.M. Wilson, HM Ambassador in Budapest, complained that it was 'negative and defeatist' (Budapest telegram No. 522 of 13 November). In the light of these and other criticisms, Mr. Cable completely redrafted the paper over Christmas 1973 (EN 2/25). The four annexes accompanying the final version are not printed.

[2] *V. ibid.* Mr. Amery's instructions were confirmed in a commissioning minute from Mr. Goulding to Mr. Cable of 20 July 1973 (Annex A).

[3] Mr. Goulding's minute (*v. ibid.*) specifically asked with regard to the Eastern European countries: 'Do we want them to break away from Soviet domination and align themselves with the "captitalist" countries of Western Europe, assuming (a big assumption) that this were possible in political and economic terms? Or would it suit us better for them to remain within a liberalised Soviet system, or constitute a kind of *cordon sanitaire* between Western Europe and the Soviet Union? What are the implications, in either case, for the future of Germany? Should we for instance incline to favour a continued Soviet occupation of East Germany and hence of Poland while looking

Eastern Europe, for the purposes of this paper, is defined as comprising the countries of the Warsaw Pact minus the Soviet Union.

Assumptions

2. This paper considers possible developments in Eastern Europe on the assumption that there will be no fundamental change, during the next ten years, in the wider pattern of East–West relations: that Western Europe will continue on the path of integration, will remain in defence partnership with the United States and will retain a basic minimum of cohesion and self-confidence in its adversary relationship with the Soviet Union; that the United States will maintain at least parity of strategic power with the Soviet Union, and that there will be neither upheaval nor major change of direction in the Soviet Union. Within this pattern of external forces operating on Eastern Europe, significant shifts in emphasis are nevertheless likely if present trends continue. The military balance in Europe will tip further in favour of the Soviet Union and Transatlantic unity may be further eroded. Moreover, the problems of energy, from which the largely self-sufficient Soviet Union will suffer little, may check the economic growth of Western Europe and slow the process of integration. At best, the magnetic attraction which Western Europe has exercised upon the countries of the East will no longer be reinforced by a rise in material prosperity as rapid as that of the previous decade. At worst, economic depression and its social repercussions might dim the lustre of Western Europe while increasing the economic dependence of Eastern Europe on the Soviet Union. The strength and potential influence of the Soviet Union are thus likely to increase relatively to those of Western Europe.

II British Interests in Eastern Europe

3. The first step towards identifying desirable developments in Eastern Europe has to be an assessment of British national interests. These are of four kinds:

(a) *Security*. The countries of Eastern Europe belong to a hostile military alliance, to which they contribute regular forces over a million strong, including some 14,000 tanks and 2000 combat aircraft. They also assist the unfriendly activities of the Soviet Union by the supply of arms to client states as well as in the fields of diplomacy, intelligence and subversion. The more these countries assert their national independence vis à vis the Soviet Union, the less reliance the Soviet Union will be able to place on their support for Soviet interests or for Soviet pressure upon other Eastern European countries and upon Western Europe. The advantages offered by such developments need, however, to be weighed against the risk of their provoking Soviet counter-measures which might not be confined to Eastern Europe. Even without their Warsaw Pact allies, for instance, Soviet forces on the northern and central fronts exceed those of NATO.

forward to a greater independence for the Danubian and Balkan countries?' In addition, Mr. Amery suggested that the Office should 'as a matter of some urgency' consider what threats might emerge to the stability of Yugoslavia and Austria if instability should follow the death of Marshal J.B. Tito, Yugoslavia's Federal President.

(*b*) *Economic.* The countries of Eastern Europe together account for only 2% of British trade, a proportion that has not significantly varied over the last two decades. For the Community as a whole it is less than 4%. The limited ability of the East Europeans to earn foreign exchange will restrict the scope for any future increase in this trade. But opportunities are better in some countries than in others and could be enlarged by new factors such as the increased attractions of Polish coal, the reduction of present obstacles to agricultural imports or the growth of 'industrial co-operation' schemes. A recession in the non-socialist world could also increase the relative attractions of the Eastern European market. Looking further into the future, the Eastern European economies may be better placed than ourselves to maintain their rates of economic expansion in difficult world conditions. In any event, Eastern Europe will be of growing importance in world commodity markets, especially grain, possibly also in western financial markets and institutions. The prospects for British trade would be improved by greater national independence in Eastern Europe, economic liberalisation and better relations with the West.

(*c*) *The Community Element.* Our partners in the Community, though commercial rivals, share our interest in seeing Eastern Europe develop in the direction of greater national independence and closer contact with the West. This interest is reinforced by domestic political pressures that may incline some of our partners towards greater concessions in the supposed interest of détente (and even of political liberalisation in Eastern Europe) than we might consider desirable. For this reason, as well as to promote the integration of the Community, it is a British interest to develop a common policy among the Nine vis à vis Eastern Europe. These considerations may call for greater British concern with Eastern Europe than might be demanded by purely British interests.

(*d*) *Repercussions on the Soviet Union.* The kind of developments in Eastern Europe intrinsically most favourable to British and Western interests—greater national independence, internal liberalisation and increased contacts with the West —will tend to reduce Soviet ability to bring pressure on Western Europe and may ultimately stimulate some degree of beneficial change in the Soviet Union. But they might, if pressed too far, be seen by the Soviet Union as a threat to the status quo and to basic Soviet interests. Insofar as this increased the risk of Soviet aggression or pressure against Western Europe, major change or pronounced instability in Eastern Europe would not be in British interests. In the last resort Eastern Europe must always be less important, for good or ill, to Britain, than is the Soviet Union. But the choice is not likely ever to be presented in so stark a form and it is clear that our policies can have more influence in Eastern Europe than in the Soviet Union.

III THE SCOPE FOR AUTONOMOUS CHANGE IN EASTERN EUROPE

4. Given the existence of a British interest, albeit limited and qualified, in change in Eastern Europe, the first step is to consider what kinds of change are likely and, only thereafter, to examine the potential contribution of British or Western European policies.

The Impulse for Change

5.   Eastern Europe is an inherently unstable area, in which external armed force has, on three occasions within the last twenty years, been required to repress explosions of the latent popular impulse for major political change. This impulse, which exists even within the ruling classes of all these countries, has two main objectives: a contented population and (with the probable exception of Bulgaria) greater national independence. Their attainment is widely seen as requiring the loosening of Soviet domination and the reform of the Communist system, a conviction reinforced by the living example—more visible to Eastern Europeans than to Russians—of Western Europe. Here countries of similar size and cultural traditions, having avoided these two constraints, are seen to have achieved much of what East Europeans want for themselves. The intermediate position success-fully maintained by Yugoslavia has also had some influence elsewhere in Eastern Europe.

6.   The last decade has seen significant, though not continuous or uniform, progress towards both objectives in all Eastern European countries. So long as there is official encouragement for an atmosphere of détente and of increased contacts with the West, the autonomous impulse towards change may be expected to grow still further. Indeed it is this prospect which has led Moscow to intensify economic integration and to tighten ideological discipline throughout the Warsaw Pact in the last eighteen months.

The Constraints on Change

7.   The ability of Eastern European countries to move in these directions will, however, remain subject to severe constraints: the vested interest of Government and Party hierarchies in the maintenance of Communism and their own power; their consequent dependence on the Soviet Union; their suspicion of political and in some cases economic innovation; their concern about manifestations of nationalism; and their anxiety—especially strong in the GDR—about the lure of the West. This caution in the leaderships will be reinforced at the popular level by suspicion of the FRG and sometimes by dislike of certain aspects of Western society. Moreover, all questions of ideology or military security apart, consider-able changes would be needed to reduce the economic dependence of Eastern Europe on the Soviet Union and to forgo the benefits this can bring. These internal factors help to restrain the forces of change within each country. They would, however, probably be inadequate but for the external pressure exerted by the Soviet Union.

8.   Although Eastern Europe presents many problems for the Soviet Union, Soviet ascendancy there could not now be challenged without serious detriment to its prestige and to the domestic authority of the Soviet leadership. Eastern Europe is now a vital Soviet interest for several fundamental reasons. Strategically it permits the Soviet Union to maintain a forward defence posture and to ensure the continued division of Germany. Politically it strengthens the Soviet Union's leverage in European affairs. Nor are Soviet interests confined to the preservation of Eastern Europe as a Soviet sphere of influence. The maintenance of Com-munism in Eastern Europe is no less important for the domestic authority of the

Soviet Communist Party (CPSU). Ideologically, moreover, Eastern Europe (even without Romania) provides the necessary majority of ruling parties in the contest between the CPSU and the Chinese Communists. At a lower level, Eastern Europe makes a useful contribution to the Soviet economy and Soviet diplomacy. It can be taken as axiomatic therefore that the Soviet leaders will go to great lengths to control change in Eastern Europe and to keep Western—and Chinese—influence there to a minimum. According to circumstances, however, they may sometimes prefer repression and sometimes a degree of concession and flexibility. Judging from past experience the Soviet Union may be willing to tolerate a degree of internal liberalisation (as in Hungary) or of independence in foreign affairs (as in Romania) but not both together.

The Likely Outcome

9. These constraints will not necessarily prevent one or more Eastern European countries from attempting larger or faster changes than now seem likely to be acceptable to the Soviet Union. There could be further upheavals in Eastern Europe and the Soviet Union might find these more difficult to repress than hitherto. Nevertheless, given the growing relative strength of the Soviet Union and the increasing political sophistication of Eastern European leaders, the prospects that change will continue to be kept under control—even if it sometimes proceeds by bursts of innovation followed by periods of repression—now seem rather greater than before. The sort of change which could occur, in most favourable circumstances, is considered, sector by sector, in Annex B.[4] This amounts to a progressive softening of the sharper edges of Communism, but not to the disappearance of any of its fundamental characteristics.[5] Even this kind of change will probably not be continuous or consistent. A country which goes a long way in one area may feel the need for added restraint in others. In some countries there may be retrogression, as in Poland after 1956 and Czechoslovakia after 1968. Annex C suggests some possible variations from one country to another.[6]

10. The picture is one of continuing Soviet supervision—reinforced, in the

---

[4] See note 1 above. Annex B was entitled 'What could happen in Eastern Europe: sector by sector'.

[5] Annex B (*v. ibid.*) predicted that the preservation of the leading role of the Communist Party was likely to remain the 'essential Soviet test of soundness in Eastern Europe'; that the Party must above all retain control over internal security, the armed forces, the economy and the media; and that any country stepping outside these guidelines was 'likely to face severe Soviet pressure to reverse the trend'. It considered that Soviet forces would remain in Eastern Europe to uphold Soviet interests, and that, where foreign policy was concerned, Romania's position probably represented 'the extreme limit of independence available to any country within the Soviet system'. On the other hand, the Annex suggested that economic reform was a field where deviation from Soviet norms was comparatively easily disguised and easy to justify by local considerations, and that this would tend to favour trade with the West by encouraging joint ventures and the use of cost-efficient technology.

[6] Annex C (see note 1 above) considered likely developments in Eastern Europe on a country-by-country basis. It foresaw the continuation in Poland of rapid economic progress and relatively liberal domestic policies, with church/state relations remaining the largest political problem.

Northern tier and Hungary, by the presence of Soviet troops. There will be strains, but both Eastern European and Soviet leaders will try very hard to suppress or defuse these situations before military measures are needed. Pursuit of détente with the West will be accompanied by prophylactic steps at home. In terms of standards of living, political tolerance and vigour of intellectual life, the countries of Eastern Europe will continue to advance faster than the Soviet Union. There will be some further progress towards economic decentralisation. Links with the West, including industrial cooperation and direct Western invest-ment, are likely to develop further, especially in the cases of Romania, Hungary and Poland. There is scope for the Romanians to consolidate their special position in CMEA and the Warsaw Pact. But they, and the other five, will be hard put to extend their independence within either body. None of the Eastern Europeans is likely, by the early Eighties, to have achieved the independence of Moscow or the relaxation of Communism enjoyed by present-day Yugoslavia.

IV The Impact on British Interests of Change in Eastern Europe
11. The kind of change envisaged in paragraph 10 above would be welcome, but not of major importance. It would facilitate the efforts of British business-men and diplomats, reduce occasions for friction, increase the opportunities for the exercise of British influence on marginal issues, e.g. the attitude of Eastern European governments on international problems not directly related to East–West confrontation. It might even further reduce, in Soviet eyes, the reliability of their East European allies. But it would leave the countries of Eastern Europe as at least potential enemies of Britain: ideologically hostile and likely to give some support (even if this now needed greater Soviet pressure) to Soviet diplomacy, espionage, subversion and propaganda. On the other hand, to the extent that the Soviet Union had to accept, on the part of East European governments, a certain softening of ideological commitment and of resistance to Western influences, it is arguable that this new permissiveness might also begin to infect the Soviet Union itself. The fear of such infection has been plausibly suggested as an important motive for the violent Soviet reaction, in 1968, to change in Czecho-slovakia. The range of Eastern European contacts with different levels of Soviet society, and hence their potential influence, will probably continue, throughout the coming decade, to be much greater than the opportunities open to Western Europeans. And any resulting change in Soviet attitudes could be very important both to Britain and to Western Europe as a whole.

Accelerated Change
12. The further change proceeds in this direction, provided it does not provoke Soviet intervention to reverse the process, the greater would be the potential advantages to Western Europe. Romania is an example of an Eastern European country that has succeeded in moving faster and farther than can have been at all welcome in Moscow. If another East European country were to get away with something similar, Soviet authority would suffer throughout Eastern Europe and perhaps even at home. These consequences would, in themselves, be advantageous to British and Western European interests, but they are also reasons

for regarding Soviet toleration of any dramatic departures from orthodoxy as unlikely, particularly in countries adjacent to Western Europe. And an attempt at change that was frustrated by the Soviet Union would in some ways be worse than no change at all. Admittedly the jolt to wishful thinking might be salutary for Western Europe and the Western Alliance. But Western European impotence to prevent Soviet armed intervention would again be demonstrated; progress elsewhere in Eastern Europe would be checked; international tension and Soviet hostility towards Western Europe would increase. There could even be some danger of wider repercussions if the Soviet Government thought it necessary to excuse their intervention as being directed against Western subversion—a real risk in the event of trouble in East Germany. The advantages to be expected from accelerating change in Eastern Europe thus diminish as the uncertain limit of Soviet toleration is approached. And the threshold of Soviet tolerance for change in Eastern Europe is likely to be lower if this change appears to be the result of Western influence rather than of internal pressures.

V British Policy towards Eastern Europe

13. *Present Policy.* These considerations are reflected in British policy, which has recently been stated in the following terms: with the exception of Bulgaria,[7] the association of the East European states with the Soviet Union seems to us unnatural and in the long run unstable. We have no ambition to turn East European peoples against their governments, but we try to practise policies which make it easier rather than harder for those governments to exercise whatever degree of independence from Moscow they may feel to be in their power. This involves above all treating each East European country (in spite of much evidence to the contrary) as a fully sovereign entity with an international status in its own right. We try to push the political dialogue beyond the conventional level to a point where views are exchanged of which the Russians are not aware and would definitely not approve. In trade, we want the maximum of direct contact with end-users in Eastern Europe. Industrial cooperation serves to ensure that Western rather than Soviet technological standards are regarded throughout Eastern Europe as the goal to aim at. In cultural activities we try to offer the East Europeans the maximum contact, subject to limited resources, with the heritage of civilisation which they too regard as their own. We do not expect dramatic events, e.g. that Romania will walk out of the Warsaw Pact or Hungary out of COMECON. But we believe that Western Europe can play a role by showing sympathy and patience, against the day when events may weaken the Soviet grip upon Eastern Europe or when the links binding those countries to Moscow may become less vital to Soviet security.

Cost Effectiveness

14. It has been argued that this policy is about the minimum needed to sustain

---

[7] 'Bulgaria' was, according to Annex C, 'sharply distinguished from her Eastern European neighbours by her unique desire for an ever closer embrace with the Soviet Union.' Indeed, it was thought doubtful whether Bulgaria was economically viable without substantial Soviet support.

the present trend towards national independence and progress in Eastern Europe. It not only complements the similar efforts of our Western European partners, but ensures that our influence (to the extent that influence is attainable in Eastern Europe) is kept abreast of theirs. In 1972/73 the support of this policy cost HMG £2.8 million (Annex D),[8] a little more than corresponding efforts towards either the European Neutrals, Australasia or the Far East where governmental efforts are complemented by a large network of individual and institutional contacts. This is not an extravagant amount, even if the gains expected are modest. If drastic cuts had to be made in British expenditure in support of foreign policy as a whole, Eastern Europe would scarcely deserve a high priority for exemption, but the case for any immediate reduction in effort is not obvious.[9]

Possible Increase in Effort

15. Prima facie, it might even be contended that additional efforts are needed to counteract the probable decline—because of economic depression in Western Europe and the increasing relative strength of the Soviet Union—of Western European magnetism. The difficulty here is that some of the most promising expedients—credits and investment to increase trade and reduce Eastern European economic dependence on the Soviet Union—would cost money that will, for some years to come, be increasingly needed to finance British imports of energy and essential raw materials. Even the lesser sums needed to expand BBC[10] broadcasts, information work and cultural activity whether in isolation or to exploit any gains from the Conference on European Security and Cooperation —will be hard to come by in the foreseeable economic climate. Moreover, it must be doubtful whether increased British efforts alone could actually exert a significant influence either on the autonomous forces for change already operating in Eastern Europe or on the constraints that hold these forces in check. Indeed, to the extent that British efforts could exert such influence, this would become obvious both to Eastern European Governments and to the Soviet Union and might thus prove counter-productive.

16. It is arguable, therefore, that insofar as increased Western efforts are needed, and are able, to counter what Mr. Dubcek[11] called 'the dark and real power of international factors ... limiting the possible pace and form of our own political development', this reinforcement should be sought from better coordination of the policies of the Nine, rather than from purely British exertions. Such

[8] See note 1 above. Annex D tabulated expenditure in support of foreign policy during 1972–73.

[9] Sir N. Henderson was particularly critical of an earlier draft of the planning paper which he considered 'too negative' about the opportunities that could be available to the UK in Eastern Europe. In a letter to Mr. Cable of 19 December 1973 he contended that what was required was 'something more subtle than the yardstick of immediate cost-effectiveness'. It was, he believed, a matter of 'diplomacy, of exploiting by human skill and ingenuity the opportunities open to us, and to do so in order to exert our presence' (EN 2/25).

[10] British Broadcasting Corporation.

[11] Mr. A. Dubcek was First Secretary of the Central Committee of the Communist Party of Czechoslovakia during 1968–69. The Soviet invasion of Czechoslovakia in August 1968 brought an end to his reforming policies.

improved coordination is, in any case, likely to be needed merely to cope with the problems that could arise from autonomous developments in Eastern Europe. These could range all the way from a sudden change that left the Soviet Union uncertain whether intervention was desirable to a minor proposal for cooperation with the EEC. In each case a prompt and united response from the Nine would be markedly more effective than the kind of disarray which followed the latest Arab-Israeli war.[12] Conversely, it could be undesirable, and even dangerous, if each of the Nine remained free to respond individually and spontaneously to certain contingencies: the FRG to disturbances in East Germany, for instance. Of course, there are severe limits to what can be expected of even greatly improved coordination: the Nine are neither militarily nor economically capable, in the last resort, of preventing the Soviet Union from doing what it likes in Eastern Europe. But, in lesser problems, they might exercise more influence together than individually. And, if their relative economic advantages are destined to diminish, any decline in Western European magnetism might be offset by increased unity in policy and diplomacy.

VI PROSPECTS FOR A COMMON WEST EUROPEAN POLICY

Obstacles

17. These are considerable. France, Italy and the FRG all want to pursue the national policies to which they have devoted considerable efforts, partly from commercial motives, but also under domestic political pressures of a kind not matched in Britain. In France Gaullist mystique and the existence of a large Communist Party combine to invest relations with Eastern Europe with a special value. Italy, too, has a large Communist Party and the FRG, themselves not immune from left-wing influence, also have an emotional stake in East Germany that has wider repercussions. Some of our smaller partners put more faith than we do in the potential contribution of relations with Eastern Europe to the cause of general détente. Then both the Soviet Union and the East European governments can be expected to obstruct the development of a common Western European policy: it is in their interest to play off members of the Nine against one another. Finally, a common West European policy can only achieve maximum effectiveness if it is coordinated with NATO and the United States—a concept particularly unwelcome to the French Government.

Opportunities

18. Nevertheless the picture is not entirely black. The CSCE has been an example of effective coordination, not merely among the Nine, but on a wider Western basis. The Community's Common Commercial Policy, though eroded

---

[12] The nine EC member states, having failed at the outbreak of the fourth Arab-Israeli war on 6 October 1973 to speak with a united voice, issued a joint statement on 6 November calling for Israel to relinquish the Palestinian territories occupied since 1967 and to respect the rights of the Palestinians. Differences were subsequently to re-emerge amongst the Nine in their reaction to the Arab oil embargo and cooperation with the US on energy matters. Cf. No. 56, note 3.

by bilateral agreements and so far commanding little enthusiasm, is due to come into force by the end of 1974, by which time it may have been more precisely defined. There is some chance of the Nine agreeing to produce a companion paper on the European Identity vis à vis the East to complement that on relations with the United States. Moreover, the very fact that the process of European integration is encountering difficulties in other fields strengthens the arguments for greater efforts in this area, where Britain can well afford a strongly communautaire position. These arguments are also reinforced by the opposition from Eastern Europe and the Soviet Union, which demonstrates that the present state of affairs suits their interests better than those of Western Europe.

Content of a Common Policy
19. This should include:

(a) *Increased Political Cooperation.* Once agreement has been reached on basic principles (the European Identity paper),[13] we should press for stricter application of the obligation (the second Luxembourg Report)[14] for prior consultation among the Nine before any of them take major steps in bilateral relations with Eastern European countries. We should also encourage discussion in the political cooperation machinery of likely future problems in connection with Eastern Europe and perhaps even contemplate a degree of contingency planning. So far as possible these measure should be supplemented by wider liaison within the North Atlantic Alliance.

(b) *Common Commercial Policy.* We should try to ensure that the Community discharges its commitment to develop an effective CCP to enter into effect by the end of 1974. As a minimum this should include agreement on credit terms and an obligation to clear with the Community any further bilateral agreements on economic cooperation with Eastern European countries.

(c) *Wider Relations between the Community and Eastern Europe.* The ideal solution from our point of view is that East European countries should deal with the Community like any other third parties. We could accept some form of EEC/CMEA relationship if it would facilitate this. We should show ourselves open to Eastern Europe and ready to discuss their trade problems on a basis of effective (rather than formal) reciprocity. Special benefit would accrue to Britain from further liberalisation of Eastern European agricultural exports to the Community.

Advantages of a Common Policy
20. To the extent that we could achieve these aims, we should have advanced the integration of the Community and increased the collective bargaining

---

[13] See No. 51, note 15.

[14] This second report on European Political Cooperation (see Volume II, No. 1, note 26), adopted by the Foreign Ministers of the EC member states on 23 July 1973, committed member-governments not to decide their definitive policy in any new external contingency without having first consulted their partners.

strength of Western European countries vis à vis Eastern Europe and, more importantly, the Soviet Union. There is no reason why particular British interests should suffer thereby. In view of the doubtful prospects for the British economy in the coming years, we stand to lose, rather than gain, by the continuation of unrestricted competition in Eastern Europe with our Western European partners. Moreover, we have a special interest in loosening the restraints imposed by the EEC on our ability to import cheap food from Eastern Europe. We should not be deterred from pursuing these policies by the argument that some aspects of them will be unwelcome in Eastern Europe, for the ultimate source of these objections is the Soviet Union. The only specifically East European argument against a programme that would offer their countries both commercial and political advantage is that any consequent enhancement of the status of COMECON would increase Soviet influence in Eastern Europe. This risk should not deter us from paying this price, if it does prove necessary, for the other advantages of a common policy.

Risks of a Common Policy
21. The real danger to British interests is rather that our Western partners might wish to give the political aspects of a common policy a colouring that was unduly conciliatory towards Eastern Europe and, by extension, towards the Soviet Union. There is already an insidious tendency to suppose that, by responding to the expressed wishes of Eastern European governments (some of which are probably prompted by the Soviet Union), we shall thereby be advancing détente and improving the prospects of lasting peace and stability in Europe. It is true that, the more a common policy becomes a reality, the more we may be inhibited from independently pursuing a harder line than that of some of our European partners. But it also seems likely that we shall be better able to restrain their tendencies within the context of a common policy than by pursuing an independent line likely to become decreasingly effective with the decline of our relative economic strength. A common West European policy might be 'softer' than we would wish, but it would certainly be less dangerously so than the kind of Ostpolitik which might be pursued by a future government of the FRG that had become disillusioned by the prospects for Western European unity.

VII CONCLUSION AND RECOMMENDATIONS

The Outlook and the Scope for influencing it
22. In the absence of fundamental changes in the external environment, the most likely prospect for Eastern Europe during the coming decade is of further, but controlled progress towards greater independence of the Soviet Union and some relaxation of the rigidities of the Communist system. This would be beneficial to British and Western European interests, though the advantages would not be of major importance unless they also helped to promote some softening of Soviet attitudes towards the West and even a degree of internal liberalisation in the Soviet Union. This is unlikely in the coming decade.
23. Faster change in Eastern Europe (and the possibility of further upheavals

cannot be excluded) would only be welcome if it was durable, which depends on Soviet toleration. The Soviet Union could, and probably would, intervene forcibly to reverse any dramatic assertion of national independence or departure from Communist orthodoxy. This might strike a useful blow against wishful thinking,[15] but it would check progress throughout Eastern Europe; would not advance British or Western European interests; and might even increase the Soviet threat to the security of Western Europe.

24. The impulse for change in Eastern Europe is autonomous and Western European policies can do little to control its effect or to inhibit the major constraint on progress—Soviet power and determination to maintain Communism and their own hegemony. But the example of Western Europe is one of the incentives to change in Eastern Europe. Western European governments can thus help to maintain the momentum of change by adopting an attitude of interest and understanding and by giving sympathetic responses to Eastern European efforts to develop closer and more independent contacts with the West.[16]

Recommendations

25. There is little scope for the further extension of purely British efforts in this direction and no need to modify present British policy. This should be maintained pending the development of a common Western European policy towards Eastern Europe. The objectives of such a policy—and its potential advantages—would primarily be to promote the integration and increased effectiveness of the EEC, including Western European ability to make an united response to new problems, or even crises, in Eastern Europe. To the extent that such a policy met British commercial desiderata, it would also serve purely British interests.

26. Improved relations with the governments of Eastern Europe and discreet encouragement of official and national aspirations to greater independence and ideological flexibility are desirable insofar as they are compatible with more important objectives: the pursuit of Western European integration, of British economic needs and of the maintenance of peace and stability in Europe. But British interests in Eastern Europe are insufficient to justify the diversion of resources from more remunerative employment or the running of risks.

---

[15] This clause reflected views expressed by Mr. Wiggin in a minute to Mr. Cable of 4 January. 'It is', Mr. Wiggin noted, 'not cynical to suggest that events such as Hungary in 1956 and Czechoslovakia in 1968 had a salutary effect in reminding the West of the danger of lowering one's guard ... I think it worth introducing the thought somewhere in the paper that, if and when the Soviet Government decide that they have to resort to armed intervention again, this would at least serve to make the West more conscious of defence and less attracted by détente; and this in turn is likely to be a factor influencing the Soviet Government in the direction of comparative restraint in cases of doubt.'

[16] In a minute of 11 January, which he wrote after reading an earlier draft of this planning paper, Mr. Amery argued that, in view of the threat which the Russians could pose to Albania and Yugoslavia after the departure of President Tito, 'our first priority in Eastern Europe' should be the preservation of their independence from the Soviet Union. He further suggested that the West should encourage Greece, Turkey and Yugoslavia to develop their relations with strategically-

important Bulgaria, and that the MBFR talks might offer an opportunity to 'shift the Russians from Hungary'. But when on 12 February this minute and the planning paper were considered by the Planning Committee, Sir T. Brimelow (PUS since November 1973) made plain his disagreement: 'On balance, he thought Mr. Amery's proposals for a more activist attitude towards the Balkans and Hungary were not realistic: the situation in the Balkans was so complex that a reconciliation between Bulgaria and Yugoslavia or Albania and Yugoslavia was unlikely; and the Hungarian Government's policy did not permit much in the way of our developing relations in the direction favoured by Mr. Amery.' Sir T. Brimelow's views were confirmed in discussion, and it was agreed that Mr. Amery's idea on MBFR and Hungary 'offered no solution' (minutes of the 53rd meeting of the Planning Committee, 12 February).

No. 55

Paper by Mr. Amery

[EN 3/548/1]

Confidential   FCO, *28 February 1974*

Policy towards the Soviet Union and Eastern Europe [1]

1.   I have spent much of my time in the last year or so on our relations with the Soviet Union and the so-called 'Socialist countries' of Eastern Europe and in the last nine months have made official visits to Romania, Yugoslavia, Poland and Hungary as well as a second allegedly 'non-political' shooting weekend in Poland. I have not yet taken up invitations to visit Czechoslovakia, Bulgaria and the Soviet Union. But it may possibly be useful if I set down some of my personal impressions and conclusions to date.

2.   The USSR is an economically backward and constitutionally authoritarian empire governed by a strongly entrenched and privileged 'establishment' consisting of the Bureaucracy, the Army and the Technocracy. As such it is subject to all the normal imperatives which decide the policies of a Great Power which is also a 'have not' power.

3.   It is concerned with its security and therefore seeks vassals or allies along its frontiers or where this has not yet proved possible at least neutrals over whom it has influence. The 'socialist' countries and Finland, India and Afghanistan fit into one or other of these categories; China, Turkey and Iran do not. It is concerned to prevent the build up of any potential hostile power group (NATO, EEC, CENTO or Japan). But it also abhors a vacuum and therefore seeks to fill one where it occurs. For geographical reasons it has inherited the traditional Czarist aspirations towards an outlet on the North Sea, the Mediterranean and the Persian Gulf. As its economy has developed and its consumer public become more

---

[1] Mr. Amery sent this paper to Sir A. Douglas-Home under cover of a minute of 28 February, in which he explained that he had originally intended it to serve as a discussion paper for the forthcoming biennial conference of Ambassadors to the Soviet Union and Eastern Europe. On 9 March Mr. Acland noted on Mr. Amery's minute: 'Sir Alec Douglas-Home was not able to see this paper before the Conservative Government resigned. It should be entered for the record.' Cf. No. 57, note 1.

demanding so it has grown more concerned with securing access to raw materials and markets. Its present rulers have also accepted that it cannot hope to emerge from its present backwardness without enlisting the cooperation of the more advanced technology of the West. They are aware that super-power status requires an economic base. As one of the two super powers it is naturally intent not to become subordinate to the other. By the same token it is ready, given the opportunity to do so safely, to become the world leader. Such a power would always be a dangerous factor in international relations, as indeed the old Czarist Empire was, all the more so since its internal stability is constantly threatened by social, economic and national or minority tensions.

4. But the danger is compounded by the fact that the USSR is also a theocratic state and the head of a universal creed—Communism—dedicated to the cause of world revolution.

5. The Soviet leaders may or may not be convinced in their hearts of the truth of communist doctrine or the inevitability of the communist revolution. But for individual leaders to admit to such doubts would be to play into the hands of their rivals at home and abroad in the struggle for power. And in any case even the sceptics among them must recognise that the communist myth is essential to their collective survival.

6. Communism is the basis of Soviet legitimacy. It is the justification of the privileges enjoyed by the establishment, and the excuse for their abuses of power, past and present. The Communist party is the cement—part Church, part free-masonry, part Mafia—which binds the establishment together. Communism is also the focus of loyalty to Moscow's Empire over other nations both within and outside the Soviet Union—much as the Crown or the Church or the Khalifate have been to other Empires in the past.

7. Soviet policy claims to make a distinction between State and Party in inter-national affairs. It asserts simultaneously the possibility of cooperation between Communist and non-Communist states and the impossibility of compromise between Communist and non-Communist systems. In fact political realities make this distinction untenable. Communist parties in non-Communist countries are an important arm of Soviet State policy, potentially if not always in practice. They are a force for disruption in potential adversary countries (e.g. France and Italy) and for extending influence where this may seem desirable (e.g. Finland, Aden or Cyprus). Thus even if the Soviet leaders had no wish to support a world revolution (and the prospect of a Communist Germany or even a Communist Japan must be daunting to some at least of the Moscow establishment) they would still need to cherish other Communist parties as instruments of state policy.

8. This has inescapable and embarrassing implications for Moscow. It makes it difficult for the Soviets to refuse to give some encouragement to local Com-munist movements, at any rate the Moscow-oriented ones. In the process it makes the Soviet Union appear a potentially hostile power to any non-Communist state, even if the Soviets have no immediate intentions against that state.

9. It would be hard enough to achieve a genuine détente with a powerful but 'have-not' Muscovite Empire which laid no claim to universalism; though this might be achieved on a basis of spheres of influence and trade agreements. But

it is virtually impossible to do so with an Empire whose 'establishment' depends for its own survival on its allegiance to and encouragement of a revolutionary doctrine and movement which have the overthrow of other established states and their subordination to Moscow as their declared aim.

10. If the Soviet leaders could accept the concept of 'convergence'—the idea that the evolution of industrialized societies will in due course transform both the socialist and the capitalist systems—without revolution—into a single system having characteristics of both—the problem might be solved.

11. Yugoslav and Romanian leaders already accept this concept. Some Polish leaders are prepared to consider it at least in private. For the Soviet leaders to do so, however, would be to undermine the legitimacy of the Soviet dictatorship at home and the basis of their Empire abroad. Their moral authority over their subjects would be gravely compromised. Only force would remain.

12. It may yet come to that. Already the discrediting of Stalin, the Yugoslav and Chinese schisms, and the need to suppress the Hungarian and Czech heresies by force have all gravely weakened Moscow's claim to infallibility and hegemony. But it still retains enough authority not to have to rely on force alone. If and when it reaches that point it will be doomed.

13. There is substantial evidence that the present Soviet leadership believe— as Malenkov and Khruschev may have done before—that some temporary accommodation with the Industrial West (USA, Europe and Japan) is necessary to the development of the Soviet Union and to their own political survival. It is possible that over time such accommodations may so water down the Communist faith that like Christianity or Islam before it will lose its dynamism. But, for the present, such accommodation is seen in Moscow as purely tactical—a pause for consolidation before the offensive is resumed—and the might of the military and KGB establishment as well as other indicators suggest that the policy of 'détente' is by no means irreversible.

14. Against this background it would be naive to believe that a stable relationship can be established with the Soviet leaders. Agreements there can be over trade, credits and cultural exchanges. Concessions in one area may be bargained against concessions in another. Resources could conceivably be diverted from defence provided the balance of power was not affected or the Soviet ability to adopt military options impaired. But so long as the Soviet Union and its allies continue to form a Communist Empire centred on Moscow the dynamic expansionist imperatives in Soviet policy seem likely to continue. Their relationship with the rest of the world, including China and Yugoslavia, will be one of truce, not peace.

15. The circumstances of the other 'socialist' countries are very different. This can perhaps be seen by a glance at each of them in turn.

Yugoslavia

16. Yugoslavs often boast, with their tongues only partly in their cheeks, that the 'world is divided into East, West and Yugoslavia'. Certainly their present independence from Moscow scarcely needs stressing. The old Partisan establishment which set up the regime is slowly giving way to a new technocracy. But

old and new alike repudiate the authority of Moscow. They claim, ideologically, to stand for the right of each country 'to find its own way to socialism'. In practice they seem at times more intent on standing up for the right of each country 'to find its own way *back* from Socialism'. Trade, tourism and personal taste have already linked Yugoslavia closely to the West. With the self-confidence built up over the 25 years since he broke with Stalin, Marshal Tito may affect a relaxed attitude towards the Soviet danger and describe his people as a 'hedgehog' which no invader could hope to digest. But the younger generation of leaders are more conscious of a Soviet threat to this independence after Tito, and, if they had to choose, the majority of the establishment, to say nothing of the people, would almost certainly opt for Europe. They seem not the least interested in the fostering of world revolution; and if they have external aspirations at all these are probably limited to the extension of their influence into Bulgaria and possibly Albania.

17. The issue of convergence has long since been buried in Yugoslavia. The country abounds in a variety of economic experiments all of which claim to be basically socialist but some of which are frankly syndicalist or even capitalist. Few Yugoslav political leaders would insist in private on the ideological incompatibility of the kind of system they are seeking to evolve with that of the mixed economies of Western Europe.

Romania

18. The Romanian leaders surprised me by the virulence of their denunciation of Soviet policy, of the Soviet establishment and even of the Soviet leaders personally. They were quite open about their sympathy for the Yugoslav and Chinese regimes and seemed anxious for close association with Western Europe. They were also keen on promoting a Balkan grouping which would include two NATO countries (Greece and Turkey) as well as two from the Warsaw Pact (Romania and Bulgaria) and two neutrals (Yugoslavia and Albania).

19. The Romanian regime is certainly authoritarian; and it has sometimes been said that they have been able to pursue a relatively independent foreign policy only by conforming to Communist orthodoxy at home. There may be some substance in this explanation but there is also a strong authoritarian tradition in Romania going back to the origins of the State; and this has been reinforced since 1918 by the need to keep control over a large and probably disaffected Hungarian minority. It is in any case clear that the Romanian establishment has rejected the infallibility and hegemony of Moscow. They also seem to have accepted the concept of convergence. When I asked Vice President Bodnaras about convergence he answered that the concept was unacceptable. Prime Minister Maurer, whom I saw the same afternoon, took the opposite line. In the course of a journey between Moldavian monasteries two days later, Ambassador Popa,[2] who had been present at both conversations, told me he had sought clarification. He was, he said, authorised to tell me that Maurer's view represented the official consensus and that Vice President Bodnaras had misunderstood my question!

[2] Mr. P. Popa was Romanian Ambassador in London.

20. Men of President Ceausescu's[3] generation are not of course old-style communists imported from the Soviet Union. But it is striking that old guard Communists like Bodnaras and Maurer who came back in the baggage train of the Red Army have succeeded in maintaining their position by adopting Romanian nationalism as their basic political platform as distinct from loyalty to Moscow. Their past may still make them talk of their commitment to a 'Communist society', though it is interesting that Bodnaras' son studied in Britain before doing his military service and is now doing so again.

Poland

21. The Polish establishment cannot aspire to the same freedom as their colleagues in Yugoslavia or Romania. There is a substantial Soviet garrison in Poland, and the Polish leaders are bound to profess and practise conformism with Moscow's line in foreign affairs. But most of the old guard internationalist and largely Jewish Communist leadership who came back into Poland with the Red Army have gone. The young technocrats who run things today make little secret of the fact that they are communist for two main reasons. First because the alternative to Polish communism would be Russification and perhaps even Russian colonisation. Secondly, because having grabbed very large areas of Germany and driven out the German population, they really are scared of German 'revanchism' and see in Russia the power most likely to protect their territorial gains. But even short official visits such as mine suggest very strongly that the Polish leaders' commitment to Moscow—and even perhaps to Communism—is a matter of calculation and not sentiment, in some ways, perhaps, not unlike the commitment of the Vichy leaders to Hitler during the Second World War.

22. The Polish leaders do not enjoy the complete allegiance of their peoples to the same extent as the Yugoslavs. But they have managed to gain a measure of acceptance on the ground that they are doing the best they can as Poles for Poland in the present circumstances. They have avoided the collectivisation of the land. One Polish junior minister told me that while convergence was still regarded as heresy we would see a big change on this issue in Poland and even in the Soviet Union if we would wait only a few years for the younger generation of technocrats to come to the top.

23. Polish fear of the Germans is so strong that the Polish leaders would almost certainly prefer the continued division of Germany to a united neutralist or even Communist Germany. Their influence in Moscow. such as it is, is therefore likely to be exercised against any Soviet expansionism into Western Germany, should such a trend develop.

Hungary

24. Hungarian foreign policy is a caricature of Soviet foreign policy. When I asked a Hungarian Deputy Prime Minister to explain the contrast between his country's orthodox foreign policy and its comparatively liberal economy, he replied 'we are a small country and have no ambition to overstep our shadow'.

---

[3] Mr. N. Ceausescu was President of Romania.

He went on to explain that Hungary was too small a country to make its influence felt in the international field but that they wanted to run their economy in their own way. This requires total obedience to 'Big Brother' in international affairs.

25. But Hungary's past associations with the West, like those of Poland, are very strong. Moscow's moral authority in Hungary will probably never recover from 1956 and the present leaders recognise that they can only make themselves at all acceptable to their people by pursuing as liberal an economic policy as possible. If there is a national Hungarian foreign policy at all—and any reference to it is quickly discouraged—it is probably directed towards the eventual recovery of Transylvania. There may even be some in Budapest who hope that Romanian independence will lead the Soviets one day to back Hungary's latent claims in Transylvania.

26. I have not been to Czechoslovakia, Bulgaria or Albania since they became Communist.

27. Albania repudiated its allegiance to Moscow on [*sic*] 1961. In Czechoslovakia the moral authority of Moscow has been broken by the events of 1967. It can probably never be restored though a Communist establishment may be tolerated if, like the Hungarian establishment, it manages to satisfy to some extent the material appetites of the people.

28. The Bulgarian case is rather different. There are strong Pan-Slav and Russophil traditions in Bulgaria and although there are no Soviet forces there the Bulgarian Communist Party has never really deviated from the Moscow line. The Soviets, moreover, have helped to keep the Macedonian issue alive as a source of conflict between Bulgaria and Yugoslavia.

29. It is however worth remembering that before both the First and Second World Wars Bulgaria accepted regimes that were basically anti-Russian (both anti-Tsarist and anti-Soviet) and that the Bulgarian Peasant Party—numerically by far the strongest party in the country between the wars—was dedicated to the concept of a south Slav Union of Slovenes, Croats, Serbs, Macedonians and Bulgarians. Something like 20,000 Bulgarian peasants were killed in the suppression of Stambulisky's regime in the 1920's. This ideal of a South Slav Union continued in the forefront of the Bulgarian Agrarian Movement, of the Zveno group of officers (Veltchev and Ghiorgiev)[4] and of a section of the Macedonian revolutionary movement (Protoguerov).[5] This concept had echoes too in the Bulgarian Communist Party and was discussed between Tito and Secretary

[4] The Zveno group of officers was a supra-party pressure group, founded in 1927 and aimed at regenerating the Bulgarian nation. Pro-Zveno officers, led by Colonels D. Velchev and K. Georgiev engineered a *coup d'état* in May 1934. Following another *coup* in September 1944 Colonel Georgiev was appointed Bulgarian Prime Minister with Colonel Velchev as Minister of Defence.

[5] The Macedonian Revolutionary Movement was associated with the Internal Macedonian Revolutionary Organisation (IMRO), which had originally sought Macedonia's 'liberation' from Ottoman rule. General A. Protogerov, a right-wing member of IMRO, signed the May Manifesto in 1924, which committed IMRO and the Macedonian Federalist Organisation to the establishment of a Balkan federation.

General Dimitroff[6] on more than one occasion. It is difficult to believe that given the relative prosperity and freedom prevailing in Yugoslavia the ideal of a South Slav Union had altogether disappeared from Bulgarian minds.

General

30. Even very superficial visits to the 'socialist' countries—such as mine —leave one in no doubt of the privileges enjoyed by the Communist leaders. To visit Tito's private zoo, to take the salute of an honour guard of Hungarian beaters after a pheasant shoot, or to attend a shooting lunch in the Polish forests— the guests wrapped in furs around a bonfire while servants in thin mess jackets and patent leather shoes served a five course meal in a temperature 10 degrees below zero—these are interesting indicators that the satellite establishments already have a lot to lose. Even more agreeable was to hear a Polish gamekeeper —dressed as a colonel—discuss the respective shooting ability and sporting characters of socialist grandees like Krushchev, Kosygin, Gierek,[7] Ceausescu and Tito—the latter, according to him, by far the best shot of them all. They might have been so many Edwardian noblemen and I was sorely tempted to send him a copy of 'Lady Chatterley's Lover'! But the political point is that the non-Soviet Socialist leaders have built up a position of power and privilege that in Yugoslavia and Romania is independent of the backing of Moscow, while in Poland and Hungary it exists as much by appeasement of local pressures as by allegiance to the Soviets.

31. Of course in Poland, Czechoslovakia and Hungary the establishment does rest in part on Soviet bayonets, while in Romania, Yugoslavia, Albania and Bulgaria it relies on its own physical resources to maintain itself in power. In all cases, however, its acceptability depends to a considerable extent on its economic performance. Hence the importance for most of the 'socialist' countries of trade with the European Community—Eastern Europe's traditional market.

32. As a block the COMECON absorbs some 60% of the exports of the non-Soviet socialist countries. Some 17% go to Western Europe and the balance (23%) to third markets (the table in the Annex gives the details on a country by country basis).

33. The comparable figures for the Soviet Union are 59%, 10% and 30%.

34. For the European Community trade with non-Soviet Eastern Europe is not important, about 2% of Europe's total trade compared with only 1% to the Soviet Union. For Eastern Europe however this trade is of great importance. A recession in the West would tend to drive the socialist regimes back on to the COMECON thus increasing their dependence upon Moscow and upon each other and probably necessitating the adoption of less liberal policies at home. The Eastern European countries distrust the COMECON, which they regard as an instrument of Soviet policy. They thus have a political as well as an economic incentive to increase their trade with Western Europe.

[6] Mr. G. Dimitrov, leader of the Bulgarian Communist Party, was Prime Minister of Bulgaria during 1946–49.

[7] Mr. E. Gierek was First Secretary of the Central Committee of the Polish United Workers' Party.

35. Then there is the question of cultural orientation. Yugoslavia is wide open to Western influence through the media, tourism and the export of labour. The consequences can be clearly seen in the streets of cities like Belgrade or even Titograd, in Montenegro, where fashions in dress and hairstyles are distinctly Western.

36. Poland has strong cultural ties with the West through the Catholic Church—the churches seem more crowded than any even in Spain and it is striking how fresh flowers have been laid even on little wayside altars. Poland's tourist attractions are limited but its universities seek to develop Western contacts—the professor who showed me round Krakow University was a former secretary of General Sikorski[8]—and Poles established abroad are welcomed as visitors for the sake of the link with the West as well as for the hard currency they bring.

37. Hungary has developed a flourishing tourist trade mostly with Austria and Germany. The Hungarian press indeed has recently been warning Hungarians of the pernicious Western influences which are spreading with the growth of tourism.

38. Romania is geographically more remote from the West and more closed to foreign tourism, but as an island of Latin culture largely surrounded by Slavs it continues, as in the past, to stress its cultural links with Western Europe and particularly with France. By the same token there is a fairly vigorous resistance to cultural links with the Soviet Union. Romanians in official positions have told me proudly that they have forgotten how to speak Russian!

39. Taken together therefore it is reasonable to conclude that economic interest, cultural inclinations and the personal interest and ambitions of the different 'socialist' establishments lead their members, in varying degrees, to maintain or to seek as much independence as possible from the Soviet Union. Their Communism is conventional and conformist rather than messianic.

40. What conclusions should be drawn from all this?

41. It would be idle to think in terms of a 'roll back' on Dulles[9] lines. But from the point of view of Western security and the world balance of power there would seem to be advantage in helping the others to increase their independence insofar as this is possible.

42. How can this be done?

(i) The first condition is to maintain and build up the strength of the Atlantic Alliance. The 'socialist' countries must never be allowed to feel that the Russians are likely to be the winning side.

(ii) The second condition is to develop the prosperity and unity of the European Community. A prosperous and united Europe will act as a magnet on the Eastern European countries. Equally, a recession in Western Europe will turn

[8] General W.E. Sikorski headed the Polish Government in exile during 1939–43.

[9] Mr. J.F. Dulles was US Secretary of State, 1953–59. During his first two years in office he advocated a foreign policy aimed at liberating Eastern Europe from Soviet domination and rolling back Communist power.

them back to the Soviet Union. Seeing how important trade with Europe is to the Eastern countries, it may be worth giving serious consideration to ways of promoting this trade even at some marginal cost to ourselves. In all this we shall have to watch carefully the development of relations between the European Community and the COMECON. The latter is largely an instrument in Soviet hands and it would not serve our interests to allow the Soviets to control the pattern of trade between Eastern and Western Europe too closely.

(iii) Sustained progress towards European political union and, in the context of anxieties over American withdrawal, defence union will be very important. Much the strongest card in Soviet hands, apart from the presence of the Red Army, is the genuine fear entertained by Poland, Czechoslovakia and indeed Yugoslavia of German 'revanchism'. If West Germany is seen to be closely locked into a European Community, East European countries will feel themselves that much less dependent on the Soviets.

(iv) It has been a point of Soviet dogma to stress the division of the world into two systems (the Socialist and the non-Socialist). The concept of non-alignment is admitted only as a temporary political half-way house. But with the schism between China and the Soviet Union and the revival of Western Europe and Japan, most East Europeans are increasingly attracted to the idea of a polycentric world system. They may find it ideologically easier to associate with, and ultimately perhaps to converge with, a European Community which has a distinct identity than to switch over from the Soviet camp to an Atlantic community. We need to define the European Community's identity in relation to the Soviet superpower just as we have done in relation to the American superpower.

43. In all this it may be worth trying to determine certain priorities both in time and importance.

44. Yugoslavia and Albania have already opted out of the Soviet sphere. Tito's death could create circumstances which threatened the independence of either or both; and this could have serious repercussions for Western Europe's Adriatic and Mediterranean interests. The first priority therefore should be to consider how to safeguard the independences—different in character though they be—of Yugoslavia and Albania. This could call for economic, political and even military initiatives from the West.

45. If Yugoslav independence can be maintained Bulgaria could become the most vulnerable of the Soviet satellites, surrounded as it is on three sides by countries totally independent of the Soviet Union (Yugoslavia, Turkey, Greece) and to the North by Romania the most independent of the Warsaw Pact countries. The Bulgarian regime is very loyal to Moscow but Bulgaria's neighbours, and in particular Yugoslavia, are in a position to give encouragement to independent tendencies that may exist under the surface in Bulgaria. In this context we might also give discreet support to Romanian ideas for a Balkan grouping. I have made a point, in talks with Turks, Romanians and Yugoslavs, of asking whether Bulgaria should be regarded as a Russian 'gubernaya' which is rather the assessment we have tended to form. Bulgaria's neighbours, though far from sanguine, seemed slightly less pessimistic.

46. Moving to North-Eastern Europe, we are brought up sharply against the German question. It is extremely unlikely that the Soviets will withdraw from East Germany except in the context of a major internal disruption at home or a major shift in West German policy. We should therefore reckon with a continuing Soviet military presence in East Germany; in Poland, through which the Soviet lines of communication with East Germany lie; and probably, after the events of 1968, in Czechoslovakia, which also has a common frontier with Western Germany. We cannot, therefore, think in terms of working in these two countries for the same degree of independence of Moscow as exists already in Yugoslavia and Albania and might be achieved in Bulgaria. By fostering trade and contacts, however, with both Poland and Czechoslovakia, we can help to undermine their value as advanced posts of Soviet imperialism in Europe. Nor should we under-rate their own influence on their Soviet allies. By virtue of their population, skill and technology, both should be capable not just of acting as intermediaries with the Soviets, but sometimes of exercising influence on them. This is a role which the Poles, at least, seem anxious to play, and which the Czechs may aspire to later.

47. Between the countries south of the Danube and the northern tier of East Germany, Poland and Czechoslovakia lie Hungary and Romania. There is no Soviet garrison in Romania and the Romanians have already achieved a remarkable degree of national independence considering that they have a common frontier with the Soviets. This independence is something which we should endeavour to maintain and so far as possible enlarge by trade and political contacts. Western ability to defend Romania against the Soviets is negligible, though our influence could grow rapidly if Bulgaria were to become more independent than it is today.

48. Hungary achieved a short lived independence in 1956 and still enjoys, despite the presence of a Soviet garrison, a relatively liberal regime at home. It will not be easy now to prise out the Soviet military presence, though MBFR may still offer a possible lever. From the point of view of Yugoslav and Austrian security, as distinct from the balance of force on the Central European Front, this would be something worth paying quite a price to secure.

49. To sum up, I would conclude that we should give our first priority to maintaining the independence of Yugoslavia and Albania. A second but high priority should be to seek to draw Bulgaria into the Yugoslav camp.[10]

50. We should seek to help Romania retain its present degree of independence and seize any opportunity of bringing about a reduction or withdrawal of the Soviet garrison in Hungary.

51. We should accept the division of Germany (and perhaps welcome it until European Union is much further advanced than it is today). We have therefore

---

[10] In a letter to Sir T. Garvey of 1 March Mr. Bullard observed that he had made a number of suggestions on an earlier draft of Mr. Amery's paper, most of which had been incorporated. But, he added, Mr. Amery had not felt able to accept his 'two main points': that the independence of Albania and Yugoslavia carried different implications for Western interests; and that the present and future situation in Bulgaria did 'not warrant the suggestion that our second priority in Eastern Europe should be to draw Bulgaria into the Yugoslav camp'.

to accept the continuing Soviet presence in Poland and Czechoslovakia but should seek to strengthen our links with these two countries and to use their influence to promote our interests in Moscow.

52. Except for Yugoslavia, where events could move rapidly, the policy outlined here would be a gradual and evolving process proceeding more or less step in step with our own success in building up the European Community both in prosperity, political union and ultimately power. It is perhaps just as well that the process should be gradual. If it were rapid it could well lead to Soviet countermoves, since the growing independence of the Eastern European states could well have some chain reaction among the different nationalities inside the Soviet Union itself. If by contrast the process is gradual it may lead to the gentle decline of the Soviet Empire into a Soviet Commonwealth with its own Arnold Smith and Marlborough House![11]

[11] Mr. A.C. Smith was Secretary-General of the Commonwealth from 1965–75. The Commonwealth Secretariat is located at Marlborough House.

No. 56

Letter from Sir E. Peck (UKDEL NATO) to Sir J. Killick

[*WDN 21 / 1*]

Confidential   BRUSSELS, *8 March 1974*

Dear John,

The Importance of NATO for the UK

1. As I suggested on the telephone, your visit to NATO on 14 March will enable you to get a first hand impression of NATO and enable you to judge the right moment to imprint the importance of the Alliance to the UK on the minds of our new Ministers. I think you agreed that NATO is important rather than urgent, since the first direct impact of NATO on our new Ministers will only be either on the appearance of President Nixon for the signature of the Atlantic Declaration on 25 April (if that proves to be the precise date)[1] or, in the defence field, the Defence Secretary's appearance first at the Nuclear Planning Group meeting fixed for Bergen, Norway, on 11–12 June and (subject to confirmation) the subsequent Eurogroup and DPC meetings in Brussels on 13 and 14 June respectively.

[1] Dr. Kissinger had called on 23 April 1973 for a rejuvenation of the transatlantic relationship. Once it became clear that the nine EC states would have to negotiate a separate declaration on economic matters with the USA, the NAC set to and produced a draft declaration which largely met American *desiderata* in the defence field. HMG was privately informed that President Nixon was thinking tentatively of a visit to Europe during the week beginning 23 April, and Dr. Luns suggested that the Alliance should plan for a NATO summit meeting on or around 25 April to celebrate the Alliance's 25th anniversary (brief for Sir J. Killick under cover of minute from Mr. Lever of 8 March).

2.   What follows is not intended to be in any way a brief for Ministers[2] but an attempt to set down afresh and without benefit of reference to back papers, a short assessment of the value of NATO to the United Kingdom in present circumstances.

3.   The fact that NATO has succeeded in preserving the peace in Europe for the past 25 years only too easily leads to its deterrent value being taken for granted. It is consequently difficult to propagate the NATO image in certain NATO countries and while it is desirable to give it a polish up with certain extraneous matters like the Committee on the Challenges to Modern Society (CCMS) and the Science Committee, one should never lose sight of the fact that the NATO partnership is essentially a matter of collective defence against a Soviet threat which has in recent years become less of an imminent military threat than of a political threat backed by increasing military force. It follows that any reduction in the military strength of the Western side, outside MBFR, will increase the potential of the Soviet political threat. Already Soviet military strength, particularly on the Naval side, is on the increase and will soon outstrip NATO; and with Soviet personnel costs representing only 30% of their defence budget (compared with NATO's 60%), their scope for increased military capability is very much greater.

4.   The importance of NATO to the UK's security was well recognised by Ministers of the present Government when they were previously in office; and indeed they reshaped the UK defence programme in such a way that, with the reduction of our overseas commitments to small detachments mainly in Singapore, Hong Kong and the Caribbean, over 90% of the British defence effort is now directly or indirectly committed to the support of NATO. There is, therefore, not much scope for further retrenchment without impinging directly on our commitments to NATO. Reductions on any scale would be very damaging both to the Alliance and to the UK's role in it, both now and potentially as a major element in any future European defence grouping. We have in the past been highly critical of the Danes, the Dutch, the Belgians and the Canadians as, at various stages in recent years, they have been obliged, under the NATO rules, to explain to SACEUR and the other Allies their proposals for restructuring their forces, while maintaining their commitments to NATO. Even though our own record hitherto both in terms of financial sacrifice and 'sharp end' contribution is good, any relaxation—particularly at the 'sharp end'—will be viewed by them as justification of their past reductions, and encouragement to go further in the same direction.

5.   Reductions would also be very hard to reconcile with the current European efforts to reassure the United States that the Europeans play a full part in their own defence and would moreover be harmful to the work of the Eurogroup in which the UK plays a leading role and from which we have gained such valuable prestige. Controlled reductions are another matter and this is what the Alliance seeks to achieve in the MBFR talks at Vienna, where, for sound political and

---

[2] Mr. Callaghan was appointed Foreign and Commonwealth Secretary in the new Labour Government on 5 March. See No. 13, note 1.

military reasons, it is intended that Phase I should be confined to US and Soviet forces only.

6.   In short, NATO's defence must be credible, the more so because détente is in the air; with various East/West negotiations in progress the need not to lower our guard is all the more important. Under the umbrella of the US nuclear guarantee, the strategic doctrine of flexible response requires a fairly high conventional threshold, if it is not to dwindle into a nuclear trip-wire, which is no longer acceptable in the present era of US/Soviet nuclear 'sufficiency'. There is undoubtedly scope for better use of the resources devoted to defence to achieve more effective results (e.g. no cost/low cost measures; European co-ordination; specialisation among the smaller nations and so on) but this improvement in the dividend from defence investment is needed in any event and is not an easy means for reducing total budgets.

7.   Apart from the provision of collective means for physical security and the peripheral peaceful matters mentioned in para. 2 above, the biggest current benefit from NATO is *consultation*. In the defence field, two major examples are (a) the Nuclear Planning Group, which is intended to share nuclear thinking in a restricted circle of Defence Ministers, to keep the Germans happy and to provide a forum in which the US can keep the Allies informed of the nuclear balance, and (b) the consultations on SALT which take place in the full North Atlantic Council with the French present. But a third area is now being revitalised and this is the field of political consultation. NATO is the only political forum where Europeans and Americans can talk in an intimate circle and where an agreement to disagree among friends need not, and should not, be considered as an adversary-partner relationship. The machinery already exists, but it can only function effectively if there is adequate political will at the back of it. As a result of the recriminations over the Middle East which have grumbled on since October, 1973,[3] the US has learnt to some degree the importance of consulting with her Allies but as Kissinger has repeatedly stressed, consultation is a two-way street. If the Europeans are convincingly to comment on American propositions, it is incumbent on them not to pursue their own courses too far without taking soundings with the Americans. Naturally the degree to which advice is accepted is another matter but an exchange of comments in NATO is likely to go more than half-way to achieving understanding of mutual objectives. An ounce of advance consultation can, as the Americans have learnt, go a long way to avoiding

---

[3] As Sir E. Peck more fully explained in his NATO Annual Review for 1973 (dated 10 January 1974), it had soon become apparent during the Arab-Israeli War of October 1973 that the US interest in protecting Israel and deterring the Soviet Union diverged from the essential European interest in Arab oil. 'Consequently', he noted, 'on the one hand the Americans felt aggrieved that they were not receiving full support from their Allies over facilities for the airlift to Israel; and on the other the European Allies, while complaining of lack of consultation, of a breach in the policy of *détente* and of deals behind their backs, were in fact resentful that the Americans expected them to support a policy which had not been explained to them and that their need for Arab oil was being subordinated to automatic loyalty to the US. The declaration of a world-wide alert for US forces during the momentous night of October 24–25 was the event which shook NATO' (WDN 1/2). Cf. Kissinger, *Years of Upheaval*, pp. 545–613.

a ton of recrimination later: this goes for Europeans too, and the UK with a closer understanding of the American scene can play a role in this.

8. It was of course Kissinger himself who spoke firmly in favour of improved Alliance consultation at last December's Ministerial meeting (as you will yourself recall) and the meeting which you are to attend here next week is the result of a proposal which he then made.[4] Especially in the past few weeks, Kissinger has also been sounding off in all directions about the development of European identity in opposition to the United States. This came out strongly in his meeting with the NATO Council on 4 March and in subsequent press briefings. All of this is naturally aimed first and foremost at the French. The Americans—quite rightly from their point of view—see a strong and unfortunate contrast between the draft Atlantic Declaration, which should emerge as a proposition agreed among the 15, and the US/Nine declaration which (if it ever emerges at all) will be the outcome of an essentially bilateral negotiation. The forum which NATO provides for political consultation is the only place where we are likely to be able to resolve the contradictions between the growing pains of political co-operation among the Nine and the need to re-establish Atlantic partnership on a sound basis.

9. To sum up, NATO has been an effective shield in the past: it will be needed as such in the future, all the more so with the siren song of Détente as an inducement to drop our guard on the Western side. The growth of the European Community has lent a new dimension to the trans-Atlantic relationship; if properly handled this can only be to the advantage of all partners. Détente and Deterrence need to be complemented with a requirement for Consultation, Cohesion and Credibility laid upon all partners to the Alliance in the name of Defence against a threat which is as much political as military.[5]

> Yours ever,
> EDWARD PECK

[4] Sir J. Killick was due to participate in a reinforced meeting of the NAC on 14 March. The idea for such a meeting stemmed from a suggestion made by Dr. Kissinger in December 1973 that 'Senior Officials from capitals, perhaps Political Directors, might join the Council in permanent session following NATO Ministerials and at regular intervals, both to pursue matters raised by the Ministers and to consider other points of mutual interest'. Only the French had opposed the suggestion. They, according to Mr. Lever (see note 1 above), 'regarded it as a plot to dilute European political cooperation [see Volume II, No. 1, note 26] by bringing in the Americans through the back door and to establish some sort of Atlantic counterweight to the meetings of Political Directors in the Political Cooperation machinery'.

[5] In a letter to Sir E. Peck of 12 March, Sir J. Killick pointed out that while the Office had not yet had time 'to get to grips with Ministers on many detailed questions', Sir E. Peck's letter would be a 'valuable quarry to draw on when making submissions'. With regard to the new Government's defence programme, Sir J. Killick observed: 'I think we would agree with all you say but we must be under no illusion that the Government does not intend to put into effect what was said in the election manifesto on this front. It is clear to me that this will be not just a matter of defence policy but of financial stringency.'

No. 57

Letter from Mr. Bullard to Sir T. Garvey (Moscow)

[EN 2/18]

Confidential   FCO, *3 May 1974*

Trends in the Soviet Union and Eastern Europe

I had hoped that round about this time we should be sitting down with HM Ambassadors from Eastern Europe to take stock of the general situation since we last met in the spring of 1972.[1] Now that our Conference is cancelled, I should like to seek your views and those of other posts. The view at the departmental level, in brief, is that the course of events during the last 2 years has borne out the darker rather than the brighter side of the assessment made at that time.

Present situation

I will take the CSCE first. As one of those who argued that the Conference would enable at least some of the East European governments to flex their muscles and cut a figure on the international stage, I have to admit that this has not happened, apart from some Romanian activity which (as explained below) has come to seem rather peripheral to the main stream and has often not been helpful from our point of view. In retrospect the course of events seems even more obvious now than it did at the time. The Russians seriously underestimated the importance of the preparatory talks in Helsinki and the effectiveness of Western co-ordination. They therefore lost many of the opening skirmishes. They pulled themselves together in the spirit of 1941, and issued firm directives to their allies for Stage II. During the last 6 months in Geneva they have preserved tight discipline and conducted their side of the argument with great skill and persistence, with the object at least of giving no more away and if possible of regaining ground lost. Put another way, the Russians offered a certain price at Helsinki in order to get their conference, and are trying to avoid paying it in full. This is the kind of pitched-battle diplomacy where the Russian characteristics can be used to best advantage. The Soviet negotiating team is well on the way to a final result giving them most of what they wanted on the Declaration of Principles without committing themselves to anything significant in the way of freer movement of persons, information and ideas. The West has been prevented from building as they had hoped on the Final Recommendations which the Russians accepted in Helsinki as the price for Western agreement to a Conference.[2]

---

[1] See Volume I, No. 95. Plans to hold the biennial Conference of HM Ambassadors in the Soviet Union and Eastern Europe on 4–8 March (cf. No. 55, note 1) were abandoned because of the General Election (see No. 13, note 1). In a submission to Sir J. Killick of 14 March Mr. Bullard recommended that the Conference be arranged for 24–28 June. But, as Mr. Callaghan explained in telegram No. 194 to Moscow of 27 March 'pressure for economies' compelled him to postpone the gathering indefinitely (EN 2/1).

[2] See Cmnd 6932, pp. 143–57 and Volume II, Nos. 69 and 79.

The role of the East Europeans in all this has not been very distinguished. The Romanian fireworks have fizzled out, or rather have been allowed to splutter away harmlessly in a corner. The Poles, on whom some of us pinned hopes, have put up a dismal show.

Then there is MBFR. From the outset of the negotiations the Russians have played a predominant, almost exclusive, role on the Eastern side, and the proposals which they tabled last November in the name of the Warsaw Pact bear the stamp of Russian authorship. You will have seen Clive Rose's despatch of 17 January[3] about the first round of the negotiations, but I cannot resist quoting a passage from paragraph 14:

'Like actors in a play, the individual non-Soviet Eastern participants may be given a part to act, and may even be permitted a limited degree of ad-libbing. But they all speak from the same basic script, which they did not write. The East Germans, although privately agreeable and even civilised, are the only ones so far to include in their plenary statements, any genuinely polemical passages, while their Allies have consistently adopted tones of sweet reasonableness. The Poles have occasional well-rehearsed attacks of frankness and indiscretion. The Czechoslovaks provide a chorus of dutiful orthodoxy, and the Hungarians and Bulgarians have walk-on parts only. The Romanians provide the light relief; anxious to display their independence without suffering its penalties.'

I do not want to conduct a complete *tour d'horizon*, but I will just mention the special session of the UN General Assembly.[4] If you read the summaries of the speeches, you will have noticed that only the Romanians among the Warsaw Pact did anything else than produce a dutiful echo of the Soviet themes.[5]

We do not know the precise mechanism through which this co-ordination is established. There is the annual gathering in the Crimea, which Çeaucescu appears to have rejoined. Warsaw Pact summit meetings are fairly infrequent, and it is clear that there was a good deal of argument behind the scenes at the Political Consultative Committee in Warsaw last month. But the phrases about strengthening cohesion and deepening co-ordination, and about the role of the Warsaw Treaty organisation as the centre for co-ordination of its foreign policy, which appear respectively in the Soviet and the GDR party-government statements issued after the meeting, illustrate the kind of pressures which the Pact is able to bring to bear upon its members. Then there is COMECON. We are

[3] See No. 11.

[4] The Sixth Special Assembly of the UN General Assembly (UNGA), of 9 April–2 May, was convened to study the problems imposed on developing countries by the rising cost of raw materials. Participants proclaimed their united determination to work for the establishment of a New International Economic Order which would redress existing injustices and make it possible to eliminate the widening gap between the developed and developing countries. See *Resolutions adopted by the UNGA during its 6th Special Session*, Supplement No. 1 (A/9559).

[5] See *Official Records of the Sessions of the UN General Assembly*, Sixth Special Session Plenary Meetings, A/PV 2213 and A/PV 2240.

approaching the season of 5-year Plans, and there seems a very good chance that these will this time be brought out more or less all together, instead of straggling out over a period of 2–3 years as happened with the plan for 1970–75. Finally I am sure we were right to attach importance to the network of ideological co-operation agreements, which seem all the more sinister because none of them has even been published. The tightening of the Soviet screw all over Eastern Europe in the last 2 years is unmistakable.

The situation inside the individual countries seems to be no more encouraging:

(*a*) *USSR.* The Soviet Union has so far absorbed without much difficulty the challenges of détente, whether in the form of external invasions (tourists, businessmen, foreign radio broadcasts) or internal dissent. The dissident movement indeed has been virtually destroyed through repression, emigration and its own divisions. Yet the Soviet authorities still behave as if some of these activities, if permitted to proceed unchecked, could really threaten the security of the Soviet State. It has been suggested that this is really why the USSR Academy of Sciences had postponed its anniversary celebrations. On the offensive side, we are becoming accustomed to the strident sound of the voice of Ponomarev[6] prophesying doom for all societies west of the River Elbe. This appears to cause no practical problems despite its inconsistency with the theme of long-term economic co-operation. It does not take the publication of a second volume of questionable memoirs by Khrushchev[7] to remind us how far the situation has travelled backwards in the 10 years since he fell. Despite all this, the Soviet preoccupation with Soviet-US relations continues to enjoy a matching response from the Administration in Washington.

(*b*) *Poland.* We have all noticed the encouraging trends, e.g. the expansion in Polish foreign trade, its re-orientation towards the West (will this last?) and the rapid advance in the standard of living. But these are consequences of the Gomulka/Gierek change-over[8] rather than of East/West developments, and the political aspirations which accompanied the economic reforms of 1970 and 1971 have all been disappointed. It is unthinkable now as ever to criticise the Soviet Union in print in Poland, a principle which I gather may cause the Joseph Conrad anniversary celebrations this year to be cancelled or curtailed. (Anniversaries are a two-edged lightning conductor.) If the acid test is the performance of Polish representatives abroad, that of Olszowski[9] in London last month was discouraging. His main desire seemed to be to spin out the reading of his prepared text so as to leave the least possible time for impromptu discussion in which he might conceivably have said something unorthodox.

---

[6] See No. 53, note 1.

[7] See Strobe Talbott (ed.), *Khrushchev Remembers. The Last Testament* (Boston: Little, Brown and Co., 1974). The second, like the first, volume of these memoirs was based on typescript transcribed from audiotapes, and some Western scholars were sceptical about its authenticity.

[8] Mr. Gierek had succeeded Mr. W. Gomulka as First Secretary of the Central Committee of the Polish United Workers' Party in December 1970. See Volume I, No. 59, note 2.

[9] Mr. S. Olszowski was Polish Foreign Minister.

The recent changes amongst Polish Ministers seem to have a complicated background, but the results included the placing of foreign trade under the management of a man hitherto closely involved with the CMEA, and the exit of one who had sponsored a draft law for mixed-capital Polish-Western joint ventures in Poland.[10] I am not surprised to hear that some observers suspect pressure from Moscow. There has also been a marked tightening of central control over the media, a reminder that Poland's abdication of freedom of manoeuvre on international issues has perhaps bought her less independence in internal affairs than is sometimes thought.

(c) *Hungary.* We have long since accepted Hungarian orthodoxy abroad as the price of some eccentricity at home. There can be no better apostle of orthodoxy than Puja,[11] now Foreign Minister after his years as deputy to Peter. In Hungarian foreign policy we must look forward to a period of conformity without even the superficially idiosyncratic element of Peter's personality.[12] In Hungary too there have been changes of personnel. At the very least these suggest that there will be a more cautious implementation of the New Economic Mechanism, which the Russians can only welcome. I personally would go further and say that the changes mark a partial retreat from the objectives which had come to be associated with the NEM,[13] and the Russians had some hand in this.

(d) *GDR.* Our bilateral relations with the GDR have, of course, undergone a major change during the last two years. The East Germans have adopted a pragmatic and non-polemical approach. Widespread international recognition during 1973 did not have much discernible effect on the GDR's domestic policies. Indeed the price it paid for recognition in terms of greater freedom of movement between the two German states has led to a slight tightening of the screw rather than the reverse. GDR foreign policy continues to follow Soviet policy at least as rigidly as any other East European power. The slight differences that occasionally reveal themselves over Berlin and 'German' questions are interesting pointers to the USSR's and GDR's differing interpretations of their interests. But I would not wish to make too much of this. There is no doubt who is in overall control.

(e) *Czechslovakia.* As we approach the sixth anniversary of the Warsaw Pact invasion, things look as black as ever. The lists of political prisoners are still long, and the lists of persons suffering penalties in employment for their political views much longer. This no doubt accounts for the low quality of Czechoslovak performance in all fields. The delay in grasping the nettle of

[10] In April 1974 Mr. K. Olszewski, the former Polish Minister of Shipping, became Minister of Foreign Trade and Shipping.

[11] Mr. F. Puja became Hungarian Foreign Minister in 1974. He was First Deputy Foreign Minister during 1968–73, and Secretary of State for Foreign Affairs during 1973–74.

[12] Mr. J. Péter was Hungarian Foreign Minister duirng 1961–73.

[13] Hungary's New Economic Mechanism was initiated in 1966 and left producer companies with greater freedom to determine their own short-term plans on the basis of market forces.

finding a successor to President Svoboda[14] suggests that the authorities are approaching even this little fence with extreme trepidation.

(f) *Romania*. Some of the panache seems to have gone out of the Romanian challenge in the last couple of years. Çeaucescu strikes even more exaggerated attitudes but, in an international situation that has greatly changed, he matters less than he used to. It seems somehow symbolic of Romania's sidestep from the centre of the stage that the recent personality changes in the Romanian régime appear to have parochial origins.

(g) *Yugoslavia*. I am not really speaking of Yugoslavia in this letter and I speak from ignorance. Dugald Stewart[15] has argued that the pattern of Yugoslav internal and external policies is cyclical and that the tide may be about to turn away from the disciplinarians. The earlier return to discipline was, of course, the result of internal events rather than of Russian pressure. But to the outside observer Tito does seem to be trimming his sails to the same wind as his East European colleagues, even if for different reasons.[16] His last speech pooh-poohed the danger of 40,000 Soviet troops in Hungary, while representing the naval manoeuvres of a few American and Italian ships in the Northern Adriatic as a monstrous example of NATO pressure. It seems a very long way from the atmosphere of Tito's visit to the United States in the autumn of 1971 and the joint communiqué signed then with President Nixon.[17]

(h) *Bulgaria* Few people have cherished any very bright expectations of Bulgaria. But a Romanian said to us recently that he was staggered at the flattery of the Soviet Union contained in the documents of the recent Bulgarian Party Conference—it sounded to him more like 1954 than 1974. If it were not for Bulgaria's geographical separation, the question of incorporation into the USSR might well be a serious issue.[18]

Explanation

8. In searching for explanations of these trends, I do not think we need reproach ourselves at having brought the result upon ourselves. Bahr may say that one effect of the CSCE has been to promote a renaissance of the blocs, but granted Soviet and Warsaw Pact objectives, the co-ordination on our side was necessary and on theirs inevitable. Only the Romanians were prepared to show a degree of independence, and their initiatives were often such that the

---

[14] Mr. L. Svoboda was President of Czechoslovakia during 1968–75.

[15] HM Ambassador, Belgrade.

[16] In a letter to Mr. Bullard of 7 May Sir D. Stewart observed that he considered 'weakness and disarray in Western Europe to be the main, and at times ... virtually the only serious danger to Yugoslavia's balance'.

[17] President Tito visited the United States during 28 October–2 November 1971. See *Public Papers of the President of the United States: Richard Nixon* (Washington: GPO, 1972), pp. 1070–2.

[18] Mr. Bolland commented on this that he did not think that Bulgaria's geographical separation was the principal factor inhibiting its incorporation into the USSR. 'It is', he added, 'surely to Moscow's advantage, at this stage, that Bulgaria should remain an apparently independent and sovereign state' (letter to Mr. Bullard of 23 May).

West could not support them. I am not sure where to put the weight as between 3 possible ways of describing the situation: that the opportunities for Eastern Europe at the CSCE never really existed, that they did exist but were not grasped, or that the East Europeans tried to grasp them but were prevented by Moscow. I suggest that elements of all three were involved. Certainly I think we may have been guilty of misjudging the threshold of Soviet tolerance. We always said that the Soviet view would prevail against any of its allies 'in the last resort', but this point seems to have been reached rather earlier than some of us expected.

9.   I would also mention 3 contributory factors:

(*a*)   The US/Soviet special relationship. It is only 18 months since the then PUS opposed the use of the term 'bilateralism', because he thought it implied an unwarranted degree of community of interest between Washington and Moscow.[19] Nowadays the only doubt is whether 'condominium' is too strong.[20] I need not discuss the effects of this in Western Europe, but in the East it must have contributed to the general rallying of stragglers towards the pole of attraction in Moscow. Certainly it must have contributed to the decline in the significance of the Romanian challenge.

(*b*)   The energy crisis has greatly strengthened the economic lever which the Russians have always possessed, although they cannot be entirely happy about its broader international effects on their own external trading and financial arrangements. All over Eastern Europe the planners must be asking themselves what will be the price of Soviet oil and other raw materials after 1975 when the present arrangements expire. It is not surprising that the East European countries which are dependent largely on the Soviet Union in this respect (which means all of them except Romania) have been paying special attention to their relations with Moscow in the last 6 months especially.

(*c*)   A connected factor is the weakness of Western Europe. We were quite right to say that a dynamic and vigorous European Community would act as a magnet to the countries in the East which had any stirrings of independence. We were perhaps not quite so punctilious in adding the converse, that a weak and obviously unsuccessful Community would send the iron filings drifting

---

[19]   On a minute from Mr. Bullard to Sir T. Brimelow of 27 November 1972, entitled 'Bilaterism', Sir D. Greenhill noted American 'present methods have put the wind up the alliance who now read into US/Soviet contacts a more sinister interpretation than, I believe, is justified' (ENS 3/304/1).

[20]   In a letter to Mr. Bullard of 20 June Mr. A.M. Simons (Counsellor, HM Embassy, Washington), expressed surprise at the use of the term 'condominium' to describe the community of interest between the United States and the Soviet Union. 'At the present time', he observed, 'the Americans, who are preoccupied with their internal problems, are in no mood to seek to establish control over other people's affairs—with or without Soviet assistance—as would be implied by the literal meaning of the term "condominium".' Mr. Bullard was evidently not convinced. In a minute to Mr. B.J.P. Fall (First Secretary, EESD) of 9 July he noted that 'one has the clear impression that the Soviet-US relationship has steadily thickened and deepened, and that its special and exclusive character has become ever more marked, to the point where doubt is now being cast even on the concept of a triangle with Peking as the third corner'. And while he admitted that the 'traditional

back into Moscow's magnetic field. The weakness of the United States, though of a different kind, has not helped either.

Lessons to be Learned

10. The first necessity is for us all to agree on the interpretation of these events, and I have no doubt that the replies to this letter will contribute to the process.

11. We should then look at our own expectations. I think these need not so much to be revised as scaled down or re-phased. I have read through the Country Assessments Sheets and the 'Bahr brief'[21] without finding anything that I should want to withdraw, but any implication of early results is clearly out of place. Nor should we encourage any private hopes for Albania and Bulgaria. It is not a question of seeking to draw Bulgaria into the Yugoslav orbit, but of whether Yugoslavia may float into that of the Soviet Union at some future stage.

12. Finally, I would mention two specific lessons. The first concerns the value of bilateral relations with the individual countries of Eastern Europe. I have already said that the Polish performance at international conferences has been undistinguished but throughout the last 18 months the Poles have been useful and even rewarding people to talk to. I was struck by their Foreign Minister's remark to the Secretary of State about the need to institutionalise the political dialogue.[22] Perhaps bilateral East/West contacts will soon be due for a productive second innings, under the benign umbrella of whatever multilateral platitudes come out of the CSCE. I have always thought there was much sincerity in the argument, first put to us I think by the Czechoslovak Deputy Foreign Minister Ruzek in April 1973, that a suitable declaration on Item II will strengthen the hand of those in Eastern Europe who are trying to resist the built-in pull of the COMECOM system. The same is surely true under other items also.

13. Secondly there is the question of trade. It has long been obvious that trade with the East is small in proportion both to the whole and also to the resources of private and official money and time devoted to it. We normally quote the figure of 3% of British exports, but if the March pattern is repeated the percentage may in future be less than this. I cannot see Eastern Europe and/or the Soviet Union making any substantial contribution to the vast increase in British exports which will have to be achieved if the British balance of payments is to be rectified. It may be more a question of preventing 7 or 8 Communist countries from joining the number of those who already find Britain a soft market for their manufactured products, owing to the weakness of our native production and the lack of

---

American carelessness in the use of language, or incompetence at the game of Communicopoly, [had] played its part', he considered it difficult to contest the conclusion that the nature of the US/Soviet relationship would 'increasingly cause the leaders on both sides (even those less in love with their own ideas and talents than Dr. Kissinger) to overlook the interests of their allies unless these [were] steadily represented to the 2 superpowers' (ENS 3/304/1).

[21] See No. 49.

[22] Mr. Olszowski visited the UK during 8–10 April. He told Mr. Callaghan that 'Poland viewed Great Britain as one of her most important partners for cooperation', and proposed 'a system of regular consultation' between his Ministry and the FCO (record of conversation between Mr. Callaghan and Mr. Olszowski on 10 April, ENP 3/548/5).

resistance here to foreign goods. These considerations reinforce our traditional view of the Communist countries as a group who have it in their power to do us a good deal of harm if we let them, but not to do us very much good.

Procedure

14. I hope you and other recipients will feel free to comment at whatever length and in whatever way you wish, copying to all posts listed below.[23] I will await replies and then perhaps attempt a summing up. There is no particular deadline—the answers to this letter will form a helpful counterpoint to the review of relations with the Soviet Union and Eastern Europe which the Secretary of State has asked Mr. Hattersley to conduct, and on which we are now engaged.[24]

J.L. BULLARD

[23] Not printed. Cf. No. 67, note 1.
[24] See No. 66.

No. 58

Report by Joint Intelligence Committee (A) on the Soviet Threat[1]

JIC (A) (74) 17

Secret. *UK Eyes Only*   CABINET OFFICE, *6 May 1974*

Summary

1. This paper considers the principal threats posed by the Soviet Union to the United Kingdom and Western Europe over the next 5 years. It falls into two parts. Part I reviews current and likely Soviet policies in the fields of principal interest to us. Part II identifies the Soviet threat in the light of the foregoing and of our assessment of British interests.

PART I: SOVIET POLICIES

2. Soviet external policy seeks certain general objectives: to maintain the security of Soviet and Warsaw Pact territory; to consolidate the Soviet position as a super-power; to extend Soviet influence and reduce Western and Chinese influence; and to promote Soviet leadership of the world Communist movement. It partakes of the cautious quality of the Soviet leadership but reflects their confidence in Soviet military and industrial strength.

3. The principal Soviet foreign policy preoccupation is the relationship with the United States. This is a relationship of underlying antagonism, but masked by Soviet strategic caution and by the striking development of Soviet/United States bilateral relations over the last 3 years. This special bilateral relationship offers the Soviet Union a number of advantages, notably reasserting the primacy

[1] Only the summary of this report is printed here.

of US/Soviet relations, promoting an atmosphere of détente suitable for the prosecution of Soviet policies in Western Europe, giving access to Western technology and giving opportunities for wedge-driving between the United States and its allies. The relationship is subject to some strains, notably over the SAL negotiations: the Russians currently have a major programme of new strategic nuclear weapons which they may be unwilling to impede.[2] The relationship may be at greater risk when Brezhnev leaves the scheme; but on balance we think that it and the policy of détente associated with it serve Soviet interests well and are sufficiently institutionalised for the main elements to survive changes in the Soviet leadership in the short term. However, we see this participation in bilateral dealing as essentially tactical on the part of the Russians and as not affecting their basic philosophy of longer-term objectives.

4. In Europe the Russians seek to consolidate their position in the East while leaving themselves maximum opportunity to influence events in the West, in particular to encourage withdrawals of US troops and to prevent greater West European cohesion in the political and defence fields. The atmosphere of reduced vigilance associated with East/West negotiations, the current economic pressures on Western Europe arising in particular from the oil crisis, and the political divisions within Europe and the Atlantic Community will all provide the Russians with encouragement. At the same time the steady improvement of the Soviet military position of strength as against NATO continues unabated and NATO's northern and southern flanks are particularly vulnerable.[3] The Soviet long-term objective is a Western Europe from which United States defence cover has been largely withdrawn, which remains divided, and which, like Finland, exists under the shadow of Soviet military strength and is increasingly compelled to adjust its policies accordingly. Brezhnev apparently considers that given 10 to 15 years of détente the Soviet Union should be in a position to dictate the terms of its foreign policy.

5. In the Far East the Soviet Union has as neighbours two major powers, China and Japan, upon whom it can exercise only limited influence. China in

[2] The Main Report stated that the Soviet Union, having achieved nuclear parity with the USA, was currently engaged in a very large programme of new strategic nuclear weapons, equipped with Multiple Independently Targetable Reentry Vehicles (MIRVs), which should be ready for deployment in the 1970s. It had very large conventional forces which had been considerably improved in quality over the last few years, and a growing potential for intervention abroad, both airborne and seaborne. The Soviet navy was growing rapidly, including increasing numbers of nuclear-powered carriers, and was being deployed over a steadily expanding area. The Report estimated that the Soviet economy was capable of sustaining the present rate of growth in military expenditure (i.e. 4–5% per annum), and that in the late 1970s there would be an increase in expenditure on arms procurement and the introduction into the Soviet armed forces of new weapon systems presently under development.

[3] Main Report asserted: 'They [the Russians] have always sought assurance in numbers but are now adding quality to quantity: there have been more qualitative and quantitative increases in Soviet forces in the Central European sector over the last 5 years than over any corresponding previous period.' The Russians were also assumed to have grounds for hoping that their attainment of strategic parity with the USA, increasing US introversion and possible strains within the Atlantic Alliance, would 'erode the credibility of the United States nuclear guarantee to Europe'.

particular is likely to remain a profound anxiety for the Soviet leaders. They have resisted the temptation to seek a military solution while China is still weak in modern weapons. They follow a 'long haul' policy, exerting their superior resources to contain China and to reduce her influence as far as possible, while waiting for the day, after Mao's[4] death, when it may be possible to improve Sino/Soviet relations on terms satisfactory to the Soviet Union. Soviet preoccupation with China affects Soviet policies throughout the world and is on the whole to the advantage of the West.

6. In the Third World, the Russians pursue an opportunist policy, availing themselves of the openings provided by the era of decolonisation, their own willingness to supply selective economic aid and sophisticated military equipment, and any political influence accruing from their increasing naval deployment. They have sought to formalise their relations with selected Third World States by means of treaties, probably in the hope of deriving thereby a more lasting foundation for their presence by building up local political influence. But the US/Soviet relationship restricts Soviet options in the Third World; the Russians have less to offer the developing countries in aid than the West; and less in terms of example than the Chinese.

7. Their most spectacular encroachments have been in the Middle East, where despite setbacks in Egypt, there remains a formidable Soviet effort at stake. At the same time certain serious weaknesses in the Soviet Middle East position have recently become more apparent, deriving, inter alia, from Arab nationalism and increased self-confidence, the inherent instability of the area and the restraints imposed by the US/Soviet relationship. Their behaviour during and since the Middle East war of October, 1973 indicates that despite many ambiguities in their policy, the Russians remain anxious to avoid a further outbreak of major hostilities and the renewed danger of confrontation with the United States which this would bring. Recent Soviet policy in the Middle East has not been conspicuously successful. But the area retains its strategic importance for the Russians; they retain important levers there and will certainly continue their efforts to maximise their influence.

8. In the oil crisis the Russians have played a cautious role. Although they have encouraged Arab countries to take control of their own resources and have given some propaganda support for the use of oil as a political weapon, they had little influence on the oil embargo and none on the rises in oil prices. While they have some cause for satisfaction in the economic and political impact of the oil crises on the West and Japan their own oil position is not invulnerable in the longer-term and they are increasingly unable to meet the oil needs of their Warsaw Pact allies.

9. In the Indian Sub-continent the position of special advantage given the Russians by the Indo/Soviet Treaty and the Indo/Pakistan war of 1971 has not brought them very great practical benefits and with the normalisation of relations between the three States of the Sub-continent the opportunities for United States

---

[4] Mr. Mao Tse-tung was Chairman of the Central Committee and *Politburo* of the Chinese Communist Party.

and Chinese influence are likely to increase. In South East Asia the Russians seek to increase their influence in the context of the Sino/Soviet dispute and also to benefit from any Western withdrawals; but they are unlikely to become more than one element in any balance of power in the area.

PART II: THE NATURE OF THE SOVIET THREAT

10. The threat posed by the Soviet Union must be analysed by reference to the account above and also by reference to our assessment of British interests, which, though widely spread, centre on the West European and Atlantic area. Fundamentally the threat arises from the Soviet leaders' commitment to struggle by all means short of war and their sense of historical mission as convinced Communists, supported by the national ambitions and strength of the Soviet state.

11. On the military side, we do not see the Soviet Union launching a deliberate military attack on the West in the period under review. Nevertheless, Soviet military power will threaten our security in a number of ways. In particular in an era of nuclear parity and of United States reduction of a number of its overseas commitments, Soviet superiority in conventional arms is likely to have serious political implications for Western Europe, by reducing Western confidence and facilitating Soviet politico/military pressure. Soviet naval and military strength is also likely to give the Russians added opportunities for acquiring influence outside Europe.

12. On the economic side, the Soviet Union is less well placed, given the greater flexibility of capitalist economies and Soviet deficiencies in various areas of applied technology and in the consumer sector. But they are able to mobilise their efforts for priority goals and to maintain a rate of growth which compares favourably with that of most advanced Western countries. They stand to benefit from any economic quarrels in the free world, from pressures on the Western and Japanese economies arising from the oil crisis and from their own considerable supplies of raw materials.

13. In another aspect of the struggle, we expect the Soviet Union to intensify its world-wide campaign of propaganda, espionage and subversion, and to exploit the deceptive atmosphere of security engendered by détente. There are some 850 identified or suspected Soviet intelligence officers under official cover in Western Europe.[5] Soviet agents of influence and sympathisers seek to influence Western policy making and undermine Western resistance to Soviet aims. West European Communist parties retain a basic loyalty to Moscow and Ireland offers the Soviet Union further opportunities.

14. The real Soviet threat, however, derives not from these individual factors in isolation but from their combination. Essentially the threat is that the Soviet

[5] The Main Report noted that the greatest number of these were in France. It added that the Soviet intelligence services were seeking to restore their presence in the UK following the expulsions of 1971, but that the policies of ceilings and visa refusals to known intelligence officers had had an inhibiting effect, especially on the re-establishment of a KGB presence. The opening of a Soviet Embassy in Dublin was, however, seen as offering 'new opportunities for "third country" operations' against the UK.

Union, by using political, economic, subversive and military means of influence and relying on its own consistency of purpose and any infirmities on the part of the West, may acquire such a position of dominance in vital areas that it will be able to achieve many of its objectives without resort to hostilities. We identify two danger areas: Western Europe; and that part of the Third World lying to the south of the Soviet Union, in particular the Middle East and Indian sub-continent.

15. Of these, the threat in Western Europe is unquestionably the more serious. In essence it is a threat of politico-military pressure. The Russians are able to use the policy of détente to soften up the West while maintaining their long-term aims and improving their military strength. In these conditions of détente, Western Europe may be gradually deprived of credible United States support without providing a substitute of its own and without making the efforts to develop political co-operation and to maintain a credible defence posture which will be necessary if Soviet influence and pressures on Western Europe are to be repelled. The threat derives as much from Western inaction and divisions as from Soviet design; but we doubt whether these shortcomings will be remedied.[6] We therefore foresee a period of danger in the immediate future and fear that the Soviet Union may significantly improve its position in Europe in the period under review.

16. Specifically we expect the Russians to strengthen their persuasions that efforts to improve political and military co-operation in Western Europe are superfluous and provocative; and to offer the alternative of 'all-European' co-operation and better bilateral relations by individual states with the Soviet Union. At the same time pressures within NATO countries for reduction in defence effort are likely to grow. Subsequently the Soviet Union can argue that the effective defence of Western Europe is no longer possible; urge that safety should be sought in accommodation rather than collective resistance; and seek to detach the weaker members of NATO from the alliance. We cannot be sure of the precise form of events but current trends are greatly in Soviet favour.

17. The second danger area, that part of the Third World lying to the South of the Soviet Union, will remain one of steady Soviet effort, but even in the Middle East the dangers from Soviet activities are less acute than in Western Europe and some corrective forces operate. There may well be striking Soviet successes in particular countries. Nevertheless we expect this to be a patchy performance, in which success will be interspersed with setbacks, and we doubt whether by itself it will give the Soviet Union the lasting influence that will be needed fundamentally to improve its world position.

---

[6] The Main Report explained that Western Europe's maintenance of credible conventional defences would require a higher level of defence expenditure than governments were at present prepared to undertake. 'And', it continued, 'in the political context, the maintenance of close political ties between Western Europe and the United States, which is in the interests of both, requires a commitment to consultation and mutual trust which is not always evident on either side of the Atlantic.'

No. 59

Sir T. Garvey (Moscow) to Mr. Callaghan

No. 507 Telegraphic [ENS 3/548/2]

Confidential   FCO, *15 May 1974, 4.14 p.m.*

Repeated for information Saving to Warsaw, East Berlin, Prague, Budapest, Bucharest, Sofia, Washington, Bonn, Paris, UKDEL NATO, UKREP Brussels, UKMIS Geneva, UKDEL Vienna, Belgrade.

Your tel[egram] No. 308:[1]

Anglo-Soviet Relations

1. I had meant to postpone reply until after seeing Kosygin. But since he has put me off till 10.00 hours local time tomorrow (being tied up with Jalloud this afternoon)[2] I submit following comments off the cuff.

2. I am in no doubt that it is right to take Soviet initiative seriously. But we need to mind our eye.

3. Soviet attitude to ourselves has, on my reading, evolved in recent months roughly as follows:

(a) Having kept us in doghouse for 18 months they recognised by mid-1973 that, as members of enlarged EEC (then as they thought moving towards harmonisation of foreign policies and eventually joint defence policy), it was worth getting back on some sort of terms with us; not least because we could be a nuisance in CSCE and MBFR;

(b) Hence invitation to your predecessor and moves towards 'normalisation' in December 1973;

(c) But notion that Britain was worth cultivating receded in face of fall-out from Middle East War (oil prices, intra-EEC and trans-Atlantic tensions),[3] subsequent industrial and balance of payments difficulties in UK, election and uncertainties of parliamentary situation;

---

[1] In this telegram of 15 May Mr. Callaghan referred to Mr. Lunkov's meetings with Mr. Wilson on 7 May, during which Mr. Lunkov had conveyed the wish of the Soviet leadership to re-establish the relationship which they had enjoyed with the Prime Minister when he was last in office, and with himself on 10 May, when Mr. Lunkov had said that the Soviet leadership wished to 'raise relations to a higher level'. Mr. Callaghan stated in the telegram that he intended to treat the Soviet initiative seriously and that he proposed 'to make a substantial effort over the next six months to improve Anglo-Soviet relations' (cf. Volume II, No. 79, note 4).

[2] On 16 May Sir T. Garvey discussed with Mr. Kosygin prospects for the forthcoming meeting of the Anglo-Soviet Joint Commission in London (record of meeting, 16 May). Major A.S.A. Jalloud was Libyan Prime Minister.

[3] Mr. Wilson's minority Labour Government was committed to renegotiating the UK's terms of entry into the EC. This, and the sceptical attitude adopted by Mr. Callaghan towards further political and economic integration, set Britain apart from its European partners in the spring of 1974. Meanwhile, differences between the USA and Europe persisted over their attitudes towards the Arab-Israeli conflict and the Arab oil embargo.

(*d*) Since then they have left us to stew and concentrated on grander designs with US, Federal Republic and France. Though stakes are much higher in Soviet/US game (notably SALT, Arab/Israel) common elements of all approaches have been summit meetings, jumbo-sized co-operation deals and (hopefully) consummation of Soviet Westpolitik.[4]

4. Their past two weeks whirlwind wooing of HMG coincides with their deepening uncertainty about future of their preferred partners. Brandt and Pompidou have gone. Nixon, even from Moscow, looks fairly rocky.[5] In my view main Soviet motive in their pursuit of us is to find a partner who might crack the front in Geneva, facilitating triumphant summit conclusion of CSCE operation, providing a success for Soviet 'peace' policy which Brezhnev (though not yet desperately) needs and enabling them to ride out, in better order, the pause which seems likely to supervene until Americans, French and Germans have sorted themselves out.

5. They know our proclivity for commerce and probably reckon that, given our economic difficulties and the opportunities (which they exaggerate) of cashing in on current UK political situation, they may with luck find in us a willing accomplice.

6. Concretely, what they will hope to get out of us is:

(*a*) Assent to a CSCE Summit in Helsinki this summer;
(*b*) No more hair splitting about human contacts and Basket 3;
(*c*) Dismantlement of ceiling on Soviet represensations [*sic*] in London and reconstitution of London-based intelligence network.

7. In exchange they will hold out prospect of expansion of bread and butter export business plus a glimpse of some very large contracts, one or two of which (on experience of others) would quite likely mature.

8. A deal on these lines could not, as seen from here, represent a worthwhile bargain for HMG. Our problem thus becomes one of opening up the game and exploiting such opportunities, notably commercial, as are offered without (your para. 3) 'paying a price that is not justified'.[6]

[4] Sir T. Garvey reported in Moscow telegrams Nos. 478 and 479 of 10 May that a 'period of stocktaking by [the] Soviet leadership would not be surprising'. But he expected Mr. Brezhnev's policies 'substantially to survive' any such reappraisal. *Détente* policy, he noted, was 'firmly rooted in Soviet national interest', risks to internal security had been successfully contained, the course of CSCE was satisfactory to Soviet interests, Western difficulties were multiplying sufficiently to argue against need for more active Soviet encouragement, and the Soviet economy was in reasonable shape (ENS 2/1).

[5] See Volume II, No. 79, note 3. In Moscow telegram No. 479 (*v. ibid.*) Sir T. Garvey remarked with regard to Soviet *détente* policy: 'So long as content remains unchanged, there is no tangible reason why Brezhnev's own position should be weakened. But it looks, particularly if Watergate claims its victim, as though there will have to be a pause for reconnaissance.'

[6] Mr. Callaghan noted in telegram No. 308 (see note 1 above) that it seemed that the Russians hoped to secure British support for, or at least acquiescence in, some of their international positions,

9. Of points in your proposed message[7] a 'constructive' reply to Lunkov's points on CSCE is the least easy. He made no bones about what he was after and I can add little to what I said on this to Gromyko (my tel. No. 499).[8] Vienna talks (6(b)) are indeed the touchstone (SALT apart) of Soviet intentions.

10. By way of signalising the high level dialogue and 'statement of approach' (6(c) and 6(d)), we should need a new style, and new language, from what has gone before. Following elements, in ascending order of magnitude, may commend themselves:

(*a*) Periodical talks on specified (geographical and functional) subjects. We have already put forward several proposals, which could be reactivated;

(*b*) Establishment of high-level Anglo-Soviet consultative machinery (compare Soviet-Canadian 'protocol on consultations' and parallel Franco-Soviet and other arrangements);

(*c*) Dating of visits already agreed in principle, but leading up to an invitation to Brezhnev to come to London;[9]

On that occasion (or on Mr. Wilson's earlier visit here) conclusion of a document on 'principles governing Anglo-Soviet relations'.

11. This programme would put us on equal terms with our competitors, show that HMG are doing something new, and leave us better placed to deal with the 'snares and difficulties' (your para. 3) if and when we encounter them.[10]

especially at the CSCE. 'For my part', he continued, 'I shall judge these issues on their merits. I have no intention of paying a price that is not justified, but on the other hand I shall not be prejudiced against any proposal they may make merely because of its origin.'

[7] Mr. Callaghan wanted to respond to the Soviet leadership with a message that might, as he put it in paragraph 6 of his telegram (*v. ibid.*), include: (a) 'constructive replies' to points made by Mr. Lunkov on CSCE; (b) a reference to the Vienna talks 'to indicate that [he regarded] these as having no less importance'; (c) a passage on the Middle East and/or other international questions 'to establish the principle of an Anglo-Soviet high-level dialogue on such matters'; and (d) a statement of HMG's own approach to Anglo-Soviet relations with more concrete suggestions than the Russians had presented.

[8] See Volume II, No. 81, note 7.

[9] During his meeting with the Prime Minister on 7 May, Mr. Lunkov expressed the hope that Mr. Wilson would visit Moscow 'before long' (see note 1 above). The invitation to Mr. Gromyko to visit London was also subsequently 'revalidated' (Moscow telegram No. 498 of 14 May).

[10] Sir T. Garvey was due to return to London for the meeting on 20–22 May of the Anglo-Soviet Joint Commission (cf. No. 37, note 13, and No. 42, note 2). Mr. Bullard proposed in a minute to Sir J. Killick of 13 May that this would afford them the opportunity to discuss what instructions he might receive for a future meeting with Mr. Gromyko.

No. 60

Letter from Mr. Dobbs (Moscow) to Mr. Bullard
[*EN 2/18*]

Confidential   MOSCOW, *29 May 1974*

Dear Julian,

Trends in the Soviet Union and Eastern Europe

1.   We have been giving thought to the various issues raised in your letter of 3 May[1] and in particular to two cardinal propositions in your analysis, namely 'the tightening of the Soviet screw all over Eastern Europe in the last 2 years' and 'how far the (domestic) situation has travelled backwards in the 10 years since he (Khrushchev) fell'. I am not sure that we would have stated either quite so forcibly as you have done, although in the one case this may be because our information is insufficient, and in the other, because it is a question of value judgement as much as objective assessment.

2.   On the question of the 'Soviet screw', it is particularly difficult to separate the real from the apparent. Of the three explanations for lack of Eastern European initiative at the CSCE which you put forward in paragraph 8 of your letter, I would give most weight to the first, namely that the opportunities never really existed.[2] It follows from this that I do not regard public statements about 'strengthening cohesion and deepening coordination' as necessarily indicative of the screw being tightened. The recent phase of alliance diplomacy has brought unity of foreign policy on the Eastern side into the public spotlight, but the proposition that it has enhanced it substantially remains to be proven. Apart from Romanian waywardness (and I could agree with all you say about the way in which this had been neutralised) I can think of no successful example of Eastern European independence specifically in the field of foreign policy since the establishment of Soviet hegemony over the area (certainly not episodes such as the Rapacki plan).[3] It is not that the Eastern European governments have totally failed to make their views heard. But I would argue that their efforts have only

---

[1] No. 57.

[2] In a letter to Mr. Bullard of 4 June Mr. R.J.M. Wilson observed, with regard to dealing with Communist countries in a multilateral forum, 'where the Eastern Europeans appear jointly with the Russians (e.g. CSCE or MBFR) what happens in practice is that the Eastern Europeans (with maverick exceptions like the Romanians) are forced to become obedient puppets of the Russians and any tendencies on their part to show a spirit of independence are promptly squashed'. Mr. T.F. Brenchley, HM Ambassador in Warsaw, likewise emphasised that for the Party leaderships in Eastern Europe 'the basic and overriding reality of their situation [remained] their total dependence, for survival, on the Soviet Union' (letter to Mr. Bullard, 7 June).

[3] This plan, promoted by the Polish Foreign Minister Mr. A. Rapacki, and first advanced in the UN on 2 October 1957, foresaw a ban on the production and storage of nuclear weapons in Poland, Czechoslovakia, the FRG and the GDR. The proposal was later taken up by the Soviet Government.

really succeeded in modifying a Soviet diktat when they have tended towards preservation of a *status quo*, rather than its alteration, e.g. until recently, GDR back-pedalling on relations with the FRG.

3. The tightness or otherwise of the screw is probably better judged by the degree of Soviet interference in the internal affairs of the countries involved. The network of ideological agreements to which you refer is certainly indicative of a desire to maintain, and in some cases, reimpose conformity. It would be interesting to know to what degree, if at all yet, these agreements have filtered through to everyday life in the participating countries. The absence of any real innovations in the internal policies of the Eastern European countries over the last two years, and, in the case of Hungary's NEM, apparent regression,[4] are certainly consistent with the picture you have painted, but I am still not sure whether the evidence is sufficient to prove your point. As I said at the outset, however, our information here may be insufficient.

4. Finally there is the CMEA, where, as you point out, certain concrete steps on the path towards fuller integration are being implemented. Although everything at present being undertaken is mentioned in the Complex Programme adopted in July 1971,[5] I think it would be fair to argue that apparent success in maintaining the schedule outlined therein is indicative of a certain closing of the ranks. We may be in a better position to assess the degree of success after this year's session of the CMEA, at which the draft plan of integrational measures for 1967–80 is to be considered. The movement towards internal economic orthodoxy in Hungary should perhaps be seen in this context—until some conformity of internal pricing is hammered out, financial integration is not going to get very far.

5. We would agree with your reference in paragraph 9(b) to the strengthening of the Soviet economic lever, although I would add the pedantic rider that it is not so much the price as the quantity of oil and raw materials, which will be crucial. The main point is that the rise in world prices will make it extremely costly for the Eastern Europeans to look elsewhere; the rise in Soviet prices, though substantial, is unlikely to be of quite the same order.

6. To turn now to the point made in paragraph 7(a) about internal retrogression in the Soviet Union since the fall of Khrushchev. It is certainly true that the cultural and artistic atmosphere has grown staler the longer the Brezhnev régime has lasted. But there is something of an optical illusion in the appearance of retrogression. Liberalism was not the characteristic feature of the Khrushchev period, although there were periodic explosions of something very like it (with equally combustive reversions, e.g. the Pasternak affair).[6] The end of the

---

[4] But Mr. R.J.M. Wilson pointed out in his letter of 4 June (see note 2 above) that it was not by any means established that the Hungarians were definitely retreating from the NEM and that the Russians had had a hand in this.

[5] The Complex Programme for the Development of Socialist Economic Integration was approved at the 25th session of the CMEA at Bucharest on 27–29 July 1971.

[6] When in October 1958 the Soviet author Boris Pasternak accepted the Nobel Prize for Literature for his novel, *Dr. Zhivago*, he was denounced in the Soviet Union as an enemy of socialism. A mounting campaign of abuse culminated in his expulsion from the Soviet Union of Writers and

Khrushchev period was such a moment and is, therefore, a somewhat misleading point of comparison. Since the dissident movement which was spawned by this last liberal episode had not yet got under way, it is a matter for conjecture how the Soviet body politic at that time would have dealt with it. My own guess is that Khrushchev's reaction would have been as heavy-handed as that of his successors. The chief contrast seems to me to be between the extreme volatility of Khrushchev and the drab consistency of his successors.

7. I doubt, incidentally, whether many Russians outside the worlds of literature and the theatre look back on the early 60s with much nostalgia. Both bread and circuses, not to mentions flats and consumer durables, have become very significantly more plentiful since Khrushchev's day, and most city dwellers, at any rate, would probably agree, if asked, that they have never had it so good.

8. The points raised in the final section of your letter seem chiefly applicable to the Eastern European posts.

Yours ever,
J.A. Dobbs

it was suggested that he should be deprived of his Soviet citizenship. He subsequently withdrew his acceptance of the award and made a public apology for his conduct.

No. 61

Mr. Callaghan to Sir T. Garvey (Moscow)

No. 350 Telegraphic [ENS 3/548/2]

Priority. Confidential FCO, *3 June 1974, 12.20 p.m.*

M[y] I[mmediately] P[receding] T[elegram].[1]

Following is text of message from me to Mr. Gromyko.
Begins
The British Government have taken careful note of the message from the Soviet leadership which your Ambassador in London delivered to me on 10 May,[2] and also of what was said to HM Ambassador in Moscow by yourself and by the Soviet Prime Minister on 14 and 16 May respectively.[3] My colleagues and I are much encouraged by these conversations, by the signature of Anglo-Soviet intergovernmental agreements on long-term economic co-operation and on the protection of the environment, and also by the results of the third session of the Anglo-Soviet Joint Commission held in London from 20–22 May. We have the

[1] In this telegram of 3 June Mr. Callaghan instructed Sir T. Garvey to seek an interview with Mr. Gromyko to deliver orally the following personal message, the text of which was on the lines discussed with Sir T. Garvey during his recent visit to London (cf. Volume II, No. 85, note 1).

[2] See No. 59, note 1.

[3] *V. ibid.*, note 2, and Volume II, No. 81, note 7.

clear impression that the Soviet Government wish to improve the quality and to raise the level of Anglo-Soviet relations. This is also the desire and intention of the Government of the United Kingdom. You will know that Mr. Wilson, and a number of us who have served in successive Labour Governments, have worked hard in the past to create a safer, more productive and more durable relationship with the Soviet Union on the basis of mutual respect and mutual advantage. Such is still our objective and we believe that the present time offers wider and more hopeful possibilities of moving towards it than have existed for many years.

2.   As your Ambassador said to me, it would help us to achieve this objective if we could go at least some way towards reconciling the British and Soviet positions on important international questions. One of these is the CSCE. You will know from Mr. Lunkov how much importance we attach to this Conference and, in particular, to the third item of the agenda and military confidence-building measures. Like you I am disappointed that there is so far so little to show for all the months of hard work in Geneva. I had hoped to see the third stage of the Conference held before the end of July. But time is now very short, and it is quite clear to me that it will be impossible to do this unless a great deal more progress can be made very soon. The next few weeks will be critical. We for our part intend to work constructively to achieve such progress and I hope that all the participants in the Conference will do the same.[4]

3.   An event of no less importance in our eyes is the Conference in Vienna on the Mutual Reduction of Forces and Armaments and Associated Measures in Central Europe. There is no disagreement about the general objective of the negotiations which is, in the words of the agreed communiqué issued after the preparatory consultations, to contribute to a more stable relationship and to the strengthening of peace and security in Europe. After so many years of military confrontation it is perhaps not surprising that there are differences of view between us about how this objective should be achieved. But I am confident that, with patience and perseverance, it will be possible to arrive at agreements which are fully in conformity with the general objective and with the principle of undiminished security for all.

4.   A third area of great concern to us both is the Middle East. I know you will agree that in the next stage of the diplomatic process it will be the duty of each of us to use influence where it can most effectively be brought to bear in favour of a settlement. We shall be doing this, and I feel sure that your own greater weight will be brought to bear in the same constructive direction.

---

[4] During a meeting with Mr. Callaghan and Mr. Bullard in London on 23 May Sir T. Garvey said that he thought the Russians were 'looking for a point in the Western front where they might be able to break in'. They had recently lost their top-level contacts in Bonn and Paris, and this was essentially why they had been behaving so agreeably towards Britain during the last month. 'Specifically', he maintained, 'they hoped to secure British assistance in obtaining a Third Stage of the CSCE at summit level, in winding up the remaining problems in Basket III without embarrassment to the Soviet Union, and in raising or abolishing the ceilings imposed on the Soviet establishment in Britain in September 1971.' Mr. Callaghan stated with regard to the level of Stage III that 'if the United States wanted a summit in the larger interests of détente, he would not resist it' (minute from Mr. Alexander to EESD of 30 May).

5.   The recent nuclear explosion in India is another significant development, as depository powers for both the Non-Proliferation Treaty and the partial Test Ban Treaty our two Governments share a special interest in this event. We are both working for the forthcoming Non-Proliferation Treaty Review Conference.[5] I should be interested to know what you think about the implications of the Indian test explosion for the Non-Proliferation Treaty.[6] One may ask how this event may effect the prospects for further accessions to this Treaty and for further proliferation of nuclear weapons.[7]

6.   As regards our bilateral affairs, the framework for improved relations already exists. The visit of Academician Kirillin to Britain last month and the third session of the Anglo-Soviet Joint Commission have, I hope, marked the end of a period during which the trend in Anglo-Soviet trade has been less than satisfactory.[8] It goes without saying that scientific and technological cooperation too are of great importance as a factor in Anglo-Soviet relations. In the cultural field, the recent review of the first year of operation of the current programme has shed a useful light on certain difficulties which it was becoming increasingly difficult to explain to academic institutions in both countries. I hope that here too we have finally put behind us a difficult period which has existed for too long.

7.   As to political contacts, I expect you would agree that the main channel for these must be our respective diplomatic missions. I admire the wide range of contacts which your Ambassador in London has built up in a short time, and I feel sure that your officials are ready to assist Her Majesty's Ambassador in established contacts no less wide. I hope particularly that Sir Terence Garvey may be given an opportunity of meeting Mr. Ponomarev, who made a great impression upon me when I met him in Moscow two years ago.[9] I should like to make the fullest use of our two Ambassadors in ensuring that you and I remain in close

[5] The Nuclear Test Ban Treaty was signed by the UK, the USA and the USSR on 5 August 1963. The same three powers signed the Nuclear Non-Proliferation Treaty (NPT) on 1 July 1968. Signatories of the NPT agreed not to transfer nuclear weapons to non-nuclear states and International Atomic Energy Authority safeguards were to be used to inspect nuclear plants designed for peaceful purposes. The treaty, which came into effect in 1970, also provided for five-yearly review conferences. See *Treaty Series*, No. 88 (1970), Cmnd 3683 (London: HMSO).

[6] India became the world's sixth nuclear power when on 18 May it conducted a successful underground test in the Rajasthan desert.

[7] In Moscow telegram No. 601 of 5 June Sir T. Garvey queried the relevance of his referring to the Middle East and the Indian nuclear test in conversation with Mr. Gromyko. Mr. Callaghan replied in telegram No. 362 to Moscow of 6 June that it was not his intention that Sir T. Garvey should engage in substantive discussion of these subjects; that would follow in later exchanges.

[8] Mr. Callaghan told Sir T. Garvey on 23 May (see note 4 above) that 'ideally he would like Britain to have the same relationship with Moscow as the United States enjoyed, i.e. one in which no illusions were harboured but substantial trade deals were possible'. Mr. Bullard 'questioned whether the relationship between politics and trade was quite so direct as sometimes suggested'.

[9] The second and third sentences of this paragraph were deleted at Sir T. Garvey's request. In Moscow telegram No. 601 (see note 6 above) Sir T. Garvey observed with regard to this passage: 'I am all for buttering Lunkov up but, seen from this end, this lays it on a bit thick.' He added, with regard to Prof. Ponomarev, 'it seems to me bad style for HMG to be soliciting the appointment in a message from Foreign Minister to Foreign Minister'.

touch from now on. I am also ready to instruct senior officials from the Foreign and Commonwealth Office to meet with your specialists on particular subjects if you agree with me that this would be useful. You may think that the Middle East and the Indian sub-continent would be particularly suitable for discussion. If the experiment is successful, I would hope that it could be repeated from time to time, and I am willing to consider, if you wish, whether these contacts might be placed on a regular institutional basis.

8. I have one further idea which I have already mentioned to your Ambassador. I believe it would be useful if Parliamentary contacts could take place between Britain and the Soviet Union more frequently and at a higher level than has been possible under the auspices of the IPU.[10] If possible, I should like to devise some way of bringing in also non-Parliamentary figures of distinction from the press, industry, the Trade Unions and other fields. We have such arrangements with some other countries and I have long thought it a gap in our relations with the Soviet Union. If you are attracted to these ideas, I will instruct Sir Terence Garvey to pursue them with the appropriate Soviet organisations.

9. Finally, I note with pleasure that certain important invitations have recently been renewed and accepted. Events will show us in which order these visits could most conveniently take place. I shall hope to be in touch with you further about this before long. Meanwhile I send you my best wishes for your own continued health and for the success of your activities in pursuit of the goals which we have in common.[11]

Ends.

[10] Inter-Parliamentary Union.

[11] Sir T. Garvey delivered this message to Mr. Gromyko on 7 June (cf. Volume II, No. 85, note 1). In Moscow telegram No. 626 of 7 June Sir T. Garvey noted that Mr. Gromyko's comments 'were mainly unremarkable and did not go beyond familiar, if rather discursive, restatements of known Soviet positions'. The Russians, as Mr. Callaghan reminded Mr. Gromyko when he visited Moscow in February 1975 (see No. 74), did not reply to this message: Mr. Gromyko then said he was sorry, but he 'had not understood that an answer was expected' (minute of 28 February 1975 from Mr. Bullard to the Private Secretary, ENS 3/540/2).

No. 62

Sir T. Garvey (Moscow) to Mr. Callaghan

[*ENS 3/304/1*]

Confidential   MOSCOW, *12 June 1974*

Summary ...[1]

Sir,

US–Soviet Relations

1.   President Nixon is to visit the Soviet Union on 27 June for the third in the present series of US–Soviet Summit Meetings.[2] It may be helpful, on the eve of this event, to attempt a review of the present state of US–Soviet relations as seen from Moscow.

2.   The uncertainties surrounding the forthcoming Summit have been less acute than those which were created on the eve of the President's visit to Moscow two years ago by the mining of Haiphong Harbour.[3] The question-mark this time has lain only over the President's position and authority in his own country. Public Soviet commitment to the visit has not faltered and recent speeches by such unlikely advocates of US–Soviet harmony as Ponomarev (ideologist)[4] and Andropov (Chairman of the KGB) have reaffirmed its importance and desirability. During the two years which have elapsed since the removal of the obstacle of Vietnam, the central importance in the USSR's foreign policy of its relationship with its fellow super-power has become more obvious, more freely admitted and less conditional. Wading through the massive and benevolent coverage accorded by the Soviet media to the recent visit by Ponomarev and his Supreme Soviet delegation to the United States,[5] it took an effort to recall that less than three years ago the same media were delivering daily and bitter assaults on American 'aggression', 'provocation' and other political misdeeds across the globe.

3.   The political turn-around has, moreover, released and enabled ordinary Soviet citizens to express an instinctive rapport which, whether or not it is reciprocated, they feel with the people of another vast and powerful country with a frontier tradition. The travelling American exhibition on 'Recreation and Tourism' aroused extraordinary interest and enthusiasm not only in Moscow but in the provinces (and may have helped to inspire Schcherbitsky's[6] hostile reference

---

[1] Not printed.

[2] President Nixon visited Moscow during 27 June–3 July. He had previously met Mr. Brezhnev in Moscow in May 1972 and in Washington in June 1973.

[3] In May 1972, following a major North Vietnamese offensive against the South, the US announced a total blockade of North Vietnam and the mining of Haiphong Harbour.

[4] See No. 53, note 1.

[5] Prof. Ponomarev led a delegation of eight members of the Supreme Soviet to Washington during 19–29 May.

[6] Mr. V.V. Schcherbitsky was Premier of the Ukrainian SSR.

at a recent Plenum of the Ukrainian Party to 'a wide campaign of propaganda for bourgeois democracy and the American way of life'). Those still sceptical of the transformation not only of the content but also of the atmosphere of Soviet-US relations would have been hard put to maintain their doubts during the rapturous ovation given to the Roger Wagner Chorale's rendering of 'America' to a packed house in the Tchaikovsky Hall earlier this month.

4. It is perhaps worth recapitulating the underlying reasons for this transformation. Reports from this post have reflected my belief that present Soviet policy towards the USA is not dictated by the personal views of Mr. Brezhnev —though these have had much influence in the matter—but is firmly anchored in Soviet national interest. I would therefore expect it to continue, whatever the changes in form and style, under any successive Soviet leadership, for as long as the US administration is prepared and allowed by Congress to meet the Soviet Government half way.

5. The constant objective of Soviet policy is to reinforce the USSR's security, and to facilitate the USSR's ambitions, by altering the balance of forces in the world in the Soviet favour. To this end the régime seeks to convert Russia's enormous resources—both natural and human—into ever more imposing economic strength. Possibly the single most important threat to such a purpose would be a resumption of a spiralling nuclear arms race with the USA which, although with a less tractable population, has twice the Soviet Union's GNP. The Soviet leaders realised that if this nuclear competition was to be contained the climate of East–West relations would have to undergo a fundamental change, from mutual suspicion to acceptance, on the Western side, of the Soviet Union in its new guise of a powerful nation interested more in consolidation than in expansion and more in economic co-operation than in subversion. The 'peace programme' of the 24th Party Congress in 1971 was designed to serve this purpose.[7] Particularly during the past three years, Mr. Brezhnev has devoted a major part of his political activity to its execution. This shift in Soviet strategy ante-dated but was encouraged by the reappraisal of US foreign policy by President Nixon and Dr. Kissinger at the time of America's disengagement from Vietnam and resulted in the Summit Meeting in Moscow in May 1972 at which both Mr. Brezhnev and Mr. Nixon put their names to a statement on the Basic Principles of Relations, the first of which stated: 'They will proceed from the common determination that in a nuclear age there is no alternative to conducting their mutual relations on the basis of peaceful coexistence …'.[8]

6. The crucial importance to the new relationship of a nuclear understanding is evidenced by the series of agreements signed in May 1972 and June 1973 which comprise the Treaty of Limitation of Anti-ballistic Missiles, the Interim Agreement of the Limitation of Strategic Offensive Weapons,[9] the Agreement on the Prevention of Nuclear War, and the Agreement on the Basic Principles of Negotiations of Further Limitation of Strategic Offensive

[7] Cf. Volume I, pp. 325–6.

[8] See Cmnd 6932, pp. 130–2.

[9] *V. ibid.*, pp. 122–30.

Arms.[10] When assessing the durability of these agreements it is important to bear in mind that negotiations in these areas were in progress with President Johnson and Defence Secretary Macnamara before Mr. Nixon's election. This underlines the long-term nature of Soviet policy in this sphere, and suggests that it will almost certainly survive Mr. Nixon, if the worst—from the Soviet point of view—happens, and he is impeached.

7. Trade and economic co-operation is the other area in which the Soviet Union has hoped to obtain direct benefits from improved relations with the United States. The main Soviet requirement is US technology and, perhaps even more importantly, US capital. For the scale of development, in particular of energy resources, that the Russians have in mind, the United States is one of the few markets in the world capable of absorbing the quantities of raw materials and energy with which the Russians wish to pay for imported technology and capital.

8. I nevertheless share the view expressed by my predecessor that the Soviet Union sees the benefits to be obtained from trade with the US at least as much in political terms, as a means of underpinning their new relationship, as it does in economic. The long-term, large-scale commitment of US technology and capital in the Soviet Union would help to inhibit the reversion by a future US administration to a more hostile stance towards the Soviet Union. A recent major article in *Pravda* to mark the fifth anniversary of the 1969 World Conference of Communist Parties listed four requirements for 'making international détente irreversible'. One of them was: 'Imparting material content to the already existing international treaties and agreements by developing large-scale economic, scientific, technological and cultural co-operation among all the states concerned, irrespective of their differing social systems.' The underlying political motivation is thus made explicit. Dr. Kissinger's policy of securing relations between the US and the Soviet Union by means of a network of minor agreements which create a vested interest in the maintenance of a stable *status quo* is one to which I believe the Russians also subscribe.

9. Against this background, the course of the US–Soviet relations since the last Summit Meeting between President Nixon and Mr. Brezhnev in the United States in June last year has been both eventful and instructive. Although there have been several moments when the warmth of Soviet public treatment of the subject has temporarily cooled, I think it is true to say that, in important matters of foreign policy, the Soviet Government's actions had been determined by the over-riding desire not to put the new relationship with the US into jeopardy.

10. In this respect the Middle East has undoubtedly provided the Soviet government with the biggest problem. I suggested in my despatch of 26 February[11] that East–West, and specifically US–USSR understanding, carried greater

---

[10] See Grenville, pp. 540–2.

[11] In this despatch Sir T. Garvey concluded that there 'was little doubt in the minds of observers' in Moscow that while Soviet actions were dictated 'by an essentially pragmatic appraisal of how best to preserve their Middle East interests without jeopardising their East/West interests, it was the latter concern which mattered most' (NFX 3/303/1).

priority for the Soviet leadership both during the 6–25 October period and subsequently, than their Middle East interests. This is undoubtedly still true. But they have had to swallow some rather bitter pills, and there have been instances where the expression on Soviet faces has very clearly revealed the nasty taste. Mr. Brezhnev spoke forcefully about 'ersatz' plans in a scarcely veiled condemnation of Dr. Kissinger's activities. The galling part about it all for the Soviet leadership is that for all their wooing of President Assad,[12] they must still regard the last 6 months as a period of setbacks in their Middle East interests, especially in Egypt, while US diplomacy, and Dr. Kissinger personally, march on from strength to strength. Soviet reaction to each step along the way, including the recent Syrian/Israeli disengagement,[13] has seemed to be to come grudgingly to terms with the inevitability of Dr. Kissinger's success, while working hard not only to scramble on board the wagon at the last moment but to pretend that they have had at least one hand on the reins. They believe (and I should guess rightly) that in the last analysis a durable Middle East settlement cannot be got without their acquiescence. Russian apprehensions are doubtless still lively; but I would expect the Soviet leadership's concern for the continuing health of the Soviet-US relationship to impose limitations on their willingness to interfere too obstructively. Paradoxically, one of the more durable and least desirable effects of the Middle East war on US–Soviet relations has been to evoke adverse criticism from what they consider to be a significant and vocal part of the US academic establishment about the genuineness of Soviet détente policies. These groups, the 'new liberals', have been attacked by Soviet commentators as 'enemies of détente', financed by the Pentagon.

11. On the trade front in 1973, the Russians have been faced with a double disappointment. Not only has the Jackson/Vanik Amendment to the Trade Bill prevented the President from keeping his part of the June 1973 bargain (MFN treatment for the Soviet Union in return for Soviet settlement of outstanding lease-lend debts and an understanding on Jewish emigration) but the Vanik addition to the Jackson Amendment has effectively cast a shadow over the future of Export-Import Bank credits which will be essential for the completion of the major co-operation projects now under discussion between US firms and the Soviet Union.[14] It is a further sign of the Soviet desire to maintain good relations

[12] Lieut.-Gen. Hafiz al-Assad was President of Syria.

[13] Dr. Kissinger assisted in brokering two Arab-Israeli disengagement agreements in 1974: that between Israel and Eygpt of 18 January, which permitted Egyptian forces to return to the east bank of the Suez Canal, and that between Israel and Syria of 31 May, by which the Syrians returned to the main town of Quneitra.

[14] In October 1972, following the Soviet Government's imposition of a substantial 'exit tax' on emigrants, Democrat Senator H. Jackson sponsored an amendment to the US Trade Reform Bill which precluded the granting of most favoured nation (MFN) status to any communist country restricting emigration. Mr. C. Vanik introduced a similar measure into the House of Representatives. Partly in response to the repressive policies pursued by the Soviet Government towards political dissidents, Senator Jackson and his allies maintained their stance on trade with the Soviet Union throughout 1973, and in June 1974 threatened to restrict credit facilities provided by the US Export-Import Bank to the Soviet Union. Cf. Volume II, No. 45, and No. 110, note 4.

that these reverses have not provoked bitter attacks on US trustworthiness. The Russians have, however, left no doubt where their real interest lies. They look to the US Administration to underpin the political relationship by facilitating credits for major deals. The point was made directly to US parliamentarians and businessmen by Foreign Trade Minister Patolichev during his visit to the US in February and reinforced in May by Politburo member Ponomarev to the Senate Foreign Relations Committee. They may have been given some encouragement by the recent agreement between the Export-Import Bank and a consortium of commercial banks to raise a $360 million credit for the purchase of US equipment for the construction of a fertiliser plant in the Soviet Union. Although straight trade has, in percentage terms, increased very significantly over the last two years, total US–Soviet trade in 1973 at $1400m. (more than 70% of which was accounted for by Soviet imports of US grain and soya beans), was still less than total US-FRG trade. For all the talk of great contracts, the only one actually to be signed since the last Summit Meeting has been with Mr. Armand Hammer, President of Occidental Petroleum, for the building of a new Trade Centre in Moscow.

12. Soviet-US interests have also been involved in varying degrees in the two major multilateral negotiations now in progress in Europe—CSCE and MBFR. In the CSCE, which is of key presentational importance to the Soviet détente policies, the US has adopted a relatively passive rôle. It is worth recalling that Soviet agreement to the initiation of force reduction negotiations was originally linked to agreement by the Americans to the affirmation in the June 1973 Summit Communiqué that both sides would make efforts to bring the CSCE to a successful conclusion and perhaps at the highest level. This balance of interest appears to have been maintained. I would expect President Nixon to come under heavy pressure during his forthcoming visit from Mr. Brezhnev to agree to 'persuade' his Western European allies to drop their 'unrealistic' demands over human contacts and exchanges of information and move rapidly to a summit level conclusion of the CSCE. Indeed, in your recent conversation with him in Washington, Mr. Rush said that the Americans had dangled the prospect of a summit Stage III in front of the Russians in order to get results.

13. There has been successful resistance in the MBFR talks to initial Soviet attempts to achieve bilaterally with the Americans a rapid agreement which would have perpetuated at a lower level the present disparity of forces between the Warsaw Pact and NATO. For the moment the Russians appear to be in no hurry. It may be that they have come to the view that too rapid a withdrawal of US forces might be the one thing that could possibly galvanise the Western Europeans into a new defence grouping based on the EEC, although recent developments in the Community must have given them some reassurance on that score. Once the CSCE is out of the way, however, and if (despite the latest reverse suffered by Senator Mansfield and his amendment)[15] domestic pressures in the US for troop reductions abroad revive, I would expect a reversion to earlier Soviet tactics, directed towards the inclusion of the nuclear forward-based systems

[15] In the spring of 1974 both houses of the US Congress rejected amendments, including one moved by Senator Mansfield, for the reduction of American forces abroad.

aspects of MBFR in SALT II. If they succeed, the Russians will then be in a position to let the MBFR talks run slowly into the sand without any initiative on their part to break them off.

14. Without detailed information on the SALT II Talks, I am not a position to assess whether the Russians are prepared to strike a reasonable bargain by the end of this year.[16] All that can be said from Moscow is that in 90 per cent of all commentaries on US–Soviet relations, pride of place is given to a strategic understanding. Equally there has been a sharp public reaction to Mr. Schlesinger's recent defence review,[17] as well as to the voting of funds by Congress for research and development for a new nuclear submarine and an improved strategic bomber. The fact that as a preparation for the present Summit Meeting it is thought necessary to press ahead fast with bilateral discussions on the principle of an Underground Test Ban Treaty[18] demonstrates the importance which the Soviet Union attaches to having something under the nuclear heading ready for signature at the Summit.

15. Two other areas in which Soviet/US interests touch importantly, though tangentially—Sino-American and US-Western Europe relations—have been relatively quiescent, as far as the Russians are concerned, during the past year. Although US initiatives with China remain important for the Russians, the relatively slow development of the Peking-Washington dialogue, contrasted with the large amount of bilateral business conducted between the Soviet Union and the US, has had a reassuring effect. As far as Western Europe is concerned the rift between the US and its allies which began to appear during the Middle East war was clearly a welcome development to the Soviet leadership. However, apart from praising M. Jobert[19] and France's 'courageous' stand against US oil monopoly interests, there was little that the Soviet Union could, or needed, to do.

16. Finally, Watergate raises problems for the Russians too. During the past year they have been driven to acknowledge, understand and finally to evaluate the problem. For Mr. Brezhnev, whose style in foreign affairs has been to seek to establish rapport with a chosen interlocutor, the removal of Mr. Nixon following the death of President Pompidou and the resignation of Chancellor Brandt would not only be a personal set-back but, more importantly would revive uncertainties over future US policy. The Russians are well aware that Mr. Nixon

[16] The Geneva-based Strategic Arms Limitations Talks (SALT II) had made little progress since their resumption in September 1973, and a visit by Dr. Kissinger to Moscow in March failed, despite his expressed hope for a 'conceptual breakthrough', to end the deadlock. See Kissinger, *Years of Upheaval*, pp. 1006–31.

[17] Mr. Schlesinger called in the Defense Department's annual report to Congress of 3 March for a rough balance in strategic nuclear weapons in opposing forces in central Europe and in the navies on the high seas, and for more options with which the US could respond to the Soviet nuclear threat.

[18] See Cmnd 6932, pp. 187–90.

[19] The former French Foreign Minister had been particularly critical of US conduct during the recent Middle East war, and in a speech to the French National Assembly of 12 November 1973 he denounced the USA for not consulting its allies and for its monopolising the Middle Eastern peace settlement whilst Europe was left 'a forgotten victim of the conflict'.

and Dr. Kissinger have consistently been ahead of Congressional and public opinion in pursuing a policy of détente with the Soviet Union. It is of interest, as a reflection on their evaluation of the US domestic scene, that so far the Soviet public line has been one of undeviating support for the President against the enemies, who have been portrayed as trying somehow to use the 'so-called Watergate Affair' to undermine his position and attack his policy of improving relations with the Soviet Union. Nevertheless, there have recently been signs that a contingency plan has been put into effect which involves cultivating bipartisan support for US–Soviet rapprochement. The treatment given Senator Kennedy's travels in the Soviet Union in April[20] and Ponomarev's recent public relations exercise in the US[21] are examples. The Soviet hope must be that should Mr. Nixon fall, Mr. Ford[22] would retain Dr. Kissinger and that the main lines of US policy, sustained by bipartisan support, would continue as before.[23]

17. If the Soviet Union now attaches central importance to its relations with the United States, what are the policy implications for us and for our partners in the EEC and NATO? I can offer only the unstartling conclusion that the improvement of communication between the two super-powers and their clearer identification of their common interests increases still further the importance of keeping our own and Western Europe's lines to the US Administration open, operative and free from atmospheric crackle. The Americans must be helped to retain a clear understanding of the coincidence of their and our vital interests and to keep this well in mind in their dealings with the Soviet leadership.

18. Finally, the visit itself. The big prize of a full SAL II Agreement is not to be had. But since the June 1973 Agreement did not call for one until the end of 1974,[24] this need not necessarily be represented as a failure. Indeed, although this is for Her Majesty's Ambassador in Washington to judge, it is arguable that in his present domestic situation a SAL II Agreement signed by President Nixon might have a more difficult passage through Congress than it deserved. The 'threshold agreement' on underground tests, if it materialises, will no doubt be suitably decked out as a further historic step along the road to security in the nuclear age. In general terms, however, from the Soviet point of view enough must be done

---

[20] On 21 April Senator E. Kennedy became the first US politician ever to address students at Moscow University. According to one account the interpreter declined to translate some of the Senator's remarks about the desirability of free emigration on the grounds that Senator Kennedy 'was tired and wished to conclude' (letter from Mr. N.H.R.A. Broomfield (First Secretary, HM Embassy, Moscow) to Mr. Fall of 24 April).

[21] See note 5 above.

[22] Mr. Ford succeeded to the Presidency when, under threat of impeachment over the Watergate affair, President Nixon resigned on 9 August.

[23] In a minute to Sir J. Killick of 24 June Mr. Bullard commented on Sir T. Garvey's despatch and Dr. Kissinger's recent explanation of US policies at NATO's Ottawa summit of 18–19 June (see No. 64): 'What comes out very strongly from both sides is that each requires, expects and intends the special relationship [US/Soviet] to continue, notwithstanding setbacks … I think this assumption has to be the basis of all planning and forecasting on East–West matters.' Cf. Cmnd 6932, pp. 182–6.

[24] See Grenville, p. 540.

at the meeting with President Nixon to enable the Soviet Government to present it as being in the same category as the previous two 'historic meetings' in May 1972 and June 1973. To this end additional agreements are likely to be signed, probably including a long-term trade agreement. Especially after earlier uncertainties, however, Mr. Brezhnev's foremost objective for the Soviet-US Summit is that it should duly take place and thus sustain momentum in the improvement in Soviet-US relations. If it also produced agreements of substance, particularly in the strategic and commercial fields, he will regard these as a useful bonus.[25]

19. I am sending copies of this despatch to Her Majesty's Representatives at Washington, Bonn, Paris, Helsinki, Cairo, Tel Aviv, Damascus, to the North Atlantic Treaty Organisation, Brussels, to the Office of the United Nations and other International Organisations at Geneva, to the European Communities, Brussels and to the United Kingdom Delegation to the Negotiations on Mutual Reductions of Forces and Armaments and Associated Measures in Central Europe, Vienna.

I have, etc.,
TERENCE GARVEY

[25] Mr. Bullard observed in his minute of 24 June (see note 23 above) that Sir T. Garvey endorsed the view advanced by Sir J. Killick that the 'Soviet objective of "making détente irreversible" [was] the mirror-image of Dr. Kissinger's policy of creating a vested Soviet interest in stability through a network of mutually beneficial agreements'. As to which side would be the most successful in tying the other's hands, he added: 'In so far as this whole "spider's web" argument requires the creation of lobbies and pressure-groups, I cannot help thinking that an Administration in Washington will tend to be more vulnerable to these than Brezhnev or his successors in Moscow.'

No. 63

Sir P. Ramsbotham (Washington) to Mr. Callaghan
[ENS 3/304/1]

Confidential   WASHINGTON, *21 June 1974*

Summary ...[1]

Sir,

Détente—On the Eve of President Nixon's Second Visit to Moscow

My predecessor, writing soon after President Nixon's visit to Moscow in 1972, discussed the United States Administration's theory of 'engagement' as applied to United States/Soviet relations.[2] According to this theory, the Russians were to be

[1] Not printed.

[2] In a despatch of 15 November 1972 Lord Cromer explained President Nixon's view that 'the aim of a stable international order, the object of the containment policy, must be pursued through the positive means of negotiation instead of confrontation'. Mr. W. Rogers, the then US Secretary

involved with the United States in a web of activities designed to develop a vested Soviet interest in cooperation in international affairs. Since then meetings between the President and Mr. Brezhnev have shown signs of becoming an annual event and, despite his domestic difficulties, Mr. Nixon will be keeping an appointment in Moscow on the 27th of June. It may be useful, therefore, to review the achievements of the policy and the prospects. While what follows was written before I had seen Sir Terence Garvey's despatch (DR 270/74) on US–Soviet relations of the 12th of June,[3] I am glad to see that the views from Washington and Moscow are not dissimilar.

2. The achievements of that first Moscow summit were not negligible. Agreements signed then and later—notable among the later agreements was that on the Prevention of Nuclear War of the 22nd of June 1973[4]—have led to US–Soviet contacts at many official levels and in unprecedentedly wide areas. Sensibly, specific but soluble problems involving the two countries have been tackled first. Where, as in the Strategic Arms Limitation Talks (SALT), the matter was too complicated for comprehensive solution at one bite, a portion (like anti-ballistic missile deployment) was isolated to be dealt with definitively, and provisional steps were agreed to control the other main element, the development of offensive missiles. A qualitative change in the overall relationship of the Soviet Union and the United States has undoubtedly occurred. Given these achievements and the prospect for further advances, how is it that the view is frequently met in the United States, that *détente* with the Russians is a sham? Why, indeed, are Soviet, as well as United States spokesmen, on the defensive; taking credit for past achievements while stressing the difficulty of reaching solutions to the far more intractable problems that remain? Have the basic objectives of the two sides changed since 1972 or are the underlying compulsions still there?

3. An immediate reason for the change in tone and in tempo is that the problems that remain are more complicated and fundamental than those that have been solved: the under-brush has been cleared away and the two sides are now tackling the wood itself. But the American attitude has been affected by other considerations. For example, the Soviet wheat deal in 1973, in which the Russians are popularly believed to have outsmarted the United States Government and to have purchased subsidised wheat in such large quantities that the price of bread was driven up for the United States domestic consumer, has caused Americans, within Congress and in the country generally, to question whether the Administration was sufficiently hard-headed in its dealings with the Russians.[5] Similar apprehensions, not necessarily justified, have also been heard about the SALT I agreement, the argument being that the United States deliberately gave the Soviet

of State, described this process of building 'a web of mutual interests and involvements whose very existence [would] become an incentive to the Communist powers to maintain a constructive relationship' as a policy of 'engagement' (AMU 2/3). Cf. Volume I, No. 97.

[3] No. 62.

[4] *V. ibid.*, note 10.

[5] See Kissinger, *Years of Upheaval*, pp. 246–8.

Union an advantage at that time, expecting reciprocal concessions in SALT II; and that these show no signs of materializing.

4. Perhaps more significantly, the October 1973 crisis in the Middle East, where the super-powers came closer than at any time since the Cuban missile crisis to being embroiled militarily, has raised the question whether, in matters of peace, as of trade, the Russians could be trusted not to press an advantage.[6] Soviet involvement on the Arab side (including, it is widely held, their later encouragement of the Arabs to maintain the oil boycott, and doubts about their attitude to Dr. Kissinger's meditation) has appeared to many Americans to be actively hostile to United States interests and contrary to the Russians' under-taking in the Declaration of Basic Principles signed in Moscow in May 1972,[7] not to obtain unilateral advantage at United States expense. The continuing Soviet military build-up in Europe feeds such anxieties. The intensification of repression in Soviet internal policy—the obverse of *détente* abroad—has been widely criticised here and has raised doubts about the morality of United States representatives hobnobbing with Soviet leaders. The view that the promotion of freedom abroad should be an aim of United States policy, has a long history and the issue of Jewish disabilities in the Soviet Union is one which arouses wide-spread sympathy. There is, therefore, sentiment on the side of supporters of Senator Jackson's amendment to the Trade Reform Bill, which would link action by the Soviet Government in this field to the grant to the Soviet Union by the United States of Most Favoured Nation status and of credits. But there would, in any case, be reluctance in some quarters to grant what some would depict as commercial favours to the Russians.[8]

5. The *impasse* over trade and credits illustrates the Administration's problems in fulfilling undertakings to the Russians in conditions where it lacks the support of Congressional and public opinion. It also reflects the fact that the Americans and the Russians have different goals and values, and that they are, and are seen to be, in direct competition for influence in many parts of the world. Optimists who considered that *détente* implied *entente* have been disappointed. Nonetheless, the leaders of the two countries have managed to lower the level of tension to the point where more frequent official contact is possible, indeed normal: and parallel—if not cooperative—efforts can be made in the search for political solutions. This is a valuable development although—as seen from Washington —the day when the Russians may be willing to be drawn into a cooperative endeavour to preserve international stability is still far off, despite the terms of the Agreement on the Prevention of Nuclear War which have so worried the French Government. Soviet approaches to the Americans for joint intervention in crisis situations have, at best, been scouted by the Americans, suspicious of the Russians' motives and anxious about the likely reactions of the NATO allies. (At worst, last October, the proposal for joint military action coupled with the threat of unilateral Soviet action otherwise, was met by rejection and military alert.)

[6] See No. 56, note 3.

[7] See Cmnd 6932, pp. 130–2.

[8] See No. 62, note 14.

6. This caution on the part of the United States is matched, American observers believe, by reduced eagerness on the part of the Russians. This is partly due to the fact that the Russians seem here to have attained their initial objectives. In Eastern Europe they have secured acknowledgement of the *status quo* and especially of the division of Germany. Recognition of the GDR has been achieved. Western Europe, the implications of whose many governmental changes and financial weakness are likely to be under review in Moscow, poses no military threat. Even the least sanguine Soviet analysts are likely to conclude that the overall European situation has some compensation for them, in that prospects for the development of political and military unity have been set back. The capitalist world as a whole faces financial and monetary problems, the result of inflation and, specifically, of the cataclysmic rise in the cost of energy, which will tax its ingenuity and fasten its attention on its own affairs. As for China, where Mr. Nixon's visit must have aroused fears that United States-Chinese relations would develop to Russian disadvantage, recent developments will have been reassuring. The Chinese precondition to further rapprochement with the United States has been made clear, that there must be progress over Taiwan; and for its part the United States, having extricated itself from 20 years of immobilism, is content with the modest level of contact with China so far achieved. For all these reasons then, as the Americans see it, the Russians may well see less cause for urgency than a year or two ago.

7. Yet the advantages both for the Americans and the Russians in consolidating and building on their improved relations remain. For the Americans, there is the basic need to reduce the dangers of confrontation which, in an era of nuclear parity, could lead to the devastation of the United States. There is also the hope of achieving a reduction in defence expenditure at a time when such expenditure, apart from intrinsic objections to it, is becoming increasingly difficult in political terms. Though there are differing emphases, these aims are largely common to both American political parties, to all factions in the Congress and to public opinion. Similar imperatives must operate on the Soviet side, though the circumstances differ. Specifically, in the United States' view, despite recent hints by Russian spokesmen of an intention to develop Siberian resources on their own, there will be little chance of the Russians narrowing the gap between Soviet and Western economic performance, unless they secure access, over a long period, to Western technology and finance. The task of Soviet economic managers will be made more difficult if no agreement can be reached, to limit the production and deployment of new strategic weapons and if, as a consequence, the quantity of resources preempted by defence is undiminished. But in the long-term, the basic security problems remain: the inherent opposition of the two systems; the need to ensure United States' acquiescence in what the Russians may regard as their proper sphere of influence (an argument that applies also, *mutatis mutandis*, to the United States); and their fear of China. As an underpinning to these considerations, the Americans, rightly or wrongly, set great store by Brezhnev's personal commitment to peace, which they believe derives from his experience on the Eastern front during the Second World War. As he

put it in his speech on the 14th of June '… the improvement in Soviet-American relations must go on … one must not also mark time'.[9]

8.   Both sides then may, for their different reasons, be approaching the outstanding problems with greater deliberation and caution. Nevertheless, while the final solution of those problems may be less urgent, the way in which the approach to their solution is handled will have immediate effects. Failure to make significant progress in SALT II, for example, could lead to new American programmes for strategic armaments, designed to 'match' the Soviet efforts, with the risk of escalating competition in this field. It should be in the interest of both sides to avoid such an outcome. But the difficulties have proved insurmountable so far. Mr. Nixon and Mr. Brezhnev may well have to content themselves with more modest goals when they meet in Moscow on the 27th of June: at best, a statement of the principles on which a MIRV[10] limitation agreement should subsequently be negotiated; an agreement to limit the scale of underground nuclear tests; and various technical and scientific research agreements. Failure to reach even these targets would strengthen the conviction of those in the United States who doubt whether the Russians are interested in genuine *détente* and who wish to preserve full United States autonomy in defence matters. But success, particularly in the field of MIRVs, would be a feather in Mr. Nixon's cap, something for which his critics profess to fear he might be ready to pay too big a price. According to United States sources, however, the Russians, who are well aware of the weakness of President Nixon's domestic position have not apparently sought to exploit this in negotiation. Moreover, any agreements the President brought back would be subject to the closest scrutiny in the Senate and elsewhere, where his critics are strongly represented. If he attempted to 'cut corners' in order to achieve something in Moscow to bolster his domestic position, he would quickly be exposed. Both he and Dr. Kissinger must be aware of this: indeed there is a school of thought here which believes that, in some respects, the President would be quite happy with only a limited agreement on SALT, in order to show that he had given nothing away.

9.   Sir Terence Garvey, in his despatch of the 12th of June,[4] has described Russian reactions to Mr. Nixon's domestic troubles and has suggested that Mr. Nixon's removal from office would revive Soviet doubts over future United States

---

[9] Moscow telegram No. 665 reported Mr. Brezhnev's pre-election speech of 14 June, in which the Soviet leader affirmed: 'One of the most important foreign policy events in recent years has been the turn-around in earnest relations between the Soviet Union and the USA … Progress in this is obvious … the improvement in Soviet-American relations can and must continue' (ENS 2/1).

[10] The development and deployment of these multiple warheads (see No. 58, note 2) complicated the pursuit of arms control since it meant that negotiators could no longer afford to concentrate on numbers of missiles launchers. By the terms of the SAL I Agreement of May 1972 (see Cmnd 6932, pp. 127–30) the US had acquiesced in having substantially fewer missile launchers than the Russians largely because its monopoly of MIRVs offset that disadvantage. But by 1974 the US administration was seriously worried by the prospect that new Soviet missiles equipped with MIRVs would raise the 'throw-weight' of Soviet Intercontinental Ballistic Missiles (ICBMs) to five or six times the US equivalent.

policy. His analysis accords with that of most American observers who argue that the Russians, in their concern for stability, will deal with whoever is in office in the United States, recognising, as we all must, the need to do business with the government of the day. President Nixon is a man with whom they have had business-like contacts in the past and whose continued commitment to *détente* cannot be doubted, though his failure so far to carry out his undertaking on Most Favoured Nation status must reduce his credibility in Russian eyes, however little practical value that status may now hold for them. No likely successor would be an improvement from the Soviet point of view. So despite the difficulties on both sides, the visit will go forward.

10. It is possible that there could be dangers here for the allies of the United States, who might find issues of moment to them being decided by the super-powers over their heads. The temptation to the US to make a deal, by conceding a point of little interest to them but of direct concern to the Europeans, might prove irresistible, especially to a President to whom a foreign success that would confound domestic critics would be a boon. So far, to their credit, both Mr. Nixon and Dr. Kissinger have resisted that temptation. It is true that whatever Mr. Nixon does in the field of *détente* will incur criticism at home, either for his being too soft in the pursuit of a success, or too tough in order to maintain the support of his right-wing on the Hill. That is the Watergate dimension. But in this case it operates to ensure caution, since of the two it is the need to keep his right-wingers happy which will be dominant. That said, it is only fair to make the point that, in my judgment, neither the President nor Dr. Kissinger have allowed domestic considerations to cloud their judgment of the substance of foreign policy. They have played straight with us over *détente*. For example, though I believe Mr. Nixon might personally welcome a Third Stage of the CSCE at the summit level, and though Dr. Kissinger would, I am sure, prefer to avoid difficulties with the Russians over what he considers to be peripheral issues, the Administration has been meticulous in its consultation of the Europeans on the point and has deferred to our views. I believe that they are, and will continue to be, alive to the need to carry the Allies with them. For our part, we must keep them up to the mark.

Conclusion

11. The policy described by my predecessor remains valid. As Mr. Nixon himself said, speaking to the United States Naval Academy on the 5th of June: 'Slowly and carefully over the past five years we have worked with the Soviet Union to resolve concrete problems that could deteriorate into military confrontation. And upon these bridges we are erecting a series of tangible economic and cultural exchanges that will bind us more closely together.' That remains the policy, despite the difficulties and discouragements. Progress may prove slower now than in the earlier days. Both sides may have reasons for caution. But it is significant that neither the Middle East war, nor the virtual exclusion of the Russians from the subsequent disengagement negotiations have stopped it. Both sides have strong reasons to persevere. It is in our interest that they should.

12. I am sending copies of this despatch to Her Majesty's Representatives in

Moscow, Paris, Bonn, the UK Delegation to NATO, Berlin, East Berlin, Warsaw, Prague, Budapest, Bucharest, Sofia, Belgrade, Peking and Ulan Bator.

I have etc.,
PETER RAMSBOTHAM

No. 64

Mr. Callaghan to Sir P. Ramsbotham (Washington)
No. 1374 Telegraphic [*WDN 21/4*]

Priority. Secret   FCO, *21 June 1974, 4.20 p.m.*

Repeated for information to Moscow, Routine to UKDEL NATO, Paris, Bonn, UKMIS Geneva (for CSCE delegation), UKDEL Vienna, UKDIS [*sic*] Geneva.

NATO Ministerial Meeting Ottawa 18/19 June: [1]
President Nixon's visit to the Soviet Union

1.   At the restricted session in the afternoon of 18 June Dr. Kissinger gave a comprehensive 'preview' of the President's forthcoming visit to the Soviet Union. He prefaced his remarks by saying that he proposed to speak with great frankness and that he relied on the allies to respect his confidence. He was accompanied by Rumsfeld [2] and Sonnenfeldt only.

2.   He was delighted that the President would be visiting Brussels before Moscow. Détente was no substitute for the Alliance. People should shed any unjustified fears they might have that the United States Government would consciously jeopardize their allies' interests, or would seek to cover new ground in areas of general allied concern, without full prior consultation. Nevertheless, if only for reasons of Western public opinion, it was essential to continue to work for real détente, to search for alternatives to confrontation, and to seek to bring the strategic arms race under control. If military technology continued to expand at a geometric rate security would not be enhanced: on the contrary the danger of military confrontation would increase.

3.   He was under no illusions about Soviet motives. The Soviet interpretation of détente differed from that of the West. Even so, the commitment of Soviet leaders to détente as they interpreted it did impose an 'element of restraint' on their actions. This did not mean that the Soviet regime would not go on seeking to build up their armed forces. Nor did it mean that other crises might not arise, as events in the Middle East had shown. But the pursuit of détente did improve the prospects of both 'crisis avoidance' and 'crisis limitation'. And where the Middle East was concerned, some of the problems which had arisen could

---

[1] NATO Foreign Ministers gathered in Ottawa to mark the Alliance's 25th anniversary with the issue of a substantial document reaffirming their common commitment both to the Alliance and to the aims and ideals set forth in the North Atlantic Treaty. See Cmnd 6932, pp. 182–6.

[2] Mr. D.H. Rumsfeld was US Ambassador to NATO, 1973–74.

arguably be attributed not to Soviet intransigence but to Soviet restraint. Most of the Arab Nations were currently critical of the Soviet Government on the grounds that in the name of détente, they had refused the Arabs all the military help they needed. In saying this he was basing himself on Arab sources, not Soviet ones.

4. He was sceptical of the over-simplified theory that there were 'good' and 'bad' elements in the Kremlin, with only the former favouring détente. He believed that the present Soviet leadership had a heavy collective investment in détente. But if their policy again failed to pay any dividends, the leadership might well succumb to pressures to go into reverse, and the effects might well be severe. He did not believe that the Soviet leadership were interested in 'peace' as an abstract concept. It was very much in the interest of the whole Alliance to create the maximum incentives for the Soviet leadership to pursue a moderate course and not to leave them with a sense of complete frustration deriving from avoidable actions on the Alliance's part.

5. He did not propose to discuss the CSCE or MBFR in restricted session. These were very much subjects for the whole Alliance, more appropriately discussed in plenary. Whatever the President might say on them while in the Soviet Union would be based on the Alliance consensus, not on any bilateral considerations. It was his intention to leave the President in Moscow after the official talks had concluded in order to brief the Alliance on them in Brussels early in July. He hoped also to have the opportunity to brief some of his colleagues individually in their own countries.

6. Dr. Kissinger then gave an account of certain specific subjects which the President expected to discuss while in the Soviet Union, namely:

(*a*) SALT[3]
(*b*) Possible agreement limiting underground nuclear tests.[4]
(*c*) Possible agreement banning 'environmental warfare'.[5]
(*d*) Economic, technical, and industrial cooperation, etc.[6] His comments thereon, and answers to specific questions are described in the four following telegrams.

---

[3] Dr. Kissinger said that the gaps between the US and Soviet positions were too wide to permit the conclusion of a comprehensive SALT II agreement at the forthcoming Moscow summit. According to Mr. Callaghan, the 'only possibility of specific progress he [Dr. Kissinger] foresaw in the early future was an "extension" of SALT I for two or three years coupled with some agreement on the limitation of MIRVs' (telegram No. 1375 to Washington of 21 June, ENS 3/304/1).

[4] After outlining the technical and political obstacles to such an understanding, Dr. Kissinger stated the American experts were presently in Moscow discussing a limited agreement banning tests in a certain range (telegram No. 1376 to Washington of 21 June, ENS 3/304/1).

[5] Dr. Kissinger thought in Moscow they would do no more than discuss this idea (telegram No. 1377 to Washington of 21 June, EMS 3/304/1).

[6] Dr. Kissinger was particularly critical of the US Congress's obstruction of a trade agreement with the Soviet Union, but foresaw some kind of arrangement on cooperation in this sphere (telegram No. 1378 to Washington of 21 June, ENS 3/304/1).

7. In conclusion, Dr. Kissinger repeated that the President would be embarking on his visit to the Soviet Union with no illusions. The Soviet leadership believed in 'objective factors', not least in military strength. The policy of the United States Government was to seek to build up a network of relationships designed to encourage moderation. But the United States Government were expecting no spectacular results to emerge during or immediately after the visit. The Allies need fear no surprises and should not expect any startling announcements.

8. Many delegation leaders, and the Secretary-General, expressed their appreciation of Dr. Kissinger's exposé. In so doing I said that the magnitude of the problems which he had described, notably in the SAL field and also in that of nuclear testing, were to some extent beyond the range of the rest of the Alliance including the United Kingdom, for all that we had a degree of expertise. Politically I agreed generally with Dr. Kissinger's conclusions. But we should remember that the Soviet Union, with about half the United States GNP, spends at least as much as the United States on its armed forces. One could but hope that the Soviet leadership would come to spend less on arms and more on the welfare of their people. For even moderately contented people were not apt to be keen on military adventure. But actual Soviet policies made it essential to maintain our defences in Europe, not least the conventional United States presence there. (Dr. Kissinger nodded assent.)

9. I added that I was sure the Council would wish to give Dr. Kissinger a mandate, not that he needed it, to pursue his policies as he had described them, as a trustee for the Alliance and for the peace of the world.

10. Several Ministers asked Dr. Kissinger for his estimate of the impact of the Chinese factor on Soviet attitudes. His comments thereon may be summarised as follows:

(*a*) Historically, the intensification of Soviet-American relations had preceded the United States 'apertura' towards China. But he had no doubt that the wish to avoid confrontation on two fronts was a significant factor in Soviet political attitudes towards the West, even though the Soviet Union lacked neither the men nor the equipment to man both fronts.

(*b*) In the strategic field, the Chinese factor exerted both a positive and negative effect on Soviet thinking. Positively, it was an inducement to the Soviet leadership to negotiate seriously. Negatively, the Soviet leadership were apt privately to ask for 'bonuses' because of the problems they faced with others, unnamed.

11. In view of Dr. Kissinger's emphasis on secrecy, addressees should treat this and the following telegrams as being for the information of themselves and senior members of their staff only.

12. See M[y] I[mmediately] F[ollowing] T[elegram]s (not to all).[7]

---

[7] See notes 3, 4, 5 and 6 above.

No. 65

Minute from Sir. J. Killick to Sir. T. Brimelow
[*ENS 3/304/1*]

Confidential. Eclipse   FCO, *15 July 1974*

US–Soviet Relations

1.   I assume that the Secretary of State's understandable injunction that we should not let critical comment on the outcome of the Moscow visit[1] get to the press does not mean that we must not formulate a clear assessment of the position for our own internal purposes. The following is mine, in the light of the things said at Ditchley last weekend[2] (where I found some of my non-official American friends privately pretty critical of Dr. Kissinger's methods and approach. Even Cy Weiss[3] was at pains to say he had some differences with Hal Sonnenfeldt, which means in fact with Dr. Kissinger). I do not see any grounds for amending what I said in my minute of 4 July[4] commenting on the pre-visit despatches from Moscow and Washington.

2.   To take the positive side first, I agree very much with the assessments made from Moscow. In brief:

(*a*)   The relationship has now taken on an appearance of 'reasonable maturity and stability'. The continuation of these exchanges seems assured.

(*b*)   The further creation of a network of mutual vested interests has continued, with some welcome and healthy diminution of past somewhat frenzied attempts to find spectacular agreements to sign on each occasion. This latest meeting was more of a 'working' occasion, although certain significant new agreements were reached.

(*c*)   There seems again to have been some collateral progress on matters such as Jewish emigration, as well as incidental benefit in terms of freer exchange of basic technical information related to strategic arms and nuclear testing and

---

[1]   i.e. the visit of President Nixon to the Soviet Union (see Nos. 62 and 63).

[2]   During the weekend of 12–14 July Sir J. Killick attended at Ditchley Park one of a series of study group meetings devoted to examining the meaning and effect of *détente*.

[3]   Mr. Seymour Weiss was a member of the State Department's Policy Co-ordination Staff. In July he was appointed US Ambassador to the Bahamas.

[4]   In this minute to EESD, written after reading Nos. 62 and 63, Sir J. Killick stated that while he agreed generally that Soviet policy towards the USA was firmly anchored in Soviet national interest, he was inclined to feel that there was more room than Sir T. Garvey seemed to believe for 'quite significant changes—quantitative if not qualitative'. He also argued that a concerted EC approach to relations with the Soviet Union would make more sense than a bilateral one. 'But', he added, 'even a concerted European approach would fall short of the truly "global" approach (both geographically and in terms of e.g. overall strategic military capability) which is the distinguishing feature of the US/Soviet relationship, and which makes it so difficult for the two, and for other countries, to distinguish clearly between legitimate pursuit of special "superpower" interests and "condominium".'

of the impact on the Soviet scene of Western information media, including the President's television address.

3.　This list is probably not exhaustive. However, my main concern is to bring out my disquiet at certain other aspects which I find disturbing. Broadly, I agree very much with the leading article in the *Neue Zürcher Zeitung* of 7 July, which states the principle that if a politician is to retain credibility, he should 'say what is, and not say what is *not*'. The Russians do a great deal of the latter. President Nixon seems to have joined them. As the *Neue Zürcher Zeitung* says, this amounts to an illusory assessment of the position and prospects. Specifically:

(*a*)　In the communiqué, the Americans have once again lent their names to the concept of 'peaceful co-existence',[5] this time without the qualifications which were included elsewhere in the 1972 Statement of Principles, and which were then cited in defence of this American gift to Soviet propaganda, although there is admittedly still a clear link with the Principles.

(*b*)　The formula about CSCE used in the communiqué is, as we have analysed it, almost pure Soviet doctrine.[6] Although Dr. Kissinger used a quite different (and more nearly standard Western) formula in his press conference in Moscow, and has assured us that the US side does not consider it has given anything away, it is the communiqué which the Russians will henceforth use. The Americans do not seem to have gained anything in return for using Soviet language; we do not know what they may in addition have said to the Russians. They have always told us that CSCE is, for them, anything but an 'outstanding event' of 'historical significance'. The Russians will certainly now believe, with some justice, that they have a potential, if not an actual, ally in bringing CSCE to an end on something much closer to their own terms.

(*c*)　Since his return from Moscow, President Nixon has talked as though he regards détente as already irreversible, and has even referred to the establishment of a basis for 'permanent peace'. Not only does this fly in the face of the facts (and even Mr. Brezhnev has not gone so far), but it is in total contradiction to Dr. Kissinger's expressed views. For example, he told the NATO Council that détente could not survive unless there was some restraint on Soviet defence spending.

4.　Since we have hitherto been assured that neither the President nor Dr. Kissinger has any illusions, who is fooling whom? There are already some signs of a split between the two (*Sunday Telegraph* of 14 July)[7] and this was foreseeable last December, as the President's anxiety to use foreign policy to bolster his domestic position seemed likely to clash with Dr. Kissinger's strategy and tactics.

[5]　See *Public Papers: Nixon*, 1974, pp. 571–2.

[6]　See Volume II, Nos. 89 and 91.

[7]　David Adamson, the newspaper's Washington correspondent, reported growing concern in the US capital over signs of a rift between President Nixon and Dr. Kissinger following the publication on 13 July of the Final Report of the Senate's Watergate Committee (*The Sunday Telegraph* of 14 July, p. 1).

The rift between the latter and Mr. Schlesinger over SALT is already apparent.[8] However this may be, I do not suppose that the Russians are fooled, although they will no doubt try to extract all they can, and for as long as they can, from the President.

5.   The danger, as I see it, lies in the effects of the President's exaggerated line on US and other public opinion. It can obviously give a boost to Mansfieldism and to trends in Europe towards reductions in the defence effort. On the other hand, it risks equally strengthening the hands of those in the US who are sceptical of détente, and who can prevent or inhibit further progress in important directions, whether in trade and economic cooperation or in SAL. American business is already sceptical enough. These effects, which are not necessarily mutually exclusive, could involve setbacks for Mr. Brezhnev and for Soviet confidence in the US, the establishment of which, in the longer term, is one of Dr. Kissinger's main aims. So I find it very difficult to see what useful purpose is served in either US domestic or foreign policy terms by what the President has done. I do not even exclude some growth in scepticism about détente in Europe; for example if 36 heads of state or Government meet to sign a lot of paper which many people will regard as inadequate in terms of Basket III.

6.   Unfortunately, the last trend, even if it emerges, seems unlikely to lead to any willingness to contemplate the improved defence effort in Western Europe which is called for if the Soviet Union is not to emerge significantly stronger in political terms, from all this—even if, or perhaps especially if, Brezhnev survives it. In this connexion, I begin to find Dr. Kissinger's obsession with SAL somewhat morbid.[9] I do not seek to belittle the importance of the problem, but some of his more apocalyptic deductions from any failure to reach US/Soviet agreement seem open to question (as Mr. Thomson acknowledges in his minute of 12 July).[10] At the same time MBFR is on the 'back burner' in his mind, and there seems to have been no useful discussion in Moscow of either this or of the Middle East which, with SAL/MBFR are (I suggested in my minute of 4 July) the main foreseeable threats to the continuation of the process of US/Soviet

---

[8]   See Kissinger, *Years of Upheaval*, pp. 1157–9.

[9]   As expected, during the Moscow summit no new permanent agreement on offensive missiles was reached. The two sides did, however, agree to work towards a new arrangement dealing with both quantitative and qualitative limitations. In a despatch of 10 July Mr. Dobbs reported that Dr. Kissinger appeared to have achieved in SAL, 'not the "conceptual breakthrough" for which he was hoping in March, but a qualitative breakthrough in communication and mutual perception between the two strategic super-powers'. See No. 62, note 17.

[10]   Mr. Thomson observed in this minute to Mr. Acland that Dr. Kissinger must have found the Russian line in his recent Moscow talks 'discouraging though probably not hopeless'. If, however, Dr. Kissinger failed to achieve a bargain with the Russians in the next few months whereby they limited their MIRV development in exchange for a continuation of the SALT I limits on numbers and types of nuclear launchers, Mr. Thomson thought this would increase the possibility of strategic instability and lead to a continuation of the strategic arms race at a fairly strong pace. 'My conclusion', he added, 'is that there is little we can do in this situation except to keep close to both the Americans and the Europeans in SALT matters, to guide our Allies towards a sensible nuclear package in MBFR and to the extent we can, help Dr Kissinger to pursue his original SALT policy' (DP 11/2).

détente.[11] Presumably SAL has priority as *the* subject which justifies the super-power bilateral relationship.

7. I begin to wonder if we should start thinking privately about the possible consequences of a breakdown in the US/Soviet relationship, with or without the disappearance of the President and/or Dr. Kissinger.[12] Would this necessarily imply anything other than a reversion to the situation before May 1972? Could Western Europe, in such circumstances, continue to pursue a détente policy of its own in East–West relations? How effective could this be unless on the basis of fully-concerted European Community action? Would the latter imply a more effective European defence policy and effort?

8. P.S. This was all written before Cyprus,[13] which also contains the seeds of a US–Soviet clash.

[11] Sir J. Killick argued in this minute (see note 4 above) that he could not see how the process of US/Soviet *détente* could be successfully continued until and unless 'essential equivalence' in the strategic sphere could be permanently established. He also felt that it would be politically impossible for the Russians to sit back and do nothing in the Middle East, and that a fresh crisis there could seriously threaten the development of the Soviet/US relationship.

[12] After President Nixon's resignation on 9 August (see No. 62, note 22), Dr. Kissinger remained Secretary of State and, until October 1975, National Security Adviser.

[13] On 15 July Greek-officered units of the Cyprus National Guard overthrew the Government of President Makarios of Cyprus, and five days later Turkish forces landed on the northern coast of the island (cf. Volume II, No. 97, note 2). British reactions to the ensuing international crisis will be documented in a subsequent volume.

No. 66

Paper by Mr. Hattersley for Mr. Callaghan

[*ENS 2/20*]

Confidential   FCO, *30 July 1974*

Relations with the Soviet Union and Eastern Europe

Introduction

1. You asked me to examine the current relations between Great Britain and the countries of Eastern Europe. A subsequent minute from Mr. McNally[1] described how you would like that examination to be conducted. Mr. McNally's minute referred both to your speech in the House of Commons on 19 March ('We shall look for opportunities to build a safer and more productive relationship

[1] Mr. T. McNally was Political Adviser to Mr. Callaghan. In a minute of 25 March Mr. McNally reminded Mr. Hattersley that during a recent visit to Bonn Mr. Callaghan had 'announced his determination to seek an improvement in East/West relations in general and Anglo/Soviet relations in particular'. The minute further stated that, with this in mind, Mr. Callaghan wanted Mr. Hattersley to prepare a general position paper.

with the Soviet Union')[2] and to comments on the same subject during your visit to Bonn.

2. I was asked to examine the present state of MBFR negotiations, assessing in particular the British negotiating position and any difference between that position and the attitude of our allies, and to make a similar examination of progress within the CSCE. I was also asked to assess the state of bilateral relations between Great Britain and the Soviet Union placing particular emphasis on the prospects for increased trade and comparing, where appropriate, our record with that of our allies.

3. I have had a number of discussions with Sir John Killick and members of the Eastern European and Soviet Department and the Western Organisations Department.[3] A number of papers have been provided for me, some of which are annexed to this paper.[4]

4. A good deal of time was spent in discussing Soviet motives. Although there was some disagreement over the details of departmental analysis, there was a general agreement that Soviet policy was intentionally inimical to Great Britain and her Western allies.[5] There was, however, substantial disagreement about what response is appropriate to the accepted Soviet position. I fear that too often in the past the Foreign Office has confused the maximisation of British interests with the minimisation of the interests of the Soviet Union. A paper related to this point was prepared by Mr. Orchard and is attached at Annex A.[6] I do not claim that Mr. Orchard is in general support of the point above but you will see from his paper that whilst he predicts that 'Soviet foreign policy will, for as long as we can foresee, be formed by an ideology which dictates hostility towards the West' he discusses the possibility of Soviet self-interest being 'stimulated and encouraged by the West' in a way which serves the British purpose better than the maintenance by the West of a purely defensive posture.[7]

---

[2] *Parl. Debs., 5th ser., H. of C.*, vol. 870, cols. 858–9.

[3] Work on the paper began following an Office meeting convened by Mr. Hattersley on 8 April. Mr. Bullard observed in a minute to Mr. Goulding (Private Secretary to Mr. Hattersley) of 24 April: 'I believe that the successful conduct of relations with the East requires from Britain not so much the adoption of some grand strategy, but the skilful and patient assembly of small ingredients in the right proportions and at the right moments.'

[4] Not printed.

[5] 'It is', Mr. Bullard observed in a minute to Mr. Murrell of 23 April, 'part of our standard doctrine that one of the basic aims of Soviet foreign policy is progressively to change the balance of power in favour of Socialism' (ENS 2/1). But in a letter to Sir T. Garvey of 14 June he noted that, while Mr. Hattersley found it difficult to argue with the 'standard British analysis of Soviet objectives', Mr. McNally was 'more inclined to see Soviet aims in Western Europe as merely the mirror image of Western objectives in Eastern Europe'.

[6] In his paper at Annex A, a minute to Mr. Bullard of 14 June, Mr. Orchard expressed his personal belief that the West could 'get onto a footing of improved and, lastingly better, relations with the Russians', and that this should now be attempted 'in case Russian preponderance increases or their present relatively reasonable behaviour changes'.

[7] 'Any conceptual framework for new policies or improving old ones should', Mr. Orchard observed, 'not "revisit" the philosophies of 1949 but attempt to abolish remnants of former "containment" and "cold war", put in political and temporal perspective the constructive as well

5. I take the view that traditionally the Foreign Office has believed that adequate protection against military and coercive pressures from the Soviet Union and her allies could only be obtained by adopting a purely defensive posture. The assumption accepted in too many minds is that protection of British interests requires a policy which is static in two senses. First, there is a reluctance to move from the established position, even on the details of policy. This has produced a tendency for other Western European countries to be in the forefront of detente. That tendency has been reinforced by the second assumption, namely the belief that it is dangerous to initiate policies towards Eastern Europe rather than to react against initiatives that are from them. I believe that our best interests may be served by activity.[8]

6. One unavoidable inhibition of UK initiatives is the need to remain a loyal and responsible member of the Alliance. It would be intolerable were we to seek to promote new individual policies which were either against the interests of our allies or constructed without reference to them. But whilst we must march in step with the Alliance there is no reason why we should not influence the pace at which the entire formation moves. I believe we should play a more creative and constructive role within our partnerships. In part this would be achieved by altering the details of some of our policies. But we need to make it clear that we no longer regard ourselves as the sheet anchor of defence against the hurricane of detente. That was certainly the role Lord Carrington believed Britain should occupy within the Alliance. We need to make it clear both internally within the government and privately to our allies that that is no longer our position.

7. Detente can be pursued in two ways: first within the multilateral negotiations set up for the purpose, and secondly through bilateral initiatives. I turn first to the two East/West negotiations in which Britain is directly involved.

Conference on Security and Cooperation in Europe
8. As you know we are now engaged on a review of the Western position following Dr Kissinger's initiative on the subject.[9] We hope thereby to obtain a clearer idea of our objectives and what can realistically be achieved. When Dr Kissinger was last here you gave him a list of 'general objectives' for CSCE

---

as the adversary elements in Soviet intentions and place strategic doctrines in a context of "détente", realistically understood.' He further proposed that future Western policies be based on two main themes: (a) the enlightenment of Soviet self-interest and provision of 'incentives for its development and permanence'; and (b) the reinforcement of incentives 'with a network of agreements and institutions which could inhibit adversarial behaviour and enlarge Soviet responsibilities'.

[8] In a minute to Mr. Goulding of 4 June Mr. Bullard noted that they might have to consider how best to convey to Mr. Hattersley the point that there had been 'a certain continuity in British policy towards the East which transcend[ed] changes of Government in London'. He added: 'To seek for "new" attitudes and initiatives may be an understandable emotion, but it confuses the issue by obliging officials to ransack their minds and cupboards for types of action which have never previously been thought to be in the British interest, but which would now be so represented. Naturally these do not exist.' A note by Mr. Goulding of 11 June indicated that Mr. Bullard made his points openly to Mr. Hattersley at a meeting on 10 June.

[9] See Volume II, No. 89.

(Annex B).[10] That list should be regarded as a statement of aims. Many (perhaps most) of the objectives can be realised. But failure to achieve all that the paper sets out should not be regarded as failure for this stage of the Conference. In the meantime it may be worth looking at the four outstanding issues which most concern Britain. (I think we can now assume that the declaration of principles will be broadly satisfactory):

   i   Basket III
   ii   Military confidence-building measures
   iii The level at which the final stages of the Conference should be held
   iv How the work of the Conference should be continued

   9. *Basket III.* We must face the fact that we are unlikely to get all or even most of what we want. The problem is that the Russians maintain that the accumulation of small improvements in personal freedom that Basket III would involve is an attempt to erode the authority of the Soviet Government and mount a propaganda exercise against the Soviet system. We have in the past insisted that a judgement about the success of the CSCE must be based on what we can achieve in Basket III. I am sure we must continue to press for the best result possible, including using our bargaining card of an eventual summit meeting a great deal more toughly than President Nixon seemed to use it during his recent visit to Moscow. But we should be careful not to judge the Conference by its failure to produce results which it was never reasonable to expect. To do so would make it more difficult to build in future on such modest progress as is eventually achieved.

   10. *Military Confidence-Building Measures.* In the discussion on the declaration of principles, the West has already accepted the Eastern proposal that the inviolability of frontiers should be one of the 10 principles guiding the behaviour of European states. It will however be confirmed elsewhere that frontiers can be changed by peaceful means and by agreement. We had hoped that following this understanding on inviolability of frontiers, the Russians might be willing to make concessions on questions of interest to the West. There has been no sign of such willingness.[11] Apart from Basket III, discussed above, little progress is being made on confidence-building measures. The Russians have categorically refused to consider the prior notification of major military movements. The Americans are also opposed to this measure, although they are at present prepared to lend some tactical support to it to preserve Western cohesion. Nor has there yet been real progress on the prior notification of major military manoeuvres, though the differences between East and West look bridgeable. However it is the usual Soviet practice to delay concessions until the last minute. I am sure that we must continue to work to get what we can from our proposals, tactically over the prior notification of movements and substantially on the prior notification of manoeuvres.

   11. *The Level of the Third Stage.* The formal Western position has been all along

[10] Not printed, *V. ibid.,* notes 7 and 9.
[11] Cf. Volume II, Nos. 72 and 78.

that the level of Stage III should depend on the results of Stage II. In fact most of us have been ready to admit that the eventual decision on the level of the third stage will be taken in the light of other factors as well, including the state of East/West relations generally at the time. President Nixon has long been out in front of the other allies on this point. He is probably less concerned with the success of the CSCE than with the failures of his own Presidency.[12] While I am opposed to a summit declaring a bogus triumph and deeply reluctant to become a party to an exercise designed to improve President Nixon's deteriorating reputation, we are I think agreed that it is inconceivable that we should stand out against a proposed summit meeting. The mere existence of the CSCE in the form of multilateral East/West dialogue is an achievement which 10 years ago would have seemed impossible. Its direct results may prove small, but the spin-off could be considerable. There is of course the risk that by creating the impression that detente has moved further and faster than it really has, we shall encourage dangerous complacency in the West. However I believe a properly managed summit could avoid such a danger.

12. *Follow Up.* This brings me to the question of the arrangements to continue the work of the Conference after it is over. If the Conference is a failure then there will be nothing to follow-up. But if we assume a modest result there would be advantage in having some forum in which we can build on whatever has been achieved, not least because the idea of a Consultative Committee was conceived (although in different circumstances) by the last Labour Government. I do not believe the machinery should be too formal, nor comprehensive. Meetings could take place in different capitals as the Romanians have advocated. They could be related to a probationary period on the lines of the Western proposal. But the probationary period should not be as long as three years. We should play an active part in working for such a solution on these lines. As the results of our recent approach in Washington show, much hard work will be needed to carry the Americans with us.[13]

13. I am conscious that this account is somewhat discouraging. So far the CSCE has been mainly notable for its by-products. At the Conference itself there has been, in spite of everything, an interesting multilateral dialogue from which both sides—and perhaps still more the neutrals—have learnt a lot. The notion that the nations of Europe could sit down to discuss freer movement of peoples, ideas and information would have seemed bizarre only five years ago. Secondly, the Nine have developed the habit of working together at the Conference, and have become, partly because the Americans held back, the mainspring of the Western effort. Throughout the long months of bargaining the Nine have stuck together and place a high value on their continued cooperation. I am sure we should continue to play our full part in this common effort. It is perhaps the most successful example of Political Cooperation and one which the Americans have welcomed from the start.

14. *Mutual and Balanced Force Reductions.* Potentially this area of detente offers

[12] *V. ibid.*, Nos. 77 and 89.
[13] Cf. Volume II, No. 80.

more practical prospects than the CSCE. The issues with which it is concerned have more serious and direct application: the prospect of security and the actual materials by which security is preserved. They have to be examined in the knowledge that the United Kingdom is certain (under a Labour Government) to make substantial reductions in defence expenditure; that some of these reductions must be made within NATO; that *several* of our NATO allies are contemplating reductions in their European forces. There is clearly much to be gained from a successful MBFR which includes at an early stage reductions by all NATO nations. This means that the MBFR talks should reach a successful conclusion in sufficient time to enable the reductions under consideration by members of the Alliance to take place within the MBFR framework.

15. Our predecessors saw themselves as a NATO 'sheet anchor' on MBFR. They wanted on the one hand to help the Americans cope with internal pressures for reductions, and on the other to draw attention to the dangers and dissuade the Europeans from jumping too quickly on to the bandwagon. But the alternative to reckless progress is not necessarily the 'deadlock' or 'snail's pace' which the head of our delegation to the MBFR talks told me was a fair description of the current state of play. And I believe Britain could do more, within the Alliance, to help the negotiations along.

16. I am not, of course, suggesting that we should be on the look out for possible Western concessions, nor that we should regard it as the responsibility only of the Western side to ensure results. We must bear in mind that MBFR affects the interests of our European allies, and especially the Germans, even more closely than our own. We should therefore be careful not to press upon our allies obligations affecting their forces or territories which they are unwilling to accept. That said, our interest is in making progress in the negotiations and in involving ourselves in any reductions which emerge.

17. Moreover the interests of the Alliance require that the negotiations should be successful. It is worth noting that the CDS [14] believes that 'the danger is, given the inevitably slow pace of these complex negotiations, that Western Governments on both sides of the Atlantic will lose patience and undermine our negotiating stance by going for unilateral reductions'. We must ensure that the negotiations do not get so bogged down as to cause this to happen.

18. We need therefore to consider how to instil greater momentum into the talks. Although informal discussions between delegations have enabled the two sides to explore each others' position in a useful way, real negotiations have yet to begin, and it seems unlikely that much progress will be made unless both sides show greater flexibility.

19. The Russians have so far shown virtually none. Many believe that they are waiting for the CSCE to be got out of the way before getting down to serious business. But whether this is right or not, I believe they have their own reasons for wanting MBFR to succeed: they have a vested interest in the maintenance of stability backed by the presence of both super-powers in Europe; they would probably welcome anything which inhibited the development of new defence

[14] Chief of the Defence Staff.

arrangements in the West in the event of American disengagement and at the same time gave a measure of permanence to their own arrangements in Eastern Europe; and they might, at least in the long run, welcome a reduction of forces for the same sort of reasons as ourselves.

20. For our part an MBFR result on the basis of something like the Allied proposals would enable us, as you once said in the House of Commons, to sleep more soundly at night. The question is to distinguish the essential from the inessential parts of the Allied position. There are some points, for example the need to resist 'national sub-ceilings', on which no concessions could be made; but there would be little progress if we remained committed to all the details of our proposals of 20 November 1973.

21. The response of the Warsaw Pact countries to these proposals has shown that their two main concerns are;

(*a*) to ensure that all Western participants, not just the Americans, are committed to reduce their forces from the outset;
(*b*) to bring air forces and nuclear weapons within the scope of the negotiations.

We have already gone some way to meet the first of these preoccupations. As far as reductions of non-US NATO participants are concerned, our negotiators have already offered a series of assurances about the link between our suggested two phases of MBFR. These include the important statement that in the event of a satisfactory Phase I agreement (including the concept of a common ceiling) the ground forces of all non-US Western direct participants (excluding Luxembourg) would be reduced in Phase II. We should be prepared to strengthen these assurances, perhaps even to the point of eventually blurring the distinction between the two phases of MBFR so as to provide for something like the staged implementation of a single agreement.

22. We should also be prepared to be forthcoming about the inclusion of nuclear weapons. The repeated impression I received in the United States was that the American Government increasingly accepted that a nuclear 'make-weight' would be needed to persuade the Soviet Union to accept disproportionately large reductions in its ground forces. (The present Allied proposal is that the first phase of MBFR should consist of a reduction of 68,000 men and 1,700 tanks on the Soviet side and a reduction of 29,000 men on the American side.) If, as we are told, the Soviet Union is massively superior on the ground and slightly inferior in the nuclear area, we ought to be able to construct an acceptable asymmetrical model including nuclear weapons, and thus avoid an outcome whereby the weaker opponent became yet more weak as a result of proportional reductions.

23. The details and timing of the inclusion of a nuclear element in MBFR will need careful working out and we must continue to work closely with the Germans and Americans on it. But 'working with' does not mean following behind them. I think it will be necessary, for reasons of public presentation and to avoid setting a dangerous precedent for SALT, to have some element of

reciprocity in nuclear reductions. But this would not mean that nuclear reductions would have to be equal; it might for example be possible to negotiate a freeze on certain Soviet systems in return for Western reductions in equivalent systems.

24. If, as I suggest, we can show flexibility in two of these areas (eventual reductions by all direct participants and nuclear weapons), not necessarily in the immediate future but when the time seemed right, I think we might have the key to real progress. We may find it necessary to modify the details of our ground force proposals. We are not for example wedded to the figure of 700,000 which we have proposed for a ground force common ceiling, and it may be that a different form of parity—e.g. a common ceiling on the overall total of ground and air force manpower—might be more palatable to the Russians. But we should stick to the idea of a common ceiling on ground forces, even if sweetened by other inclusions. It is what Kissinger has called 'the iron pole' of the negotiations. Once we let go of it we would put our whole position at risk. It is moreover politically attractive; it can be justified in terms of the agreed objective of 'contributing to a more stable relationship'; and I think that there is a reasonable prospect that the Russians may be brought to accept it.[15]

25. The British approach to MBFR is of course only part of the Allied approach. We have to work out things with our allies, and in particular the Americans and Germans, before putting proposals to the Russians. But an approach on the lines set out above would, I think, enable us to play a more active part in the discussions within the Alliance. It would also better reflect the realities of our own national interests, and incidentally remove any ground for accusations that we were the foot-draggers in the Western camp.

Bilateral Relations

26. The Soviet Union is susceptible to the style adopted by the West. If we are to improve bilateral relations it will be necessary for us to show a visible enthusiasm for detente. This implies both improved relationships and increases in trade. Mr. Kosygin told Sir Terence Garvey that 'the last Government had not paid enough attention to the development of economic relations. It was a competitive world and given Britain's lack of desire to cooperate the Soviet Union had to go elsewhere.'[16] A great deal of time and effort will have to be spent promoting personal contacts and mounting individual efforts.

27. One of the most significant areas in which such initiatives can be mounted is the area of Ministerial and official visits. There is no doubt that Eastern European countries take such visits extremely seriously and regard them as an indication of good faith and enthusiasm.[17] Fortunately they will often accept

[15] In a minute to Sir J. Killick of 2 August Mr. Bullard pointed out that he did 'not share Mr Hattersley's confidence that the Soviet Union [might] find it advantageous to sign an agreement on MBFR'.

[16] Record of meeting between Mr. Kosygin and Sir T. Garvey on 16 May enclosed in letter from Mr. B.G. Cartledge (HM Counsellor in Moscow) to Mr. Bullard of 20 May (ENS 3/548/2).

[17] Mr. Bullard noted in a submission to Sir J. Killick of 21 March regarding the development of bilateral relations with East European countries: 'The dilemma is that relations with the socialist states require a high input of governmental effort to compensate for the lack of contact through

senior Civil Servants as substitutes for Ministers, other than the Secretary of State. There is very considerable scope for increased visits at what the Soviet Union and its allies call Deputy Foreign Minister level. The Foreign Office should try positively to encourage visits to and from Eastern Europe by Ministers associated with trade. We should ask the Department of Trade, the Department of Energy, the Department of Industry and possible the Ministry of Agriculture to consider with us a scheme of carefully planned visits to Eastern Europe for their Ministers and senior officials.

28. In preparing this policy we ought to realise that the influence we have on Eastern Europe and their relationship with us is bound to be affected by their judgement of the political and economic strength of the UK. You will have seen intelligence reports and other assessments of the Soviet Union's reaction towards the policies of the new Labour Government. Any demonstrations that we remain a strong partner in NATO, a close ally of the United States or a permanent member of the EEC and that we are solving the Irish crisis will encourage Eastern European countries to take us more seriously. It may be that we can never achieve the special position enjoyed by France, Germany and the United States in our trade and political relationships with the USSR and its allies. But we can avoid some of the self-inflicted wounds which are caused in part by our inability to solve our economic difficulties and in part by what has been our ambivalence towards the United States and may now become our detachment from the EEC. A firm position in all our Western partnerships will be an important ingredient in establishing a successful relationship with Eastern Europe.

29. Whilst it is important to stimulate British industry into increasing normal commercial initiatives with Eastern Europe, the problems of doing business with state trading countries are such that the Government must give a lead to private industry and organise its progress towards improved exports. Formal discussions with the CBI[18] followed by an FCO/DOT[19] sponsored conference on 'Trading with Eastern Europe' might well start the ball rolling. But a single initiative will not in itself be sufficient. We need to create within the Government a mechanism by which progress can be monitored and, where necessary, further stimulated. Perhaps the Foreign Office should chair an official committee which could co-ordinate continued activity on this front. Alternatively we could take up the idea of a National Trade Corporation which Sir Rudy Sternberg has mentioned to you and which is at present under study in the Department of Trade.

30. One view, of course, is that the possible increase in trade with the Soviet Union and its allies is so small that time and effort might be more profitably spent on other countries who are more receptive to our trade initiatives. To that argument there seem to me to be two answers. The first is that if Britain is to surmount its economic difficulties industry and government must find the time

private channels: but that exchanges have a built-in tendency to develop beyond what is feasible for the diaries of British Ministers, or appropriate to the state of relations with the country concerned' (EN 2/4).

[18] Confederation of British Industry.

[19] Department of Trade, successor department to the DTI.

and energy to mount trade initiatives in every possible field. The second is that trade promotion with Eastern Europe ought to contain a second benefit as well as its commercial advantage, namely the relaxation of tension, the promotion of detente and therefore the prospect of reduced armament budgets which would provide advantages to the UK not obtainable through increased trade with South America or Iran.

31. Because of the constitution and organisation of Eastern Europe, it is likely that the most favourable response to attempts to achieve improved bilateral relations will come not from the Soviet Union itself but from its Eastern European allies. But there are certain rules which ought to govern our attempts to improve bilateral relations with all members of the Warsaw Pact. The first is the understanding that whilst we should, and must, talk about the general plan for improving East/West relations the real success of the plan will be determined by the methodical application of small initiatives, each of which is carefully worked out to ensure that it is particularly suitable for the country at which it is directed. At Annex C is a list of 'nuts and bolts' prepared by the Department.[20] I recommend that each one of these initiatives be pursued as part of our overall strategy.

32. You included in my remit the task of comparing Britain's trade record with Eastern Europe with that of her Western allies. A table at Annex D[21] shows that our regular adverse balance compares most unfavourably with the success achieved by the United States, Germany and France. I find myself unable to judge whether their success and our comparative failure is wholly the result of factors outside our control or whether the undoubted natural advantages that those countries enjoy have been maximised by their governments at a time when governments in the UK were failing to minimise our disadvantages. Certainly the British trading position looks worse than it is because many of the raw materials we import from the Soviet Union are later exported in a semi manufactured state. Certainly the United States has achieved trading success because of its size; Germany has a favourable balance because of its geographical position; France has done well because of her willingness to abandon the Alliance position in a way which would be wholly unacceptable to the United Kingdom. Notwithstanding that, however, I believe that application of the right spirit and the right detailed policies could improve our trading record, as it could improve the political atmosphere that exists between the UK and Eastern Europe.[22]

---

[20] Annex C lists political visits to the Soviet Union and Eastern Europe for which dates had to be fixed; visits by Ministers from other Government Departments which might be stimulated; technical agreements which might be signed; and other projects which might be encouraged or followed-up.

[21] See note 4 above.

[22] In a letter to Mr. Dobbs of 18 July Mr. Bullard explained that Mr. Hattersley had dropped from his paper three points which officials had earlier contested: 'that we fall into the error of supposing that every Soviet move forms part of their unflinching pursuit of the goal of world Communism; that success or failure in trade with the East is caused exclusively by political attitudes; and that in the mass expulsions of September 1971, we lost far more than we gained'.

Conclusion

33. The construction of a 'policy' for improved East/West relations is a difficult exercise. The result has little shape and no intellectual elegance. It can only consist of the definition of an objective, the statement of a strategy and a list of large and small initiatives which are united by the single fact that they contribute to the objective's achievement. The policy objective you defined in the House in March: 'a safer and more productive relationship with the Soviet Union'.[23] The strategy I advocate is the acceptance that British self interest is often best served by activity and a willingness to initiate movement rather than respond to the proposals and policies of others. The initiatives I advocate appear in those parts of the body of the paper which deal with CSCE and MBFR (paragraphs 8 to 25) and in Annexes B and C.[24]

---

[23] See note 2 above.

[24] Mr. Callaghan noted on the paper that he accepted Mr. Hatterley's 'line of approach' and that he would be glad to follow up his conclusions and proposals regarding MBFR and bilateral relations (minute from Mr. P.J. Weston (Assistant Private Secretary) to Mr. Hattersley of 27 August). He also agreed that they should be guided by the 'themes' suggested by Mr. Orchard (see note 7 above). But at a meeting called by Mr. Hattersley on 9 September to consider the next steps, the general feeling was that nothing could be done until the domestic situation (an impending General Election) had been clarified. Meanwhile, Mr. Hattersley endorsed Mr. Bullard's suggestion that he (Mr. Hattersley) should propose to Mr. Callaghan a short conference of Heads of Mission in Eastern Europe in the autumn. 'This', Mr. Bullard concluded in a letter to Sir T. Garvey of 10 September, 'is a rather foggy outcome to what has throughout been a rather foggy exercise. I hope that in practice it will prove satisfactory.'

In a letter to Sir T. Garvey of 21 November, written in answer to a complaint from the Ambassador that he had not yet seen Mr. Hattersley's paper, Mr. Bullard observed that the status of the paper was 'a little ambiguous'. Mr. Hattersley had promised officials that they should be given a chance to express dissenting views, either to him in connexion with the final draft or direct to Mr. Callaghan. This had not, however, happened, and the paper still contained 'quite a lot with which officials disagreed'. As a result Mr. Callaghan had never heard the counter-arguments. 'I am not', Mr. Bullard added, 'particularly anxious to give Mr. Hattersley's paper the status of accepted policy, and for this reason I have not circulated copies abroad. The importance of Mr Hattersley's efforts, in my view, lay in the fact that he became convinced of the need to be more active towards Eastern Europe, and in the practical steps which have now been set in motion following his meeting with the Secretary of State on 4 November.' These 'practical steps' included the organisation of Ministerial visits to and from the Soviet Union (minute from Mr. Weston to Mr. Bullard of 5 November, EN 3/548/2).

No. 67

Letter from Mr. Bullard to Sir T. Garvey (Moscow)

[*EN 2/18*]

Confidential   FCO, *31 July 1974*

My dear Terence,

Trends in the Soviet Union and Eastern Europe

1.   I am grateful for the 12 very interesting replies which I received to my letter of 3 May.[1] It may be convenient if I try to draw the threads together before the summer break.

2.   I should say first of all that my letter was not meant to be a complete substitute for the Conference of Ambassadors. The questions raised in the reply from Bonn are indeed very well worth discussing,[2] together with many others which did not find a place in my restricted theme.

3.   I accept the point made in several replies that if there is disappointment with the part played by the East European countries at the CSCE, it is because some of us pitched our hopes on this point unrealistically high. Paragraph 10 of Anthony Elliott's letter of 11 July[3] sets out in pretty unanswerable form the arguments of self-interest which have discouraged the East Europeans from taking a more independent line. His adjective 'cynical' must certainly figure in any list of common characteristics of the East European régimes. The CSCE has been highly instructive for everybody. It seems to me that each side has been a good deal more successful in its defensive or negative than in its offensive or positive aims. The West has not succeeded in opening up significant gaps between the East European states, or between these states and Moscow; nor are we likely to open many of the gates of which President Kekkonen spoke at the first stage in Helsinki;[4] nor is there going to be much improvement of the procedures for the handling of personal cases, circulation of foreign newspapers etc. On the other side, the Russians have not had much success in splitting NATO, nor in creating the exaggerated euphoria in the West which we at one time feared (there is more boredom than anything else) nor in canonising their one-sided definition

---

[1] See No. 57. By 31 July replies had been received from the British Embassies in Belgrade, Bonn, Bucharest, Budapest, Moscow (No. 60), Paris, Prague, Sofia, Warsaw and Washington, UKDEL Vienna (No. 16) and UKMIS Geneva.

[2] Amongst the subjects that Sir N. Henderson would have liked to have seen a conference discuss were, according to his reply of 29 May (see No. 16, note 8): the 'balance-sheet' of *Ostpolitik*; West Berlin and the workings of the Quadripartite Agreement; and Soviet aims towards the Germanies.

[3] In this letter Mr. Elliott stressed with regard to the CSCE that the Soviet Union's East European allies 'would not step out of line with the Russians in any field unless there [was] a divergence of interest and they [saw] a real potential gain'. They were, Mr. Elliott thought, well placed to know how limited the Russians intended the practical results of the CSCE to be, and therefore had 'good reason to be cynical about it'.

[4] Mr. U.K. Kekkonen was President of Finland. Cf. Volume II, No. 42.

of détente. The only one of the positive Soviet objectives which seems likely to be achieved is the consolidation and semi-legalisation of the *status quo*—multi-laterally, I mean, since they had already secured this bilaterally through the FRG's Eastern treaties. Even this is to some extent a paper tiger, since outside Germany there is no serious wish to change the *status quo* anyway.[5]

4. If neither East nor West has achieved its ends, what are we to say of the neutrals? Having re-read Derick Ashe's very persuasive letter of 9 July[6] I am prepared to concede that I was too hard on Romania. After all, the Romanians have given the world the principle of rotation and the phrase 'outside military alliances'—both innovations which have been more helpful on the whole to the West than to the East. Perhaps Romania should also take some credit for the principle of consensus, although there may have been no serious alternative to this. I certainly acknowledge that if the Romanian challenge to Moscow looks less conspicuous, it is at least partly because this has become part of the accepted landscape of Europe. But Soviet acceptance of Romania as 'our France' may pigeonhole the problem in more senses than one.[7] I see no sign of any part of the Romanian example being copied by her neighbours, any more than the Yugoslav example has caught on elsewhere in Eastern Europe during the last 25 years. The racial and linguistic distinctness of Romania perhaps makes it easier for the rest of the régimes in Eastern Europe to draw aside their skirts from Ceausescu's experiment. When you come down to it, the Romanian policy of partial non-cooperation with the Warsaw Pact and their very selective participation in CMEA may be as important as anything Ceausescu is doing in the political field—especially in times like the present, when the lack of instant and unquestioned land communications between the Soviet Union and the frontier of the Warsaw Pact in Bulgaria is surely far more serious for Soviet generals than the 'Economist' was prepared to concede in its article on this subject 3 weeks ago.

5. I will not go over the ground country by country. I acknowledge the justice of many of the points made by individual posts. My own letter was an attempt to take a general and very summary view. I recognise in particular the justice of

---

[5] In a minute to Mr. S.J.L. Wright (EESD) of 27 August Sir T. Brimelow commented on the file containing Mr. Bullard's correspondence with HM Ambassadors in Eastern Europe: 'Many thanks. An interesting file. But were we in the FCO ever enthusiastic about the CSCE, or sold on the MBFR? The view of Mr Michael Stewart [Secretary of State for Foreign and Commonwealth Affairs, 1968–70] was that we could not afford to appear negative, which is not the same thing as being optimistic or enthusiastic.' Mr. Bullard added on 2 September: 'I believe that in some quarters expectations went further than this.'

[6] Mr. D.R. Ashe was British Ambassador in Bucharest. In his letter to Mr. Bullard of 9 July he argued that while Romania's conduct in the CSCE and the MBFR talks might be 'peripheral to the main stream of events', there was still 'some advantage for the Western cause in having Romania with her non-conformist ideas at these meetings rather than just another docile member of the Eastern bloc'. And he felt that the Romanians should be given credit for the 'courage and success of their general resistance to Soviet pressure'.

[7] Mr. Ashe observed (*v. ibid.*) that Soviet influence in Romania was surprisingly limited. 'Certainly', he reported, 'the Soviet Embassy say that it is, ruefully shrugging off Romania as "our France" in NATO/Warsaw Pact terms.'

Frank Brenchley's point about the divergence of attitudes between the peoples and the régimes in Eastern Europe[8] (not exactly a new thought, but it gets lost sight of from time to time), and I like Eddie Bolland's phrase about the brighter side continuing very slowly to grow larger on the dark Communist moon.[9]

6. As to the future, I agree with Frank Brenchley that all we can do is plug away with bilateral relations and wait and see. I share John Wilson's impression that the East Europeans will always speak more freely in bilateral than in multilateral meetings.[10] On Basket III in general, the East Europeans have all been saying privately that the problem is not with them but with Moscow. While they have publicly lined up with the Russians at CSCE itself, we can only hope to develop relations under this heading more fully with them than with the Soviet Union once the Conference is over. It may be a long time before anyone proposes a repetition of the CSCE on anything like the same scale, although I would not bank on this. But I sense a general acceptance of my thought that the Conference may prove to have given us a 'benign umbrella' under which bilateral contacts can continue to flourish. I do not think any of this is inconsistent with the Secretary of State's thoughts about continuing machinery.

7. In another sense, however, the multilateral phase of détente is evidently going to continue. The workings of the EEC are increasingly impinging on our own relations with the countries of Eastern Europe, Romanian tomatoes and Polish bacon being only 2 most recent examples, and beef an example of another kind. In his visits to Eastern Europe John Killick has noticed a definite fear that the EEC will in practice turn out to be a selfish economic animal, whatever the protestations of its individual members. (This point is often put in the form that the policies of the Community are harder towards Eastern Europe than those of its individual members, or alternatively that Community policies can be no more than the lowest common denominator of individual policies.) A similar trend is discernible in Comecon. The Sofia meeting seems to have given a new impulse to integration within CMEA,[11] but this would not be acceptable to the East European members if it were not for the advantages (pointed out by Frank Brenchley) of relative insulation from the typhoon now blowing in the markets of the free world. We must surely hope that some sort of relationship will continue

---

[8] In his letter of 7 June (see No. 60, note 2) Mr. Brenchley stated that it went without saying that the majority of people in the satellite countries would welcome greater independence from the Soviet Union. But, he added, party leaderships, uncertain of popular loyalty and cautious and defensive in their approach to most problems, surely must see their best hopes for their personal survival in office 'in close cooperation with and reliance on the Soviet Union—the only force that in the final analysis can sustain them'.

[9] Mr. Bolland argued in his letter to Mr. Bullard of 28 May (see No. 57, note 18) that Bulgaria's development and the 'practice of *détente*' made Bulgaria more stable and a more peaceful and cooperative member of the international community. 'Thus', he wrote, 'as I see recent trends here, the brighter side continues very, very slowly to grow larger on the dark Communist moon.'

[10] See No. 60, note 2.

[11] The CMEA held its 28th session in Sofia during 18–21 June. Special urgency was accorded to cooperation in fuel and power supply, and the unification of Eastern Europe's electricity grid and the development of exchangeable power supplies were approved.

between the members of the Community and those of Comecon, so as to minimise the damage which would result to both Western interests and the cause of true détente if the incompatibility of the 2 systems were allowed to work itself out unchecked.

8. I had hoped to be in a position by now to say something more definite about future British policies. The Cyprus crisis[12] has not after all prevented Mr. Hattersley from finalising his paper on relations with the East,[13] but this has not yet been considered by the Secretary of State or discussed with officials. Meanwhile, the Soviet performance over Cyprus has not, I think, been without effect on thinking here.[14] In any case we face a period of 2 or 3 months during which the Parliamentary situation here will make it pointless to discuss new lines of policy, and difficult even to pursue existing ones.[15] This illustrates the problem which we in London face in drawing up any kind of logical scheme for East–West activities to match the document which, for example, the Poles have told us that they put together every autumn for the coming year. It surely follows that when favourable conditions exist, we ought to make the maximum use of them. I think we can claim to have done this throughout 1973, and perhaps 1975 will be another such year. A Conference of Ambassadors in say November, by which time the political situation here will presumably have been clarified, could fit in quite well with this. At some stage in the process we must review all the Country Assessment Sheets, starting with those for posts which are due to be inspected first.[16]

9. I owe Nicko Henderson an answer to his paragraph 7, about trade.[16] I think that during recent years the exaggeratedly political explanation of the ups and downs in East–West trade which one hears from time to time may have forced me into a more extreme position than it is really possible to hold. I agree entirely with the points made in John Wilson's letter of 5 June, quoting his Commercial Secretary,[17] and I hope that he and others may accept the line of the enclosed general summary of the problem which I prepared in June with the help of the DOT for inclusion in Mr. Hattersley's paper (where it was not in fact used). It is one thing, however, to acknowledge the relevance of the political climate to trade; quite another to endeavour deliberately to manipulate the former for the supposed benefit of the latter.[18]

10. I hope to deal separately with Murray Simons' points about the US–Soviet relationship.[19]

11. I have found this a very useful exchange of views, and I am grateful for the time which busy Ambassadors have devoted to it.

Yours ever,
J.L. BULLARD

[12] See No. 65, note 13.

[13] No. 66.

[14] Soviet diplomats were particularly critical of the declaration which, following the Turkish military intervention in Cyprus, the British helped mediate between Greece and Turkey at Geneva. The Russians obstructed the early meeting of the UN Security Council on 30 July to discuss its implementation, and on 31 July Mr. Hattersley warned Mr. Lunkov that HMG would 'regret and

resent' any Soviet action at the UN which would make it more difficult to achieve a constitutional settlement of the crisis (telegram No. 521 to Moscow of 31 July, WSC 2/522/2).

[15] Since the February General Election no party had had an overall majority in Parliament.

[16] In a letter of 29 May (see note 2 above) Sir N. Henderson drew attention to what the Russians might hope to secure from trade, the importance of it to them, and the extent to which the direction of trade could be deflected for political reasons.

[17] In this letter Mr. Wilson cited the views of Mr. A.J. Payne (First Secretary (Commercial), HM Embassy, Budapest) that total British export figures were made up of the turnover of individual companies, many of which achieved in Eastern Europe a significant percentage of their total sales, and that this was an area in which the help of Government services was needed and more appreciated than elsewhere.

[18] In his enclosed draft summary note Mr. Bullard remarked that although it was self-evident that trade flourished better in a warm political climate than in a cool one, 'political factors [were] not easily quantified ... and [seemed] not to be the main determinant of trade'. Sir T. Garvey commented on this point, in a letter to Mr. Bullard of 20 August, that he thought it possible to identify certain features which, 'if not strictly "quantified"', at least contributed to a preciser understanding of the political factors governing Soviet commercial behaviour. 'Size of contracts awarded is', he maintained, 'an obvious indicator.' But, he added, the 'commercial prizes are never likely to be high enough for UK economic self-interest to become the primary determining factor in our political relationship with the Soviet Union'.

[19] See No. 57, note 20.

No. 68

Letter from Sir J. Killick to Sir P. Ramsbotham (Washington)

[ENS 3/304/1]

Confidential. Eclipse   FCO, *4 September 1974*

Dear Peter,

Isolation versus Hegemony

1.   We have read your despatch of 2 July[1] with the greatest interest. (Nicholas Gordon Lennox[2] has explained that the delay in thanking you for it in no way implies the contrary).[3] It arrived at precisely the right moment, when we were

[1] In this despatch, 'Isolation versus Hegemony', Sir P. Ramsbotham focussed on Dr. Kissinger's concern that Europe had misunderstood the direction of the political and economic forces affecting US foreign policy, and his assertion that Europeans had more to fear from a resurgence of isolationism in the USA than from an American attempt at hegemony, such as the French claimed to perceive. Sir P. Ramsbotham concluded that although there were 'isolationist tendencies' in the USA, even with a Democrat-dominated Congress and, possibly after 1976, a liberal-Democrat President, a return to the full-scale isolationism of the 1930s was unlikely. 'As for hegemony', he observed, 'in the sense that it means leadership, it is surely desirable that the United States should exercise this, in partnership with her European allies. In the sense that it implies a desire to impose her will regardless, I agree with Dr Kissinger that this is not a threat' (AMU 2/2).

[2] Lord N. Gordon Lennox was Head of North America Department.

[3] Lord N. Gordon Lennox explained to Mr. R.H.G. Edmonds (AUS) in a minute of 19 August that action on Sir P. Ramsbotham's despatch had been delayed by leave absence and the Cyprus crisis.

engaged in a vigorous discussion within the Office about the problems with which it deals. We were indeed on the point of writing to you to sum up the correspondence between Julian Bullard and Murray Simons (Bullard's letter of 3 May to Garvey[4] and Simons' reply of 20 June refer) about US/Soviet relations.[5] I propose to deal with the issues raised in that correspondence in this letter.

2.   In Bullard's letter he mentioned Denis Greenhill's objections to the word 'bilateralism' to describe the US/Soviet relationship and to the development of that relationship over the last eighteen months. He added: 'Nowadays the only doubt is whether "condominium" is too strong a word to describe it.' Murray Simons expressed surprise at this and it may be useful if I set out in more detail what we had in mind.

3.   We had come to the conclusion even before the Presidential transition that 'condominium' *is* too strong a word to describe the actual US/Soviet relationship, whether before or since the latest Summit Meeting of the two leaders. The emphasis by the Nixon/Kissinger team on their bilateral relationship with the Russians is not surprising—as you say, it is inevitable that the approach of two super powers to international problems, and their relations towards each other, should differ, and differ widely, from that of middle-ranking powers with narrower interests, although Washington may sometimes see these interests as narrower than they really are. It is also to be expected that Dr. Kissinger will see diplomatic problems principally in terms of their implications for the super-power relationship, which has become, and for the foreseeable future will remain, the yardstick of American foreign policy.[6] To take the most recent example, I am sure you will agree that he saw, and still sees, the Cyprus crisis in important respects in these terms. But it is abundantly clear from my talk with him on 27 August that he continues to reject any suggestion from the Soviet side of joint action in crisis situations such as this.[7] It is also to be expected that Kissinger will regard himself as the best—and perhaps the sole—judge of how the United States should deal with the Soviet Union, and with major crises affecting US interests. Sometimes he will do this to the point of forgetting or deliberately overlooking the fact that Europe is also trying to deal with the Soviet Union on many of the same questions, and that major crises affect European interests too. This leads him to expect that Europeans will keep out of certain affairs until and unless he decides that they have a rôle to play which will assist his activities, and not merely get in the way. This attitude showed very clearly during the

---

[4]   No. 57.

[5]   *V. ibid.*, note 21.

[6]   In a minute to Sir J. Killick of 7 August Mr. Cable argued that while the view of the two superpowers 'getting together in any real sense to rule the world' was a French bogey that should be dismissed, Dr. Kissinger regarded the 'adversary relationship' with the Soviet Union as the 'overriding international problem' whose management took priority over other considerations and constituted the touchstone for determining US policy on issues the British and others were inclined to judge on their intrinsic merits.

[7]   During talks with Sir J. Killick in Washington on 27 August regarding Cyprus, Dr. Kissinger stated that the US 'would "in no circumstances" act as joint guarantor with the Soviet Union of any Cyprus settlement' (Washington telegram No. 2820 of 27 August, WSC 1/16).

negotiations following the Middle Eastern war,[8] and is at the bottom of much of the recent private and public criticism—e.g. over the Europe/Arab dialogue— which he has levelled at the Europeans.[9] Similarly, he may from time to time expect America's allies to soft-pedal other subjects, such as CSCE, when this suits his purpose.

4.   One of the main difficulties in dealing with him is that he is not always willing, or conscious of the need, to give a sufficient explanation of his require-ments. His methods of operation, and particularly his emphasis upon personal diplomacy and secrecy, inevitably lead to justifiable complaints about lack of consultation, and to exaggerated suspicions of his motives (which, to judge from his remarks about Europe's relations with the new Greek Government, are reciprocated!) The extent of the sheer muddle caused by his working methods should not, I think, be underestimated. Moreover the bureaucratic machine beneath him, often unused to and ignorant of his thinking, frequently proves unable to help straighten things out. I was very struck, at my meeting with him on Cyprus on 27 August,[10] by the evident fact that a good deal of what he was saying to me was also being heard for the first time by many of his officials. But I accept that Kissinger has made a genuine effort to improve his lines of com-munications with the Allies since last October, even if his methods of consultation often mean no more than that the Allies are informed.

5.   The CSCE provides a particularly good example of Allied difficulties in working with him. The United States delegation to NATO played by far the largest part in drawing up the paper which formed the substance of the Western position in the opening stages of the Conference (the contribution of the Nine when they entered the game was largely confined to tactics and organisation). It was therefore surprising to hear from Dr. Kissinger in Ottawa that the Americans had never wanted the CSCE, that they regarded it as a mistake, and that they had only gone along under pressure from the Europeans.[11] He has an extra-ordinary capacity for refining his thinking without always seeming to notice that he has done so; perhaps the activity of the US delegation to NATO reflected only the attitude of the 'bureaucracy'. At all events, Kissinger seems to have forgotten, or conveniently overlooked, that US agreement to CSCE was the price he had to pay for the Soviet commitment to MBFR. In any case, the US/Soviet com-muniqué after the Moscow summit endorsed, presumably with his agreement, the Soviet view of the 'historic significance' of the CSCE; and this is on the face of it incompatible with the line which the Americans were taking in Ottawa and

---

[8] Sir P. Ramsbotham suggested in his despatch of 2 July (see note 1 above) that the action of the USA and the Soviet Union in seeking to regulate the affairs of the Middle East, an area with which other powers were vitally concerned, 'might be thought to approximate more closely to the posture of a diktat which the Chinese or the French like[d] to draw'. But this he considered a 'distortion' since the Europeans had lost their capacity to influence either Arabs or Israelis, and Dr. Kissinger 'had no choice but to carry the burden alone'.

[9] Cf. Volume II, No. 81, note 6.

[10] Cf. note 7 above.

[11] See Volume II, No. 89, note 3.

before. The Moscow communiqué was a good deal closer to the language of the Warsaw Pact communiqué of mid-April than to that of Ottawa. Inevitably this led to suspicions of a sell-out amongst America's allies which Dr. Kissinger's subsequent explanations (which amounted to saying 'never mind the communiqué, listen to what I am telling you') have not entirely allayed.[12]

6.   The American performance in Moscow over the CSCE has to be set beside other doubts about Dr. Kissinger's tactics. At first he went out of his way to present his approach to relations with the Soviet Union in the context of triangular politics, emphasising that he would be doing business with Moscow from a cool distance and with a hard head. The less than evident strength of the US-Peking axis has however weakened the American hand, and thrown a spotlight on the US-Moscow axis. The United States' bargaining position was probably further weakened (though not necessarily seriously) by Nixon's need for international success as his chances of avoiding or surviving impeachment diminished.

7.   The current American analysis of Soviet policy is not quite clear to me. Kissinger in Ottawa criticised 'some Western politicians' for taking a tough line towards the Soviet Union, and emphasised the risk that the Russians might return to a harder line in East/West relations.[13] I do not know of any evidence which would support this idea, and the general Western assessment (as expressed for example at the APAG[14] meeting at Sesimbra[15] in June) would surely be that the Russians have in the short term no reason to depart from their present policies towards the West, and indeed no real alternative to these. The Soviet reaction to Nixon's departure and to Ford's accession strongly supports this view. If the Americans have reason to think differently they should make a better job of explaining their view to us. It is their failure to do so which caused Allied confidence to waver.

8.   Kissinger is presumably still focussing on SALT, and on what he sees as the need—publicly emphasised in Moscow—to get agreement in the next 18 months. During his visits to NATO and to London following Moscow he showed what seemed to me to be an almost morbid preoccupation with the subject—and with the consequences of failure to reach agreement. He told the NATO Council that he did not see how détente could survive unless there were some restriction on Soviet military spending. When he speaks of the Russians returning to a harder line in East/West relations, does he perhaps mean 'being more obdurate in SALT'? If so, the question arises how far Soviet willingness to sign a satisfactory SALT agreement will be affected by progress on other questions on the East/West agenda, such as the CSCE. My answer to this would be that a series of major rebuffs for the Russians in their dealings with the West might affect their *Westpolitik* sufficiently to strengthen the hands of those in the Soviet Union who do not like SALT; but that it would be wrong to assume that Western concessions at the CSCE or elsewhere would have a positive effect on SALT. The Soviet military

[12] *V. ibid.*, No. 89.

[13] *V. ibid.*, note 8.

[14] NATO's Atlantic Policy Advisory Group.

[15] A fishing village and resort on the Costa de Lisboa, Portugal.

establishment are surely going to insist that SALT are handled on their merits, as they see them. I suspect that Kissinger's personal inclination is rather different, and that—a new President and a new Congress permitting—he would like to make everything smooth sailing for the Russians on what he may see as peripheral issues during the eighteen months which are held to be crucial for SALT. If so, the result would be in effect to extend the US/Soviet special strategic relationship into fields which are less legitimately and clearly bilateral, and—in the absence of American reassurance—to increase the anxiety of her allies.[16]

9.   I accept the conclusion of your despatch that 'in the sense that hegemony means leadership, it is surely desirable that the United States should exercise this in partnership with their European allies'. I am less certain that 'in the sense that it implies a desire to impose their will regardless … it is not a threat'. There are good *a priori* reasons why we can accept US assurances of good faith to their allies in their dealings with the Soviet Union. Broadly speaking, American objectives ought to coincide with our own so far as our ultimate security is concerned. But it is in all our best interests that the Americans should see that these simple truths command general acceptance in Europe, and that 'partnership' should not in practice become a relationship in which the junior partner always defers to the senior when they disagree. When it comes to substance, furthermore, as I suggest in the preceding paragraph, other important European interests do seem to be put under some threat when Kissinger subordinates them to his major objective.

10.   Nor is there any certainty that Kissinger's tactics will always suit us. Our experience of working with him in the past gives us cause for concern that there may too often be a tendency not to explain his views adequately, and to ignore or fail to give a proper hearing to Allied points of view. We cannot do much about this, except to continue to work as closely as we can with and on him and his team (as you have been doing so successfully) in the hope that he will recognise that it would be a mistake to overlook the interests of America's allies for the sake of marginal or tactical advantages in his negotiations with the Soviet Union. I believe he is ready to listen to those who are prepared to argue with him clearly and cogently.

11.   When we started drafting this reply we wondered whether one of the main immediate dangers lay in the possibility of exclusive American concentration on détente (the *locus classicus* is Nixon's speech in July on his return from Moscow).[17] It is this sort of thing which fans European suspicions and makes people use emotive phrases such as US/Soviet Hegemonism. We can no doubt expect an improvement under Ford: as you pointed out in your telegram No. 2628,[18] he has

---

[16]   On the US domestic debate on SALT II, Sir P. Ramsbotham wrote (see note 1 above): 'We cannot expect to influence this debate and the United States must be the best judge of its security, on which our own depends. But we can, I think, reasonably assume that no United States Administration will settle for arrangements which, in the eyes of their defence experts, would jeopardise the safety of the United States.'

[17]   Cf. *Public Papers: Nixon*, 1974, pp. 578–82.

[18]   In this telegram of 8 August Sir P. Ramsbotham reported that in foreign affairs Mr. Ford would no doubt leave a great deal to Dr. Kissinger. Sir P. Ramsbotham thought that Mr. Ford would

less reason than Nixon to plug the achievements of détente and may be less ready to push specific measures in support of détente through Congress, if they arouse too much opposition there. We shall be interested to see how far he inclines towards Pentagon thinking on issues such as SALT. On the other hand, he will certainly wish for the time being to maintain continuity with Nixon's foreign policy, upon which he has laid so much stress. It is too early to guess how his own rather simple views on foreign affairs may evolve, and what specific effect his concern to cooperate with Congress, in particular, may eventually have on Kissinger's policies. We shall no doubt get a better view in some months, after the Congressional elections. But we should welcome whatever preliminary thought you may have in the meantime.

12. I was grateful for your clear analysis and conclusions about the growth of isolationism. It shows how very little substance there was, or is, in Kissinger's dire warnings to the Europeans about the risk of its resurgence. The antithesis between Isolationism and Hegemony is clearly a false one. It is all the more false because both words are emotive, and neither fits the facts. No-one I think here would suggest, Jobert-like, that the United States is somehow hell-bent on achieving a partnership with the Soviet Union to rule the world, and to keep her less powerful allies in their highly subordinate place. But the present leadership of the United States and the way in which Dr. Kissinger exercises it, makes it clear that the 'genuine partnership' is one in which the United States is very much the senior, and the Europeans the junior.[19]

13. It would be nice if we could avoid the use of words which carry undesirable overtones. It is the Europeans who indulge themselves by the use of the word 'hegemony' and the Americans who keep so loosely referring to 'isolationism'. The latter phenomenon might perhaps better be described as a desire for significant withdrawal from overseas commitments and the role of world policeman. Two things strike me about it. The first is that insofar as an American administration continues to pursue an active foreign policy it must presumably to some extent be swimming against a tide of grass-roots opinion which must be reflected in the Congress. It will be interesting to see what the mood of the Congress is following the mid-term elections; I imagine that it is common ground that President Ford is liable to be more responsive to it than Kissinger might like in some respects.[20] The second point is that I do not see how the further development

---

in principle want to continue with *détente* and the new policy towards China, though it was doubtful if he would be willing to expend much credit in Congress on pushing forward *détente* against domestic opposition. 'In consequence', he added, 'we might well see a period of marking time in United States-Soviet relations' (AMU 1/2).

[19] Yet, as Sir P. Ramsbotham noted in his despatch (see note 1 above), the once fashionable view that Europe and Japan were becoming economic superpowers in their own right had been dealt a severe blow by the energy crisis, which had underlined the strength of the USA and the vulnerability of Europe and Japan. Events had demonstrated divisions within the EC, which had been exposed 'as being still an agglomeration of states of differing interests and strengths rather than a cohesive unit'.

[20] Sir P. Ramsbotham had assumed that, whatever the outcome of the Watergate affair, Dr. Kissinger would remain 'the decisive voice' in formulating US foreign policy. He also reminded

of the US relationship with the Soviet Union will in fact enable the United States to become less involved in the outside world, although this is presumably Kissinger's aim. I have no doubt that the Soviet intention is to expand its world influence as an equal of the United States and to establish what might fairly be called a dual hegemony in managing world affairs. There is a wealth of evidence—most recently over Cyprus—of Soviet attempts to move the United States in this direction. I cannot totally exclude the possibility that they might succeed at least in some areas—functionally if not geographically. This will surely *ipso facto* commit the United States more deeply in the outside world. On the other hand, if the relationship does not prosper, the Soviet Union will certainly not give up its attempts to expand its influence and, except in the now unlikely event of the United States acquiring a President of the McGovern[21] type, no American administration will surely be able to afford to allow the Soviet Union to continue its expansion of its influence unchallenged.

14. I much look forward to the continuation of this correspondence. Perhaps we might aim at reviewing the situation first following Kissinger's visit to Moscow in October[22] and secondly following the mid-term elections if there is any significant identifiable new mood in the Congress.

Yours ever,
JOHN KILLICK

Mr. Callaghan (*v. ibid.*), 'it should not be forgotten that, despite Watergate (and indeed as the reaction to Watergate has shown) the United States remains a moralistic, moralising, if not always a moral, nation. The Puritan ethic is still there; and the concept of American responsibility to help others worse off in the world has not disappeared, even though it may be less prominent than before.'

[21] Senator G.S. McGovern was Democrat candidate in the US Presidential elections of 1972.

[22] On 22 October, the day of Dr. Kissinger's departure for Moscow, Sir P. Ramsbotham reported in Washington telegram No. 3443 that the Secretary of State was leaving 'in an atmosphere less febrile and more measured in its expectations of any progress in détente than that which surrounded President Nixon's trip in the summer'. And according to Sir P. Ramsbotham, Dr. Kissinger's intentions about the linkage between SALT, MBFR and CSCE remained opaque. 'He should', Sir P. Ramsbotham insisted, 'not be allowed to ignore West European sensitivity on this score, but neither should the West Europeans overlook the possibility that he may succeed in using the concept of linkage to Western advantage. If his talks in Moscow develop satisfactorily, Kissinger may quite possibly explore with the Russians the implications for SALT and MBFR of introducing nuclear systems into the latter, but we have been assured that the US stand on FBS's will remain unchanged.'

No. 69

Sir T. Garvey (Moscow) to Mr. Callaghan

[*ENS 2 / 1*]

Confidential   MOSCOW, *18 September 1974*

Sir,

Détente and Secretary-General Brezhnev

1.   Americans, as reported in Sir Peter Ramsbotham's despatch of 15 August,[1] are asking themselves whether détente as practised by President Nixon's Administration was in the interests of the United States of America. Russians, though less prone to heart-searching in public, have I believe, grounds for at least entertaining similar doubts about its impact on the interests of the Soviet Union.

2.   One does not have to be what the analysts are pleased to call a Soviet hardliner to note that all is not as it should be. Even for those not wedded to economic autarky, the commercial content of détente demanded a considerable act of faith. Interdependence may imply 'US dependence on Soviet raw materials': it also implies Soviet dependence on US technology and hardware. The act of faith would be easier to make if more specific engagements were demonstrably being fulfilled. But, on one important point, the Russians may reasonably consider they have been let down. One of the original bargains struck by President Nixon in 1972 was that in return for the payment of outstanding lend-lease debts, Soviet goods entering the USA should receive Most Favoured Nation treatment. However, as a result of amendments by Messrs. Jackson and Vanik to the Trade Bill, not only has MFN not been granted, but more importantly from the Soviet point of view, US firms find it increasingly difficult to obtain Ex-Im Bank credits for bi-lateral trade with the Soviet Union.[2]

3.   Besides, the suggestion that, in order to help the US Administration over its internal difficulties, an annual quota of (at least) 45,000 Soviet Jews should be granted exit visas amounts to a massive intervention in Soviet internal affairs. The proposal would have more credibility in Soviet eyes were it not clear that, with the current level of unemployment in Israel, the Israeli Government would have the greatest difficulty in accommodating such a number. The Jewish case is dangerous too as an example to other minority groups. The Volksdeutsche (both the Volga Germans and those from the Baltic States) are now organising themselves into pressure groups on the same lines as the Soviet Jews and clearly hope that by means of pressure through Bonn they will be allowed to emigrate. If they

---

[1] In this despatch Sir P. Ramsbotham pointed out that President Nixon's June visit to Moscow had intensified the debate in the USA over the merits of *détente*. He explained that, while the majority of Americans still supported the search for *détente*, there was considerable criticism of detailed aspects of the policy, such as the export of grain to the Soviet Union and the forging of other economic links at a time when the Soviet authorities were repressing dissidents, curtailing free speech and restricting emigration (AMU 2/2).

[2] See No. 62, note 14.

succeed, who comes next? In the context of Basket III in the CSCE negotiations, pressure from a number of Western countries has been mounting in an evident attempt to force the Soviet Union to adopt bourgeois standards and practices in the field of human contacts and access to information as a precondition for agreeing to a 'satisfactory' declaration of principles and a summit level conclusion to the conference. In the Middle East détente has not brought peace by condominium. US influence has increased markedly since the end of the October War and there is danger that the Soviet position, based on years of effort and investment, may be undermined.

4. I cite the above points, which are not exhaustive, merely to indicate that the Soviet Government too has a *prima facie* case for reassessing, if it were so inclined, the assumptions of the policy of détente, and possibly for adopting a less 'cooperative' attitude to the West in general and the United States in particular. But I can find no signs of such inclination, and I do not believe that any such change of course is likely.

5. Détente, in the Soviet view, is a long term policy. It is a phase of peaceful coexistence in which the Russians, by contributing to the reduction of tension and thereby reducing the risk of having to engage in another massive spasm of defence expenditure, hope to buy a period of relative international stability during which they can make economic progress both by the rational deployment of their own resources and through beneficial cooperation with the technologically more advanced countries. The Russians cannot, however, be expected to sacrifice to détente vital state interests such as the preservation of internal stability or an adequate degree of political and strategic influence in, for example, the Middle East. Concern for vital Soviet interests is not a monopoly of the 'more cautions and suspicious forces in the Soviet régime' but is, I am sure, shared equally by Brezhnev and those closest to him.

6. For this reason I would take issue with those in the United States and elsewhere who transpose to the Soviet political scene their own differentiation between 'hawks' and 'doves', putting Brezhnev at the head of the latter. Seen from Moscow, Soviet policy is based on a realistic assessment of Soviet national interest.[3] No-one in the Kremlin needs to be given a helping hand in executing it. But there are objective limits to unhelpfulness on the part of the Western powers, in particular the United States. I would judge that for as long as the United States show that they are not intent on undermining internal order in the Soviet state or in its Eastern European clients, or starting on another lap of the arms race with the object of regaining a position of complete strategic superiority, a collapse of the present growing *modus vivendi*, due to unilateral United States action, seems unlikely. Indeed, even though the Soviet propaganda

---

[3] Sir J. Killick endorsed this analysis. In a letter to Sir T. Garvey of 20 September he recalled that he had a 'slightly sharp exchange' with Dr. Kissinger on this subject when he visited London in December 1973, and that he had found Dr. Kissinger's answer 'less than convincing' when asked whether he regarded Mr. Brezhnev 'as the best Secretary-General we have'. Sir J. Killick noted that he had heard some stories privately about Dr. Kissinger's 'somewhat emotional belief in his personal relationship with Brezhnev'. Moreover, he added, 'I must also confess that I have not so far convinced our Secretary of State of this line'.

machine makes much of Senator Jackson, Zionists, and militarists, the leadership may draw comfort from the fact that US public opinion polls, which they quote regularly, appear to show a consistent majority in support of détente and, as reported, even US politicians of both parties appear to be concerned more with debating the means than with questioning the end.[4]

7.   I am copying this despatch to Her Majesty's Representatives at Washington, Paris, Bonn, UKDEL NATO, East Berlin, BMG Berlin, Helsinki, Warsaw, Prague, Budapest, Bucharest, Sofia, Belgrade, Peking and Ulan Bator.

> I have, etc.,
> TERENCE GARVEY

[4] Sir J. Killick found it difficult to think what line of policy would suit Soviet interests better than that currently pursued by Mr. Brezhnev. He wrote to Sir T. Garvey (*v. ibid.*): 'On a broader time-scale, I cannot see Brezhnev and his colleagues abandoning détente so long as they are able to assure themselves and the country at large that in a general sense it has lubricated the wheel of history (in their determinist sense) and will continue to do so better than any other known product.'

No. 70

Minute from Sir. J. Killick to Mr. Bullard

[*ENS 3/304/1*]

Confidential. Eclipse   FCO, *24 September 1974*

Dr. Kissinger and Détente

1.   Here are some preliminary comments on Dr. Kissinger's statement to the Senate Foreign Relations Committee on 19 September.[1]

2.   In general, it contains less codswallop and special pleading than I had expected. The whole tone is sober in its expectations of détente and a far cry from Mr. Nixon's hyperbole in terms of irreversibility and the prospects for an era of permanent peace. There is much in the detail with which we can agree and perhaps one should turn first to Section IV which sets out a balance sheet of progress so far. Even here one has reservations. As regards the durability of America's alliances, Dr. Kissinger, whether sincerely or not, asserts that they have become more stable because of the removal of 'the fear that friendship with the United States involved the risk of unnecessary confrontation with the USSR'. The fact is I fear that alliances may now be undermined because of a new worry that US friendship with the Soviet Union involves the risk of the sacrifice of at least some of the important interests of the allies of the US. Secondly, one is bound to be sceptical of the assertion that there are new possibilities for positive

[1] On 19 September Dr. Kissinger told the Foreign Relations Committee of the US Senate, which had been holding hearings on *détente*, that there could be 'no peaceful international order without a constructive relationship between the United States and the Soviet Union' (*Department of State Bulletin*, 14 October 1974, pp. 505–19.).

US/Soviet cooperation in global interdependent issues like science and technology, the environment and energy. I do not know whether Dr. Kissinger is just being cynical in parroting what Mr. Brezhnev says or whether he is simply betraying his ignorance of the facts of life in these areas, in which the prospects for real cooperation are very superficial.

3. I note also that Dr. Kissinger repeats his favourite trick of reducing to the absurd the arguments of his critics in order to demolish them. Thus, he says in Section IV that the temptation to combine détente with increasing pressure on the Soviet Union will grow, and 'such an attitude would be disastrous'. Elsewhere he says 'we cannot demand that the Soviet Union in effect suddenly reverse five decades of Soviet and centuries of Russian history'. He also implies that his critics seek to justify each agreement with Moscow only when unilateral gain can be demonstrated—through striving for strategic superiority, systematically blocking benefits to the Soviet Union or transforming the Soviet system by pressure. I am not aware that any serious American or other politician is trying to do any of these things; they are seeking to ensure that concessions are matched by counter-concessions.

4. At the same time, Dr. Kissinger tries to take credit for the suspension of the Education Tax on Soviet emigrants,[2] for the increased volume of Jewish emigration, for the attention given to hardship cases submitted to the Soviet Government and for the prospects of further diminution of obstacles to emigration and hardship to emigrants. The fact is surely that these achievements would not have been possible had it not been for Senator Jackson and for the linkage established by him with trade arrangements with the Soviet Union—tactics which Dr. Kissinger strongly criticised elsewhere as having been adopted 'not until after the 1972 agreement' (how could they have been adopted earlier when there was no legislation before Congress?), as casting doubt on US reliability as a negotiating partner, as inflating the significance of trade and as transforming the 'hoped-for results' of policy into pre-conditions. On this last particular point one inevitably has serious doubts about the approach of a man who is willing to make significant and binding concessions whose reciprocal results are no more than 'hoped-for'.

5. Finally, on trade he argues that the laws of mutual advantage must operate or there will be no trade. He begs the question how to establish commercial advantage for the US in trade with the Soviet Union and appears to suggest only that it may 'leaven the autarkic tendencies of the Soviet system, invite gradual association of the Soviet economy with the world economy, and foster a degree of interdependence that adds an element of stability to the political equation'. I would agree within realistic limits, but the difficulty is that these are political returns which American business and capital are unlikely to invest in, at least at the sort of significant level which offers any real hope of achievement.

6. As I had expected, Dr. Kissinger devotes disproportionate space and a good deal of emotion to the question of strategic arms. I believe that this reflects his own thinking, and is not just a matter of presentation for Congressional

[2] See H. Kissinger, *Years of Renewal*, pp. 128–35 and pp. 255–60.

consumption. He says—rightly as regards the US—that 'in the nuclear age the relationship between military strength and politically usable power is the most complex in all history'. My own belief is that the Soviet Union is still capable of the use of nuclear blackmail, whatever the position of the US may be. Dr. Kissinger acknowledges elsewhere that Soviet foreign policy is conducted 'in a gray area heavily influenced by the Soviet conception of the balance of forces ... Soviet diplomacy ... is never determined in isolation from the prevailing military balance'. While I would accept that the main Soviet aim is and is likely to remain the avoidance of confrontation with the United States, it is by no means to be excluded that Soviet foreign policy aims will be pursued by the exploitation of Soviet nuclear military power in areas where such confrontation is unlikely— including Western Europe if it ever comes to the point of significant US withdrawal or disengagement.

7.   As regards the bilateral strategic relationship, I find his remarks full of internal inconsistences [*sic*] and doubtful propositions. He talks awesomely of each side having the capacity to destroy civilisation as we know it and of the failure to maintain equivalence jeopardising our survival. At the same time he sees the enormous destructiveness of weapons and uncertainties regarding their effects as combining to make the massive use of such weapons increasingly incredible. In a nutshell, they could mean the end of the world—but they are by their nature increasingly unlikely to mean the end of the world! Also, at present levels of nuclear arsenals, he argues, it becomes difficult to determine what combination of numbers and technology would give one side a militarily and politically useful superiority. Yet the appearance of inferiority—whatever its actual significance—he says can have serious political consequences. But he does not say what. And despite his apocalyptic forecasts of the end of the world if the arms race continues, he says the United States, if driven to it, will sustain it and in all likelihood emerge from it 'with an edge over the Soviet Union in most significant categories of strategic arms'. The benefits of this would, he acknowledges, remain elusive and indeed both sides might be worse off than before. Again he does not say how.

8.   Where we can agree with him is that the American people can be asked to bear the cost and political instability of such competition, doomed to stalemate, only if it is clear that every effort has been made to prevent it. He still fails to convince me that it will be the end of the world if it is not prevented. (I have not yet seen the text of his speech to the General Assembly, which goes off on a new tack.)[3]

9.   In all this Dr. Kissinger does not appear to share our assessment that the pursuit of détente is perceived in Moscow as serving Soviet interests. He claims that 'the changing situation [the loss of Moscow dominance in the Communist world] *and US policy* seem to have encouraged the Soviet leaders to cooperate at least in a temporary lessening of tension with the West', and goes on to argue that it is for the United States to 'provide as many incentives as possible' to keep the Soviet Union on the patch of peace and individual wellbeing. In his familiar argument about the network of relations between the Soviet Union and the West he talks of the development of Soviet self-interest in fostering the entire process

[3] See Records of the 29th Session of the UNGA, A/PV 2238, pp. 59–63.

of relaxation of tension. In short, he still appears to believe that the traffic will not bear much, if any, effective pressure on the Soviet Union and that the continuation of the pursuit of détente is essentially dependent upon the United States staying on the present course as determined for it by him.

JOHN KILLICK

No. 71

Letter from Mr. Bullard to Sir T. Garvey (Moscow)

[*ENS 2/1*]

Confidential   FCO, *4 October 1974*

My dear Terence,

The Soviet Union and Détente

1.   I enclose a copy of my Department's not very original contribution to the papers being prepared for a possible new Government in London next week.[1] This was written 10 days ago, since when I have been wondering whether we may be entering a new phase in East–West relations. The evidence is not exactly ample, and indeed I am only aware of the following:

(*a*)   The unhurried approach of the Soviet delegation to the resumed Stage II of CSCE. This could indeed be tactical, or a move to establish a link between the CSCE and MBFR (as Gromyko has now proposed to Dr. Kissinger),[2] or there is the Yugoslav story that the Russians want to fit in the Conference of European Communist Parties before Stage III of the CSCE.[3] But there could also be deeper causes.

(*b*)   Gromyko's speech to the UN General Assembly.[4] Like Mr. Richard,[5] I was struck by the serene and Olympian tone of this speech, from the first sentence with its echoes of Anna Karenina to the magisterial summing up of priorities at the end. Gromyko speaks as if he were conscious of moving at a level of

---

[1] Mr. Wilson announced on 18 September the holding of a General Election on 10 October. The EESD paper (not printed) pointed out that, although Anglo-Soviet relations had been through a frosty period, 'latterly there had been a visible thaw'. Amongst the FCO's 'broad objectives' it listed the patient pursuit of *détente*, 'but not at the expense of security, and while guarding against the Russians exploiting their superior strength in questions affecting British interests' (RS 3/9).

[2] See Volume II, No. 100.

[3] *V. ibid.*, No. 99.

[4] See, *A/PV 2240*, pp. 100–6.

[5] Mr. I.S. Richard was UK Permanent Representative to the UN at New York. In UKMIS New York telegram No. 1167 of 24 September he wrote of Mr. Gromyko's speech: 'There were almost no polemics. I almost had the impression of a Red Indian chieftain coming, at a formal gathering, to smoke a pipe of peace with his opposite number. The lesser tribesmen might have been gathered round to listen in, but one chief was really only interested in addressing the other. The message

power and experience where nobody in his audience can touch him. There is a sense of detachment in face of even the most pressing of the world's problems, almost as if Gromyko thought that the Soviet Union was not affected by them.

2. Not everybody here sees these two pieces of evidence in quite this light, and some see them in no particular light at all. But, as I see it, the events of the last year must have greatly strengthened the streak of self-reliance and self-sufficiency (to avoid such emotional words as autarky and isolationism) which has always been so strong in the Russian national character. Brezhnev has seen 3 glittering figures in the West, each of them prominent in détente, vanish within the space of a few months.[6] Their places have been taken by 3 comparatively unknown quantities for Moscow. President Ford's first public statements did not mention the Soviet Union and détente, any more than they mentioned Europe. President Giscard is going to concentrate on giving a new impetus to 'Europe' and on putting the French economy right. Schmidt and Genscher talk of continuity in relations with the East, but their interest centres more on the technicalities of Berlin, inner-German relations and the German minority in the USSR than on the broad themes of ex-Chancellor Brandt. (There is a lecture this term at the LSE[7] entitled 'The End of Ostpolitik'.) On top of these political events, the Russians have become aware of the totally new economic scene which is so well described in your despatch of 25 September.[8] (This has gone to be printed, and we were very grateful for it.)

3. In the face of such a year, the instinctive reaction in Moscow could perhaps have been on the following lines:

'Détente was always a mixed blessing for the Soviet Union. Russia was expected to pursue it consistently, but Western countries felt free to change their leaders every few years, with or without elections, and every change of face spelt a possible change of policy towards the East. Our special relationship with Washington did not save us from being totally upstaged by America over the Middle East, and even by decadent tumbledown Britain over Cyprus.[9] The grand design of the CSCE has degenerated into a procedural wrangle over square brackets and dots. The 6th Special Session of the UN General Assembly came close to promulgating the dangerous doctrine that the poor countries of the world have some kind of *a priori* claim upon the rich.[10] To quote Uncle

was: we have no intention of rocking our boat; let us meet again, in a year's time, and on a similar ceremonial occasion.'

[6] See Volume II, No. 79, note 3.

[7] London School of Economics and Political Science.

[8] In this despatch Sir T. Garvey examined the impact of the energy crisis upon the USSR's international position. He concluded that the 'shift in power' in the world had left the Soviet Union relatively unscathed, adding: 'In that the bargaining strength of the developed West has been weakened, the Soviet Union's bargaining position vis-à-vis the West is *ipso-facto* strengthened. I think that the Russians would like it to stay that way, without further deterioration, which would incapacitate the West as a commercial and technological partner' (ENS 5/1).

[9] No. 67, note 14.

[10] See No. 57, notes 4 and 5.

Matthew:[11] "Abroad is unutterably bloody and foreigners are fiends". Does Russia really need the outside world? We have most of what we require at home, and as regards the rest, we are even better placed than before to pick and choose from what the rest of the world has to offer. Our economy has its weaknesses, but it has been praised by Mr. Kenneth Tynan[12] in the correspondence columns of 'The Times'. In any case we have plenty to do at home. The next Five-Year Plan will be of exceptional importance, and the 25th Party Congress cannot be more than 18 months off. We have to stage-manage parallel events throughout the Warsaw Pact and COMECON—apart from Romania, which has characteristically gone ahead with its own docments and its own Congress next month. Some of the East European leaders are looking a bit past it, and even in Moscow we do not feel immortal. Détente has had a good run of 3½ years since the 24th Party Congress. It is time to stop bothering about far-off countries of which we know nothing, and to concentrate on events at home and within the Soviet empire.'

4. We were already thinking on these lines before we read Moira Cunynghame's article in the 'Financial Times' of 1 October.[13] David Lascelles[14] tells us that her sources were Soviet, although he does not know to whom precisely she had been talking. Lascelles himself got much the same impression during his recent trip to the Soviet Union. He sensed a feeling of bewilderment at the new array of Western leaders and thinks that the Russians will retire into their shells until the picture in the West becomes clearer. After his stops in Tokyo and Washington, Lascelles also had the distinct impression that Japanese and American interest in Siberian development had diminished, while the Russians for their part (cf Shasin's[15] press conference) were perhaps less happy about mortgaging part of their natural resources in order to get these out of the ground more quickly with the help of Western technology.

5. If the interpretation in paragraph 3 above is anywhere near correct, the question arises whether we are merely witnessing a wobble or change of gear in a more or less continuous line of Soviet policy towards the West, or whether East–West relations have (so to speak) rounded a bend and entered a new reach of the river. It could even be, to use a still more dramatic metaphor, that the tide of détente has actually passed its flood. Ted Orchard has sometimes spoken of a fairly short period during which the Soviet Union would be both interested in détente and weak enough to need it, so that the West might have only a fleeting opportunity of enmeshing the Soviet Union in constructive East–West arrangements. Could it be the case that this opportunity came and went during the years 1971 to 1973? (Even

---

[11] A character created by Nancy Mitford. See her novel, *The Pursuit of Love* (London: The Reprint Society, 1947), p. 131.

[12] British author and drama critic.

[13] In this article Mary Cunynghame argued that events during the last six months had forced the Soviet Union to reappraise its foreign policy and economic plans (*The Financial Times*, 1 October, p. 7).

[14] Banking Editor of *The Financial Times*.

[15] Mr. V.D. Shasin was Soviet Minister for the Oil Industry.

if the answer is Yes, I am not suggesting that the West should have 'tried harder', which could only have meant making more concessions, during those years.)

6.   To some extent all this involves the question what view we should take of the situation within the Soviet leadership. I have copied to you our recent exchange of telegrams with UKDEL NATO about a possible discussion of this subject in that forum.[16] As you know, we have traditionally remained sceptical in the face of 'evidence' (usually taking the form of unsupported statements by Soviet and East European officials) of threats from hard-liners to Brezhnev's policies and position. But if there is anything in the theory that Soviet policy has carried out a course correction in recent weeks, one can imagine the question being asked in Moscow whether the leader who has made an international reputation in the last 3 years will serve equally well for the next 3, and whether new policies would not be better implemented by a new man. I suppose Brezhnev has every intention of taking the rostrum at the 25th Party Congress, and it looks at the moment as if only death or a serious illness could prevent this: the stories about his ill health and aged appearance continue, but so does his busy schedule. Yet recent events may have given a new twist to the old question of who are Brezhnev's likely successors and what policies they will follow.[17] I touched on this in paragraph 9 of the note enclosed with John Killick's letter to you of 20 September[18] but the possibility of a neo-isolationist generation taking over in Moscow in a year or two is a slightly new thought.[19]

[16] In telegrams No. 220 and 221 to UKDEL NATO of 2 October Mr. Callaghan referred to a possible NAC discussion of Dr. Kissinger's most recent exposition to the Senate Foreign Relations Committee of his analysis of *détente*. He suggested that the NATO Group of Experts on Eastern Europe and the Soviet Union should consider: (1) the extent to which *détente* depended on Mr. Brezhnev's leadership; (2) a Soviet balance sheet of *détente*; (3) Soviet alternatives to *détente*; and (4) the likely consequences of changes in Soviet foreign policy.

[17] Sir T. Garvey considered *détente* a 'collective policy' with which Mr. Brezhnev had been careful to associate his *Politburo* colleagues. 'There is', he noted, 'no reason to suppose that a change in policy is more likely after Brezhnev's departure than before it. If there is a change it will almost certainly result from a revaluation of perceived advantage to Soviet state interests rather than from a change in personalities' (Moscow telegram No. 1224 of 10 October).

[18] See No. 69, note 3. In this minute to Sir J. Killick of 21 May Mr. Bullard listed a number of possible successors to the present Soviet leadership, remarking that the 'line-up could easily be otherwise' and that it was far from certain what foreign policy line they would pursue in office. He added that: (1) although many believed that a new Soviet Government would have little choice but to continue the 'Brezhnevian policies of détente in the West, firmness in the East and opportunism in the Third World', Brezhnev's successors would be the first Russians to take office in a country that was already a superpower, and might therefore 'be more willing to take risks than he was'; (2) some argued that, judging by experience, 'a new Soviet leadership tend[ed] to act cautiously and by consensus, producing a single leader only some years later'; and (3) there was a theory that the next generation of Soviet leaders would not be prepared to give the security apparatus the free hand it had hitherto enjoyed and that 'a second round of de-Stalinisation could be in prospect'.

[19] In a letter to Mr. Bullard of 23 October Mr. I.J.M. Sutherland, who had recently been appointed Minister in HM Embassy, Moscow, observed that the possibility of the present Soviet leadership being replaced by 'neo-isolationists' must be conditional on: (1) the radical transformation of the doctrine of peaceful coexistence; (2) the USSR abandoning its interest in 'maintaining and improving its strategic posture on the global scale vis à vis the United States and its allies'; (3)

7.   I concede that there may be much less dramatic interpretations of the present Soviet stance. A radical change from détente to neo-isolationism would go against currents in Soviet society which we have hitherto regarded as very strong, and indeed against the general direction of Soviet foreign policy for some years past. The tone of Gromyko's speech to the General Assembly was pretty much the one he had adopted with Sir A Douglas-Home in December 1973, and after so many slippages the timing of Stage 3 of the CSCE is a good deal less important for Brezhnev than the level of it. Certainly he will want to hold the boat steady in the run-up to the 25th Congress, so that we may expect a relatively uneventful year or 18 months from now. But when the Congress opens, Brezhnev will want to be in a position to present his policies over the whole 5-year period as consistent and successful, and to seek a mandate for their extension into the future. In other words one would expect détente to remain the Soviet watchword, even if it is perhaps given a less active interpretation.[20]

8.   Lastly, there is the question of the implications of all this for the West. In Dr. Kissinger's eyes, for excellent reasons, the crucial question is SALT. The rest of us do not operate on this plane, and the tête-à-tête note in both Kissinger's and Gromyko's speeches in New York is only a reflection of the way in which 'bilateralism' has been strengthened by the events of the past year, economic as well as political.[21] But we should perhaps be re-thinking (yet again) what exactly Britain wants from the Soviet Union, in both the negative and the positive sense. The enclosed paper pitches our desiderata deliberately low—you may think too low. We could consider this when the Country Assessment Sheet for the Soviet Union comes to be re-written in preparation for next year's inspection—by which time, as you know, I hope that we shall have had an encounter with our new Ministers at a Conference of Heads of Missions.

Yours ever,
J.L. Bullard

its foregoing the pursuit of increased political influence over the countries of Western Europe; and (4) its becoming indifferent to 'the possible expansion, in the longer term, of Chinese influence in Asia'. He saw no evidence of these conditions having been fulfilled. 'Moreover', Mr. Sutherland added, 'to balance a decline in ideological motivation in the field of foreign policy, there is a calculated acceptance that super-power status automatically implies certain global responsibilities.'

[20] In his letter of 23 October (*v. ibid.*) Mr. Sutherland noted: 'The momentum of détente, as seen by the Russians, may have slowed down. This can partly be explained by the normal summer pause and partly because it takes two to make détente. From the Soviet side, however, the recent signals that they are willing to continue the policy still seem constant.'

[21] In a letter to Mr. Bullard of 23 October Sir T. Garvey expressed his concern lest Dr. Kissinger's thinking on *détente* obscure a 'very real distinction in the Soviet mind between the various strands of their détente policy', particularly the degree of importance which the Russians attached to strategic matters. 'It is', he noted, 'this element in Dr Kissinger's handling of the US/Soviet relationship that could be most troublesome for America's allies, if it led him to include in a general US/Soviet bargain points which are not likely to affect Soviet responses on nuclear strategic matters but which may be of importance to the United States' allies.'

CHAPTER IV

The New Phase
27 November 1974–7 December 1976

No. 72

Sir T. Garvey (Moscow) to Mr. Callaghan

[*ENS 3/548/2*]

Confidential   MOSCOW, *27 November 1974*

Summary ...[1]

Sir,

Anglo-Soviet Relations

I approach the forthcoming visit of the Prime Minister and yourself to Moscow[2] in the spirit of two comments from your own lips. You spoke in the House of Commons on 19 May of developing a 'safer and more productive' Anglo-Soviet relationship:[3] and you told the Soviet Ambassador on 5 November that you hoped that the visit would be a 'landmark'.[4]

2. The seven years which have passed since a British Prime Minister last visited the Soviet Union[5] have, for a variety of reasons, most notably Britain's response to the Czechoslovak events of 1968 and the expulsion of the 105 Soviet spies in 1971, not been a productive period in Anglo-Soviet relations. Your predecessor's visit to Moscow in December 1973[6] was conceived, by both parties, as drawing a line under the past. The Soviet Government were in my belief ready, at the beginning of this year, to turn the page: but the economic and electoral situation in the UK gave them pause. Following the October election they are

---

[1] Not printed.

[2] As a result of the General Election on 10 October Mr. Wilson's Labour Government was returned to power with an overall majority of three in the House of Commons. When Mr. Lunkov called at 10 Downing St. on 16 October to convey Mr. Brezhnev's congratulations, Mr. Wilson said that he now felt able to take a rather longer look ahead at Anglo-Soviet bilateral relations, and that he wished to take up the Soviet Government's earlier invitation to visit Moscow (record of a conversation between Mr. Wilson and Mr. Lunkov at 3.40 p.m. on 16 October, ENS 3/548/1: cf. No. 59, note 9). By mid-November it had been agreed that Mr. Wilson and Mr. Callaghan would visit the Soviet Union early in the new year.

[3] This is evidently a reference to Mr. Callaghan's statement of 19 March. Cf. No. 66, note 2.

[4] Record of a conversation between Mr. Callaghan and Mr. Lunkov at 4.30 p.m. on 5 November (ENS 3/548/10).

[5] See Volume I, No. 2.

[6] See No. 52.

now, in my belief, ready to move forward again, so that conditions for erecting a 'landmark' may reasonably be held to exist.

3. Your speeches in the Foreign Affairs Debate of 19 March and the Debate on the Address of 30 October[7] establish the broad framework in which the Government seek an improvement of relations with this country. You spoke on the earlier occasion of the close alliance with the US, involving the closest co-operation and interdependence in defence matters, which required to be supplemented by parallel co-operation on matters of trade, money and energy. You spoke too of Britain's natural affinity with the other countries of Western Europe including the member States of the Community; and of the Government's aim to intensify the system of political consultation and co-operation among the Community countries. This aim, as you made plain, neither obstructed nor was obstructed by the Government's concurrent pursuit of improvements in the UK's terms of accession to the Community. I have thought it well to identify these two constants—the American alliance and our links, however defined, with our West European neighbours—at the outset since they serve to define one boundary of our field of operation.

4. Other defining factors are to be found in the disparities of objective and nature between the Soviet Union and the UK.

5. In developing their bilateral relationships nations seek to identify, and build on, areas of shared interest and common objectives, so far as possible isolating and containing areas of conflicting interest and disagreement. The latter, for reasons partly of history, and partly of ideology are, in the Anglo-Soviet case, quite considerable. The Russians have been taught to believe that their duty is to hasten the demise of social systems other than their own. History tells them that Western Europe, the cradle of capitalism, sought to strangle the Soviet revolution and Germany has twice this century inflicted terrible damage on them. Having now successfully interposed between itself and the Western Europeans a protective cushion of subservient States, the Soviet Union would like to see a Western Europe acquiescent towards itself, and not too closely tied to the US, but which is at the same time fragmented politically—a Europe susceptible to economic pressures and to political pressure backed by Soviet military strength. The British interest, by contrast, lies in a cohesive Western Europe and a strong Atlantic Alliance, from the security of which as you told the House of Commons on 30 October we are able to give a high priority to the problems of *détente*.[8]

6. Besides, the definition which the Soviet leaders give to *détente* limits the scope of co-operation and the depth of contacts in which we and our allies can usefully engage. The range of permissible contacts has been extended and the areas in which the Russians recognise that co-operation is possible and advantageous have broadened. Through the 'unproductive' period in Anglo-Soviet relations, it has been difficult for us to utilise such opportunities and in some bilateral fields we have perforce been less venturesome than our allies. We have, as will appear below, some ground to catch up. But the limits imposed upon us

[7] See note 3 above, and *Parl. Debs., 5th ser., H. of C.*, vol. 880, cols. 239–41.

[8] *V. ibid.*

as upon our allies are still relatively narrow. In the eyes of the Soviet leaders, *détente* is not open-ended, nor do they admit that the concept is applicable within the Soviet Union itself. Convergence is an ugly word in their vocabulary. Theirs is an increasingly prosperous but still a relatively closed society and one of the leaders' primary current concerns is to conserve the social attitudes and patterns of thought on which the stability of Soviet society and the perpetuation of their and the Party's authority are held to rest. As an illustration, some two weeks ago, President Podgorny identified 'political agnosticism' and the 'consumer mentality' as meriting special discredit and urged his listeners to show intolerance of alien ideas. When they say that intensification of the ideological struggle is an integral part of the concept of *détente* the Soviet leaders have the home front as much in mind as the external world.

7.   We must also take account of the disparity of scale. It goes without saying that in terms of power, only the US can treat with the Soviet Union as an equal, independently if necessary from the support of allies or friends. Other Western countries can effectively advance or defend their interests only from within the security of our alliance. Within this generalisation, however, there are gradations. Some, through history or geography or both, enjoy specific advantages which, in lesser though not in greater matters, increase both their scope for manoeuvre and the Soviet interest in cultivating them. Towards Western Germany for example, the Soviet attitude rests on a substratum of fear of an eventual resurgence of power and ambition, combined with respect for existing German economic strength and ingenuity. The past record and future potential of France as a well-tried source of discord within the Atlantic Alliance entitles her, in Russian eyes, to special attentions and favours—the latter, admittedly, sometimes more optical than concrete. Japan occupies what might prove to be a key position in the Sino-Soviet relationship and is suited by geography and resource requirements to participate in the development of Siberia's natural resources.

8.   The reality that the UK does not possess any comparable or similar claim on Soviet attentions is apt to be obscured by memories of a time, when, as allies against Nazi Germany, the UK and the Soviet Union spoke as equals—memories which the Russians were in the habit of reviving when it suited them as an anti-German gambit, but about which they are more reticent since the advent of *Ostpolitik*. The institutional relics of a period in which the discrepancy of scale was less marked, such as the British role as a depository Power for the Nuclear Test-Ban and Non-Proliferation Treaties,[9] our share of the quadripartite responsibility for Germany and Berlin and our Co-Chairmanship of the Geneva Conferences on Indo-China can nevertheless still constitute distractions from current reality and encourage misapprehension of the true substance of the Anglo-Soviet relationship of 1974. Substance the relationship certainly has: but its composition and scale has changed.

9.   Although the British claim on Soviet attention is less powerful and more difficult to define than that which the Germans, French and Japanese can command, we are by no means without cards in our hand. Our strongest card is

[9] See No. 61, note 5.

the influence which the Russians think we can still exercise not over the Soviet Union and its allies but over our own friends and their policies. Indeed, as a member of NATO and of the EEC we do have the capacity to influence the policy-formation and decisions of the Western nations in political, strategic and economic fields of vital concern to the Soviet Government. In many contexts what the UK does through the two delegations in Brussels—or for that matter in Vienna and in Geneva—may have more impact on the Soviet Government than what we say or do in London or Moscow. Soviet recognition of this fact and a realisation of the indirect damage which ostracism of one member of the Nine could do to their relations with other members of the European Community, and with the Community as a whole, had, I think, a good deal to do with the decision of the Soviet Government in mid-1973, to draw a line under the affair of the 105 officials expelled from London and to take the initiative in normalising relations.

10. It follows that such leverage as we possess in Moscow depends in the final analysis on the maintenance of our influence in West European and transatlantic counsels. It also depends as you said in the House of Commons on 30 October in a wider context, 'on how we handle our domestic affairs and overcome our domestic weaknesses'.[10] The interdependence of our foreign and domestic affairs has a particular relevance to the view that the Soviet Government takes of Britain. Their estimate of our future economic capacity and stability obviously sets a limit, irrespective of political preference, on the extent to which we can expect to increase our trade when they are seeking to spend as much of their available foreign exchange as possible on large-scale advanced-technology contacts in the framework of long-term economic plans. Moreover, as we are constantly reminded in the Press and on the television screen in Moscow, the present ills of the West in general, and of Britain in particular, are regarded with smug satisfaction and as confirmation of what the Soviet textbooks have said for so long about the crisis of our economic system. If we are to command attention on political as well as economic issues, it is essential that we should demonstrate to the Soviet leaders the strength and seriousness of our endeavours to surmount these problems, domestically and internationally.

11. In drawing attention to these limits to the scope for improving Anglo-Soviet relations, I am not suggesting that we should seek to restrict the agenda for the discussions which you and the Prime Minister will have in Moscow during your impending visit; only that our objective and expectations should be related to the realities of a disparate relationship and what I conceive to be the Russians' view of their own place in the world. Indeed I see advantage in exploring the Soviet leaders' views on a very broad front. Speaking to the Soviet Ambassador in London on 5 November you referred to some of the topics which you wished to raise.[11] This despatch is not the place for writing a draft agenda, but the

---

[10] *Parl. Debs., 5th ser., H. of C.,* vol. 880, col. 231.

[11] See note 4 above. Amongst the possible topics for discussion which Mr. Callaghan had mentioned to Mr. Lunkov were: a summit meeting at the conclusion of the CSCE; peaceful nuclear explosions; the Soviet attitude towards the Indian Ocean; the prospects for SALT; and the Middle East.

considerations just mentioned suggest that it should find room for an account of how we view the international scene and perhaps for discussions on aid and world commodity problems—topics which have not figured prominently in recent encounters between Soviet and West European leaders.

12. But of equal, and perhaps greater importance is the momentum which the visit can provide to the bilateral, particularly the commercial aspect of our relationship.

13. Foreign trade is a small part of Soviet economic activity—under 4 per cent of GNP. Two-thirds of Soviet trade is with other CMEA countries. The UK, with the FRG, Japan, France, Italy and the US, are the six principal supplier and customer countries in a closed, planned, limited, convertible currency system. Soviet imports from the latter five countries have been at least doubling every five years. In the early 1960s the UK was the Soviet Union's leading supplier. We retained not lower than third place until 1969, when we slipped to fifth. In 1973, the sharp rise of imports from the US—even excluding grain—thrust us into sixth place. In the 10 years to 1973, but mainly since 1968, the UK share of this market fell from over 20 to under 8 per cent and the value of our exports has stagnated at around £100 million a year: the volume has actually contracted. The reasons for this decline are partly political and partly economic. As the Soviet Union moved towards the normalisation of relationships with former enemy countries and adversaries in the cold war, the development of frustrated but natural economic ties became respectable. Soviet convertible-currency purchasing power has traditionally been limited by the narrow base of Soviet exports and the scarcity of surplus production, reinforced in recent months by substantial windfall profits on oil and gas exports. It was probably inevitable that a major share of the growth in trade should have gone to the FRG, Japan, France, Italy and, ultimately, the US. At the same time British policies and attitudes—on Czechoslovakia, our firm stance in defence matters and the 1971 expulsions—also strengthened the hand of those in Moscow who held that doing business with our competitors would yield more useful political results.

14. If it was a Soviet political aim to consolidate trade with our newly admitted competitors, there were also strong economic reasons. West Germany was the key source of large-diameter pipe, and remains willing to be paid in gas. The UK automobile industry was too pre-occupied with its own problems to wrest from the Americans, Germans, Italians and French new major Soviet contracts in this field. Had the British economy been stronger we should have done better, though not enough to retain the advantageous position of the early '60s. British business-men, moreover, with longer experience of the difficulties of this market have perhaps been more disillusioned than their less experienced and latterly more successful competitors.

15. But the balance of Soviet economic interest may not continue to be served by leaving Britain on the sidelines. Since mid-1973, following the Soviet decision to re-activate the political relationship, there has been a revival of major business. Contracts worth well over £200 million have been concluded. As deliveries flow in 1975–76 the trade figures should at last show a rise in exports to a rate of perhaps £150 million to £200 million a year. There are good prospects that, subject to

competitive prices and credits, such business will continue to come to UK firms at the rate of up to £200 million a year. There is some prospect of larger deals on a compensation basis e.g. in timber and pulp, and, conceivably, in civil aircraft engines and oil. The decision to hold the Olympic Games in Moscow in 1980 presents opportunities in the construction and tourist industries. On the other hand, the Soviet market is narrow and specialised. It competes for UK resources for which demand is high in easier markets. And our high rate of price inflation is now seriously undermining our power to bargain with a monolithic and selective customer. In the past few months it has been increasingly difficult to elicit quotations from British firms. But we must create conditions here in which an upturn of trade can take place. The French and American examples suggest that a target can be useful. Soviet trade with the six countries is likely to continue at least to double every five years. Indeed during the 1976–80 Plan growth could be faster if the Soviet Union retains the advantageous terms of trade arising from current commodity prices. Doubling of our own exports in, say, three years would not in my view be a realistic target, given lead times for major business. But trebling the value of our exports in five years, to restore our market share to about 10 per cent, would not be an impossible goal.

16. The Russians will demand a price for commitment to such a joint target. Specifically, they are likely to look for advantages in the form of a favourable agreement on export credit; 'non-discriminatory' access to the British market including a renewed undertaking on most-favoured-nation treatment on lines that have been set by the examples of France and the FRG; probably agreement to an increase in the staff of the Soviet Trade Delegation; and a less troublesome system of granting visas to Soviet business visitors. But our competitors face similar demands, and have by no means conceded all of them. So the prospects for our increased trade are unlikely to depend very directly upon what we offer in these areas, and in so far as we do, we should press for reciprocal concessions —for example better facilities for British business representatives in this country. In general the Soviet attitude to forward commitments will depend to a much greater extent upon how they assess the quality of the Anglo-Soviet relationship and most of all on the degree of assurance they have that British industry can deliver and at competitive prices.

17. The formal framework for development of business relations exists in the 10-year Co-operation Agreement of May 1974[12] and the 1968 Technological Co-operation Agreement.[13] But this legal framework, at present provided in the Temporary Commercial Agreement of 1934[14] and the Long-Term Trade Agreement of 1969,[15] has not yet been adjusted to align with the application of

---

[12] This agreement, signed on 6 May by Mr. P. Shore (Secretary of State for Trade) and Mr. M.R. Kuzmin (Soviet Deputy Minister of Foreign Trade), foresaw the preparation of 'concrete programmes' on scientific and technical cooperation and economic and industrial cooperation. See *Treaty Series* No. 43 (1974), Cmnd 5659.

[13] See *Treaty Series* No. 59 (1968), Cmnd 3710.

[14] See *Treaty Series* No. 11 (1934), Cmd 4567.

[15] See *Treaty Series* No. 92 (1969) Cmnd 4132.

the EEC's Common Commercial Policy towards State trading countries from 1 January, 1975.[16] The Soviet Government are likely to raise soon the question of the trading relationship between us in these matters.

18. Soviet attitudes to the UK both as a trading partner and as a Power with a future in the world's councils are also a function of their assessment of our technological skill and capacity for innovation. The realisation that despite the great advances in the volume and quality of production achieved in the past 15 years, there is still a wide gap between their standards and those of the US and the West is a major motive in Soviet *détente* policies. Their plans for narrowing this gap and increasing the range and quality of goods available to the consumer involve some concessions to the principle of the international division of labour, but so far as trade with their free-foreign-exchange partners is concerned, the emphasis is on collaboration involving the means of production. And the plant and processes they are seeking to import are of the most advanced design. Hence the importance they attach to technological and scientific co-operation. The balance in terms of technological transfer and commercial advantages must be carefully weighed; in some fields and for certain types of very large projects the Russians will not look to the UK and it would be a waste of effort to try to persuade them otherwise. But in others, the benefits of exchange need not and should not be one way. In this context the long-term 'Concrete Programme' provided for in the Ten-year Co-operation concluded in May 1973 provides a vehicle for the identification of specific areas where it is agreed that collaboration may be mutually beneficial. There is a parallel long-term programme for scientific co-operation. Neither will of themselves generate trade but both provide for increased contacts between officials, specialists, and scientists which should increase our knowledge of Soviet intentions and enable us to take opportunities which might otherwise be missed. Both programmes will gain in authority if they can be signed during the Prime Minister's visit. There is also scope for intensifying co-operative efforts within the existing agreement on Agricultural Research, in the plans for exchanges and joint projects in pure science, fusion research and in environmental protection and through the proposed reciprocal medical agreement.

19. There is room for greater activity and imagination in Anglo-Soviet cultural relations. The marked lull since 1971, has been enlivened only to a modest degree by the Prospect Theatre Company's tour last spring and by an exhibition of British water-colours in the Hermitage which is due to open next month; and, in a negative sense, by the visit of the Bolshoi Ballet to London this summer.[17] We now need to plan a series of events and exchanges which will make an impact. I appreciate that this cannot be a time for lavish expenditure but the size and quality of our cultural programme—and here every item must be planned and sponsored

[16] See No. 37, note 6.

[17] The Bolshoi Ballet's summer season at the Coliseum theatre, London, was marred by periodic public demonstrations about the treatment of Soviet Jews. As a result of incidents inside the theatre, culminating with the throwing on to the stage of tin tacks on 27 June, the Russians protested to the British Embassy in Moscow and to the FCO.

officially—is one of the indices by which our standing is judged. The exhibition of Turner's paintings which has been the subject of negotiations with the Russians for some time would provide one major item; there is at last a good prospect that this will finally materialise in October 1975, and we must ensure that it is seen in Moscow as well as Leningrad. Negotiations on a new Anglo-Soviet Cultural Agreement are due to take place in late February 1975, and we should use the momentum engendered by the Prime Minister's visit to promote such negotiating aims as the elimination of recurrent snags in educational exchanges and the adoption of an expanded programme of cultural exchanges which is both imaginative and realisable.

20. As the Department are aware from current correspondence, I believe that there would be advantage in a prudent expansion of our contacts with a key sector of the Soviet establishment with which our relations are at present confined to superficial formalities, namely the Soviet Armed Forces. This is not a question of senseless jollification between potential adversaries but a means of improving our knowledge and, through access to people and establishments normally barred to attachés, of informing ourselves about a sector of Soviet society which plays a very significant part in the promotion and execution of policy. Proposals for a modest programme of exchanges are on the table and agreement on them would be a useful addition to the corpus of work transacted during the visit.

21. Despite and within the limits outlined earlier in this despatch there is, in my view, considerable scope for an increase in constructive activity in developing the Anglo-Soviet relationship. This is not just a matter of keeping up with the other West Europeans but, as I have said, an important means of maximising the weight of our opinion in the counsels of our friends and in the conduct of negotiations, including those currently in progress in Geneva and Vienna, which touch serious British and Western interests. It is also a question of renewing and revitalising contacts with a country with the power to influence events in every quarter of the globe at a time when its society is changing and its leaders are beginning to realise, in some fields at least, the necessity for co-operation in an increasingly inter-dependent world. We should not be afraid, in carrying this process forward, of adopting a style of our own. It is likely to be more effective if our style is workmanlike rather than grandiloquent, our emphasis on substance rather than on atmospherics; discussions and the documents for the Prime Minister's visit should reflect this approach, which I believe will command respect.

22. I am sending copies of this despatch to Her Majesty's Representatives at Washington, Bonn, Paris, Warsaw, Prague, Budapest, Bucharest, Sofia and East Berlin and to the UK Permanent Representative on the North Atlantic Council.

I have, etc.,
T. GARVEY

No. 73

Sir T. Garvey (Moscow) to Mr. Callaghan

No. 65 Telegraphic [ENS 3/548/2]

Confidential   MOSCOW, *16 January 1975, 8.20 am*

1.   I was very grateful for time you gave me on Monday evening.[1] For memory purposes I summarise as follows thoughts that I wished to leave with you, and earlier with Mr. Wilson, and with your advisers.

2.   I see visit as having two main aims.

(*a*)   to improve tone and atmosphere of Anglo-Soviet relations,[2] and
(*b*)   to achieve a substantial increase of UK trade

I regard these as attainable though success is not a foregone conclusion.

3.   We shall need to do both things, for they hang together in the Soviet mind. We shan't get (b) without (a).

4.   The Russians do not regard good relations with us as essential. They can get on without us. Their principal Western partner is the United States (this remains true, notwithstanding subsequent pull back on carrying out the trade agreement): and in Europe France and FRG provide all that is needed.

5.   Accordingly if we are to get anywhere we shall need to work our passage. The argument turns on how long and hard we shall have to work. They have made their intentions pretty plain in their handling of our pressure for assurances on Brezhnev's participation:[3] that, they imply, will depend on the view they form between now and 13 February of the likely quality of the visit.

6.   In this preparatory phase we have two hazards to avoid. First, that of seeming to suck up to them so assiduously that they lose all respect for us. But,

---

[1]   On 3 January Mr. Y.A. Semenov (Minister Counsellor in the Soviet Embassy in London) confirmed that 'Moscow was ready to receive a visit' from Mr. Wilson and Mr. Callaghan during 13–17 February (letter from Mr. P.R.H. Wright (Private Secretary to Mr. Wilson) to Mr. Weston of 3 January). Sir T. Garvey subsequently returned to London for consultations, including a meeting with Mr. Callaghan on the evening of Monday, 13 January.

[2]   Mr. Callaghan informed Sir T. Garvey in telegram No. 61 to Moscow of 17 January that he and Mr. Wilson believed that the time and circumstances were right for the 'turning of a new page in Anglo-Soviet relations'. He proposed as subjects for bilateral settlement during or soon after the visit: (1) a protocol on consultations; (2) the establishment of a better basis for Anglo-Soviet trade and economic and industrial cooperation; (3) a parallel improvement in arrangements for scientific and technical cooperation; (4) the signature of 'concrete programmes' covering (2) and (3); (5) the setting up of an Anglo-Soviet Round Table; (6) the signature of a health services convention; (7) cultural exchanges; (8) supersonic air traffic routes; and (9) miscellaneous Anglo-Soviet exchanges. Working parties of British and Soviet officials would, he hoped, be established to prepare joint recommendations on various problems such as business representation and new embassy buildings.

[3]   As Sir T. Garvey explained to Mr. Suslov on 3 January, Mr. Semenov's communication regarding the visit was obscure in so far as it made no reference to the invitation having come from the 'Soviet leadership' to which Mr. Wilson attached importance (Moscow telegram No. 8 of 3 January).

secondly, if we allow them to conclude that we have learnt nothing and forgotten nothing, they will draw the consequences and no good will be done, including no Brezhnev.

7. I think our best chance lies in an approach having following components:

(i) early tabling by us of a UK draft joint statement in language designed to signal the change of atmosphere which we seek to create during and as the result of the visit. We may call it a 'communique' or a 'joint statement': but I prefer the latter as the Russians will in either case regard it as a formal document setting the tone for Anglo/Soviet relations for the year ahead and probably longer.[4]

(ii) separate prior agreement to the outline of the commercial package. The DOT have got good ideas on this: it is important that we should succeed in persuading the Russians to send a Vice-Minister to London at the end of January to get on with this.

(iii) identification by ourselves of the political concessions that can't be made everything else being regarded as in greater or lesser degree negotiable. My own short list of sticking points are MBFR, the readmission of the 105 spies, monkeying with Brussels tariff arrangements, and any suggestion of doing more at a CSCE summit than signing final documents.[5]

8. It is to be expected that Russians will at some stage turn rough and nasty as they did with Schmidt and Genscher in November.[6] They will desist if firmly faced.

9. I can offer you no definite assurance that this approach will come off or indeed that it will suffice to bring Brezhnev in. Having allowed the ill-health story to run as far as they have, they can always extricate him by telling us at the last moment that he is sick.[7] I think however that if we can kindle their interest, and keep it alive between now and the day, we have a chance worth taking of success in the terms I have outlined.

---

[4] Telegram No. 62 to Moscow of 17 January stated HMG's preference for a joint statement, signed by Mr. Wilson and Mr. Brezhnev, which would demonstrate the significance of the visit. A British draft joint statement was sent to Moscow on 21 January, but the Soviet counter-draft of 5 February was, according to a minute by Mr. Bullard of 7 February, 'a scissors and paste job ... using more scissors than paste'.

[5] British officials soon deduced that concessions in the CSCE and on MBFR would be the required prerequisite for expanded trade (minute from Mr. Bullard to Mr. Morgan of 4 February).

[6] Herr Schmidt and Herr Genscher arrived in Moscow on 28 October for two days of talks with Mr. Brezhnev. During these discussions the Russians strongly resisted West German demands that a series of bilateral agreements then awaiting signature should include West Berlin.

[7] There were rumours towards the end of 1974 that Mr. Brezhnev was seriously ill. As it subsequently emerged, he was recovering from a stroke.

No. 74

Record of meeting between Mr. Wilson and Mr. Brezhnev in
St. Katherine's Hall, the Kremlin Palace at 6 p.m.
on Thursday, 13 February 1975

[*PW 9/303/5*]

Secret

Present:

The Prime Minister	Mr. L.I. Brezhnev
Foreign and Commonwealth Secretary	Mr. A.N. Kosygin
HE Sir Terence Garvey	Mr. A.A. Gromyko
Sir John Hunt[1]	Mr. I. V. Arkhipov[2]
Sir John Killick	Mr. M.R. Kuzmin
Mr. R.T. Armstrong	Mr. A.M. Aleksandrov[3]
Mr. J. Haines[4]	Mr. A.I. Blatov[5]
Mr.T McNally	HE Mr. N.M. Lunkov
Mr. J.L. Bullard	Mr. V.P. Suslov
Mr. B.G. Cartledge[6]	Mr. V. Sukhodriev
	(Interpreter)

After opening words of welcome, *Mr. Brezhnev* noted that the Conservative Parliamentary Party had just elected a woman as their leader.[7] This would give Mr. Wilson somebody to woo. *Mr. Wilson* said that their relationship had started with a honeymoon period. On Mrs. Thatcher's first day as Leader of the Opposition he had paid her a visit in her room in the House of Commons as a gesture of courtesy. The fighting would start next week.

Mr. Brezhnev said that his colleagues had already extended a welcome to Mr. Wilson and expressed their satisfaction at his visit. He wanted not simply to associate himself with these sentiments but also, for political reasons, and in view of his long-standing relationship with Mr. Wilson, to express his personal satisfaction. The Central Committee of the Communist Party of the Soviet Union, together with the whole of the Party and the Soviet people, had a positive attitude to the United Kingdom, and contacts between working classes of Britain and Russia went back to the beginning of the Russian Revolution.

He suggested that at these meetings there should be no delving into the past. There had been ups and downs in the Anglo-Soviet relationship, though the

---

[1] Secretary to the Cabinet.

[2] Vice-Chairman of the Council of Ministers of the USSR.

[3] Assistant to Mr. Brezhnev.

[4] Chief Press Secretary to the Prime Minister.

[5] Assistant to Mr. Brezhnev.

[6] Mr. Bullard's successor as Head of EESD.

[7] On 11 February Mrs M. Thatcher was elected Leader of the Conservative Party.

Soviet leadership had always welcomed Mr. Wilson's visits. This meeting was taking place at a time when many different events, both positive and negative, were taking place in the world. He believed that either the Soviet side or the British side were bound to touch on all the most important issues in world affairs. In the first instance, they should discuss the question of strengthening and developing the relationship between Great Britain and the Soviet Union. He looked forward to strengthening co-operation between the two countries and reinforcing the struggle for peace. No doubt their meetings would touch on economic matters, but the most important issues to discuss were political matters. The Soviet Government had no strict protocol or agenda to suggest. He hoped that the discussions would be entirely free. He himself would talk freely, frankly and confidentially, as he conducted his discussions with his colleagues and with other foreign visitors. In this he spoke for all his colleagues; the Soviet leadership undeviatingly pursued a single line.

In speaking about political affairs, the meeting should not ignore economic co-operation, which was a factor contributing to greater political co-operation. In recent years the two countries had registered certain progress in that field; but neither side could say that in any field we had exhausted the possibilities for the United Kingdom, the Soviet Union and our peoples.

Mr. Brezhnev hoped that Mr. Wilson's stay would be pleasant, and that it would be hallmarked by a new step forward in improved Anglo/Soviet relations and economic ties. If during these meetings they talked diplomatically, there would not be enough time for all that had to be discussed; so they should talk politically, with concrete and clear views and propositions. That was the best way to use the time available and to find solutions for the problems.

Mr. Brezhnev suggested that, if issues arose on which it was not possible to reach a common viewpoint in the main discussion, they could be handed over to Ministers of the two sides for further discussion. Equally, matters relating to economic co-operation could as necessary be delegated.

The Prime Minister thanked Mr. Brezhnev for his very warm and kind welcome, and expressed his pleasure at meeting Mr. Brezhnev and seeing him looking so fit.[8] The welcome accorded to him on his arrival had been a very moving experience, with the troops, the music, many members of the Soviet Cabinet, many ordinary people, and the flags waving in the breeze. *Mr. Brezhnev* interjected that the troops at the airport were, of course, designed, all hundred of them, for attacking Europe. *The Prime Minister* said that he would not propose mutual reductions in troops at airports. At the airport Mr. Kosygin had recalled that the British and Soviet flags had waved together in time of war. Now we needed to see them wave together in the struggle for lasting peace and security. He agreed with Mr. Brezhnev that these meetings should not delve into the past. As he has

---

[8] Cf. No. 73, note 7. In guidance telegram No. 33 of 21 February, which outlined the results of, and significance attached by the FCO to, the Moscow visit, Mr. Callaghan observed: 'Brezhnev's performance was in all essentials normal by comparison with that before his illness. Of his political health there could be no doubt. He was self-assured and as dominant as ever. It was our clear impression that his détente policy remains valid in all essentials and will be continued' (MTW 10/303/1).

said, there has been ups and downs in the Anglo/Soviet relationship; but now we sought a new phase.[9] In these discussions both sides should work for a fresh start, together with a more fruitful and constructive basis for the Anglo/Soviet relationship. The key note for the talks should be Mr. Brezhnev's word 'positive'. The conversations should deal with possibilities for strengthening and developing the bilateral relationship over a wide range of subjects, and with contacts between the two Governments on world affairs during this important phase of international conferences and studies. In the field of bilateral matters, there should be discussion of what could be done to increase trade and industrial co-operation and participation in joint ventures, including the development of the Soviet Union's vast raw material resources, as well as of its technological and scientific manufacturing interests. There would also be possibilities of co-operation in cultural and scientific matters to discuss, including co-operation in medical research. Proposals had been made for closer co-operation on the military side. He understood that a considerable number of documents were or would be ready for signature at the end of these meetings. Turning to international affairs, the Prime Minister said that, as co-depositories with the Soviet Union of the Nuclear Non-Proliferation Treaty, the British Government would like to discuss measures to reduce the risk of spread of nuclear weapons and of competition between countries in nuclear weapons.[10] The two sides should consider what they could do together at the Review Conference in May on these matters, and on chemical warfare, biological warfare and so on.[11]

Heads of Government or their experts could review progress in various international conferences, including the Conference on the Law of the Sea,[12] in which the British and Soviet Governments held positions very close to one another. They could review progress in the talks in Vienna (on Mutual and Balanced Force Reductions) and in Geneva (on the CSCE). Progress had been slow in the Geneva talks: there had been some improvement in recent weeks, but that had not yet gone far enough. The Secretary of State and he were keen to be able to join with the Soviet Government and other Governments in a summit conference later

---

[9] Mr. Callaghan later explained in guidance telegram No. 33 (*v. ibid.*) that the central British objective had been 'to make a fresh start in Anglo-Soviet relations through personal contact with the Soviet leaders at the highest level'. Yet, as Sir T. Garvey pointed out in Moscow telegram No. 208 of 7 February, the Russians knew very well that when the British spoke of a 'new start' they had in mind the removal of the 'blight cast on bilateral relations by the affair of the 105', and while there was evidence that they would entertain the 'new start' thesis, they were determined to exact payment in the form of a political Joint UK–Soviet Statement which accepted their formulations on 'peaceful coexistence', *détente* and the CSCE (ENS 3/548/2).

[10] See No. 61, note 5.

[11] On 17 February Mr. Wilson and Mr. Brezhnev signed a Joint Anglo-Soviet Declaration on the Non-Proliferation of Nuclear Weapons, which welcomed the progress achieved in recent years in limiting strategic arms and nuclear weapons tests, and affirmed that the UK and the USSR 'aimed at the discontinuance of all test explosions of nuclear weapons for all time'. See *Soviet Union No. 1 (1975), Visit of the Prime Minister for Foreign and Commonwealth Affairs to the Soviet Union 13–17 February 1975*, Cmnd 5924 (London: HMSO, 1975), pp. 26–27.

[12] See No. 16, note 13.

this year and thought that, if it was possible to make enough progress, in coming weeks, it should be possible to hold the conference in the summer, and thus combine a meeting which would improve security of all the peoples of Europe with opportunities for the leaders of the conference to acquire a healthy sun tan.

In conclusion, the Prime Minister said that he would leave it to *Mr. Brezhnev* to suggest how these discussions should be organised. After Mr. Brezhnev had invited the British side to suggest a couple of topics for discussion, the *Prime Minister* invited the Foreign and Commonwealth Secretary to take a lead.

The Foreign and Commonwealth Secretary said that the problems he found himself thinking most about were how we should continue the struggle for peace, and how the world could find enough food and energy for its peoples and for the development of prosperity. The food situation was one that was going to concern all of us. It was becoming increasingly difficult to find enough fertiliser at prices which the developing countries could afford. So far as he knew there had been no recent developments of new and higher-yielding strains of cereals. In the meantime world population grew with remorseless speed. The World Food Council was something to which all of us would have to pay increasing attention. There was to be a special conference at the United Nations General Assembly in September, and those who thought about these matters should go to that conference prepared to speak about them.

The primary producing countries were increasingly likely to insist on arrangements which assured a fair return for their products. On the other side those who depended on those products would need greater assurance of stability of price and supply. Mr. Callaghan recalled that Labour Governments had always been interested in commodity agreements, and he believed that there was a possibility of a common approach with the Soviet Government. The prospect of deepening consultation on these matters was one way of bringing about a more easy exchange of views between the two Governments than in the past.

But overriding these problems was the question of world peace. The British Government had noted with sympathy and understanding the development of the Soviet Union's relationship with the United States. The progress made on the talks on strategic arms limitation[13] had been extremely welcome to Britain. So far as the British Government was concerned, the progress of détente could be made as irreversible as human beings could make it. It was their impression that there was great desire both in the United States and in Europe that this progress should be deepened and strengthened.

Mr. Kosygin interjected that the impression did not harmonise with increased military expenditure in the United States. *The Foreign and Commonwealth Secretary* thought there was no inconsistency: the United States Government could show that the Soviet Union was also increasing its military expenditure, even though that did not mean that the Soviet Union did not have pacific intentions. *The Prime Minister* remarked that defence was very expensive these days.

The Foreign and Commonwealth Secretary continued that the British Government believed that the Geneva talks on the CSCE could be brought to an end in a

---

[13] See No. 20, note 16.

relatively short time. He had studied the texts carefully, and thought that, when they appeared in a final and complete document, they would have an important effect on opinion in Europe, because they would represent a setting down for the first time of principles of considerable importance. There were differences between the British Government and the Soviet Government in their approach to these matters and on particular points in the texts. Given goodwill and readiness to be flexible on all sides it should be possible to reach agreement. The British Government was ready to make its contribution to that end.

Mr. Brezhnev said that he could find nothing to which he could object in what the Foreign and Commonwealth Secretary had said. But he wished to add one point of principle. He did not think that it was right at the present time to talk about peace and security in such general and abstract terms. The peoples of the world were becoming increasingly close to one another, and there was nothing they cherished more than peace. He would be prepared to talk to the Prime Minister in a very concrete way on these matters. He did not deny the importance of the food problem. But we must face the fact that another five years would go by, and the problem would still not be solved. The United Nations would take the matter up, and probably set up some kind of conference. The Soviet Government would be prepared to talk to the British Government, and join in proposals to such a conference. But the main question was peace, and we must talk about it in a concrete way.

The Prime Minister had referred to the Geneva talks on the CSCE. These questions had been under discussion for five years, and military expenditure was still rising. We talked about security and co-operation, and we spent more and more on arms. We should look closely and in concrete terms at the position which each of the various participating countries took as these matters were discussed during these meetings. Food was important, but in the end it too depended on peace. If there was tranquillity in Europe, it would be easier to resolve all the other problems.

The Prime Minister had said that he favoured an early completion of the CSCE at a summit conference. That was what the American Government had been saying; that was what Herr Schmidt had said, and Signor Moro[14] in a recent message to the Soviet Government. Everybody was in favour of bringing the conference to a conclusion. But we seemed to be unable to do so. Instead of getting together to sign an agreement, people were digging around in the Third Basket, discussing tourism and questions of opening up a bar or a café in someone else's country. No-one mentioned that the United States Secretary for Defence had just sent two brigades armed with nuclear weapons to West Germany.[15] These weapons were not ICBMs, so that they were not covered by the Strategic Arms Limitation talks; but if you were killed it did not make any odds what kind of weapon it was you were killed by. We should not try to avoid these more complex problems.

[14] Sig. A. Moro was Italian Prime Minister.

[15] The *communiqué* issued at the end of a Ministerial meeting of NATO's Defence Planning Committee on 10–11 December 1974 announced the US intention to form the equivalent of two new brigades in Europe by the re-allocation of personnel from supporting functions.

The Soviet Government knew that the voice of the United Kingdom carried considerable weight. They had never regarded Great Britain as a third rate country; they had always heeded Britain's voice, as that of a major and well developed country. He would be very ready to sign the documents to which the Prime Minister had referred; but they would not solve the main problem. If we could have a stable peace we could have far fewer submarines and fewer bombers—and at 10 million roubles each that was no mean consideration. If the United States sent two brigades armed with nuclear weapons into West Germany, the Soviet Government would be entitled to send similar troops into East Germany, Poland, Czechoslovakia and Hungary; and that would not be nuclear proliferation as the arms would be under Russian control.

So we were walking round and round in circles. We should be concrete and talk about important matters. We should not waste our time in the fine print of Third Baskets, of integrity of States, of inviolability of frontiers and so on. There was a debate going on at present on the size of the zone in which all manoeuvres should be announced. This was not a serious matter, if there were hundreds of nuclear installations in Western Germany. If the United States were prepared to take away those installations, the Soviet Government would be prepared to proclaim the movement of even a single regiment right up to the Urals. What people were really worried about was the possibility of a terrible catastrophe, as a result of which the entire race could perish. He knew what war meant; that was why he was dedicated to strengthening peace. That was the policy handed down by Lenin and that was what mattered, not bars and cafés. If the Prime Minister and the Foreign and Commonwealth Secretary were guided by the motive of strengthening peace, they would be welcomed by all the 15 million members of the Communist Party in the Soviet Union and indeed all of the Soviet People.

The Prime Minister said that his visit with the Foreign and Commonwealth Secretary had the full support of the British Labour Party, though they could only claim just over 6 million members, and was backed with the goodwill of the British people, as Ambassador Lunkov knew. The British people were hoping for productive results from this meeting.

The Prime Minister reverted to the British Government's desire for an early summit conference on security and co-operation in Europe. While he had not been following the Geneva negotiations in detail, he knew that there were a few big confidence-building measures on which we should be able to agree. Mr. Brezhnev had spoken of the Third Basket: the questions involved might seem small in relation to the major issues of world peace, but they were part of the stuff of life for ordinary people. Mr. Brezhnev had also spoken of the proposed agreement on inviolability of frontiers. This was an issue of vital importance to Germany. The Prime Minister's understanding was that it was possible to reach agreement about the words to be used, but not about under which heading those words should come. This was surely a matter which could be resolved by mutual agreement, even if it meant putting the words in more than one place. The time had come to take these matters up in Geneva, to make possible a summit conference at Helsinki or wherever else might be agreed.

Mr. Brezhnev said that the question of voluntary changes of frontiers without the use of force was one on which the Soviet Government had made proposals which were being discussed at Geneva. But this question of peaceful change of frontiers should be separated from that of inviolability of frontiers. If people wished to change their frontiers, they were free to do so. There had been endless arguments at Geneva about where to put the wording to which the Prime Minister had referred. Some of the participants were clamouring for formulae which would order people to change their frontiers. No solution had so far been found for this matter.

The Prime Minister said that the British Government would not support forced changes of frontiers; they would support inviolability of frontiers. He repeated that it should be possible to find some way of settling the problem of where to put this wording: it was the thought that mattered, not the exact place in which it was set in a document. *The Foreign and Commonwealth Secretary* said that this was not a matter which the two Governments could settle in Moscow. He understood the Soviet Government's argument for not including the words in question under the third principle. It would be helpful for him, when the time came for him to discuss the matter with others who were greatly concerned, to know where in the view of the Soviet Government the words should go.[16]

The Foreign and Commonwealth Secretary hoped that Mr. Brezhnev would not underrate the importance of the Third Basket. At the Helsinki Conference there had been a statement of intention to settle upon the principles of human rights. The Third Basket was an attempt to channel the general sentiment in particular directions: it was about the quality of peace. These questions mattered to people as they went about their ordinary work and life, and were of great concern to the people in the West. The success of the conference would be judged by the outcome, and he was glad to note that a good deal of progress had been made.

The Foreign and Commonwealth Secretary confirmed that the United States was now replacing some support troops in Western Germany by two brigades, though he could not confirm that these brigades were armed with nuclear weapons. But we could not forget on the other hand that Soviet tanks in Europe out-numbered those of the Western Powers by 3 to 1. This did not mean that he thought that the Soviet Union was going to attack Western Europe; but the fact of the disparity remained. If we could get down to real talks in Vienna there would be a chance of results that would enable us all to reduce expenditure on defence.

Mr. Brezhnev said that it was rather strange that the Foreign and Commonwealth Secretary should say that he did not know the views of the Soviet Government on the appropriate place for a phrase about voluntary change of frontiers. The Soviet Government's representative had tabled proposals in Geneva, about which it was his business to know. *The Foreign and Commonwealth Secretary* said that, if those proposals were the Soviet Government's last word and the other Powers concerned had said their last words, it was difficult to see how the issue was to be resolved. *Mr. Brezhnev* said that the Soviet Government did not know what was

[16] Cf. Volume II, No. 112.

the British Government's last word. *The Foreign and Commonwealth Secretary* said that the British Government was not in the lead on this matter, in which others were more deeply concerned.

Mr. Brezhnev said that, if anybody was concerned, it was the Federal Republic of Germany. In that connection he would ask whether it was better to deal with the SPD or the CDU.[17] The Prime Minister knew what the situation was in the Federal Republic of Germany: he was a statesman, and he had been around in this business for 30 years, longer than Mr. Brezhnev himself. Mr. Brezhnev said that he respected Herr Brandt very much for his sense of realism. History would evaluate him rightly, as a realistically thinking man, who endeavoured to look into the future. He had respected Chancellor Schmidt, whom he had recently received in Moscow. He held President Giscard d'Estaing in deep respect; the President had assured him of his dedication as President to the policies of President Pompidou in international matters. He might have some problems on the domestic front; in these the Soviet Government did not interfere. But on several matters of principle he held a very clear position, and for that he deserved respect.

Mr. Brezhnev said that he had so far had only one meeting with President Ford, but it was a meeting of fundamental importance. He had liked President Ford very much, as (judging from their approval of the outcome of the meeting) had the entire Soviet leadership. But Mr. Wilson would know the situation in the United States as well as or better than he did. He thought that President Ford was having a hard time, with an economic crisis, 7 million unemployed, mounting inflation, rising military expenditure, and no signs of finding a way out.

Reverting to the talks on CSCE, Mr. Brezhnev recalled that Mr. Callaghan had said that the Third Basket was necessary and useful. The Soviet Government did not dispute that. He had said that the Soviet Union had more tanks in Europe than the Western European Powers, but the Soviet Government was prepared to sign a document on the inviolability on frontiers which in fact meant the prevention of war; so he did not see that the numbers of tanks had any relevance. *Mr. Callaghan* interjected that he had only mentioned the matter because Mr. Brezhnev himself had talked about the two United States brigades in Western Germany.

Mr. Brezhnev recalled that he had met President Pompidou several times, first as President de Gaulle's Prime Minister and later as President in his own right. It was he who had suggested to President Pompidou that soldiers were soldiers, and went out and had exercises, so why should the Soviet Army not invite the French Army to see their manoeuvres. President Pompidou had said that he thought that that was very good. But, when this was taken up at Geneva, it had been expanded to terrible proportions requiring notification of everything that was done right up to the Urals. The talks had gone on for three years without any solution; that could not be right.

The time was now 8.15 p.m., and Mr. Brezhnev suggested that the meeting should be adjourned until tomorrow. He proposed that the Treasurer of the Labour Party should sign a cheque to the Soviet Government for £4½ billion

---

[17] *Christlich Demokratische Union*/Christian Democratic Union.

sterling. The Soviet Government would be prepared to sign an agreement on that instantly.

The Prime Minister said that unfortunately the Treasurer of the Labour Party had not brought his cheque book with him.[18]

On the CSCE, the Prime Minister said that the British Government understood the position of the Soviet Union on the matters to which reference had been made. He believed that there was no difference in principle between the two Governments, and suggested that the Foreign and Commonwealth Secretary and Mr. Gromyko should have a further word, to see if they could arrive at a satisfactory solution to suggest at Geneva.

The Prime Minister went on to propose that, when the meeting was resumed the following morning, discussions should begin on bilateral matters. There was a certain amount of work still to be done, to which the Ministerial meetings could give a push (what he described, to the amusement of the Russian side, as a 'pinok').[19] After that they could turn to non-proliferation, or whatever else the Soviet Government might wish to raise.

The Prime Minister then raised the question of what should be said to the Press. The talks themselves were confidential: he suggested that the Press should simply be given an indication of subjects discussed, without any briefing on the tenor of the discussions. *Mr. Brezhnev* then caused the interpreter to read a ready prepared Soviet draft statement to the Press, which indicated that the discussions had concentrated on strengthening peace and security, improving *détente* and co-operation, in Europe and elsewhere, the need for constructive co-operation between Britain and the Soviet Union, and the desire for a new impetus between Britain and the Soviet Union in such matters as trade.

The Prime Minister noted the Soviet statement, and agreed that British briefing should be on corresponding lines.

Mr. Brezhnev agreed that the meeting should resume on bilateral questions the following morning. It would also be necessary to finalise documents for signature on 17 February (when Mr. Gromyko would be absent since he had to meet Dr. Kissinger in Geneva). It might therefore be useful for members of the British and Soviet sides to meet to take a further look at the various drafts which had been prepared.

The Prime Minister welcomed Mr. Brezhnev's proposals as constructive and positive. On the question on non-proliferation he said that the British Government would like to get more substance into the draft; but that was something which could be discussed when the meetings were resumed.

The meeting was adjourned at about 8.20 p.m.

---

[18] Mr. Brezhnev returned to this matter during his final meeting with Mr. Wilson on 17 February. He then said that he understood Mr. Kosygin had since proposed that the amount should be increased to £6 billion, but that Mr. Callaghan had said that Britain had 'overemployment' and could not afford such a contribution. Mr. Wilson replied that the British side had assumed that 'this could be forgotten as a matter of the merest detail'. Mr. Brezhnev opined that Mr. Wilson and Mr. Callaghan had been too busy looking at paintings to concentrate on these 'important matters' (record of meeting between Mr. Wilson and Mr. Brezhnev in the Kremlin on 17 February).

[19] Colloquial Russian for a 'kick'.

No. 75

Minute from Mr. G. Foggon[1] *to Mr. Bullard*

[EN 5 / 1]

Confidential   FCO, *14 February 1975*

Soviet Westpolitik after the CSCE: the Trade Unions

1.   I should like to comment on your minutes of 8[2] and 28 January.[3]

2.   There is not the least doubt that the rehabilitation of Soviet and East European trade unions in the eyes of some leading Western trade unionists after the events of 1969 represents a considerable victory for the Soviet AUCCTU,[4] who have throughout masterminded the various contacts. From a situation in 1969, after the invasion of Czechoslovakia, when an invitation to the AUCCTU to send a delegation to Britain was angrily withdrawn and contact broken off, we have moved to an position of regular bilateral and multilateral exchanges with, at the apex, the second East–West major trade union gathering taking place at Geneva at the end of this month. I do not regard the principal importance of these events as resting on the meetings themselves. In my view, these East–West trade union meetings achieve at one and the same time a weakening of resolve among trade unionists here to resist Communist infiltration and disruption and a reassurance to trade unionists in Eastern Europe and Soviet Russia that their particular brand of trade unionism is accepted as 'good coin' by their Western confreres.

3.   But it is the first of these which I think is the most important in our domestic affairs. For more than half a century our trade unions have been exposed to Communist attempts to infiltrate and control. There was a great conflict over this in the 1920s. (George Lansbury,[5] who today would presumably be a member of the Tribune Group, said in 1924 'The left-wing is no more prepared than the workers' movement as a whole to be bored or manipulated from King Street,[6] or

---

[1] Overseas Labour Adviser, FCO.

[2] In this minute to Sir J. Killick, 'Soviet Westpolitik after the CSCE', Mr. Bullard predicted a renewed Soviet effort, after the conclusion of the CSCE, to mobilise Western public opinion to press governments to fall in with Soviet ideas about an all-European security system, economic cooperation, a freeze on armed forces in central Europe, and resistance to further EC integration. This, he thought, would involve attempts by East European Communist parties to intensify their contacts with Western social democrats and the vigorous development of East/West trade union contacts (ENS 2/1).

[3] Mr. Bullard suggested in this minute to Mr. Foggon that an immediate tactical aim of Eastern trade unions was to get themselves accepted as interlocutors on equal footing with trade unions in the West. He feared that, if British trade unionists thought that by making things easy for the Russians in this respect they would reap benefits of a purely trade union kind, the results from the FCO's point of view 'could be anything from disappointing to disastrous' (ENS 2/1).

[4] All Union Central Council of Trades Unions of the USSR.

[5] Labour Party Leader, 1932–35. He founded *The Daily Herald* in 1919 and edited it until 1923.

[6] The headquarters of the Communist Party of Great Britain (CPGB) were located at 16 King Street, London, WC2.

for that matter from Moscow'). As recently as 1948/49 the General Council of the TUC was circulating to affiliated unions, pamphlets such as 'The Tactics of Disruption: Communist Methods Exposed'. There remained a core of strong anti-Communist feeling within the General Council of the TUC until the death 3 years ago of Les Cannon of the ETU.[7] It was he indeed who moved at Congress in 1969 the motion to withdraw the invitation to the Soviet trade union delegation to visit Britain. Here and there there are sporadic attempts to expose and combat Communist infiltration in the unions but the will to press these home is sapped by the absence now of any lead from the General Council of the TUC. As for the media, it is instructive how much space has been given to the Shrewsbury Two[8] and how little space was given to the trial of the two East Kilbride officials of the AUEW[9] who last year faked an entire branch election in order to make possible the election of a Communist to the AUEW Appeals Board and were given heavy sentences.

4. So far as intentions are concerned, nothing has changed in my view since the early guidance issued to Communists overseas by the Soviet leaders in 1926: 'The Communist Parties, particularly in circumstances obtaining in the West, would be unable to develop and grow in strength if they lacked the earnest support of the trade unions and their leaders. Only a party able to maintain broad contacts with trade unions and their leaders, able to establish a real proletarian contact with them can win the majority of the working class in its country.' Nor have tactics changed: the creation of factions, fronts and groups within the unions, stimulation of unofficial disputes and the exploitation of the apathy of the ordinary trade union member. Against this background of long-term objectives deeply rooted in Communist theology, the statement made by Mr. Brezhnev on 24 April 1967 has a particular significance, both in the political and trade union spheres:

> Experience teaches, in particular, that the 'cold war' and the confrontation of military blocs, the atmosphere of military threats, seriously hampers the activity of revolutionary democratic forces. In conditions of international tension in bourgeois countries the reactionary elements become active, the military raise their heads, anti-democratic tendencies and anti-Communism are strengthened. And, conversely the past few years have shown quite clearly that in conditions of slackened international tension, the pointer of the political barometer moves left. Certain changes in relations between communists and social democrats in certain countries, a noticeable falling off in anti-Communist hysteria, and the increase in the influence of Western European Communist parties is most directly correlated with the reduction in tension which has taken place in Europe.

[7] Mr. L. Cannon was formerly General President of Electrical Trades Union (ETU) and a member of the TUC General Council.

[8] Two militant trade unionists charged and subsequently imprisoned in connexion with violence used during the picketing of building sites in Shrewsbury and Telford in 1972.

[9] Amalgamated Union of Engineering Workers.

5. The Secretary of State made the point at his meeting with the International Committee of the TUC last week that what was important was to know what your objectives were when you started to talk with the Russians; the Russians were always clear about what they wanted. The objectives described by Mr. Hargreaves at the meeting of the Overseas Labour Consultative Committee and referred to by you in your minute of 28 January[10] represented, I think, only a personal view of Mr. Hargreaves. The TUC position has been somewhat differently presented in the report of a recent TUC delegation to Hungary and Czechoslovakia:

> It was not the time to press for agreement between trade union organisations in Eastern and Western Europe on broad international issues, since many changes in attitudes were required, and the best for the moment was to avoid those issues which might divide. As for joint action, much caution was required. For example, TUC operations in regard to South Africa would certainly not be helped by a general campaign, though there might be some scope in respect of Chile, for example, for parallel action. It would be best to avoid misunderstanding and suspicion and let common understanding grow through cautious contacts.

Given the political objectives of the Eastern trade unions in any contacts with the West, I should think that this is a formula that would suit the East very well.

6. This whole background of growing contacts and much publicised smiling photographs of Western and Eastern European trade union leaders such as those which appeared after the Automobile Workers Conference in London in January, produces an atmosphere where anyone who complains about the dangers of Communist infiltration or of growing East–West trade union contacts is either accused of 'seeing Reds under the bed' or reverting to the 'Cold War'. The American fraternal delegate at last year's Congress at Brighton had a very rough time when he came to those passages in his fraternal speech which criticised the Soviet system and Soviet trade unions.

7. Some observers claim to see some shift to the right; but, for example, the emergence of Mr. John Boyd[11] as No. 1 candidate for the Secretaryship of the AUEW over his Communist opponent stems not from a change of spirit but from the adoption against the opposition of left-wingers on the Executive, of the postal ballot. TASS,[12] led by Mr. Ken Gill, the new Communist member of the General Council of the TUC, is opposing the postal ballot and the left wing in the AUEW are seeking to revert to the old easily manipulated Branch arrangements.

---

[10] See note 3 above. Mr. Bullard cited Mr. A. Hargreaves, the Head of the International Department of the TUC, as having expressed the TUC's hope that 'they would be able to move to a position in which they could influence conditions affecting Eastern European workers who were now becoming commercial competitors'.

[11] Mr. Boyd, a former Chairman of the Labour Party and a 'moderate' union leader, defeated his 'broad left' opponent in a postal ballot for the post of General Secretary of the AUEW in May 1975.

[12] Technical, Administrative and Supervisory Section of AUEW.

8.   In short, I think it is an unfortunate consequence of the new friendliness between our unions and those of Eastern Europe, however carefully formulated these meetings might be and however much they are confined to technical subjects, that they make the task of Communist infiltration and manipulation of our unions and shop stewards' organisations that much easier.[13] They also therefore make the job of getting the Social Contract[14] to stick that much harder; and trade union support for remaining in the EEC so much more difficult to win.[15]

9.   I think we must nevertheless do our best to provide more background briefing material for these meetings as recommended by Mr. McNally. I have sent some IRD[16] material to the TUC about Soviet and East European working conditions for possible use at this month's Geneva meeting[17] and it will be interesting to see if it is used. It may be timely to review our briefing arrangements after the results of the Moscow meetings have been assessed?[18]

[13] Sir J. Killick thought Moscow more interested in pursuing its ends through British trade unions than through links between Communists and the Labour Party. But he assumed that the Russians saw Britain in a different category from its Western neighbours, 'on a presumed assessment that our influence is declining both within Europe and more generally and that we are perhaps best left for the moment to stew in our own juice' (minute to Mr. Bullard of 9 January, ENS 2/1).

[14] The notion of a 'social contract' between Government and trade unions had become a dominant political and industrial issue during the second half of 1974. With the object of curbing domestic inflationary pressures, wage restraint was to be coupled with economic and social reform.

[15] The Labour Party had promised in its manifesto for the General Election of October 1974 that within a year the British people would decide 'through the ballot box' whether the UK should stay in the EC on terms to be renegotiated by the Labour Government, or reject them and leave the Community. On 22 January the Government announced it was bringing in a Referendum Bill and, after the passage of the necessary legislation, a referendum on the issue was held on 5 June. Although the Labour Party remained deeply divided on the question, the Prime Minister publicly supported continued EC membership, and electors voted by more than 2–1 in favour of it.

[16] Information Research Department of the FCO.

[17] An East/West trade union conference was held in Geneva during 28 February–1 March.

[18] On 20 February Mr. Bullard noted on this minute: 'This is very plain and important, and in line with what we have observed from EESD as regards Soviet objectives in Western Europe. I understand that certain meetings may be initiated next week.'

No. 76

Sir T. Garvey (Moscow) to Mr. Callaghan
[*ENS 3/548/2*]

Confidential   MOSCOW, *4 March 1975*

Summary ...[1]

Sir,

Anglo-Soviet Relations: The Prime Minister's visit and the 'New Phase'

The visit of the Prime Minister and yourself to the Soviet Union from 13–17 February has been described by Mr. Kosygin as historic. This despatch seeks to analyse the results for the UK and the Soviet Union and to make suggestions about our policy in the 'new phase'.

Background

2.   The visit followed seven lean years in Anglo-Soviet relations, caused first by the invasion of Czechoslovakia in 1968, and our reaction thereto, and intensified by the British expulsion of Soviet spies in 1971. While Britain was a forerunner in *détente* policies in the early '60s and played an active role in the Quadripartite negotiations on Berlin and in the Conferences in Geneva and Vienna, our bilateral relationship with the USSR had come by the end of the period to look very much out of joint with the times. When your predecessor visited the Soviet Union in December 1973, both sides were ready to draw a line under the past but not yet to launch a new spirit in our relations.[2] In trade, where we seemed to be suffering from some Soviet political discrimination, we had begun to take steps towards a new phase. In May 1974 this bore fruit in a 10-year Agreement on Economic, Industrial, Scientific and Technological Co-operation.[3] But the Parliamentary situation in Britain delayed our initiative for a top-level political visit.

The visit itself

3.   The immediate run-up did not seem auspicious. We had to haggle with the Russians about the dates of the visit and the terms of the announcement. In negotiating about the programme, and the documents to be signed, the Russians were unforthcoming and slow. The build-up in the Soviet media was minimal.

4.   But the visit itself was a sharp contrast. As soon as you arrived in Moscow, and we learned that Mr. Brezhnev would participate, it was clear that the talks were likely to go well. Mr. Brezhnev attended three sessions, the Kremlin lunch and the signature of the documents. The atmosphere in the Ministerial

---

[1] Not printed.
[2] Cf. No. 52.
[3] See No. 72, note 12.

discussions was excellent. The treatment in the Soviet Press, and even more on television, was exceptional in its warmth, extent and duration; while for the first two days it was above all about Mr. Brezhnev's participation, the Anglo-Soviet story quickly acquired its own momentum which still has not spent itself in the Soviet Press. The bargaining between officials about the terms of the Joint Statement was predictably tough and it lasted into the final night of your stay. But progress was steady and only one point remained for settlement on the final morning. We obtained all the documents we wanted. Six were signed in Moscow: the Joint Statement,[4] which is very substantial as communiqués go; the Protocol on Consultations;[5] the two detailed Long-Term Programmes on Economic and Industrial Co-operation; and Scientific and Technical Co-operation;[6] the Agreement on Medical Co-operation;[7] and the Declaration on Nuclear Non-Proliferation.[8] The Credit Agreement was concluded during the visit but signature was left for a subsequent exchange of letters.[9]

How we did

6.   We have succeeded in ending the barren period in Anglo-Soviet relations by re-establishing personal contact at the highest level as a normal feature of these relations. This was confirmed by the acceptance by Mr. Brezhnev, Mr. Kosygin and Mr. Gromyko of invitations to visit the UK; and by the conclusion at our initiative of the Protocol on Consultations which provides that Foreign Ministers or their representatives shall meet in principle at least once a year. The seven documents we concluded were ample demonstration that the Soviet Union had been persuaded of the seriousness of our desire to build up a productive political relationship based so far as possible on co-operation in areas that matter and not just on atmospherics. We also achieved Soviet endorsement of language which should give the right kind of impetus to the expansion of Anglo-Soviet trade. While we did not obtain mention of a numerical target, the Joint Statement refers not only to a 'substantial increase in the level of trade over the next five years' but also to the achievement of a better balance, which means a reduction in the long-standing Soviet surplus. There is also mention of an expected increase in contracts for British machinery and equipment and specific reference to important projects in the Soviet Union in which British firms might participate. This, and especially the Long-Term Programme on Economic and Industrial Co-operation and the new Credit Agreement, gives us a formal framework for Anglo-Soviet trade which is fully comparable with that of our Western

---

[4]   See Cmnd 5924, pp. 1–7.

[5]   *V. ibid.*, pp. 24–25.

[6]   These programmes foresaw, among other things, the exchange of scientific and technical information, the organisation of lectures, symposia, conferences and specialised exhibitions. *V. ibid.*, pp. 11–23.

[7]   *V. ibid*, pp. 8–10.

[8]   See No. 61, note 5.

[9]   The new credit arrangements with the Soviet Union involved £950 million for new contracts with British firms at rates of interest comparable to those offered by other Western countries.

competitors in the Soviet market. We were able to agree on a Joint Statement reflecting the importance of the visit and establishing guidelines for the future development of relations. We had also aimed to set out our views on important international questions and if possible to influence Soviet views. The Prime Minister and you were able to do much to achieve at least the first half of this objective.

7.   Finally we were aiming to set out a British view of *détente* and to ascertain whether Soviet thinking had evolved away from a concept which included ideological struggle and the development of the class war in non-Communist States. We cannot claim to have gained detailed new insight into Soviet views. But we did confirm our assessment that Soviet *détente* policy continues despite the recent collapse of the Soviet-US Trade Agreement.[10] And we did obtain, in two of the documents, a definition of peaceful co-existence which equates it to co-operation alone and applies it to relations between States irrespective of their social systems.[11] This will not change Soviet practice. But it has advantages. The definition excludes the overtones about the ideological struggle with which over the years Soviet theorists have saddled the concept; and the word 'irrespective' makes it theoretically applicable to Soviet relations with other Socialist States and thus in logic denies the Brezhnev doctrine. The new definition also has practical utility: its existence will enable us in future to mention peaceful co-existence in bilateral documents with Communist countries and thus to remove a long-standing irritant which we have had very frequently to face when negotiating with members of the Warsaw Pact.

8.   We also achieved an objective of a more general kind. The Russians, especially in the voluminous Press comment, have recognised the existence of the 'new phase'.[12] Indeed, they went further: in his speech on 17 February, the Prime

[10]   Senator Jackson's supporters succeeded, during the autumn of 1974, in securing the inclusion in the US Trade Act of provisions which would, in effect, have made the Soviet Union's most-favoured-nation status and its access to US credit dependent on its policy towards the emigration of Soviet Jews. On 10 January the Soviet Government formally rejected such terms.

[11]   In a speech delivered at a Kremlin luncheon on 14 February Mr. Brezhnev emphasised the Soviet Union's determination to do all in its power 'to impart a historically irreversible character not only to international détente as such, but also towards the long term fruitful co-operation of states with different social systems on the basis of full equality and mutual respect'. He added: 'That is what we in the Soviet Union mean by peaceful co-existence'. This redefinition of 'peaceful coexistence' was welcomed by British officials, and they seized the opportunity to incorporate it in both the UK–Soviet Protocol on Consultations and the Joint UK–Soviet Statement (Moscow telegram No. 306 of 16 February). See notes 4 and 5 above and Volume I, No. 104.

[12]   The Soviet-UK statement, signed by Mr. Wilson and Mr. Brezhnev on 17 February, also referred to the 'new phase' in the two countries' bilateral relations (see note 4 above). On this Mr. Callaghan noted in guidance telegram No. 33 of 21 February (cf. No. 74, note 8): 'This is not just a question of atmosphere: we intend that it should apply to the substance of our relations, thereby placing them on a more solid and constructive basis ... It is likely that the Soviet side wished to use the visit to demonstrate their undiminished commitment to détente after the setback of their relations with the Americans. But it is nonetheless clear that the Soviet side also wished to open a new phase, in which Britain moves up alongside France and the FRG in Brezhnev's pattern of détente diplomacy.'

Minister referred to a break-through in Anglo-Soviet relations and Mr. Kosygin in reply said he agreed with everything Mr. Wilson had said. In commentaries on East–West relations, the Soviet Press now refers to the UK in the same breath as the US, France and the Federal German Republic. We may not be fully abreast of the other three countries. The US, as the other super Power, is in a category of its own; and, as I argued in my despatch of 27 November last year,[13] both France and the Federal Republic have a special importance in Russian eyes. These priorities are likely to reassert themselves. But we are no longer odd man out.[14]

How they did

9. What did the Russians obtain? The Credit Agreement is of symbolic as well as commercial value to them, since it came soon after the limits set by the US Congress on American credits had contributed to the cancellation of the Soviet-US Trade Agreement. But the Credit Agreement is a competitive necessity for us if we are to increase substantially our exports of capital goods to the USSR. Both sides have interests, albeit of different kinds, in the same result.

10. A major Soviet objective was certainly to obtain formulations in the Joint Statement implying British support for Soviet positions on international issues. Here they will consider that they achieved some success. The formulations on CSCE, on the Geneva Conference and on the Middle East[15] and on Cyprus differ from the language we had previously employed, though Mr. Gromyko would have liked to move us further on CSCE. The Russians also failed to extract the formulations they wanted on various other issues and the language agreed in the three contexts just referred to was not such as to offer much scope for causing trouble between Britain and her allies. The Russians, as anticipated, insisted on removing from the published documents various references to contacts and the exchange of information outside the framework of formal bilateral agreements and all mention of mutual responsibility for aid to the developing world. The discussion on world economic problems was, not surprisingly, one-sided and the reduction of our passage on this theme to a passing reference to exchanges of views under the aegis of the Protocol on Consultations provided confirmation (if such were needed) that one range of problems of paramount importance to the

---

[13] No. 72.

[14] Mr. Bullard listed amongst the reasons why he thought the visit could be called a 'success' its establishment of 'a British line towards the Soviet Union on which Ministers and officials are united—for the time being'. He also thought it a personal success for Mr. Wilson and Mr. Callaghan, 'perhaps especially the latter, who had his baptism of fire from Gromyko' (letter to Sir T. Garvey of 21 February).

[15] During his discussions with Mr. Brezhnev Mr. Wilson stated the standard British position on the Middle Eastern conflict: support for the relevant UN resolutions; acknowledgement of the rights of the Palestinians; continued support for Dr. Kissinger's step by step approach; and a return to the Geneva Conference only when the results of Dr. Kissinger's efforts were known. Mr. Gromyko subsequently pressed for reference in the Joint Statement to an 'immediate' resumption of the Geneva Conference, but Mr. Callaghan refused to go beyond the phrase 'at a very early date' (Moscow telegram No. 306 of 16 February).

rest of the world and by which the Soviet Union is certainly not unaffected, is still firmly excluded from their definition of co-operation.[16]

11. I believe that these Soviet gains obtained during the visit are less than the British gains referred to above. This, I am sure, is because the Russians had wider reasons for wanting a successful visit at the present time. The Soviet decision to abort the Trade Agreement with the US had been accompanied by evident concern that the world might think Moscow's policy of *détente* had been abandoned or modified. Before you came a number of statements had sought to show the contrary; but your visit was the first public opportunity to demonstrate this in action and the Russians seized it. To make the demonstration successful they built up the news coverage and were probably willing to pay a higher price. In the Soviet leadership's official summing-up of the visit, as in the Press comment before and since, the continuing and constant nature of *détente* has been emphasised. It was no doubt one of the Soviet objectives to be able to claim credit for persuading us to come round and, as I have commented in my telegram No. 351 [17] analysing this formal Soviet balance-sheet on the visit, this document gives the impression that the improvement in our relations had come about through a belated shift in British attitudes.

12. Soviet willingness to pay a price was also, I believe, related to their desire for completeness in *détente*. To silence our discordant voice in the choir of *détente* was a useful achievement for the Soviet leaders, who will wish to demonstrate at the XXVth Congress of the CPSU expected in about a year, that the 'peace policy' proclaimed at the last Congress has evoked a favourable response everywhere. They probably also wanted, by making a fanfare about better relations with Britain, to spur on the other Western participants in *détente*, such as France and the Federal Republic, to greater willingness to make concessions as the price of staying among the leaders in the race. There is also possibly a doctrinal element in their wish to improve relations across the board with all the developed countries of what the Chinese describe as the Second World. And, in the longer term, they may still harbour illusions about co-operation with the democratic Left in Western Europe.[18]

13. If these were the main external factors behind the visit's success, there was

---

[16] The original British draft of the UK–Soviet Joint Statement contained a substantial paragraph on the importance of aid and the need for a global approach to the world food situation and poverty. But this was struck out *in toto* by the Soviet side (telegram No. 45 to Belgrade of 28 February).

[17] In this telegram of 24 February Sir T. Garvey reported on the formal appraisal of the visit which had recently appeared in Pravda. That same day he commented in Moscow telegram No. 355 that by underlining the continuing and constant nature of Soviet policy, the impression was being given that the improvement in relations came first and foremost as the result of a shift in British attitudes.

[18] In his letter to Sir T. Garvey of 21 February (see note 14 above) Mr. Bullard suggested as reasons for the Russians treating the British 'so proud': (1) 'Pleased to put an end to a discordant voice in the chorus of détente, i.e. to secure our obstinate scalp at last'; (2) they saw possibilities for exploiting what had been said and agreed during the visit; (3) it would spur the French and West German leaders to do better, 'i.e. the bicycle race is back and no mistake'; (4) they wanted a 'conspicuous forum in which to re-emphasise the Soviet commitment to détente after the US Trade Agreement fiasco'; and (5) 'Brezhnev's reappearance'.

also an internal one. Mr. Brezhnev's absence from view for seven weeks before the visit was ended when he joined the first session of talks just after your arrival. He of course had his own reasons for choosing this occasion to reappear. Judging by his demeanour during the visit, he was fit enough to have appeared in public somewhat earlier. He chose not to, I am sure, because the best way to scotch all the rumours about his health, physical and political, was to reappear in full vigour for an international event lasting several days and expose himself to Western leaders, officials and journalists. Nevertheless, the Russians must have known that, by choosing this occasion for Mr. Brezhnev's reappearance, they were limiting their own freedom of action: a fiasco was no longer an option for them.

14. We were expecting the Russians to try during the visit to obtain concessions on the numerical ceilings on Soviet officials resident in Britain and perhaps even to go for some kind of dissociation by Her Majesty's Government from their predecessors' expulsion of Soviet spies in 1971. They did not try. To do so might have been to put the success of the visit at risk. It may be that the KGB wanted to do so and was over-ruled. But I think it more likely that the Russians decided not to seek retrospective contrition—or, as Mr. Brezhnev put it at the outset of the visit, not to delve into the past—but rather to work towards a larger official presence in Britain in the future. They may have calculated that the British Government, in a new and warmer phase of Anglo-Soviet relations, would find it more difficult than during the visit itself to stand firm on the numerical ceilings and on refusing visas for known spies. Soviet officials made it clear at the end of the visit that they wanted to include visas in future discussions about commercial representation in both capitals.

Next moves

15. This visit was a notable success in opening the new phase in Anglo-Soviet relations and thus setting the scene for progress on specific issues. We should move quickly to sustain the momentum and benefit as much as possible from the present atmosphere. Early action will also help us to deflect Soviet attempts to blame us for any subsequent difficulty on particular questions.[19] I have made recommendations by telegram about pressing on with the first meeting of the non-governmental Anglo-Soviet Round Table, with Parliamentary visits, with defence exchanges and with the return visits of Soviet leaders.[20] On the most important single issue, trade, the Government is in the hands of British industry, who must, by hook or by crook, be constrained to do its bit. The next critical date is the fourth session of the Anglo-Soviet Joint Commission, which the Secretary of State for Trade is to attend in Moscow in May. Many British firms have adopted a critical or disinterested attitude towards doing business here. Others which export

---

[19] Much the same point was made by Mr. Bullard in his letter to Sir T. Garvey of 21 February (*v. ibid.*). He proposed as next steps: 'Retain the initiative so as to a) define the new phase in our terms and not theirs, b) get our proposals on the table first, c) avoid criticism for lack of momentum.'

[20] In Moscow telegram No. 347 of 23 February Sir T. Garvey speculated that in view of Mr. Brezhnev's other engagements the most likely period for a return visit seemed to be December 1975–March 1976. He suggested that Mr. Gromyko might be persuaded to visit London in July 1975.

successfully to other markets have never even examined this market. It is not easy to win business and it takes time. Given the escalation in our prices, we must find an acceptable basis for concluding contracts with a country that so far has not conceded more than 10 per cent escalation on contracts for delivery over two or three years. If industry really gets going, we can look for a reduction of the gross imbalance in Anglo-Soviet trade to a ratio of perhaps two to one within two or three years. Deliveries under contracts worth more than £150 million won in the past 18 months are now beginning to swell our exports, which may rise from £110 million in 1974 to some £150 million in 1975. I believe we stand a reasonable chance in 1977 or 1978 of reaching £200 million and thus doubling our recent average.

Conclusion

16. Anglo-Soviet relations have been greatly improved. Britain is now seen world wide as an active participant in *détente*. Comment has been generally very favourable. Our standing in international affairs has benefited. We must now set in hand the hard work to produce concrete results. We should ourselves follow, and do all we can to persuade the Russians to follow, Mr. Kosygin's words on 17 February:

> 'I can express my conviction, and I say this with full responsibility, that the Soviet side will do all it can to ensure the complete implementation of the documents we have signed, to see to it that relations between our two countries strengthen and develop from year to year.'

17. We must be firm on essentials; and the new improvement in our relations despite the expulsions of 1971 may be regarded among other things as proof that firmness with the Russians can pay. We must be flexible in making the concessions that are feasible in return for a proper price. We must make the best of our new opportunity for seeing whether a Power of Britain's size can influence through frequent contact the views of the Soviet super Power on international issues. We must try to maintain through our close relationships in the West the influence outside our shores which gives us continuing importance in Soviet eyes. We must make sure that Anglo-Soviet relations do not return, through lack of effort and without very good reason, to the doldrums which have just been replaced by a relationship that is promising in important respects despite the fundamental differences which will continue to divide us.

18. I am sending copies of this despatch to Her Majesty's Representatives in Ankara, Athens, Belgrade, Bonn, Brussels, Bucharest, Budapest, Cairo, Copenhagen, Dublin, East Berlin, The Hague, Helsinki, Lisbon, Oslo, Ottawa, Paris, Peking, Prague, Reykjavik, Rome, Sofia, Stockholm, Warsaw and Washington; to the GOC[21] in Berlin; to the UK Permanent Representatives at the EEC and NATO and in Geneva, New York and Vienna.

I have, etc.,
TERENCE GARVEY

[21] General Officer Commanding.

No. 77

Letter from Sir T. Brimelow to Sir T. Garvey (Moscow)

[*ENS 3/548/2*]

Confidential.   FCO, *3 April 1975*

Dear Terence,

Anglo-Soviet Relations: The Prime Minister's visit and the New Phase

1.   The Prime Minister's visit to Moscow raised three questions of basic importance. Why did the Russians go to such lengths to make the visit successful? Who did best out of the visit? What are the consequences for the future of Anglo-Soviet relations? Your despatch of 4 March [1] addressed itself to all three questions and I agree with your conclusions.

2.   When Mr. Brezhnev, at the head of his entourage, strode into St Catherine's Hall in the Kremlin, on the evening of the arrival in Moscow of the Prime Minister and Mr Callaghan—a moment of considerable drama—it became clear that the Soviet leadership had decided to make the visit a success. Some of the journalists experienced in covering the Soviet scene who accompanied the party to Moscow made no secret of their surprise at the red carpet treatment given to the Prime Minister and the Secretary of State. Was Britain really worth it to the Russians? I am sure you are right in saying, in paragraph 11 of your despatch, that the Soviet Union had wider reasons for wanting a successful visit and that these were basically linked to Mr. Brezhnev's desire and need to reaffirm publicly, on the occasion of a visit by a major Western political figure, his continued commitment to détente. Whereas we in the FCO had not entertained serious doubts as to the Soviet Government's commitment to détente, irrespective of their repudiation of the US–Soviet Trade Agreement, the Russians themselves appear to have been nervous lest the West should conclude, especially in the light of Mr. Brezhnev's temporary absence from public view, that the Soviet Union had inaugurated a major shift in its foreign policy. I agree that there was also a strong Soviet interest in completing the pattern of Mr. Brezhnev's détente diplomacy at the Summit, by filling the void that had hitherto existed between Moscow and London. This was surely not, however, a matter of 'silencing a discordant voice' (your paragraph 12).[2] As long ago as the Debate on the Address following the General Election of February 1974, the Secretary of State had made clear HMG's wish for an improvement in Anglo-Soviet relations and for a positive approach to CSCE and MBFR. Our voice had ceased to be discordant long before the visit. On the other hand, the Soviet Government may have seen some advantage in being polite to us lest our voice might become discordant again. The importance to the leadership of launching Brezhnev into public life again

---

[1] No. 76.

[2] Sir T. Garvey accepted that this might have been better phrased. 'But', he added in a letter to Sir T. Brimelow of 8 April, 'if, as you say, HMG were singing in tune, their voice was not carrying very far.'

should also, as you say, be given due weight. From this point of view the treatment given to the first session of talks by Moscow television news on the night of 13 February was revealing. The public participation in the proceedings of all members of the Politburo present in Moscow was also striking.

3.   Although we were fortunate in the timing of the visit, we did not simply ride on the crest of the wave of the immediate requirements of Soviet external and domestic policies. I have no doubt that our initiative in tabling first drafts of the Joint Statement, of the Protocol on Consultations and of the Nuclear Non-Proliferation Declaration, well in advance of the visit convinced Mr. Brezhnev that there could be real political advantage in making it a success. In the CSCE, in MBFR and in questions of disarmament and non-proliferation we are playing a role which, on its merits, has kept alive a dialogue with Soviet diplomatists despite the post-1971 strain in our bilateral relations. Despite their irritation with us, the Soviet Government never went so far as to contend that we had ceased to matter.

4.   It was, as you point out, because the visit had an importance to the Russians outside the narrower bilateral context that when the Prime Minister and Mr. Callaghan left Moscow the balance of advantage seemed to be in our favour. I am sure the Secretary of State would not wish to make calculations of this sort, as if the Anglo-Soviet relationship were a kind of football match in which what matters is the scoring of goals. He does not think in terms of 'zero-sum games'. However, the Russians have all too often played things as if they themselves did think in those terms. They may now calculate that in the bilateral context they now have a considerable reserve of credit and that they can now begin to present cheques drawn on their account. Mr. Brezhnev's message to the Prime Minister of 8 March about the timing and level of Stage III[3] can, at least in part, be seen in this light. Ministers will certainly not wish to reject out of hand further attempts to draw on this credit. Their acceptability will become clear when we have Soviet reactions to our proposals, and Soviet proposals themselves, for follow-up to the visit. The Prime Minister and the Secretary of State, as soon as they returned to London, considered that it was as important to take the initiative in elaborating the follow-up and maintaining momentum as it had been in preparing for the visit beforehand. They did not want simply to pre-empt Soviet proposals for the follow-up, or to put Moscow on the defensive by advancing our ideas first. On the contrary, they wished to demonstrate their serious wish to build on the foundations laid in Moscow. The real measure of the visit's success and of the longer-term benefit to Anglo-Soviet relations may only become clear in the course of months and even years. But so far as we are concerned, it will be to our strategic and tactical advantage to try to impose on the further development of relations a pattern which suits us, and is not dictated from the Soviet side. This applies as much to our dealings with the Soviet Union in the wider framework of East–West relations as to our contacts on purely bilateral matters. We must look ahead to the use of our improved relationship to take initiatives if a period of active détente diplomacy follows the conclusion of the Conference on Security and Cooperation

---

[3] See Volume II, No. 115, note 3.

in Europe. The Soviet side are already launching ideas about the future course of East–West relations through appeals to West European public opinion. We on our side should be ready to build on any Western achievements in the final stage of the Conference with proposals, both bilateral and multilateral, to turn the reciprocal undertakings written into the Conference documents into reality.

5.   In bilateral relations, I think it is right to dismiss the vituperation of Mr. Shelepin and his Trade Union delegation in the United Kingdom media as a fortuitous complication.[4] His invitation from the TUC long antedated the Moscow visit. He was well aware of the likelihood of demonstrations but none-theless elected to come. It is my hope that neither the Soviet Government, nor Mr. Brezhnev personally, will choose to regard the way in which the visit worked out in practice as a setback to the development of the process which was begun in Moscow.

6.   As for the need to maintain momentum in the political field, we have for the time being done all that seems necessary or indeed possible by your action with the Soviet Ministry of Foreign Affairs on 5 March[5] and with Mr. Gromyko on 10 March.[6] The Secretary of State, at the Dublin Summit, was able to give a strong lead to our partners in returning a suitable reply to Mr. Brezhnev's message.[7] But in this country, the success of the visit will also be judged, especially by public opinion, in the light of what it does for Anglo-Soviet trade. And here we have less control than in the political field over what happens. I believe that we have done all we can to create the right conditions for an appreciable and sustained development in Anglo-Soviet trade which will benefit our balance of payments. We look to the Russians to keep to their side of the bargain as registered in the Joint Statement. I think your prognostications for the development of our trade are realistic and, if fulfilled, would certainly justify the Moscow visit in commercial terms. But the answer now lies with British industry and we should do everything possible to encourage them to grasp the opportunities presented by the 'new phase'.

7.   Your quotation from Mr. Kosygin's lunchtime speech on 17 February is the key to the immediate future of Anglo-Soviet relations. We must above all seek to

---

[4] Mr. A.N. Shelepin was Chairman of the All-Union Central Council of Trades Unions. He had been during 1958–61 Chairman of the KGB, and his invitation to attend a Trades Union Council conference at the end of March attracted a good deal of hostile comment in the British press. There were also public demonstrations against his visit.

[5] Mr. Callaghan instructed Sir T. Garvey in telegram No. 272 to Moscow of 4 March to inform the Soviet Foreign Ministry of HMG's desire to put into practice the 'systematic expansion of relations' foreseen in the UK–Soviet Joint Statement, and in particular the establishment of working parties to deal with long-standing or complicated bilateral problems. Sir T. Garvey carried out these instructions on 5 March (Moscow telegrams Nos. 383 and 384 of 5 March).

[6] Sir T. Garvey reported in Moscow telegram No. 400 of 10 March on a meeting that day with Mr. Gromyko during which the latter had said that the Soviet Government would do all it could to give 'practical realisation to what had been agreed during [Mr. Wilson's] visit'. Mr. Gromyko also stated that 'so far as he could visualise, an autumn visit by himself to London should be possible', and that it might be linked to his visit to the UN General Assembly.

[7] See Volume II, No. 115, note 5.

ensure that we and the Russians interpret the implementation of the Joint Statement and the other documents signed on 17 February in the same way (and we shall keep a watchful eye on Soviet attempts to re-write some of these documents, particularly the Joint Statement, where the Russians have already tried to claw back parts of the redefinition of peaceful co-existence that we secured from them: we shall therefore be particularly interested in your analysis of what Mr. Brezhnev himself, or his Politburo colleagues like Mr. Suslov, may have to say on this subject in their future pronouncements). We shall be backsliding from the high point of the visit if the United Kingdom and the Soviet Union adopt divergent understandings, whether in the letter or the spirit, of what constitutes good relations. We for our part shall be content not to rake up the difficulties and tensions of the past few years. The 'new phase' should be forward-looking.

8.   Our task is clear. As the Secretary of State said to Mr. Brezhnev on the afternoon of 13 February, it is not détente itself which is in question but the quality of détente. The Secretary of State wants the 'new phase' to contribute to the evolution of a relationship which will make possible the improvement of the quality of life for the British and Soviet peoples. We would like to hope that Mr. Brezhnev does too, and that the impression of sincerity he gave in expressing his desire for peace and constructive relations with the non-Communist world was more than just play-acting. Our wish to give him every reasonable chance of proving it is no less sincere.

Yours ever,
THOMAS BRIMELOW

No. 78

Letter from Sir T. Garvey (Moscow) to Sir J. Killick

[*ENS 2/1*]

Confidential   MOSCOW, *9 April 1975*

Dear John,

Soviet Foreign Policy

1.   When the Russian leaders survey the current international scene they may conclude that the tide of recent events in a number of areas is running faster in their favour. This is a recurrent theme in periodic commentaries reviewing the progress of the 1971 Party Congress Peace Programme,[1] the most recent of which, published in *Izvestia* on 29 March, is reported in a separate letter to the Department (Broomfield's letter 2/6 of 9 April).[2] And it must be recognised that

---

[1]   See Volume I, No. 67, note 11.

[2]   This is evidently a reference to a letter from Mr. Broomfield to Mr. Burns of 9 April which cited a review in *Izvestia* of 29 March of the progress made during the past four years towards the fulfilment of the 24th Party Congress Peace Policy. The article stated: 'Some of the problems which

what has happened in Viet Nam,[3] in Cambodia,[4] in Portugal[5] and in the Middle East[6] gives the Party analysts grounds for elation. But there are also some signs of concern that the repercussions of events in all these four areas may create difficulties for the general policy of détente which, as I have argued elsewhere, remains the central theme of Brezhnev's foreign policy. If these difficulties loom larger, this could become a major worry in the context of planning for the XXV Congress of the CPSU, which we believe is due to be held about April next year. The Russian leaders must be watching very closely the reactions in Washington to the recent reverses in American policy in the Middle East and South East Asia in calculating whether this will affect US attitudes towards themselves.

Vietnam

2.   After a lull following the fall of Da Nang, the Soviet central press is now reporting events prominently and regularly. The construction of events is as before: the PRG[7] in South Vietnam is dealing a just rebuff to Thieu's violations of the Paris Agreements.[8] The tone is one of gratification but not triumph. We have seen practically no mention of the possibility that Vietnam might be unified.

3.   A blow to US prestige in the developing world is a plus in Soviet eyes in the context of the struggle inherent in peaceful co-existence. But this has to be set against, at least in the short term, the risks to détente. The Russians are probably abstaining from glorification of the communist military success in case it might make things slightly easier for the US Administration with Congress. A much more serious risk for Moscow is that US public opinion, in its perplexity and revulsion about the collapse of South Vietnam, might come to question agreements with communists generally and therefore détente with the Soviet Union. A commentary in *Pravda* of 7 April identified two types of American public reaction to events in Vietnam: Reston[9] was quoted as writing that the future of US–Soviet relations would not suffer and might even improve because of the fate of Saigon; while other Americans were reported as declaring détente dead and trying to sow panic in American public opinion. The article concluded,

were in the Peace Programme have been solved, some have reached the stage of being solved and a third category remains on the agenda.'

[3]   In January the North Vietnamese launched a military offensive against South Vietnam. Their forces captured Danang on 30 March, and proceeded to occupy the whole of central Vietnam. Saigon, the South Vietnamese capital, fell to the North on 30 April.

[4]   Insurgent Khmer Rouge forces launched an offensive in January aimed at cutting off the supply route to Phnom Penh. They took the Cambodian capital on 17 April, and Cambodia's President, General Lon Nol, fled to Indonesia.

[5]   See Volume II, No. 117, note 14. A subsequent volume will deal with British reactions to revolutionary developments in Portugal.

[6]   On 23 March Dr. Kissinger left Tel Aviv following a breakdown in his efforts to negotiate the second stage of a disengagement agreement between Egypt and Israel.

[7]   The Provisional Revolutionary (Communist) Government of South Vietnam.

[8]   General Nguyen Van Thieu resigned as President of the Republic of (South) Vietnam on 21 April. The Paris Accords of 27 January 1973 had established a cease-fire in South Vietnam.

[9]   Mr. J. Reston was a columnist for *The New York Times*.

in typical *Pravda* style, that 'life itself demands the strengthening of realistic tendencies in the foreign policy of the USA, the avoidance of military adventures and the end of interference in the internal affairs of others'. The connection between the plight of South Vietnam and the bilateral Soviet-US relationship is not direct; but the Soviet leadership may well fear that it will be made by public opinion in the United States.

4.   The effects of recent events on Soviet interests in Indo-China itself are probably still unclear to the Russians. They too were probably taken by surprise by the rapid change in the military situation: the previous relationship of forces, and the accompanying US involvement had certain advantages for them. They will have to take a systematic view of where their interests now lie; which may not be easy. North Vietnam and the southern communists may soon need less military aid, and that could reduce Soviet leverage over them. Against this, they will still need economic aid and may be expected to seek good relations with Moscow as a counter-balance to Peking. Moreover, a victorious Hanoi, exerting great influence throughout Vietnam and perhaps beyond, could become a useful barrier to Chinese expansion. The Russians will be in some degree worried about the opportunity for China created by a collapse of US influence in South Vietnam and Cambodia.

Cambodia

5.   To the Russians, the fate of Lon Nol probably seems much less important, especially for détente, than the plight of Thieu. But it is no unmixed blessing for the Russians. Whatever mix of 'patriots' emerges in a new government, the Russians, who sat on the fence until too late, have few claims on their gratitude and seem unlikely to have much influence.

Middle East

6.   The Russians are no doubt pleased that step-by-step should have failed and be discredited. They had told the world (with varying degrees of conviction) that it was bound to. Sadat's[10] approach to the Soviet and US Governments to reconvene the Geneva Conference[11] has been reported in the press, as has his call for British, French and non-aligned participation. But there is no degree of urgency. As reported in my telegram No. 509, when I saw Sytenko on 2 April, he spoke of 'sooner or later' and gave no very convincing reasons for the Soviet failure to approach Arab governments in the 10 days that had passed since Kissinger's return to Washington.[12] This lack of haste reflects the real difficulties

[10] Mr. Anwar Sadat was President of Egypt.

[11] The Geneva Conference of December 1973 had explored the prospects for peace between Israel and its Arab neighbours.

[12] Mr. M.D. Sytenko was Head of the Near Eastern Countries Department of the Soviet Foreign Ministry. Sir T. Garvey reported in Moscow telegram No. 509 of 2 April that although he had found Mr. Sytenko 'invincibly optimistic of a comprehensive settlement, with "partial solutions" now out of the way, he showed no sense of urgency about resumption of Geneva Conference, and did not essay a possible date' (NFX 3/303/1).

which are involved in convening Geneva, and Sytenko seemed to have no particular plan for getting round them. There may well be genuine uncertainty as to what they should do next. Their continued advocacy of Geneva has given them a stake in the Conference's by no means certain success, and they may well find a conflict of interest between their support for the Arabs and the pursuit of détente. In the final analysis the risk to détente is potentially more important to them than the pleasure of having been proved right about step-by-step diplomacy.

Portugal

7.   I have little to add to my telegram No. 476.[13] It may not be by chance that one of the points in Cunhal's[14] election programme that *Pravda* chose to report was that ' ... the achievement of a national democratic revolution will create favourable conditions for a peaceful transition to socialism'. This does not imply an early takeover, which Moscow, I believe, cannot desire. The question is whether the Portuguese communist party, for all its traditional allegiance to the CPSU, will take its orders from Moscow; and again, whether the combined influence of the CPSU and the Portuguese communist party would suffice to prevent an upheaval for which Moscow would be blamed. I should be very interested in any indications from Lisbon on this point. Meanwhile, Portugal must be a serious headache for Moscow, both in the *Westpolitik* context and in the CPSU's relations with West European communist parties.

General

8.   Soviet handling of these several problems reflects continuing anxiety for a resounding Party Congress next year at which the Peace Programme would be seen as an unambiguous success. Defensiveness on this shows up pretty regularly in Soviet utterances: from the stress on 'all' the leadership's adherence to détente while the Prime Minister was here; to Brezhnev's passage at the Hungarian Congress on the ability of CMEA countries to defend themselves against inflation imported in the process of East–West trade; to a laboured rebuttal in *Pravda's* weekly international review article on 6 April of an alleged, and obviously far-fetched, theory that détente was responsible for the West's economic difficulties.[15]

As a footnote, I should add that all this reinforces our view in Moscow telegram No. 463[16] that there is no evidence (at least here) that Brezhnev is on his way out

---

[13] Not traced.

[14] Sr. A. Cunhal was Secretary General of the Portuguese Communist Party.

[15] On 16 April Sir J. Killick minuted Mr. Cartledge on this letter: 'I find this very persuasive. Perhaps you would coordinate a reply. In particular, it reinforces my view that we should not and need not badger Moscow publicly and directly about Portugal.'

[16] In this telegram of 21 March Sir T. Garvey expressed his surprise at references in the Western press to Mr. Brezhnev's likely retirement later in the year. 'On balance', Sir T. Garvey observed, '... the prospect of early retirement seems much too uncertain to provide a sound basis for Western strategy in CSCE' (WDW 1/23).

and will be followed by a less détente-minded successor.[17] I should be interested in any comments the Department have on that telegram.[18]

Yours ever,
TERENCE GARVEY

[17] Mr. Cartledge noted in a minute to Sir J. Killick of 5 May: 'Soviet eyes may now be turning to the horizon which, we have always assumed, lies at the end of a period of détente and relative international stability, namely that of a phase in which the Soviet state will begin to make use of the accretion of economic and strategic power which the détente period will have brought.'

[18] In a letter to Sir T. Garvey of 1 May Sir J. Killick noted that he had found himself 'very much in agreement' with Sir T. Garvey's observations. He argued: 'For détente to act as an effective constraint on the search for unilateral advantage, which is after all a continuing imperative for the CPSU, it has to be continually demonstrated to (and by) the Soviet leadership that détente brings them tangible benefits, of which the most important is the avoidance of a serious confrontation with the USA and NATO. To put it another way the leadership have to be satisfied that the interest of "socialism" and the security of the USSR would be prejudiced by the disappearance of détente.' And, he noted, if Mr. Brezhnev were to be prevented from exploiting his recent gains, 'the West must be demonstrably willing and able to stand up to the USSR in defence of its vital interests'.

No. 79

Letter from Sir. P. Ramsbotham (Washington) to Sir J. Killick

[*ENS 3/304/1*]

Confidential   WASHINGTON, *19 May 1975*

Dear John,

US/Soviet Relations

1.   In Terence Garvey's letter of 9 April to you about Soviet foreign policy,[1] he mentioned Soviet concern in case the repercussions of recent events in South-East Asia, Portugal and the Middle East created difficulties for the general policy of détente, which remained the central theme of Brezhnev's foreign policy. Garvey saw a serious risk for Moscow that US public opinion might come to question agreements with the Communists generally and therefore détente with the Soviet Union.

2.   So far, however, I doubt whether American public opinion on détente has been greatly affected by the collapse of South Vietnam. Opponents of détente have argued that, if détente is worth anything, it should have inhibited Soviet support for North Vietnam. But I can detect no general tendency in this country to make the Soviet Union a scapegoat for what is widely recognised as a failure of US policy. On 29 April Dr. Kissinger gave the Russians the benefit of any doubts by saying, in reply to a question. 'I think we received some help from the Soviet Union in the evacuation effort [from Vietnam]'. But, he added, on 5 May,

[1] See No. 78.

'on the other hand, I do not want to give the Soviet Union excessive credit for moderating the consequences that its arms brought about'. This general attitude might change if there are widespread reprisals in South Vietnam. At present, however, détente does not seem seriously at risk.

3.   Nevertheless, at a time of high political tension in the United States before the 1976 elections, the Administration will be increasingly inclined to take a close look at the détente balance-sheet, particularly if Presidential candidates, such as Jackson or Reagan,[2] bring foreign policy and détente into the arena. You will have seen Kissinger's warning in St Louis on 12 May that 'if détente turns into a formula for more selective exploitation of opportunities, the new trends in US–Soviet relations will be in jeopardy'. More pointedly President Ford, in his State of the World speech on 10 April, said: 'as long as I am President, we will not permit détente to become a licence to fish in troubled waters. Détente must be—and I trust will be—a two-way street'.

4.   But such remarks, made in the context of the present unhappy relationship between the Administration and Congress, do not indicate that the Administration has become disillusioned with its relatively equable relationship with the Soviet Union, nor that it may contemplate alternative policies. President Ford has referred to his hopes of turning the Vladivostok Agreement of 1974 into a final agreement when Brezhnev visits the US. He has called, too, for legislation to alter US statutes affecting the Russians' decision not to put into effect the 1972 trade agreement between the two countries,[3] and to build a more stable relationship with the Soviet Union.

5.   In this connection I was puzzled by the reference, in paragraph 4 of your letter of 1 May to Terence Garvey, to Brezhnev's visit to the US having been postponed at the Americans' request.[4] On balance I should have thought the postponement more likely to have been a matter of mutual convenience. There are worthwhile agreements in prospect, but there is still much work to be done on them. In any event, the reason you ascribe for the delay—namely that the

---

[2] Mr. R.W. Reagan was Republican Governor of California, during 1967–74. A favourite of conservative Republicans, in 1975 he sought nomination as Republican candidate in the US Presidential elections.

[3] The Soviet Government rejected the trade agreement on the grounds that American legislation making its implementation conditional on the easing of emigration from the Soviet Union was both discriminatory and a transgression of the principle of non-interference in the internal affairs of other countries. Cf. Volume II, No. 110, note 4.

[4] During their Vladivostok meeting (see No. 20, note 16) President Ford had invited Mr. Brezhnev to visit the USA for the signing of a SALT II agreement, and Sir P. Ramsbotham reported in telegram No. 1719 of 14 May that it was assumed in Washington that this would take place in September. But Dr. Kissinger recalls in the concluding volume of his memoirs that it had soon become clear that such a visit 'could not happen, indeed that the entire SALT process was floundering and might even collapse' (Kissinger, *Years of Renewal*, p. 302). Sir J. Killick speculated in his letter to Sir T. Garvey of 1 May (see No. 78, note 18) as to whether the reported postponement of Mr. Brezhnev's visit might in part have been due to a feeling in Washington 'of the disadvantage of a meeting in the nearer future at a time when the Americans [were] feeling weakened and vulnerable while Moscow [might] be supposed to be feeling stronger'.

Americans are feeling weakened and vulnerable in the wake of Vietnam—is, I am sure, *not* true. President Ford gave the opposite impression during his conversation with the Prime Minister on 8 May;[5] and the Administration's behaviour in the Mayaguez episode shows that the President is concerned to ram the point home.[6]

6. I am also glad to have this chance to say that I found JIC(75)13—'Wider Implications of Recent Events in Indo-China'—unwarrantedly alarmist as regards its treatment of US internal events, and the implications of these for overseas policy.[7] The echoes of the Vietnam episode are already diminishing and the Administration seems to be turning with some relief to the next tasks in hand.

7. We have, indeed, been struck by the disinclination of members of the US Administration to allow Vietnam and other setbacks for Western policy to affect the normal course of business with the Russians. They have been helped by an apparent lull in US/Soviet bilateral business. This, in turn, is sometimes attributed to failing momentum stemming from Brezhnev's state of health, and the reassertion of a degree of collegiality in the management of Soviet affairs.

8. The Americans do not have the impression that the Russians have tried to aggravate the crises in the Middle East, Portugal and South East Asia. In the last of these areas it is widely believed that the Russians are far from having things their own way; the new Communist regimes are unlikely to be amenable to Soviet direction, although they may not be as hostile to the Russians as to the West. It is also forecast that the Russians are likely to become increasingly cautious in the period before the 25th Party Congress, during which the Soviet leaders will be concerned with the problem of the succession to the General Secretaryship, and when they will need to walk the difficult path between achieving triumphs in foreign as well as domestic affairs, while maintaining enough of détente for the US to be kept in play,

9. This is not to say that any warming in the US/Soviet relationship is visible at present. There is some disillusionment with US foreign policy and with Dr. Kissinger as its leading practitioner; as a result his initiatives are regarded with suspicion. Nor is there much sign of a lessening of interest in the dark side of

---

[5] According to the British record of a White House meeting on 7 May between Mr. Wilson, Mr. Callaghan, President Ford and Dr. Kissinger, to which this evidently refers, Dr. Kissinger said that Mr. Brezhnev could not visit Washington before September, since he could not be received until a SALT agreement had been reached. 'This', he added, 'would however be possible by September' (NFX 3/304/1). Cf. Volume II, No. 124, note 6.

[6] On 12 May, following the Cambodian navy's seizure of an American merchant ship, the *Mayaguez*, and its crew, President Ford ordered the US aircraft carrier *Coral Sea* into the Gulf of Thailand. US marines were landed on the island of Koh Tang and US aircraft bombed Kompong Som.

[7] This paper of 25 April stressed that there were grounds for fearing, in the aftermath of South Vietnam's collapse, a further period of 'recrimination and guilt' in the USA and increased public disenchantment with overseas commitments. Under President Ford, the paper contended, US foreign policy would be constrained by a hostile Congress and, even after the Presidential elections of 1976, it was 'likely to be based on a more selective and less predictable concept of United States interests and responsibilities'.

Soviet internal affairs; the Russians have recently shown less concern to hide the extent of their repression of dissent. Officials here have expressed the view that the Russians' forthcoming attitude to the Prime Minister during his visit to the Soviet Union was partly due to the opportunity to demonstrate to the US that even the Americans' closest allies were anxious to provide the Soviet Union with large credits on favourable terms; consequently, American political leaders were mistaken who thought the Russians would need to make concessions in internal policy in the interest of securing US finance.

10. Brezhnev's visit is awaited without enthusiasm, but no calls for its cancellation have been made.[8] The restoration of equilibrium in the US approach to foreign affairs, as the Vietnam episode recedes, could even enable a certain warming of the atmosphere to take place beforehand.

Yours ever,
PETER RAMSBOTHAM

[8] See note 5 above.

No. 80

Mr. Sutherland (Moscow)[1] *to Mr. Callaghan*

[ENS 3/304/1]

Confidential   MOSCOW, *30 July 1975*

Sir,

Soyuz-Apollo[2]

The flight of the Soyuz and Apollo spaceships has historic significance as a symbol of the process which has taken place of international détente and improvement in Soviet/US relations on the basis of the principles of peaceful co-existence.

(From L.I. Brezhnev's congratulatory telegram to President Ford on 24 July).

The successful completion of the Apollo-Soyuz space mission has attracted world-wide attention and has, in the Soviet Union itself, been given almost unprecedented coverage on television and in the newspapers. I enclose an annex to this despatch a report on the technical and scientific aspects of the mission prepared by Dr. Thynne, Scientific Counsellor at this Embassy. However, since the Soviet leadership clearly see the flight mainly as a political rather than a scientific event, it is also worth examining it from that viewpoint.

[1] Mr. Sutherland was *Chargé d'Affaires.*

[2] On 17 July the US Apollo and Soviet Soyuz spacecraft docked in outer space in the first-ever such joint venture between the two countries. The spacecraft remained docked for 44 hours and crews visited each other's capsules.

2.   Internationally, the Soviet leaders will calculate that Soviet prestige has been enhanced by acting publicly on the world stage as equal partners of the US. The flood of congratulatory telegrams from the leaders of their Eastern European allies, from the UN Secretary-General and even from Mr. Gairy of Grenada,[3] which were faithfully reproduced in *Pravda* and *Izvestia* bear witness to this. The main foreign policy message has been that the flight was a shining example of co-operation between States with different social systems and a proof that, in certain spheres, *détente* has already been achieved. In his first greeting to the Soyuz 19 and Apollo crews following their launches, Brezhnev put it in the following terms:

> The relaxation of tension and positive changes in Soviet/American relations have created conditions for the first international space flight. New opportunities are opening up for an extensive fruitful development of scientific ties between the countries and peoples in the interests of peace and the progress of the whole of mankind.

3.   The publicity generated by the Soyuz/Apollo mission is likely to be prolonged by the Russians for some time to come. There are plans for the Soviet cosmonauts to visit the US and for a return visit to the Soviet Union by the American astronauts. There may be a world tour. All this will provide a good copy for the Soviet Press in writing up the benefits to be obtained from a policy of peaceful co-operation and co-existence.

4.   The occasion has also been used to emphasise the pre-eminence of Brezhnev as the undisputed leader of the Soviet Union where matters of national prestige are concerned. One has only to recall that it was Kosygin who signed the agreement to undertake a joint manned flight during President Nixon's visit in May 1972 to see how completely Brezhnev has taken over the centre of the stage in international affairs. And in the spectrum of foreign relations the US has become his special concern. Following the precedent of the telegram he sent to President Ford on the 30th anniversary of the ending of the war in Europe, it was Brezhnev alone who exchanged congratulatory telegrams with President Ford on this occasion and it was he alone who sent a greeting to the cosmonauts after their successful launch. Indeed, the desire to pay special tribute to Brezhnev's role in the mission produced some odd incidents like the curiously clumsy ploy of printing in all Soviet papers, immediately after the Soyuz launching, an old photograph of Brezhnev talking to Leonov—but not Kubasov[4]—as if the astronauts had, without a moment's delay, come to report to their leader and inspirer. The effect was somewhat spoilt by photograph elsewhere in the paper of the cosmonauts climbing out of their capsule in the fields near Karaganda.

5.   But unlike the majority of Soviet international initiatives the Soyuz-Apollo project appears to have genuinely captured the imagination of the Soviet people and to have been followed with considerable popular excitement. It must be

[3] Mr. E. Gairy was Prime Minister of Grenada.

[4] Mr. A. Leonov and Mr. V. Kubasov were Soyuz crew members.

remembered that this was the first time that the Soviet public had been allowed to see a live launch from the cosmodrome in Baikonor and a landing of any sort inside the Soviet Union. It is also worth bearing in mind that public education on the Soviet space programme over a long period coupled with a strong native tradition in mathematics and the physical sciences probably meant that the flight was watched by a surprisingly high number of those to whom the concepts and jargon were familiar. I would suspect that the effect of this more open approach has done a great deal for self-esteem throughout the country. Whatever the leaders may proclaim, the average Russian has a healthy scepticism about claims to technological parity with the West, in particular the US. The sight of Soviet and American astronauts working together in space may have done more to make claims of, for example, nuclear parity credible, than all the slogans and speeches directed to this end.

6.   Popular enthusiasm was fostered by a campaign which, at times, had more in common with Madison Avenue than with the normal practice of the State Advertising Agency, Gosreklama. A number of Western firms were called in to help. Revlon collaborated with local perfume makers to produce a Soyuz perfume. Philip Morris helped local producers to market Soyuz-Apollo cigarettes. There were Soyuz-Apollo badges and stamps; an official song was printed with music on the back page of *Izvestia*; and the obligatory poem was composed by the unofficial Poet Laureate, Yevtushenko. It is true that the inexperience of the Soviet publicists in mounting a display of this sort was evident on a number of occasions. The flight controllers and the commentators at the space centre at Kalingrad were not in the same league as their American counterparts at Houston in terms of ability to explain what was going on and to fill the time allocated on television. The *Pravda* correspondent at Houston felt constrained to comment on the favourable reaction of American viewers to the 'elegance' of the cosmonauts' wives while the official Tass report of the Soyuz landing stated proudly that the whole sequence had been shown on colour television. But in general it was an able public relations performance in a field and on a scale with which the Russians have hitherto been unfamiliar.

7.   In order to carry out the joint operation and to achieve this degree of publicity the Russians were obliged to relax their usual security precautions. The launch and landing were shown live on Soviet television. The American Ambassador, Mr. Stoessel, his Scientific Attaché and a representative of NASA[5] were allowed to see the Soyuz launch at Baikanor. In the months of preparation the Americans learned a considerable amount about the organisation and execution of the Soviet programme. But the relaxation of the rules was strictly limited. Mr. Stoessel was not permitted to stay overnight at, or to see more than a very small part of the military complex in which the launch site is located. No Western journalists were allowed to attend nor to visit the space control centre at Kalingrad outside Moscow where only a small and strictly controlled group from NASA were admitted. Nevertheless, the confidence bred from having passed their first public examination with relatively flying colours should encourage the

[5] The US National Aeronautics and Space Administration.

Russians to reduce their over-insurance in matters which, in the West, are regarded as open to scrutiny.

8. Another sign of the Soviet desire not to appear to play second fiddle to the Americans was the attention devoted to the Salyut orbital station which was in space at the same time as Soyuz and Apollo. Scientific investigation apart, I suspect that a major reason for the extended Salyut programme was to compensate for the disparity in numbers of astronauts, size and manoeuvrability between the Apollo and Soyuz spaceships and to pre-empt publicity in the final stages of the Apollo flight. The fact that Salyut was brought back to earth only two days after Apollo tends to confirm this.

9. For Brezhnev it has been a fortunate coincidence that the successful Soyuz-Apollo mission has immediately preceded the Summit conference of the CSCE in Helsinki—where no doubt he will point to US–Soviet space cooperation as an example of the sort of international, multilateral cooperation which the CSCE is intended to foster. In terms of relations with the US in areas of primary importance, the space success may not have a direct bearing upon the outstanding difficulties in the SAL talks which will be taken up by President Ford and Brezhnev in Helsinki.[6] If, however, a solution is not found and if in consequence a US–Soviet Summit does not take place this autumn the contrast with the present fulsome reporting on the US will be that much greater. Criticism of Senator Jackson, Mr. Schlesinger and the 'enemies of *détente*' has been largely suppressed in this general euphoria about co-operation and a friendship in space. But I suggest that this may be a temporary lull. In the 25 July issue of *New Times* Mr. Arbatov, Head of the Institute of the US and Canada, returned at length to the attack on the US Defence Secretary.

10. On occasions in international affairs it has to be accepted that form is more important than substance. The Soyuz-Apollo mission will certainly be remembered more for its symbolic political value than for its contribution to science. But it would be wrong to write it off as one Western observer has done simply as '*bon cinéma pour les vacances*'. It has demonstrated in a spectacular way that the Super Powers can co-operate in as strategically an important a sphere as outer space, and the total secrecy on the Soviet side in all such matters is not necessary. There are signs of Soviet interest (see paragraph 14 of the Annex) in co-operating in the US Shuttle programme which may indicate that the Russians see both political as well as scientific advantage in a further spectacular manned project with the Americans. But whether, when it comes to the point, the Americans will decide that the balance of advantage in the technological field is so heavily weighted in favour of the Russians as to rule this out, remains to be seen.[7]

[6] At a NATO briefing in Washington on 7 August Mr. Hyland told Allied representatives that during the CSCE summit in Helsinki Mr. Ford and Mr. Brezhnev reviewed the stage reached in the SAL negotiations and concluded that they were in agreement in principle on five issues. The main outstanding issues were verification, cruise missiles, the Backfire bomber and the definition of heavy and light missiles. There was an unstated understanding that a SALT agreement should be in prospect before Mr. Brezhnev next visited the USA (Washington telegrams Nos. 97 and 98 Saving of 8 August).

[7] In a letter to Sir T. Garvey of 18 August Sir J. Killick wrote, with regard to this despatch, that

11. I am sending copies of this despatch to Her Majesty's Ambassadors at Washington, Paris, Bonn and UKDEL NATO.

I have, etc.,

I.J.M. SUTHERLAND

he agreed that the Soyuz-Apollo operation 'was primarily, perhaps even exclusively, a political exercise … the British press certainly treated it as an exercise in public détente diplomacy'. Sir J. Killick added: 'I believe that if one result is to give the Soviet public greater self-confidence (as opposed to bombast based on suspicion and inferiority complex) in the USSR's standing relative to the USA, it will be of benefit to us all.'

No. 81

Minute from Mr. Cartledge to Mr. Morgan

[*ENS 2/1*]

Confidential   FCO, *14 October 1975*

Brezhnev, The European Communist Parties and Detente[1]

1. The Department have recently been engaged in a dialogue with HM Embassy in Moscow about those aspects of Soviet policy which, it is fair to assume, are in the forefront of Brezhnev's mind as he begins the run up to the 25th Congress of the CPSU, now only four months away. Copies of parts of the correspondence are attached below.[2] It may be helpful to summarise the main conclusions which it has produced.

2. Brezhnev is likely at present to have three dominant preoccupations:

(i) relations with the West European Communist parties and the difficulties in convening a conference of European Communist parties;[3]
(ii) the significant loss of momentum in the promotion of global Soviet interests; and
(iii) the problems of the Soviet economy.

Relations with Western Communist Parties
3. Soviet ideologists have covered a great deal of paper in recent months discussing the correct tactics for Western CPs[4] to employ in exploiting the 'crisis of capitalism.' The Portuguese revolution has to some extent cut across these

---

[1] Mr. Callaghan noted on this minute: 'Very helpful thank you. Sauvagnargues [the French Foreign Minister] commented to me on how old the Soviet Leadership seemed & he didn't expect any adventures.'

[2] Not printed.

[3] See Volume II, No. 99, note 3.

[4] Communist Parties.

theoretical deliberations and Soviet ideas have had to be adapted to take account of it. At the same time, the Italian and Spanish Communist Parties, in particular, have proclaimed with striking precision their commitment to a fully 'democratic' form of socialist society, including the plurality of political parties; their ideas appear to enjoy some support in other Western CPs. A major *Pravda* article of 6 August by K. Zarodov[5] has been widely interpreted in the West as an attack on the respective gradualist approaches and popular front strategies of the Italian and French CPs; and as an endorsement of the anti-democratic tactics of the Portuguese communists.[6] Brezhnev's much-publicised meeting with Zarodov on 17 September has been depicted as authoritative endorsement for this approach.[7]

4. There has been speculation in the West, particularly by American analysts (including some in the State Department) that Brezhnev and his colleagues in the Soviet leadership may have become impatient with the constraints of détente and that, consequently, Western CPs are being given their head and encouraged to adopt a more militant line.

5. We believe that this interpretation is wrong; and that both the Zarodov article and Brezhnev's meeting with its author were designed not so much to support one Party or to condemn another but simply to assert the authority of the CPSU, in a confused political situation, as the only authorised interpreter of Lenin, whose prescriptions must be shown to be applicable to all situations and of permanent validity.[8] The *Pravda* article, nevertheless, has produced further discord between the CPSU and the leading Western CPs at a time when relationships within the European Communist movement are already under strain as a result of Soviet efforts to convene a European Conference of Communist Parties.[9]

[5] Mr. K.I. Zarodov was Chief Editor of the magazine, *Problems of Peace and Socialism*.

[6] In his *Pravda* article Mr. Zaradov criticised Communist parties abroad which were prepared to 'dissolve' themselves in alliances with Social Democratic parties, and he argued that the only way to true socialism was through the hegemony of the proletariat. But Sir T. Garvey contested the views expressed in an article published in *The Guardian* of 18 September, 'Russia rekindles the Cold War'. He insisted in Moscow telegram No. 1267 of 19 September on the 'duality of Soviet policy', adding: the 'main preoccupation in next 6 months is to get a SALT II agreement, a Washington summit and a Party Congress where external successes of peace policy may take some limelight off unsolved domestic problems. These priorities do not rule out concurrent playing of dirty tricks but latter will not wittingly be allowed to foul up main objective.'

[7] Mr. S.J.L. Wright interpreted Mr. Zarodov's meeting with Mr. Brezhnev on 17 September (reported in Moscow telegram No. 1271 of 20 September) as evidence of Mr. Brezhnev's putting his own authority behind the CPSU's position on the debate over Communist strategy. 'With the forthcoming Conference of European Communist parties in mind', Mr. Wright observed, 'he [Mr. Brezhnev] may well be trying to discourage Western Parties from publicly questioning the authority of the CPSU in the Communist movement' (minute to Mr. Cartledge of 19 September).

[8] In a minute to Mr. Cartledge of 8 October, Mr. D.I. Miller (Research Department) observed with regard to Mr. Zaradov's article and other similar pieces in the Soviet press: 'When all is said and done, the ground rules of the World Communist Conference still apply, i.e. that each party chooses, in accordance with circumstances, a peaceful or non-peaceful path of transition to socialism ... What may be new is the emphasis which Zaradov and others place on the uninterrupted nature of this transition.'

[9] See note 7 above. In a letter to Sir T. Garvey of 10 October Mr. Cartledge wrote with regard

The Yugoslavs and the Romanians, as well as a number of Western parties, are strongly opposed to the emergence from such a conference of any binding document or programme. The latest indications are that the conference may eventually go ahead, although perhaps not (as the Russians would have liked) before the 25ᵗʰ Party Congress of the CPSU. But if it does take place, with a respectable attendance, it is likely to produce only a very general and anodyne document which will in itself testify to the limitations of the CPSU's authority over other Parties; and which will not constitute as effective an instrument as the Russians would have liked for the further prosecution of Soviet Westpolitik in Europe.

The balance sheet of détente

6.   During the first half of 1975, the Soviet leadership could derive encouragement from a number of international developments favourable to their interests. These included the collapse of US policy in Indo-China, the seeming failure of Dr. Kissinger's step-by-step approach in the Middle East, the apparent disintegration of NATO's southern flank,[10] and the onward march of the PCP[11] in Portugal.[12] In the last quarter of the year, the picture looks rather different. The Chinese have seized the initiative in SE Asia,[13] US policy has achieved a major success (owing nothing to the Russians) in the Middle East,[14] the erosion of NATO's southern flank appears to have been stemmed[15] and the PCP has suffered at least a temporary reverse in Portugal. In many of the major issues preoccupying the rest of the world—the new international economic order, energy and petrodollars—the Soviet Union is either standing on the sidelines or has nothing constructive to say. China seems to have more appeal for the non-aligned. Gromyko's claim that no international problem can be solved without the participation of the USSR seems to be exaggerated, at least for the present. Above all, the SAL II negotiations have been prolonged by serious difficulties, thus reducing

to the projected conference: 'It is beginning increasingly to look as if this venture, presumably designed to put another feather in Brezhnev's cap for the 25th Party Congress and to put steam behind an important element in Soviet Westpolitik, was quite seriously misconceived.'

[10]   The repercussions of the Cyprus conflict (see No. 65, note 13), including Greece's departure from NATO's integrated military structure and a US arms embargo on Turkey had, along with political changes in Portugal and Spain, appeared to risk exposing the Alliance's southern flank.

[11]   Portuguese Communist Party.

[12]   See Volume II, No. 117, note 14, and No. 138, notes 2 and 11.

[13]   The People's Republic of China had recently established diplomatic relations with Thailand and the Philippines and was consolidating its ties with Cambodia. The Russians had not yet been invited to reopen their Embassy in Phnom Penh and were evidently having to work hard to maintain their influence in North Vietnam and Laos.

[14]   On 4 September, largely as a result of Dr. Kissinger's mediation, Egypt and Israel concluded a new interim accord providing for an Israeli withdrawal from Sinai and the establishment of a new UN buffer zone.

[15]   The Greeks were, as Mr. Miller reported in a minute to Mr. Cartledge of 25 September, 'quietly renegotiating their base agreements with the United States', and the Americans were hopeful of lifting their arms embargo on Turkey.

the chances of a Brezhnev/Ford summit in Washington before the end of the year.[16]

7.   At a time when Soviet strategic military power has never been greater, therefore, and when the Soviet Union could have been expected to exploit Western difficulties to good effect, the promotion of Soviet interests across the globe seems to have slowed to a halt.[17]

8.   Some voices in the Soviet establishment may be asking whether Soviet national interests are not on balance suffering as a result of the constraints which détente policies impose—whether, in fact, the détente game is worth the candle. We think that the majority response in the Politburo must be that it is—just. The over-riding Soviet objective of maintaining a sufficiently stable international climate to make a revival of the arms race unlikely and increased economic cooperation with the West possible is still being achieved. Failure to bring about a satisfactory SAL II agreement and an indefinite postponement of Brezhnev's visit to the US would significantly darken the picture and, perhaps, cause the Russians to take a further hard look at their policy options. Conversely, the achievement of a SAL II accord and a triumphal Brezhnev visit to Washington in, say, January would provide a dramatic vindication of Brezhnev's policies on the eve of the 25th Party Congress.[18] For the time being, we expect these policies to be maintained and to form the basis of the new foreign policy programme which will now be under preparation for unveiling at the Congress.

The Soviet economy

9.   Although very little of the relevant evidence is as yet firm, it seems probable that a substantial shortfall in the Soviet grain harvest for 1975 must take some of the lustre off the economic report which Brezhnev will make to the 25th Congress. Substantial purchases of American grain will have their effect on the already disappointing Soviet balance of payments situation and, consequently, on the desired expansion of Soviet imports of Western technology during the period of the new Five Year Plan which is shortly to be announced.

[16]   See No. 80, note 6.

[17]   Mr. Cartledge wrote to Sir T. Garvey on 10 October (see note 9 above): 'In the Middle East, in South East Asia and in Latin America Soviet power and influence are either static or in regression. In Western and Southern Europe, opportunities arguably ripe for exploitation are being neglected in the interests of détente. (Does the current disposition of Soviet theoreticians to play down the acuteness of the "crisis of capitalism" owe anything to the reluctance of the political leadership, in the interests of détente, to do anything about it?).'

[18]   In a minute to Mr. Hibbert of 24 October Mr. Cartledge observed: 'Quite apart from the inherent Soviet dislike of the obligations imposed by Basket III and a consequent natural inclination to play them long, it is conceivable that Brezhnev may now see a need to adjust his posture on détente, for internal reasons during the run-up to the 25th Party Congress and to sharpen the Socialist profile of Soviet policy. Brezhnev would certainly like to have, before the 25th Party Congress in February, a visit to Washington and a second SAL Agreement. But neither can be taken for granted and if in the event they do not materialise, political détente may well seem to have lost some of its momentum: this could complicate the presentation of foreign policy at the 25th Party Congress' (ENS 3/548/15).

Brezhnev

10   These problems, in combination, amount to a formidable complex of difficulties for even the most vigorous and active statesman to tackle. Although Brezhnev has been much in the public eye recently—greeting the American astronauts and turning out at the airport for both Honecker[19] and President Assad—he is not, so far as we know, yet able to put in a full working day. HM Embassy in Moscow have argued, very cogently, that a Party Congress would be the least convenient occasion on which to announce a change of leadership; and it is also true that Brezhnev would be reluctant to appear to admit failure by stepping down at a time when Soviet fortunes are clouded. The question of whether the Soviet leadership as a whole will feel comfortable in facing a period of significant difficulty under an ailing General Secretary must, however, remain open.[20]

11.   Research Department agree.[21]

B.G. CARTLEDGE

[19]   Herr E. Honecker was First Secretary of the Central Committee of the Socialist Unity Party of the GDR.

[20]   At the beginning of 1975 Mr. Brezhnev had been forced by ill-health to renounce all public engagements for a period of six weeks, and at the Helsinki CSCE summit he had appeared competent but subdued. Rumour had it that he intended to retire at the 25th CPSU Conference scheduled for 24 February 1976.

[21]   On 15 October Mr. Morgan noted at the bottom of this minute: 'According to to-day's *Times*, the Italian Communist paper *l'Unità* yesterday foreshadowed a Soviet climbdown at the E. Berlin preparatory meeting over the nature of the document to emerge from a European Party Congress—i.e. it will not be a binding directive. This source is biased, of course, but it tends to confirm the conclusion above.'

No. 82

Letter from Sir. T. Garvey (Moscow) to Mr. Cartledge

[*ENS 2/1*]

Confidential   MOSCOW, *21 October 1975*

Dear Bryan,

The Soviet Balance Sheet of Détente

1.   Thank you for your clutch of letters on various aspects, internal and external, of the prospects for next February's XXVth Party Congress.[1] On the theme of CSCE and Westpolitik, I think we are almost wholly in agreement and

[1]   See No. 81, note 9. Other letters included in this 'clutch' were one from Mr. Burns to Mr. Mallaby of 3 October and another from Mr. Cartlege of 9 October acknowledging recent communications from the Moscow Embassy on the ongoing debate on Soviet foreign policy. Research Department papers on this subject were also sent to Moscow.

I reserve comments for the promised despatch.[2] On Brezhnev's health Iain Sutherland wrote to you on 15 October.[3] Since then the Secretary General has told the French press and the world that he has a cold. This may well be true, but further clinical speculation is not very rewarding. Certainly there has been a filthy cold around. In this letter I prefer to consider the general thesis set out at length in your letter of 10 October[4] that, whereas six months ago with détente policies in full flood, Brezhnev could look forward to a series of policy successes which could be proclaimed as such at the Congress, the momentum has now been lost, that the advancement of Soviet interests through these policies is slowing to a halt and that he must now view the outcome with considerably reduced confidence. You argue from this that some Russians must be questioning the correctness of those policies and also that, given the Secretary General's uncertain state of health, unless some notable successes intervene between now and February, the Congress could see changes in the leadership. This is a thesis which I see is now widely accepted in the British press.

2.   Confining attention for the moment to the field of foreign policy, there is no doubt that the balance sheet as seen from Moscow has changed in the past six months. I agree with the assessment of the position at the beginning of the year set out in your paragraph 12,[5] although I think that the Russians had for some time expected the British to say 'yes' to Europe. The change in Soviet fortunes since then was summarized briefly in my telegram 1253 of 15 September[6] which indeed contained the main message of your paragraph 13.[7] But not all the sugges-

[2] No. 85.

[3] Mr. Sutherland noted in this letter that the evidence of Mr. Brezhnev's recent activities tended to support the Embassy's view that his health could hold until February 1976. In that case, Mr. Sutherland thought he was most unlikely to be replaced at the CPSU Congress, and that thereafter he was 'likely to stay on for a matter of months or even a year or two' (ENS 1/3).

[4] See No. 81, note 9.

[5] *V. ibid.* In this and the subsequent paragraph Mr. Cartledge quoted from a minute from Mr. Miller to Mr. Wright of 25 September which listed as reasons why the Soviet leadership should have had considerable cause for satisfaction in the early summer of 1975: (1) the collapse of US policy in Indo-China; (2) the suspension of Dr. Kissinger's mission to the Middle East; (3) the seeming imminence of a second SAL agreement; (4) the repercussions of the Cyprus problem on NATO; (5) the possibility of the British referendum going against the UK's continued membership of the EC; (6) the deadlock in the MBFR; (7) the situation in Portugal; (8) the prospective successful conclusion of the CSCE; and (9) the likelihood of a Conference of European Communist Parties.

[6] In this telegram Sir T. Garvey pointed out that although the Russians were well pleased with the recent course of their *détente* policy, Mr. Gromyko was conscious that the Helsinki proceedings had had a mixed reception, and that widespread scepticism about Soviet intentions persisted. Other Russian worries were, he thought, the Soviet Union's exclusion from the Middle East peace process, the impact of the revolutionary events in Portugal on Western opinion, and a bad harvest, which was a blow to Soviet prestige and a drain on their reserves.

[7] Again quoting from Mr. Miller's minute (see note 5 above), this paragraph pointed out that the Soviet Union's failure to take maximum advantage of favourable international circumstances suggested 'a certain immobilism in current Soviet foreign policy which [could] be ascribed either to the long-term détente strategy or else to sheer indecision'. The Soviet Union's potential advantage had either been neutralised or turned to its disadvantage: (1) in south-east Asia, where

tions listed in Research Department's analysis are ones of which the Russians could take advantage. The Referendum is a case in point. The delay over the European Conference of Communist Parties may have been deliberate while CSCE was got out of the way.[8] Soviet inaction on MBFR was almost certainly deliberate. On CSCE they acted very decisively in the last weeks at Geneva and achieved the long-wanted Helsinki Summit. It therefore seems mistaken to suggest that the record demonstrates immobilism or sheer indecision on the part of the Russians.

3.   On the later developments listed in your para 13:

(i) The Russians will never have expected US withdrawal from Indo-China to be an unmixed blessing. But I think you over-state their problems in Vietnam, at least to the extent that China's are greater, as shown by the coolness of Le Duan's visit to Peking.[9] Traditional Vietnamese distrust and fear of China must surely suggest that the Russians will be able to maintain a good deal of influence in Hanoi. But Cambodia, I agree, is a Soviet setback.

(ii) Agreed.

(iii) I fully agree that the Russians must be terribly frustrated at their exclusion from Kissinger's Sinai success. But they are not altogether out of the game, as indicated by Assad's brief visit to Moscow.

(iv) SALT II is the key outstanding problem. The Russians are still present-ing an optimistic front in their press, e.g. by describing Brezhnev's visit to Washington as 'forthcoming'.

(v) Agreed.

(vi) I do not see why the Russians cannot continue for some time yet to stone-wall on MBFR, in the confident expectation that the West is preparing a new move.

(vii) The Helsinki summit, we must not forget, was in itself a major success for the Russians and Brezhnev personally. I strongly agree that implementation of Basket III is a headache for them. But it may not become an acute one for some months yet, perhaps not until after the Congress.

(ix) [*sic*][10] I agree that events in Portugal have given the Russians worries with-out successes on the ground. See my tel[egram] no. 1253.

the US withdrawal had led to increased Sino-Soviet rivalry; (2) elsewhere in Asia, particularly India and Bangladesh; (3) in the Middle East where Dr. Kissinger had achieved a further disengagement agreement between Egypt and Israel; (4) in the protracted SAL II negotiations; (5) in the Mediterranean, where developments in Cyprus had not damaged NATO as seriously as might have been expected; (6) in the MBFR negotiations, where the Russians now risked charges of opposing 'military détente'; (7) in the CSCE context, given public cynicism in the West over the results of *détente* and the difficulties to which the implementation of Basket III measures was likely to give rise; and (8) in Portugal, where the Communists had lost much of their influence.

[8] See Volume II, No. 99, note 3. The Conference opened in East Berlin on 29 June 1976.

[9] Mr. Le Duan was Secretary-General of Lao Dong, the Vietnamese Workers' Party. His visit to China during 22–28 September seemed to reveal divergences between China and Vietnam particularly with regard to their relations with the Soviet Union.

[10] Portugal, the eighth item in paragraph 13 of Mr. Cartledge's letter, was incorrectly listed as ninth.

4.   The general balance of successes and failures in foreign affairs in the period since the last Congress could still, in my view, be represented as one of success for Soviet policy and for Brezhnev. He could point, in particular, to the Helsinki Summit itself, to the international recognition of the GDR and the fulfilment of a good number of points in the 'Peace Programme'. As regards very recent developments, there have been two since you wrote which can be chalked up as at least partial successes. First is the Soviet/GDR Friendship Treaty involving a strong reaffirmation of close bilateral relations and of the Brezhnev doctrine without mention of German reunification and, thus far at least, without visible harm to détente.[11] Secondly, and of major importance, it now looks as if the Conference of European Communist Parties will take place before next February. It is true that the Russians may have settled for an anodyne final document confined to the subject of détente and the independence of individual Communist parties,[12] but this should be sufficiently effective to counter the kind of charges which might be made at the Congress or elsewhere on the lines suggested in your paragraph 10.[13] The Giscard d'Estaing visit may not have achieved as much as the Russians (or the French) had hoped but I have no evidence that it has seriously rocked the boat.[14] Brezhnev may also be able to point, though perhaps not at the Congress, to a long-term grain/oil agreement with the Americans.

5.   Thus, the overall situation, even on events this year alone, is reasonably good. But SALT II, as you say and as I said in my tel[egram] no. 1253 of 15 September, is crucial.[15] If agreement is secured and Brezhnev goes to Washington, the leadership will be able to claim a major success story. That might well enable attention at the Congress to be diverted to foreign policy and other positive things and away from the bad harvest and the more general failure in agriculture. This effect might actually be enhanced if the Conference of Communist Parties and Brezhnev's visit to Washington had been brought off in December and January, shortly before the Congress: (a Soviet official has told my US colleague that the

[11]   The preamble to this treaty, signed on 7 October, confirmed both countries support for the 'consolidation and protection' of 'socialist gains'. See *UN Treaty Series* (New York, 1985), Vol. 1077, pp. 76–92.

[12]   Cf. No. 47.

[13]   Mr. Cartledge argued in paragraph 10 of his letter that Mr. Brezhnev had, in trying to convene a Conference of European Communist Parties, set a deadline by which inter-party ideological differences would have to be resolved and made himself vulnerable to the charge of putting the external authority of CPSU at risk. Even if Mr. Brezhnev settled for a loose, generalised and non-binding Conference document, Mr. Cartledge thought 'the efficacy of an important strand of post-CSCE Soviet policy [would] have been considerably reduced'.

[14]   The rather chilly political atmosphere surrounding President Giscard d'Estaing's visit to Moscow during 14–19 October seemed to suggest that the halcyon days of Franco-Soviet friendship were over.

[15]   Sir T. Garvey argued in his telegram No. 1253 (see note 6 above) that if SALT II were achieved in 1975 and the Conference of European Communist Parties was brought off, the Russians could then claim at their party Congress in February a major success for their *détente* policy. 'But', he added, 'if SALT II should come unstuck and Brezhnev did not go to Washington, while President Ford visited Peking, Soviet peace policy would lose much of its shine.'

Brezhnev visit would be convenient right up to mid-January). I agree that a very great deal depends on SALT and we cannot yet foresee how the overall achievement, domestic and external, will be presented in February.

6. I suggest, however, that we can already point to two probabilities:

(*a*) It will be difficult to drop the pilot until SALT II is decided and the Conference of European Communist Parties is over, unless Brezhnev's health collapses meanwhile. That implies that Brezhnev will stay until December or January, which would be too near the Congress for a change of leader. We remain convinced that, for procedural and other reasons, a change of leader at the Congress itself is very unlikely. So it seems possible to forecast, as a best bet but no certainty, that Brezhnev will stay until after the Congress, with or without SALT II.

(*b*) The 'peace policy' is based on Soviet interests, notably the need to avoid confrontation with the USA and the need for Western technology and credits. This point is developed in our paper for the Heads of Mission Conference next month. Even without SALT II, the interests behind the détente policy would persist. Even without SALT II, a forward policy of active support for Western Communist Parties in sight of power would be likely to upset seriously the USSR's relations with the USA and thus undo what has been done to reduce the risk of confrontation. It thus seems that militant actions are a dangerous option, although more militant talk about the 'crisis of capitalism' is not excluded.

7. I conclude, for the moment, that the balance of results from the 'peace policy' is not bad and would be good with SALT II; that SALT II might enable the leadership to divert attention at the Congress from the rotten harvest; that Brezhnev, barring a medical collapse, is likely on balance to hold on until after the Congress; and the abandonment of the 'peace policy' is hardly on the cards.

Yours ever,
TERENCE GARVEY

No. 83

Minute from Mr. McNally to Mr. Cartledge
[*EN 2/6*]

Confidential   FCO, *11 November 1975*

No Armistice in the War of Ideas [1]

Like you, I found Sir Terence Garvey's despatch of 21 October on the Ideological Struggle[2] fascinating reading. So much so that I am tempted to put pen to paper.

2.   One of the more irritating habits of what, for want of a better word I will call the 'hard liners' as far as East/West relations is concerned, is the tendency to assume that the differences between themselves and those who advocate a more flexible approach is one of perception. They (the 'realists') perceive the Soviet Union for the threat that it is to our security and our way of life. We (the dupes and woolly minded idealists) are easy prey for the machinations of Soviet propaganda. What actually divides us is not perception but differing views of how to meet a commonly discerned threat. Happily, Sir Terence's despatch escapes from the 'hard line' straight-jacket and thus poses us the problem in just the right way to enable us to discuss policy and tactics in a rational manner.

3.   I was told early in my Foreign Office career that the basic FCO approach to Anglo-Soviet relations was that they could go to hell in their way, if only they would let us go to hell in our way. If that in fact was ever FCO policy it was doomed to failure, since its inherent passivity automatically hands the initiative over to the Soviet Union on a permanent basis and condemns the West to forever chasing the hares of Soviet choosing.

4.   The policy which the Secretary of State has tried to develop aims at conducting our relations on two levels. First, we want genuinely to improve relations with the Soviet Union, both in terms of trade and in terms of better political understanding which would, as far as possible, eliminate misunderstandings or miscalculations. The second aim must be to provide a counter strategy within the framework of détente to the ideological struggle.

---

[1] During the foreign affairs debate in the House of Commons on 10 November Mr. Callaghan stated with reference to the CSCE that there had been no overnight end to East/West tensions. 'There are', he continued, 'great ideological differences and there is no armistice in the war of ideas. That war will go on between the Soviet Union and those who espouse the ideology of the Soviet Union and the rest of the free world' (*Parl. Debs. 5th ser.*, H. of C., vol. 899, cols. 937–38).

[2] In this despatch of 21 October, 'Living with the Russians. The ideological struggle—myth and machinations' (copied to Mr. McNally by Mr. Cartledge on 5 November) Sir T. Garvey argued that the 'ideological struggle' was a 'compound of myth and machinations', but that the field in which it could safely be pursued by the Soviet Union had narrowed because of the possession by both sides of nuclear weapons, East/West economic interdependence and *détente*. 'The limitations', he concluded, 'have come about in every case through the Soviet Union's confrontation with the facts of international life and deepening involvement with other nations not subject to the Soviet writ. The more that confrontation and involvement imposes revisions of the myth, the less compelling will the myth become.'

5.   The critics of détente always duck two fundamental questions, and they are what they precisely think the West has given away by the détente exercise, and how would they have conducted relations with the Soviet Union over the last ten years in such a way as to enhance our security? I myself see it as nothing but healthy and safe that we have in recent years recognised some of the realities concerning central Europe which emerged from the Second World War. It is a particular bonus that the FRG has managed to educate its people in these realities without a violent lurch to the Right. We are at least in the position now of facing up to the Soviet threat with our own policy secure in logic and not in fantasy.

6.   Neither do I think, as is so often asserted, that the détente exercise has weakened Western Europe's willingness to defend itself. It is true that economic pressures tempt Western European governments to solve problems of resource allocation by making do with a little bit less commitment. But this is a matter of political judgement. It is not in response to any mass public pressure. Part of the problem is that NATO appears to want to fulfil a role in the public mind which is unattainable. It seems to want to be loved, revered and respected like a favourite village Bobby. Defence organisations do not excite that kind of affection. NATO would be far better to settle for a reputation as a fit and efficient guard dog, respected for doing the job it is supposed to do competently. In fact, rather than weakening the defence of Western Europe, détente has positively contributed to NATO effectiveness by giving the United States administration the breathing space in which to resist isolationist pressures in American in the Vietnam and immediate post-Vietnam era.

7.   Given that Sir Terence's analysis is right, that NATO's efficiency and the balance of nuclear terror has removed the military option from Soviet strategy, he is probably also right in assuming that the ideological struggle will be a continuing factor in Soviet policy. The question then surely becomes 'How do we respond to the ideological struggle?'

8.   Firstly, we should respond to it by having an ideology of our own. I very much welcome Sir Terence's statement in paragraph 3 that 'We also heartily desire change in Soviet society and the others that emulate it. We wish to see them humanised, brought under the rule of law and their citizens to know, to speak and to move.' This need not involve balancing crudity with crudity in terms of front organisations and grotesque propaganda, but in a perpetual willingness to stand up for and speak up for the values and freedoms in our society which we believe to be its essential strength. That is why I have favoured on-going machinery for the CSCE. The Soviets have always had the opportunity to interfere in our internal affairs. Basket III means that how they treat *their* citizens is now firmly on the agenda for international discussion and we should never allow them to remove it.

9.   Equally, I think we should be much more confident about our ability to deal with Soviet initiatives. Too often in the past the standard Western response to a Soviet proposal has been to turn it down out of hand, simply because it is a Soviet proposal. This leaves in the public mind a positive/negative picture. It is essentially a defeatist response in that it assumes that the Soviets will succeed in any strategy or ploy, and that the West is incapable of turning the tables.

10. It is equally true of language. I know that the Humpty Dumpties of the Kremlin often expropriate a word or a phrase and then make it mean exactly what they want it to mean. But surely the Prime Minister is right in resisting this philological imperialism, especially when it is the English language that is being violated.

11. Sir Terence's paragraph 12 on the changing Soviet attitudes to Western economies and Western technology[3] also deserves deeper strategic consideration. Of course there is a degree of impudence in the Soviet bargaining for technology. But the emergence of a middle class and the rising expectations which Sir Terence chronicles in themselves circumscribe the range of political options for the Soviet leadership. Expectations can be deferred and belts tightened in a dictatorship, but not with complete immunity as can be seen by the events in a number of satellite countries (most recently Poland).[4] There is a case to be made that growing Soviet dependence on western technology and on Western products to meet the rising expectations of the Soviet people is in itself a kind of Finlandisation in reverse. I am not taking this to extremes. I merely state it as a constraint on their total freedom of action in terms of the ideological struggle.

12. Neither should we see the ideological struggle purely in terms of East/West relations. When I was in New York recently Ivor Richard mentioned that one of the happier sights for him was the glum faces of the Soviet delegation during the 7th Special Session.[5] The fact is, as Ivor pointed out, that on this key issue of North/South relations, the Soviets have nothing to say. We should not be afraid of reminding some of our critics in the Third World of this—or for that matter, the Soviets themselves. This point was underlined to me recently in a talk with a Soviet diplomat who talked disparagingly about the Third World's request for a new economic order, said that this was a matter for the 21st century, and that the first call on Western technology should be the Soviet Union, where *real* potential existed. We should be putting the Soviet Union on the spot in the run-up to UNCTAD IV,[6] both to stifle their own propaganda and to put our own efforts in to more favourable perspective.

13. We also have the China card to play. It is an aspect of our policy which I

---

[3] Sir T. Garvey reasoned in paragraph 12 of his despatch (*v. ibid.*) that since the Soviet Union was not free to introduce a market economy, which might respond more speedily to rising consumer expectations than their present centralised planning system, the Russians had 'hit on the expedient ... of accelerating the development of the Soviet economy by using Western technology and Western credits to make the goods which indigenous technology [could not] yet devise and indigenous resources [could not] finance'.

[4] Food shortages had only recently triggered an angry public reaction in Poland.

[5] The Seventh Special Session of the UN General Assembly was held during 1–16 September on international economic cooperation and development. The resolution unanimously approved on the final day outlined measures for improving the lot of poorer countries. These aimed at expanding and diversifying trade and opening up markets of the wealthier nations to developing countries, and emphasised the need to curb excessive fluctuations in commodity markets and the importance of ensuring stable export earnings through compensatory financing.

[6] The Fourth UN Conference on Trade and Development was held in Nairobi in May 1976. It adopted a resolution calling for commodity stabilisation agreements backed by a common fund.

know has not been fully developed by the present Government, but to which we could devote greater thought in the run-up to the Secretary of State's own visit to China next year.

14. Sir Terence is right that the future is not plain sailing. The ideological struggle may yet become increasingly intense and indeed physical in Portugal, Spain, Italy, France and Yugoslavia.[7] But if that is to be the case, it is more necessary than ever that our own strategy should be that of a positive war of movement —advancing our own ideas, challenging theirs. We must make it abundantly clear that an ideological struggle has truth and consequences for the Soviet Union and is not simply an open invitation to use the Western democracies as an ideological punch ball. Sir Terence's timely call to the colours will involve us in battles more subtle and sophisticated than those of the Cold War era.[8] But they are battles which I have every confidence we can win, so long as we do not fall into the old English habit of fighting the next war with the battle plan and prejudices of the last.[9]

TOM MCNALLY

[7] 'Western societies', Sir T. Garvey observed (see notes 2 and 3 above), 'could lose the "struggle" by a simple failure of the will to maintain their material defences, their internal cohesion and their diplomacy. For we have noted that doctrinal revision reflects changes in the Soviet Union's perception of its real interest: the best, indeed the only, way of enforcing such changes is by keeping our own end up.'

[8] Sir T. Garvey explained in his despatch (*v. ibid.*): 'The ideological struggle is a two-way process. If the Russians seek to promote change in Western societies, so do we also heartily desire change in Soviet society and the others that emulate it. We wish to see them humanised, brought under the rule of law and their citizens permitted to know, to speak and to move. Else why did we spend all those months in Helsinki and Geneva arguing about Basket III?'

[9] In a letter to Sir T. Garvey of 5 November Mr. Cartledge expressed his agreement with Sir T. Garvey's view of the continuing relevance of the Russian nineteenth-century experience for Soviet foreign policy. 'It is my own belief', he wrote, 'that one powerful motivation in that policy is the will to complete the consolidation of a central position on the world stage for the Russian nation which was frustrated by Tsarist incompetence in the closing decades of the last century and in the early decades of this.'

No. 84

Record of the Conference of HM Ambassadors in Eastern Europe and the Soviet Union: Second Session, Tuesday, 18 November 1975[1]

[EN 2/12]

Confidential

Item II: British Objectives, Defensive and Offensive, in Relation to the Soviet Union and Eastern Europe

1. *Sir T. Brimelow* opened the discussion on this subject by quoting from a recent telegram (Moscow tel[egram] no. 1459) Soviet press comment on this year's conference of the CPGB:[2]

> The Helsinki conference opens a new stage in the struggle for peace and détente in Europe. At the same time it does not signify ideological détente and the perpetuation of capitalism in Western Europe. In all capitalist countries the struggle for advancement towards Socialism will intensify in step with the deepening of the crisis of capitalism.

2. Sir T. Brimelow went on to say that, in the past, the UK had had offensive aims towards the Soviet Union. He instanced our intervention in Russia after the First World War. However, we had not then been strong enough to eliminate communism. Since the Second World War, and not withstanding John Foster Dulles, we had been content to live with the Soviet Union because we were unwilling to attempt to use force against her. However, this did not exclude attempting to get Western ideas known in the Soviet Union. Mr. Callaghan had said in the House of Commons that there was no armistice in the war of ideas.[3] The struggle of ideas would continue.[4] However, we were on the defensive in

---

[1] The Conference of HM Ambassadors in Eastern Europe and the Soviet Union met in London during 17–19 November. The first session on 17 November was devoted to discussion of Item I(a), 'Soviet and Warsaw Pact Objectives and Policies in Europe after the CSCE'. Item I(b), 'Relations between the Soviet Union and Eastern Europe', and Item III, 'The Instruments of British Policy', were considered respectively on the mornings of 18 and 19 November.

[2] According to this telegram of 18 November, *Pravda* had included the following passage in its summary report of the opening speech by Mr. G. McLennan, CPGB General Secretary, to his party's 34th Congress (ENS 13/1).

[3] See No. 83, note 1.

[4] This point was put forcibly in EESD's Conference paper, 'The Warsaw Pact Countries after CSCE: Opportunities, Problems and Priorities through Western Eyes'. The paper argued that the West should seek to deploy the Final Act to its advantage in the 'ideological struggle'. It asserted that there was no point in continuing to tell the Russians that the 'ideological struggle' was inconsistent with policies of *détente* and that it should be suspended. 'The West', the paper maintained, 'should make use of the opportunities, created in the first place by the circumstances of détente but enhanced by the existence of the Final Act of the CSCE, to make the contest more equal by widening and improving the channels through which Western ideas and objective information about the West can reach the citizens of the Soviet Union and Eastern Europe'.

regard to the Soviet Union's growing military strength. It was arguable that the West was unduly alarmed at the end of the Second World War. At that time the Soviet Union had enough on its plate and subsequent apparently offensive actions, for example against Prague, were really defensive. The Soviet Union might welcome communist governments in France and Italy, but had no intention of intervening. Despite their apparently aggressive policies, the only territorial gains which the Soviet Union had made since the war were in an unimportant area on the frontiers of Mongolia. The Soviet Union argued that change in capitalist societies was inevitable and would continue until those societies were ripe for communism without outside intervention. This argument became more difficult to sustain when NATO had to be taken into consideration. However, the Soviet Union would probably continue to rely on events to secure its ends. In the past the Soviet Union's helping hand had been generally ineffective.

3. Sir T. Brimelow concluded his introduction by saying that it was true to say that the West was on the defensive. The West's present economic difficulties were a gift to communism.[5] But the crisis was exaggerated; production in the West had declined to 1972 levels, but this did not represent collapse. In NATO, détente was seen as an objective in its own right, and not as a means for undermining the Soviet Union, but nevertheless détente did hold dangers for the Soviet Union. He then asked Sir J. Killick[6] to introduce the afternoon's topic.

4. *Sir J. Killick* said that Article V of the North Atlantic Treaty[7] was the key to NATO, despite the many attempts made to flesh out other sections of the Treaty. NATO was essentially about defence. The Soviet military threat to the West still existed and therefore deterrence was still necessary, despite efforts towards détente. A deterrence capability was, however, more important as a means to self-reassurance than for defence against the Soviet Union. It was not a question of convincing the Soviet Union that we were prepared to use nuclear weapons, but rather of convincing Moscow that we would not unless compelled to. It was for this purpose that the NATO Triad existed: the United States' (and to a lesser degree the UK's and France's) second strike capability; the ability to use tactical nuclear weapons (in this area NATO's capability was more than adequate, though he thought that the concept of the selective use of tactical weapons was impractical); and conventional weapons. The position as regards this third element in the Triad was unsatisfactory. Although in terms of the offensive-defensive ratio, NATO had a certain capability, there was a considerable

---

[5] EESD's paper (*v. ibid.*) noted with regard to the impact of the economic crisis: 'At the very time when the economic difficulties besetting most Western societies have become critical and, consequently, the purely economic pressures on defence budgets most acute, the problem of demonstrating to Western opinion the vital necessity for maintaining defensive force levels has become more urgent and complex.'

[6] Sir J. Killick was appointed UK Permanent Representative to NATO in October 1975.

[7] By Article V of the North Atlantic Treaty of 4 April 1949 the parties agreed that an armed attack against one or more of them in Europe or North America should be considered an attack against them all, and that consequently they would 'assist the party or parties so attacked' by taking forthwith, individually and in concert with other parties such action as was deemed necessary, including the use of armed force, to restore and maintain the security of the North Atlantic Area.

imbalance of ground forces. This imbalance was usually described by NATO as intolerable, though in his view it could be lived with.

5. Turning to the possibility of Soviet military activity, Sir J. Killick said that the Soviet Union would need complete certainty of success before it would embark on military activity. To avoid this, it was necessary to ensure that there was no decoupling of the United States from Europe and that NATO retained the option of a first use of nuclear weapons, in the event of its losing the conventional battle. But these were not urgent problems. Even if no effective Western defence capability existed, there was no evidence of the Soviet Union's wishing to occupy Western Europe. However, the NATO Triad would continue to be necessary in the foreseeable future, until we had passed through the various intermediate phases leading to true détente. Even if détente placed constraints upon the Soviet Union, the question arose of what use the future Soviet leadership would make of a Soviet military capacity which was growing both absolutely and relatively. All this was the justification for keeping up the West's guard. Ideally, NATO should control both the arm upholding the defence shield and the hand proffered in détente. This control had operated in the CSCE, but now did not exist outside the MBFR negotiations and the CSCE follow-up on confidence-building measures. The question still remained, however, of why the West should maintain its guard if Soviet aggression was ruled out. The answer was that the Soviet Union exploited its increasing military strength to threaten war for political ends. Given this continuing attempt to exploit Western populations' fear of war, NATO's role lay in crisis management. There were many situations in which this role could be played: the Soviet Union's continuing desire to recapture Yugoslavia;[8] Berlin, where the Quadripartite Agreement had not resolved the problem and the 3 powers and NATO still had an obligation to stand firm; Cyprus; and the Middle East. Soviet policies were global, for example their maritime activities. And were therefore of concern to NATO (in this context Sir J. Killick remarked that the present Conference ran the risk of being too Euro-centric).[9]

6. Developing the theme of NATO's crisis management rôle, Sir J. Killick said that NATO was not of course solely responsible for crisis management. The Moscow-Washington axis would remain the key factor and other Western powers might wish to intervene. Nevertheless, NATO could bring the various threads together. The Middle East crisis of 1973 had demonstrated that NATO was not like the Warsaw Pact;[10] the United States could not force its allies into line as could the Soviet Union. This factor increased NATO's importance for crisis

---

[8] A Conference paper prepared by HM Embassy, Belgrade, entitled 'Yugoslavia after Tito: a threat to European Stability', stated that it seemed 'most improbable' that the Russians would invade Yugoslavia within the next two or three years. But, it concluded: 'It would be folly to assume that they will not take advantage of any opportunity which a divided Yugoslavia might give them.'

[9] During the first session of the Conference on 17 November Sir T. Garvey argued that the Russians 'could further be brought to accept a safer and more manageable world, providing they were guaranteed super-power status, a voice in every continent and parity of esteem'. He added: 'In all this, the US Alliance was crucial to us' (record of the Conference of HM Ambassadors in Eastern Europe and the Soviet Union, 17 November).

[10] See No. 56, note 3.

management, since it provided a forum within which the allies could provide mutual reassurance and the smaller member states could be satisfied that their interests were not being ignored. A situation could arise in which political leaders and public opinion would have to show great resolution, given the Soviet Union's readiness to exploit the threat of nuclear war. The CSCE Final Act would not deter the Soviet Union in any way. If governments and peoples in the West were to be held firm, they would have to be convinced that the military capability existed to resist the Soviet Union. Hence the need for NATO's second strike capability. NATO's conventional capability was also a part of this guarantee. In the sort of situation envisaged, there would always be the risk of miscalculation. If this happened, NATO had to retain the ability to respond flexibly while a solution was sought by diplomacy in the hope that the Soviet Union could be persuaded to desist. The EEC was not equipped for a crisis management rôle; it lacked a centre for political decision making and the necessary military machinery. Its rôle, therefore, could only be theoretical. Sir J. Killick said that a further paradox faced NATO, namely that in countries like Greece and Portugal the emergence of democratic régimes had weakened the Alliance. Although it was attractive to be able to say that NATO must oppose totalitarianism, both of the right and the left, the chief threat came from the left, which was often an extension of the Soviet Union, whereas the right frequently provided solid allies.

7.   Turning to the use of NATO in offence, Sir J. Killick said that NATO was not effective as a means to carry the message of the West into the enemy camp. NATO was only concerned with the Soviet Union's external behaviour. The EEC might, however, be able to contribute something in this area. Concluding, Sir John Killick said that much of the West's current difficulties fell outside the competence of NATO. The OECD,[11] the International Energy Agency and national governments held the answers to many problems. While he had welcomed the recent NATO Summit as an opportunity to exchange views, it had provided few solutions, but much hand-wringing over economic problems. A repetition of this would only demonstrate weakness.

8.   *Sir T. Brimelow* said that the basic problem was that in market economies the operation of the economy was not intended to produce any specific rate of growth, which was a result rather than an objective. In the same way, the rate of inflation was also a residual. Recently the Western economies had produced low rates of growth and, in some cases, high rates of inflation. In contrast, the Soviet economy grew at a planned rate. In consequence it was possible for the rate of expansion of military expenditure to be almost proportional to the economy's rate of growth. In Europe, in conditions of high inflation, Governments became alarmed by high public sector borrowing and as a result the defence budget suffered. Rising expectations in the West also ensured that private expenditure would be given priority over military expenditure. The Soviet Union would maintain this advantage until rising expectations imposed a change in Soviet defence spending.[12] However, there was no sign of this as yet. In the West, it was

[11] Organisation for Economic Cooperation and Development.

[12] In his opening address to the Conference, on 17 November, Lord Goronwy-Roberts,

thought that one solution to this problem would be an arms limitation agreement with the Soviet Union, hence SALT and MBFR. But the Soviet Union had pressed for progress in the CSCE before progress in MBFR, hoping that the apparent impulse to détente provided by a successful conclusion of CSCE would weaken Western resolve to keep up with Soviet arms expenditure. This explained the lack of progress in MBFR. Sir T. Brimelow then asked Mr. Rose to speak on the subject of MBFR.

9. *Mr. Rose* said that MBFR was essentially an Alliance negotiation to a greater extent than had been the case with the CSCE. This had to be because the negotiation was between the two alliances; Western success depended on the negotiations continuing on this basis. The Western position as put to the East represented the agreed position of NATO as a whole; positions never carried a national label. There were two reasons for this. First, the basis of the Western approach was the need to correct the imbalance between the forces of the two alliances, not an imbalance of forces between individual nations The end result aimed at was therefore a common ceiling for each alliance. Second, was the need to maintain Alliance cohesion and to avoid the opportunities for Soviet wedge driving which the negotiations offered. The interests of NATO members were often different and if these differences were allowed to damage Western cohesion one of the Soviet Union's most important objectives would have been achieved and Western security correspondingly reduced. The UK's prime objective must therefore be the maintenance of Alliance cohesion. This did not exclude the UK having specifically national objectives, but these could only be sought through Alliance agreement.

10. Mr Rose then went on to outline four other UK offensive objectives. These were:

(i) to maintain the momentum of détente by extending it into the military field. This objective had been expressed by many Western leaders at the CSCE. It was the only objective which was shared to any degree by the Soviet leadership;
(ii) to secure a reduction of Warsaw Pact and Soviet ground force superiority in Eastern Europe so as to provide improved warning time should the Soviet Union take aggressive action. This improvement would be marginal but in terms of the situation envisaged the margin would count;
(iii) to maximise restrictions on Soviet activities and deployments in Eastern Europe. This presented problems of verification and reciprocity, but any degree of inhibition placed on the Soviet Union could only be of benefit to the West; and
(iv) to permit NATO to make those force reductions made necessary by

Parliamentary Under-Secretary of State for Foreign and Commonwealth Affairs, pointed out that as a result of the economic crisis during the last three years the Soviet Union had been able to strengthen its grip on the economies of the East European countries. 'Recent developments', he said, 'therefore cast doubt on one of the main conclusions of the 1972 Conference, namely that HMG should concentrate its efforts on Eastern Europe rather than the Soviet Union. We should now give greater priority to dealing directly with the "management" in Moscow' (record of the Conference of HM Ambassadors in Eastern Europe and the Soviet Union, 17 November).

economic pressures by ensuring that such reductions were reciprocated and controlled.

One major success for the West had been that since the MBFR negotiations had begun in 1973 the US Congressional pressure for unilateral force reductions had been staved off, as had other Western force reductions despite pressure on the Dutch in particular. The aim was to negotiate a basis for force withdrawals, which the UK among others would wish to make. Mr Rose then added that there was one defensive objective, namely to avoid any commitment which could damage NATO's military structure or prejudice future European co-operation on defence. Above all, national ceilings on the forces of each Western country must be avoided. All those objectives were shared to a greater or lesser extent by other members of the Alliance.

11. Mr. Rose concluded by saying that the West could not expect to impose its terms on a take it or leave it basis. Despite Western claims to the contrary, the West had made no significant concessions since 1973. If Agreement was to be reached, it could only be secured by a solution which the Soviet Union could present as an 'equal treaty'. Differences within the Alliance were more likely to emerge when the time came to identify how such a solution could be secured. As yet, there had been no difficulty. The negotiations had been co-ordinated in Vienna and Brussels and in Vienna NATO's position appeared to be monolithic. The Alliance was now considering Option III, which was intended to break the present deadlock.[13] But already differences had emerged over its contents and presentation. These differences were likely to increase. At some stage it might be necessary to decide between pressing for terms which could lead to an agreement and risking criticism of blocking the negotiations.[14] In these circumstances the guiding objective must be the cohesion of the Alliance.

12. *Sir J. Killick* endorsed Mr. Rose's view that Alliance cohesion was of paramount importance. Turning to Soviet attitudes towards MBFR, he said that the Soviet Union wished to maintain détente, but MBFR was not a major plank in the Soviet Union's and Brezhnev's policy. The Soviet Union was in part motivated by the need to meet US wishes, these however were clearly formulated. The Soviet Union was committed to complement political détente with military détente but this did not imply the use of practical means—the Soviet Union preferred more general, and empty, disarmament measures.[15] Finally the Soviet

---

[13] See No. 20.

[14] A Conference paper prepared in collaboration between Arms Control and Disarmament Department (ACDD), Defence Department, EESD and Research Department, entitled 'Military Détente: Probable Soviet Strategy and Tactics and the Western Response', argued that, although MBFR had provided Western governments with a 'useful bulwark against domestic pressures for cuts in defence expenditure', it might not continue to do so indefinitely, and that some Allied governments might have to implement force reductions pledged in their respective defence reviews with or without agreement in the talks. 'The Russians', the paper continued, 'may well calculate that in this situation there will be a growing tendency in the West to look for progress in MBFR even at the cost of settling for less than is envisaged in the present Allied reduction objectives.'

[15] The Conference paper on 'Military Détente' (*v. ibid*) argued that the 'political expectations

Union was not faced with the West's economic problems. It might in fact cost the Soviet Union more to withdraw its forces from Eastern Europe then to maintain them there, since they would then bear directly on Soviet resources, and even if the troops were disbanded rather than re-deployed, the saving would be small. Sir J. Killick doubted whether there was a real basis for agreement in the MBFR negotiations, but said that he would not dismiss them out of hand.

13. *Mr. Moreton*[16] said that the United States, and Dr. Kissinger in particular, had in the past concentrated on the SAL negotiations. These negotiations were now in difficulties and therefore officials at the working level in the State Department wished to press on with MBFR. Awareness of the problems of MBFR was now increasing at higher levels in the State Department. Sonnenfeldt had said that the United States would 'get comfortable' on MBFR in the near future.[17] Kissinger would wish to avoid differences within the Alliance and would therefore be reluctant to consider possible concessions.

14. *Sir O. Wright*[18] said that the FRG was primarily concerned to maintain the US commitment to Europe though the West German authorities were uneasy at the time of SALT I and during the Middle East crisis about US attitudes towards its European allies. The FRG was also concerned to get France 'back alongside' on defence, though it was difficult to see how this could be achieved. It was possible to speculate that the FRG saw a possible answer in the 'construction' of the EEC, by gradually transforming it into a European Union with a defence capability. This would gradually draw the French into a closer association in military matters. The FRG also hoped to maintain a defence capability in Europe, through the NRCA [*sic*][19] and other agencies. The UK's attitude appeared to be a matter for doubt to the FRG. Although the UK had voted to remain within the EEC, its subsequent acts had called into question its commitment to what the FRG had assumed to be the UK's aims. MBFR might provide a means by which the UK could demonstrate its commitment to 'the construction of Europe'.

from détente' had implications for the Russians. 'We cannot', it suggested, 'therefore discount the possibility that the need to avoid provoking a strong degree of Western disillusionment with Soviet performance in détente might bring about a change in the Soviet attitude to MBFR. There might be a greater disposition in Moscow to look to the political advantages that would accrue to the Soviet Union from reaching an agreement with the West, even at the cost of some military concession in MBFR. In a sense, this is the strongest card in the Western hand; but it has its chief relevance in the context of US/Soviet relations; and in those relations MBFR does not, at least at present, loom large.'

[16] Mr. J.O. Moreton was Minister in HM Embassy, Washington.

[17] Dr. Sonnenfeldt told Mr. Moreton on 4 November that he did not know whether a SALT agreement would be achieved before the US presidential elections of 1976. He added that whereas he had previously thought that agreement on MBFR would follow an understanding on SALT, 'conceivably this might change' (record of conversation with Dr. Sonnenfeldt enclosed in letter from Mr. Moreton to Mr. A.H. Campbell (DUS) of 25 November).

[18] Mr. J.O. Wright became a KCMG in 1974 and was appointed HM Ambassador in Bonn in October 1975.

[19] This would appear to be a typographical error and should read MRCA (Multi-Role Combat Aircraft). In 1968 London and Bonn agreed upon an Anglo-German collaborative project to equip both air forces with MRCA (later called Tornado) fighter-bombers.

15. *Mr. Preston* said that Ministers had given a lot of attention to East–West trade and cooperation; and this had involved much high-level visiting. There were three questions we should ask ourselves. The first had been raised in a despatch earlier in the year from Mr. Reddaway[20] in Warsaw, to which Sir J. Killick and Mr. Preston had replied. The question was how to be sure that the special support we gave to certain major projects when they were under negotiation, such as the Ursus deal in Poland,[21] was in the overall national interest, taking into account such matters as credit, subsidies, and obligations to counter-purchase. Were we building up industrial capacity in Eastern Europe which might be commercially or even strategically damaging in future? Might one result be to make the populations of those countries more content with the regimes they have got? The second question was whether we should give cheap credit to these countries at all. Were we giving too much in some cases, such as Poland? The preparations for the Rambouillet Summit[22] had shown that the Germans were worried about this. The third question was whether it was right for us to try to push British industry into a more active role over industrial co-operation. The DOT took a neutral view; they did not discourage the practice, and kept people informed of such opportunities as there were, but left the decisions to the commercial judgment of the firms involved.

16. There had been a considerably increased workload as a result of all the high-level visits which had taken place. Other work might have been more useful. The Eastern Europeans had a passion for new pieces of paper, which were mostly meaningless. We had recently taken a hard line with Poland in particular. They had asked for a 5-year Cooperation Agreement, similar to those they had signed with some of our partners. We had told them there was a perfectly good 10-Year Agreement in force between us and we therefore saw no need for a 5-year one. The Poles had also asked for a Long-Term Credit Agreement on the lines of that signed in Moscow in February. We had said that the case of the Soviet Union was special; but also had at the back of our mind that as we were getting near to the Polish credit limit, we would not be able to put into any such agreement with Poland a figure which would meet their wishes. The Poles also wished to see the Joint Commission elevated to full Ministerial level. Mr. Preston had persuaded the Secretary of State for Trade that this would constitute a precedent, not only for the other Eastern European countries, but possibly for the Middle East too. We had resisted all these Polish proposals, but being sensible in this meant that we were running some political and commercial risks, if our EEC partners were less robust.

---

[20] Mr. G.F.N. Reddaway was HM Ambassador in Warsaw.

[21] In September 1974 a large Anglo-Polish contract was concluded providing for the manufacture in Poland, under licence, of Massey-Ferguson-Perkins tractors and engines. This involved the modernisation and expansion of forge, foundry and production facilities at the tractor plant in Ursus, a small town just outside of Warsaw.

[22] At the instigation of President Giscard d'Estaing of France, the Heads of Government of France, the FRG, Italy, Japan, the UK and the USA met at Rambouillet from 15 to 17 November to examine ways of dealing with world economic problems.

17. On the question of whether we devoted too much time to the Eastern European market, Mr. Preston said that our exports there amounted to only 2–3% of our total exports. He had also noted that the efforts our partners had put into increasing their exports there had not resulted in any significant increase in their exports there (as a proportion of their total exports) either.

18. *Sir T. Brimelow* asked whether the effort we had devoted to trade with the USSR had been worthwhile. A leading businessman had said to him that we could have got more business in other markets.

19. *Sir D. Stewart* said that not only was Yugoslavia different in its system of economic management, but also in that there had been no surfeit of Ministerial attention to trade with Yugoslavia. He also wondered if we could be sure that our partners were wrong in providing credit as liberally as they had in response to Eastern European requests. *Mr. Preston* said that as he was not responsible for Yugoslavia he could not comment on Sir D. Stewart's remarks.

20. *Mr. Bolland* said he would welcome guidance on whether the considerable efforts we made to increase our very small trade with Eastern Europe, was misplaced, and whether it should be diverted elsewhere. But were not exports of £19m still worthwhile? The Eastern European passion for documentation was a fact of life. But they could be helpful to British missions in dealing with the bureaucracy of a centralised state. On the question of Ministerial-level Joint Commissions, he said that the Austrian Minister who chaired all the Austrian Joint Commissions with Eastern European countries, had no time for anything else. But unless he was told otherwise, he would continue to work hard, and pointed out that Schweppes had just signed an agreement with Bulgaria. *Sir T. Brimelow* said that so long as we had Commercial Departments in our Embassies, we would wish them to do the best they could. But the point Mr. Preston had raised was whether efforts elsewhere in the world might be more rewarding. *Mr. Preston* said that, as he had written to Mr. Reddaway, he thought that our efforts were worth-while, especially in view of British industry's straitened circumstances, and the work of our posts was not wasted.

21. *Mr. [R.J.M.] Wilson* wondered whether, in determining trade policy, we gave enough weight to political objectives. If, for example, we wished to reduce Hungary's dependence on the Soviet Union, and to increase her ties with the West, then trade had an important role to play. The USA certainly saw their trade with Eastern Europe in this light. Increased trade between the West and Eastern Europe could involve the USSR having to devote more resources to keep Hungary in line. Did we differentiate sufficiently between the USSR and Eastern Europe: the latter were surely more deserving of cheap credit. *Mr. Preston* wondered how realistic was the idea that we could lessen Eastern European dependence on the USSR; such a process would never be allowed to go too far, and indeed Western trade might reduce pressure on Soviet resources. We should not trade for political reasons, but should leave it to the commercial judgment of those principally involved, i.e. businessmen. As for credit, the terms of the Agreement with the USSR had not been all that cheap, and we had been obliged to match on a case by case basis. *Sir T. Brimelow* asked whether the Soviet Union

had yet drawn on our credit. *Miss Terry*[23] said hardly at all. But they had hypothecated it for future projects, and were suggesting that they could use some more. *Sir T. Garvey* agreed with Miss Terry.

22. *Mr. Reddaway* said that naturally all Ambassadors liked big contracts, and his despatch had not meant to suggest that they were not good for Embassies. But that they raised certain questions which could only be properly considered in London. As for Declarations, we need not worry too much so long as they were harmless. If the French were prepared to sign them, why not us? Naturally the drafts had to be looked at carefully, but such pieces of paper had considerable 'PR' value. Mr. Bolland's point was very valid. If an increase in the staff of a Commercial Department resulted in more business, then the work of the whole Embassy could be paid for perhaps for several years ahead. We should therefore be flexible in looking at such establishment questions. The political angle was also important: commerce gave missions the best excuse for trying to get to know the local inhabitants.

23. *Mr. Smith*[24] said he had heard some bankers say that since the Soviet Union needed more money, they should be charged the going rate, since they had to have it. But did this mean we would lose business to e.g. the French, if we took such a line? *Mr. Preston* said the answer was to make the Gentlemen's Agreement stick. *Sir T. Brimelow* said that this question had been discussed at Rambouillet, but of course not everybody was a gentleman. *Mr. Preston* said that so long as cheap credit was extended by our partners, it was difficult for us to stand out. *Mr. Reddaway* pointed out that it was we who had undercut the French in the case of the recent PVC contract awarded to a British consortium. *Mr. Preston* said that our undercutting had not been on interest rates, but possibly on the length of credit extended. But we did not have a good system for evaluating the national benefit of such terms. He and Sir J. Killick had considered the matter, but the main problem was that the precise terms of such deals were not known until the last minute. Nor could we know if the companies concerned would in fact be able to get similar deals for cash in the Middle East. One tried to make some judgment, but it was necessarily inexact. As for Eastern European addiction for pieces of paper, he took the points which had been made, but CRE's[25] staff was heavily loaded. He had indeed been told that it was overstaffed. It was not only a matter of drafting the documents but of having intensive consultations with industry about their contents, and negotiating them. The result could be that his staff had no time for commercial enquiries. But if the result of our reluctance was that our partners did better in their trade with Eastern Europe, we might have to look at the matter again. But our attitude had had the effect of stiffening Dutch resistance to recent Polish proposals for having another Cooperation Agreement. *Sir T. Brimelow* said that the negotiation of such documents had the effect of giving

---

[23] Miss P.M. Terry was appointed HM Ambassador in Copenhagen in October 1975. She was formerly attached to the Government Communications Headquarters (GCHQ) at Cheltenham.

[24] Mr. (later Sir) H. Smith was then on secondment to the Cabinet Office.

[25] The Commercial Relations and Export Division of the Department of Trade.

'swans' to those behind the Iron Curtain. In this country we would find the purse strings being drawn tighter.

24. *Mr. Moreton* said that the objective of US foreign policy was to divert resources from the accumulation of military power, and the US Government was willing to do a bit of pump priming to bring this about: to present the Soviet Union with the choice of meeting rising expectations or suffering unrest. But was the creation of a bourgeois system in Eastern Europe a good thing? Would it make their people more satisfied with the regimes they had, or more open to Western ideas? Was British policy on all fours with the Americans? *Sir T. Brimelow* said the British economy was too small to be swayed by considerations of diverting Soviet resources. We must be guided by economic benefit to ourselves, as judged by the chairman of the companies concerned.

25. *Sir T. Garvey* said he had sympathy for CRE4.[26] But given the bureaucratic structure of the Soviet administration, and the need for Ministerial cover, such documents could have a useful purpose. 'Swans' could be expensive in terms of candle ends but in the long run were probably worth it despite the trouble involved, and he hoped they would continue. He agreed with Mr. Preston about the unsatisfactory nature of calculations of the benefit of transactions in one market rather than another. But the process of getting an operation going in Soviet markets could be a matter of years, and one must take a long view. Since Ministers had willed that we should have a shot at the Soviet market, we must stick to our efforts. The USSR was in a number of short-term troubles and would have a substantial cumulative deficit for the years 1974–76. But this did not mean the whittling of our hopes and our efforts. We might see some lags in the placing of orders over the next few months, but the list of transactions under negotiation made it reasonable to expect a doubling of our visible trade with the USSR during the period of the next 5 year plan. We would just have to learn to live with the odious Soviet system.

26. *Mr. Preston* said that Ministers felt they had more freedom of action in Eastern Europe than in other parts of the world so they would be reluctant to see EEC rules on East–West trade tightened up. Some officials might like to see more Community activity in this field, but not Ministers, or indeed the French. This meant that we had a disproportionate Ministerial interest in the subject. If Ministers decided that protective action on behalf of certain industries was necessary, it would produce quite strong reactions on the part of some East European Governments. *Mr. Petersen*[27] said that, contrary to many expectations, the recent visit of a Romanian Minister to Britain at the expense of Rolls-Royce had been successful, and private industry had had to do much of the work of CRE4 in drawing up the documents.

27. *Mr. Cartledge* said it was important to identify our options correctly. We were agreed that firms were the best judges of their own interests. The task of officials was to do their best to see that our firms got into the markets with an equal chance, and preferably with an edge. So they needed all the weapons given

---

[26] *V. ibid.* CRE4 was responsible for dealing with the Soviet Union and Eastern Europe.

[27] Mr. J.C. Petersen had been HM Ambassador in Bucharest since February 1975.

to our competitors—pieces of paper, favourable credit and officials' time. If we decided that these contracts were not in the national interest and, by 'withdrawing official labour' forced UK firms to look elsewhere for business, those firms might or might not be successful in other markets. But we should remember that it was the firms themselves who went into the East European market in the first place, as a commercial judgment; nobody had forced them to do so.

28. *Sir T. Brimelow* said that Mr. Barker[28] was unable to be present, and that Mr. McMinnies[29] of IRD would speak in his place. *Mr. McMinnies* said that all the predictions which had been made at the previous Heads of Missions' Conference in the propaganda field were being borne out. Soviet propaganda had three main facets: first, disarmament in the context of military détente; secondly, continuation of the ideological and class struggle; and thirdly, exploitation of Western economic difficulties. The first of these was probably the most serious and most insidious. The Russians in particular were making a sustained effort to create a mood in favour of unilateral disarmament in Western public opinion. Two examples: […] an article in *The Times* […] which […][30] said that the Soviet Navy was shrinking.[31] This had resulted in a heated exchange of letters, which on the whole the West had won. The Russians had been obliged to bring Ivor Montagu[32] into the correspondence, which they only did when they felt themselves under pressure. A few days later TASS and Moscow Radio had put out an interview with Stan Thorne MP[33] who had said that the thousands of millions of pounds now spent on arms should be devoted to welfare. The Russians were trying to put this message around. How should we contest them? We put the stress on the growing Soviet military threat.

29. The Russians had also wheeled out the Front Organisations, who were impinging on activities all over the world, notably the WPC, the WFTU[34] and the ISC.[35] The principal topics were Chile, Portugal, Spain, Angola, anti-colonialism, anti-Zionism and the activities of multinational companies. In particular, they had made a set at the UK to test our visa defences. They had arranged a conference on Cyprus in March, and another on Chile last week, for which they had hidden behind the NUS.[36] Several quite senior IUS[37] officials had been admitted for it. A more serious threat was a forum on Disarmament to be held

---

[28] Head of IRD until November 1975.

[29] Mr. J.G. McMinnies was Deputy Head of IRD.

[30] Personal references omitted.

[31] This article asserted that that the Soviet Union had fewer ships than it had in 1958, and that all that had changed was their deployment.

[32] Mr. I. Montagu had been leader-writer of *The Daily Worker* during 1943–47, and was currently President of the Society of Cultural Relations GB/USSR and a member of the World Peace Council (WPC).

[33] Labour MP for Preston South.

[34] World Federation of Trade Unions.

[35] International Student Conference.

[36] National Union of Students.

[37] International Union of Students.

in York in March 1976. Ministers were disposed to take a more robust line over this, because it constituted a more direct threat to the national interest. IRD were working on the problem of how Ministers should defend exclusion of such people in public. There was also the question of what type of signals we could send to the Russians to show that this sort of activity was unwelcome after Helsinki. The difficulty with the Front Organisations was that the Russians would say that their activities were none of their concern. But we must show that this abuse of détente was not welcome. We must also make sure that Soviet propaganda labels did not stick and become normal language. It was not a new problem, but after Helsinki the hostile propaganda threat had increased; this was important and needed countering. *Sir T. Brimelow* said that Ministers did not want to seem to be cold warriors, after Helsinki. Not all recommendations for visa refusals were turned down, but the climate was more difficult than previously. *Mr. Cartledge* said that because the York forum was the most important one, we had been cautious about recommending refusals for less damaging gatherings prior to it. But we had found in the case of the recent seminar on Chile that we had probably been over-cautious. Ministers would have been receptive to a tougher recommendation, which was encouraging. They were fully alive to the dangers Mr. McMinnies had described. *Sir T. Brimelow* said the Secretary of State had taken a close interest in developments in Portugal, and was now very aware of Communist techniques of subversion and keen that they should not succeed there. There was not much illusion in the minds of Ministers.

30. *Sir J. Killick* said there were problems about presenting NATO in the new situation; in particular how to answer the question 'what are our Armed Forces for if they will never have to fight a war?' The answer had to be explained in terms of diplomacy and crisis management, but this was more difficult to put across. But the facts about Soviet power were coming out. Moreover much left-wing opinion in Britain was very nationalistic: those who held it did not wish to be pushed around by Moscow. In 1972 the Conference had discussed the question of Ministerial speeches. Sir J. Killick thought that the line agreed then was still valid, and perhaps applied with still greater force. *Sir T Brimelow* said that the Secretary of State for Defence had circulated to Parliament two months previously a small brochure about the shape of British defence expenditure after the defence cuts had been made. The Chief Secretary to the Treasury[38] had objected to it having been circulated without consultation with the Treasury. The Foreign and Commonwealth Secretary had said that he supported the Defence Secretary. *Sir J Killick* said the problem was not just a question of the Soviet military threat, and those who addressed it in only those terms such as certain US Generals in testimony before Congressional Committees, could weaken our case rather then strengthen it. *Mr. Smith* said it was better to concentrate on the question of Soviet military strength. *Mr. Rose* said that he was encouraged by the fact that Soviet propaganda on MBFR had failed to get through in the British press. Admittedly, there was an enormous quantity of material and the issues were complex, but he found it extraordinary that despite its plausibility to the uninitiated, there had

[38] Mr. J. Barnett.

been no disposition on the part of the British press to pick it up. What had appeared had been well-balanced, reflecting the Western position, as a result of official briefings. If the Eastern side had done more work on certain people in this country, they might have got better results in terms of publicity. *Sir T. Brimelow* said that one reason for this phenomenon was no doubt that we no longer had newspapers of record.

31. *Mr. Hibbert* said we should look ahead to the 1977 CSCE Review Conference. Ministers were already being asked in PQs[39] if certain actions of the Soviet Union and Eastern European countries were compatible with the Final Act. We were now giving *ad hoc* replies, but would need to formulate a clear line for future use, in which IRD would have a role to play. We could either begin by urging people to wait and see, and then later say publicly that such-and-such activity was not compatible with the Final Act; or alternatively we could wait until 1977 before making such pronouncements. *Sir T. Brimelow* said the Secretary of State wished to move slowly on this, and not to bludgeon the USSR immediately the CSCE was over. But by 1977 we might be in a pre-electoral situation, in which Ministers would wish to show that they could get on with the Russians, as Mr. MacMillan[40] had done in 1959.

32. *Mr. Bolland* wondered whether instead of looking at every aspect of the Final Act, we could not concentrate on particular items, perhaps in conjunction with our EEC partners. For instance, in Bulgaria the sale of Western and British newspapers would provide a suitable topic. He had asked the Bulgarians how they squared the non-availability of such papers with the terms of Basket III. The Bulgarians had said that they had no foreign exchange to buy them. Mr. Bolland had pointed out that they could be resold at a profit to the many tourists. Obviously questions such as divided families must be pursued on a case-by-case basis, but concentration on certain topics might make for more punch and cohesion amongst the allies; in Bulgaria only his US and FRG colleagues had shown much interest. We should therefore establish an order of priorities. The point about not adopting Eastern labels was important. He had been disappointed to read in the Declaration of Rambouillet[41] a reference to the 'Socialist' countries. At one time there had been a circular telling people not to describe the Eastern European countries as such. *Sir T. Brimelow* said that Ministers had been reminded of the point before the Rambouillet meeting.

33. *Sir J. Killick* asked Mr. Campbell how the Nine saw CSCE follow-up, and how their work might be brought to NATO. *Mr. Campbell* said that the Political Directors had been discussing CSCE follow up; getting agreement that the matter should be discussed at expert level had been a slow process. Some members wished to agree lengthy documents on common positions, which took a long time.

---

[39] Parliamentary Questions.

[40] In February 1959, eight months before a General Election, Mr. Macmillan had paid a celebrated Prime Ministerial visit to Moscow for talks with Mr. Krushchev. See A. Horne, *Macmillan*, Vol. II (London: Macmillan, 1989), pp. 122–32.

[41] See *The Annual Register. A Record of World Events in 1975*, ed. H.V. Hodson (London: Longman, 1976), pp. 486–87.

But these difficulties were being tackled, and we hoped guidance would emerge from the Nine. It was a slow process but it was essential to get it right. There was a general willingness, with some French reservations, to bring in the NATO allies. The French were not being too obstructive, but wished to keep their own hands free as much as possible. *Mr. Bolland* said that the Eastern side were moving much more quickly. He had heard of a meeting of European Agrarian Parties in Bulgaria whose purpose was to give support to the Helsinki Declaration. Fortunately some Western parties there had objected to the draft resolution. He had also read of an article by the Chairman of Peace and Security in Europe, suggesting a 'scientific study' of the various parts of the Final Act; this would doubtless mean a study of those parts favourable to the Eastern side. *Sir T. Brimelow* said that the point about the need for guidance was taken. *Mr. Cartledge* agreed and said that the words 'prudent and cautious' which appeared in the EESD paper for the conference applied not to the implementation of Basket III but to the pursuit of the CSCE concept as such.[42] Whereas Western achievements in the CSCE, as enshrined in Basket III, were probably incapable of improvement, in that there was unlikely to be another conjuncture of events which would induce the Eastern side to sign something better from our point of view, other parts of the Final Act were, at least theoretically, capable of being built on, and to the advantage of the East rather than the West. Moreover the Secretary of State had instructed us to play it cool, and we must establish a satisfactory basis [for] concerted action in the Nine or the Fifteen before rushing in.

34. *Sir T. Brimelow* said that discussion had shown that on our side too, it was a case of the mixture very much as before.[43] However, the discussion had not touched on the effect of inflation, recession and deficits in the public accounts on the resources available to do what we had tried to do hitherto. In Britain, the Chancellor had made it clear that because of rising unemployment, he was not willing to impose drastic cuts in public expenditure at present. When demand picked up would be the time for such cuts. In 1976–77 a 1½ cut would be required; those for the two subsequent years were not decided. Discussions with the Treasury would start soon. But it was implicit in what the Chancellor had said that there would be substantial cuts. As for defence we had had the Defence Review, which had concentrated on our role in NATO, but we had had to

---

[42] See notes 4 and 5 above. EESD's paper emphasised that the West shared with the Soviet Union a central interest in the prolongation of *détente*, 'not only in order to reduce the likelihood of nuclear war and to maintain the constraints which détente imposes on Soviet mischief-making; but also because the replacement of détente by confrontation would quickly bring to a standstill those trends in the societies of the Soviet Union and Eastern Europe which are desirable from the Western point of view.' Meanwhile, EESD thought Western governments must devote more resources to making their populations aware that their freedoms depended on the maintenance and improvement of the West's military deterrent. 'It follows', the paper concluded, 'that the Western approach to CSCE follow-up should be positive but prudent and cautious.'

[43] The Conference papers prepared by HM Embassies in Bucharest, Budapest, Prague, Sofia and Warsaw all dealt with the policies of their respective host countries towards the West and the USSR in the aftermath of CSCE, focussing on the question 'The Mixture as before or a New Prescription?'

reinforce our forces in Belize, and the situation in the Falkland Islands was dicey. In these circumstances we would have to depend on the maintenance of cooperative arrangements with the Nine or the Fifteen, since our ability to act independently would be reduced. This made for a slightly depressing forecast. Communist countries with their centralised economies could control their rates of inflation more easily, and thus provide more steady growth in industry, and especially heavy industry capable of turning out armaments. The pressures on the West were such as to make it difficult to keep up with the Armed Forces of the Warsaw Pact, In Britain, some MPs, especially on the left of the Labour Party, would be tempted to discuss the range of Government economies needed to reduce total expenditure. Defence would obviously be looked at again, and it would not be an easy matter to resist unreasonable pressure.[44]

[44] EESD's paper (see notes 4, 5 and 42 above) summarised the problems posed for Western governments by the combination of economic crisis and *détente*: 'Western societies are faced to a greater extent than at any time since 1939 with the complex task of maintaining their economic and social integrity, and their will to defend themselves, if necessary, in a relatively relaxed, non-confrontational situation.'

No. 85

Sir T. Garvey (Moscow) to Mr. Callaghan

[*ENS 3/548/1*]

Confidential   MOSCOW, *6 December 1975*

Sir,

Retreat from Moscow

1.   Long acquaintance with the Soviet Union customarily begets a blend of scholarship and pessimism. My two years in Moscow, now concluding, have been too short to achieve the one or to acquire more than a tincture of the other; and this my last despatch makes no claim to be more than a sophomore's view.

2.   It has been a rare experience to watch, even for so brief a period, the behaviour of an old empire, galvanised by revolution and lately graduated to super-power status. The Soviet Union's interests now extend to all continents and all seas. To obtain a rough idea of how the world looks to the Soviet geopolitician, turn Mercator's projection upside down and trace a curve from Kamchatka on the left, round South-East and South Asia and Africa and Western Europe, up to Archangel on the right. All that lies within this orbit, is in varying degrees, of concern to the Soviet Union. Outside it lie the Americas (though the Cuban enclave breaks the pattern), and, between the two, the great vacant spaces of the Pacific, the Indian Ocean and the South Atlantic, less vital in themselves but acquiring importance when the other super-power seeks to establish a presence there. And, for reassurance, reconnaissance has to be carried out right up to the Western Hemisphere itself. This may seem an old-fashioned blue-water view,

reminiscent of Admiral Mahan[1] and the British imperial 'life-line', and irrelevant in the era of intercontinental missiles, electronic surveillance and spy satellites. I believe nevertheless that it plays quite a large part in defining the goals of Soviet diplomacy. It is the only explanation that I can find of the compulsive expansion of Soviet naval power which causes the world so much loss of sleep.

3.　The Russians have spent the post-war years in a sustained effort to overcome their handicap in military technology and armaments. For them superpower status means parity of strength and parity of esteem with the United States. But they have found that nuclear parity, while securing them against 'nuclear blackmail', does not in itself guarantee security; and its maintenance and operation is chancy and expensive. Besides, they have other claims on their efforts and resources, including the development of their economy and the handling of potential socio-political problems at home. This, in essence, is the motivation of Brezhnev's 'peace policy', which seeks, while maintaining to the fullest extent practicable the imperial aims of old Russia and the revolutionary aims of the Marxist myth, to achieve, on terms yet to be fully agreed, a relaxation of world tension. It is a policy that makes sense in the Soviet Union's own interests. Indeed there is no credible alternative to Westpolitik for the Russians to adopt. It is right that the West should in principle respond positively to it since the nuclear holocaust promises to be our funeral as well as Brezhnev's. But the response needs to be cautious in practice, bearing in mind the saving clause about Soviet aims and the still nebulous nature of the terms of the accommodation.

4.　The Final Act of Helsinki provides as good a basis as is likely for some time to be devised for the conduct of East–West relations. The long months of negotiation in Geneva that preceded its signature obliged the Russians to tuck in several unpleasing shirt-tails so that the resulting appearance was reasonably spruce. But the shirt has ridden up again and a familiar expanse of midriff is again exposed. The Russians once more openly claim full licence to pursue the 'struggle of ideas' with all the machinations that accompany it: and are again invoking their 'duty' to champion national liberation movements to justify their adventurist, and by recent form incautious, conduct in Angola.[2]

5.　It would be a serious error if we were to suppose that we were dealing with a reformed character. Much time must pass, much effort be expended on our side and many hard lessons learned by the Russians before there can be any reasonable confidence about Soviet behaviour in the world. But we may note that, as Soviet involvement in world affairs increases, so also does the tendency to increased

---

[1] R.-Adm. A.T. Mahan (1840–1914) was an American naval officer and historian, probably best remembered for his writings on the influence of sea power on history in which he sought to demonstrate that imperial greatness and commercial prosperity sprang from the absolute command of the sea.

[2] The revolution in Portugal in April 1974 was followed by the collapse of the Portuguese colonial rule in Angola. But by the autumn of 1975 the former colony had fallen victim to a civil war between rival liberation movements. The Soviet Union offered massive military assistance to the Marxist-orientated *Movimento Popular de Libertacao de Angola* (MPLA) which, with the aid of Cuban forces, quickly established dominance over much of Angola. Meanwhile South African forces invaded the south of the country.

caution and pragmatism, qualities which the Russian Communists have inherited from their historical predecessors. This thought underlies Dr. Kissinger's conception of entangling the Soviet Union in a 'web' of shared interests. I am fully persuaded that it is a fruitful approach. Besides, as I have noted elsewhere, ideology, the Soviet Union's unique and sometimes over-rated weapon, is not immutable. It changes, generally in response to Soviet state interests; and the latter are shaped by the degree of resistance which Soviet policy encounters. The factors currently constraining the full development of Soviet designs are the need to avoid major confrontation with the US, the need to accommodate a measure of economic interdependence with the capitalist world and the problems inherent in any expansion of the 'socialist camp'. To this I would add a further element, which came out with increasing clarity during the recent Conference of East European Ambassadors,[3] namely the need to sustain the credibility of the 'peace policy'. The transition which Brezhnev propounds from 'political' to 'military' détente is as good a line as most for the Russians to take. But it cannot run only on propaganda and phoney disarmament Resolutions in the UN General Assembly. The aim of ourselves and our Allies must be to exploit and as far as possible to enhance these several constraints. We can thereby hope to hold off and eventually turn away the spectres of 'Finlandisation' and a fundamental shift in the balance of world power with which our pundits have, with more truth than falsehood, sought to terrorise us.

6.   This said, it is obvious that successful resistance to Soviet designs depends, first and foremost, upon the will and determination of Western societies, and especially Western European societies, to overcome external and internal weaknesses. So long as the American guarantee and umbrella hold we have breathing space to set our own house in order. I drew moderate comfort from the testimony given at the recent Conference about the adequacy, even though it is declining, of NATO force-levels to discourage Soviet adventures. I also noted some support for the thought that the early withdrawal of American troops from Europe did not axiomatically correspond to wider Soviet interests. Nothing however invalidates or attenuates the need for European countries to maintain, and be prepared to pay for, a credible defence. One of the contingencies which the Russians least like to contemplate is a consolidation of Western Europe extending beyond economy and commerce and into the areas of foreign policy and defence. The short-term obstacles to such consolidation are well identified. Their gradual removal would immeasurably improve our prospects of success.

7.   In the longer term we can expect changes to come in Soviet society itself. But experience suggests that we cannot bank too heavily on this and that the time-scale is likely to be a lot longer than we sometimes suppose. The 'liberalisation' of which there were hopeful signs in the decade following Stalin's fall, ran into the sand. Many of the arguments on which its prophets relied are still valid, but they still do not bite. It is wellnigh impossible indefinitely to run an economy as complex as the Russian economy has become by detailed and rigid planning of production and forecasting of demand. At some point, the unforecastable has to

³ See No. 84.

be remitted, in some degree, to the arbitrament of market forces. But modern computers and linear programming techniques have given the command economy a second wind and probably set back this development by 15 or 20 years. Likewise, it is probably still true that the Russians will never close the 'technology gap' until they let their scientists and industrialists follow their fancy a bit more. But Soviet egg-heads and technocrats, a new class recently emerged from lean living, know for the most part on which side their bread is buttered and the Party takes good care to ensure that privilege (an outstanding feature of this most unequal society) and comfortable living are closely linked to conformity. The nostalgia for 'legality' persist. It has notably humanised (despite numerous horrible black spots) the life of the common man. Two recent guests, returning to Moscow after twenty-five years' absence, have independently identified the main difference between then and now as the absence of the stench of terror. But reasons of state and reasons of ideology combine to obstruct the spread of the rule of law. The Czechoslovak example, if further evidence was required, has underlined the hazards for socialism of excessive attention to human considerations. By and large, the Party has had better success in holding the line against change than it was reasonable to predict 15 years ago. Not for nothing has Brezhnev characterised the CPSU as 'the brain, the honour and the conscience of an epoch'.

8. New factors have appeared since Khrushchev's day which may be of greater long-term importance for change. Demographic mobility, less direction of labour, the private motor-car now in mass production, the growth of cities, the re-housing of the Soviet people in high rise buildings—these things will substantially change the life of the governed and complicate the task of the Party in its mission of inculcating the virtues of patriotism, work and optimism. By contrast with ten years ago, today apathy is a more serious hazard for the Soviet Union also. Moscow and other cities are still safer places to walk around than many in the West. But delinquency and the beginnings of addiction and alienation are there. Because of the West's prior exposure to these hazards, their appearance here is represented as the result of baleful Western influence which the Party strives sedulously to exclude.

9. For all its shortcomings this is becoming a less closed society. It has given higher education to a very large number of its citizens and their perception of the world is perforce different from their predecessors'. The extraordinary capacity of the Slav character for warmth, passion and generosity, long over-laid, lives on. So too does its tendency to lethargy and feeling futile. These characteristics are all troublesome material for the social engineer. It is getting harder than it was to insulate Soviet society from external contagion. A few germs get blown in even from the pretty aseptic air of Eastern Europe. The jamming of foreign broadcasts has gone. Russians daily and with impunity listen to Western transmissions in their own language and Western languages, gaining thereby knowledge of outside events which their own press leaves unmentioned and also replays by wireless of the reporting of Western correspondents in Moscow. This is far more important in its implications than the outcome of the forthcoming haggle with the Russians over the importation of a few Western newspapers. I

believe that the flank has been turned. But we should be careful, in exploiting it, not to spoil everything by naïve cold war propaganda.

10. Some acceleration of the time-table may reasonably be expected from the change of generations and the relieving of the old guard. The leadership that supplanted Khrushchev is now close to or past seventy years of age. It is on the whole doubtful that the impending 25th Congress will bring any major change; but if anything is certain, it is that the top four or five men in the Soviet Union will be under the sod or out to grass before very long. The new leaders—still unidentified will in the main be men untainted by the excesses of Stalinism, old enough to have known the war but not the revolution. They will be no less tenacious of what they conceive to be Soviet interests then their predecessors were. They will approach the 1980s in a different spirit and a different style from the present incumbents. We would do well to spend more effort in spotting the winners and rather less on medical analysis of Brezhnev's maladies.

11. My time here has witnessed the opening of a 'new phase' in Anglo-Soviet relations following a period of frigidity and stagnation. The meeting in Moscow in February 1975 between the Prime Minister and yourself and the Soviet leaders has opened up opportunities for both sides. The Russians have watched the dissolution of the Empire and see us as a medium-sized, developed European country posing no threat to themselves but still capable, in association with others of exercising an influence disproportionate to our strength. They have a shrewd understanding of our present weaknesses, but past habits of thought inhibit them from drawing far-reaching conclusions. They still regard us as experienced and realistic in foreign affairs and as possessing special, if diminishing, capabilities in international finance, and some useful technology. The fear periodically recurs in their minds that a European Community with Britain in it might prove a serious nuisance to their plans; but, so far, it has generally receded in the light of subsequent events. Our multiple troubles in 1974 confused them a good deal and they went completely off the air for the first half of that year. Now, as President Podgorny made plain when I said goodbye to him this week,[4] they look upon Britain as a promising Western partner; less important, it is true, than the potentially revanchist Germans or the maverick French, but worth knowing all the same. They will seek from us, as the relationship develops, the removal of a series of long-term obstacles (one of them being the ceiling on the Soviet representation in London) to the propagation of Soviet influence. HMG have been right to proceed with great caution in this.

12. For ourselves the new phase offers the prospect of pursuing, hopefully but warily, that 'safer and more productive' relationship of which you spoke last winter, and of casting off some ancient attitudes which, while doing no harm to the Russians, tended to mar our style. It also offers us the prospect of competing on equal terms for a share in the industrial orders which the development of the Soviet economy can be expected to generate. This prospect is no mirage though it recedes from time to time under the pressure of unforeseen events. In the shorter term, at a time of diminished employment at home, Soviet orders are not

[4] Sir T. Garvey had his final meeting, as Ambassador, with Mr. Podgorny on 4 December.

to be sneezed at. Provided that we can remain tenacious of our own interest and advantage, I believe that the present improvement in Anglo-Soviet relations can be made, not, in the Russian jargon, 'irreversible', but at least as durable as most diplomatic arrangements.

13. I am sorry to leave Moscow at this moment when there is the prospect of much activity ahead, but it is a wise rule that the old horses should go out to grass. And thirty-seven years on the road is enough. I have much valued the confidence of Ministers, the forbearance of officials at home and the loyalty and friendship of those who have worked with me here.

14. I am sending copies of this despatch to HM Representatives at the EEC, NATO, the United Nations in New York, Washington, Bonn, Paris, Rome, Lisbon, Warsaw, Budapest, Bucharest, Sofia, Prague, East Berlin, Belgrade, Helsinki, Peking and New Delhi.

I have, etc.,
T. GARVEY

No. 86

Mr. Callaghan to Sir H. Smith (Moscow)

No. 83 Telegraphic [*MTW 121/303/1*]

Immediate. Confidential   FCO, *29 January 1976*

Repeated for information to UKDEL NATO, UKDEL Vienna, UKREP Brussels, Washington, Paris, Rome, Bonn and UKMIS Geneva.

Brezhnev's Message[1]

1. You have received by bag the improved translation of Brezhnev's message. You may like to draw upon the following guidance in any discussion which may arise with the Russians of the points which Brezhnev has made about international relations.

2. *Disarmament.*[2] The Prime Minister's views were made clear in his statement

---

[1] On 24 November 1975 the Prime Minister wrote to Mr. Brezhnev to remind him that during his February visit to Moscow both Mr. Brezhnev and Mr. Kosygin had accepted in principle his invitation to visit the UK, and to suggest that a four-day visit between mid-October and mid-December 1976 would be welcome. Mr. Wilson observed that the documents signed in Moscow 'had led to the constructive and progressively more active development of the "new phase" in Anglo-Soviet relations'. In his reply, dated 28 December and delivered to HM Embassy, Moscow, on 29 December, Mr. Brezhnev reaffirmed that he thought that the current state of Anglo-Soviet relations and the development of the world situation favoured arranging a new meeting at the highest level, and stated that specific dates for such a visit could 'be agreed on later' (ENS 3/548/9).

[2] Mr. Brezhnev's message (*v. ibid.*) referred to the Soviet leadership's deep conviction that the 'positive development' of Anglo-Soviet relations was 'inseparably linked with broadening the scope of integration of [their] two countries in the international arena'. In this context, he cited the arms limitation and disarmament proposals put by Mr. Gromyko to the UN General Assembly in

at Helsinki on 30 July.[3] Since then we have been working particularly closely with the Russians at the meetings in London devoted to improved common procedures for nuclear exports. If the Russians raise Brezhnev's initiative on weapons of mass destruction[4] you should say that it is an interesting proposal, the objective of which we share. We should be glad for further Soviet ideas on how it would be worked out.

3. *CSCE Follow-Up.* Brezhnev's insistence on full and balanced implementation of the decisions of the CSCE is a sentiment we share.[5] But it expresses in Russian eyes a belief that what matters most is the declaration of principles. Neither we nor any other Western European Government underestimate the importance of the political principles drawn up at Helsinki. They are principles on which our conduct has always been and continues to be based. Balanced implementation will therefore be easily attainable if the Soviet Government for its part can ensure that the provisions of Baskets II and III and of confidence-building measures are fully carried out.

4. *Conferences on environment, transport and energy.*[6] These proposals have a history going back at least 10 years. All three subjects have been given particular attention by the Economic Commission for Europe in Geneva. We should not wish to duplicate or waste the Commission's efforts, and the expertise built up in Geneva, by holding new Conferences elsewhere. Some of our partners may have particular difficulty if it appears that the Russians want to take these subjects out of the hands of the ECE.[7] Our attitude on all three subjects will need to be concerted within the European Community and we shall discuss the matter with them. It would be interesting to know more of what the Russians have in mind. From the language used in Brezhnev's message, it seems that he has in mind cooperation on the conversion of energy, e.g. power grids rather than on the primary sources of energy such as oil, but this is not the view of the Russians at the ECE in Geneva and it would be helpful to have further clarification on this point.

5. *MBFR.* Brezhnev does not acknowledge the latest Western offer at Vienna.[8]

September (see *Official Records of the 30th Session of UNGA, A/PV 2357*, pp. 53–65), and expressed the hope that the UK and the Soviet Union should do all they could to achieve progress in this sphere.

[3] See Cmnd 6932, pp. 216–22.

[4] In a televised election speech, delivered on 13 June 1975, Mr. Brezhnev called for an international agreement 'banning the creation of new types of weapons of mass destruction, new systems of such armaments' (Moscow telegrams Nos. 903 and 904 of 14 June, ENS 2/1).

[5] 'As regards Europe', Mr. Brezhnev observed (see notes 1 and 2 above), 'it is very important now, as we see it, to concentrate attention on implementing the Helsinki agreements and the Final Act ... in all its aspects and in its entirety, without excepting or minimising any of the provisions contained in it.'

[6] Mr. Brezhnev recalled in his message earlier proposals he had made for the holding of 'all-European congresses or inter-state conferences on cooperation in the sphere of protection of the environment, the development of transport, and power'.

[7] Economic Commission for Europe.

[8] Of the MBFR talks, Mr. Brezhnev simply wrote that progress in these negotiations was of 'common concern'. Cf. No. 27.

You should seek every opportunity to impress upon the Russians the importance of that offer and our hope that the Warsaw Pact reply will be positive and forthcoming.

6. *Critics of Détente.* In attacking unidentified Western circles,[9] this passage of Brezhnev's message diverts attention from the causes of criticism in the West of Soviet attitudes, viz the Soviet actions in Angola, Portugal etc. You should impress upon the Russians that, while we have no objection to the contest of ideas, we object strongly to efforts to promote the solution by force of political problems arising in countries far from the Soviet Union's territory. The Soviet Union cannot expect us to accept the arming of revolutionary movements on the territory of other people as a reasonable form of ideological struggle. Such activity is bound to have international repercussions and adverse consequences for détente.

7. *The North Atlantic Council Meeting.* The language in the NATO communiqué about Soviet military expenditure reflects well-known facts.[10] The conclusion of the CSCE will in no way inhibit us from pointing out that the continuing rapid growth of the forces of the Warsaw Pact threatens European stability.[11] This said, you should emphasise that the main message of the NATO communiqué was the common determination to persevere in efforts to place relations in Europe on a more stable basis.

8. *The Quadripartite Agreement.* HMG have no intention of undermining the agreement about Berlin, and know of no serious problems arising in that connection.[12] On the contrary they have taken steps to ensure that quadripartite rights are maintained, for example by their joint statement with France and the United States on 14 October that the rights and responsibility of the four powers for Berlin and Germany as a whole remain unaffected by the Soviet/GDR Treaty of Friendship.[13] At your discretion you might point out that the Treaty of

---

[9] Mr. Brezhnev observed in his message: 'certain circles in the West, and these are echoed somewhere in the East, are persistently trying in every way to criticise détente and discredit it. Indeed it is not only that they are activating a campaign of slander and dis-information but that these circles are directly counteracting the process of the increasing reduction of international tension and the yearning of the peoples for peace and cooperation. They are seeking to whip up hotbeds of tension in various areas of the world, and to interfere overtly and covertly in the internal affairs of countries and peoples.'

[10] See Cmnd 6932, pp. 289–91. In his message Mr. Brezhnev expressed his regret that the results of the NAC meeting in December 1975 had run counter to the results of the CSCE and the 'spirit of the Final Act'. He noted that participants had been more concerned with increasing their military expenditure, and that the main pretext for this had been 'the notorious myth of "the Soviet threat"'.

[11] A JIC paper of 19 September 1977 estimated 'that in 1972–76 Soviet military expenditure grew by about 5 per cent a year in real terms and absorbed 11–13 per cent of GNP, a far higher share than for any member of NATO' (JIC (77) 7).

[12] See *Selected Documents on Germany and the Question of Berlin 1961–1973*, Cmnd 6201 (London: HMSO, 1975), pp. 236–42. Mr. Brezhnev insisted in his message that *détente* was not facilitated by 'attempts from time to time to undermine previous agreements, and particular the Quadripartite Agreement on West Berlin'.

[13] See No. 82.

Friendship has significantly contributed to Western unease about détente, given its implicit reaffirmation in relation to the GDR of 'The Brezhnev doctrine' of limited sovereignty.

9.   *The Paris and Rambouillet Conferences.*[14] The world economy is facing its most serious problems since the 1930s—the non-oil producing less-developed countries being particularly hard hit. HMG would welcome a positive and constructive contribution by the Soviet Union to the solution of these problems. For your own information, Brezhnev's remarks[15] are another interesting indication, in addition to those noted in your tel[egram] No. 1572,[16] that the Russians may now realise that they are in danger of being excluded from important developments which they, as a super-power, would like to influence.[17]

[14] See No. 84, note 22. The Conference on International Economic Cooperation (CIEC) met in full session in Paris on 16–19 December 1975. It was attended by the Foreign Ministers of 19 developing and oil-producing countries, and 8 developed, counting the EC as one.

[15] 'It is', Mr. Brezhnev complained with regard to these Conferences, 'hardly realistic to search for a solution of the problems of the world economy within an unjustifiably narrow circle of states, without taking due account of the role and interests of a large part of the world.'

[16] Mr. Sutherland reported in this telegram of 8 December 1975 that although the Russians had so far stood aside from the debate on the New International Economic Order, the economic and political consequences of the shift in financial power since 1973 had been less favourable to them than anticipated, and that 'they must fear increasingly that, without their involvement, a fruitful North-South dialogue and possibly new international economic machinery could tend to limit their world influence and be inconsistent with their superpower status' (MFA 19/598/16).

[17] In a further personal message to Mr. Brezhnev despatched in telegram No. 82 to Moscow of 29 January, and delivered by Sir H. Smith on 11 February, Mr. Wilson reiterated his desire to settle the dates of Mr. Brezhnev's proposed visit to the UK. The Prime Minister also stressed the importance of maintaining the 'momentum of the process of détente'; expressed his concern about events in Angola and noted the need to ensure that the better relations they were seeking to develop in Europe were 'reflected in [their] dealings in the wider world'; and commended to Mr. Brezhnev's attention the recent offer made by Western delegates to the MBFR talks at Vienna (see note 8 above).

No. 87

Mr. Callaghan to Sir H. Smith (Moscow)

[EN 408/548/1]

Confidential   FCO, *11 March 1976*

Sir,

The Conference of HM Ambassadors in the Soviet Union and Eastern Europe, 17–19 November 1975

1.   I have read with interest the records of the Conference of Her Majesty's Ambassadors in the Soviet Union and Eastern Europe which was held in the Foreign and Commonwealth Office from 17–19 November, 1975.[1]

[1] See No. 84.

2. I have used the report of your Conference as a basis for my own thoughts on East/West relations in recent months.[2] What follows represents my view of East/West relations and of the UK's relations with the Soviet Union and the countries of Eastern Europe, in the light of the Conference's proceedings and more recent developments.[3] Your Conference was the first to be held since the Government took office; the normal pattern of biennial Conferences was interrupted by the domestic political events of 1974. The three years which have passed since the Ambassadors' Conference of 1972 have also been marked by two major and related developments in East/West relations which make this an appropriate time to take stock: the further unfolding of *détente* and the conduct and conclusion of the Conference on Security and Co-operation in Europe. These three developments—a change of Government in London, the continuation of *détente* and the CSCE—happen to make convenient headings for the points which I wish to make.

3. I was interested to see that the view was expressed during the Conference that we sometimes concentrate on Soviet objectives to an extent which leads to a defensive or even a defeatist attitude on our part. It has been my firm intention to counter this attitude by having a positive attitude to East/West relations. This does not mean that we ignore Soviet transgressions of the spirit of *détente*. Equally, so long as the Soviet Union and her Allies devote so much of their resources to armaments, *détente* must also be matched by an adequate defence capability that is sufficient to deter. But it has been and remains an objective of Her Majesty's Government, having brought to an end a period of relative stagnation in our relations with the Soviet Union, to secure a genuine improvement in those relations. We are not starry-eyed about it. We are fully conscious of the limitations which disparities of power and of belief impose. But given the complexity of the present international scene and the unthinkable consequences which could flow from misunderstandings or miscalculations, it should be the duty of every Western Government to establish the best possible lines of communication with the Russians in order to obtain the most accurate reading we can of their thinking, priorities and intentions and to ensure that they understand ours.

4. This improvement in communications cannot be brought about by exchanges of visits at the top level alone. Top level visits help to unlock valuable doors, but the purpose should be to broaden and intensify our contacts at all levels, both officially and otherwise. This is why, when I visited Moscow with the

---

[2] At the instigation of Sir T. Brimelow the Conference had drafted its conclusions in the form of a revised version of the Summary of Conclusions of the 1972 Ambassadors' Conference (see Volume I, No. 95), a copy of which Mr. Cartledge enclosed with a letter to Sir H. Smith of 8 January.

[3] Dissatisfied with Sir T. Brimelow's decision simply to revise the 1972 conclusions and evidently disappointed at the lack of Ministerial involvement in the 1975 Conference, Mr. Cartledge sought to use this follow-up despatch 'as a means of forcing Ministers to focus on a quite important discussion of a policy area to which they [said] they attach[ed] importance'. A draft despatch was sent to Private Office in January and, as Mr. Cartledge subsequently affirmed, Mr. Callaghan gave a great deal of thought to it and the result reflected 'not only his own ideas but, at many points, his own phrasing' (letters from Mr. Cartledge to Mr. Bullard of 26 January and to Sir H. Smith of 12 March).

Prime Minister in February 1975, I proposed the setting up of the Anglo-Soviet Round Table which held its first session in London last autumn.[4] It produced no dramatic new insights, but these are not to be expected all at once. Understanding, which does not necessarily mean agreement, will grow with familiarity. I was attracted by Lord Trevelyan's [5] remark, made during the Round Table session and quoted more than once during your Conference, about the value of 'a state of permanent negotiation' with the Soviet Union.[6] This is what we should aim at. We should be in a position to form our own views, at any time and in any area, about Soviet behaviour and Soviet thinking; we should never have to rely on second-hand opinions.

5. This primary objective applies equally to the development of our relations with the countries of Eastern Europe, although here our aims are slightly different. The contributions of our Ambassadors in Eastern Europe to the Conference brought out very clearly the fact that although several of the East European Governments have certain interests in common with the Soviet Union—most obviously perhaps in the case of Poland and Bulgaria—they also have specific national interests of their own which may run counter to the collective interests of the Warsaw Pact and the CMEA. In my visits to Eastern Europe, I have been impressed by the remarkable diversity of the region; and the importance of this diversity emerged clearly from your discussions in London. I believe that the British, and Western, interest lies in using the individual, national aspirations of the East European countries, especially where these diverge from *bloc* loyalties, in order to encourage their Governments gradually to enlarge the area within which they can assert separate identities. The Romanians have already shown that they can behave like Romanians and still remain in the Warsaw Pact; we should like to see the Poles being more Polish, the Czechoslovaks more Czechoslovak and even the Bulgarians more Bulgarian. The stronger this trend becomes, the harder it will be for the Soviet Union to treat the countries of Eastern Europe as a drill squad. And the more links of all kinds—economic, cultural and human—that can be developed between Eastern and Western Europe, the more difficult it will become for the Soviet Union abruptly to sever them should the Kremlin's policies swing away from *détente*. We should not deceive ourselves that the Soviet Union will be willing, at least in our lifetime, to forgo or even to relax its ultimate control of the Eastern European region. However, the development of a network of links between the two halves of Europe may serve as at least a marginal inhibition on the application of the 'Brezhnev doctrine', and this is in itself a worthwhile objective.

[4] See No 73, note 2. The Anglo-Soviet Round Table held its first session on 24–25 October 1975. The British side was headed by Mr. A.A. Schonfield, Director of the Royal Institute of International Affairs, and the Soviet side by Academician N.N. Inozemtsev, Director of the Institute of World Economics and International Relations in Moscow (minute from Mr. Cartledge to Private Secretary, 27 October 1975, ENS 3/548/8).

[5] Lord Trevelyan was British Ambassador in Moscow, 1962–65. He participated in the Anglo-Soviet Round Table discussions.

[6] Mr. McNally attributed this remark to Lord Trevelyan during the first session of the Conference of HM Ambassadors in Eastern Europe and the Soviet Union on 17 November 1975. Cf. No. 84, note 1.

6. I noted a change of emphasis from your 1972 Conference on whether we should pay more attention to the 'management' in Moscow or to Moscow's East European clients.[7] I do not think that this is a problem which should be posed. There are good reasons for developing relations with both. The increase of activity in Anglo-Soviet relations should not be at the expense of bilateral relations with the countries of Eastern Europe and I hope the pattern of Ministerial visits will underline this fact.

7. This is very obviously true in the field of trade. The point was made more than once during the Conference that the fundamental pre-condition for an effective British policy towards the Communist countries, as elsewhere in the world, is the recovery of the UK's economy. If we are to play abroad the part of which we are capable and to which our knowledge and experience entitle us, we must put our own house in order. A sharp reduction in the rate of inflation is already taking place and I am convinced that as 1976 progresses you will be able to talk to your clients with growing confidence and conviction. The development of Britain's export trade is a key factor in that recovery. The creation of healthy political relations with the State-trading countries does not in itself guarantee that we shall win orders from them; but it does mean that British firms will be able to compete on equal terms with their Western rivals and that if their prices and deliveries are right they should get their fair share of the business. The Conference brought out very clearly that the development of trade with the CMEA countries often involves a great deal of work and expenditure of time, both Ministerial and official, for frequently inadequate commercial reward; some participants were inclined to question whether the game was worth the candle. But, from the Government's point of view, every export order won, even in small markets such as Bulgaria, is a significant contribution to domestic recovery and to employment here at home.

8. We are at present dealing with domestic economic problems which still need, and will need for some time to come, sacrifice and self-discipline. There are no quick or easy answers. But I do not believe that our voice in foreign affairs need be, or should be, unduly muted during our period of difficulty, even though it is likely to continue for some time yet. We as a Government and you as the country's representatives have a duty to proclaim and defend the beliefs and principles on which our society is based. You should assert that the West, far from being a society without a future, has democratic strengths which enable it to absorb and contain the changes which are generated by a rapidly evolving industrial society.[8]

9. I am not suggesting that we should engage in a permanent slanging match with the Communist régimes. This would be unproductive. But we should show

---

[7] See No. 84, note 12.

[8] The 1975 revise of the Conclusions of the 1972 Ambassadors' Conference (see note 2 above) argued: 'Progress in détente will not cause the "ideological struggle" to wither away. This means that plain speaking about Communism and the policies of Communist governments will continue to be necessary. Discrimination is nevertheless required to ensure that the plain speaking does not degenerate into the language of the cold war.'

serious and persistent determination in specific situations, such as humanitarian cases, which will in itself demonstrate our firm attachment to the cause of the individual and his liberties. We should remember—and this emerged during your Conference—that our approach to human affairs by no means lacks its supporters even in Communist societies. I agree with Sir Terence Garvey's statement in his despatch of 21 October, 1975, on the 'Ideological Struggle' that, however much the Communists may wish to promote revolutionary change in the West 'we also heartily desire change in Soviet society and the others that emulate it. We wish to see them humanised, brought under the rule of law, and their citizens [permitted] to know, to speak and to move'.[9]

10. I was interested by the unanimous agreement which the Conference revealed on the importance of broadcasting, and specifically of the BBC's external services, as the medium through which we can best project our beliefs and our view of the world. These are views I fully support. The contest of ideas over the air is perhaps a less dramatic business now than it was in the heyday of the cold war; but with the reduction in jamming and in the constraints on listening to foreign broadcasts in Communist societies, the opportunities for the BBC's operations directed towards Eastern Europe have increased. The Department is already looking into ways in which the BBC's work can, compatibly with the need for thrift in all our overseas effort, be made more effective in relation to the countries in which you reside.

11. You will note that none of the policy objectives which I have so far identi-fied are reactive or responsive. They stand on their own feet, are valid in their own right and do not amount merely to a reaction to Soviet purposes. They would retain their validity even if Soviet policy were to move away from *détente* —although they would then become more difficult of attainment. I mention this in order to underline the fact that it is not necessary in approaching East/West relations always to take the 'Soviet threat' as the starting point. In other fields, we put our own objectives first. We should do likewise in this field as well.

12. One important area in which policy is of necessity responsive is, of course, the area of defence. I do not wish, in this despatch, to discuss current Soviet policies in any detail. I think that, despite natural differences of emphasis, a clear consensus emerged from your Conference that, although the Soviet Union's insatiable desire for the enhancement of its security will lead it to persist in attempting to adjust the balance of power in Europe and elsewhere to its own advantage, there is a degree of conflict between various facets of its own national interest which imposes important constraints on its behaviour at the present time.[10] Nobody, I believe, argued during the Conference that Brezhnev's policies

[9] See No. 83, note 8.

[10] These tensions in Soviet policy were also noted by the JIC in their 1977 report on Soviet military expenditure (see No. 86, note 11). It reasoned that poor industrial productivity and a slowing rate of expansion in the USSR's labour market gave the Soviet leadership 'a strong motive for seeking to restrain the growth of military expenditure, so that it [did] not pre-empt an even greater share of economic resources'. On the other hand, the paper asserted that 'major military programmes generate[d] their own momentum, and the interests of the military leadership and defence-related industries [were] likely to continue to carry heavy weight in decision making at the

of *détente* are other than a reflection of clearly perceived Soviet State interests—in avoiding nuclear war, in avoiding a resumption of the strategic arms race (although some would deny that it has been suspended), in giving priority to the development of the Soviet economy, in drawing on Western wealth and technology for this purpose, and in isolating China.[11]

13. Some of these interests to a large extent complement our own. The Soviet commitment to a certain level of *détente*, which they collectively produce, is very much in line with our interest. The objectives which I have outlined for British policy are more likely to be achieved in a period of *détente* than in a period of confrontation. Interest in the continuation and consolidation of *détente* cannot, however, obscure the fact that, as the Conference was reminded, the last five years have seen the greatest build-up in Soviet military power since the war.[12]

14. The Conference also focused on a number of potential flash points. The Soviet Union used an aspect of her military power, despite the potential risks, to swing the political balance in Angola.[13] I have left the Soviet Government in no doubt of my view that the spirit of *détente* places upon us all obligations to behave with restraint and responsibility. To disregard that principle, and to adopt policies which serve to prolong rather than reduce tension in the Third World, will undoubtedly damage the spirit of global *détente*. The recapture of Yugoslavia, though probably not by direct military means, remains an important Soviet objective. Berlin, to whose continuing liberty we are firmly committed as I assured Berliners during my recent visit,[14] still offers disquieting scope for East/West friction. Against this background, the paramount importance of maintaining a credible Western defence capacity needs no further emphasis; and the Conference noted the necessity for reinforcing, through NATO, the cohesion of the Western Alliance.

15. Political co-operation within NATO clearly has a vital part to play in this respect. The Conference was impressed, as I am, by the American view, which owes much to Dr. Kissinger's personal philosophy, that the purpose of *détente* is in part to control the emergence of the Soviet Union as an imperial power. This

highest level', especially given 'the paramount importance which the Soviet leaders attach[ed] to national security and military power'.

[11] The 1975 revise of the Conclusions of the 1972 Ambassadors' Conference (see notes 2 and 8 above) observed: 'The Soviet leaders appear to be relying more on the course of events and on their propaganda of détente than on active diplomacy for the modification of the balance of power in Europe. But although their tactics in Europe have been characterised by caution and some uncertainty, the Soviet leaders have given no grounds for any important revision of our assessment of their fundamental aims and strategy which are rooted in their ideology.'

[12] 'Although there is no reason at present to regard this as an indicator of increased danger of direct Soviet aggression, or as reducing the Soviet incentive to avoid military confrontation with the United States', the 1975 revise (*v. ibid.*) contended with regard to the Soviet arms build-up, 'it gives the Soviet Union a significantly increased capability of exploiting military power for political purposes. The West requires the same military capability to deter or counter this as to deter war.'

[13] See No. 85, note 2. British reactions to Soviet involvement in southern Africa will be covered in a subsequent volume.

[14] Mr. Callaghan visited Berlin during 21–22 January.

is a process in which the US, as the other Super Power, must clearly play a leading role. The Conference was also right to emphasise, however, the equal importance of effective political co-operation within the Nine. It is natural that on some issues, and indeed on some central international problems, there should be a distinctively European view which will not always be identical to that of our American friends. Our task must be to ensure that the Nine work sufficiently closely together to enable such a common view to evolve coherently, while ensuring that our lines of communication with Washington are also of the best, so that the European view may be heard.

16. NATO machinery has also played a key role in co-ordinating the Western approach to the negotiations in Vienna on Mutual and Balanced Force Reductions (MBFR), where it is vital that the Alliance should remain in step. We can harbour no illusions about the nature of Soviet objectives in the talks on MBFR which, as the Conference heard, are to secure the ratification of the Warsaw Pact's military superiority in Central Europe while weakening the defences of Western Europe and the American commitment to them. But so long as the Russians are not permitted to achieve their subsidiary aim of using the negotiations as a wedge with which to split the Alliance, there is no reason why we should not continue confidently to pursue in Vienna our own objective of exacting, as the means of extending *détente* to the military field, a reduction of Warsaw Pact force levels, the increase of restrictions on Soviet deployments in Eastern Europe and a degree of reciprocity and control in force reductions which will enable us to carry through important economies in defence expenditure without impairing our own security. Soviet willingness to pay the price we ask will be the acid test of its commitment to the military *détente* which, as the Conference agreed, is now becoming the central theme of the Soviet propaganda effort.[15]

17. I turn finally to the Conference on Security and Co-operation in Europe (CSCE). I agree with the view expressed by most participants in the Conference that the CSCE did not in itself amount to a watershed or turning point in East/West relations. Nor is it likely to result in any significant modification of the relationship between the States of Eastern Europe and the Soviet Union; the Conference agreed that in Eastern Europe we could expect no more than the mixture as before rather than a new prescription. But we should not write down the CSCE too far. The Russians appear to have been at least as defensive about the Final Act since its signature in Helsinki as they have been triumphant over its achievement. This is a measure of Western success in the long negotiations, in which the Nine can be said to have tested their political strength. But the source of Soviet discomfort was the West's willingness to put forward ideas of its own and not simply engage in 'damage limitation'. The Western achievement in

[15] The 1975 revise of the Conclusions of the 1972 Ambassadors' Conference (see notes 2, 8, 10 and 11 above) stated: 'NATO policy continues to be "defence plus détente". So far, inflation has done more than détente to increase pressures on the Governments of the European members of NATO to reduce defence expenditure. The CSCE did not in itself create in the NATO countries a euphoria which markedly increased pressures for defence cuts. Nonetheless, the combination of inflation and the general atmosphere of détente threatens to make it increasingly difficult for NATO to maintain a satisfactory balance of conventional forces in Europe.'

compelling Communist régimes to accept that the quality of life for individual human beings has a legitimate place on the international agenda should not be underestimated and it is an item which will now have an ongoing place in East/West discussions.

18. This achievement will not, however, count for much unless we show tenacity and determination in following up the provisions of the Final Act. As you know, I take the view that it will be unrealistic to expect that traditional attitudes and practices can be modified or reversed overnight. But it is nevertheless important to demonstrate to the Communist régimes that we do expect change and that we intend to press for it. I am not sanguine that we shall get much but they must be made to argue their case. *Détente* should allow us greater opportunities to protect our values and beliefs, in the hope that by doing so we may eventually help to make the Communist States less intransigent and uncomfortable neighbours in Europe. We should not recoil because there will be no armistice in the war of ideas.

19. The Final Act of the CSCE puts into our hands some new instruments and we should use them. The Department gave you, during the Conference, a preview of some of the initiatives which we are contemplating (the relevant note was annexed to the records of the Conference which you have already received). Our plans are necessarily modest, in keeping with our financial means. It is nevertheless important that they should be pursued in order to demonstrate that we have not simply put the Final Act in the cupboard.

20. The Conference recognised the necessity, in this as in other fields, for maintaining and intensifying our political co-operation within the Nine and I am encouraged by the progress which the Experts Group on the CSCE[16] has already made in this work. This will be the indispensable basis for a co-ordinated Community approach to the review meetings in 1977. These meetings will present us with some difficult choices. The Russians will want to use them to refight some of the battles which they lost in Helsinki and Geneva and to seek to transform CSCE principles into a more formal system of European collective security, complemented by pan-European projects in economic co-operation built on to Basket II[17] of the Final Act. But they have not so far shown much of their hand and I should like to keep an open mind for the time being. Of two things, however, I am already certain. The Soviet Government must not be allowed to engage us in a further marathon of European negotiations until they have first established their credentials by making material—not simply presentational—contributions to the consolidation of *détente*, both through the implementation of the provisions of 'Basket III' and by adopting a more constructive approach in the MBFR negotiations in Vienna. We must make it clear to the Russians that we regard multilateral negotiations as a means of achieving material results and not as an

[16] The signing of the Helsinki Final Act on 1 August 1975 was followed by the establishment of a European Political Cooperation Working Group on follow-up to CSCE (see Volume II, No. 1, note 26).

[17] Basket (or Item) II of the CSCE covered cooperation in the field of economics, science and technology and the environment (see Volume II, No. 137).

end in themselves, much less a substitute for real progress. Eagerness on our part to contemplate a second full-scale European Conference without any tangible evidence that the first one had borne useful fruit would be unwise in our own interest and certainly not understood by British opinion.

21. It will, I hope, be possible to arrange a further Conference for Heads of Mission in the Soviet Union and Eastern Europe in about two years' time. The intervening period is likely to be an eventful one in East/West affairs. We shall probably see a change of leadership in the Soviet Union. President Tito will, we must assume, at last leave the stage, with all the dangers and uncertainties which this event will evoke for the Yugoslav peoples. Our task will be to ensure that dramatic events of this kind do not disrupt the processes of *détente* which are, on the whole, in the British interest; but that vital Western interests are at the same time safeguarded. *Détente* is not a favour conferred by the West upon the Soviet Union, but a recognition of the mutual destructive capacity of the two world Super Powers. Alongside that reality the conflict of ideas will be continually prosecuted. It is my firm belief that our society, with all its respect for human values and the rights of the individual, has more to offer than any other in answer to that challenge.

22. I am sending copies of this despatch to Her Majesty's Ambassadors in Washington, Warsaw, Budapest, Prague, Bucharest, Sofia, East Berlin, Ulan Bator, Bonn, UKDEL NATO, Helsinki, Belgrade, UKDEL Vienna and to Her Majesty's Representatives at EEC posts.

I have,etc.,
JAMES CALLAGHAN

No. 88

Mr. Callaghan to HM Representatives Overseas

Guidance No. 66 Telegraphic [*MTW 121/303/1*]

Immediate. Confidential   FCO, *26 March 1976*

Visit of the Soviet Foreign Minister to the United Kingdom: 22–25 March 1976

1. The following account of Mr. Gromyko's visit to London is primarily for your own background information, and in any public comments you should confine yourself to the terms of the Prime Minister's written reply to Mr. Graham's [1] PQ on 25 March (Hansard Vol. 908, Cols. 238 and 239: text telegraphed to certain posts in the retract series). You may however draw at your discretion on the whole account in discussion with allied colleagues or officials of other friendly governments. Community and NATO briefings will be based on this guidance tel[egram].

[1] Mr. T.E. Graham was Labour MP for Edmonton.

General

2. The visit was in response to an invitation extended when the Prime Minister and I visited the Soviet Union in February 1975.[2]

3. The main British objective was to consolidate the improvement in bilateral relations and contacts which has resulted from the Anglo-Soviet summit of February last year. A further important aim was to re-establish firmly, as a normal feature of the Anglo-Soviet relationship, the practice of political discussions at Ministerial level, which had fallen into abeyance before the Prime Minister's visit to Moscow last year. Both these objectives can be regarded as having been achieved. The talks were conducted in a good atmosphere, free from unhelpful acrimony, and with frankness in the exposition of views from both sides. They were generally useful and constructive. Anglo-Soviet relations have regained a degree of stability which can absorb the clear expression of different opinions. At his press conference on 25 March, Mr. Gromyko described the talks as very positive. Mr. Gromyko invited me to pay a return visit to the Soviet Union and I accepted.

4. I had three sessions of talks with Gromyko, lasting some six hours in all. Mr. Gromyko also had a meeting with the Prime Minister. There were a number of more informal conversations between Gromyko and myself during the three days of the visit. The talks covered as wide a range of international and bilateral matters as time allowed.

5. Gromyko's main objective appears to have been to keep the détente current flowing against the resistances which it has recently encountered. He reaffirmed the Soviet Union's commitment to détente as defined by Mr. Brezhnev at the 25th CPSU party Congress[3] (the Soviet Foreign Minister repeatedly used Mr. Brezhnev's report as a reference point) and to the further improvement of bilateral relations with the UK on the basis of the agreements signed in Moscow in February 1975. Little attempt was made to pressure HMG into endorsing Soviet positions on international questions, although Gromyko was as tenacious as ever in expounding established Soviet policies. The negotiation of the communiqué presented relatively few difficulties. It is in fact somewhat leaner than the Soviet Foreign Ministry has usually liked. In general, Gromyko and his party gave the impression of wishing to appear as agreeable and forthcoming as possible. This made it a little easier to conduct the visit in such a way as to put the accent on the importance of restraint, patience and moderation.

International

6. On European issues, Gromyko emphasised that his Government was

---

[2] See No. 74.

[3] In his speech on 25 February Mr. Brezhnev stated that *détente* and coexistence referred to interstate relations, which meant that disputes between states were not settled by war or the threat of force. 'The détente', he continued, 'does not in the slightest abolish, and cannot abolish or alter, the laws of class struggle. None should expect that because of the détente Communists will reconcile themselves with capitalist exploitation or that monopolists become followers of the revolution.' But he also asserted that the 'strict observance of the principle of non-interference and sovereignty' was one of the 'essential conditions' of détente. See Cmnd 6932, pp. 295–304.

'rigorously observing' its Helsinki undertakings and expected other governments to do the same. He thought that Helsinki had brought 'a warmer breath' to the general atmosphere in Europe: but maintained that, at the propaganda level, 'certain circles in some countries' were impeding progress in détente. Some people were trying to play down the significance of CSCE, others had aimed their hostile propaganda at the 25ᵗʰ Party Congress: but these things would not deter the Soviet Union in its resolve to promote détente.

7. I said that there were indeed better relations between the Governments of East and West. But it was also true that, in terms of public opinion, much of the Helsinki euphoria had worn off. There were doubts and difficulties which should be frankly faced and discussed. One major example was the question of family reunification. But I also expressed my view that developments in recent months in Africa—i.e. Soviet involvement in Angola—had produced a feedback in Europe which affected the atmosphere of détente.[4] Gromyko made no comment of substance on this.

8. In answer to a question from me, Gromyko said that the Soviet Government had an open mind on the forums which would be appropriate for consideration of Mr. Brezhnev's proposals for pan-European Conferences.[5] I said that the Economic Commission for Europe (ECE) had already done useful work in the areas mentioned: I made clear that HMG were still considering their attitude in consultation with their friends and allies.

9. On MBFR negotiations, the two sides acknowledged that there remained a fundamental difference of approach between them,[6] but there was no discussion of substance.

10. There was no substantive discussion of EEC/CMEA relations.

11. There was a very full discussion of the situation in the Middle East in which both sides made clear their wish to see the achievement of a peaceful settlement as soon as possible. The talks did not reveal any significantly new points. There was no elaboration of Mr. Brezhnev's suggestion that the UK should take part in international guarantees.[7] I made it clear that HMG's position remains that they are willing to play any role in negotiations which the Parties directly concerned consider would be helpful: and, as regards guarantees, that they are willing, as a permanent member of the Security Council, to give serious consideration to any proposal made in the context of a peace settlement.

12. Gromyko was predictably critical of US diplomacy in the Middle East but this was not put over in a strident manner. He emphasised that the Soviet

---

[4] 'It was', Mr. Callaghan told Mr. Gromyko, 'an objective fact that public opinion was now more conscious of the armed might of the Soviet Union' (record of a meeting between Mr. Callaghan and Mr. Gromyko on 23 March, at 3.30 p.m. in the FCO).

[5] See No. 86, note 6.

[6] Mr. Gromyko said on the subject of the MBFR talks 'that he could not see much prospect for progress along the road so far followed by the West' (see note 4 above).

[7] The Soviet draft of an Anglo-Soviet *communiqué*, delivered to Mr. Callaghan by Mr. Lunkov prior to Mr. Gromyko's visit, had 'confirmed' both Governments' readiness to participate in international guarantees of the frontiers of all Middle Eastern countries.

Government was in favour of Israel having the right to exist and develop as an independent sovereign state. He said that the Soviet Government had grounds to believe that the PLO[8] would, in fact, be prepared to accept Israel's existence, but this was not the PLO's declared position, and he had not been asked to speak on their behalf. The problem lay in bringing about a simultaneous declaration of willingness to accept the idea of Palestinian State by Israel on the one hand and PLO acknowledgement of Israel's right to exist on the other. The Soviet view of reconvening Geneva was 'positive', but all participants, including the Palestinians, must attend from the outset. Gromyko dismissed any idea of trying to establish 'informal' talks as an alternative to Geneva. There could be no difference, he maintained, between formal and informal talks, since the points of view of the various parties concerned would hardly be any different and the problems of PLO participation would remain.

13. Gromyko said that President Sadat's abrogation, at his own initiative, of the Soviet/Egyptian Treaty, did not introduce any new element into the situation, since the treaty had already been paralysed. If President Sadat wished to try his luck in other directions, he was welcome.

14. There was also some discussion of the situation in Lebanon.[9] Gromyko agreed that it was important that the internal troubles should be peacefully resolved and not allowed to spread and give rise to a wider conflict.

15. Gromyko and I compared views on Southern Africa in the light of contacts during the preceding ten days between Ambassador Lunkov and both the Prime Minister and myself.[10] Although there are obvious differences of view concerning recent developments in Southern Africa, the discussions were constructive and should prove a value in helping to encourage restraint and responsibility by the parties directly concerned. Gromyko's statement at his press Conference on 25 April to the effect that 'the question of Angola and the countries around Angola could be resolved constructively' is a possible pointer in this direction. (The announcement by the South African Government that they will withdraw from

---

[8] Palestine Liberation Organisation.

[9] Mr. Callaghan informed Mr. Gromyko on 24 March that he had just received news that the Syrians were contemplating sending their forces into the Lebanon, and it was clear that a serious situation was brewing there (note of a meeting between Mr. Wilson and Mr. Gromyko at 10 Downing St. on 24 March at 11.15 a.m.).

[10] Mr. Wilson asked Mr. Lunkov to call at 10 Downing St. on 12 March mainly with a view to discussing the situation in Africa. During their meeting Mr. Wilson expressed his concern 'about the possibility of outside intervention in Mozambique or through Mozambique in the other southern African territories, including [White minority-ruled] Rhodesia'. The Prime Minister warned Mr. Lunkov: 'Any such intervention would bring the British Government under the very strong pressure to intervene ourselves in these territories in order to protect the white minority. The Foreign and Commonwealth Secretary had made it clear, with the Prime Minister's full agreement, that we could not consider intervening on behalf of a minority against the majority. But if there was a massacre in Rhodesia, and particularly if this had come about as a result of foreign intervention, the British Government would be under very strong pressure.' Mr. Callaghan, who was also present, emphasised 'that outside intervention in Rhodesia by troops of any colour would have a very serious effect on détente' (note of a meeting between Mr. Wilson and Mr. Lunkov at 10 Downing St. on 12 March at 11.15 a.m.).

Angola by 27 March is the immediate consequence of the use of a channel of communication during the last ten days involving both the Soviet Government and HMG. The announcement made clear that although the clarification the South Africans had sought of certain assurances came from the UN Secretary-General, the third party through whom the assurances had been received was the British Government.)

16. In more general terms, Gromyko was left with a clearer understanding of the extent of public concern in the UK and in the West generally about Soviet policies in Africa. I left him in no doubt of HMG's view that détente is indivisible, and that British public opinion is not likely to accept that détente in Europe should be immune from developments in the African continent.

Bilateral

17. The relevant paragraphs of the joint communiqué convey an accurate picture of the bilateral subjects discussed.[11] No major points of contention arose.[12] Gromyko brought with him a personal message from Mr. Brezhnev confirming the latter's acceptance in principle of the invitation to visit the UK extended to him last year in Moscow by the Prime Minister. It was agreed that the precise timing of Mr. Brezhnev's visit should be discussed at a later date. I expressed the hope that Mr. Brezhnev would be able to take up his invitation before the end of the year, and pointed out that a crowded calendar in the first half of 1977 might make it difficult to receive Mr. Brezhnev then.

Trade

18. There was a useful discussion on trade. One of the British objectives had been to underline the importance that HMG attach to the placing soon of major contracts with British industry. Gromyko volunteered at the beginning of the talks a firm and unequivocal undertaking that a decision had been reached in Moscow to take up, in the near future, the full amount (£950m), provided for under the Anglo-Soviet credit agreement signed last year.[13] This means that substantial orders can be expected to be placed shortly with British industry.

[11] The *communiqué* recorded the participants' agreement that a further meeting of officials from the FCO and Soviet Foreign Ministry should take place that year, and that visits to the UK and the Soviet Union by British and Soviet Ministers would promote cooperation in a number of fields to the mutual benefit of both countries.

[12] Mr. Callaghan told Mr. Gromyko that since his visit to Moscow in 1975 Anglo-Soviet relations 'had continued in the spirit of the "new phase"'. He added that during the preceding twelve months there had been a considerable broadening of contacts and that it was HMG's wish that this should continue. 'The British Government', he said, 'wanted détente to succeed and they were not afraid to use the word' (record of a meeting between Mr. Callaghan and Mr. Gromyko on 22 March, at 4.35 p.m., in the FCO).

[13] The Soviet Government had so far taken up only £25m of this credit. In conversations with Mr. Gromyko on 24 March Mr. Wilson said that he was pleased that the value of British exports to the Soviet Union had doubled during the last year. 'But', he added, 'we could do better than that. British businessmen were entering the Soviet market with increasing confidence, and he had been pleased to see that commercial contacts had improved immeasurably in the "new phase". Now was therefore the time for the Soviet Union to take further advantage of last year's credit' (see notes 4 and 6 above).

Conclusion

19. The visit produced no surprises and no drama. For the consolidation of the improved Anglo-Soviet working relationship, this is exactly what was needed. I agreed with Gromyko that it ought to have a steady effect on public opinion. The discussions, though free from confrontation were by no means anodyne, and were of sound practical use. On the Middle East, on Southern Africa, on the nature of détente and, bilaterally, on Anglo-Soviet trade the exchanges were substantial and of value.

No. 89

Sir P. Ramsbotham (Washington) to Mr. Callaghan

[*AMU 020/303/1*]

Confidential. Eclipse   WASHINGTON, *31 March 1976*

Summary ...[1]

Sir,

'Peace Through Strength'—US–Soviet Relations in 1976

President Ford's recent abandonment of the term détente has been represented here as of no major policy significance.[2] Nevertheless it reflects a change of atmosphere which will affect the conduct of US–Soviet relations in 1976. In this despatch, I shall examine the domestic criticism of the Administration's détente policies; discuss the US–Soviet relationship, in the wider context of the domestic debate about the US role in the world; and make some guesses about the prospects for US–Soviet relations between now and the Presidential elections in November.

2. The policy of détente—I prefer to use this term even if President Ford has temporarily discarded it—is now under more critical examination than at any time since its birth in 1969, when former President Nixon announced in his inaugural speech that 'after a period of confrontation', the US was entering 'an era of negotiations'. The Nixon/Kissinger concept of détente—the most sophisticated and determined of the many American attempts since 1945 to establish a *modus vivendi* with the USSR—was, of course, based on the assumption that a nuclear war between the Soviet Union and the US would result in mutual suicide and that both sides shared an overriding interest in minimising that danger. To this end, Kissinger embarked on the negotiation of a series of agreements, intended to slow down the pace of the strategic arms race and reduce the risk of war by accident. The Soviet Union, under Brezhnev, has seemed

---

[1] Not printed.

[2] During a television interview in Miami on 1 March President Ford said that he was dropping the word 'détente' as a description of policy towards the Soviet Union. He explained that he preferred to describe the process as 'a policy of peace through strength'.

to endorse these objectives. Hence the SALT I and the Vladivostok Agreements.

3. Kissinger also believed it essential to persuade the Russians that a greater degree of contact and co-operation with the US, and with the West in general, would coincide with their interests. He wished to keep the Allies' military guard up, while involving the Russians in a web of strategic, economic and cultural relationships. As the USSR became increasingly enmeshed, its capacity, and will, to take decisions hostile to the US would decrease; conversely, the American ability to apply leverage in order to restrain Soviet 'adventurism' would increase. Kissinger has outlined his objectives and methods in a recent series of speeches. In the first, at San Francisco, on 3 February, he summarised these succinctly: the aim of US policy was to ensure that 'the Soviet Union will always confront penalties for aggression, and also acquire growing incentives for restraint ... Our essential task is to recognise the need for a dual policy that, simultaneously, and with the equal vigour, resists expansionist drives and seeks to shape a more constructive relationship.'

Criticism (i): SALT

4. In my despatch of 15 August, 1974, I rehearsed the major criticisms of Kissinger's détente policies.[3] Since then, the scale and depth of the attack has intensified. Kissinger has increasingly been criticised by senior officers and defence intellectuals who have argued—and continue to argue—that the SALT I and Vladivostok Agreements have permitted the Russians to make strategic gains at the US expense. They point out that, since these agreements, the throw-weight of the Soviet missile force has greatly increased; silos have been hardened; new SLBMs[4] built at a frightening rate; civil defences strengthened. The fact that all this is permitted under SALT I and Vladivostok only strengthens the critics' conviction that the agreements were sloppily negotiated and that a situation is being created in which the Soviet Union will possess the strategic advantage over the US.

5. To quote Paul Nitze, the former Secretary of the Navy and SALT negotiator, in a much-publicised article in *Foreign Affairs* in January 1976, 'there is every prospect that, under the terms of the SALT Agreements, the Soviet Union will contrive to pursue a nuclear superiority that is not merely quantitative, but designed to produce a theoretical war-winning capability. Further, there is a major risk that, if such a condition were achieved, the Soviet Union would adjust its policies and actions in ways that would undermine the present détente situation, with results that could only resurrect the danger of nuclear confrontation or, alternatively, increase the prospect of Soviet expansion through other means of pressure.'

[3] In this despatch Sir P. Ramsbotham assessed the domestic opposition to Dr. Kissinger's pursuit of *détente* with the Soviet Union. He listed amongst Dr. Kissinger's critics American farmers and businessmen, who felt 'cheated' by the 1972 wheat deal with the Soviet Union and irritated by the proposal to give the Russians credit at interest rates lower than those prevailing in the USA. The 'latent Puritan conscience' of the country was also, he explained, being increasingly aroused by the Soviet Government's treatment of dissidents (AMU2/2).

[4] Submarine-launched Ballistic Missiles.

Criticism (ii): The Soviet Conventional Build-up
6.   Other critics, largely based in the Pentagon, point to the fact that while the US has reduced the overall strength of its defence establishment by 900,000 men since 1970, Soviet numbers have increased, perhaps by as many as 300,000 men. The USSR has also engaged in a vast modernisation programme intended both to improve the equipment and training of its troops and to create the capacity to intervene in strength outside Soviet borders. The Soviet Navy has grown dramatically and is now a 'blue water fleet' capable of challenging the US on the world's oceans. New bases, e.g. in Somalia, have been established. Finally, the Soviet defence budget appears to have risen to a frighteningly high level, now accounting for between 10 and 15 per cent of GNP.
7.   To what end? The answers, as the critics see them, are far from reassuring. Soviet behaviour in the Third World has increasingly strengthened the suspicions of those members of the defence establishment who believe that the possession of these greatly improved, and continuously expanding, strategic and conventional forces, poses a direct challenge to US and Western vital interests, particularly in the Third World. They argue, with rising vehemence, that the Soviet aim is to undermine these interests wherever this can be done without the risk of a direct confrontation with the US; thus slowly shifting the global balance of power against her. The fact that Kissinger accepts many of their arguments has not prevented his Right-wing critics from asserting that he is 'soft' about Soviet expansion. They adduce, as supporting evidence, Soviet failure to prevent North Viet-Namese violation of the Paris Agreements of 1973; the alleged Soviet refusal to restrain Egypt and Syria from attacking Israel in October 1973; and, with most point, recent Soviet behaviour in southern Africa.

Criticism (iii): Human Rights
8.   Unlike some, at least, of his critics, Kissinger and his immediate circle of advisers in the State Department have from the beginning been conscious of the fact that Soviet acceptance of the need to avoid global nuclear war, and to slow down the pace of the arms race, meant no slackening of the ideological contest with the West and no change in the USSR's rigid suppression of internal dissent. Thus, while the US has pressed hard, most recently within the framework of the Helsinki Final Act, for an improvement in the free flow of ideas between East and West and for private assurances of an increase in the scale of Jewish emigration from the Soviet Union, there have been few illusions at the highest level of the Administration about the prospects for rapid progress in these fields. Change would only come slowly—if at all—and as the result of continuous, firm, yet tactful, pressure.
9.   Kissinger critics have been less realistic and, perhaps, more typically American, in their quest for a sea-change inside Russia. The high hopes of 1972 and 1973 have now given way to bitter complaint: the US has been taken for a ride. She has been insufficiently tough. Kissinger has come under attack from both the Right and Left. Conservatives, led by Reagan, talk repeatedly of a 'one way street', suggesting that all the concessions had been made in favour of the Soviet Union. Jackson, powerfully aided by the Jewish lobby, has accused

Kissinger of 'moral neutrality' and of a failure to understand that US foreign policy must always be grounded in morality rather than expediency, idealism rather than *real politik*. The fact that the Jackson/Vanik Amendment of December 1974 seems to have little positive impact on Soviet emigration policies only increases the sense of bitterness and betrayal. At the same time, Kissinger is under attack from a strongly liberal majority in Congress, who suspect his secretive ways and accuse him of duplicity in the conduct of foreign policy.

Criticism (iv): Southern Africa

10. Against this background of suspicion of Soviet motives, and frustration at the way détente seems to be working in practice, recent events in Angola have confirmed the pessimists' fears and deepened their anger at the US impotence in the fact of Soviet 'adventurism'. They do not admit to surprise. What else was to be expected? In their eyes, Kissinger's apparent shock at the lengths to which the Russians, and their Cuban Allies, have been prepared to go only demonstrates his incurable naïveté. The Right have derided him as an innocent abroad, ready to succumb to a sucker punch. The intelligent Centre—epitomised by George Kennan[5]—while accepting the broad framework of his détente policies, have urged him not to equate the US vital interests, e.g. in Western Europe and South Korea, with those in areas of 'local strategic importance' such as Angola. They also remind him that 'careful attention has to be given to the nature of the tools or the allies we have to work with … It is not everyone who can be made successful, even with the greatest effort of outside aid.'

The Broader Debate: 'No More Viet-Nams'

11. But the tide against Kissinger's interventionist policies in Angola has been running strongest in the Congress. By prohibiting further US intervention, the Congress is reflecting the widespread view in the country that, to put it in simplistic terms, there must be 'no more Viet-Nams'. This does not imply that the American people would not rally behind the Administration in the face of a direct Soviet, or Soviet inspired, attack on NATO, or on a country such as South Korea, which the US is formally committed to defend. Nor does it mean a return to the isolationism of the '30s. As Kissinger put it—and few informed Americans would disagree—in his testimony to the Senate Foreign Relations Committee Bicentennial Hearings on 16 March: 'On a shrinking planet there is no hiding place … The world knows full well that no solutions are possible without the active participation and commitment of a united American people.'

12. But few Americans, apart from the extreme conservative Right, are now willing to accept the current Kissingerian view that any extension of Soviet power must now be opposed, wherever it manifests itself in the Third World. Many are also increasingly sceptical about the validity of Kissinger's repeated warnings —most recently in a speech to the Boston Council for World Affairs on 11 March—about the dangers which face the Atlantic Alliance if Communist Parties come to power, or share power, in Western Europe. His tendency to 'cry wolf'

---

[5] Professor G.F. Kennan, publicist and former diplomat.

over Portugal has weakened his qualifications as a guide through the complex maze of European politics.

13. The tide running against the Kissingerian world-view is strongest among the 'intellectuals', using the term in its widest sense to mean those who make their living in the 'knowledge industry'—the mass media (especially on the East Coast), higher education and 'think tanks', such as the Rand Corporation. They are a strong influence on members of the Congress and their increasingly powerful staffs. They are also taken seriously by the livelier minds within the bureaucracy. Many of the men and women in the 'knowledge industry' have now clearly rejected what was an article of faith for most Americans until the late 1960s: that the extension of American political and military power throughout the world —and, in particular, in the Third World—either independently, or in response to Soviet pressure, is essentially legitimate.

14. It would be misleading to imply that, in abandoning this dogma, they have ceased to dislike the Soviet political system or to uphold classical democratic values. Their objection is to any attempt to *impose* these values on others or to associate too closely with unworthy local allies. (The memory of Thieu still lingers.) For these people, the American Century, in the terms triumphantly defined by Henry Luce,[6] is over. As American power becomes increasingly difficult to apply in a multipolar world where the traditional hierarchy of states is constantly shifting, American objectives, above all in the Third World, become simultaneously harder to define and more difficult to explain. Angola has shown that the end result is likely to be confusion of purpose, disagreement between the Congress and the Administration and ineffective and fragmented American policies.

The Emergence of the Soviet Union as a Super Power

15. A further factor making for uncertainty and frustration is the emergence of the Soviet Union as a Super Power. This is now, in Kissinger's mind, the central security problem for the US. The task is to contain Soviet power without global war; to avoid both abdication and unnecessary confrontation. Unfortunately, many, perhaps most, Americans have so far failed to adjust to this new and reality. As Kissinger pointed out to the Senate Foreign Relations Committee on 16 March: 'This is not a familiar world for most Americans.' Haunted by memories of Indo-China, and cynical about the quality of their leadership in the wake of Watergate, some—such as Reagan—have reacted by reverting to old slogans (we should have 'eyeballed' them in Angola) or by attacking the Administration for its failure to prevent a process which more sensible men understood, however, reluctantly, to be inevitable.

16. The debate goes on in a thousand political meetings. Rhetoric conceals uncertainty; serious men are often silent. There are many voices, but few convincing answers. Kissinger's attempts to define the terms of the argument seem to find little echo among those members of Congress who fear the 'imperial presidency' and seem to want 'open secrets openly arrived at'. Yet there are

---

[6] American journalist and publisher.

heartening signs: the draft FY 1977 defence budget, which embodies the biggest increase in real spending since 1970, is unlikely to be drastically reduced. Senator Cranston (Democratic, California) was able to introduce a resolution into the Senate on 16 March (the text of which has been sent to your Department) broadly endorsing the Administration's détente policies; and this attracted a wide measure of support from the leadership of both parties and will probably be approved by a majority of Senators when it emerges from the Foreign Relations Committee. Good sense has not, after all, abandoned the Congress in an election year.

The Immediate Future

17. But clearly there can be no return to the over-optimistic Nixonian version of détente. The Administration's handling of the US–Soviet relationship for the rest of 1976 will be necessarily cautious and tempered by the domestic political winds. What will this mean in practical terms? First, and *pace* Governor Reagan, no resumption of an unrestricted arms race or return to the frozen climate of the Cold War. Whatever their scepticism about Soviet behaviour and motives, few Americans are political recidivists. As his primary victories in New Hampshire and Florida demonstrate, President Ford senses the central instinct of the American moderate Right—and their views are probably shared by most Democrats. They—and he—wish to preserve the 'central core' of détente, but it will be, to use Senator Humphrey's[7] phrase, 'détente without illusions': the emphasis will be on the traditional Yankee ability to strike a hard bargain.

18. Détente has already figured as an election issue, though it is not yet clear how important it will be. The electoral successes which Reagan has so far enjoyed, for example his victory in the North Carolina primary, may well be due in part to his having tapped a vein of concern among the electorate that the cumulative effect of negotiations with the Soviet Union, together with what is perceived as a weakened defence posture, may leave the US vulnerable. Reagan's campaign rhetoric has, at the least, obliged President Ford to defend his foreign policy repeatedly on the hustings, and to assert that 'peace through strength' implies that the US will remain 'second to none' in defence capability. The electoral climate also suggests that it will be difficult for this Administration to conclude any agreement on SAL without provoking strong attacks from contenders for the Democratic nomination, such as Senator Jackson; and without inviting at least rigorous public scrutiny from other Democratic nominees. The election there-fore, is a strong factor affecting the timing, and possibly the substance, of the SAL negotiations. On the other hand, as I have found in my travels throughout the country, the general public would probably welcome a SAL Agreement. Despite electoral unease about relations with the Soviet Union, there is no evidence to suggest that the policy of détente, as currently interpreted by the Ford Admini-stration, will be rejected at the polls in favour of any alternative foreign policy; nor, indeed, has any cohesive alternative so far been offered to the electorate. North Carolina is by no means typical of the US as a whole, and although the critics of détente have an audience, President Ford can still count on something

---

[7] Democrat Senator for Minnesota.

of a consensus behind his policy. Nor is it certain that foreign policy, in spite of an unusual degree of current interest, will eventually be a major issue in the November election.

19. Attempts to negotiate SALT II will therefore continue, although, as the President has recently indicated, an agreement may not come in 1976. The MBFR negotiations will be pursued, albeit in low key. The recently negotiated Grain Agreement will be honoured: it is too important to American farmers, and too useful a bargaining lever, to be easily abandoned. But elsewhere progress will be slow. Agreements will be negotiated—if at all—strictly on their merits and as part of a 'two-way street'. By postponing planned meetings of three of the intergovernmental commissions at Cabinet level, the Administration has both signalled its displeasure to the Russians over Soviet behaviour in Angola and made a small, if not particularly dramatic, genuflection to the new, tougher mood at home.[8]

Southern Africa

20. Whether the Administration can maintain this cautious line depends, to a large extent, on what the Russians and the Cubans now do in southern Africa. There is little support in the country or the Congress for activist policies in the Third World. Interest in southern Africa for its own sake was largely confined to the relatively uninfluential ranks of the African specialists in the State Department and the universities, until the US involvement in Angola focused greater attention on southern Africa in the East Coast media and on the Hill. White conservatives tend to sympathise with the (white) South Africans and Rhodesians, though they might hesitate to see the US become involved in a bitter racial conflict on their behalf. Informed and moderate blacks are worried about the degree to which the Russians and Cubans have succeeded in parading themselves as the most effective supporters of black nationalists in southern Africa. Americans, both black and white, tend to see southern Africa as someone else's problem and, in Rhodesia's particular case, Britain's. They will expect us to take the lead.

21. Against this background, Kissinger, his relations with the Congress difficult and his judgment over Angola questioned, will be unable to intervene directly in southern Africa or elsewhere, in response to a direct Soviet—or more probably—Cuban challenge, even if he wished. His private threats to 'go after the Cubans' if they were to launch a large-scale offensive against Rhodesia, and the President's public warnings to Cuba about the American reaction to new interventions in southern Africa, do not, I believe, refer to actions contemplated in Africa itself.

[8] *The Washington Post* of 16 March reported that the US Government had 'already postponed' a meeting of the Soviet-US Joint Energy Commission, and that the Russians had been told that planned meetings of the Joint Commissions on Trade and Economic Relations and on Housing would also be postponed. Sir P. Ramsbotham commented in Washington telegram No. 930 of 16 March: 'These actions are unlikely to quiet the Administration's critics, who will no doubt describe them as derisory pinpricks which, while angering the Russians, will not cause them to modify their policies in favour in Southern Africa or elsewhere in the Third World. Yet it is hard to see what more the Administration can do, given that a break-off of the SALT negotiations or an abrogation of the grain deals with the USSR are still ruled out.'

When it comes to the provision of military aid in defence of white minority régimes, or approval for US involvement on the ground, we must assume that for most Congressmen the considerations that decided their votes on Angola would apply with equal force to other parts of southern Africa. They do not believe that the US should get bogged down anywhere in the African continent; even, I suspect, in defence of US investments: and they are in a position to make their views prevail. We can expect these attitudes to heighten Kissinger's sense of frustration and occasional despair. But this is no reason for us not to go on urging him to adopt less dramatic, if more effective, African policies. I believe we have already had some success in this direction.

Conclusion

22. To sum up, I do not think we need be disturbed by the dropping of the term détente. Despite the exaggerated fears of some sections of the Western European Press—notably in West Germany—the new formula, 'peace through strength', continues to embrace Kissinger's essential policies. These have not changed. Whether the Administration's verbal sleight of hand will appease the domestic critics of their policies remains to be seen; but presumably it will have given some pleasure in Peking. The new Administration in 1977, whether Republican or Democratic, may have more domestic freedom of manoeuvre and may, therefore, be able to modify the tone in which policies towards the Soviet Union are conducted. But, barring accidents in southern Africa, the objectives laid down by Kissinger, which reflect the US long-term interests, will continue to be pursued and probably in much the same way as before.

23. Meanwhile, the wider debate about America's role in the world will go on. The task will be to evolve policies which will enable the US to respond to the Soviet challenge more flexibly and subtly than in the past; which acknowledge, but do not underestimate, the true limits of American power; which accept the inevitability of change in Africa and Asia, even if this expresses itself in radical terms; which do not condemn Americans to support régimes or political factions alien to the national ideals; and which distinguish between vital national interests and those not worth defending. I possess sufficient confidence in the American system to believe that the challenge will be met. But it will not be easy to reach a new consensus and we shall all go through troubled times along the way.

24. I am sending copies of this despatch to Her Majesty's Representatives in Moscow, Paris, Bonn, the UK Delegation to NATO, Berlin, Helsinki, East Berlin, Warsaw, Prague, Budapest, Bucharest, Sofia, Belgrade, Peking and Ulan Bator.

I have, etc.,
PETER RAMSBOTHAM

No. 90
Minute from Mr. Cartledge to Mr. D.M.D. Thomas[1]

[*AMU 020/303/1*]

Confidential   FCO, *7 June 1976*

HM Ambassador in Washington's Despatch of 31 March on US–Soviet Relations[2]

1.   I am very sorry to have taken so long to produce the comments for which you asked on Sir P. Ramsbotham's despatch on US–Soviet relations, which raises some important questions. I hope those which follow are not too late to be of any use.[3]

2.   As an account of the current debate about détente in the United States, and as an explanation of its origins, the despatch is excellent and there is nothing in it with which I would disagree. In particular, as emerged clearly from the talks which, with Mr. Rhodes,[4] I had in Washington at the end of March (when Mr. Pike[5] had just completed drafting the despatch) I entirely agree with Sir P. Ramsbotham that President Ford's semantic innovation in discarding the word 'détente' is more atmospheric than substantial. US policy has not in essence changed although both the Presidential election campaign and Soviet behaviour in Africa have dictated a deceleration in the interweaving of relations between the two superpowers. Moreover, as the despatch makes clear, Kissinger's philosophy of détente still prevails and was expounded very effectively both by him and by Sonnenfeldt in a series of speeches during the first quarter of this year.

3.   One question, however, central to the future development of US–Soviet relations, is not addressed by Washington's despatch—quite legitimately, since it has not been made explicit in the debate about détente with which the despatch is concerned. The question is that of the validity of the basic assumption underlying Kissinger's view of détente, which is summarised in paragraph 3 of the despatch: 'As the USSR became increasingly enmeshed, its capacity, and will, to take decisions hostile to the United States would decrease; conversely, the American ability to apply leverage in order to restrain Soviet "adventurism" would increase'. This has always been an attractive concept. It has been advanced with varying degrees of elaboration as a justification for the détente policies of the West against their critics and ever since President Nixon's first visit to Moscow in 1972; and it still commands general acceptance. I have never been entirely confident, however, that the premises on which the assumption is based have been adequately examined. I think that it reflects Dr. Kissinger's sometimes over-

---

[1]   Head of North America Department since May 1975.

[2]   No. 89.

[3]   This minute by Mr. Cartledge was originally meant to provide the basis of a draft acknowledgement of Sir P. Rambotham's despatch. But as Mr. Thomas explained in a letter of 5 August to Mr. R.M. Russell (Counsellor, HM Embassy, Washington) covering Mr. Cartledge's minute, the work had been 'repeatedly set aside to make room for other things'.

[4]   Mr. P.A. Rhodes was AUS and Head of the Cabinet Office Assessment Staff.

[5]   Mr. M.E. Pike was Counsellor in HM Embassy, Washington.

schematic approach to international affairs and that the attractions of its symmetry are apt to obscure its limitations in terms of the real world. Sir P. Ramsbotham's despatch throws these limitations in to clear relief.

4.   I think it is important to bear in mind that what has come to be known as 'détente' is the product of a phase of Soviet, not of Western, foreign policy. The strenuous activity of President Nixon's public relations machine in 1971–73 to some extent succeeded in establishing the opposite impression—namely that 'détente' is essentially an American initiative designed to swaddle the Soviet Union in a cocoon of negotiations and agreements which appeal to Soviet self-interest but which have the effect of inhibiting and constraining Soviet international behaviour. The United States, according to this approach, has held out certain benefits to the Soviet Union which the Soviet government needs— agreements on arms limitation, trade, grain, and access to American scientific know-how—which can be withheld if the Soviet Union fails to fulfil its own side of the bargain by respecting the interests of the US and its allies and keeping its nose out of international crisis spots. It is possible, however, to look at the recent development of 'détente' rather differently. It could be argued that, once having attained its primary objective of the 1960s, namely the achievement of something approaching strategic parity with the United States, the Soviet Union sought, firstly, to peg that parity down through SALT and then to address as its new top priority the traditional problems of the Soviet economy and the realisation of the Soviet Union's full economic potential. For this task, a degree of stability in East–West relations was essential if the newly won strategic parity was not to be upset by a renewed spasm of arms expenditure in the United States, and if East–West trade was to expand to the extent necessary to supply the Soviet Union with technological shortcuts to economic growth and development. Hence, eventually, the 'Peace Programme' of the 24th Congress of the CPSU.

5.   This shift in Soviet priorities and the inauguration of a new phase in Soviet foreign policy coincided, fortunately for the Soviet leadership, with the requirements of the American mood post-Vietnam, with President Nixon's own political ambitions and, perhaps most importantly, with Chancellor Brandt's ideals for the future security and well-being of the German people. 'Détente' therefore gathered momentum more rapidly than, perhaps, the Soviet leadership had at first thought likely. Even the Conference on European Security, which had been touted by the Russians since at least 1967, finally became a reality. From the very first, however, the Soviet leadership never made any secret of the fact that the successor to and extension of 'peaceful coexistence' which was now called 'détente' could not and would not freeze the dynamic factors which, from the Marxist point of view, underlie human and world development, namely the class struggle against 'monopoly capitalism' and the national liberation struggle against 'imperialism and colonialism'. It followed, as the Soviet leadership has always made equally clear, that the Soviet duty to assist the international working class and national liberation movements would be as strong as ever and that the Soviet Union would continue to respond to its calls. Given the change in Soviet priorities it was clear that these responses would be subordinate to the higher interests of East West stability; considerable leeway was bound to remain,

however, for Soviet activities directly or indirectly hostile to US and Western interests.

6.   The Western response to the new phase of Soviet policy has in general been to attempt to exploit the opportunities which it provides for building a permanently safer world, through agreements on disarmament and arms limitation, and to contribute to a progressive normalisation of East–West relations which in the long term might make a Soviet reversion to policies of confrontation less likely and less feasible. With these objectives in view, the West has, for example, initiated the MBFR negotiations, extracted from the Soviet Union a significant *quid pro quo* in Basket III for the satisfaction of Soviet demands from the CSCE and responded positively to growing Soviet interest in the purchase of Western technology and capital equipment. These are all valid means of achieving the West's equally valid but essentially long-term objectives. What is much more questionable is the validity and efficacy of what might be called the short term levers of détente as means of moderating or restraining Soviet international behaviour. Starting from the bottom, these levers might, according to Kissinger's theory, be said to consist of the implementation of the various agreements which the United States has concluded with the Soviet Union for cooperation in scientific and technological fields—there are, I believe, about 40 bilateral Committees of various kinds now in operation. These are in a sense the cosmetics of détente and it is difficult to believe that they are other than readily expendable by either side. The significance of President Ford's recent decision to postpone routine meetings of two such Committees lay in its public announcement rather than in the act itself; it probably produced, and was designed to produce, more of an impact on US electoral opinion that on Soviet behaviour. At the next level of significance are the 'economic levers'. These include grain sales, the provision of credit facilities and aspects of commercial policy (MFN, the operation of the strategic embargo etc). Unlike the smallest, cosmetic, levers, however, the economic levers are not wholly or readily susceptible to operation by executive decision. They require the cooperation of Congress which, in turn, is bound to reflect pressures from relevant interest groups, such as the farm lobby in the case of grain sales. Such leverage as US–Soviet economic relations provide cannot be exerted quickly, if at all (in the case of grain sales the US Administration has put its leverage in baulk by concluding a 5 year agreement with the Soviet Union) and its efficacy is in any case questionable: in the episode of the Jackson-Vanik amendment, for example, the Soviet government showed that it was not in the last resort prepared to adjust its internal policies in response to economic pressures. In that case, admittedly, the pressures were not particularly compelling since the amount of credit at stake was relatively small and the benefits of MFN treatment are more relevant to Soviet prestige than to the US Soviet trade figures. But I would question whether the application of more substantial pressures, such as the withholding of grain deliveries if this were feasible, would be likely to enjoy any greater success. This is because there will always be conservative currents of thought in the Politburo and Central Committee of the CPSU which would react adversely to any tendency by the top leadership of the day to bow to what they would describe as economic blackmail by the capitalist West. For internal reasons,

the Soviet leadership will always be more likely to enjoin the Soviet people to tighten their belts than to expose itself to charges of capitulationism from within the Party. The same would, I think, be true of such other economic levers which are in theory available to the West. Western technology is highly desirable for the Soviet Union as a means of accelerating the solution of its economic problems but it is not, in the last resort, essential: the Soviet leaders would always be more likely to forego imports from the West (assuming—and it is a major assumption— that 'the West', including Japan could be lined up to act as one in such matters) than be seen to accede to overt Western pressure.[6]

7.   This leaves the upper, 'blue chip', level of leverage: namely the superior technological and economic capacity of the United States to carry the development of strategic weaponry to a new and higher plateau and its superior capacity, in theory and for the time being, to deploy its military strength globally. The Soviet Union has shown that it is sensitive and responsive to the possibility that the West, and the United States in particular, might turn its back on the fundamentals of détente, namely the mutual self-denying ordinance of escalation in weaponry, the moratorium in the arms race and abstention from confrontational policies which might contain the seeds of nuclear conflict. The Soviet Union has, for example, behaved with conspicuous caution recently in the Middle East, whose political crises always carry the possibility that the two superpowers might be sucked in, even against their will, to a situation of confrontation. In Africa, where this possibility is clearly much more remote, the Russians have behaved much less cautiously. The Soviet Union is constantly taking the Western temperature so far as attitudes towards détente are concerned. But what makes them apprehensive is not the possibility of individual short-term set-backs in East–West amity or cooperation but a more fundamental shift in Western opinion which could lead back, as they put it, to 'the days of the cold war'. Only such a shift, in the last resort, or an international crisis threatening nuclear conflict, could affect vital Soviet interests sufficiently seriously to compel significant changes in Soviet policies. In other words, the only effective levers are the really big ones.

8.   The trouble with the big levers, however, is that they are even less susceptible to ready application by the US executive than the economic ones. The majority of the American public really wants a SALT Agreement; and, whatever Dr. Kissinger may say about 'going after the Cubans', the US Congress, with an overwhelming majority of American opinion behind it, rejects any policy which could lead to new American military involvement abroad. Congressional opinion is not likely, either, to be responsive in foreseeable circumstances to a desire on the part of the executive sharply to escalate US defence expenditure.[7]

---

[6] In a letter to Mr. Edmonds of 6 October Mr. Moreton expressed his doubts about Mr. Cartledge's comments on the 'short-term levers of détente'. He thought that the lessons of the Jackson/Vanik episode were that the Russians were prepared to go surprisingly far in order to secure trade and credit benefits, and the Soviet Union might 'on occasion be susceptible to economic pressure when this is sensitively applied'.

[7] Mr. Moreton agreed (*v. ibid.*) that the majority of the American public probably wanted a SALT agreement on the right terms and that most Americans would reject any policy likely to lead to renewed US military involvement overseas. But he also pointed out that opinion could change

9.   Looked at in Kissinger's schematic terms of levers and pressures, rewards and punishments, carrots and sticks, therefore the currently prevailing American philosophy of détente does not stand up very well to close examination as a means of controlling Soviet behaviour. The Russians demonstrated in Angola that they are capable of accurate political calculation; and the recent spate of Soviet agreements with the governments of Angola and Mozambique indicates that the Soviet government is embarking on a policy of steadily consolidating its influence in Africa.[8] Similar policies could and doubtless will be implemented in other parts of the world in which Western influence is either discredited or vulnerable and in which the Soviet Union can pose as the champion of the oppressed against the oppressor. Persistent attempts to extend Soviet influence by such means are likely to be a continuing phenomenon. Targets of opportunity will be exploited whenever this can be done without serious risk to the basic equilibrium of détente. The Soviet Union will continue to endeavour both to have its détente cake and to eat it.

10.   Given the limitations, outlined above, of Kissinger's 'enmeshment' theory, this prospect is not a cheering one. On the one hand, the Soviet superpower will continue to exert pressure on the frontiers of Western influence and to lean against any doors which it finds ajar. On the other, the American superpower, as Sir P. Ramsbotham makes clear in paragraph 14 of his despatch, is for the time being reluctant to resist these pressures by applying the only type of leverage— namely the deployment of or threat to deploy American power—which is likely to be effective. Much can certainly be done, particularly in the Third World, by responding to the Soviet challenge 'more flexibly and subtly' as Sir P. Ramsbotham suggests in paragraph 23: the United States can in theory out-trump the Soviet Union in any field of aid or technical assistance and a careful discrimination in the choice and cultivation of friends and allies should often be able to pre-empt the Soviet political challenge. But in the last resort the United States must be prepared to deploy the full extent of its power in the world and the Soviet leadership must be made to believe in the American will to do so. The answer, probably, lies in the same paragraph 23 of Sir P. Ramsbotham's despatch: as the Soviet challenge, encouraged by current American self-doubt and inhibition, grows to greater and more obvious proportions the American mood, too, will change and Congress will be prepared to allow the executive to resume the United States' full responsibilities as the democratic superpower. The Russians are doubtless well aware, in their sober and rational moments, of this probable operation of the laws of cause and effect: but they will, as always, 'push to the limit'. I think it is better to face this reality squarely than to put more faith than the facts warrant in Dr. Kissinger's intellectual model of détente relationships.

B.G. CARTLEDGE

extraordinarily quickly in the USA, especially when it was being fed a continuous stream of information about growing Soviet military strength and in response to Soviet adventurism in Angola. 'We may', he wrote, 'therefore, be witnessing a change in the public mood which, if continued, might enable a future US administration to adopt a tougher stance.'

[8] A Soviet airlift to Angola of large quantities of modern weapons had begun on 31 October 1975 and continued at an increasing tempo until March 1976. In May President S. Machel of Mozambique concluded a technical cooperation agreement with the Soviet Union.

No. 91

Letter from Mr. E.A.J. Fergusson[1] *to Mr. P.R.H. Wright*

[*ENS 020/548/3*]

Confidential   FCO, *23 September 1976*

Dear Patrick,

Mr. Brezhnev's Visit

In your letter of 8 September[2] you asked for comments on a talk between Tom McNally and Kubekin[3] of the Soviet Embassy about a possible visit to the UK by Mr. Brezhnev, and for advice on Kubekin's suggestion that the Soviet Ambassador might see the Prime Minister in the near future.

The Foreign and Commonwealth Secretary concludes from this conversation that whatever Mr. Brezhnev had originally intended, he would now consider a visit to the UK worthwhile only if he had an advance commitment from us to provide a specific political bonus for him, for example in the form of endorsement by HMG of one or more of the range of current Soviet initiatives, which include his proposals for all-European congresses on transport, energy and the environment, for a ban on the development of new weapons of mass destruction, for an international treaty on the non-use of force, and for a comprehensive test ban treaty.

While we should still like to maintain the Anglo-Soviet dialogue at the highest level, Mr. Crosland does not consider that in pursuing this goal HMG should be required to pay a new political price in this form, and he cannot identify any tangible advantage to the UK which might make such a price worthwhile. In particular the increase in our level of exports to the Soviet Union has been less than expected, and although we could press Mr. Brezhnev on this point, the prospects for a substantial resultant increase in our trade do not appear sufficiently great to justify substantial political concessions.[4]

---

[1] Private Secretary to Mr. Crosland.

[2] In this letter Mr. Wright enclosed a note by Mr. McNally of 7 September describing his conversation that day with Mr. V. Kubekin, Third Secretary in the Soviet Embassy, London. Mr. Kubekin remarked that 'there was a strong feeling on the Soviet side that Anglo-Soviet relations were somewhat in the doldrums, and indeed may have slipped back since the Wilson visit of 1975', and that the 'Soviet side could only contemplate a visit by Mr Brezhnev if it marked a new stage in the relations between Britain and the Soviet Union'. He added that the Russians would want such a visit 'to mark perhaps some new initiative on the international side (e.g. on progress towards a comprehensive test ban treaty)', and that the Russians were reluctant to name a date for the visit because they had a feeling that it would be 'no more than a "public relations exercise" and that there was no enthusiasm on the British side to think positively about Anglo-Soviet relations' (ENS 020/548/1).

[3] Mr. Cartledge noted in a submission of 14 September that Mr. Kubekin clearly enjoyed 'considerably greater authority than his rank would suggest'.

[4] In his submission of 14 September (*v. ibid.*) Mr. Cartledge pointed to the 'very disappointing level of Anglo-Soviet trade since the Moscow summit … and Soviet dilatoriness in taking up more than a small fraction of the £950 million credit agreed in February 1975'.

Mr. Crosland has considered possible initiatives which might be useful to Mr. Brezhnev and acceptable to HMG on their merits. There are one or two modest bilateral agreements on subjects such as the prevention of nuclear accidents, and the prevention of collisions at sea, though these are unlikely to add up to a package which the Russians would regard as a substantial inducement.

Other things being equal, Mr. Crosland would have felt it was a little early for the Soviet Ambassador to have a substantial meeting with the Prime Minister and he would have thought it preferable for Mr. Lunkov to engage in an exploratory exchange with him first. However, I have now heard from you that the Prime Minister is disposed to see Mr. Lunkov while he is attending the Labour Party Conference in Blackpool both because he is a senior Ambassador and because of the convenience of his presence there. In these circumstances the Prime Minister may wish to be aware of the following further points which we think that Mr. Lunkov may take the opportunity of raising.

The Prime Minister already knows of the difficulty created by a visa application for a new Counsellor in the Soviet Embassy, Kuplyakov, which the Soviet authorities have now been asked to withdraw.[5] When the Permanent Under-Secretary conveyed Mr. Crosland's decision on this matter to the Soviet Ambassador on 22 September, Mr. Lunkov raised a number of relatively minor bilateral problems, including delays in the granting of visas and the status of the Soviet Embassy's doctor. Other recent or current difficulties in our relations with the Russians include the Home Secretary's denial, with the concurrence of FCO Ministers, of a visa to one member of the Soviet delegation to a meeting of the World Federation of Scientific Workers in this country; Soviet reluctance to acknowledge serious shortcomings in their plans for new Embassy buildings in Kensington; and the refusal of permission to a Soviet research vessel, the 'Okeanograph', to call at ports on the East coast of Scotland on dates which coincided with a major NATO naval exercise. The Prime Minister will clearly not wish to be drawn into any substantive discussion of these matters with Mr. Lunkov; he might simply suggest to the Soviet Ambassador that it would evidently be timely for him to call on Mr. Crosland for a thorough discussion of Anglo-Soviet relations. As the Russians seem currently disposed to exaggerate the political significance of the present coincidence of several essentially minor problems, and to take a melancholy view of the state of Anglo-Soviet relations in consequence, it would be helpful if the Prime Minister were to emphasise the fact that on more important levels those relations are developing constructively; four Soviet Ministers (including Mr. Gromyko) have visited Britain this year and two others (the Minister of Aviation and Oil Industry) may do so; Mr. Ponomarev is to lead the Party delegation which is coming at the invitation of the Labour Party next month: military exchanges involving all three Services are developing satisfactorily; and the second session of the Anglo-Soviet Round Table, which

---

[5] Mr. Y.P. Kuplyakov had been identified as an intelligence officer and was thought likely to be the new London KGB Resident. His application for a visa, in June 1976, had therefore been refused. Confirmation of Mr. Crosland's decision not to accept Mr. Kuplyakov as Soviet Minister-Counsellor in London was conveyed to Mr. Lunkov on 22 September.

developed from a personal initiative of the Prime Minister's, is due to take place in Moscow in mid-October. The Prime Minister might also express the hope that the major contracts which have long been promised in the oil and chemical sectors will soon materialise and make an impression on the outstanding credit of £950 million extended to the Soviet Government last year, of which only £42 million has so far been taken up. Mr. Crosland considers that the Prime Minister's general line might be to emphasise the Government's desire to move forward with the development of our relationship with the Soviet Union without being blown off course by the minor squalls which occur in all bilateral relationships from time to time.

Yours ever,
E.A.J. FERGUSSON

No. 92

Submission from Mr. Cartledge on Anglo-Soviet Relations[1]
[*ENS 020/548/3*]

Confidential   FCO, *28 September 1976*

Problem

1.   The Private Secretary's letter of 23 September to Mr. Wright at No. 10[2] conveyed the Secretary of State's comments on recent conversations between members of the Soviet Embassy and Mr. Tom McNally about the possibility of a visit to the UK by Brezhnev; and, in the context of the Prime Minister's decision to see the Soviet Ambassador during the Labour Party Conference, summarised both the negative and the positive aspects of the current phase of Anglo-Soviet relations and suggested a line which the Prime Minister might take with Lunkov. It is possible that, following his discussion with the Prime Minister (if this in fact takes place)[3] the Soviet Ambassador might seek a call on the Secretary of State to talk about Anglo-Soviet relations in more detail. The currently sceptical public mood about East–West détente, and the lively interest of the media in some of the current difficulties in Anglo-Soviet relations, are likely to be reflected in Parliamentary interest in those subjects when the Commons reassemble. It would therefore be useful to have the endorsement of FCO Ministers for a general line

---

[1] This submission was addressed to Mr. Sutherland (recently-appointed AUS). It was forwarded to Lord Goronwy-Roberts and Mr. Fergusson.

[2] No. 91.

[3] Mr. Callaghan received Mr. Lunkov at 10 Downing St. on 7 October. When Mr. Callaghan pressed Mr. Lunkov on the prospect of Mr. Brezhnev and Mr. Kosygin visiting London he replied that the problem was that the Soviet leaders had 'so many invitations outstanding', and he suggested that, instead of a full Heads of Government visit, they might arrange a 'working two-day visit'. Mr. Callaghan said that would be 'very acceptable' (telegram No. 917 to Moscow of 7 October).

on HMG's attitude towards Anglo-Soviet relations which would provide a basis for draft public statements, replies to Parliamentary Questions and briefing for Ministers during the next few weeks. What should this line be?

Background

2.   Mr. Kubekin of the Soviet Embassy told Mr. McNally early in September that the Anglo-Soviet bilateral relationship was somewhat in the doldrums.[4] Kubekin may have been referring primarily to the denial of a visa to Kuplyakov, Counsellor-designate at the Soviet Embassy; there are, however, a number of other current bilateral difficulties, summarised in Annex A to this submission.[5] The Russians seem disposed to exaggerate their political significance and to take a gloomy view of the present state of Anglo-Soviet relations in consequence. In so doing they may entertain the hope that HMG may be induced to make concessions to their viewpoint on a number of international issues.

3.   Some of the bilateral problems summarised in Annex A relate to our national security: others are of a practical nature. All of them, however, should be seen as distinct from and against the general perspective of the conduct of Anglo-Soviet political and commercial relations, the substance of which has filled out considerably during the last 2 years. The most substantial prospective bilateral event would be a visit to the UK by Mr. Brezhnev, which was the subject of my submission of 14 September;[6] but, whether or not this visit materialises,[7] the recent and current level of constructive activity in Anglo-Soviet relations transcends the bilateral difficulties on which the Russians are at present disposed to harp. The positive aspect of the Anglo-Soviet relationship are summarised in Annex B to this submission.[8]

---

[4] In a letter to Sir H. Smith of 23 September Mr. Cartledge wrote that Anglo-Soviet relations were 'evidently entering one of their periodic phases of fragility'. The Soviet Embassy, he thought, were 'at present engaging in the familiar Russian tactic of maximising minor problems in order to orchestrate the theme that the British side [was] lagging behind in the development of Anglo-Soviet relations, [was] failing to practice what it [preached] and [needed] to pull its socks up'.

[5] Not printed. The current bilateral Anglo-Soviet problems listed in this annex were: (1) Soviet complaints over British delays in the issue of visas; (2) the ceilings imposed on the number of Soviet officials in London; (3) British objections to Soviet plans for new Embassy buildings in London; (4) the non-delivery of prescriptions signed by the Soviet Embassy doctor; (5) the withholding of permission for Soviet 'research vessels' to call at British ports; (6) HMG's non-ratification of the Protocol to the Anglo-Soviet Merchant Navigation Treaty of 1968; and (7) the detention of a mackerel-fishing Soviet vessel off Cornwall.

[6] See No. 91, notes 3 and 4. In this submission Mr. Cartledge recommended that Mr. Crosland should, in discussion with Mr. Lunkov, indicate a positive attitude towards a visit by Mr. Brezhnev without offering a price for such a visit.

[7] Mr. Cartledge wrote in his letter to Sir H. Smith of 23 September (see note 4 above) that hopes of a visit from Mr. Brezhnev, 'although dimmed and flickering', had 'not yet been entirely extinguished'.

[8] Not printed. In Annex B Mr. Cartledge pointed out that four Soviet Ministers had visited the UK during 1976, including Mr. Gromyko. He also noted that official exchanges had continued to 'develop satisfactorily'; that military exchanges involving all three services had taken place or were in prospect; and that visits by British businessmen to the USSR had 'maintained throughout 1976, the high level which developed after the Anglo-Soviet Summit in February 1975'.

Argument

4. A balanced assessment of the debit and credit sides of the current Anglo-Soviet ledger shows that, while the bilateral relationship continues to display its traditional vulnerability to chance upsets, it is still broadly on the course established by the meetings between Sir Harold Wilson and Mr. Callaghan and the Soviet leadership in 1975 and reaffirmed during Mr. Gromyko's visit to Britain in March 1976. Anglo-Soviet relations have been and will continue to be liable to greater atmospheric fluctuations than most of the UK's other bilateral relationships. This is due in part to the repercussions of permanent features of Soviet policy and practice: the Soviet intelligence effort, the violations of human rights and freedoms in the Soviet Union which arouse understandable hostility and concern in the UK, and the Soviet prosecution of the 'ideological struggle' which involves, as a matter of course, spasms of criticism of HMG's policies and of British society. These factors are made more inflammable by the consistently high level of interest in the Soviet Union of the part on the British media. A coincidental bunching of minor bilateral problems, against a background of increased scepticism on the part of the media and public opinion over détente and East–West relations, have at present combined to produce one of the cyclical troughs in the relationship. A successful visit by Brezhnev and a few major contracts could produce an upswing. In the meantime, HMG's policy should be to do what we can to demonstrate to the Russians that we, for our part, do not intend to be deflected from a generally positive course by a few minor problems which they are disposed to exaggerate. At the same time we are not disposed to make concessions or to take initiatives of uncertain value for the sake of improving the atmosphere.

5. There are also strong arguments at the present time for ensuring that the fabric of the Anglo-Soviet relationship is sufficiently sound and unfrayed by temporary difficulties to bear the weight of the substantial and probably contentious political exchanges with the Soviet Government which will ensue from the extension of UK fishing limits to 200 miles. These exchanges could open with a Soviet reaction to the announcement, probably in mid-October that the extension is to take effect on 1 January, 1977.[9] Thereafter, diplomatic exchanges will be taking place against a background of the risk of incidents at sea within the new limits. It is important to ensure that our lines of communication during these exchanges are not impaired by the kind of bilateral difficulty summarised in Annex A.[10]

6. These objectives might best be achieved if HMG's approach both in public statements and in discussions with Soviet officials in London and in Moscow, were to be defined on the following lines:

---

[9] On 30 October EC Foreign Ministers meeting in the Hague agreed to extend their fishing limits to 200 miles as from 1 January 1977 and to invite interested countries wishing to continue fishing in these waters to negotiate agreements. In the absence of any formal response from Eastern bloc states, the EC Council further agreed on 14 December to give them until 14 March 1977 to reply.

[10] See note 5 above.

(i) HMG's policy of working, with our Allies, for a safer and more productive relationship with the Soviet Union and of developing, to this end, improved cooperation, contacts and exchanges at all levels, remains unchanged.

(ii) In general, the British Government is satisfied with the way in which this policy is working out; momentum is being maintained in Anglo-Soviet exchanges at Ministerial, official and non-official level and the range of these contacts is being extended.[11]

(iii) One area in which there is certainly scope for more rapid progress is that of trade; HMG attach great importance to Soviet assurances that the whole of the £950 million line of credit agreed in 1975 will be taken up. British industry is now in good shape to exploit its growing interest in the Soviet market.

(iv) Temporary bilateral difficulties, whether over visas or other matters, should be kept in perspective and should not be allowed to impair the more important strands of the Anglo-Soviet relationship; that relationship is, in HMG's view, now sufficiently soundly based to bear the weight of the kind of differences of view on specific issues which are bound to arise from time to time.

[for use with Soviet officials]

(v) The FCO will deal in a constructive matter and at an appropriate working level with the various problems which the Soviet Ambassador and his staff have raised with the Department in recent months; there is no need for these relatively minor issues to sour the atmosphere.

(vi) The official talks in London which have been agreed in principle for October/November should provide an opportunity to carry forward the Anglo-Soviet political dialogue and it would be useful to reach agreement on dates soon.

Recommendation

7. I therefore *recommend* that the Secretary of State's endorsement should be sought for the general approach to the present stage of Anglo-Soviet relations outlined in paragraph 6 above; and that it should be reflected

(*a*) in ministerial statements. There are likely to be a number of Parliamentary Questions on various aspects of relations with the Soviet Union when the

---

[11] In his letter to Sir H. Smith of 23 September (see notes 4 and 7 above) Mr. Cartledge commented that in the light of adverse press treatment of a recent visit by the Czechoslovak Foreign Minister and the 'sustained blast of hostile comment' about the absence of official representation at the unveiling of the Katyn Memorial in London, Mr. Crosland was 'somewhat disenchanted with the development of our bilateral relations with the East'. Mr. Cartledge added: 'He [Mr. Crosland] is inclined to feel, I think, that the pace is becoming a little too brisk and that some loss of momentum would do no harm. I think that there is, in fact, something to be said for this: if EESD's clients had their way, the entire Cabinet would be in endless procession through the capitals of Eastern Europe.' But Mr. Cartledge also felt that there was a risk of the pendulum swinging a 'little too far' in over-reaction to the present public mood, and that EESD's purpose would be to 'restore balance'.

House reassembles and either in this context or at the first Foreign Affairs debate a general statement might be valuable.

and

(*b*) in discussion with representatives of the Soviet Government.

B.G. CARTLEDGE[12]

[12] On 30 September Mr. Sutherland noted on this submission that he agreed with Mr. Cartledge's argument and recommendation, both of which he had discussed with EESD in draft. 'The Russians', Mr. Sutherland observed, 'are saying that bilateral relations are in the doldrums. They are saying this against the background of an increased public disillusionment with détente policies, in part the result of Soviet actions and in part the consequence of unrealistic expectations generated by the CSCE.' He thought it important that the coincidence of relatively minor difficulties should not obscure the fact that the content of the Anglo-Soviet relationship remained 'substantial'. Lord Goronwy-Roberts added in a note of 2 October: 'So let us play it cool and factual … This, in fact, is consonant with the general views of the Sec. of State and the P.M. on the posture to be assumed towards Eastern Europe. Mr. Cartledge's para 6 is very useful here.'

No. 93

Planning Paper on Détente and the Future Management of East/West Relations by the Foreign and Commonwealth Office

[*RS 081/1*]

Confidential   FCO, *23 November 1976*

Summary[1]

Introduction

1. The word 'détente' has been much overworked and misused, but the gradual evolution of East/West relations away from the cold war and confrontation cannot conveniently be described by any other term. The paper attempts to define how the evolution of détente would best accord with Western interests.

The Nature of Détente

2. After the breakdown of earlier attempts to move away from sterile confrontation, both sides in the late 1960s attached increasing importance to the creation of a more stable relationship. This led to the negotiation in the 1970s of a modest *modus vivendi* based upon a common interest in the avoidance of military confrontation leading to nuclear war.

[1] This is the summary of a paper commissioned by Sir M. Palliser (PUS since November 1975) and prepared by the Planning Staff. Sir M. Palliser explained in a minute to Mr. Fergusson of 23 November covering the paper, that he had wanted 'to put into focus a subject which, after Angola, had been provoking more emotion than clarity of thought, and to provide a coherent analysis of where British interests [were] in the détente process'. The full paper was considered by the PUS's Steering Committee on 26 October and revised to take account of points then raised in discussion. In its final form, including the summary, the paper was fifty-three pages long.

3. Below this level, different countries have different interests and objectives. The *Soviet Union* sees the process of détente both as meeting state interests and as facilitating the promotion through the ideological struggle of the world-wide triumph of communism. The Soviet Union seeks to avoid a renewed nuclear arms spiral,[2] to secure access to Western technology, capital and grain, to isolate China, to retain elbow-room for the political and ideological struggle and to preserve and perhaps extend its authority on the European continent.[3] The *United States* seeks to manage the emergence of the Soviet Union as a superpower and to create a vested interest in cooperation; and eventually perhaps even to achieve a breaking down of East/West barriers. *Western Europe* shares United States interests, but attaches greater importance to East/West trade. Of the European Community countries, the FRG has special concerns arising from the division of Germany. France has sought to assert an independent personality, while the UK has aimed to play a responsible role in the formulation of overall Western policy towards the East. The *Eastern European* states seek opportunities for advantageous dealings with Western countries, access to Western markets and technology and opportunities for some assertion of national personality.

4. Recent changes in East/West relations have been changes of degree, not of kind. The nature of the Soviet and Eastern European regimes has not changed. This, together with the continuing Soviet military build-up,[4] has led to some disillusionment in the West. However, the West has not given away valuable cards, and there have been real if limited gains. Disappointment has resulted from exaggerated and unwarranted expectations.

The Current Business of Détente

5. East/West negotiations combine a cooperative approach to solving difficult problems and a confrontational approach aimed at achieving advantage. SALT lies at the heart of the détente process and the interests of both sides make it reasonable to hope for a SALT II Agreement in 1977. The CSCE embodies and exemplifies both the search for common ground and the unresolved struggle. Basket III is very important for Western public opinion, but the Russians cannot fail to see it as an exercise in confrontation. MBFR rests in part on common interests, but the Western hope of reducing the Warsaw Pact's existing advantage

---

[2] The Main Paper explained that a renewed nuclear arms spiral 'would place an additional and probably crippling burden on the Soviet economy', which already devoted 11–12% of its GNP to defence expenditure.

[3] According to the Main Paper, circumstances might arise which would tempt the Soviet Union to engage in the more active pursuit of a pan-European system within a Soviet sphere of influence. 'Failing such a temptation', Planning Staff noted, '… current Soviet objectives in Europe appear essentially defensive.'

[4] Soviet armed forces in central Europe had been systematically re-equipped with more effective and sophisticated weapons during the past five years, with the result that the qualitative advantage once enjoyed by NATO had been largely eroded. Moreover, as Planning Staff pointed out (*v. ibid.*), Soviet armed forces generally had acquired capabilities, such as immediate readiness airborne brigades and a sophisticated blue-water navy, which enabled them, as Soviet support for the Cuban intervention in Angola had recently demonstrated, to operate on a global scale.

is bound to seem confrontational to the Soviet Union. Reconciliation of the conflicting approaches will be difficult. There are common interests in some other areas of arms control (e.g. the Test Ban Treaty, the NPT), but the prospects for genuine disarmament are remote.[5]

6.   The motives behind the Soviet proposals for all European conferences on energy, transport and the environment are not entirely clear, but the West is right to be prudently unenthusiastic, and should continue to emphasise the role of the ECE.[6]

7.   The growth of East/West trade has been an important factor in the development of East/West relations, and has led to suggestions that the economy of the Soviet Union is no longer autarkic. Because of the sizeable balance of payments deficits run up by some of the East European countries, it has also led to a greatly increased level of indebtedness to the West. For the West this trade remains no more than marginal; for the Soviet Union it is sufficiently significant to be a factor in foreign policy decisions. On the other hand, the competitive aspects of Soviet foreign economic policy (e.g. in shipping and fisheries) could provoke political problems.[7] Problems have arisen from the refusal of the Soviet Union and its allies to deal directly with the Community. It would be against Western interests to allow the Soviet Union to use this as a pretext for strengthening the CMEA.

Developments which might affect Détente

8.   The next generation of Soviet leaders are an unknown factor but they are unlikely to have a changed view of essential Soviet interests. On the *American* side, Mr. Carter is more likely to change style than substance. The new leadership may see advantage in a degree of normalisation of Sino/Soviet relations, but this is unlikely to have any major effect on East/West relations over the next few years.

9.   If the West does not maintain defence expenditure, the discrepancy in resource allocation between the two sides could undermine the credibility of NATO's strategy; and defence cuts by other NATO members could make the Alliance increasingly a bilateral US/German affair. Developments in military technology, assuming that they are introduced by both sides, are not likely to confer any significant advantage on either.

10.   The superpowers could be drawn into regional crises, most obviously in

---

[5]   The Main Paper further explained that the Soviet economy had always been geared to a high level of armament production and that to reduce its size would be a difficult task. In addition, the USSR had refused to countenance the principle of inspection in its territory to ensure compliance with arms control treaties.

[6]   The Economic Commission for Europe (ECE) had a special role in the multilateral implementation of the economic aspects of the CSCE Final Act, and Planning Staff considered it in Western interests to ensure that this was not eroded through the establishment of new institutional machinery to follow up the Conference.

[7]   The Soviet merchant fleet seemed determined to gain a bigger share of world freight, often by under-cutting the rates of Western shippers; and the very considerable amount of fish caught by Soviet trawlers off the coasts of Western countries appeared likely to lead to difficult negotiations as fishing limits were extended to 200 miles. Cf. No. 92, note 9.

the Middle East, but perhaps most awkwardly in Korea. Communist participation in an Italian or French government would weaken the North Atlantic
Alliance, but would also pose problems for the Soviet Union in Eastern Europe
and in East/West relations.[8]

11. The Soviet Union will continue to find openings to exploit in some Third
World countries, but its dismal aid performance and its economic irrelevance in
the dialogue between developed and developing countries may hamper the
extension of its influence.

12. The *status quo* in Eastern Europe is inherently unstable, but there are
limits to the scope for change. There is a risk of East/West confrontation over
Yugoslavia after Tito's death.[9] Even the Soviet Union itself is not immune from
pressures for change[10] and this is the only way in which the confrontational
element in East/West relations might eventually be diminished; but the process
of change could equally lead to greater confrontation.[11]

Possible Implications for Western Policy Makers

13. The fundamental requirement is the avoidance or successful management
of crises. From the Western point of view this calls for the early identification of
situations which might tempt the Russians and for postures which leave as little
room as possible for Soviet miscalculation of the limits of Western tolerance. If
the Soviet Union does not exercise restraint, the West can choose between a
sharply destabilising and potentially dangerous reaction—e.g. calling off SALT;
a partially destabilising and probably ineffectual reaction designed to punish the
Soviet Union—e.g. restrictions on trade; or threatening to react if the Soviet
Union does not pull back—i.e diplomatic deterrence of the sort adopted by the
US in the early case of Angola.[12] The problem reduces in the end to early identi-

[8] Communist participation in Western governments would, the Main Paper suggested, increase
the already considerable problems faced by the Soviet Union in trying to control the international
communist movement, and rapid political change might destabilise *détente*.

[9] Economic difficulties, nationalist tendencies in the different republics, and divergent political
attitudes following Marshal Tito's death could, the Main Paper argued, create a situation in which
there was political tension and a danger of Yugoslavia breaking-up. The Soviet Union might then
be tempted to intervene, and that could create a 'major crisis'.

[10] In the Main Paper Planning Staff reasoned that the present Soviet régime would have to
reckon with challenges posed by the spread of Western ideas, technological change, and non-
Russian nationalism within the USSR. 'There is', they noted, 'some evidence that scientists,
technologists, and engineers on whom the Soviet Union depends for its economic progress are
calling for more freedom to exchange information and views with one another and with their
Western colleagues and are increasingly recognising the inabilitiy of their system to cope with their
country's problems.' The paper also suggested that there might be a 'prolonged period in the Soviet
economy of ever deepening difficulties', with the problems of low labour productivity, industrial
and agricultural wastefulness and poor management exacerbated by the rising expectations of the
people, and a shortage of skilled labour.

[11] Indeed, Planning Staff thought it difficult to see 'any way apart from Western acceptance of
Soviet hegemony, i.e. "Finlandisation", by which the confrontational element in East/West relations
might eventually be eliminated'.

[12] The Main Paper referred to Angola as 'a good example of a situation where the interests of

fication of situations which might tempt the Russians and the devising of sets of signals which would make it clear to them that Soviet misbehaviour would have serious consequences. Bilateral contacts can make a useful contribution in this area.

14. Threats to cut off existing trade are less likely to influence Soviet behaviour than steps to encourage the belief that Soviet restraint would facilitate increased trade of the sort which the Soviet Union wants. Western countries need better coordination of their credit policies. The European Community could develop more common policies towards the Soviet Union.

15. Détente cannot be stable if it is not carried into the armaments field and there is a strong case for making MBFR the proving ground for détente.[13]

16. The development of bilateral relations at many levels will continue to be a major element in the détente process. Western countries should continue to expand bilateral links and contacts, perhaps differentiating between individual Eastern European countries.

17. Despite the limited prospects of success, the West should continue to promote the freer movement of people and ideas through steady pressure for the implementation of Basket III and otherwise. Broadcasting to the Soviet Union and Eastern Europe is particularly important. The main target will always be the Soviet Union, but it could be influenced via developments in Eastern Europe.

Western Coordination

18. The West can achieve its objectives in East/West relations only by maintaining its cohesion and firmness of purpose. Of the points examined in Section IV, crisis management is an area in which the lead has to be taken by the US. Careful pursuit of consultation within NATO is important. The need for greater Western coordination in economic policies is already recognised, and work is in progress both in the OECD and in the Community. The degree of importance to be attached to MBFR, and the tactical handling of the promotion of freer movement of people and ideas, are already matters of continuing discussion between Western countries. In general none of the ideas discussed in Section IV calls for new UK initiatives; but they could contribute to the UK input to intra-NATO and intra-Community discussions which are already in train.

the two sides were not clearly defined and where the Soviet Union was able to exploit an unprepared situation'.

[13] Planning Staff contended with regard to MBFR (*v. ibid.*): 'There should be no question of the West putting itself under time or any other pressure to achieve results for their own sake. The West also needs to be in a position to counter Soviet attempts to deny the real disparities in numbers of combat troops and heavy equipment, especially tanks, which exist in Central Europe. The pressure should be on the Soviet Union to make concessions in order to make its own advocacy of détente convincing. If MBFR is brought more to public attention maintenance of an adequate Western defence effort will incidentally be made easier.'

No. 94

Record of a Meeting on Détente held in the Foreign and Commonwealth Office on 7 December 1976 at 9.30 am

[*RS 081/1*]

Present:

FCO

Rt. Hon Anthony Crosland MP	Rt. Hon Lord Goronwy-Roberts
Mr. John Tomlinson MP[1]	Sir M. Palliser
Mr. Sykes	Mr. Butler[2]
Mr. Hibbert	Mr. Sutherland
Mr. Fretwell[3]	Mr. Moberly
Mr. Wilberforce	Mr. Lipsey[4]
Mr. Fergusson	Mr. Crowe[5]
Mr. Beetham[6]	Mr. Prendergast[7]
Mr. Meyer[8]	

Cabinet Office
Mr. Rhodes

Arms Control

1. Referring to the Planning Staff paper 'Détente And The Future Management Of East/West Relations'[9] *Mr. Crosland* said that he could see that détente had led to a *modus vivendi* between East and West and had defused tension. This was a good thing. But were there any doubts about the benefits to the West of SALT and MBFR Agreements? *Mr. Sykes* said that there would be clear advantages for the West so long as the agreements were achieved on satisfactory terms. An MBFR settlement that put a ceiling on individual national contributions would of course be bad; and in that case it would be better to have no agreement at all. The SALT II negotiations presented no problems for the West. A SALT III agreement, which would cover forward based systems, including British weapons systems, would create greater problems. Some people thought that the

---

[1] Parliamentary Under-Secretary.

[2] Mr. M.D. Butler was DUS.

[3] Mr. M.J.E. Fretwell was AUS.

[4] Mr. D. Lipsey was Political Adviser to Mr. Crosland.

[5] Mr. B.L. Crowe had, since March, been Head of Planning Department.

[6] Mr. R.C. Beetham, formerly First Secretary in HM Embassy, Helsinki, had recently been appointed as an Assistant Head of EESD.

[7] Mr. W.K. Prendergast was Assistant Private Secretary to Mr. Crosland.

[8] Mr. C.J.R. Meyer was First Secretary in the FCO.

[9] No. 93. Mr. Crosland expressed his general approval of this paper and it was subsequently circulated to all FCO departments and all posts overseas (Planning Staff circular of 15 December).

Americans would be tempted to sell their European allies down the river in this negotiation. These fears had been unfounded; so far the Americans had behaved impeccably in safeguarding the interests of the Western Europeans. But the moment might come in SALT III negotiations when the Americans would put us under pressure to take some very awkward decisions.

2. In reply to a question from Mr. Crosland, Mr. Sykes said that our public position on MBFR was good. He agreed with Mr. Hibbert that we should have to add something to our position soon; but this would have to await the new American Administration. *Sir M. Palliser* asked how we proposed to overcome the problem of the French. *Mr. Wilberforce* said that this would be done in two stages. First, we were not counting the French forces in the overall figures. Secondly, we did not have to worry about the inclusion of the French forces in the common ceiling until we were much nearer an agreement. *Mr. Crosland* asked when the next session of the Vienna talks would take place. *Mr. Wilberforce* said that there would first be the Christmas recess and we would then have to wait for the new American Administration to get into the saddle in January. There was unlikely to be any alteration to the West's negotiating position until Easter.

3. *Mr. Crosland* asked whether the Russians were more interested in pushing MBFR or SALT. *Mr. Wilberforce* said that, like the Americans, they were more interested in the SALT talks. *Lord Goronwy-Roberts* said that the Russian strategy was to sit tight at the MBFR talks and to await a break-through in the SALT negotiations. *Mr. Crowe* said that if we were to make progress in arms control, we had to find areas of mutual benefit. We had not yet reached this point at Vienna. *Mr. Moberly* questioned the Planning Paper's description of the MBFR talks as '*the* proving ground' of détente. Would it not be more accurate to describe them as '*a* proving ground'? *Mr. Hibbert* said that it was simply a question of putting the accent on the military dimension because that was where we wanted to make progress. *Mr. Crosland* and *Lord Goronwy-Roberts* asked whether it was right to refer to the Vienna talks in the draft of the Secretary of State's NATO speech as the 'touchstone' of détente.[10] If the Russians did not want to make progress on MBFR, we were unlikely to get anywhere on détente. Lord Goronwy-Roberts added that the point was that we should make an effort to push the Russians at Vienna. But there would only be value in doing this if we had the Americans with us. *Mr. Hibbert* said that the Soviet Union's preponderance in conventional forces in central Europe was a destabilising factor. We could not take the process of détente to a satisfactory conclusion as long as it existed. We should emphasise in our propaganda the Russians' failure to reduce their conventional forces in Europe. We should point out that the West was making every effort to further détente; but that we would not get anywhere until there was a reduction in the level of

---

[10] Mr. Crosland was due to address the regular half-yearly meeting of NATO Foreign Ministers in Brussels on 9–10 December. The draft of the speech here referred to has not been traced in FCO records, but a later draft in Mr. Crosland's private papers includes the following statement: 'We must leave the public in no doubt that phrases about détente will count for little unless there is a safer strategic relationship between East and West. We have to hammer away at the theme that the true index of progress towards détente must be the extent to which the Soviet Union is willing to contribute to progress in SALT and MBFR.'

conventional forces in Europe.[11] This did not mean however that we had to link progress on CSCE matters with the progress on MBFR. *Sir M. Palliser* said that this was a point which we should work into Mr Crosland's NATO speech. It was important that the public should be aware of the true situation. The existing draft of the speech was good; but it needed simplifying and 'vulgarizing'. *Mr. Fergusson* said that Mr. Crosland's speech would be given in restricted session and would not be circulated outside. Mr. Crosland said that he might well want to draw on the text for subsequent public speeches and that he wanted to get the drafting right first time round. The passages on MBFR in the draft should therefore be 'vulgarized'.

East–West Economic Relations

4. *Mr. Crosland* said that there was nothing in the Planning Staff's paper to refute Schmidt's thesis that the present balance of East/West economic relations was one-sided and favoured the Soviet Union. *Mr. Butler* said that the Soviet aid performance was very poor. Schmidt's thesis that the West was losing twice over i.e. by carrying the burden of aid to the developing world and by providing subsidised credit to the Soviet Union, was true. On credit, we could improve things by tightening up the Gentleman's Agreement.[12] Our aim should be to turn this into a formal agreement that would cover all OECD countries and not just the present seven states that were a party to it. Hitherto the French had opposed all efforts within the EEC to co-ordinate credit policies, although all other member-states were agreed that this was desirable. Mr. Butler was hopeful that with the appointment of Mr. Barre as Prime Minister there might be a change of policy.[13] If we could reach a common position within the Community it would help promote a wider agreement among OECD countries. *Mr. Crosland* said that there was evidently no disagreement around the table on this. There should be a pithy reference to economic relations with the Soviet Union in his NATO speech. Figures illustrating the comparative aid performance of the Soviet Union and the Western countries could also be inserted. *Mr. Butler* wondered whether

---

[11] The same point was made by Sir J. Killick in UKDEL NATO telegram No. 16 (saving) of 14 December, in which he recorded some personal impressions of recent Ministerial meetings in Brussels. 'In short', he observed, 'we must somehow make credibly clear that not just Belgrade, but the whole process of détente (its achievements as well as its future development) is at stake unless the present Soviet military build-up is at least halted.'

[12] Planning Staff argued in their Main Paper (see No. 93, note 1) that although the Russians needed trade with the West much more than the West needed trade with the USSR, they had been able to exploit competition between Western countries and play one off against the other. The most striking example of this had been in competition between Western governments to improve national shares of East/West trade by arranging credit terms beyond those which firms would normally find justifiable. Canada, France, the FRG, Italy, Japan, the UK and the US had concluded a Gentlemen's Agreement in July 1976 on minimum credit and repayment terms. But while the Agreement's guidelines were in theory world-wide, the French had so far appeared reluctant to apply them to trade with the USSR and other Eastern European states.

[13] M. R. Barre, who was formerly French Minister of Foreign Trade, was appointed French Prime Minister on 26 August.

NATO was the right forum. A general statement of principles might be more in order. It was in any case very difficult to quantify the transfer of resources to the East. We did not have full statistics; and it was hard to make a comparison with subsidised credit to other areas. A clearer picture might emerge from the OECD study which the Americans had initiated. *Sir M. Palliser* suggested that we might inject into the NATO speech the thought that so long as the Soviet Union regarded aid as primarily a matter of supplying second-rate weapons, this was bound to raise questions about their attitude to détente. There was the further point that in subsidising credit to the Soviet Union the West appeared to facilitate this process.

Basket III and the Final Act

5.　*Mr. Crosland* said that he had begun by being cynical about Basket III. This view had been challenged by those who argued that:

(*a*)　CSCE had helped people to emigrate and to be reunited with their families; and
(*b*)　it had had a positive effect on Eastern European public opinion who were always encouraged by the least measure of liberalisation.

Was this true?

Mr. Hibbert said that, judged by its visible successes, progress on Basket III had been very small. But the Final Act also brought unquantifiable benefits because it was potentially of great value to dissenters. The Warsaw Pact countries had all published the Final Act. The text was in circulation and its importance lay in the quiet and unseen influence that it had on the peoples of Eastern Europe. The process was of course very slow; there would be no dramatic break-throughs. But we had to keep up the pressure on the Russians to implement in full the provisions of Basket III. *Mr. Rhodes* said that if we did not keep up the pressure, we would lose a trick by leaving the Eastern Europeans with the impression that Basket III no longer mattered to us. *Mr. Sutherland* said that the real value of the Final Act lay in its being a document to which all the Eastern European governments had themselves subscribed. It was also valuable to people who were not necessarily dissenters as such, but who were aware of the need for evolution in their societies. *Mr. Sykes* argued that Basket III had a role to play in pushing the Soviet Union towards a more consumer-oriented society. *Lord Goronwy-Roberts* said that the lack of success so far in getting the Russians to implement Basket III showed that it went to the heart of their system. If the Russians were to make major concessions on Basket III their whole system would change. As a democratic society we had to keep up the pressure. Only the other day Mr. Ben Whitaker MP had asked Mr. Luard[14] whether we were monitoring the Soviet Union's performance. If we were to give up on Basket III this would have a very bad effect on Eastern Europe, especially in key countries such as Czechoslovakia.

[14]　Mr. E. Luard was Parliamentary Under-Secretary of State for Foreign and Commonwealth Affairs.

6. *Mr Crosland* said that there was a strong anti-détente feeling on the Opposition benches in the House. Was it true that FCO officials did not share the Tories' view? *Mr. Hibbert* said that the Opposition was simply taking short-term profits from a long-term problem. It was important to put pressure on the Russians: but we had to judge the degree and direction of pressure right. The Jewish lobby for instance overdid things; if we were to emulate them we should be involved in continuous polemics with the Russians. We had to up-hold the Final Act. But we should not press to the point of damaging other interests in our relations with the Soviet Union by building up excessive acrimony in areas where the Russians could not possibly give way. The problem was very difficult it was a question of constantly adjusting the pressure to circumstance.

7. *Mr. Sykes* said that in considering détente it was worth noting that the Russians had always had greater problems with their satellite states when East/West relations were good. *Mr. Hibbert* added that before the Helsinki Conference officials had been worried that CSCE would make Western public opinion unduly receptive to Soviet propaganda. The opposite had in fact happened. This showed that our relatively low profile had paid dividends. The public had not swallowed the much more strident noises made by the Communists.

8. In conclusion, *Mr. Crosland* said that it was worth taking a good deal of trouble over his NATO speech and that it should reflect the PUS's 'vulgarising' theme. *Mr. Butler* said that if the speech was going to deal with economic questions it needed to bring out the increasing number of points of friction in economic relations between East and West like fisheries, shipping rates and dumping. *Mr. Crosland* said that he would like to end his NATO speech on a philosophical note. He wanted to take up a point made in a recent Encounter article by Hugh Seton-Watson[15] about the Soviet Union being the last remaining old style imperialist power.[16] He might also refute George Kennan's most recent article arguing against détente.[17]

PLANNING STAFF DEPARTMENT

[15] Professor of Russian History at the School of Slavonic and East European Studies.

[16] In this article, 'George Kennan's Illusions. A Reply', *Encounter*, Vol. xlvii, No. 6 (Nov. 1976), pp. 24–35, Professor Seton-Watson asserted: 'The Soviet Union is the last remaining great imperialist power, and most of its colonial subjects are Europeans.'

[17] See George Urban, 'From Containment to Self-Containment. A Conversation with George F. Kennan', *Encounter*, Vol. xlvii, No. 3 (Sept. 1976), pp. 11–43. In this interview Mr. Kennan was particularly critical of the CSCE at Helsinki and its 'fatuous declarations'. Mr. Crosland told the NAC on 9 December that the Helsinki Final Act was 'symbolic but it was not the core of détente'. He added that 'security in the face of increasing Russian strength', and the 'field of economic relationships', were both more immediately important: NATO should seek greater stability in the East/West military balance, and should 'show up the disparity between Soviet peaceful protestations and their military build-up'. Finally, after referring to southern Africa, where he thought it 'axiomatic that Russia wanted to extend her influence', he said that he agreed with General A. Haig (Supreme Allied Commander Europe) 'that the Soviet Union should now be regarded as an imperialist power' (UKDEL NATO telegram No. 441 of 9 December, DPN 060/13).

NATO and Warsaw Pact : Conventional Ground Forces in Europe, 1973[1]

	IMMEDIATELY AVAILABLE			AFTER REINFORCEMENT (a)		
	NATO	WARSAW PACT	NATO: WP	NATO	WARSAW PACT	NATO: WP
NORTH NORWAY (NATO: WP forces facing this area)	(c)	(b) (c)	(g)	(c)	(c) (f)	(g)
Divisions/Div Equivalents	1/3	2 (e)	1 : 6.1	2	5	1 : 2.5
Manpower in Divisions	5,000	22,850	1 : 4.5	20,000	57,100	1 : 2.8
Main Battle Tanks in Divisions (h)	20	376	1 : 18.8	70	940	1 : 13.4
Field Artillery in Divisions (d)	18	288	1 : 16.0	100	720	1 : 7.2
BALTIC (DENMARK, SCHLESWIG HOLSTEIN, Central and Southern NORWAY: WP forces facing this area)	(c)	(b) (c)	(g)	(c)	(c) (f)	(g)
Divisions/Div Equivalents	2 1/3	11	1 : 4.7	6	13	1 : 2.1
Manpower in Divisions	32,000	101,150	1 : 3.1	110,000	124,000	1 : 1.1
Main Battle Tanks in Divisions (h)	350	2,228	1 : 6.3	400	2,604	1 : 6.5
Field Artillery in Divisions (d)	200	2,228	1 : 4.3	450	1,1164	1 : 2.5
CENTRAL REGION (The Elbe to the Alps, excluding France and French forces in the FRG: WP forces facing this area)	(c)	(b) (c)	(g)	(c)	(c) (f)	(g)
Divisions/Div Equivalents	23 1/3	68	1 : 2.9	26 2/3	78	1 : 2.9
Manpower in Divisions	350,000	658,300	1 : 1.8	500,000	768,100	1 : 1.5
Main Battle Tanks in Divisions (h)	4,200	19,727*	1 : 4.6	4,800	21,593	1 : 4.4
Field Artillery in Divisions (d)	1,800	6,672	1 : 3.7	2,100	7,968	1 : 3.7

* Including up to 3,000 recently identified

NOTES
   a. 'After reinforcement' has been taken as M[obilisation] + 45 [days].
   b. Forces in Eastern Europe and in the Western USSR.
   c. In general, smaller air portable and maritime units have been omitted on each side. Amphibious forces are not included. However, in the 'after reinforcement' column the Canadian air/sea combat group has been included for North Norway and the United States Reforger 'divisional equivalent' for the Central Region. Possible United Kingdom reinforcements have been excluded.
   d. Field artillery over 100 mm. Multiple rocket launchers are counted as a single tube.
   e. More troops could be deployed immediately if the Warsaw Pact did not respect Swedish and Finnish neutrality.
   f. It is presumed that the Warsaw Pact would be the aggressor in any conflict in Europe. As such it could choose its moment to begin mobilisation, and thus gain a lead over NATO. It could also concentrate its forces locally against NATO, and its superior supply lines would give an advantage in reinforcement capability.
   g. These ratios should not be taken as indicating the balance of forces at the outbreak of any hypothetical hostilities. As noted in f. above, the Warsaw Pact has significant advantages in mobilisation and reinforcement over NATO. It must be assumed that the Warsaw Pact would have achieved a measure of mobilisation before that of NATO got under way, and would choose its moment for attack at the point at which it was both ready to attack and had the greatest advantage over NATO. The NATO: Warsaw Pact ratio would therefore be more in the Warsaw Pact's favour at the moment of attack than either of those shown in the table.
   h. Excludes light tanks.

[1] Annex A to a report by the Joint Intelligence Committee (A) of 18 June 1973 on the strength of Soviet forces in central Europe (JIC (73) 21).

APPENDIX II

Report by the Joint Intelligence Committee

JIC (75) 28

Secret   CABINET OFFICE, *22 December 1975*

The Increasing Capability of Soviet Forces in Central Europe

PART I: SUMMARY AND CONCLUSIONS [1]

Introduction

1. This Report examines the considerable improvements in the Soviet theatre forces in Central Europe (defined here as East Germany, Poland and Czechoslovakia) over the period 1970–75, with special reference to the 12 months ending August 1975. It supersedes JIC (74) 29 dated December 1974,[2] which covered the period 1969–74.

Summary

2. The Soviet theatre forces in Central Europe, as defined above, consist of 3 Groups of Forces totalling 27 divisions and 3 Tactical Air Armies (a fourth TAA—in Hungary—is also of some relevance to the Central European theatre).[3] The total of 27 divisions has remained unchanged since 1968, but it is assessed that increases within them have resulted in an enhancement of their combat strength which is the equivalent of 6 complete pre-1968 divisions. In the air forces (including those in Hungary) increased effectiveness is assessed as equating to the addition of 4 complete pre-1970 air regiments.[4]

3. Within the past 2 or 3 years there have been some notable exceptions to the previous Soviet practice of postponing the deployment of new ground forces equipments to the Groups of Forces until they have been in service for some time in the USSR.

4. There have been some very significant improvements in ground forces equipment, particularly in tanks, infantry combat vehicles, self-propelled guns and towed artillery, obstacle-crossing equipment, air defence, logistics and nuclear delivery systems. A number of the advantages of quality once enjoyed by NATO have disappeared or are fast disappearing and in some fields the Russians may now be in the lead. In the past 12 months there has been no slowing up in the pace of deliveries, and there are indications that the arrival of some new types of equipment is imminent. Both conventional and nuclear capability have improved. Conscripts are in general better educated and with improved training this has enabled them to keep pace with the demands of modern

[1] Part II, the Main Report, is not printed.

[2] Not printed.

[3] The Main Report noted that Soviet forces in central Europe, together with the non-Soviet Warsaw Pact forces stationed in East Germany, Poland and Czechoslovakia and with reinforcements in the western USSR, represented 'more than half the total ready theatre forces of the Warsaw Pact from the NATO borders to the Pacific'. They also included 'the great majority of high-quality Warsaw Pact ground and air forces'.

[4] 'By electing to introduce these improvements on a piecemeal basis within units', the Main Report explained, 'rather than in the form of additional formations, the Russians have contrived to avoid much of the public apprehension which would have been aroused in the West by more obvious methods.'

equipment. East German, and to a lesser extent Polish and Czech forces are showing signs of benefiting from these developments.[5]

5. During the last 5 years major re-equipment of the Soviet air forces has considerably improved their tactical nuclear capability and has enhanced to an even greater degree their ability to undertake conventional offensive operations. As in the ground forces, deliveries of new equipment have been very considerable. 300 replacement new-generation aircraft have been delivered since 1973. These have increased Warsaw Pact capability to embark on a large-scale counter-air campaign while retaining the ability to provide close air support and air defence as required. Air-to-surface missiles based on modern guidance techniques are under development in the USSR. Helicopter holdings have tripled. Aircrew training has some shortcomings; steps are in hand to rectify this, but it could be some years before the full potential of new equipment is developed.

6. Non-Soviet Warsaw Pact air forces are undergoing a slower modernisation programme.

7. The capability and survivability of air command and control facilities (for both air and ground forces) are being improved.

8. The changes in the Soviet Groups of Forces and in their Tactical Air armies during the 1970–75 period reflect a deliberate act of Soviet policy.

9. The Russians appear to be giving a degree of preference, in their modernisation and reorganisation programme, to the Groups of Forces in Central Europe as opposed to Soviet forces elsewhere. In general, we believe that the changes which have been and are still taking place in these forces are traceable to the growth since about 1970 of a Soviet view that if hostilities break out they will not necessarily escalate immediately to the nuclear stage, i.e. that there may be a period of conventional warfare. However we consider that it would be an oversimplification to conclude that the Russians have selected conventional war as the preferred option. Evidence which might be advanced to support this conclusion can equally be regarded as relevant to their concern with certain phases in a nuclear war. We continue to believe that Soviet theatre forces in Central Europe are structured for, and capable of undertaking, the whole spectrum of combat operations; that the Russians regard Central Europe as the decisive continental theatre of war with NATO; and that the quality and organisation of their forces is now such as to provide the option of conducting a conventional campaign without full reinforcement from the Western USSR.

Conclusions

10. We conclude–

(*a*) The capability of Soviet theatre forces in Central Europe has very considerably increased since 1970.

(*b*) Earlier deployment of new ground forces equipment to the Groups of Forces, and more intensive modernisation of these Groups in comparison with Soviet ground and

---

[5] The Main Report argued that recent improvements in the calibre of Soviet forces reflected a growing awareness in Moscow 'that their [forces'] quality, as well as their strength, [could] contribute to the politico-military pressures the Russian leaders [might] hope to exert on NATO and on neutral countries'.

air formations elsewhere, indicate an enhanced Soviet desire to strengthen them both relatively and absolutely.

(*c*) There is a growing Soviet belief that escalation to the nuclear stage may not immediately follow the opening of conventional hostilities. At the same time, Soviet theatre forces in Central Europe are designed for, and capable of undertaking, the full spectrum of combat operations.

(*d*) The Russians continue to regard Central Europe as the decisive continental theatre of war with NATO. They have a developing capability to mount a large-scale counter-air campaign against NATO's tactical air effort on the outbreak of hostilities.

R. A. SYKES
CHAIRMAN, ON BEHALF OF THE
JOINT INTELLIGENCE COMMITTEE

APPENDIX III

Mr. R.J. O'Neill[1] (Vienna) to Sir G. Howe[2]

[*DZM* 081/1]

Confidential   VIENNA, *17 February 1989*

Summary ...[3]

Sir,

MBFR: What did we achieve?

1. The first answer to that question is, exactly what we set out to achieve. On the Western side, the immediate background to the start of the negotiations was Senator Mansfield's call for cuts in United States forces in Europe. The steering brief[4] sent to this Delegation in October 1973 described MBFR as 'primarily an exercise in damage limitation', and stated our general aim as 'to be seen ... to be working seriously for a lowering of the level of armed forces ... while maintaining undiminished security for all'. More than fifteen years later, the negotiations have ended without an agreement; there has been no reduction in United States forces in Europe; the Warsaw Pact has itself announced unilateral reductions and withdrawals of forces; and the burden of unreduced military expenditure has made its contribution to the crippling of the Soviet economy which is Gorbachev's[5] greatest single problem.[6]

2. The formal ending on 2 February of the Vienna negotiations on Mutual Reductions of Forces and Armaments and Associated Measures in Central Europe (MBFR), the first negotiations ever to address mutual reductions in land forces, nevertheless offers the opportunity also for a more self-critical look at MBFR, and at the pitfalls and potential for conventional arms control generally. Earlier this month, both East and West agreed that MBFR should be concluded on a positive note, in order not to mar the opening of the new negotiation on Conventional Armed Forces in Europe[7] which is to follow hard on the heels of MBFR. In the final speeches delivered on each side, there was therefore talk of MBFR as a valuable learning process, from which both sides had profited. That is true; but the present conventional military superiority of the Warsaw Pact in Central

---

[1] HM Ambassador, Vienna, and Head of the UK Delegation to the MBFR talks, 1986–89.

[2] Secretary of State for Foreign and Commonwealth Affairs, 1983–89.

[3] Not printed.

[4] No. 9.

[5] President M.S. Gorbachev was General-Secretary of the CPSU, 1985–91.

[6] In fact this had been evident as early as 1977. As a JIC report on Soviet military expenditure then noted (see No. 86, note 11), despite 'a slowdown of economic growth, a very high share of GNP [had] continued to be allocated to military programmes, depriving the civilian economy of resources, particularly in the R[esearch] and D[evelopment] and engineering sectors and in infrastructure, which might otherwise have been used to promote long-term economic growth'.

[7] The Conventional Forces in Europe (CFE) talks opened in Vienna on 6 March. Involving the sixteen NATO and seven Warsaw Pact members, the negotiations had begun at the instigation of the Vienna review conference of the CSCE in the previous January.

Europe is not primarily a matter of intellectual interest: it is the main military threat facing the member states of NATO. It requires action to contain, and then to reduce the threat to our security. If we are serious in what we say about the conventional threat from Warsaw Pact superiority, we need to find some way to make the Warsaw Pact bring down the level of its forces to an acceptable and controlled number.

3. Progress on arms control depends above all on favourable political circumstances, and on the existence of the political will to reach an agreement—on each side, and at the same time. In MBFR there was no moment when both sides really wanted an agreement, except on such one-sidedly favourable terms as to be unnegotiable; and for a number of years neither side was ready for an agreement at all. In fact, MBFR did well to survive the ups and downs in East/West relations between 1973 and 1989 with only a single temporary suspension for wider political reasons for a few weeks in early 1984, over the announcement of INF[8] operational deployment in Western Europe.[9] Out of years of what was, on the surface, often only too like stage-fighting, a good deal of significance was achieved in MBFR. In 1973, the conventional arms agenda was a clean slate, and not only concepts but also the practical arrangements for implementing arms control measures had to be worked out. Fifteen years later, we could point to explicit acceptance by the Warsaw Pact of the need to eliminate disparities 'where these exist', and acceptance of parity at lower levels of forces as a shared aim. We would also point to acceptance of the need for ceilings on residual force levels after reductions, acceptance that these ceilings must be expressed numerically, and that there should be an adequately detailed exchange of data regarding the residual forces, and acceptance also of the need for effective verification, including on-site inspection.

4. The Warsaw Pact participants had also come to accept the Western case for measures designed to promote the general goal of increasing security and stability. Indeed, a number of confidence-building measures which were first explored in MBFR, notably for challenge inspection of major military exercises as of right, were adopted at the Stockholm Conference in September 1986,[10] and have already been in operation for two years. If we succeeded in educating the Warsaw Pact states in their approach to arms control, we also learnt much on the NATO side through our own work, and through the insights which MBFR gave us into Warsaw Pact thinking. The final tribute to MBFR, albeit expressed only tacitly, was the Mandate for the new negotiation on Conventional Armed Forces in Europe which was agreed in mid-January. The general aims and

---

[8] Intermediate-range Nuclear Forces.

[9] In late 1983, the Soviet Union broke off disarmament talks in Geneva over the US' decision to deploy American ground launched cruise missiles and Pershing IIs in the UK, West Germany, Italy, Belgium and the Netherlands. Both the INF talks and the Strategic Arms Reduction Talks (START) were suspended. The MBFR negotiations themselves were adjourned on 15 December, with no date agreed for their resumption. However, on 22 January 1984 it was announced that the talks would resume in March.

[10] The Stockholm Conference on Confidence and Security-Building Measures and Disarmament in Europe (CDE) began in January 1984 and ended in September 1986. In the Stockholm Declaration of 19 September 1986, the thirty-five participating states (the US, Canada and all the European states except Albania and Andorra) agreed upon procedures for the notification and observation of military manoeuvres, and for troop movements above certain levels, from the Atlantic to the Urals.

principles reflected in the Mandate, which have come to be viewed almost as common-place in arms control, were in fact points hard won by the West in argument in MBFR. By the time the Warsaw Pact was ready to think seriously about conventional arms control, however, the moment of MBFR had already passed.

5. When Gorbachev made his first call for conventional arms control from the Atlantic to the Urals in East Berlin in April 1986, the Soviet Union must have been starting to face up to the need for defence cuts which emerged finally in Gorbachev's subsequent announcement in December 1988 of reductions of 500,000 in the size of the Soviet armed forces (five tank divisions from the MBFR area). The scope of the MBFR negotiations had however become too modest to be the vehicle for so large a design. Equally, MBFR no longer looked bold enough for NATO. In the face of continuing difficulties over formulating proposals which might command any hope of success, the participating governments in MBFR had for ten years been scaling down the size of reductions they were ready to offer, or demand. In 1975, the West had put forward in MBFR the reduction of a complete Soviet tank army (68,000 men and 1,700 tanks) in return for the withdrawal of some 29,000 US troops, 36 Pershing launchers, 54 dual capable aircraft and 1,000 nuclear warheads.[11] By December 1985, in response to earlier Eastern minimalist proposals, and with the hope of drawing the East into discussion of a modest first-phase agreement, the West was proposing only the reduction of 5,000 US troops in return for the withdrawal of 11,500 Soviet personnel, with no armaments at all. The real significance of this last proposal lay in the ceiling it would then have placed on the total size of manpower in the area, some two million men, and the provision for stringent verification of that ceiling. The provisions for verification must have gone well beyond what Soviet military thinkers were then prepared to contemplate, and the reductions proposed were insignificant. There was no will on either side to try again. As a result, as interest grew in both East and West in serious negotiations on arms control, MBFR was relegated for its last three years to a highly unsatisfactory half life. Neither side was negotiating seriously, yet neither side wished to be seen to be bringing the negotiations to an end; and both had a requirement to appear still to be talking.

6. If the emphasis had been from the start on greater stability as the primary aim, and a lower level of forces as a secondary goal, something that could both follow from and contribute to greater stability but hardly an adequate end in itself, we might have got off to a better start. Moreover, there was a fundamental incompatibility between the nominal commitment of both sides to seeking mutual reductions, and the actual Western aim of seeking to avoid unilateral United States withdrawals from Europe (i.e. in fact maintaining NATO force levels) and the corresponding Eastern aim of contractualising a force relationship which was significantly in the East's favour.

7. Because the western participants regarded MBFR at the outset primarily as a means of helping the United States to avoid reductions, the emphasis was placed on United States reductions, and these were equated with Soviet reductions. The United States was accordingly given a dominant role on the Western side. The consequences were never entirely satisfactory. This leading United States role was not exercised lightly and it led to strains within the Western camp. These were kept under control by a strict discipline within the Western coordinating Ad Hoc Group, based on the principle of

[11] See No. 27.

collectivity, but at some cost. The conventions of United States leadership and of a right of veto theoretically possessed by everyone but in practice most frequently exercised by the United States, meant that MBFR became largely the playground of the super-powers. Under the particular circumstances of MBFR this handing over of the leading role to the United States was perhaps inevitable, but in future negotiations the preservation of the unity of the Alliance will require procedures which combine the cohesion which we had on the Western side in MBFR together with a flexibility which we certainly did not have, and without according to any one NATO partner a dominant position.

8. MBFR made its contribution to East/West relations, through providing the only multilateral forum for regular contact on security questions throughout more than fifteen years. It provided the basic arms control background for a whole generation of politico-military experts in both NATO and the Warsaw Pact. It has made a substantial contribution to the development of thinking on arms control in all the participating states. Out of the years of debate a measure of common ground has been established between East and West, and this consists very largely of Western ideas, and propositions argued long and persistently by the Western participants in Vienna. That is the Western achievement in MBFR.

9. As we move into the next phase of East/West talks on conventional arms control we shall need to face, if we are serious, an issue that we never really had to address in MBFR: are we prepared, in the interests of enhanced security, to accept changes in our own force levels which will perhaps require some restructuring, in return for gaining something more important from the Warsaw Pact? This means taking a dynamic not a static view, and looking at what the situation of both sides would be after implementation. It also means balancing reductions in forces against potential gains in other areas, such as effective verification and limitations. I do not believe that calculations of this kind cannot be made. No arms control agreement will be possible in which NATO has paid no price at all: the Warsaw Pact will also need to point to something gained, and this will not necessarily cost us very much. If there is a single personal conclusion I draw from MBFR, it is the need for imagination, and a real will to achieve an agreement which contains a fair balance of benefit to each party. Without both of these, we can well spend another fifteen years without result.

10. I am sending copies of this despatch to Her Majesty's Ambassadors in NATO and Warsaw Pact capitals, to the United Kingdom Representative to the North Atlantic Council at Brussels, to the Leader of the United Kingdom Delegation to the Conference on Disarmament in Geneva, and to the Ministry of Defence.

I am Sir
Yours faithfully
R.J. O'NEILL

APPENDIX IV

Songs from the MBFR Song-book

On his return from Vienna in November 1974 Mr. Tickell noted, with regard to the camaraderie he had witnessed between Eastern and Western delegates to the MBFR talks, they 'even [had] a song-book for use in the evenings' (No. 19). The origins of this MBFR song-book lay in the very difficulties delegates had experienced in establishing a social rapport. Sir C. Rose later recalled that the failure of 'orthodox' dinner parties to break the ice (the Soviet delegates had claimed that 'all Russians [were] equally proletarian and [did not] indulge in such bourgeois activities') had forced Western diplomats to consider more imaginative ways of avoiding protracted periods of stilted conversation with their Warsaw Pact colleagues. It was, in fact, Mr. Dean who 'hit upon the idea of singing together'. With the concurrence of Mr. Khlestov, (described by Sir C. Rose as 'an opera singer manqué'), the singing sessions became a regular feature of the diplomatic social scene. Under the direction of Mr. Dean, national songs from all of the participating countries were assembled into one volume and, as illustrated below, a few were 'adapted' with MBFR-themed lyrics. Although the Austrian and foreign press corps soon heard rumours of these choral gatherings, the singing diplomats were careful to ensure that no copies of the song-book fell into journalistic hands: 'This [was] probably', Sir C. Rose observed, 'the only example of a "NATO" document which never leaked—and of course it was in the interests of East and West that it shouldn't … the press would no doubt have had a field day if they had managed to get hold of it.' [1]

Oh, When These Bloody Talks Are Over
(Tune: *Oh, What a Friend We Have in Jesus*)

Oh, when these bloody talks are over,
Oh, how happy I shall be.
I will spend my life in clover.
No more plenaries for me.

No more Ad Hoc Group on Sundays.
No more guidance we must quote.
We won't have to tell the Chairman
How our spokesman should emote.

No reporting to the Council.
No more formulations fine.
Let them print it in *Die Presse*,
No more talking, just more wine.

When next the merry widow dances
And sings her way across the stage,
We will be back home in capitals
Trying to earn an honest wage.

Refrain:
Oh when these bloody talks are over,
Oh, how happy I shall be.

The Negotiators
(Tune: *The Whiffenpoof Song*)

From the tables down at Grinzing,
To the place where Kreisky dwells,
To the dear old Plenaries we love so well

Sing the 'negotiators' assembled
With our glasses raised on high
And the magic of our singing casts its spell.

Yes, the magic of our singing
Of the songs we love so well
'*Stenka Ryazin*', and '*The Dienstmann*' and the rest

We will advance our agreed positions,
While life and breath shall last,
For we think that our proposal is the best.

We are poor little emissaries
who have lost our way
Baa, baa, baa

We are little plenipotentiaries
who have gone astray,
Baa, baa, baa.

Gentlemen negotiators off on a spree
Doomed from here to eternity
May God have mercy on such as we,
Baa, baa, baa

---

[1] Letter from Sir C. Rose to the Editors of 28 October 1999.

Index of Main Subjects and Persons

This index is designed to be used in conjunction with the Chapter Summaries. References in this index are to page, rather than document numbers.